NEW PERSPECTIVES ON

Adobe® Flash® Professional CS5

COMPREHENSIVE

NEW PERSPECTIVES ON

Adobe® Flash® Professional CS5

COMPREHENSIVE

Luis A. Lopez
Robin M. Romer

COURSE TECHNOLOGY
CENGAGE Learning™

Australia • Brazil • Japan • Korea • Mexico • Singapore • Spain • United Kingdom • United States

COURSE TECHNOLOGY
CENGAGE Learning

New Perspectives on Adobe Flash Professional CS5, Comprehensive

Vice President, Publisher: Nicole Jones Pinard

Executive Editor: Marie L. Lee

Associate Acquisitions Editor: Brandi Shailer

Senior Product Manager: Kathy Finnegan

Product Manager: Leigh Hefferon

Associate Product Manager: Julia Leroux-Lindsey

Editorial Assistant: Jacqueline Lacaire

Director of Marketing: Cheryl Costantini

Senior Marketing Manager: Ryan DeGrote

Marketing Coordinator: Kristen Panciocco

Developmental Editor: Robin M. Romer

Content Project Manager: Jennifer Feltri

Composition: GEX Publishing Services

Art Director: Marissa Falco

Text Designer: Althea Chen

Cover Designer: Roycroft Design

Cover Art: © Veer Incorporated

Copyeditor: Troy Lilly

Proofreader: Vicki Zimmer

Indexer: Rich Carlson

For product information and technology assistance, contact us at
Cengage Learning Customer & Sales Support, 1-800-354-9706
For permission to use material from this text or product, submit all requests online at **www.cengage.com/permissions**
Further permissions questions can be emailed to
permissionrequest@cengage.com

Some of the product names and company names used in this book have been used for identification purposes only and may be trademarks or registered trademarks of their respective manufacturers and sellers.

Adobe®, Dreamweaver®, Flash®, InDesign®, Illustrator®, and Photoshop® are either registered trademarks or trademarks of Adobe Systems Incorporated in the United States and/or other countries. THIS PRODUCT IS NOT ENDORSED OR SPONSORED BY ADOBE SYSTEMS INCORPORATED, PUBLISHER OF ADOBE® DREAMWEAVER®, FLASH®, INDESIGN®, ILLUSTRATOR®, AND PHOTOSHOP®.

Disclaimer: Any fictional data related to persons or companies or URLs used throughout this book is intended for instructional purposes only. At the time this book was printed, any such data was fictional and not belonging to any real persons or companies.

Library of Congress Control Number: 2010934026

ISBN-13: 978-0-538-45319-6

ISBN-10: 0-538-45319-2

Course Technology
20 Channel Center Street
Boston, MA 02210
USA

Cengage Learning is a leading provider of customized learning solutions with office locations around the globe, including Singapore, the United Kingdom, Australia, Mexico, Brazil, and Japan. Locate your local office at:
international.cengage.com/global

Cengage Learning products are represented in Canada by Nelson Education, Ltd.

To learn more about Course Technology, visit **www.cengage.com/course technology**

To learn more about Cengage Learning, visit **www.cengage.com**

Purchase any of our products at your local college store or at our preferred online store **www.cengagebrain.com**

Printed in the United States of America
1 2 3 4 5 6 7 8 9 14 13 12 11 10

Preface

The New Perspectives Series' critical-thinking, problem-solving approach is the ideal way to prepare students to transcend point-and-click skills and take advantage of all that Adobe Flash Professional CS5 has to offer.

In developing the New Perspectives Series, our goal was to create books that give students the software concepts and practical skills they need to succeed beyond the classroom. We've updated our proven case-based pedagogy with more practical content to make learning skills more meaningful to students.

With the New Perspectives Series, students understand *why* they are learning *what* they are learning, and are fully prepared to apply their skills to real-life situations.

"This text engages students by providing workplace scenarios designed to help them personally connect with the concepts and applications presented. The new visual overviews greatly enhance each tutorial as they provide a snapshot to the lessons."
—Paulette Comet
The Community College of
Baltimore County

About This Book

This book provides comprehensive coverage of the new Adobe Flash Professional CS5 software, and includes the following:
- Hands-on instruction of the newest features of Flash Professional CS5, including the new Text Layout Framework (TLF) text engine, Motion Editor, Bone tool, 3D transformations, Code Snippets panel, Adobe Media Encoder CS5, and Adobe Device Central CS5
- Coverage of both ActionScript 2.0 and ActionScript 3.0 programming and incorporates the use of ActionScript, code snippets, preloaders, components, and video
- How to create content for mobile devices and test it using Adobe Device Central CS5
- Overview of the learning objectives assessed with the Rich Media Communication using Adobe Flash Professional exam

New for this edition!
- Each session begins with a Visual Overview, a new two-page spread that includes colorful, enlarged screenshots with numerous callouts and key term definitions, giving students a comprehensive preview of the topics covered in the session, as well as a handy study guide.
- New ProSkills boxes provide guidance for how to use the software in real-world, professional situations, and related ProSkills exercises integrate the technology skills students learn with one or more of the following soft skills: decision making, problem solving, teamwork, verbal communication, and written communication.
- Important steps are highlighted in yellow with attached margin notes to help students pay close attention to completing the steps correctly and avoid time-consuming rework.

System Requirements

This book assumes students have a default installation of Adobe Flash Professional CS5, Adobe Flash Player 10, Adobe Media Encoder CS5 with the Xvid codec installed (free download is available from www.xvid.org), Adobe Device Central CS5, and a current Web browser. The screen shots in this book were produced on a computer running Windows Vista Ultimate with Aero turned on and, for a browser, Internet Explorer 8. If students use a different operating system or browser, their screens might differ from those in the book.

The New Perspectives Approach

Context

Each tutorial begins with a problem presented in a "real-world" case that is meaningful to students. The case sets the scene to help students understand what they will do in the tutorial.

Hands-on Approach

Each tutorial is divided into manageable sessions that combine reading and hands-on, step-by-step work. Colorful screenshots help guide students through the steps. **Trouble?** tips anticipate common mistakes or problems to help students stay on track and continue with the tutorial.

VISUAL OVERVIEW

Visual Overviews

New for this edition! Each session begins with a Visual Overview, a new two-page spread that includes colorful, enlarged screenshots with numerous callouts and key term definitions, giving students a comprehensive preview of the topics covered in the session, as well as a handy study guide.

PROSKILLS

ProSkills Boxes and Exercises

New for this edition! ProSkills boxes provide guidance for how to use the software in real-world, professional situations, and related ProSkills exercises integrate the technology skills students learn with one or more of the following soft skills: decision making, problem solving, teamwork, verbal communication, and written communication.

KEY STEP

Key Steps

New for this edition! Important steps are highlighted in yellow with attached margin notes to help students pay close attention to completing the steps correctly and avoid time-consuming rework.

INSIGHT

InSight Boxes

InSight boxes offer expert advice and best practices to help students achieve a deeper understanding of the concepts behind the software features and skills.

TIP

Margin Tips

Margin Tips provide helpful hints and shortcuts for more efficient use of the software. The Tips appear in the margin at key points throughout each tutorial, giving students extra information when and where they need it.

REVIEW

APPLY

Assessment

Retention is a key component to learning. At the end of each session, a series of Quick Check questions helps students test their understanding of the material before moving on. Engaging end-of-tutorial Review Assignments and Case Problems have always been a hallmark feature of the New Perspectives Series. Colorful bars and brief descriptions accompany the exercises, making it easy to understand both the goal and level of challenge a particular assignment holds.

REFERENCE

TASK REFERENCE

GLOSSARY/INDEX

Reference

Within each tutorial, Reference boxes appear before a set of steps to provide a succinct summary and preview of how to perform a task. In addition, a complete Task Reference at the back of the book provides quick access to information on how to carry out common tasks. Finally, each book includes a combination Glossary/Index to promote easy reference of material.

Our Complete System of Instruction

Coverage To Meet Your Needs

Whether you're looking for just a small amount of coverage or enough to fill a semester-long class, we can provide you with a textbook that meets your needs.

- Brief books typically cover the essential skills in just 2 to 4 tutorials.
- Introductory books build and expand on those skills and contain an average of 5 to 8 tutorials.
- Comprehensive books are great for a full-semester class, and contain 9 to 12+ tutorials.

So if the book you're holding does not provide the right amount of coverage for you, there's probably another offering available. Go to our Web site or contact your Course Technology sales representative to find out what else we offer.

CourseCasts – Learning on the Go. Always available...always relevant.

Want to keep up with the latest technology trends relevant to you? Visit our site to find a library of podcasts, CourseCasts, featuring a "CourseCast of the Week," and download them to your mp3 player at http://coursecasts.course.com.

Our fast-paced world is driven by technology. You know because you're an active participant—always on the go, always keeping up with technological trends, and always learning new ways to embrace technology to power your life.

Ken Baldauf, host of CourseCasts, is a faculty member of the Florida State University Computer Science Department where he is responsible for teaching technology classes to thousands of FSU students each year. Ken is an expert in the latest technology trends; he gathers and sorts through the most pertinent news and information for CourseCasts so your students can spend their time enjoying technology, rather than trying to figure it out. Open or close your lecture with a discussion based on the latest CourseCast.

Visit us at http://coursecasts.course.com to learn on the go!

Instructor Resources

We offer more than just a book. We have all the tools you need to enhance your lectures, check students' work, and generate exams in a new, easier-to-use and completely revised package. This book's Instructor's Manual, ExamView testbank, PowerPoint presentations, data files, solution files, figure files, and a sample syllabus are all available on a single CD-ROM or for downloading at http://www.cengage.com/coursetechnology.

SAM: Skills Assessment Manager

SAM is designed to help bring students from the classroom to the real world. It allows students to train and test on important computer skills in an active, hands-on environment.

SAM's easy-to-use system includes powerful interactive exams, training, and projects on the most commonly used Microsoft Office applications. SAM simulates the Office application environment, allowing students to demonstrate their knowledge and think through the skills by performing real-world tasks, such as bolding text or setting up slide transitions. Add in live-in-the-application projects, and students are on their way to truly learning and applying skills to business-centric documents.

Designed to be used with the New Perspectives Series, SAM includes handy page references, so students can print helpful study guides that match the New Perspectives textbooks used in class. For instructors, SAM also includes robust scheduling and reporting features.

WebTUTOR

Content for Online Learning
Course Technology has partnered with the leading distance learning solution providers and class-management platforms today. To access this material, visit www.cengage.com/webtutor and search for your title. Instructor resources include the following: additional case projects, sample syllabi, PowerPoint presentations, and more. For students to access this material, they must have purchased a WebTutor PIN-code specific to this title and your campus platform. The resources for students might include (based on instructor preferences): topic reviews, review questions, practice tests, and more. For additional information, please contact your sales representative.

Acknowledgments

I want to extend my gratitude to all of the members of the New Perspectives Team who made this book possible, especially Leigh Hefferon, Product Manager, for her attention to detail, and her support and patience as she guided this project. Thanks also to Jennifer Feltri, Content Project Manager; Marisa Taylor, GEX Publishing Services; and Christian Kunciw, Manuscript Quality Assurance Supervisor, and the MQA team for this edition, Danielle Shaw, and Susan Whalen.

Special thanks to Robin M. Romer, co-author and Developmental Editor, for her outstanding writing, editorial, and organizational skills that helped make this project a success. As always, it has been a pleasure to work and collaborate with her.

To my wife, Gloria, and my daughter, Alyssandra, my heartfelt thanks for their love, patience and support which make writing possible.

And, finally, this book is dedicated to my mother, Guadalupe, for her love throughout the years.
– Luis A. Lopez

Many thanks to the dedicated editorial and production team at Course Technology. Marie Lee, Executive Editor, for the continued opportunity to part of your team. Leigh Hefferon, Product Manager, for making the management of this entire project seem effortless. Jennifer Feltri, Content Project Manager, and Marisa Taylor, Senior Project Manager at GEX Publishing Services for shepherding the book through the production process. Christian Kunciw and his band of testers for their thorough review of the tutorials. Elizabeth Pannell and Kenneth Sigler for their careful and helpful feedback during the development of this text.

Very special thanks to Luis A. Lopez. As always, it's a joy to work with you. Your dedication, thoroughness, and talent for making the complex seem simple are a real inspiration.

Much love to my family for their constant support. A huge thank you to Brian and Jake for their patience and endurance.

– Robin M. Romer

BRIEF CONTENTS

FLASH

TABLE OF CONTENTS

TUTORIAL **1**

Introducing Adobe Flash Professional CS5

Exploring the Basic Features of Flash

OBJECTIVES

Session 1.1
- Explore the types of Web media created in Flash
- Compare vector graphics and bitmap graphics
- Learn how Flash media are displayed in a Web page
- View Flash files in a Web browser
- Start Flash and explore its main workspace components

Session 1.2
- Change the view of the Stage
- Display the grid, rulers, and guides
- Change a document's settings
- Work with strokes, fills, and colors
- Compare drawing modes
- Select and modify objects
- Use Flash Help

Case | *Admiral Web Design*

Admiral Web Design, founded in 2001, is a fast-growing Web site design and development company that specializes in building Web sites for small- to medium-sized businesses and organizations. This innovative Web design company has a growing list of clients from various industries, including a national sports equipment company and a local seafood restaurant. The company's rapid growth and success have largely been due to its energetic and creative staff.

Admiral Web Design is owned by Gloria Adamson and Jim Torres, both graduates of a Web design and multimedia program at a local college. The other full-time employees are Aly Garcia, Chris Johnson, and Raj Sharma. Gloria handles the bulk of the business decisions and oversees the Web site design and development projects. Jim is responsible for marketing and manages the company's finances. Aly is the graphic designer, and Chris and Raj are the site designers responsible for developing the content for the clients' Web sites. You will help Aly develop graphics and animations using Flash.

STARTING DATA FILES

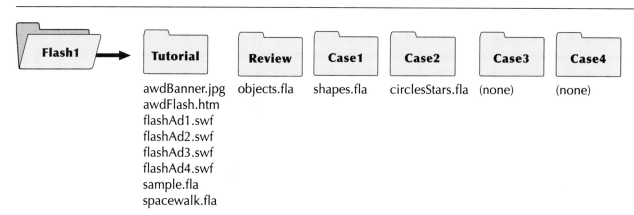

Flash1 → Tutorial
awdBanner.jpg
awdFlash.htm
flashAd1.swf
flashAd2.swf
flashAd3.swf
flashAd4.swf
sample.fla
spacewalk.fla

Review
objects.fla

Case1
shapes.fla

Case2
circlesStars.fla

Case3
(none)

Case4
(none)

SESSION 1.1 VISUAL OVERVIEW

The **Application bar** lists menu categories such as File, Edit, View, Insert, and Help, which include commands to access most of the Flash program features.

The **page tab** identifies the open document and is used to navigate among open documents.

The **Edit bar** displays the current scene number, the Edit Scene button, the Edit Symbols button, and the Zoom control.

The **Stage** is the area where you create, import, and assemble all the graphic objects that are part of a Flash document.

The **pasteboard** holds objects that are not part of the viewable Stage and that move onto or off the Stage as part of an animation.

The **playhead** is a marker that indicates which frame is currently selected in the Timeline.

The **Document window** is the main work area that consists of the pasteboard and the Stage.

The **Timeline** displays and controls the layers and frames that make up an animation and organizes the objects that are part of the document.

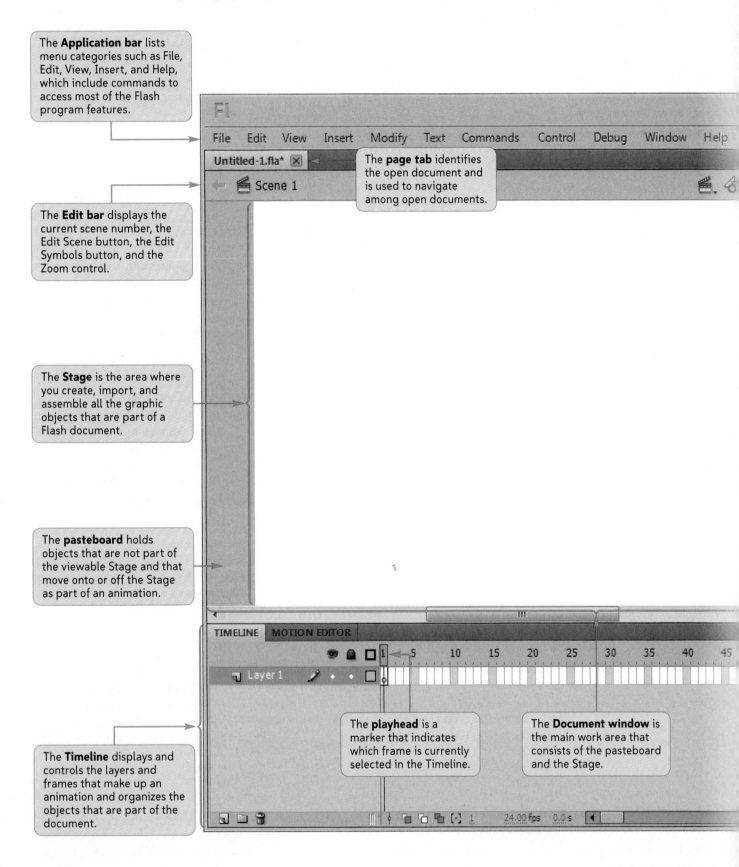

THE FLASH WORKSPACE

The **workspace switcher button** is used to select or reset the workspace layout. This figure shows the workspace in the Essentials layout.

Two or more panels displayed together form a **panel group**.

A **panel** contains controls for viewing and changing the properties of objects such as vector and bitmap graphics. The panel name appears in its tab.

A **dock** is a collection of individual panels or panel groups. Click a button once to open the panel; click it again to close the panel.

The **Property inspector** provides easy access for reviewing and modifying the most common attributes of the currently selected tool or object.

The **Tools panel** contains the Flash tools, such as the tools for drawing and painting lines and shapes, selecting objects, changing the view of the Stage, and choosing colors.

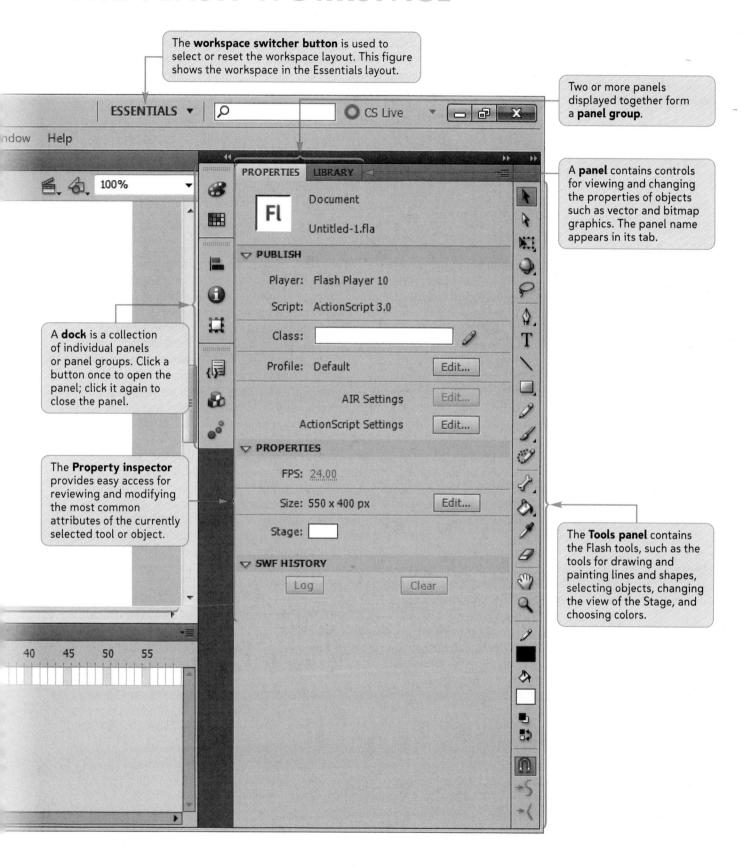

Reviewing Types of Web Media

Web pages are made up of text, graphics, animations, sounds, and videos. These elements are referred to as **Web media**. The different types of Web media are created by a variety of programs, and then pulled together to work as a cohesive whole on a Web page through **HTML (Hypertext Markup Language)**, the underlying code used in creating Web pages. The most common types of Web media besides text are graphics and animations, which can be created in Flash.

Adobe Flash Professional CS5 (Flash) is a software program used to create visually exciting and interactive components, such as animated logos and online interactive advertising, to enhance the clients' Web sites. Flash was originally designed to create small, fast-loading animations that could be used in Web pages. Over the years, Flash has evolved into an advanced authoring tool for creating interactive Web media that range from animated logos to Web site navigational controls and interactive Web sites. Flash can also be used to develop engaging content for mobile devices.

Bitmap and Vector Graphics

A **bitmap graphic** is a row-by-row representation of every pixel in the graphic along with each pixel's color. A **pixel** is the smallest picture element on the monitor screen that can be controlled by the computer. A 100×100-pixel bitmap graphic is simply a grid containing 10,000 colored pixels. As a result, resizing a bitmap graphic creates unattractive side effects. If you enlarge a bitmap graphic, for example, the edges become ragged as the pixels are redistributed to fit the larger grid. You cannot easily take a bitmap graphic apart to modify only one portion of the image. Bitmap graphics, however, provide blending and subtle variations in colors and textures. A common bitmap graphic is a digital photograph. You can also create bitmap graphics using imaging software such as Adobe Fireworks or Adobe Photoshop. The most common file formats for bitmap graphics used in Web pages are JPEG (Joint Photographic Experts Group), GIF (Graphic Interchange Format), and PNG (Portable Network Graphics).

A **vector graphic** is a set of mathematical instructions that describes the color, outline, and position of all the shapes of the image. Each shape is defined by numbers that represent the shape's position in the window in which it is being displayed. Other numbers represent the points that establish the shape's outline. As a result, vector graphics scale well, which means you can resize a vector image proportionally and the quality remains the same. Vector graphics also appear uniform regardless of the size or resolution of the monitor on which they are displayed. Individual shapes within a vector graphic can be modified independently of the rest. Vector graphics excel at sharp lines, smooth colors, and precise details. Vector graphic files are generally smaller than bitmap graphic files and take less time to download. Common examples of vector graphics are images created in drawing programs such as Adobe Illustrator as well as images created in Flash.

Figure 1-1 shows an image of a fish as a bitmap graphic (top) and as a vector graphic (bottom). The bitmap graphic becomes distorted when enlarged, whereas the vector graphic retains its quality.

INSIGHT

Combining Bitmap and Vector Graphics

Designers often import bitmap graphics into Flash and combine them with vector graphics. For example, bitmap images such as photographs often appear as the background to Flash vector graphics and animations. They tend to soften the overall effect and add realism to Flash graphics. Using a bitmap graphic in a Flash document is best when you are developing an advertisement or banner for a business's or professional organization's Web site. You should also edit the bitmap graphic in an image-editing program such as Adobe Photoshop to reduce its size to match the size of the Flash document. Using large bitmap graphics will cause the resulting Flash graphic to download very slowly.

Figure 1-1   Comparison of bitmap and vector graphics

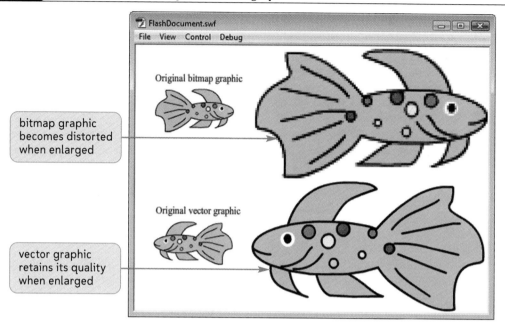

Bitmap and Vector Animation

Animation is a series of still images displayed in sequence to give the illusion of motion. Think of a flip book. Each page shows the same image with a slight alteration. When the pages are fanned or flipped quickly, the image appears to move. Animation can be accomplished with both bitmap and vector images.

Bitmap animation is created by putting a sequence of bitmap images into one file and playing back the sequence. The playback of the bitmap images produces a perception of motion. Each change the viewer sees requires changing the colors of pixels in the frame. A lot of information is required to keep track of all of the pixel changes even for small images of short duration. The amount of information that must be stored increases dramatically for larger display sizes, longer sequences, or smoother motion. Because of the importance of rapid transmission over the Internet, bitmap motion graphics are usually limited to small display sizes and short sequences.

Vector animation lists shapes and their transformations that are played back in sequence to produce the perception of motion. The information required to describe the modification of shapes in a vector animation is usually less than the information required to describe the pixel changes in a bitmap animation. Also, vector graphics are resolution-independent, which means that they always appear with the optimum on-screen quality regardless of image size or the screen resolution. As a result, increasing the display size of the shapes in a vector animation has no effect on the file size.

Developing Web Media in Flash

Flash allows developers to create media-rich elements that integrate with Web pages and that download quickly. Flash graphics also have streaming capability, which allows animations to start playing even before they download completely. Web media created in Flash are called **documents** and can include text, static images, sound, video, and animations. Flash animations are created from a series of graphic objects such as lines, shapes, and text that are then sequenced. The graphics created in Flash are primarily vector graphics but can include bitmap graphics. Flash supports many import formats so that developers can include media from a broad range of sources including Photoshop and Illustrator files. In addition, you can export Flash graphics and then reference them in HTML files created with Web site development software such as Adobe Dreamweaver.

Decision Making: Using Media in Flash Documents

As you develop Flash documents, you'll have to make many decisions about what media elements to include. A completed Flash document can include many types of media: from silent, still imagery to motion graphics with sound and interactivity as well as elements that incorporate video. You can also add sound—as sound effects, voiceovers, or music—to any element within a Flash document. You can choose to have sound play all the time, be activated by a mouse click, be turned on and off by the user, or be synchronized with events in your document. You can also incorporate video into a Web page as part of a graphic or animation and add controls to the video elements to enable the viewer to manage the video playback. Keep in mind the document's purpose and its intended audience as you decide which media to include in a Flash document. Making good decisions about what to include will help to ensure that the Flash documents you create effectively accomplish your intended goals.

Like other media files, a Flash file must be referenced in an HTML page file to be viewed in a Web page. You can publish the HTML files and references automatically from within the Flash program. You can also insert the reference manually or create your own HTML file to reference and control the Flash file.

While developing content using Flash, you work with a Flash authoring document, referred to as an **FLA file**, which has the .fla file extension. When you're ready to deliver that content for viewing by end users, you publish the Flash document as a **SWF file** (often pronounced "swiff file"), which has the .swf file extension and can be displayed in a Web page. For example, if the Flash document in which you create and develop an animation for the Admiral Web Design Web site is named awdBanner.fla, the published file with the finished animation would be named awdBanner.swf. The SWF file is also called a **Flash movie**.

The SWF file plays in an HTML file in a Web browser using the **Flash Player plug-in**. All current versions of the major Web browsers come with the Flash Player plug-in installed. Besides allowing Flash documents to be viewed in your browser, the Flash Player plug-in provides controls for zooming in and out of the document, changing the document's quality, printing the document, and other functions.

Another element of Flash is ActionScript, a scripting programming language that enables you to add interactivity to buttons and other Web media that users can click or select to control the Flash graphics or animation they are viewing. You will learn more about ActionScript in later tutorials.

Viewing Flash SWF Files

Aly wants you to look at several examples of Flash SWF files she has created and placed on the Admiral Web Design Web site. You do this by opening the Flash Web page in a Web browser. If the Flash Player plug-in is installed, the streaming capability of a Flash file allows the player to begin playing the animation as soon as enough of the file has been downloaded.

To view Aly's sample Flash SWF files in your browser:

1. On the taskbar, click the **Start** button 🌀, and then click **Internet Explorer**. The Web browser opens, displaying the default home page.

   Trouble? If you don't see Internet Explorer on the Start menu, type Internet Explorer in the Start Search box, and then click Internet Explorer. If you still don't see Internet Explorer, press the Esc key until the Start menu closes, and then ask your instructor or technical support person for assistance.

Trouble? If you are using Mozilla Firefox or a different Web browser, open that browser, and then modify any Web browser steps in these tutorials as needed.

2. If the Internet Explorer menu bar is not displayed, click the **Tools** button, point to **Toolbars**, and then click **Menu Bar**.

3. On the menu bar, click **File**, and then click **Open**. The Open dialog box opens.

4. Click the **Browse** button, navigate to the **Flash1\Tutorial** folder included with your Data Files, click **awdFlash.htm**, click the **Open** button, and then click the **OK** button. The Admiral Web Design sample page appears in the browser window. This page contains several examples of Flash SWF files.

Trouble? If you don't have the starting Data Files, you need to get them before you can proceed. Your instructor will either give you the Data Files or ask you to obtain them from a specified location (such as a network drive). In either case, make a backup copy of the Data Files before you start so that you have the original files available in case you need to start over. If you have any questions about the Data Files, see your instructor or technical support person for assistance.

Trouble? If a dialog box opens stating that Internet Explorer needs to open a new window to display the Web page, click the OK button.

Trouble? If the Information Bar indicates that your Internet Security settings block the active content in the Admiral Web Design sample page, you need to allow blocked content in this instance and whenever you open a Web page in these tutorials. Click the Information Bar, click Allow Blocked Content, and then click the Yes button in the Security Warning dialog box.

5. Right-click one of the animations on the page. The context menu with the controls for the Flash file opens.

6. On the context menu, point to **Quality**. The submenu opens. See Figure 1-2.

Figure 1-2   Sample Flash SWF files

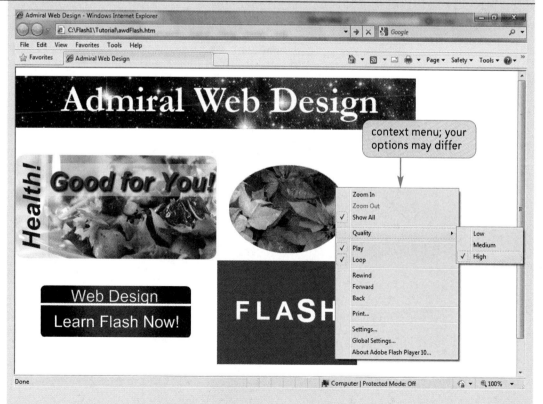

Trouble? If the text or graphics appear in different locations on your screen, you're probably using a different Web browser. The page layout can differ slightly when viewed with different Web browsers.

▶ **7.** On the context menu, click **Play** to remove the check mark. The command is deselected and the animation stops.

▶ **8.** Right-click an animation, and then, on the context menu, click **Zoom In**. The graphic's magnification level increases.

TIP

When the graphic is magnified, the pointer shape is a hand and you can drag the graphic to see different areas.

▶ **9.** Use the context menu controls to rewind, zoom out, and step forward and back through the animation.

▶ **10.** On the browser title bar, click the **Close** button ▬x▬. The browser window closes.

Trouble? If a dialog box opens, prompting you to close all of the tabs, click the Close Tabs button.

Starting Flash

When you first start Flash, or when the program is running but no documents are opened, the Welcome screen appears. The Welcome screen provides access to the most commonly used actions such as opening a recently used file, creating a new Flash document, or creating a document using a template. After you open a document or create a new one, the Flash program window appears.

To start Flash and open a new Flash file:

▶ **1.** Click the **Start** button 🔵 on the taskbar, click **All Programs** on the Start menu, and then click **Adobe Flash Professional CS5** on the All Programs menu. The Flash program window opens and displays the Welcome screen.

Trouble? If you do not see Adobe Flash Professional CS5 on the All Programs menu, look for and click an Adobe folder, and then click Adobe Flash Professional CS5. If you can't find Adobe Flash Professional CS5 in an Adobe folder, press the Esc key twice to close the Start menu, and then double-click the Adobe Flash Professional CS5 program icon on your desktop. If you still can't find Adobe Flash Professional CS5, ask your instructor or technical support person for help.

Trouble? If the Adobe Product Activation dialog box opens, this is probably the first time Flash was started on this computer. Click the appropriate option button, click the Continue button, enter the information requested, and then click the Register button. If you do not know your serial number or need further assistance, ask your instructor or technical support person.

▶ **2.** If necessary, on the Application bar, click the **Maximize** button 🔲 to maximize the Flash program window.

▶ **3.** In the Create New section of the Welcome screen, click **ActionScript 3.0**. An untitled Flash file window opens.

Trouble? If the Welcome screen is hidden, on the Application bar, click File, click New to open the New Document dialog box, click ActionScript 3.0 in the Type box on the General tab of the New Document dialog box, and then click the OK button.

The Flash program window, called the **workspace**, contains elements such as toolbars, windows, and panels that you can arrange to suit your work style and needs. Flash has several preset workspace layouts, including Designer, Developer, and Essentials. Each preset workspace reflects a different way of working with Flash based on the type of project you are creating or your preferred organization. The default arrangement of the Flash elements is the Essentials workspace. The workspace can be customized, which means you can rearrange the elements. The figures in these tutorials show the Flash workspace in the Essentials layout. You'll reset the workspace to the Essentials layout.

To reset the Essentials workspace layout:

1. On the Application bar, click the **workspace switcher** button, and then click **Reset 'Essentials'**. The Flash workspace resets to the default Essentials layout.

2. On the Application bar, click **Window**, and then point to **Toolbars**. The menu of available toolbars opens.

3. Verify that **Main** and **Controller** do not have check marks next to them and that **Edit Bar** has a check mark next to it. If necessary, click a command to add or remove the check mark; otherwise, press the Esc key twice to close the menu.

Previewing Documents

As you develop a Flash document, you should preview it to check the results of your changes. You can preview your work in Flash in several ways. You can preview or play the document's animation within the Flash workspace, publish the file to play in a separate Flash Player window, or publish it to play in a Web page in your default Web browser. Previewing the document in the Flash workspace is the quickest method, although some animation effects and interactive functions work only in the published format.

You will open Aly's spacewalk.fla document, and then preview the simple animation from the Flash workspace.

To preview the spacewalk.fla document in the Flash workspace:

1. On the Application bar, click **File**, and then click **Close**. If a dialog box prompts you to save changes, click the **No** button. The document closes and the Welcome screen appears.

2. On the Application bar, click **File**, and then click **Open**. The Open dialog box opens.

3. Navigate to the location where you store your Data Files, open the **Flash1\Tutorial** folder, click **spacewalk.fla** in the file list, and then click the **Open** button. The spacewalk.fla document opens on the Stage, and its name appears in the page tab.

   Trouble? If the spacewalk.fla file does not include the .fla extension in its filename, your computer's operating system is not configured to display file extensions. Click spacewalk in the file list.

4. On the Application bar, click **File**, and then click **Save As**. The Save As dialog box opens.

5. Navigate to the **Flash1\Tutorial** folder included with your Data Files if necessary, type **spacewalkNew** in the File name box, and then click the **Save** button. The document is saved with the new name, which appears in the page tab.

6. On the Application bar, click **View**, point to **Magnification**, and then click **Show All**. The entire document is visible. See Figure 1-3.

| Figure 1-3 | The spacewalkNew.fla document |

new filename appears in the page tab

Stage and pasteboard display the entire document

playhead moves through the timeline as the animation plays

you might see different colors

7. On the Application bar, click **Control**, and then click **Play**. As the animation plays, notice that the Timeline tracks the animation's progress. You will learn more about the elements in the Timeline later in the next session.

Another way to preview the animation in the Flash window is to play the animation manually by **scrubbing**, or dragging the playhead back and forth through the frames. Scrubbing is useful when testing an animation during development. You can also preview the published file in a separate Flash Player window or in a browser window.

To preview the published file in Flash Player and a browser:

1. On the Application bar, click **Control**, point to **Test Movie**, and then click **in Flash Professional**. Flash creates a file in the SWF format, opens it in a separate window, and then plays it with Flash Player. See Figure 1-4.

TIP

You can also test the movie by pressing the Ctrl+Enter keys.

Figure 1-4 **The spacewalkNew.swf document playing in Flash Player**

SWF file plays in
a separate Flash
Player window

2. On the Flash Player window title bar, click the **Close** button [X]. The Flash Player closes and you to return to the Flash document.

> **Trouble?** If the Flash program closes, you probably clicked the Close button on the Flash Application bar. Restart Flash and reopen the spacewalkNew.fla file.

3. On the Application bar, click **File**, point to **Publish Preview**, and then click **HTML**. The default browser on your computer opens and the SWF file plays in the browser window. See Figure 1-5.

Figure 1-5 **The spacewalkNew.swf file playing in a Web browser**

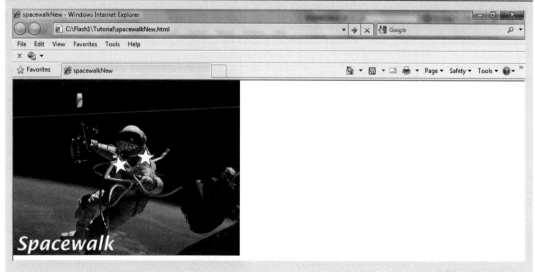

> **Trouble?** If the animation does not play in your browser window, allow blocked content. If the animation still doesn't play, start your Web browser, then open the spacewalkNew.html file located in the Flash1\Tutorial folder.

4. On the browser title bar, click the **Close** button [X] to close the browser window and return to Flash.

Exploring the Workspace Components

The main components of the Flash workspace are the Stage, pasteboard, Timeline, Tools panel, and panels.

Stage

A graphic object must be on the Stage to appear in the final document, whether that object is static or animated. The Stage shows only the objects that are visible at a particular point in an animation. In fact, the Stage in Flash is just like the stage in a dramatic production. As the production progresses, actors appear and disappear, and move around from place to place on the Stage. In Flash, different objects are visible on the Stage at different times during playback. As the animation plays, objects might appear or disappear, change position, or change appearance.

Pasteboard

When you complete a Flash document and publish it to view it on a Web page, only the objects and portions of objects on the Stage appear. Objects and portions of objects in the pasteboard are not shown. You can place a graphic in the pasteboard and then animate it to move onto the Stage.

PROSKILLS

Teamwork: Using the Pasteboard

Creating a Flash document is often a collaborative process involving the client, designers, artists, writers, and others. This group approach can lead to ideas, questions, and eventually decisions that need to be recorded and communicated to the entire team. During development, the pasteboard is a convenient storage area for notes like this. You can use the pasteboard to place instructions or comments that you and team members can use as a reference or guide while working with the Flash document. These notes are visible only in Flash and will not appear in the published document. However, you should still use clear and concise writing; correct grammar, spelling, and punctuation; and appropriate and professional language so that team members easily understand your intended meaning. The pasteboard is also a good place to store graphic objects until you are ready to add them to the Stage. For example, you might display an alternate version of a graphic on the pasteboard for other team members to review. Effective communication among team members can prevent having to rework parts of the Flash document. Strong teamwork is one key to a successful project.

Timeline

Flash documents are divided into frames similar to a motion picture film. Frames represent units of time, and appear in rows along the Timeline. Every column represents one frame. Each frame can contain different images or different states of the same image. The Timeline is used to coordinate and control the timing of the animation by determining how and when frames are displayed. As the animation is played over time, the playhead moves from frame to frame and the contents of each frame appear in succession, achieving the perception of motion. The animation in the spacewalkNew.fla document contains 60 frames, as you can see by the numbers in the Timeline header.

The Timeline also controls layers. The layers are listed in a column on the left side of the Timeline. Each row represents one layer. The frames for that layer are shown to the right of the layer name. You can place different objects on the different layers. When you draw or change something on a layer, only the contents of the active layer are changed. The objects on the other layers are not affected. The animation in the spacewalkNew.fla document contains four layers.

To explore the Timeline in the spacewalkNew.fla document:

1. Scrub the playhead by dragging it back and forth along the Timeline header. The animation on the Stage changes based on the content of the different frames. See Figure 1-6.

Figure 1-6 | **Animation played by scrubbing**

animation as it appears in Frame 50

drag the playhead to manually play the animation

animation has four layers

animation has 60 frames, as shown in the Timeline header

2. In the Timeline header, click **Frame 35**. Frame 35 is the current frame, and its contents appear on the Stage. See Figure 1-7.

Figure 1-7	Frame selected in the Timeline header

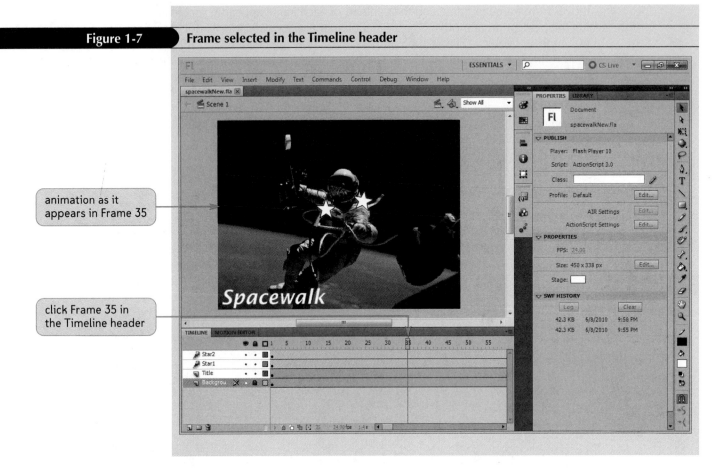

animation as it appears in Frame 35

click Frame 35 in the Timeline header

Tools Panel

The Tools panel includes a variety of tools that you use to create graphics and animations in a Flash document. The first area of the Tools panel contains tools to select and modify graphic images in a Flash document. The second area contains tools to create and modify the lines both straight and curved, shapes such as rectangles and ovals, and text that make up the graphic images of a Flash document. The third area contains tools to fill in shapes with color, to copy color from one object to another, and to erase parts of an object. The fourth area contains tools for moving and magnifying the view of the Stage, neither of which affects the way the Flash graphic is displayed to the end user. The default tools and their corresponding button and shortcut are described in Figure 1-8.

Some tools have modifiers that change the way a specific tool functions. The modifiers appear at the bottom of the Tools panel when the tool is selected. For example, when you select the Zoom tool, the Enlarge and Reduce modifier buttons appear so you can choose whether the Zoom tool magnifies or shrinks the view of the Stage.

Figure 1-8   **Tools panel**

Tool Name	Button	Shortcut Key	Function
Selection	↖	V	Selects objects in the Document window; you must select an object to modify it
Subselection	↖	A	Modifies specific anchor points in a line or curve
Free Transform	▦	Q	Moves, scales, rotates, skews, or distorts objects
3D Rotation	◐	W	Rotates movie clips in three-dimensional space
Lasso	◯	L	Selects individual objects or a group of objects
Pen	✒	P	Draws lines or curves by creating anchor points that connect them; clicking draws points for straight lines; clicking and dragging draws points for smooth, curved lines
Text	T	T	Creates and edits text
Line	╲	N	Draws straight lines (strokes) of varying lengths, widths, and colors
Rectangle	▭	R	Draws rectangles of different sizes and colors
Pencil	✎	Y	Draws lines and shapes in a free-form mode
Brush	🖌	B	Paints fills with brush strokes
Deco	🎨	U	Applies a pattern, such as a grid or vine fill, to an area or fill
Bone	🦴	M	Links objects so that animations applied to one object also affect the linked objects
Paint Bucket	🪣	K	Fills enclosed areas of a drawing with color
Eyedropper	💧	I	Picks up styles of existing lines, fills, and text and applies them to other objects
Eraser	▱	E	Erases lines and fills
Hand	✋	H	Moves the view of the Stage and pasteboard
Zoom	🔍	Z	Enlarges or reduces the view of the Stage and pasteboard
Stroke Color control	▪		Sets the stroke color from the color palette
Fill Color control	▫		Sets the fill color from the color palette
Black and white button	▪		Sets the stroke color to black and the fill color to white
Swap colors button	⇄		Swaps the current stroke and fill colors

INSIGHT

Using the Tools Panel Effectively

As you create documents in Flash, you will frequently use the tools in the Tools panel. Always double-check at which tool is selected before you click an object on the Stage to ensure that you will be making the changes you intend. The pointer changes to reflect the function of the tool that is currently selected, providing a visual cue or reminder of which tool is active. For example, when the Zoom tool is selected, the pointer shape is a magnifying glass. A good practice to prevent unintended changes is to click the Selection tool after you use any of the other tools in the Tools Panel.

You'll use some of the tools in the Tools panel to modify the spacewalkNew.fla document.

To use the Tools panel to modify the spacewalkNew.fla document:

1. On the Application bar, click **Control**, and then click **Rewind**. Frame 1 is again the current frame.

2. In the Tools panel, click the **Selection** tool ▶ to select it, if necessary.

3. In the pasteboard to the lower-left of the Stage, click the star. The star is selected and the path of the star's animation is displayed. See Figure 1-9.

| Figure 1-9 | Star selected in the pasteboard |

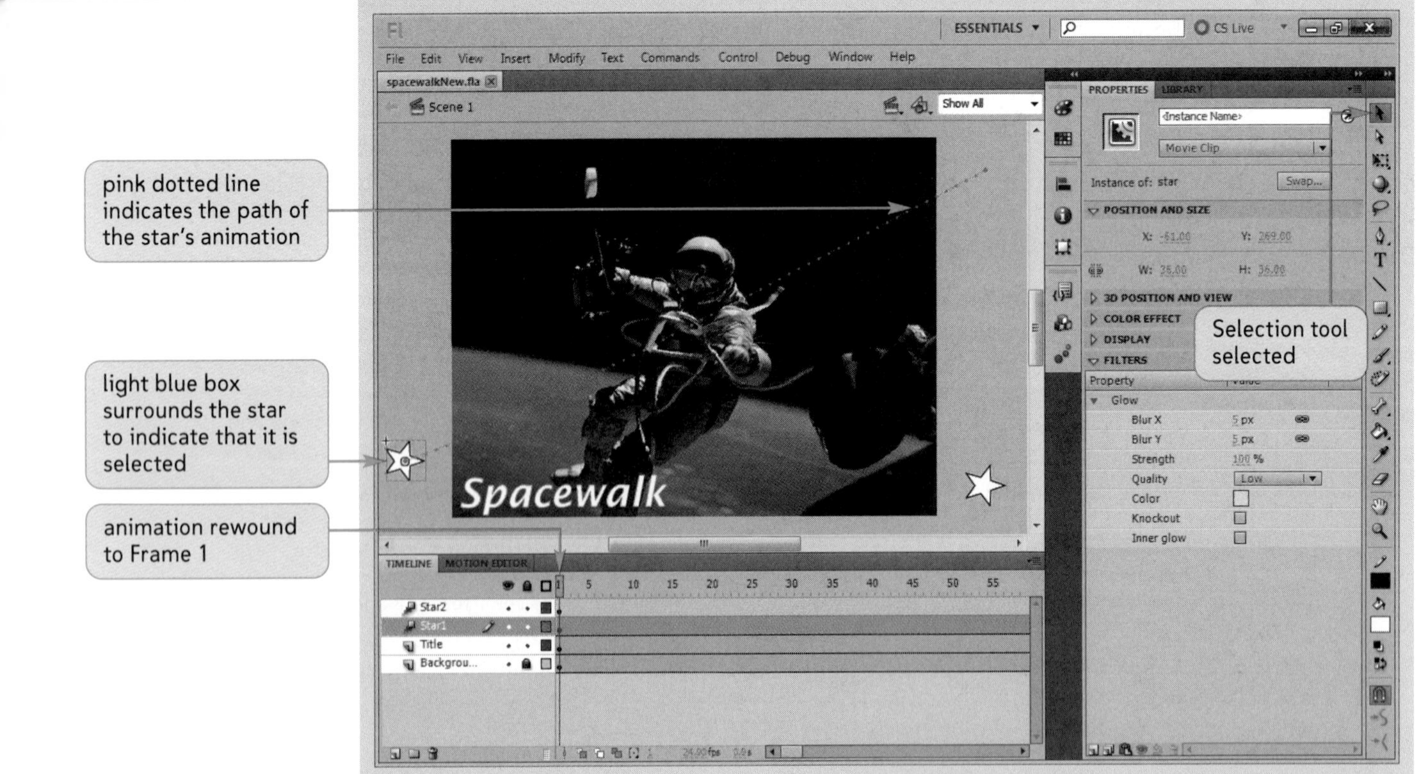

pink dotted line indicates the path of the star's animation

light blue box surrounds the star to indicate that it is selected

animation rewound to Frame 1

Trouble? If the rest of the document fades, you probably double-clicked the star and entered a different editing mode. On the Edit bar, click the Scene 1 link.

4. Drag the selected star up toward the top of the pasteboard just to the left of the Stage. This new location is now the starting point for the star animation. The star's animation path is modified based on the animation's starting point. See Figure 1-10.

| Figure 1-10 | Star's new animation path |

selected star in new location on the pasteboard

star's animation path shifts to reflect the new starting point

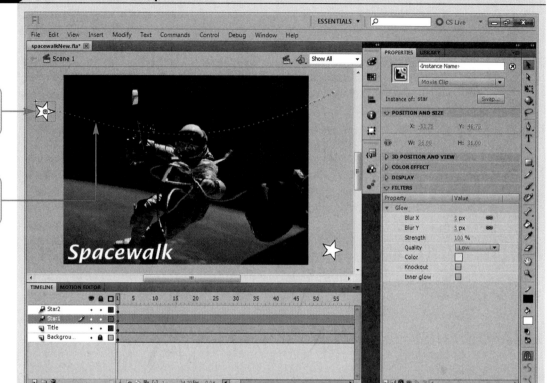

5. On the Application bar, click **Control**, and then click **Play**. As the animation plays, you can see how the star's path changed based on the different starting point.

Panels

Flash puts most of the controls you need into panels that are available as you work. Flash includes panels for aligning objects, transforming objects, and mixing and selecting colors. The Window menu lists all of the available panels. Any panel with a check mark next to its name appears in the workspace.

You can organize the panels according to your preference. You can close a panel you don't use often, reposition panels to better fit how you work, and minimize or collapse panels to icons to minimize the space they occupy in the workspace. You can also move a panel into another dock or panel group or create a free-floating panel by moving it onto the workspace.

You work with panel groups in much the same way. You can close, reposition, minimize, or collapse a panel group. You can move a panel group to a new location in a dock or create a free-floating panel group. You can also stack free-floating panels as one unit. A minimized panel group has only its panel tabs visible. In a collapsed panel group, each panel appears in the dock as a button, which you click to expand or collapse that panel.

Commonly used panels can be accessed using the docked panel bar on the workspace. You click a panel's icon to open the panel, and then you click the icon again or the Stage to close the panel.

REFERENCE

Organizing Panels and Panel Groups

- To display or hide a panel, on the Application bar, click Window, and then click the panel name.
- To move a panel, drag and drop its tab into another dock or panel group or the workspace.
- To collapse or expand a panel group, click its title bar.
- To move a panel group, drag its title bar to another location in a dock or in the workspace.
- To minimize or maximize a dock, click the Collapse to Icons button or Expand Panels button in the upper-right corner of the dock.
- To select a preset panel arrangement, on the Application bar, click the workspace switcher button, and then click a preset workspace.

You will work with the panels in the spacewalkNew.fla document.

To collapse, expand, and reposition panels:

▶ 1. Click the **LIBRARY** panel tab. The Library panel moves to the front of the panel group. See Figure 1-11.

| Figure 1-11 | Library panel |

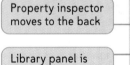

Property inspector moves to the back

Library panel is the active tab

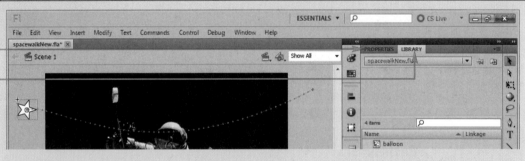

▶ 2. On the Application bar, click **Window**, and then click **Movie Explorer**. The Movie Explorer panel opens as a free-floating panel.

▶ 3. Drag the **LIBRARY** panel tab to the Movie Explorer panel title bar and drop the panel when the blue highlighted line appears around the Movie Explorer panel. The Movie Explorer panel and the Library panel are now grouped as a free-floating panel group. See Figure 1-12.

Figure 1-12   **Free-floating panel group**

Movie Explorer panel opened in a free-floating panel

Library panel moved into the panel group

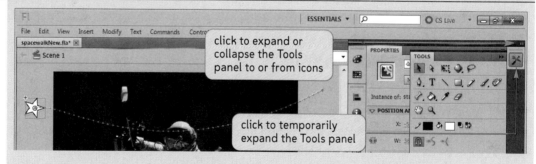

4. In the upper-right corner of the dock above the Tools panel, click the **Collapse to Icons** button ⏩. The Tools panel collapses to icons. Panels collapsed to icons minimize the amount of occupied space.

5. In the dock, click the **Tools** button ✂. The Tools panel expands temporarily so that you can select a tool. See Figure 1-13.

Figure 1-13   **Tools panel expanded**

click to expand or collapse the Tools panel to or from icons

click to temporarily expand the Tools panel

6. In the dock, click the **Tools** button ✂ again. The panel collapses to an icon.

7. On the Application bar, click the **workspace switcher** button (labeled ESSENTIALS), and then click **Designer**. The panels are docked along the right and left sides of the workspace with the Timeline and Document window at the center. See Figure 1-14.

TIP

After you customize the panels, you can save the workspace layout to quickly rearrange the panels to that layout.

Figure 1-14   **Workspace in the Designer layout**

Timeline

Tools panel

Property inspector

click to select a workspace layout

pasteboard and Stage

panels

▶ **8.** On the Application bar, click the **workspace switcher** button (labeled DESIGNER), and then click **Essentials**. The panels return to their previous layout.

▶ **9.** On the Application bar, click the **workspace switcher** button (labeled ESSENTIALS), and then click **Reset 'Essentials'**. The panels are arranged in the default Essentials layout.

Property Inspector

The contents of the Property inspector change to reflect the selected tool. When you click the Selection tool in the Tools panel, the Property inspector displays information about the document such as its Publish settings, the background color, or the frame rate. When you select an object on the Stage, such as the star, the Property inspector displays properties specific to that object, such as the object's name, its horizontal and vertical location on the Stage, and its width and height.

You'll use the Property inspector to view the star's properties.

To view information about the star in the Property inspector:

▶ **1.** On the Application bar, click **Control**, and then click **Rewind**. Frame 1 is the current frame.

Be sure to select the Selection tool so you don't make unintended changes to the object.

2. In the Tools panel, click the **Selection** tool , if necessary. The Property inspector displays information about the spacewalkNew.fla document. See Figure 1-15.

| Figure 1-15 | Property inspector for the Selection tool |

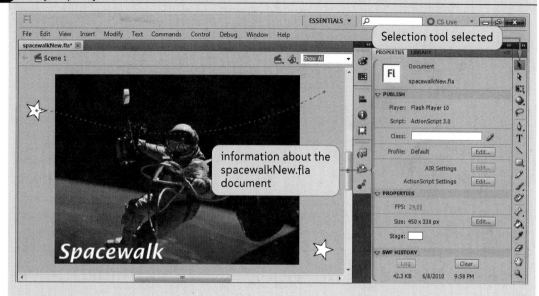

3. In the pasteboard, click the star located to the left of the Stage. The star is selected, and information about the star appears in the Property inspector.

You can also use the Property inspector to reposition the star as well as change its dimensions. The values of the X and Y coordinates in the Property inspector represent the horizontal (X) and vertical (Y) positions of the star relative to the upper-left corner of the Stage. The W and H values represent the star's width and height dimensions.

To use the Property inspector to change the star's position and dimensions:

TIP

If only the section names are visible in the Property inspector, you need to expand the sections. Click the section name to expand a collapsed section or collapse an expanded section.

1. In the Position and Size section of the Property inspector, click the **X** value to select it, type **50**, and then press the **Enter** key. The star is repositioned horizontally.

2. In the Position and Size section of the Property inspector, click the **Y** value to select it, type **200**, and then press the **Enter** key. The star is repositioned vertically. See Figure 1-16.

Figure 1-16   Star repositioned on the Stage

3. In the Position and Size section of the Property inspector, click the **Lock width and height values together** icon ⬚, if necessary, to change it to locked ⬚.

4. In the Position and Size section of the Property inspector, point to the H value. The pointer changes to 🖑.

5. Drag the hand pointer to the left to change the height value to 15.0. The width (W) value adjusts proportionally to the new height value and the star gets smaller. See Figure 1-17.

Figure 1-17   Hand pointer used to set object's size

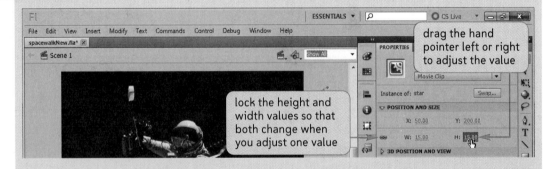

6. On the Application bar, click **Control**, and then click **Go To End**. Frame 60 is now the current frame.

7. Click the star located to the right of the Stage to select it.

8. In the Position and Size section of the Property inspector, point to the W value, and then drag the hand pointer to the right to change the width value to 60. The H (height) value adjusts proportionally to the new width value and the star gets bigger.

Trouble? If the Position and Size section of the Property inspector is not shown, you might have selected the animation's path instead of the star. Click the star again to select it and repeat Step 8.

▶ **9.** On the Application bar, click **Control**, and then click **Play**. The animation plays and you can see the effect of the changes you made to the star's properties.

During the animation, the star starts in its new position and moves to its end position as before. The star gradually changes dimensions. Because you changed the dimensions of the star only in Frame 1 and Frame 60, Flash adjusted the rest of the frames to change the star to its larger dimensions in the final frame.

You are done with the spacewalkNew.fla file. You will save and then close it.

To save and close the spacewalkNew.fla file:

▶ **1.** On the Application bar, click **File**, and then click **Save**. The changes you made to the spacewalkNew.fla file are saved.

▶ **2.** On the Application bar, click **File**, and then click **Close**. The file closes and the Welcome screen appears.

So far, you have learned about Web media and viewed sample Flash documents. You also learned about the main components of the Flash workspace and how to work with panels. In the next session, you will change the view of the Stage, learn how graphic objects drawn in Flash interact and how to select and group objects.

REVIEW

Session 1.1 Quick Check

1. What are the two basic types of graphics?
2. How does a bitmap graphic store image data?
3. Vector graphics store information as a set of _____ instructions that describes the color, outline, and position of all the shapes of the image.
4. What type of graphic becomes distorted when enlarged?
5. What is animation?
6. True or False. A completed Flash document can include anything from silent, still imagery to motion graphics with sound and interactivity as well as elements that incorporate video.
7. While developing content in Flash, what is the file extension of the Flash authoring file?
8. Where do you position the objects that will appear in the document?
9. Which panel changes to display different options depending on the tool or object selected?

SESSION 1.2 VISUAL OVERVIEW

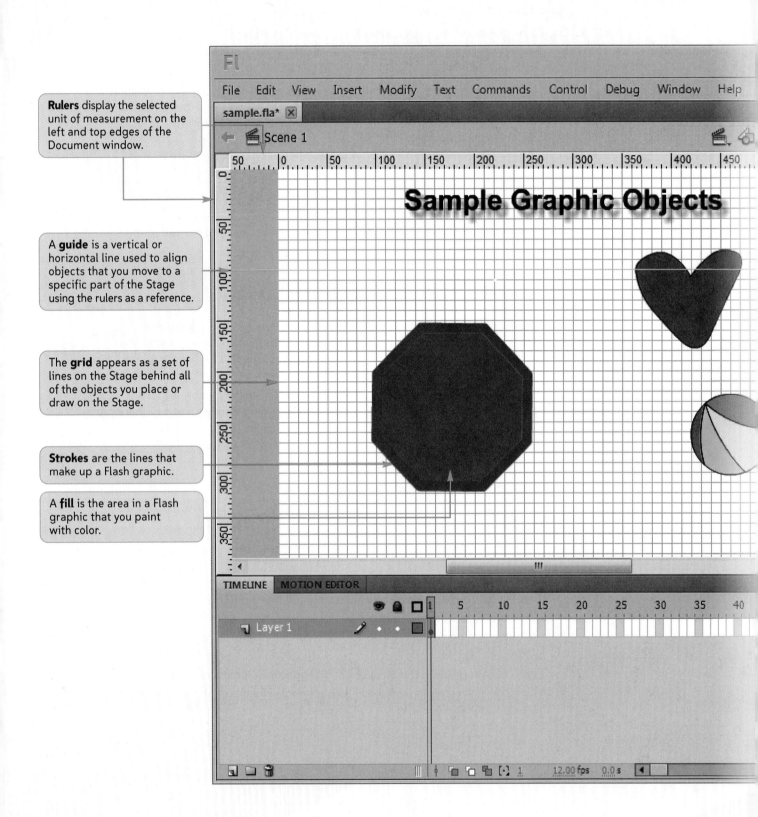

Rulers display the selected unit of measurement on the left and top edges of the Document window.

A **guide** is a vertical or horizontal line used to align objects that you move to a specific part of the Stage using the rulers as a reference.

The **grid** appears as a set of lines on the Stage behind all of the objects you place or draw on the Stage.

Strokes are the lines that make up a Flash graphic.

A **fill** is the area in a Flash graphic that you paint with color.

Sample Graphic Objects

GRAPHIC OBJECTS AND COLORS

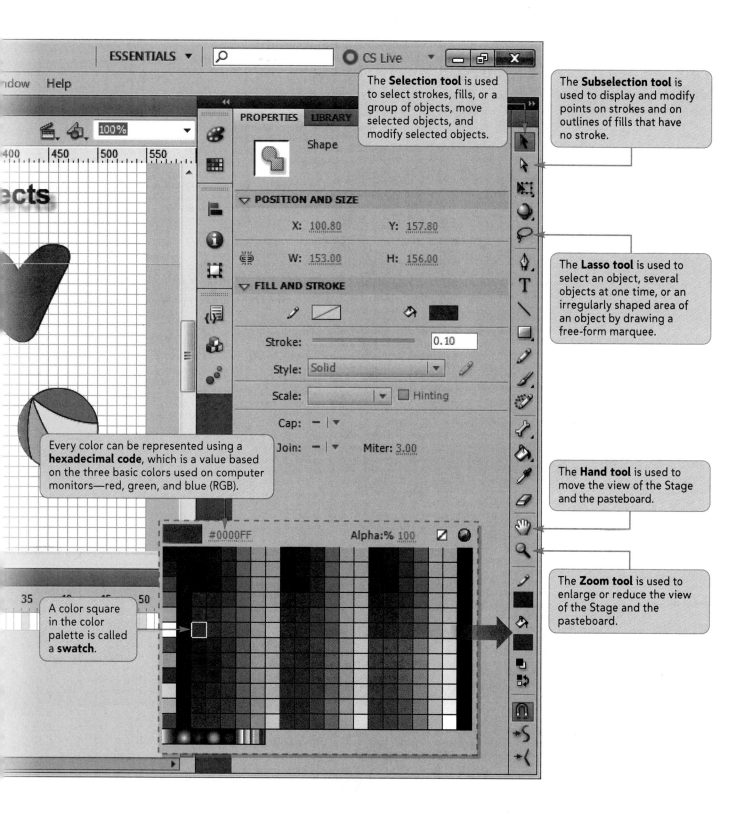

The **Selection tool** is used to select strokes, fills, or a group of objects, move selected objects, and modify selected objects.

The **Subselection tool** is used to display and modify points on strokes and on outlines of fills that have no stroke.

The **Lasso tool** is used to select an object, several objects at one time, or an irregularly shaped area of an object by drawing a free-form marquee.

Every color can be represented using a **hexadecimal code**, which is a value based on the three basic colors used on computer monitors—red, green, and blue (RGB).

The **Hand tool** is used to move the view of the Stage and the pasteboard.

The **Zoom tool** is used to enlarge or reduce the view of the Stage and the pasteboard.

A color square in the color palette is called a **swatch**.

Changing the View of the Stage

As you develop graphics on the Stage, you will need to change the view of the Stage. You can adjust the magnification level and move different parts of the Stage into view. You can also display the grid, rulers, and guides to assist you as you draw or align graphics, and you can change a document's properties.

Magnifying and Moving the Stage

The Zoom tool adjusts the magnification level of the Stage and pasteboard. The Zoom tool includes the Enlarge and Reduce modifiers, which set the Zoom tool to increase and decrease the magnification level, respectively. You can click the Zoom tool on the part of the Stage or pasteboard you want to enlarge or reduce. You can also select an area by dragging the pointer over an area of the Stage to draw a marquee around it. A **marquee** is an outline that encloses an area to be selected.

Another way to adjust the magnification level is with the View menu. It has commands to zoom in and out, set the magnification to a specific percentage level, fit the Stage to fill the Document window, show all the contents of the current frame (Stage and pasteboard), and show frame to make the entire Stage visible. A quick way to select these magnification settings is with the Zoom control on the Edit bar.

REFERENCE

Changing the View of the Stage

- In the Tools panel, click the Zoom tool.
- In the Tools panel, click the Enlarge or Reduce modifier.
- Click a part of the Stage (or drag the pointer to draw a marquee around the part of the Stage to enlarge or reduce).

or

- On the Application bar, click View, and then click the appropriate command (or on the Edit bar, click the Zoom control, and then click the appropriate command).

or

- In the Tools panel, double-click the Hand tool.

You'll try various ways to change the view of the Stage. You will use a document that contains objects Aly has drawn in Flash.

TIP

You can also click the Open button on the Welcome screen to open the Open dialog box.

To open the sample.fla document and change the magnification:

1. On the Application bar, click **File**, and then click **Open**. The Open dialog box opens.

2. Navigate to the **Flash1\Tutorial** folder included with your Data Files if necessary, click **sample.fla** in the file list, and then click the **Open** button. The sample document opens in the workspace.

3. On the Application bar, click **File**, and then click **Save As**. The Save As dialog box opens.

4. Navigate to the **Flash1\Tutorial** folder included with your Data Files, type **mySample** in the File name box, and then click the **Save** button. The document saves with the new name. You do not need to type the .fla extension when saving a document; Flash enters the file extension for you.

5. On the Timeline's title bar, click the **panel menu** button ▼≡, and then click **Close Group**. The Timeline panel group closes.

6. On the Edit bar, click the **Zoom control arrow**, and then click **50%**. The view of the Stage changes.

7. In the Tools panel, click the **Zoom** tool 🔍, and then, if necessary, click the **Enlarge** modifier button. The pointer changes to and will magnify any object you click.

8. On the Stage, click the middle of the fish object twice. The magnification level increases each time you click. The fish is centered in the Document window each time you click it. See Figure 1-18.

Figure 1-18 **Magnified fish shape**

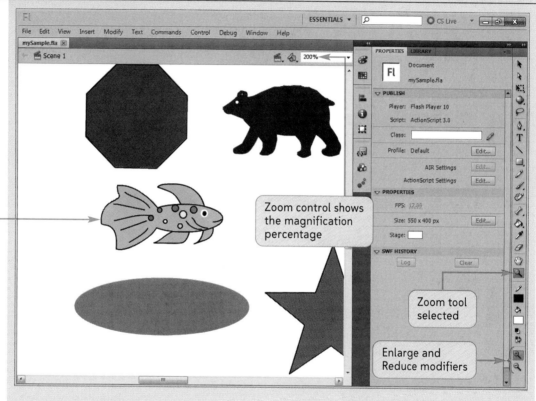

fish shape enlarged and centered in the Document window

Zoom control shows the magnification percentage

Zoom tool selected

Enlarge and Reduce modifiers

After you magnify the view of the Stage, some graphic objects shift out of sight. You can move the Stage without changing the magnification level by using the Hand tool to drag the part of the Stage you want to see into view. You'll shift the beach ball graphic into view.

To use the Hand tool to view the beach ball graphic on the Stage:

1. In the Tools panel, click the **Hand** tool. The pointer changes to as you move it over the Stage.

2. Drag the Stage to the left until you see the beach ball in the middle of the Document window. See Figure 1-19.

Figure 1-19   Stage view shifted

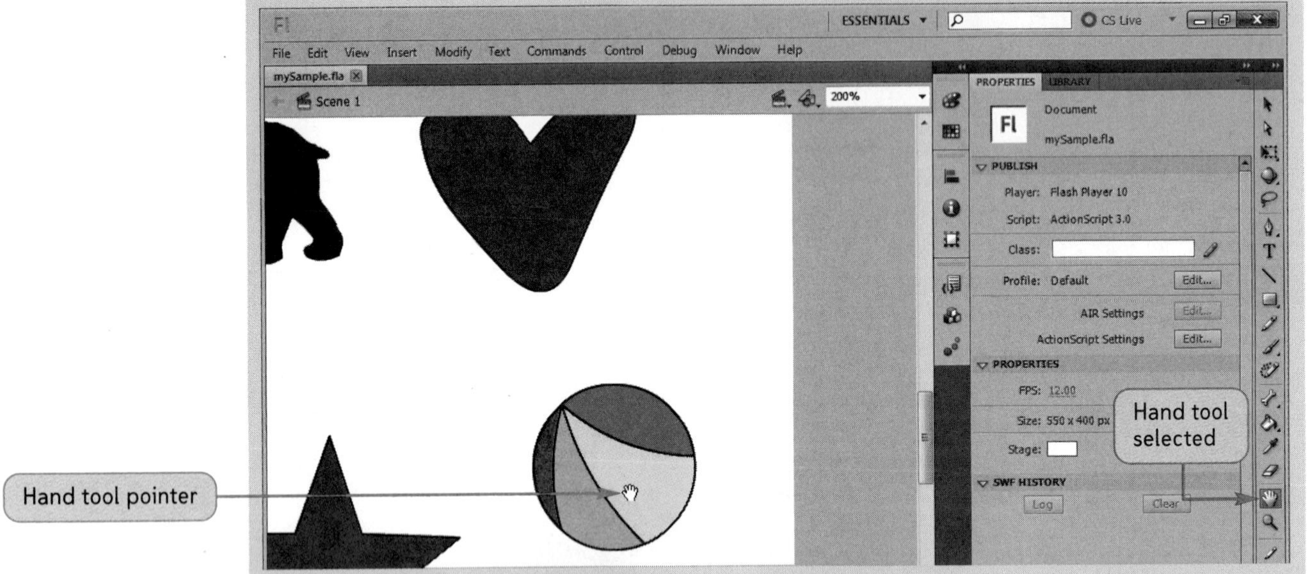

Hand tool pointer

Hand tool selected

> 3. In the Tools panel, click the **Zoom** tool 🔍, and then click the **Reduce** modifier button 🔍. The pointer changes to 🔍.

> 4. Click the center of the beach ball, and then click the center of the bear. The magnification level of the Stage reduces each time you click.

> 5. In the Tools panel, double-click the **Hand** tool 🖑. The magnification level of the Stage is enlarged to show all of its contents centered in the Document window.

Displaying the Grid, Rulers, and Guides

The Stage includes grids, rulers, and guides, which help position objects as you create documents. You can lay out objects on the Stage more precisely if you display the grid. The grid is not part of the document. It is only visible as you develop the document. You can customize the grid from the Grid dialog box. For example, you can select a color for the grid that is different from the document's background color to make the grid easier to see, and you can change the spacing between the lines. You can also select the Snap to grid option to make objects attach to the grid as you move or draw them on the Stage. Snapping enables you to more accurately align objects vertically or horizontally. Changes you make to the grid are saved with the currently active document.

You will display the grid in the mySample.fla document.

To display and edit the grid for the mySample.fla document:

> 1. On the Application bar, click **View**, point to **Grid**, and then click **Show Grid**. A check mark appears next to the command and the grid is displayed on the Stage. See Figure 1-20.

| Figure 1-20 | Grid displayed on the Stage |

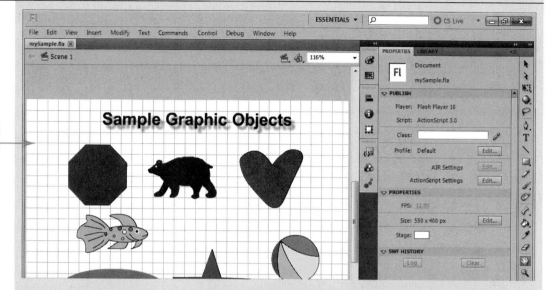

grid appears on the Stage behind the objects

2. On the Application bar, click **View**, point to **Grid**, and then click **Edit Grid**. The Grid dialog box opens so you can modify how the grid appears on the Stage. See Figure 1-21.

| Figure 1-21 | Grid dialog box |

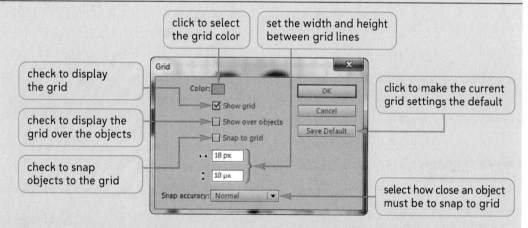

click to select the grid color

set the width and height between grid lines

check to display the grid

click to make the current grid settings the default

check to display the grid over the objects

check to snap objects to the grid

select how close an object must be to snap to grid

3. Click the **Color** control. The color palette opens and the pointer changes to ✎.

4. Click the **black** color swatch in the first column, first row of the color palette. The grid changes to black.

5. Click the **Snap to grid** check box to insert a check mark. Objects will now snap to, or align with, the nearest grid line when you move or draw them.

6. Click the **OK** button. The Grid dialog box closes, and the grid reflects the settings you selected.

INSIGHT

Measuring in Pixels

You can use various units of measurement in Flash, including inches, points, and centimeters. Because most elements in Web pages are measured in pixels, you should also use pixels to express the width and height values of Web graphics. A pixel, short for picture element, is the Flash default unit of measurement. Pixels represent the smallest picture element on the monitor that can be controlled by the computer. Each pixel is composed of three colors, red, green, and blue.

As you develop graphics, you might want to display rulers. Rulers are helpful in placing objects on the Stage according to specific coordinates. The unit of measurement indicated on the rulers, such as pixels, is specified in the Document Settings dialog box.

When the rulers are displayed, you can create vertical or horizontal guides. To create a guide, click a ruler and drag a line onto the Stage. If you drag from the top ruler, a horizontal guide is created. If you drag from the left ruler, a vertical guide is created. You can edit the guides to change their color to make them easier to see against the background, snap objects to them, and lock them into place. Guides, like the grid, are visible only while you are working with the document. Guides can be created whether or not the grid is displayed.

You will create guides in the mySample.fla document. You need to display the rulers first.

To display the rulers and create guides in the mySample.fla document:

1. On the Application bar, click **View**, and then click **Rulers**. The rulers appear along the left and top sides of the pasteboard.

2. In the Tools panel, click the **Selection** tool to select it.

3. At the top of the pasteboard, click the **horizontal ruler**. The pointer changes to.

4. Drag the pointer down to approximately 105 pixels on the vertical ruler. The horizontal guide you created snaps to the closest grid line. See Figure 1-22.

Figure 1-22	Horizontal guide

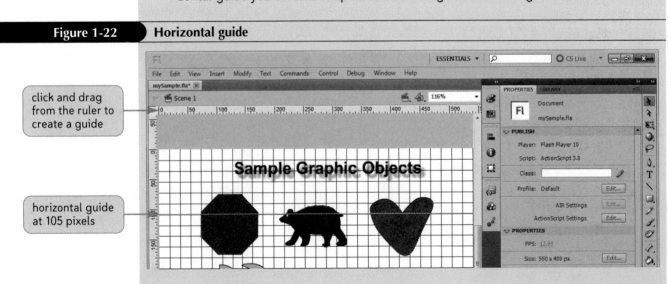

click and drag from the ruler to create a guide

horizontal guide at 105 pixels

5. Click the vertical ruler and drag the pointer to the right to approximately 105 pixels on the horizontal ruler. The vertical guide you created snaps to the closest grid line.

6. On the Application bar, click **View**, point to **Guides**, and then click **Edit Guides**. The Guides dialog box opens, so you can modify the guides, such as by changing the guide color. See Figure 1-23.

Figure 1-23   Guides dialog box

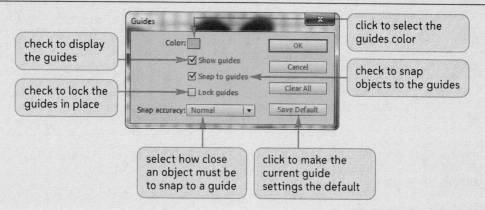

check to display the guides

check to lock the guides in place

click to select the guides color

check to snap objects to the guides

select how close an object must be to snap to a guide

click to make the current guide settings the default

7. Click the **Color** control. The color palette opens and the pointer changes to ⬧.

8. Click the **red** color swatch located in the first column, seventh row of the color palette. The guide changes to red.

9. Click the **OK** button. The Guides dialog box closes.

Changing the Document Settings

Every document in Flash has certain properties such as title, description, Stage size, background color, frame rate, and ruler unit. Title and description are embedded within the SWF file and can be used by search engines to categorize Flash content on the Web. The other document settings are set at default values when you open a new document. For example, by default, the Stage size is 550 pixels wide by 400 pixels high, the Stage background color is white, the frame rate is 12 frames per second, and the ruler units is pixels. (The frame rate specifies how many frames in an animation are displayed in one second.) You change these default properties in the Document Settings dialog box. Changes you make in the dialog box are reflected on the Stage.

Aly wants you to modify the mySample.fla document's settings by changing its background color. The dimensions, frame rate, and ruler units are fine with the defaults.

To change the mySample.fla document's background color:

1. On the Application bar, click **Modify**, and then click **Document**. The Document Settings dialog box opens. See Figure 1-24.

Figure 1-24   Document Settings dialog box

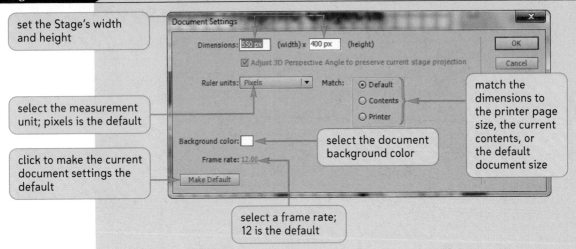

set the Stage's width and height

select the measurement unit; pixels is the default

click to make the current document settings the default

match the dimensions to the printer page size, the current contents, or the default document size

select the document background color

select a frame rate; 12 is the default

TIP

You can also open the Document Settings dialog box by clicking the Edit button in the Property inspector.

2. Click the **Background color** control. The color palette opens and the pointer changes to 🖉.

3. Click the **gray** color swatch located in the first swatches column, third row of the color palette.

4. Click the **OK** button. The dialog box closes, and the Stage has a gray background color.

5. Click the pasteboard, if necessary, to display the document settings in the Property inspector. You can also change the document's background color in the Property inspector.

6. In the Property inspector, click the **Background color** control, and then click the **white** color swatch located in the first column, sixth row of the color palette. The Stage returns to a white background.

7. On the Application bar, click **File**, and then click **Save**. The changes you made to the document are saved.

You no longer need the rulers, grid, or guides. You'll hide them for now. Hiding the guides removes them from view but they will appear in the same place when you show the guides again. Clearing the guides deletes any guides that are on the Stage.

To hide the rulers, grid, and guides:

1. On the Application bar, click **View**, and then click **Rulers** to hide the rulers.

2. On the Application bar, click **View**, point to **Grid**, and then click **Show Grid** to hide the grid.

3. On the Application bar, click **View**, point to **Guides**, and then click **Show Guides** to hide the guides.

Working with Objects in Flash

The drawing and painting tools available in the Tools panel include the Line, Pen, Pencil, Oval, Rectangle, Brush, and Deco. These tools allow you to create the lines, shapes, and patterns that make up the images in a Flash document. Before using these tools, it's important to understand how the objects you draw behave and how you can change their basic characteristics, such as their color. In particular, you need to be aware of how shapes or lines you draw interact with existing shapes or lines.

Creating Strokes and Fills

When drawing objects in Flash, you create strokes and fills. Strokes can be straight or curved. They can be individual line segments or they can be connected together to form shapes. The Flash drawing tools provide a great deal of flexibility so you can draw almost any type of line you need. Fills can be enclosed by strokes.

Before you draw a shape, such as an oval or a rectangle, you can specify whether you want the shape to have a stroke, a fill, or both, as shown in Figure 1-25. For example, you can draw a circle that has both a fill and a stroke. You can draw a circle that has a fill but has no stroke. Or, you can draw a circle with a stroke but no fill.

Figure 1-25 **Sample shapes with fills and strokes**

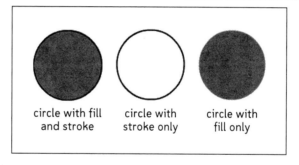

circle with fill and stroke   circle with stroke only   circle with fill only

Drawing and Grouping Objects

Flash provides two modes for how objects created with the drawing tools such as the Pencil, Line, Oval, and Rectangle tools interact: the Merge Drawing mode and the Object Drawing mode. By default, Flash uses the Merge Drawing mode. The drawing mode you use depends on how you want the objects to interact.

With the **Merge Drawing mode**, objects drawn or moved on top of other objects merge with or segment the existing objects. (Objects on the same layer are not considered to be on top of or below one another.) For example, when you draw a line through an existing shape such as a circle, the line is split into line segments at the points where it intersects the circle. The circle is also split into separate shapes. These line segments and split shapes can be moved individually. If you draw or move a fill on top of another fill of the same color, the two fills merge and become one shape. If you draw a fill of one color on top of another fill of a different color, the new fill cuts away the existing fill.

With the **Object Drawing mode**, the drawn shapes are treated as separate objects and do not merge with or alter other objects on the same layer. When you draw an object using the Object Drawing mode, a blue outline appears around the object on the Stage. Figure 1-26 shows how drawn objects interact in each mode.

Figure 1-26   **Comparison of the drawing modes**

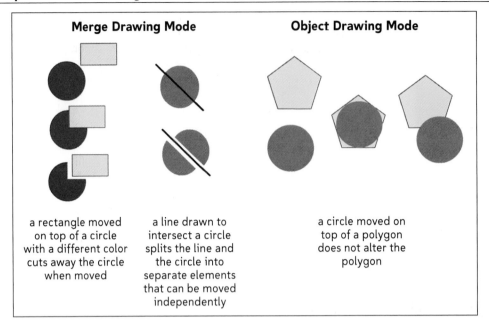

To prevent objects drawn in the Merge Drawing mode from impacting each other, you can **group** them, which treats two or more elements such as a stroke and a fill as one entity. A thin blue rectangle outlines the grouped object when it is selected. Grouped objects are on top of non-grouped objects so they do not alter or merge with other objects. To modify a grouped object, you must enter group-editing mode. You can then edit the individual objects within the group. When editing the objects within a group, the rest of the objects on the Stage are dimmed, indicating they are not accessible, as shown in Figure 1-27. After you finish modifying the individual objects, you exit group-editing mode.

Figure 1-27   **Grouped object in group-editing mode**

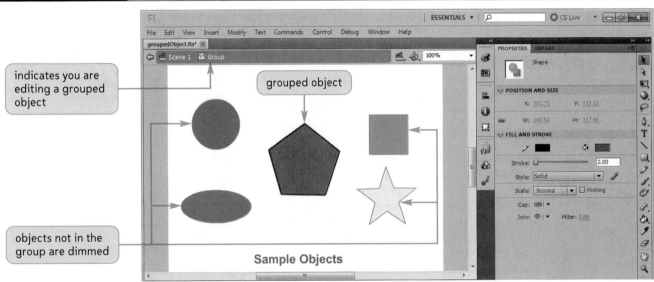

PROSKILLS

Problem Solving: Grouping Fills and Strokes

Objects created in Flash can become quite complex, involving multiple strokes and fills. After you finish creating an object, it is easy to inadvertently shift a line or fill. This problem is especially prevalent when you want to move or resize the object. You must be sure to select all the strokes and fills that make up that object. One way to avoid the problem of accidentally changing one part of the object is by grouping the strokes and fills together. When grouped, you can easily resize or move a complex object at any time without having to modify or select the strokes and fills within the object individually.

You'll group the objects that make up the fish in the mySample.fla document.

To group the fish in the mySample.fla document:

1. In the Tools panel, click the **Selection** tool ▶, if necessary.

2. Draw a marquee around the fish graphic. The fills and strokes that make up the graphic are selected and a dotted pattern appears on the fish.

3. On the Application bar, click **Modify**, and then click **Group**. A blue rectangle appears around the fish, indicating it is a grouped object. See Figure 1-28.

Figure 1-28 **Grouped strokes and fills**

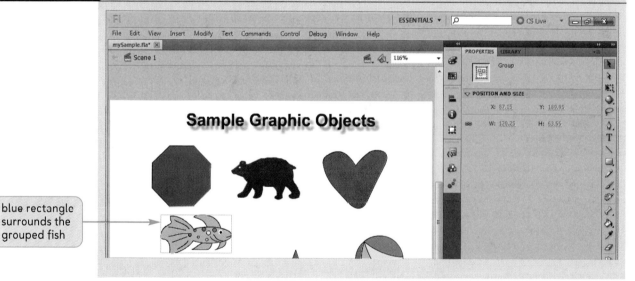

blue rectangle surrounds the grouped fish

Using the Color Controls and the Color Panel

All strokes and fills can be drawn with different colors. You can specify the colors before you draw strokes and fills or you can change the colors of existing strokes and fills. The simplest way to change the color of a stroke or fill is by using the Stroke color or Fill Color control in the Tools panel. Each of these controls opens a color palette from which you can select a particular color. By default, the color swatches in the color palette are the 216 **Web-safe colors**. These colors were developed to display the same on both Internet Explorer and Netscape Navigator browsers as well as on both Windows and Macintosh operating systems. Today's computer monitors can display many more than the 216 Web-safe colors, so most graphic programs still use the Web-safe colors but aren't limited to only those 216 colors.

Using Hexadecimal Codes

Every color has its own hexadecimal code. The hexadecimal code (such as #00FF00 for green) is based on the three basic colors used on computer monitors: red, green, and blue, referred to as RGB. The first two digits represent the amount of red, the next two digits represent the amount of green, and the last two digits represent the amount of blue. Values for each two-digit pair range from 00 to FF, which are numbers based on the hexadecimal numbering system. These three color values combine to form the color. If you know the hexadecimal code for the color you want to use, you can enter its value in the box above the color swatches in the color palette.

You can also select colors using the Property inspector. When a stroke or fill tool is selected in the Tools panel or an existing stroke or fill is selected on the Stage, its color controls appear in the Property inspector. These controls work the same way as the Stroke Color and Fill Color controls in the Tools panel.

Finally, you can select colors using the Color panel. In this panel, you can use the panel's color controls to open the color palette, you can enter a color's hexadecimal value, or you can create custom colors.

You'll change the color of the strokes in the fish.

To change the stroke color for the grouped fish object:

1. Double-click the fish graphic. The contents on the Stage are dimmed except for the fish, indicating you are in group-editing mode.

2. Draw a marquee around the fish graphic to select it, if necessary. The strokes and fills of the fish are selected.

3. In the Property inspector, click the **Stroke Color** control to open the color palette, and then point to the **red** color swatch located in the first column, seventh row of the color palette. See Figure 1-29.

Figure 1-29   Stroke Color control in the Property inspector

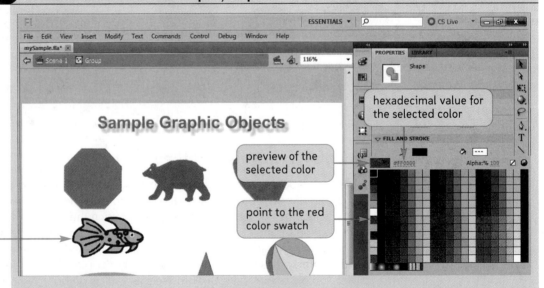

strokes and fills are selected

hexadecimal value for the selected color

preview of the selected color

point to the red color swatch

4. Click the **red** color swatch. The strokes on the fish are red. See Figure 1-30.

Figure 1-30 Fish stroke color changed

click to exit group-editing mode

other objects are dimmed

stroke of fish is red

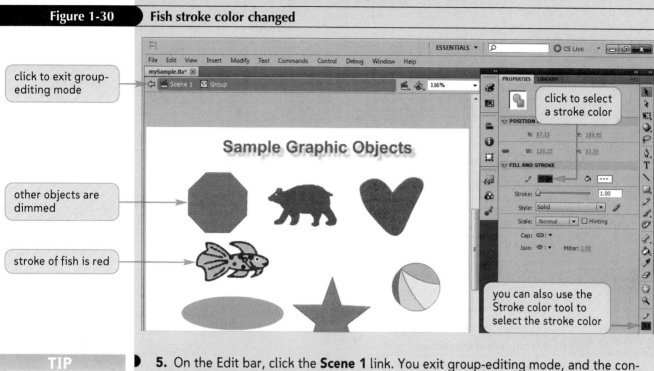

5. On the Edit bar, click the **Scene 1** link. You exit group-editing mode, and the contents on the Stage are no longer dimmed.

Selecting Objects

Before you can change the characteristics of a graphic object on the Stage, you must select the object. You can use the Selection, Subselection, and Lasso tools in the Tools panel to select part of an object, the entire object, or several objects at one time. You'll use these tools, especially the Selection tool, frequently as you create graphics.

Selection Tool

With the Selection tool, you select an object by clicking it and you select an object's stroke and fill by double-clicking or by dragging the pointer to draw a marquee around the object, which is also useful for selecting more than one object at a time. When you select a graphic object, a dot pattern covers it to indicate the object is selected. Some selected objects, such as text blocks, have a rectangular outline instead of a dot pattern. You can move a selected object to a new position by dragging it with the Selection tool. To change an object's shape with the Selection tool, deselect the object, move the pointer to one of the object's edges or corners, and then drag to reshape the object. The pointer changes based on the object you are modifying. If you move the pointer to a corner of a star shape, for example, the pointer changes to ↖, as shown in Figure 1-31.

Figure 1-31   **Selection tool modifying an object**

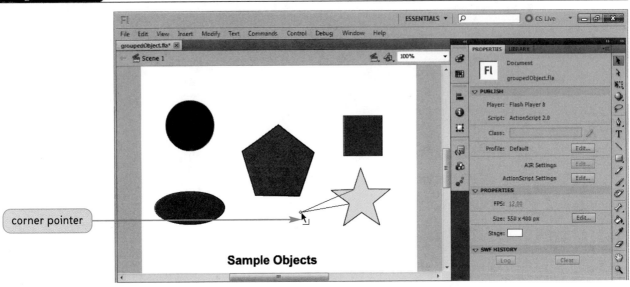

corner pointer

The Selection tool, like many of the tools in the Tools panel, has modifiers that change the way it works. The Selection tool includes the Snap to Objects, Smooth, and Straighten modifiers, which are shown in Figure 1-32.

Figure 1-32   **Selection tool modifiers**

Modifier Icon	Modifier	Description
🧲	Snap to Objects	Snaps selected objects to other objects when they are moved close together
+S	Smooth	Smoothes the selected line or shape outline
+(	Straighten	Straightens the selected line or shape outline

You will use the Selection tool to select and modify the graphics in Aly's sample document.

To select and modify objects with the Selection tool:

1. In the Tools panel, click the **Zoom** tool 🔍 and then click the **Enlarge** modifier button 🔍.

2. On the Stage, click the purple octagon. The octagon is enlarged and centered in the Document window.

3. In the Tools panel, click the **Selection** tool.

4. Click the center of the purple octagon and drag it to the right just before the bear. The octagon's fill is separated from its stroke and the dot pattern indicates the fill is selected. See Figure 1-33.

Figure 1-33 | **Octagon's fill and stroke separated**

stroke remains in its original location

fill moved to the right and selected

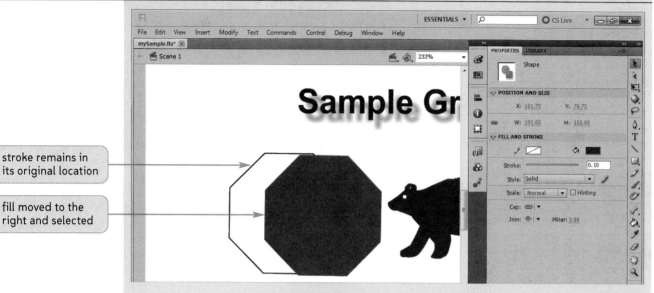

TIP

You can also undo a change by pressing the Ctrl+Z keys.

5. On the Application bar, click **Edit**, and then click **Undo Move**. The octagon's fill moves back to its original location.

6. Click a blank area of the Stage to deselect the octagon's fill.

7. Double-click the purple octagon. Both the fill and stroke of the octagon are selected.

8. Drag the selected octagon to the right. The stroke and the fill move together.

9. Click a blank area of the Stage to deselect the octagon.

Next, you'll use the Selection tool to change the shape of the octagon.

10. Move the pointer over the top stroke of the octagon until the pointer changes to. You'll use the Selection tool to change the shape of the octagon.

11. Drag the stroke of the octagon away from the center of the octagon to change its shape (but do not release the mouse button). See Figure 1-34.

Figure 1-34 | **Octagon's shape being changed**

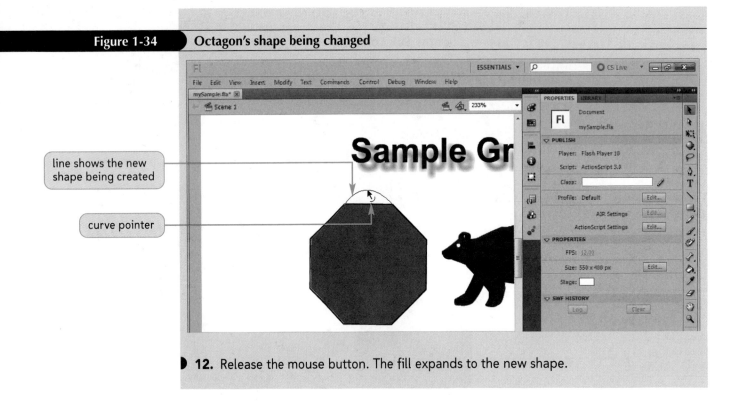

line shows the new shape being created

curve pointer

12. Release the mouse button. The fill expands to the new shape.

Subselection Tool

The Subselection tool is used to display and modify points, referred to as **anchor points**, on strokes and on the outlines of fills that have no stroke. The strokes and fills can then be modified by adjusting these points. If you click and drag an anchor point on a straight line segment, you can change the angle or the length of the line. If you click an anchor point on a curved line, **tangent handles** appear next to the selected point, as shown in Figure 1-35. You can change the curve by dragging the tangent handles.

Figure 1-35 | **Curve's anchor points and tangent handles**

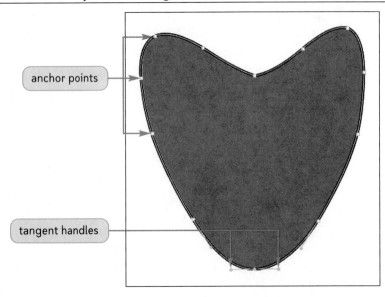

anchor points

tangent handles

REFERENCE

Using the Subselection Tool

- In the Tools panel, click the Subselection tool.
- On the Stage, click an object's stroke or its fill outline to display its anchor points.
- Drag the anchor points or tangent handles to modify the stroke or fill outline.

You'll use the Subselection tool to select and modify objects in the mySample.fla document.

To use the Subselection tool to modify the star and oval:

1. In the Tools panel, click the **Hand** tool to change the pointer to the hand pointer, and then drag the view of the Stage until the star is in the middle of the Document window.
2. In the Tools panel, click the **Subselection** tool. The pointer changes to the subselection pointer. You'll use this tool to display the star's stroke anchor points.
3. On the Stage, click the stroke of the star. A thin blue outline surrounds the star, and square anchor points appear on the star's corners and points.
4. Drag the anchor point in the star's top point away from the center of the star (but do not release the mouse button). See Figure 1-36.

Figure 1-36 Star's shape being changed

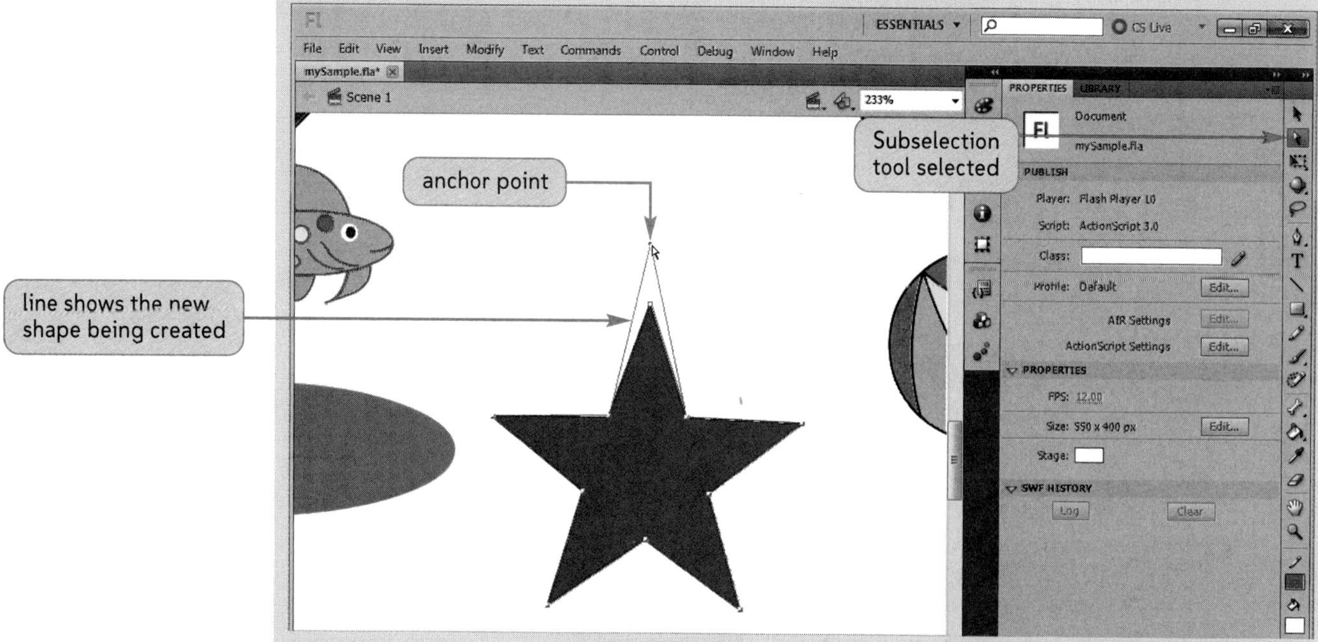

5. Release the mouse button. The star's fill expands to fill the new shape.
6. In the Tools panel, click the **Hand** tool to change the pointer to the hand pointer, and then drag the view of the Stage until the dark green oval is in the middle of the Document window.

▶ **7.** In the Tools panel, click the **Subselection** tool , and then click the oval's out-line. Anchor points appear along the oval's outline.

▶ **8.** On the Stage, click the anchor point at the bottom of the oval's outline. Because this is a curved outline, tangent handles appear. You use a tangent handle to modify the oval.

▶ **9.** Drag the left tangent handle of the bottom anchor point down to change the oval's shape. The fill expands to fit the new shape. See Figure 1-37.

Figure 1-37	Modified oval with tangent handles

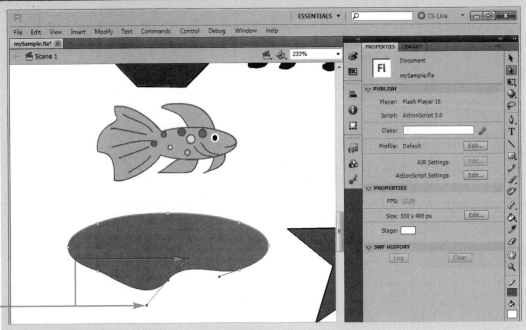

tangent handles

Lasso Tool

If you need to select part of a fill or a stroke, which you cannot do with the Selection or Subselection tools, you can use the Lasso tool. The Lasso tool is used to select an object, to select several objects at one time, or to select an irregularly shaped area of an object by drawing a free-form marquee. You can move the selection or apply other effects to it such as changing the color of all the selected fills at one time.

You will use the Lasso tool with the objects in the mySample.fla document.

To select objects with the Lasso tool:

▶ **1.** In the Tools panel, double-click the **Hand** tool . The entire Stage becomes visible.

▶ **2.** In the Tools panel, click the **Lasso** tool . The pointer changes to when moved over the Stage. You use this tool to select multiple objects at once.

▶ **3.** Drag the pointer to create a free-form marquee that includes parts of the modi-fied star, the beach ball, the heart, and the bear (but do not release the mouse button). See Figure 1-38.

Figure 1-38   Free-form marquee

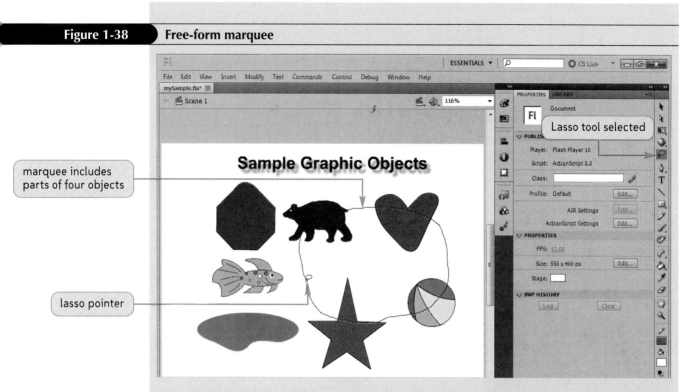

marquee includes parts of four objects

lasso pointer

Trouble? If you cannot create a free-form marquee, the Polygon Mode modifier is probably selected in the Tools panel. Click the Polygon Mode modifier button in the Tools panel to deselect it, and then repeat Step 3.

4. Release the mouse button. All of the selected areas appear with a dot pattern.

5. In the Tools panel, click the **Fill Color** control to open the color palette, and then click the **yellow** color swatch in the first column, tenth row of the color palette. The fill color of the selected areas in the star, beach ball, heart, and bear change to yellow. The strokes are not affected because they are not fills. See Figure 1-39.

Figure 1-39   New fill color for the selected areas

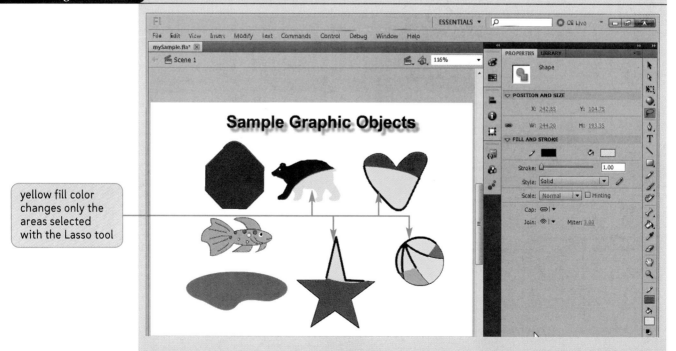

yellow fill color changes only the areas selected with the Lasso tool

6. On the Application bar, click **File**, and then click **Save**. The mySample.fla document is saved with all the changes.

Getting Help in Flash

The Flash Help system is useful for finding information about features in Flash as you work with a document. The Help system is organized topically. The left pane of the Adobe Community Help window contains a search option. The Help content is displayed in the right pane of the window.

The left column of the Help system's content pane shows the list of available categories. The first category is Using Flash Professional CS5, which contains the Help information for most of the features of Flash. The rest of the categories contain information about more advanced features. Clicking one of these initial categories displays subcategories in the right column of the content pane, which, when clicked, display additional Help categories in the left column. When a category in the left column is clicked, a list of topics is displayed. Each topic can be clicked to display a table of contents for the topic, as well as its associated help information. You can navigate the Help system by clicking any of the categories or topics. You can also use the Previous and Next buttons to navigate between topics.

A Search feature is available in the left pane of the Help window. You can search by a keyword or phrase to display a list of related topics. The search can be limited to the Flash Help system or can include other resources from the Adobe Web site.

TIP

To expand a category's list of topics, click the plus symbol to the left of the category name. To collapse the list, click the minus symbol to the left of the category name.

REFERENCE

Using the Flash Help System

- On the Application bar, click Help, and then click Flash Help (or click a panel menu button, and then click Help).
- Click a main topic category, and then click a subcategory to display.
- In the left column of the content pane, click a category to display its associated topics, and then click the desired topic.
- In the right column, read the topic information.
- Close the Adobe Community Help window to close the Help system.

You'll use the Flash Help system to obtain more information about the Property inspector.

To use get more information about the Property inspector:

1. On the Application bar, click **Help**, and then click **Flash Help**. The Help system opens in the Adobe Community Help window.

Trouble? If the Adobe AIR setup dialog box displays, click the Update button, and then click the Finish button when the update installation is complete.

Trouble? If the Updating: Adobe Help dialog box displays indicating an update is available, click the Download later button.

Trouble? If the Local Content Update dialog box opens indicating an update is available, click the Cancel button.

2. If necessary, on the Adobe Community Help window title bar, click the **Maximize** button to maximize the window.

Trouble? If an Adobe product other than Flash appears in the content pane, click the Home icon at the top of the content pane, and then click the Flash icon to display the Flash Help content.

▶ **3.** On the menu bar, click **View** and then click **Hide Search Panel**.

▶ **4.** If necessary, click the small arrow in the yellow box on the lower-right corner of the window to hide the Other versions list.

▶ **5.** In the left column, click **Workspace** to display a list of topics. See Figure 1-40.

Figure 1-40 **Flash Help system**

click an arrow to go to previous or next window

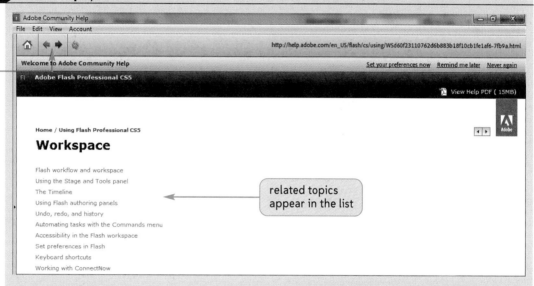

related topics appear in the list

▶ **6.** In the list of topics under Workspace, click the **Using Flash authoring panels** topic. Topics related to the panels appear. See Figure 1-41.

Figure 1-41 **Help topic selected**

TIP

To display information associated with a specific panel, click the panel menu button, and then click Help.

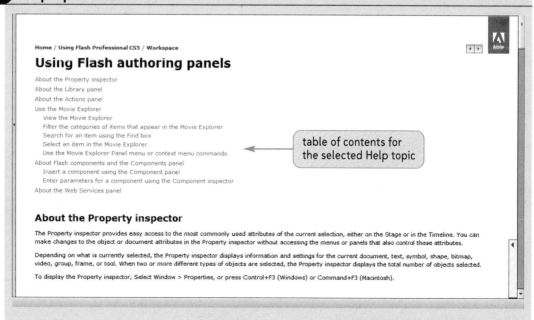

table of contents for the selected Help topic

7. Click the **About the Library panel** topic. The information for this topic appears in the right column. See Figure 1-42.

Figure 1-42   About the Library panel Help topic

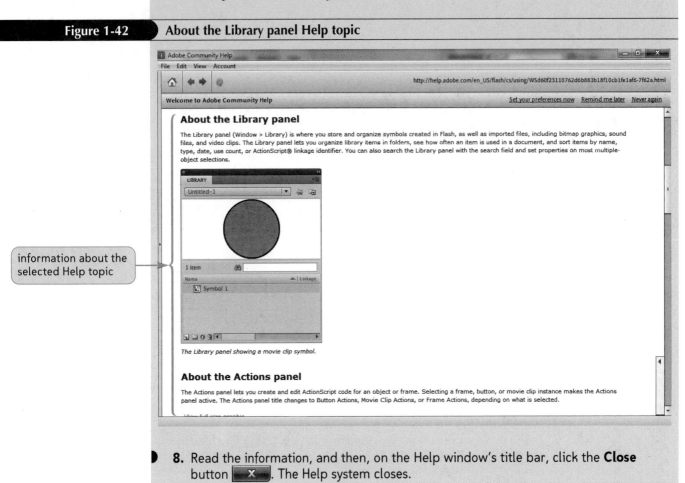

information about the selected Help topic

8. Read the information, and then, on the Help window's title bar, click the **Close** button [X]. The Help system closes.

Closing a Document and Exiting Flash

After you finish working with a document in Flash, you should close it. If you haven't already saved the document before you try to close it, Flash prompts you to save the file.

To close the mySample.fla document and exit Flash:

1. On the Application bar, click **File**, and then click **Close**. The mySample.fla document closes and the Welcome screen appears.

   Trouble? If you are prompted to save the file, you might have inadvertently made changes since the last time you saved. Click the No button.

2. On the Application bar, click **File**, and then click **Exit**. The Flash program exits.

TIP

You can also close a document by clicking the Close button in the page tab and exit Flash by clicking the Close button in title bar.

In this session, you learned how objects interact when they are drawn or moved over each other on the Stage. You selected and grouped objects, and you worked with the strokes, fills, and colors of objects. You also used the Help system.

REVIEW

Session 1.2 Quick Check

1. True or False. Rulers display the selected unit of measurement on the left and bottom edges of the Document window.
2. How do you change the background color of the Stage?
3. What is the difference between strokes and fills?
4. True or False. If you draw a blue oval on top of an ungrouped red rectangle drawn in Merge Drawing mode, the rectangle will not be modified.
5. True or False. Grouped objects cannot be edited.
6. What are two ways to use the Selection tool to select the stroke and the fill of an oval at the same time?
7. What tool do you use to select parts of several objects at the same time?
8. How can you find topics containing an exact phrase in the Help system?

Practice the skills you learned in the tutorial using the same case scenario.

PRACTICE

Review Assignments

Data File needed for the Review Assignments: objects.fla

Aly wants you to work with some of the tools in Flash and to change the document settings by modifying the objects document. You will use these skills to develop graphics for Admiral Web Design's clients.

1. Open the **objects.fla** file located in the Flash1\Review folder included with your Data Files and then save the document as **objectsNew.fla** in the same folder. Reset the workspace to the Essentials layout. Hide the Timeline and change the magnification level to Show Frame.

2. Display the rulers and the grid.

3. In the Tools panel, click the Selection tool. Double-click the red circle to select both its fill and stroke, and then move the red circle to the lower-right corner of the Stage so that it is approximately 450 pixels from the left of the Stage and 325 pixels from the top of the Stage.

4. In the Tools panel, click the Lasso tool. Drag around the beach ball and the green oval to select both shapes. Make sure no other shapes are selected. Click the Fill Color control in the Property inspector, and then click a light pink color in the color palette. The fills in the beach ball and the oval change to light pink.

5. With the Lasso tool, draw a marquee around the tree to select both its leaves and its trunk. Group the tree's strokes and fills.

6. In the Tools panel, click the Zoom tool and, if necessary, click the Enlarge modifier button. Click the kite twice to increase the magnification level.

7. In the Tools panel, click the Selection tool, and then click the stroke representing the kite's tail to select it. Click the Stroke Color control on the Property inspector, and then click the red color in the color palette. The kite's tail color changes to red.

8. Change the magnification level of the Stage to Show Frame.

9. Move the pointer to the top stroke of the blue rectangle. Use the curve pointer to drag the stroke slightly down toward the center of the rectangle to create a curved edge. Repeat to curve each of the other three sides of the rectangle toward its center.

10. Click the vertical ruler and drag the pointer to the right to approximately 150 pixels on the horizontal ruler to create a vertical guide. Click the pink oval to select it and then move it so that its left edge aligns with the vertical guide.

11. In the Tools panel, click the Subselection tool, and then click the heart shape's stroke to display its anchor points. Drag any anchor points to reshape the heart. Click an empty area of the Stage to deselect the modified shape.

12. In the Property inspector, click the Background color control, and then click a light yellow color in the color palette to change the background color of the Stage.

13. Save and close the document. Submit the finished document to your instructor.

Use the skills you learned to modify a Flash document for a pet resort.

APPLY

Case Problem 1

Data File needed for this Case Problem: shapes.fla

Katie's Pet Resort Katie Summers is the owner of Katie's Pet Resort, a full-service boarding facility for cats and dogs. The resort's services include a pet grooming salon, boarding facilities for cats and dogs, an animal hospital, and a gift shop. The resort also hosts training classes to teach customers how to train their pets. To help promote the pet resort, Katie hired John Rossini to develop a Web site. The site will include graphics and animation in addition to text. John wants to use Flash to develop the elements for the site. John asks you to explore a sample Flash document to become more familiar with the program.

1. Open the **shapes.fla** file located in the Flash1\Case1 folder included with your Data Files, and then save the document as **shapesRevised.fla** in the same folder. Reset the workspace to the Essentials layout and set the zoom magnification to Show All.

2. Display the rulers and the grid. Drag a horizontal guide from the top ruler to the grid line about 200 pixels from the top of the Stage.

3. Use the Selection tool to move both the fill and stroke of the triangle to the left side of the Stage. The bottom side of the triangle should rest on the guide.

4. Select all of the baseball, group its strokes and fills, and move the grouped baseball to the right of the triangle. The baseball's bottom edge should rest on the guide.

5. Move the cube to the right of the baseball and place it so that its center is on the guide.

6. Select all of the basketball, group its strokes and fills, and then move the grouped basketball to the right of the cube. The basketball's top edge should rest below the guide.

7. Select the red pentagon shape (both its fill and stroke), and then move the pentagon to the right of the basketball so that its bottom side rests on the guide.

8. With the pentagon still selected, use the Stroke Color control in the Property inspector to change the pentagon's stroke color to green.

9. Use the Selection pointer to curve the top sides of the pentagon toward its center.

10. Change the triangle's fill color to brown and its stroke color to red.

11. Change the baseball's fill color to yellow and its stroke color to gray. (*Hint*: Edit the baseball in group-editing mode.)

12. Change the basketball's fill color to pink.

13. Save and close the document. Submit the finished document to your instructor.

Use the skills you learned to modify a Flash document for a local zoo.

APPLY

Case Problem 2

Data File needed for this Case Problem: circleStars.fla

Alamo City Zoo   The Alamo City Zoo, established in 1965, provides animal exhibits for San Antonio and the surrounding area. The zoo is open year-round and has special exhibits throughout the year. Alamo City Zoo staff also work with local schools to arrange field trips and guided tours for students. Janet Meyers, zoo director, commissioned Alex Smith to develop Flash graphics for the Alamo City Zoo Web site. Alex asks you to explore how objects interact with each other in Flash.

1. Open the **circlesStars.fla** file located in the Flash1\Case2 folder included with your Data Files, and then save the document as **circlesStarsNew.fla** in the same folder. Reset the workspace to the Essentials layout and set the Stage magnification to Show All.

2. Using the Selection tool, drag the red circle on the lower-left side of the Stage to overlay the left side of the blue circle. Click a blank area of the Stage to deselect the circle. Select the red circle again, and then move the circle back to the lower-left side of the Stage. Part of the blue circle has been cut away.

3. Drag the red circle on the upper-left side of the Stage and place it on the green circle. Click a blank area of the Stage to deselect the circle. The red circle is behind the green circle. Move the green circle to the upper-left side, and then deselect it. Neither circle changes.

4. Point to the bottom of the red circle on the upper-left side of the Stage, and then use the curve pointer to drag the line up slightly to curve it. Repeat this step to modify

the bottom of the green circle. Both objects are modified in the same manner with the Selection tool.

5. Select the fill of the star on the upper-right side of the Stage. Then select the star on the lower-right side of the Stage. Each star's selection is displayed differently.

6. Deselect the star, point to the left point of the star on the lower-right side of the Stage, and then use the corner pointer to drag the star's point to the left slightly. Repeat this step to move the left point of the star on the upper-right side of the Stage. Both objects are modified in the same manner with the Selection tool.

7. Record what you think are the differences and similarities between the two star objects. Also record why you think the circle shapes interact differently with each other.

8. Save and close the document. Submit your answers from Step 7 and the finished document to your instructor.

Customize the Flash workspace for a gardening store.

CHALLENGE

Case Problem 3

There are no Data Files needed for this Case Problem.

Westcreek Nursery Alice Washington is the owner of Westcreek Nursery, a specialty store providing a variety of trees, plants, flowers, and gardening accessories. Alice attributes her success over the last 10 years to her focus on customer service. Customers can look through the nursery's inventory in a relaxing and inviting environment. Friendly and knowledgeable staff provide expert advice and answers to customers' gardening questions.

Alice contracted Amanda Lester to update the store's Web site. As other local nurseries have developed Web sites, Alice wants to make sure her store's Web site stays current and remains an effective marketing tool. You'll help Amanda develop Flash graphics for the Web site. She wants you to customize the Flash workspace and arrange the panels you will use regularly. You will also look for information in the Flash Help system.

1. Create a new Flash document, and then reset the workspace to the Essentials layout.

2. On the Application bar, click Window, and then click Behaviors to open the Behaviors panel as a free-floating window. Move this window slightly to the left by dragging the panel's tab or title bar. Open the Movie Explorer panel.

✚ **EXPLORE** 3. Group the Movie Explorer and Behaviors panels into one window. (*Hint*: Drag the Movie Explorer panel from its window and into the Behaviors panel's window.)

4. Open the Align panel, and then drag it into the window with the Behaviors and Movie Explorer panels. All three panels are grouped.

✚ **EXPLORE** 5. Click the Collapse to Icons button above the Property inspector and Library panel. Drag the left edge of the panel dock to the right to reduce the width of the dock and display the panels as icons only.

✚ **EXPLORE** 6. On the Application bar, click the workspace switcher button, and then click New Workspace. Type **myLayout** in the Name box, and then click the OK button.

7. Reset the workspace to the Essentials layout.

8. On the Application bar, click the workspace switcher button, and then click myLayout, which appears in the list of panel layouts. The panel arrangement reflects the changes you made.

9. Close the free-floating panel group with the three panels.

✚ **EXPLORE** 10. Delete the saved layout. On the Application bar, click the workspace switcher button, and then click Manage Workspaces. In the Manage Workspaces dialog box, click myLayout, and then click the Delete button. Click the Yes button to confirm you want to delete the workspace layout, and then click the OK button.

11. Find out more about the Align panel. Open the Flash Help system and click Using Flash Professional CS5.

12. In the list of help categories in the left column, expand Creating and Editing Artwork to view its list of subcategories. Expand Moving, arranging, and deleting artwork to display its list of topics.

13. Click Arranging objects to display its help contents. In the contents list, click Align objects to display the help information about using the Align panel to align objects. Read the information for aligning objects. Record the basic steps for aligning objects. Close the Help window.

14. Submit your answers to your instructor.

Explore drawing in Flash and Web Media for a nonprofit organization.

RESEARCH

Case Problem 4

There are no Data Files needed for this Case Problem.

Missions Support Association   Brittany Hill is the current president of the Missions Support Association, a nonprofit organization of citizens in the San Antonio and south Texas area. The association is an advocate for the San Antonio Missions National Historical Park, which preserves the Spanish missions that were established in the eighteenth century. The association provides a forum for its members to volunteer time in support of the park and to meet and learn about the history of the missions.

Brittany hired Anissa Ellison to improve and maintain the association's Web site. She wants to add new graphics and animation to the site to improve its appeal to the association members. Anissa plans to use Flash to develop the new elements for the site. She wants you to review information about drawing shapes and some of the tools used to draw graphics and then view examples of Web media.

1. In the Flash Help system, click the Creating and Editing Artwork category.

2. Click the Drawing subcategory, and then click the About drawing topic to display its contents.

3. In the About drawing contents list, click Vector and bitmap graphics. Read the information about vector graphics and bitmap graphics. Record the definitions found in the Help topics for vector graphics and for bitmap graphics.

4. Scroll to the top of the page and click the Next button in the upper-right corner of the page to display the Drawing modes and graphic objects topic. In the contents list, click Merge Drawing mode. Read the information about the Merge Drawing mode and the Object Drawing mode.

5. Scroll to the bottom of the page to the Overlapping shapes topic. Read the information about overlapping shapes.

6. Scroll to the top of the page, and in the navigation links click the Drawing link to return to that category. Click the Draw simple lines and shapes topic. In the contents list, click the Draw with the Pencil tool topic and read its associated information.

7. Scroll to the top of the page, click the Creating and Editing Artwork link to return to that category, and then click Reshaping objects. Click Reshape lines and shapes, and in its contents list, click the Reshape a line or shape topic. Read the information displayed. Record the difference between reshaping an end point and a corner. Switch to Flash.

🔷 EXPLORE

8. On the Application bar, click Help, and then click Flash Support Center. The Flash Help window displays the Flash Help and Support Web site. To view a video, tutorial, or sample, click its link. View, listen, or read the information provided and for the samples, experiment with any interactive components, if available. To return to the center's home page, use the Previous button. As you navigate to some of the samples,

study and compare the animation effects you see. Listen for sound effects, music, and voiceovers. See if you can distinguish between bitmap and vector graphics.

9. In your browser, open the home page for the Flash Kit site at www.flashkit.com. Review the various examples of Flash graphics and animations displayed on the home page. Look for a list of hyperlinks, usually located at the top of page. In this list of hyperlinks, explore several of the categories such as Movies, Tutorials, and Gallery. Note how the various examples make use of animation, colors, sound, and pictures.

10. Close any open files without saving. Submit your answers to your instructor.

ENDING DATA FILES

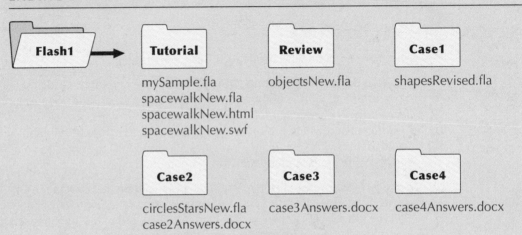

Flash1 →

Tutorial
mySample.fla
spacewalkNew.fla
spacewalkNew.html
spacewalkNew.swf

Review
objectsNew.fla

Case1
shapesRevised.fla

Case2
circlesStarsNew.fla
case2Answers.docx

Case3
case3Answers.docx

Case4
case4Answers.docx

OBJECTIVES

Session 2.1
- Draw lines, curves, ovals, and rectangles
- Apply stroke and fill colors
- Modify strokes and fills
- Transform graphic objects

Session 2.2
- Create text blocks
- Export a graphic for use in a Web site
- Use the History panel
- Create symbols and instances of symbols
- Organize symbols in the Library panel
- Apply filters to symbol instances and text

Drawing Shapes, Adding Text, and Creating Symbols

Creating and Exporting a Banner

Case | *Admiral Web Design*

Admiral Web Design focuses on designing easy-to-use, informative, and effective Web sites that meet the specific needs of its clients. One client is Jenny's Oyster Hut, a seafood restaurant that has won numerous local and national awards for its special dishes, customer satisfaction, and contributions to the community during its 10 years of operation. Owner Jenny Emerson wants Admiral Web Design to develop a new banner for the restaurant's Web site that promotes the restaurant's tenth anniversary celebration. You will work on this banner with Aly and Chris.

During the planning meeting, Jenny said that she wants a colorful banner with graphic images depicting a scene related to the sea. Aly suggested that the banner include graphics of a beach scene with sand, the ocean, some fish, and several lines of text. Chris agreed that this banner will blend well with the current design of the restaurant's home page. Jenny liked the idea and approved Aly's final sketch of the new banner. You will use Flash to create the banner according to Aly's sketch.

As you create the banner for Jenny's Oyster Hut in Flash, you will use the drawing tools, text tools, and tools for modifying graphic objects. You will select and apply colors. You will modify existing graphics, create new graphics, and then export the banner for use on the restaurant's Web site.

STARTING DATA FILES

Flash2 → Tutorial | Review | Case1 | Case2 | Case3 | Case4

jennys.htm   banner.fla   (none)   (none)   (none)   (none)
sports.fla

SESSION 2.1 VISUAL OVERVIEW

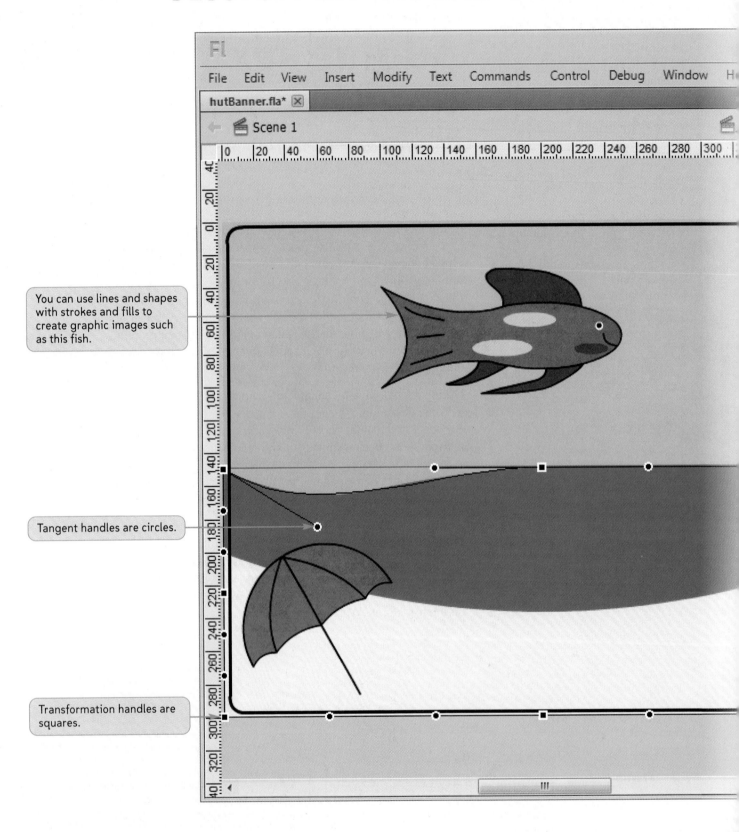

You can use lines and shapes with strokes and fills to create graphic images such as this fish.

Tangent handles are circles.

Transformation handles are squares.

THE DRAWING TOOLS

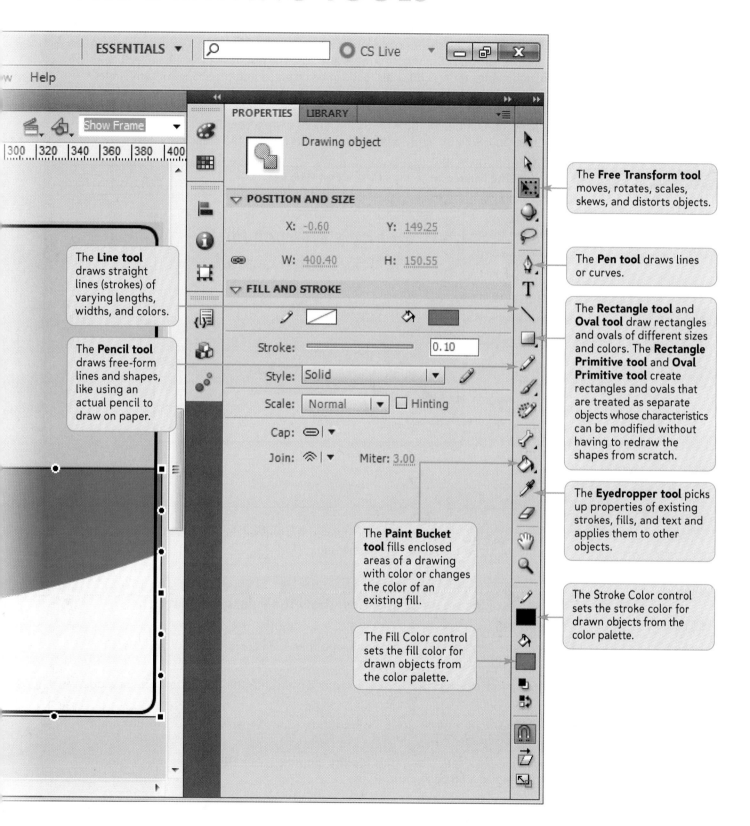

The **Line tool** draws straight lines (strokes) of varying lengths, widths, and colors.

The **Pencil tool** draws free-form lines and shapes, like using an actual pencil to draw on paper.

The **Free Transform tool** moves, rotates, scales, skews, and distorts objects.

The **Pen tool** draws lines or curves.

The **Rectangle tool** and **Oval tool** draw rectangles and ovals of different sizes and colors. The **Rectangle Primitive tool** and **Oval Primitive tool** create rectangles and ovals that are treated as separate objects whose characteristics can be modified without having to redraw the shapes from scratch.

The **Eyedropper tool** picks up properties of existing strokes, fills, and text and applies them to other objects.

The Stroke Color control sets the stroke color for drawn objects from the color palette.

The **Paint Bucket tool** fills enclosed areas of a drawing with color or changes the color of an existing fill.

The Fill Color control sets the fill color for drawn objects from the color palette.

Drawing Lines and Shapes

When working with Flash, you will often create graphic images from scratch. You can draw lines and curves and free-form shapes. Enclosed areas of shapes can be filled with a color. You can draw shapes of various sizes and colors. Ovals, rectangles, and polygons can include strokes, fills, or both strokes and fills. The primitive tools create rectangles with modifiable corners and ovals that can be changed into pie shapes or semicircles.

Figure 2-1 shows Aly's sketch of the banner you will create for Jenny's Oyster Hut. You will use a variety of drawing tools as you create and modify the fish, background graphics, frame, and umbrella. You will use the guides to help you draw and align objects on the Stage. You will also apply a drop shadow effect to graphic objects and text.

Figure 2-1	Sketch of the banner for Jenny's Oyster Hut Web site

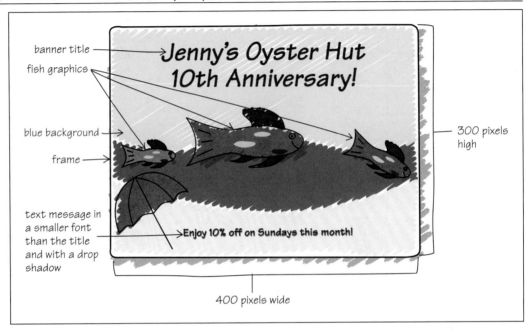

You are ready to begin creating the banner. You will set the document properties, display the rulers, and then save the banner file.

To set the document properties, show the rulers, and save the document:

1. On the Application bar, click **File**, and then click **New**. The New Document dialog box opens with the General tab active.

2. Click **ActionScript 3.0**, if necessary, and then click the **OK** button. The new document opens.

3. Reset the workspace to the Essentials layout, and then close the Timeline and the Motion Editor.

4. On the Application bar, click **Modify**, and then click **Document**. The Document Settings dialog box opens.

5. In the Dimensions area, type **400** in the width box, press the **Tab** key to select the value in the height box, and then type **300**. The document dimensions are set according to the banner sketch.

6. Click the **Background color** control to open the color palette, and then click the **light blue** color swatch (#66CCFF) in the second column from the right, sixth row of the color palette. The background color is set to light blue, as shown in the sketch. You'll leave the frame rate at 24 frames per second and the ruler units at pixels.

7. Click the **OK** button. The dialog box closes and the document changes to match the document settings.

8. Change the zoom magnification to **Fit in Window**, and then display the rulers. The document enlarges to fill the pasteboard and the rulers appear along the top and left of the pasteboard. See Figure 2-2.

| Figure 2-2 | New document properties |

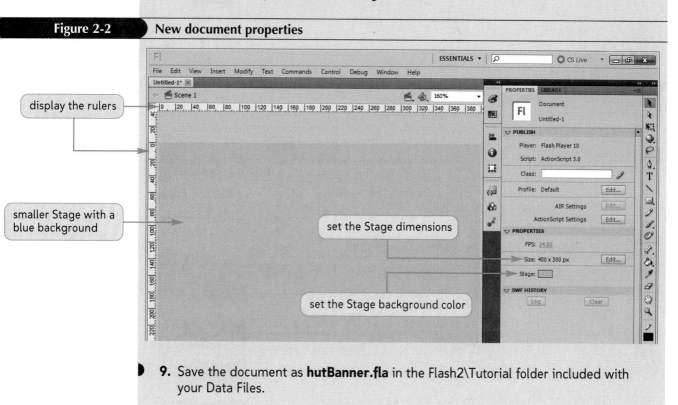

display the rulers

smaller Stage with a blue background

set the Stage dimensions

set the Stage background color

9. Save the document as **hutBanner.fla** in the Flash2\Tutorial folder included with your Data Files.

Using the Oval, Rectangle, and PolyStar Tools

Drawing simple shapes is easy with the Oval, Rectangle, and PolyStar tools. These tools all work in a similar manner. As you drag the pointer for the selected tool on the Stage, the size of the drawn shape changes until you release the mouse button. When you use the PolyStar tool, you choose whether to draw a polygon or a star. You can also indicate the number of sides the shape will have, which can range from 3 to 32. For star shapes, you can also specify the value of the star point size, which can range from 0 to 1. A number closer to 0 results in narrower star points, and a number closer to 1 results in wider star points, as shown in Figure 2-3.

Figure 2-3   **Star shapes with different point sizes**

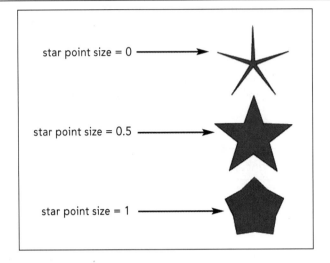

You can use the Oval and Rectangle tools to draw a perfect circle or a perfect square when the Snap to Objects modifier is selected. As you draw with the Oval or Rectangle tool, a small solid ring appears next to the pointer to let you know when you have drawn a perfect circle or a perfect square.

When you select the Rectangle tool, the Rectangle Options appear in the Property inspector. The Rectangle corner radius boxes represent the number of pixels by which to round the corners of the rectangle shape. You can enter a value for one or more corners of the rectangle. The Lock corner radius button locks all corner values to be the same as the value entered in the upper-left corner radius box. A negative value creates an inward corner, a 0 value results in a squared corner, and a higher value produces a more rounded corner, as shown in Figure 2-4.

Figure 2-4   **Rectangles with different corner radii**

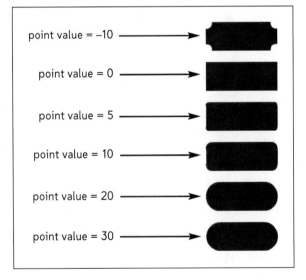

PROSKILLS

Problem Solving: Selecting a Drawing Mode to Create Graphics

Creating graphics is like solving a puzzle. You need to define how you want the graphic objects you draw to interact with each other. Then, you must determine the appropriate drawing mode based on the results you want to achieve. If you want to create graphic shapes that combine to form one shape, draw them using the Merge Drawing mode. If you want to keep the shapes you draw separate from each other, use the Object Drawing mode. You can also switch between drawing modes as you draw the graphics.

As you draw graphics, you may find that the various shapes and lines you draw interact with each other in undesirable ways. For example, you may need to draw a complex logo consisting of shapes of various colors. As you draw and rearrange these shapes, overlapping shapes can cut away at underlying shapes. To avoid this problem, select the Object Drawing mode before you start to draw. In this mode, you can easily arrange objects without having them interact with other objects.

Sometimes you need to draw a complex logo in which you combine various shapes of the same color into one larger shape, such as a drawing a rectangle, an oval, and a circle to form one final shape. In this case, select the Merge Drawing mode so that the various shapes combine into one shape.

Another problem you may encounter is when you need to draw a shape other than a standard rectangle, oval, star or other polygon. For example, you may need to draw a rectangle with a circular area cutout from one side of the rectangular shape. In this situation, select Merge Drawing mode. Draw the rectangle, and then draw a circle of a different color overlaid on the side of the rectangle. When you select the circle and delete it, the area on the rectangle covered by the circle will be cut out leaving the desired shape.

So, before you begin drawing, think about how the parts of the graphic work together and the results you want to achieve. Then determine the drawing mode you need to use. This upfront planning helps you to avoid unexpected results and eliminates the need to spend extra time redrawing a graphic.

You will draw rectangles in the banner's background for the beach and ocean and around the banner to frame all the graphic elements. As indicated in Aly's sketch, the frame rectangle will have a stroke, no fill, and rounded corners. You will draw the background graphics using the Object Drawing mode so that they won't merge with the fish you will create.

To draw the ocean rectangle:

1. Drag a horizontal guide from the horizontal ruler to approximately 150 pixels from the top of the Stage, and then drag another horizontal guide from the horizontal ruler to approximately 200 pixels from the top of the Stage.

2. In the Tools panel, click the **Rectangle** tool ▣, and then click the **Object Drawing** button ⊙, if necessary, to select it. The rectangles you draw will not merge with other shapes.

3. In the Rectangle Options section of the Property inspector, click the **Reset** button to set the Rectangle corner radius values to 0, if necessary. The rectangle you draw will have square corners.

4. In the Property inspector, click the **Fill Color** control ▨ ▬ to open the color palette, and then click the **blue** color swatch (#0000FF) in the first swatches column, ninth row. The rectangle you draw will be blue.

5. In the Property inspector, click the **Fill Color** control to open the color palette, click the **Alpha** value and drag to the left until the Alpha value is 50. The reduced Alpha value of the fill color will make the rectangle partially transparent.

6. In the Property inspector, click the **Stroke Color** control to open the color palette, and then click the **No Color** button. The rectangles you draw will not have an outline.

7. Draw a rectangle for the ocean by dragging the pointer from the left side of the Stage at the top guide to the lower-right corner of the Stage. A partially transparent, blue rectangle without an outline fills the lower part of the Stage. See Figure 2-5.

Figure 2-5   **Rectangle for the ocean**

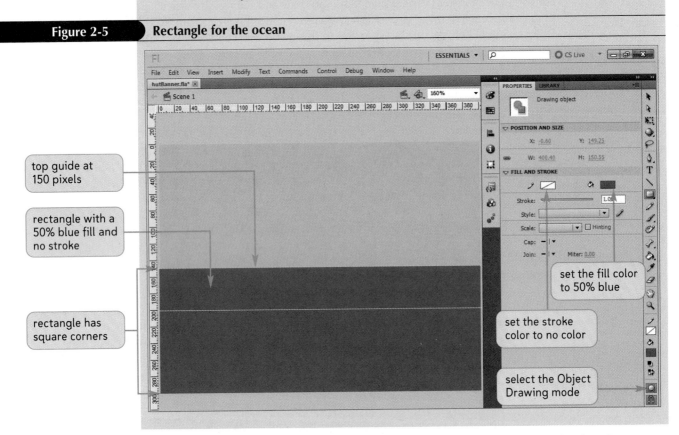

top guide at 150 pixels

rectangle with a 50% blue fill and no stroke

rectangle has square corners

set the fill color to 50% blue

set the stroke color to no color

select the Object Drawing mode

The second rectangle you draw will represent the beach. You need to deselect the ocean rectangle, and then change the fill color in the Color panel.

To draw the beach rectangle:

1. In the Tools panel, click the **Selection** tool , and then click in another area of the Stage to deselect the blue rectangle.

2. In the Tools panel, click the **Rectangle** tool to select it.

3. In the Property inspector, click the **Fill Color** control to open the color palette, click the **light yellow** color swatch (#FFFFCC) in the last column, second row from the bottom of the color palette, and then change the Alpha value to **100%**, if necessary. The yellow fill is for the sand.

4. Make sure the stroke color is set to no color. The beach rectangle will not have a stroke.

5. Draw a rectangle from the left side of the Stage at the lower guide to the lower-right corner of the Stage. An opaque light yellow rectangle with no stroke covers the lower portion of the Stage. See Figure 2-6.

Figure 2-6 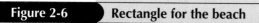 Rectangle for the beach

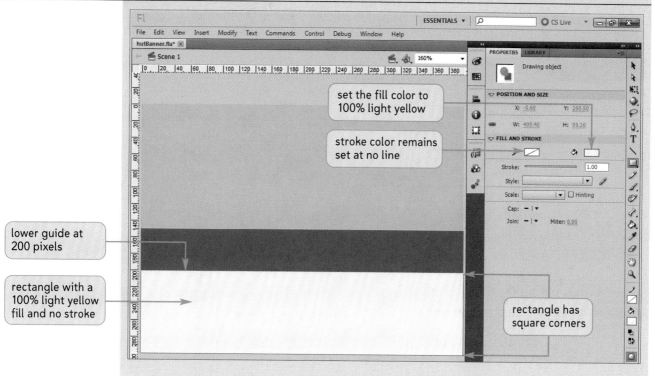

set the fill color to 100% light yellow

stroke color remains set at no line

lower guide at 200 pixels

rectangle with a 100% light yellow fill and no stroke

rectangle has square corners

You will draw another rectangle to frame the banner. This rectangle will have a black stroke color and no fill color. It will also have rounded corners and a stroke height of 2.

To draw the frame rectangle:

1. In the Tools panel, click the **Selection** tool, and then click an empty area of the Stage to deselect the beach rectangle.

2. In the Tools panel, click the **Rectangle** tool, and then, in the Property inspector, click the **Stroke Color** control to open the color palette and click the **black** color swatch (#000000) in the first swatches column, first row of the color palette. The rectangle will have a black stroke.

3. In the Property inspector, click the **Fill Color** control to open the color palette, and then click the **No Color** button. The rectangle will not have a fill color.

4. In the Property inspector, make sure the stroke style is set to **Solid**, double-click the value in the **Stroke height** box, type **2**, and then press the **Enter** key. The stroke size is set to 2.

5. In the Rectangle Options section of the Property inspector, if necessary, click the **unlock** icon for the Rectangle corner radius to change it to a lock icon.

▶ **6.** In the Rectangle Options section of the Property inspector, double-click the upper-left **Rectangle corner radius** value to select it, type **10**, and then press the **Enter** key. The value for each corner is set to 10.

▶ **7.** In the Tools panel, click the **Snap to Objects** modifier button 🔝 to deselect it, if necessary, so the rectangle won't snap to the edges of the Stage.

▶ **8.** Draw a rectangle from just inside the upper-left corner of the Stage to just inside the lower-right corner of the Stage. See Figure 2-7.

Figure 2-7   **Rectangle for the frame**

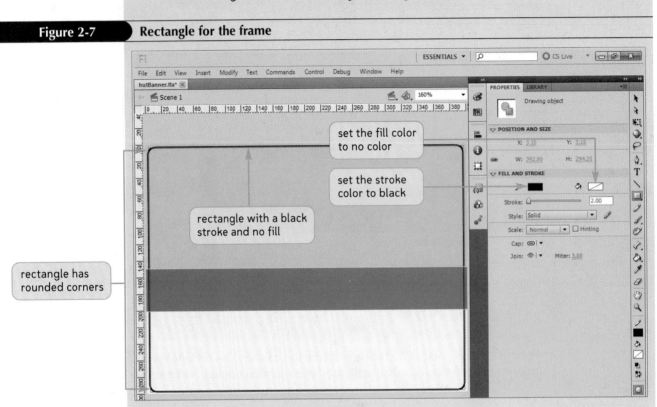

You will modify the yellow rectangle to more closely resemble the beach graphic that Aly sketched. You'll do this by curving the top side of the rectangle using the Selection tool. You will hide the guides because you won't be using them.

To hide the guides and modify the yellow rectangle shape:

▶ **1.** On the Application bar, click **View**, point to **Guides**, and then click **Show Guides**. The guides disappear.

▶ **2.** In the Tools panel, click the **Selection** tool ▶, and then click an empty area of the Stage to deselect the frame rectangle. You will modify the light yellow rectangle using the Selection tool.

▶ **3.** Move the pointer to the upper-middle side of the light yellow rectangle until the pointer changes to ▶, and then drag the top of the rectangle down about 45 pixels to curve it, but do not release the mouse button. See Figure 2-8.

Figure 2-8 **Curved rectangle created using the Selection tool**

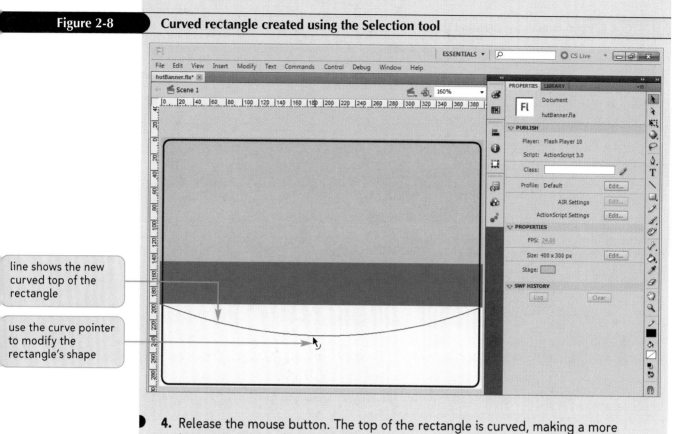

line shows the new curved top of the rectangle

use the curve pointer to modify the rectangle's shape

4. Release the mouse button. The top of the rectangle is curved, making a more interesting shape for the beach.

Next, you will create the fish in the center of the banner that Aly sketched. You'll draw a large oval for the body of the fish and a rectangle that you will modify to become the fish's tail. You will use the Merge Drawing mode so that the two shapes combine into one. Guides will help you draw these shapes.

To draw the fish:

1. On the Application bar, click **View**, point to **Guides**, and then click **Show Guides**. The guides appear on the Stage.

2. Drag the top guide up to approximately 50 pixels from the top of the Stage, and then drag the bottom guide up to approximately 90 pixels from the top of the Stage.

3. Drag a vertical guide from the vertical ruler to approximately 150 pixels from the left of the Stage, and then drag another vertical guide from the vertical ruler to approximately 250 pixels from the left of the Stage. See Figure 2-9.

Figure 2-9   **Guides for creating the fish**

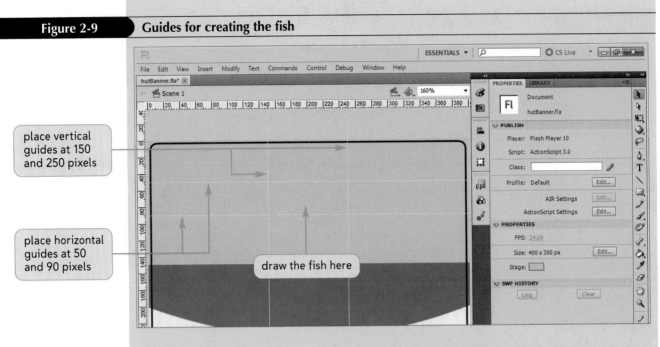

place vertical guides at 150 and 250 pixels

place horizontal guides at 50 and 90 pixels

draw the fish here

  ► **4.** In the Tools panel, click and hold the **Rectangle** tool ⬛ to open the pop-up menu, and then click the **Oval** tool ⬤. The pointer changes to +.

  ► **5.** In the Tools panel, click the **Object Drawing** button ⬤ to deselect it. Merge Drawing mode is now in effect.

  ► **6.** In the Property inspector, if necessary, click the **Stroke Color** control 🖊▱ to open the color palette, and then click the **black** color swatch (#000000) in the first swatches column, first row of the color palette.

  ► **7.** In the Property inspector, enter **1** in the Stroke height box, and then make sure the Stroke style is set to **Solid**.

  ► **8.** In the Property inspector, click the **Fill Color** control 🖊▬ to open the color palette, and then click the **red** color swatch (#FF0000) in the seventh row, first swatches column from the left. The fish body you draw will be red with a black stroke.

  ► **9.** Draw an oval from the upper-left corner of the rectangular area formed by the guides to the lower-right corner of the rectangular area formed by the guides. See Figure 2-10.

Figure 2-10   **Oval for the fish body**

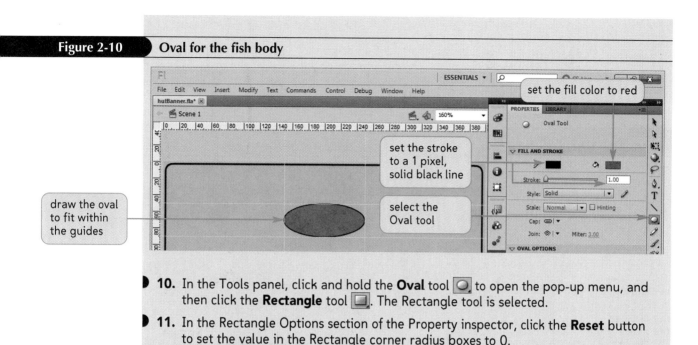

draw the oval
to fit within
the guides

set the fill color to red

set the stroke
to a 1 pixel,
solid black line

select the
Oval tool

10. In the Tools panel, click and hold the **Oval** tool to open the pop-up menu, and then click the **Rectangle** tool . The Rectangle tool is selected.

11. In the Rectangle Options section of the Property inspector, click the **Reset** button to set the value in the Rectangle corner radius boxes to 0.

12. Draw a rectangle starting approximately 40 pixels from the top of the Stage and 100 pixels from the left of the Stage, and ending approximately 100 pixels from the top of the Stage and 170 pixels from the left of the Stage. See Figure 2-11.

Figure 2-11   **Overlapping oval and rectangle shapes**

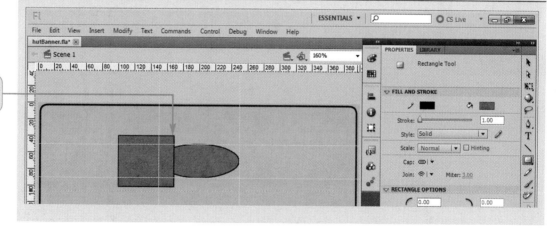

rectangle overlaps
the oval

You will use the Selection tool to modify the two shapes so that they more closely resemble the fish Aly sketched. The right corners of the rectangle will connect to the oval, and the sides of the rectangle will be curved. You will clear the guides because you don't need them anymore.

To modify the oval and rectangle shapes:

1. On the Application bar, click **View**, point to **Guides**, and then click **Clear Guides**. The guides are removed from the Stage.

2. In the Tools panel, click the **Snap to Objects** modifier button to select it.

3. In the Tools panel, click the **Selection** tool 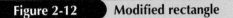, drag the upper-right corner of the rectangle down until it snaps to the upper edge of the oval, and then drag the lower-right corner of the rectangle up until it snaps to the lower edge of the oval. See Figure 2-12.

Figure 2-12 Modified rectangle

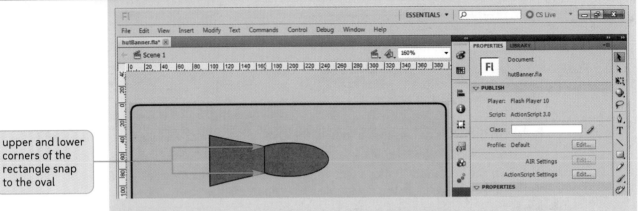

upper and lower corners of the rectangle snap to the oval

4. Move the pointer to the stroke on the left side of the modified rectangle shape until the pointer changes to ⬏, and then drag the line slightly to the right.

5. Drag the top line down slightly to curve it; drag the bottom line up slightly to curve it.

6. Click the right side of the modified rectangle to select it, and then press the **Delete** key. The unneeded stroke is removed. See Figure 2-13.

Figure 2-13 Rectangle sides modified

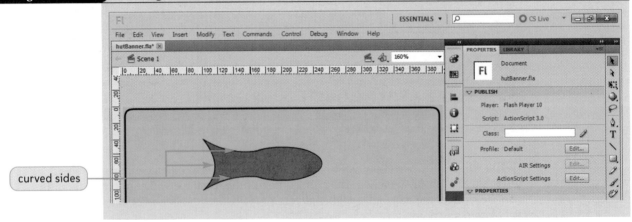

curved sides

The modified rectangle and oval resemble a fish shape. You are ready to draw the eye for the fish. You'll also draw several oval spots on the fish. To do this, you will use the Oval tool.

To draw the eye and oval spots on the fish:

1. In the Tools panel, click the **Zoom** tool 🔍, make sure the **Enlarge** modifier button 🔍 is selected, and then click the right side of the fish shape once to zoom in.

2. In the Tools panel, click and hold the **Rectangle** tool ▢ to open the pop-up menu, and then click the **Oval** tool ⬭. The pointer changes to ╋.

3. In the Property inspector, click the **Stroke Color** control ✏️▱ to open the color palette, click the **No Color** button ⬚, click the **Fill Color** control 🪣▬ to open the color palette, and then click the **white** color swatch (#FFFFFF) in the first swatches column, sixth row of the color palette.

4. Draw a small circle on the upper-right end of the fish shape for the fish eye, and then draw three ovals of different sizes on the fish body. You will change the color of the ovals later in this session. See Figure 2-14.

Figure 2-14   Fish with eye and oval spots

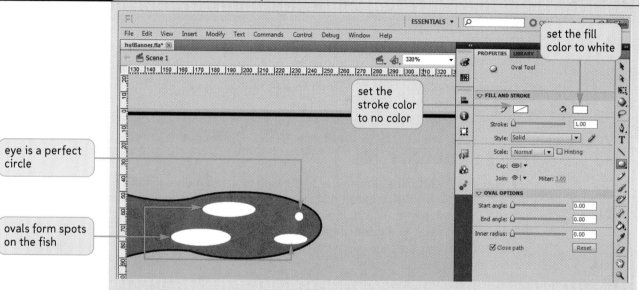

eye is a perfect circle

ovals form spots on the fish

set the stroke color to no color

set the fill color to white

5. In the Tools panel, click the **Snap to Objects** modifier button 🧲 to deselect it. Having the modifier off will make it easier to draw a small circle for the pupil of the fish eye.

6. In the Property inspector, click the **Fill Color** control 🪣▬ to open the color palette, and then click the **black** color swatch (#000000) in the first swatches column, first row of the color palette.

7. Draw a smaller circle inside the eye to represent the pupil. See Figure 2-15.

Figure 2-15   **Pupil added to fish eye**

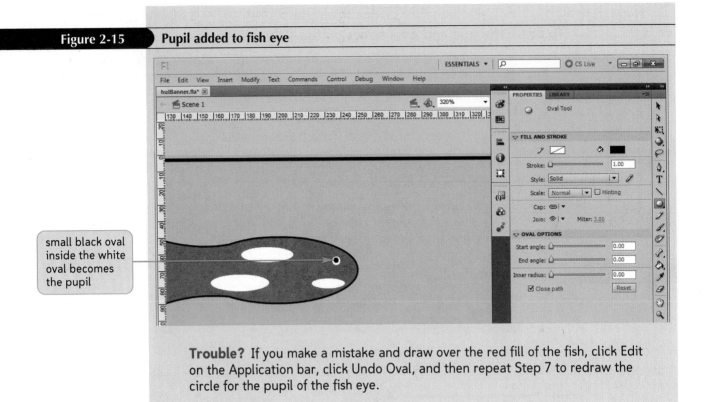

small black oval inside the white oval becomes the pupil

Trouble? If you make a mistake and draw over the red fill of the fish, click Edit on the Application bar, click Undo Oval, and then repeat Step 7 to redraw the circle for the pupil of the fish eye.

Using the Pencil Tool

The Pencil tool works in a similar way to the Line tool, but it doesn't limit you to drawing straight lines. Instead, you can draw free-form shapes as if you were using an actual pencil to draw on paper. As with the Line tool, you can select a color, height, and style for the lines drawn with the Pencil tool. The Pencil Mode modifier in the Tools panel lets you control the way lines appear as you draw them. Figure 2-16 summarizes the options for this modifier.

Figure 2-16   **Pencil Mode modifier options**

Modifier Button	Option	Description
	Straighten	Helps straighten the lines you draw
	Smooth	Smoothes the lines and curves you draw
	Ink	Provides minimal assistance as you draw

You will use the Pencil tool to add fins, a mouth, and tail lines to the fish.

To add the fins, the mouth, and lines to the fish:

1. In the Tools panel, click the **Pencil** tool to select it.

2. In the Tools panel, click the **Pencil Mode** modifier button to open the menu of options, and then click **Smooth**. The Smooth option for the Pencil Mode modifier ensures that the lines you draw are smooth.

3. In the Property inspector, make sure the stroke color is **black** (#000000), the stroke height is **1**, and the stroke style is **Solid**. The stroke color, height, and style are set for drawing lines for the fins, mouth, and tail.

4. Draw a fin on the top side of the fish and two fins on the bottom side. See Figure 2-17.

Figure 2-17 **Fins drawn on the fish**

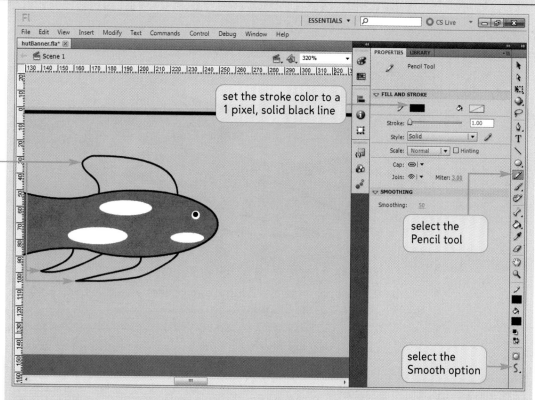

draw the fins with the Pencil tool

set the stroke color to a 1 pixel, solid black line

select the Pencil tool

select the Smooth option

5. In the Tools panel, click the **Zoom** tool 🔍, make sure the **Enlarge** modifier button 🔍 is selected, and then click the center of the fish shape once to zoom in.

Be sure that the fin strokes connect to the fish body strokes so that you can later fill the enclosed fin shapes with color.

6. In the Tools panel, click the **Selection** tool 🔧, click the **Snap to Objects** modifier button 🧲 to select it, move the pointer to the left endpoint of the lower-right fin stroke until the pointer changes to ▾, and then drag the endpoint so that it snaps to the stroke representing the body of the fish. See Figure 2-18.

Figure 2-18   Endpoints of the fins connected to the fish's body

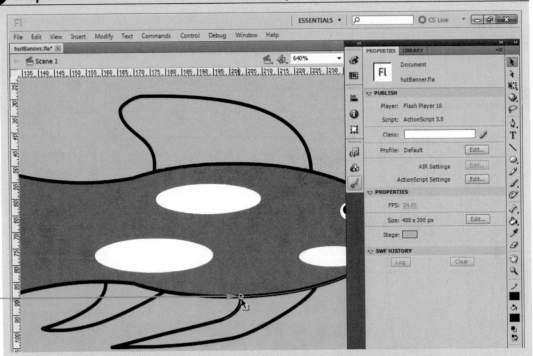

drag the endpoint of fin stroke to connect to the fish body stroke

7. Repeat Step 6 to connect the endpoints of the other fins to the fish's body.

8. On the Edit bar, click the **Zoom control arrow**, and then click **400%** to zoom in to the contents of the Stage.

9. In the Tools panel, click the **Pencil** tool to select it, make sure the **Smooth** modifier option **S.** is selected, and make sure the stroke is set to **1** pixel, **solid black** line.

10. Draw a small curved line for the fish's mouth from right below the eye to the stroke in the lower-right side of the fish, and then draw three short lines in the tail section of the fish. See Figure 2-19.

Figure 2-19   **Fish with fins, mouth, and lines**

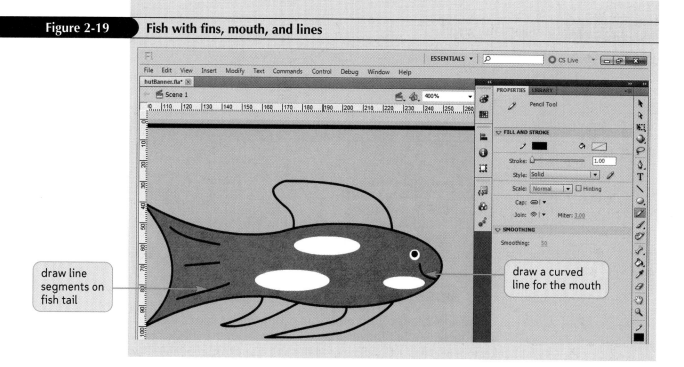

draw line segments on fish tail

draw a curved line for the mouth

Changing Strokes and Fills

After you draw an object, you can still change its stroke and fill. You can change the stroke's color, height, or style, and you can change a fill's color. You can even add a fill or a stroke to an object that doesn't have one or the other. Based on Aly's sketch of the banner, the oval shapes and the fins on the fish should be areas of color.

To keep the various parts of the fish together, you will group them. This way, you can easily modify or create copies of the fish graphic as a whole. You can still modify individual elements of a grouped object in group-editing mode.

To group the fish graphic:

1. On the Edit bar, click the **Zoom control arrow**, and then click **Show Frame** to view all the contents of the Stage.

2. In the Tools panel, click the **Selection** tool, and then draw a marquee around the entire fish to select all of its parts.

3. On the Application bar, click **Modify**, and then click **Group**. The graphic elements are grouped. A thin rectangular line surrounds the grouped object to show it is selected. See Figure 2-20.

TIP
You can also press the Ctrl+G keys to group selected elements.

Figure 2-20   Grouped fish graphic

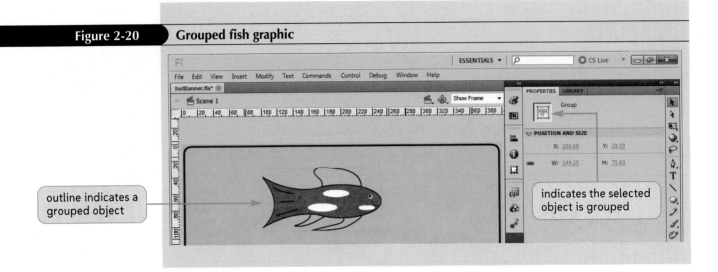

outline indicates a
grouped object

indicates the selected
object is grouped

Using the Paint Bucket Tool

TIP

The Ink Bottle tool changes the attributes or properties of a stroke or applies a stroke to an object that has no stroke.

The Paint Bucket tool changes the color of an existing fill or adds a fill to an enclosed area that does not have a fill. The fill color is selected with the Fill Color control. The Paint Bucket tool also has a Gap Size modifier and a Lock Fill modifier. The Gap Size modifiers—Don't Close Gaps, Close Small Gaps, Close Medium Gaps, and Close Large Gaps—determine how the tool will paint areas that are not completely enclosed. The Lock Fill modifier extends gradient and bitmap fills across multiple objects.

You will use the Paint Bucket tool to fill the spots on the fish with bright colors.

To add fills to the fish:

1. Double-click the grouped fish graphic to enter group-editing mode, and then click another area of the Stage to deselect the fish, if necessary. In group-editing mode, you can modify each part of the fish independently.

2. In the Tools panel, click the **Paint Bucket** tool . The pointer changes to .

3. In the Tools panel, click the **Gap Size** modifier button to open the pop-up menu, and then click **Close Medium Gaps**. With this Gap Size modifier, you can use the Paint Bucket tool to paint areas that are not completely enclosed.

4. In the Property inspector, click the **Fill Color** control to open the color palette, and then click the **purple** color swatch (#660066) in the sixth column from the right, third row of the color palette.

5. Click inside the white oval at the bottom of the fish body to apply the fill color. The fish has a purple spot. See Figure 2-21.

Figure 2-21 | **Fill color applied with the Paint Bucket tool**

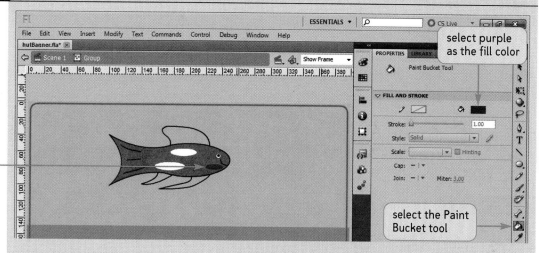

oval shape is purple

Trouble? If a padlock icon appears next to the paint bucket pointer, the Lock Fill modifier is selected. This does not affect the way the Paint Bucket tool works. Continue with Step 6.

6. In the Property inspector, click the **Fill Color** control to open the color palette, click the **light pink** color swatch (#FFCCFF) in the second column from the right, bottom row of the color palette, and then click the left white oval on the fish body. The spot changes to light pink.

7. Click the top white oval on the fish body to apply the same color. The spot changes to light pink.

Using the Eyedropper Tool

The Eyedropper tool copies the properties of a fill or stroke from one object and applies them to the fill or stroke of another object. You can also use the Eyedropper tool to copy the properties of a text block and apply them to another text block. When you select the Eyedropper tool, the pointer changes to ✐. If you move the eyedropper over a stroke, the pointer changes to ✐ to indicate that you are about to copy the stroke's attributes. After you click the stroke, the pointer changes to ✐, which indicates that you can apply the copied stroke attributes to another object. If you move the eyedropper over a fill, the pointer changes to ✐, indicating that you are about to copy the fill's attributes. After you click the fill, the pointer changes to ✐, and you can click another object to apply the copied fill attributes. The pointer includes a padlock ✐ when the Lock Fill modifier is selected.

REFERENCE

Using the Eyedropper Tool

- In the Tools panel, click the Eyedropper tool.
- Click the stroke or fill whose attributes you want to copy.
- Click the stroke or fill to which you want to apply the copied attributes.

Based on to Aly's sketch, the fins of the fish need to be the same color as the bottom oval spot on the fish. You will use the Eyedropper tool to copy the fill color of the spot to the fins.

To copy the color from the bottom spot to the fins:

▶ **1.** In the Tools panel, click the **Eyedropper** tool 🖊. The pointer changes to 🖊.

▶ **2.** Click the purple fill color in the bottom spot of the fish. The pointer changes to ◇ or ◇, depending on whether the Lock Fill modifier is selected, to indicate that you can apply the purple color to another part of the fish.

▶ **3.** Click the blank area enclosed by the top fin. The top fin now has the same color as the bottom spot of the fish. See Figure 2-22.

| Figure 2-22 | Fill color copied from the purple oval to the top fin |

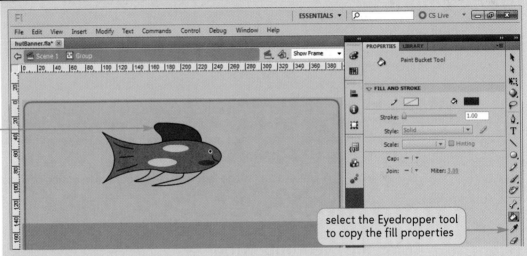

top fin now has same color as bottom fish spot

select the Eyedropper tool to copy the fill properties

▶ **4.** Click in the bottom fins. The purple fill color is applied to them.

▶ **5.** On the Edit bar, click the **Scene 1** link to exit group-editing mode.

Using Primitive Tools

The primitive tools create rectangles and ovals that you can modify without having to redraw the shapes. For example, after you draw a rectangle with the Rectangle tool, you cannot change the roundness of the rectangle's corners. However, if you create a rectangle with the Rectangle Primitive tool, you can modify the rectangle's corners by changing the values in the Rectangle corner radius boxes in the Property inspector. Similarly, after you draw an oval with the Oval Primitive tool, the Property inspector provides several controls for modifying the oval. You can specify the angles of the oval's starting and ending points to create a pie or semicircle shape. You can specify a percentage of the oval's fill to create a doughnut shape. You can also set whether the oval's path is open or closed. An open path results in an oval shape with no fill when the start and end angles are not 0. Reset returns the oval to its original size and shape. Figure 2-23 shows shapes drawn with the Rectangle Primitive and Oval Primitive tools.

Figure 2-23   **Shapes drawn with the primitive tools**

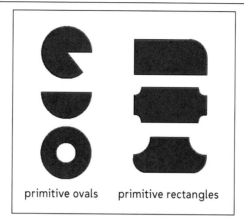

primitive ovals   primitive rectangles

You can convert a primitive shape to a drawing object to further modify the shape, just as if you had drawn the shape in Object Drawing mode. If you convert a primitive shape into a drawing object, the object is no longer a primitive shape and the primitive tool controls are not available in the Property inspector.

Aly's sketch shows that the banner still needs the umbrella. You will use the Oval Primitive tool to draw the semicircle that forms the umbrella.

To create the umbrella:

1. In the Tools panel, click the **Selection** tool [ ], and then drag horizontal guides to about 150 pixels and 250 pixels from the top of the Stage.

2. Drag vertical guides to about 50 pixels and 150 pixels from the left of the Stage. You'll use the guides as you create the umbrella.

3. In the Tools panel, click and hold the **Oval** tool [ ] to open the pop-up menu, and then click the **Oval Primitive** tool [ ]. The Oval Primitive tool is selected.

4. In the Property inspector, set the stroke color to **black** (#000000), if necessary, and set the fill color to **red** (#FF0000). The stroke and fill colors are set.

5. In the Property inspector, make sure the stroke height is **1** and stroke style is **Solid**.

6. In the Oval Options section of the Property inspector, click the **Reset** button to reset the oval options.

7. Drag ╂ inside the square formed by the guides to create an oval. See Figure 2-24.

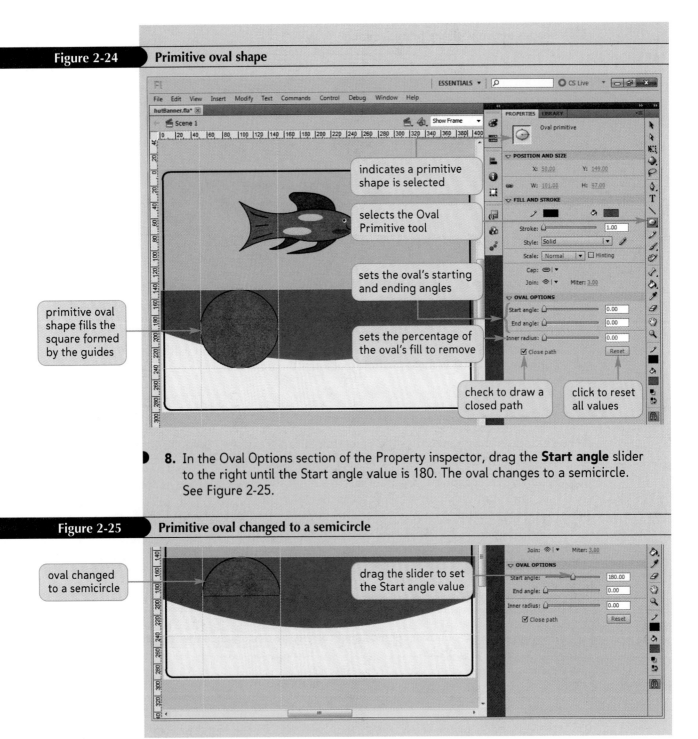

Figure 2-24 Primitive oval shape

indicates a primitive shape is selected

selects the Oval Primitive tool

sets the oval's starting and ending angles

primitive oval shape fills the square formed by the guides

sets the percentage of the oval's fill to remove

check to draw a closed path

click to reset all values

8. In the Oval Options section of the Property inspector, drag the **Start angle** slider to the right until the Start angle value is 180. The oval changes to a semicircle. See Figure 2-25.

Figure 2-25 Primitive oval changed to a semicircle

oval changed to a semicircle

drag the slider to set the Start angle value

So that the semicircle more closely resembles an umbrella, you'll use the Line tool to draw lines on the umbrella and the pole.

To draw lines on the umbrella:

1. In the Tools panel, click the **Selection** tool, and then double-click the semi-circle shape. The Edit Object dialog box opens, indicating that Flash must convert the shape to a drawing object.

Trouble? If the Edit Object dialog box doesn't open, the warning was disabled for your installation, and the program switches to Drawing Object mode. Continue with Step 3.

2. Click the **OK** button. The program switches to Drawing Object mode.

3. In the Tools panel, click the **Line** tool ◥, and then make sure the stroke color is **black** (#000000), the stroke height is **1**, and the stroke style is **Solid**.

4. In the Tools panel, click the **Snap to Objects** button 🧲 to select it, if necessary.

5. Draw three lines on the semicircle, as shown in Figure 2-26, for the umbrella frame.

Figure 2-26   Lines added for the umbrella frame

draw three lines on the semicircle

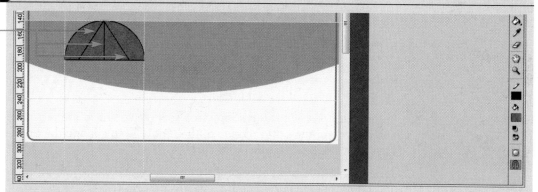

TIP

To draw a straight line, hold the Shift key as you draw with the Line tool.

6. Draw a vertical line from the midpoint at the bottom edge of the semicircle to the bottom guide for the umbrella pole. See Figure 2-27.

Figure 2-27   Line added for the umbrella pole

draw a straight line for the pole

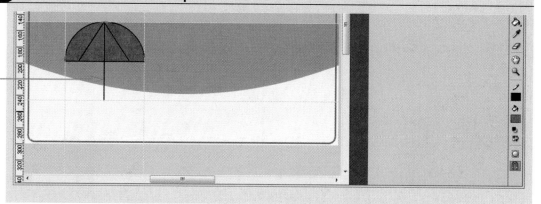

Based on Aly's sketch, two of the lines that make up the umbrella frame should be curved, and the bottom edge of the umbrella should be curved. You will use the Selection tool to modify these lines.

To modify the lines on the umbrella:

1. In the Tools panel, click the **Selection** tool ▸.

2. Using the Selection pointer ▸▫, point to the line on the left side of the umbrella until the pointer changes to ▸⌣, and then drag the left line slightly to the left to curve it.

3. Drag the line on the right side of the umbrella slightly to the right to curve it. See Figure 2-28.

Figure 2-28   **Lines modified with the Selection tool**

curved lines on
the left and
right sides of
the umbrella

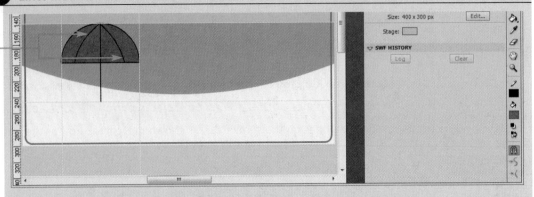

4. In the Tools panel, click the **Zoom** tool 🔍, make sure the **Enlarge** modifier button 🔍 is selected, and then click the umbrella once to zoom in and center the umbrella on the Stage. The increased magnification makes it simpler to modify the bottom edge of the umbrella.

5. In the Tools panel, click the **Selection** tool ▶, point to the first line segment on the left side of the bottom edge of the umbrella to change the pointer to ▶↓, and then drag the line slightly up to curve it.

6. Repeat Step 5 to drag each of the other three line segments at the bottom edge of the umbrella to curve them. See Figure 2-29.

Figure 2-29   **Modified line segments**

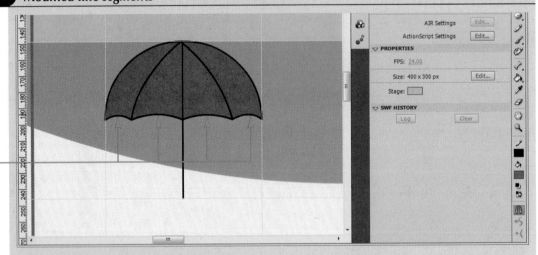

curved line
segments at
the bottom of
the umbrella

7. On the Application bar, click **View**, point to **Guides**, and click **Clear Guides**. The guides are removed from the Stage.

8. On the Edit bar, click the **Scene 1** link to exit Object Drawing mode.

Using the Free Transform Tool

You can modify the strokes and fills of objects you draw in ways other than just changing their colors. The Free Transform tool allows you to modify objects. You can transform a particular stroke or fill, or you can transform the entire object at once. When you select an object with the Free Transform tool, a bounding box with transformation handles surrounds the object. These handles are different from the anchor points you used with the Subselection tool. The anchor points modify individual curves, lines, or shapes. The transformation handles on the bounding box affect the entire object.

Transforming an Object Using the Free Transform Tool

- In the Tools panel, click the Free Transform tool.
- Select the object to transform.
- In the Tools panel, click a modifier.
- Drag the transformation handles on the bounding box to modify the object.

As you move the pointer near a transformation handle on a bounding box handle, the pointer changes to indicate how the object will be modified when you drag that handle. For example, when you point just outside a corner handle, the pointer changes to ↻, indicating that you can rotate the object by dragging the corner. The Free Transform tool also has several modifiers in the Tools panel, which are described in Figure 2-30.

Figure 2-30   **Free Transform tool modifiers**

Button	Modifier	Description
↻	Rotate and Skew	Freely rotates an object by dragging a corner handle or skews it to a different angle by dragging an edge handle
⬔	Scale	Changes the size of an object by dragging a corner or edge handle
◰	Distort	Repositions the corner or edge of an object by dragging its handle
◩	Envelope	Displays a bounding box with points and tangent handles that you can adjust to warp or distort the object

Aly's sketch shows the umbrella angled in the sand and a wavy line for the top of the blue rectangle that represents the ocean. You will use the Free Transform tool to reposition the umbrella and modify the blue rectangle.

To reposition the umbrella and modify the blue rectangle:

1. On the Edit bar, click the **Zoom control arrow**, and then click **Show Frame** to set the magnification level so you can see all of the Stage.

2. Click the umbrella to select it, if necessary.

3. In the Tools panel, click the **Free Transform** tool ▦, and then click the **Rotate and Skew** modifier button ↻. The bounding box and transformation handles appear around the umbrella.

TIP

Transformation handles are squares and tangent handles are circles.

4. Drag a corner transformation handle counterclockwise to tilt the umbrella to the left, and then drag the umbrella to position it in the lower-left corner of the banner.

5. On the Stage, click the blue rectangle. The ocean rectangle is selected and transformation handles appear around the edge of the rectangle.

6. In the Tools panel, click the **Envelope** modifier button ◩. Tangent handles appear on the bounding box.

Trouble? If the Envelope modifier button is not visible, click the Collapse to Icons button ▸▸ above the Tools panel, click the Tools button ✂, and then click the Envelope modifier button ◻. Click the Expand Panels button ◂◂ to expand the Tools panel.

▸ 7. On the top of the rectangle, drag the far left tangent handle down to create a curve. See Figure 2-31.

Figure 2-31	Curve created by dragging a tangent handle

curved line

tangent handle

rotated umbrella

Free Transform tool

bounding box

▸ 8. On the top of the rectangle, drag the far right tangent handle down to create a curve. See Figure 2-32.

Figure 2-32   Second curve created by dragging a tangent handle

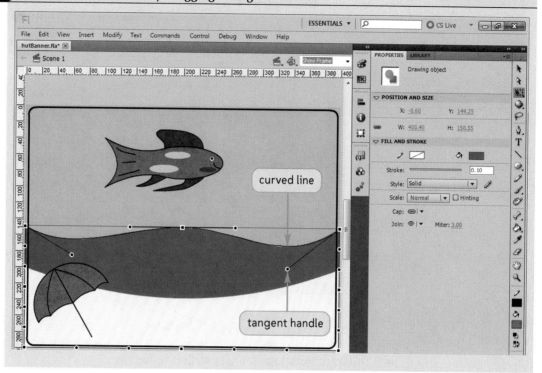

Aly's sketch shows a smaller fish swimming to the right of the fish you already drew. Instead of drawing a smaller fish from scratch, you'll copy the existing fish, and then use the Free Transform tool to resize and rotate the copied fish. You will also reposition the first fish.

To copy, reposition, resize, and rotate the fish:

1. In the Tools panel, click the **Selection** tool ![selection tool], and then click the fish. The grouped fish is selected.

2. On the Application bar, click **Edit**, and then click **Copy**. The fish is copied to the Windows Clipboard.

3. On the Application bar, click **Edit**, and then click **Paste in Center**. A copy of the fish appears in the center of the Stage.

4. Drag the copy of the fish to the right side of the Stage so that half of it is below the ocean line, and then drag the first fish down toward the ocean. See Figure 2-33.

Figure 2-33   **Repositioned fish**

5. In the Tools panel, click the **Free Transform** tool [icon], and then click the copied fish. A bounding box with transformation handles appears around the selected fish. You want to reduce the size of the copied fish.

6. In the Tools panel, click the **Scale** modifier button [icon]. When you drag a corner handle, the fish will be resized.

7. Drag a corner handle to reduce the size of the fish to about half its original size.

8. In the Tools panel, click the **Rotate and Skew** modifier button [icon], and then move the pointer near a corner handle. The pointer changes to [icon].

9. Drag the corner handle clockwise to rotate the fish so that it appears to be swimming downward. See Figure 2-34.

Figure 2-34   **Scaled and rotated fish**

Trouble? If the fish in your banner are in a different location than shown in Figure 2-34, you need to reposition them. Drag the fish as needed to match the locations shown.

▶ **10.** Save the banner.

INSIGHT

Transforming Objects Precisely

When you want to make very specific changes to an object, the Transform panel provides precise control over how you modify the object. In the Transform panel, you can enter specific values in pixels to resize an object. You can also enter values in degrees to rotate an object or skew an object horizontally or vertically. If you want to try different transformations without affecting the original object, you can make a copy of an object and then apply a transformation to the copied object.

In this session, you used the drawing tools to create and modify the graphics on the banner, including the fish, the umbrella, and the background. You modified fill colors, stroke colors, heights, and styles. You also scaled and rotated the fish and umbrella. Aly is pleased with the fish, the umbrella, and the background graphics. In the next session, you will add the text to the banner.

REVIEW

Session 2.1 Quick Check

1. True or False. When drawing a shape with the Oval tool, you can draw a perfect circle when the Snap to Grid modifier is selected.
2. How can you draw a rectangle with rounded corners?
3. The _____ tool can be used to draw pie shapes and half circles.
4. The _____ modifier helps straighten lines you draw with the Pencil tool.
5. Describe how to use the Eyedropper tool to copy a stroke's attributes to another object.
6. Which tool can you use to add a fill to an enclosed area that has no fill?
7. Which modifier can be used with the Free Transform tool to resize a selected object?
8. True or False. The Free Transform tool is used to modify an object's gradient fill.

SESSION 2.2 VISUAL OVERVIEW

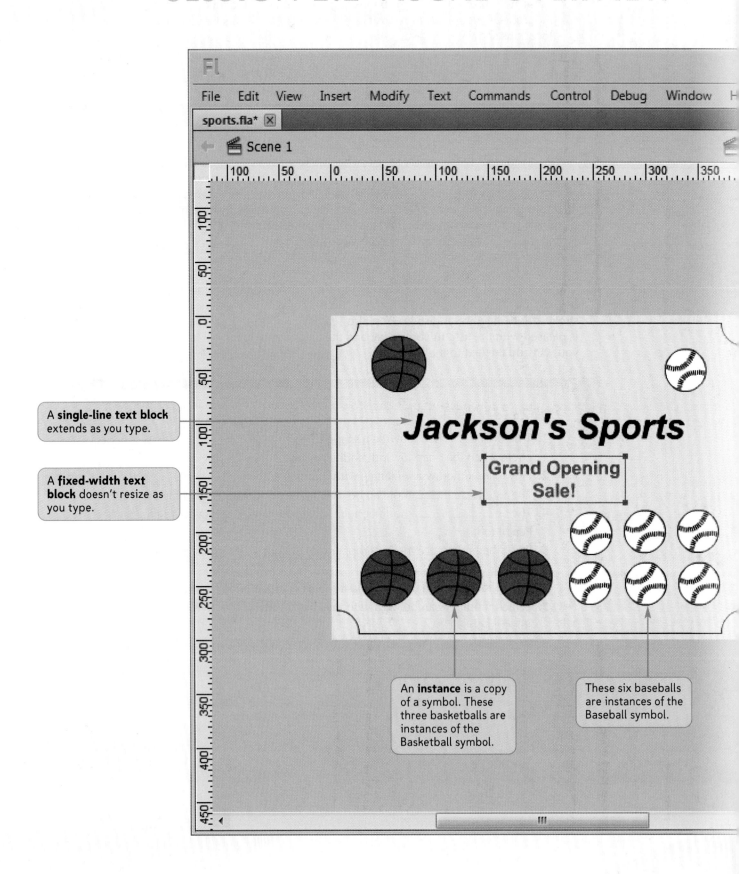

A **single-line text block** extends as you type.

A **fixed-width text block** doesn't resize as you type.

An **instance** is a copy of a symbol. These three basketballs are instances of the Basketball symbol.

These six baseballs are instances of the Baseball symbol.

TEXT BLOCKS AND SYMBOLS

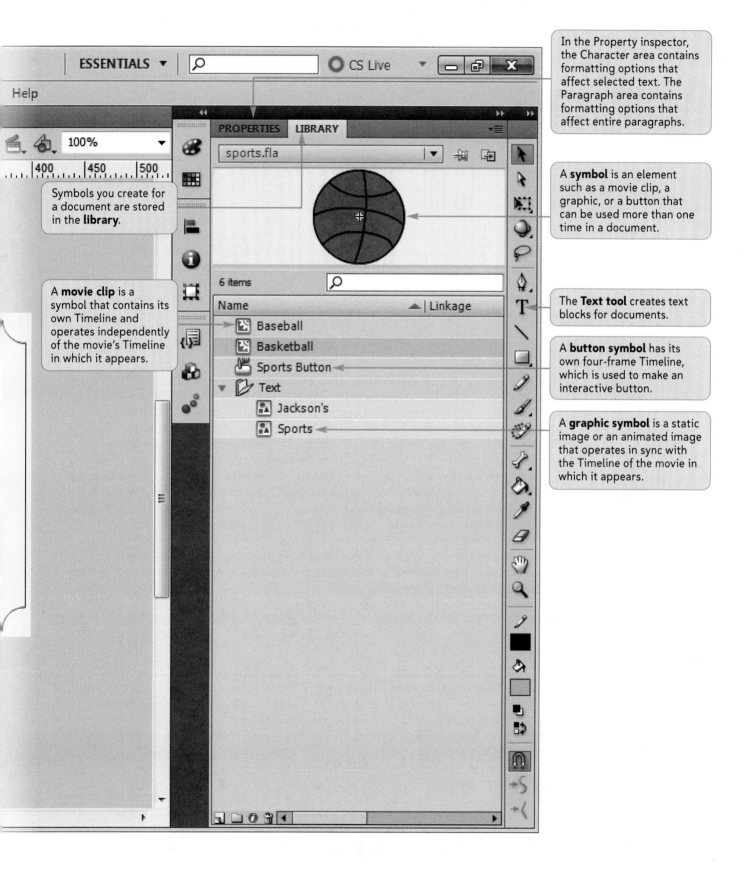

In the Property inspector, the Character area contains formatting options that affect selected text. The Paragraph area contains formatting options that affect entire paragraphs.

Symbols you create for a document are stored in the **library**.

A **symbol** is an element such as a movie clip, a graphic, or a button that can be used more than one time in a document.

A **movie clip** is a symbol that contains its own Timeline and operates independently of the movie's Timeline in which it appears.

The **Text tool** creates text blocks for documents.

A **button symbol** has its own four-frame Timeline, which is used to make an interactive button.

A **graphic symbol** is a static image or an animated image that operates in sync with the Timeline of the movie in which it appears.

Adding Text

Graphic images do not always communicate the message you are trying to convey. Many images and animations also include text. In Flash, you can create text blocks in a variety of colors, sizes, and fonts. By default, Flash uses the **Text Layout Framework (TLF) engine** to create text. The TLF engine provides extensive formatting options, including the ability to create columns of text and to link text blocks. Text created using the TLF engine is called **TLF text**.

The TLF engine creates Read Only, Selectable, or Editable text blocks. A **Read Only text block** cannot be selected or changed. The text in a **Selectable text block** can be selected but not changed. The text in an **Editable text block** can be selected and changed by the user. You will work with Read Only text blocks in this tutorial.

You can also create text using the **Classic Text engine**, which creates static, dynamic, or input text blocks. A **static text block** is an object that contains text entered when you create the document but does not change after you publish the document. A **dynamic text field** is an advanced feature where text is updated as a result of programming instructions within the SWF file or with information from a Web server when the document is published and displayed in a Web browser. A **field** is a unit of data such as a person's age or phone number. An example of a dynamic text field is one that displays up-to-the-minute sports scores retrieved from a Web server. Dynamic text fields can also display the results of a calculation based on values entered into input text fields. An **input text field** allows the user to enter text in forms or surveys.

TIP

Text blocks can be arranged in columns so that text flows from one column to the next.

Using the Text Tool

The Text tool can create fixed-width text blocks or single-line text blocks. If the width of the text block is fixed, the text wraps to create new lines as needed. A fixed-width text block has a square handle in its upper-right corner when created as Classic Text, and square handles on both its left and right sides when created as TLF text. The square handles indicate that the width of the text block will remain fixed. As you type, the words wrap to the next line when you reach the right margin of the block. A single-line text block has a round handle on the upper-right corner when created as Classic Text and on the lower-right corner when created as TLF text. The round handles indicate that the width of the text block extends as you type.

TIP

You can drag the round handle of a single-line text block to adjust its width, changing it to a fixed-width text block.

After you create a text block, you can move it using the Selection tool. You can also resize, rotate, and skew the text block using the Free Transform tool. The font, font size, text fill color, text styles, alignment, and other text properties are specified in the Property inspector. You can set these properties before you type the text, or you can select existing text and then change the properties.

INSIGHT

Anti-Aliasing Text

To improve readability, Flash uses a rendering engine that provides high-quality, clear text in Flash documents. **Anti-aliasing**, which is part of the rendering process, smoothes the edges of text displayed on the computer screen. Anti-aliasing is especially effective when using small font sizes. When text is selected on the Stage, the Font rendering method list in the Property inspector provides two methods: Anti-alias for animation and Anti-alias for readability. Select Anti-alias for animation when the text will be animated to create a smoother animation. If the text will not be animated, select Anti-alias for readability, which improves the legibility of the text.

You will use the Text tool to add two text blocks to the banner: one at the top of the banner and one at the bottom. You will set the Property inspector options before you create each text block.

To add a single-line text block to the top of the banner:

1. If you took a break after the previous session, make sure the hutBanner.fla document is open, the workspace is reset to the Essentials layout, the Timeline is closed, and the zoom magnification is set to Show Frame.

2. In the Tools panel, click the **Text** tool ⊤. The pointer changes to ⊤, indicating that you are working with text.

3. In the Property inspector, make sure **Classic Text** is selected as the Text engine, and **Static Text** is selected as the text type. Before you type the banner text, you'll set the text properties.

4. In the Character section of the Property inspector, set the Family to **Arial**, drag the Size value to change the point size to **28**, and set the Color to **maroon** (#660000), sixth column from the right, first row.

5. In the Property inspector, click **PARAGRAPH** to expand the paragraph properties, if necessary, and then click the **Align center** button ≡ to apply the center style.

6. Click in the top area of the Stage to create a single-line text block, type **Jenny's Oyster Hut**, press the **Enter** key to move the insertion point to the next line, and then type **10th Anniversary!**.

7. In the Tools panel, click the **Selection** tool ▶, and then, if necessary, drag the text block to center it at the top of the Stage.

8. In the Character section of the Property inspector, set the Style to **Bold Italic**, and make sure the Anti-alias setting is **Anti-alias for readability**. See Figure 2-35.

Figure 2-35   **Text block for the top of the banner**

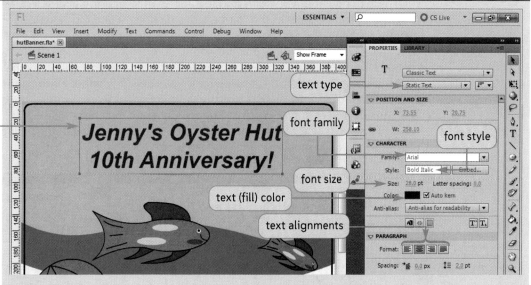

9. Click an empty area of the Stage to deselect the text block.

You will create a second text block at the bottom of the banner. Before you create the second text block, you'll change the text properties in the Property inspector.

To add a single-line text block to the bottom of the banner:

1. In the Tools panel, click the **Text** tool $\boxed{\text{T}}$.

2. In the Character section of the Property inspector, set the font family to **Times New Roman**, set the size to **16**, and set the text fill color to **dark red** (#990000) in the second swatches column from the left, seventh row of the color palette. Center alignment remains in place from the previous settings.

3. Click the bottom of the Stage in the light yellow beach area to create a single-line text block, and then type **Enjoy 10% off on Sundays this month!** in the text block.

4. In the Tools panel, click the **Selection** tool 🡕, and then drag the text block to the right of the umbrella's pole.

5. In the Character section of the Property inspector, set the style to **Bold** and make sure the anti-alias setting is **Anti-alias for readability**.

6. Click the pasteboard to deselect the text block, and then save the banner.

TIP

You can also press the V key to select the Selection tool in the Tools panel.

Checking the Spelling of Text

Flash can check the spelling of text you add to a document. The Check Spelling command verifies the spelling in each text block in the document. It can also check the spelling of text in other parts of the document, such as symbol names and layer names. Symbols are covered in the next session and layers are covered in Tutorial 3.

Before you use the Check Spelling command, you can specify options in the Spelling Setup dialog box. Under Document options, you specify which text areas to check, such as the content of text fields and the names of layers. You also select which built-in dictionaries to use, such as the Adobe terms dictionary and the American English language dictionary. The personal dictionary is a file that Flash creates on your hard drive to which you can add words that are not in the Adobe or language dictionaries but are spelled correctly, such as a company name. You can also edit your personal dictionary after it is created. In the Checking options, you specify whether Flash ignores or finds specific character types such as words with numbers or words with all uppercase letters. You can also select options such as Suggest phonetic matches to have Flash provide a list of suggestions when it encounters a misspelled word. You can then choose one of the suggested words to replace the misspelled word.

REFERENCE

Setting Options for the Spelling Checker

- On the Application bar, click Text, and then click Spelling Setup.
- In the Spelling Setup dialog box, select the desired options.
- Click the OK button.

You will set the spelling checker options before checking the spelling of text in the banner.

To set the spelling checker options:

▶ **1.** On the Application bar, click **Text**, and then click **Spelling Setup**. The Spelling Setup dialog box opens. See Figure 2-36.

Figure 2-36   ▶ Spelling Setup dialog box

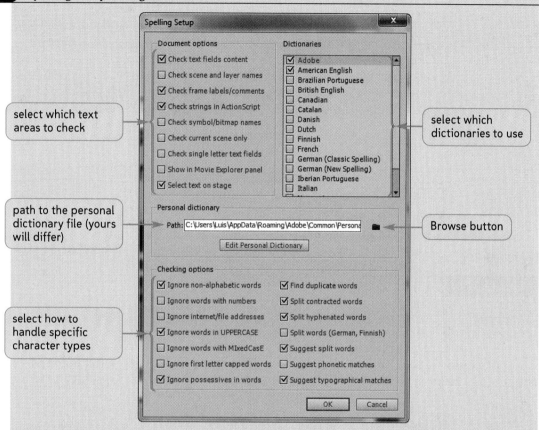

▶ **2.** In the Document options, click the **Check text fields content** check box to check it, if necessary.

▶ **3.** In the Dictionaries box, click the **American English** check box to check it, if necessary.

▶ **4.** In the Checking options, make sure that the **Ignore possessives in words** check box is checked.

▶ **5.** Click the **OK** button. The Spelling Setup dialog box closes.

When you check the spelling in a document, the Check Spelling dialog box opens if Flash finds a word that is misspelled or is not in its dictionaries. Depending on the options you selected in the Spelling Setup dialog box, the Check Spelling dialog box might offer suggestions for replacing the word. You can choose to ignore, change, delete, or add the word to your personal dictionary. The Check Spelling dialog box also shows in what element of the document the word not found is located, such as in a text field, a scene name, or a layer name.

PROSKILLS

Written Communication: The Importance of Correct Spelling

Having a misspelled word in a Flash movie can detract from the message or idea you are trying to promote. So, take advantage of the spelling checker in Flash to ensure that the text in your documents uses standard spelling. Keep in mind that the spelling checker only compares words in the document with words in the selected dictionaries. If a word is incorrect in context but is spelled correctly, the spelling checker will not detect it. Think of homonyms such as *they're*, *there*, and *their* or easily mistyped words such as *form* and *from*. So, because the spelling checker may not catch every error, be sure to review your work carefully. As a final check, it's a good idea to ask someone who isn't working on the document to proofread the text. This will help to ensure that your finished product is error free, leaving the audience free to focus on the intended message of the Flash movie.

You will check the spelling of the text in the banner.

To check spelling in the banner:

▶ 1. On the Application bar, click **Text**, and click **Check Spelling**. The Check Spelling dialog box opens, indicating the first word not found in the selected dictionaries. The word not found in the Check Spelling dialog box is 10th. See Figure 2-37.

| Figure 2-37 | Check Spelling dialog box |

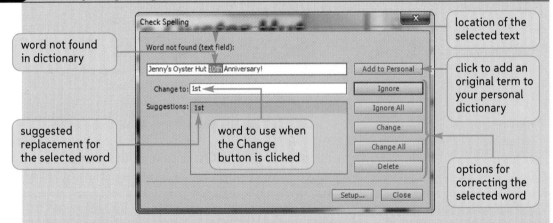

Trouble? If a different word is found, you might have another word spelled incorrectly. If the word is spelled correctly, click the Ignore button. If the word is not spelled correctly, click the correct spelling in the Suggestions box or type the correct spelling in the Change to box, and then click the Change button. Repeat until 10th is the word not found.

▶ 2. Click the **Ignore** button. A dialog box opens, indicating that the spelling check is complete.

Trouble? If other words are not found, they are not in your selected dictionaries. If the word is spelled correctly, click the Ignore button to ignore the suggestion and leave the original spelling. If the word is spelled incorrectly, click the correct spelling in the Suggestions box or type the correct spelling in the Change to box, and then click the Change button to replace the word not found.

▶ 3. Click the **OK** button.

Exporting a Graphic for Use on the Web

A document you create in Flash is saved in the FLA format. This format contains all of the different elements you create in Flash. To revise the document, you open the FLA file. To place the image in a Web page, however, it needs to be published or exported.

Publishing a document will be covered in more detail in Tutorial 3 when you add animations to documents. A published document is in the SWF file format and is called a Flash movie. It requires the Flash Player plug-in to play in a Web browser.

When you create a document banner that doesn't have animation, such as Jenny's Oyster Hut, you can export it instead of publishing it. **Exporting** means that the program converts the document into another file format, such as GIF, JPG, or PNG, which do not require a plug-in to display in a Web page. Exporting also combines all the individual elements of a document into one graphic. You cannot edit the individual elements of the image in an exported file. To edit the image's elements, you must go back to the corresponding FLA file. After you export a document into a GIF, JPG, or PNG file format, it can be placed in a Web page.

You'll export the banner into the JPG file format so it can be used on the restaurant's Web site.

To export the banner to the JPG file format:

▶ 1. On the Application bar, click **File**, point to **Export**, and then click **Export Image**. The Export Image dialog box opens.

▶ 2. Navigate to the **Flash2\Tutorial** folder included with your Data Files, if necessary. The banner will be saved in that location with the name hutBanner.jpg.

▶ 3. Click the **Save as type** button to open a menu of file formats, and then click **JPEG Image (*.jpg, *.jpeg)**. The banner will be saved in the JPG file format. See Figure 2-39.

| Figure 2-38 | Export Image dialog box |

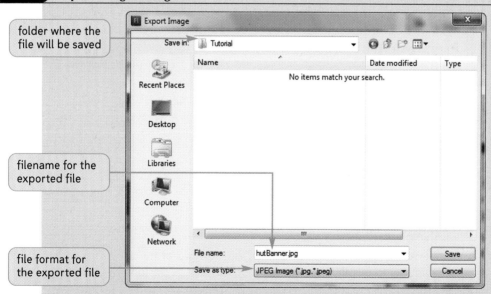

folder where the file will be saved

filename for the exported file

file format for the exported file

▶ 4. Click the **Save** button. The Export JPEG dialog box opens with additional options and settings, including the document's dimensions and resolution.

▶ 5. Click the **Include** button, and then click **Full Document Size**, if necessary. This option makes the exported JPG image the same size as the Flash document. The Minimum Image Area option might reduce the size of the exported JPG image based on the content on the Stage.

6. In the Quality box, enter **80** for the quality of the exported image. You'll accept the rest of the default settings.

7. Click the **OK** button. The banner is exported as a JPG file.

8. Save the banner.

Chris created a Web page with the HTML code needed to display the hutBanner.jpg image. You will preview this Web page in a Web browser.

To preview the hutBanner.jpg file in a Web browser:

1. Start **Internet Explorer** or another Web browser. (If you are using a different Web browser, modify Steps 2 through 4 as needed.)

2. On the Internet Explorer menu bar, click **File**, and then click **Open**. The Open dialog box opens.

Trouble? If the menu bar is not visible, you need to display it. Press the Alt key to display the menu bar, and then repeat Step 2.

3. Click the **Browse** button, navigate to the **Flash2\Tutorial** folder included with your Data Files, click the **jennys.htm** file, and then click the **Open** button.

4. Click the **OK** button. The Web page opens in the browser, and the hutBanner.jpg file appears as part of the page. See Figure 2-39.

| Figure 2-39 | Web page with the exported banner image |

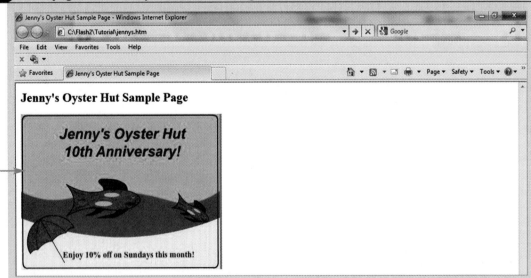

exported
hutBanner.jpg file
displayed in the
Web page (your
banner image might
differ slightly)

Trouble? If a dialog box opens, indicating that the browser needs to open a new window to display the Web page, click the OK button.

5. Close the browser.

Using the History Panel

The **History panel** holds a record of the steps performed in the current document. After you open or create a document, each step is recorded and displayed in the History panel with an icon that reflects the particular step. The History panel displays only the steps for the current document. If you switch to another document, the History panel shows the steps taken in creating or editing that document. A document's history is maintained until you close the document or clear its history. You can also save selected steps by creating a command based on those steps. The command can then be used in the same document or in another document and is available each time you use Flash. From the History panel, you can replay, undo, and save the recorded steps.

You will use the History panel as you work with a document Aly created for another Admiral Web Design client, Jackson's Sports.

To use the History panel with the sports.fla document:

▶ **1.** On the Application bar, click **File**, and then click **Open**. The Open dialog box opens.

▶ **2.** Navigate to the **Flash2\Tutorial** folder included with your Data Files, if necessary, and then double-click the **sports.fla** file. The Jackson's Sports banner opens.

▶ **3.** On the Application bar, click **Window**, point to **Other Panels**, and then click **History**. The History panel opens.

▶ **4.** If the History panel appears on top of the document, drag the History panel by its title bar to the left side of the document.

Before you can work with the document, you need to unlock the layers in the document. You do this by using the Timeline.

▶ **5.** On the Application bar, click **Window**, and then click **Timeline**. The Timeline appears.

▶ **6.** In the Timeline, click the **Lock or Unlock All Layers** icon 🔒 to unlock all the layers. A step labeled Lock Layers appears in the History panel.

▶ **7.** In the Tools panel, click the **Selection** tool ▶, and then click the **Jackson's Sports** text block to select it. The Change Selection step appears in the History panel.

▶ **8.** In the Property inspector, change the Text (fill) color to **blue** (#0000FF) in the first swatches column, ninth row of the color palette. The letters in the text block change color, and this step appears in the History panel. See Figure 2-40.

Figure 2-40 ▶ History panel with the current session's steps

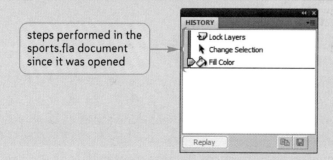

steps performed in the sports.fla document since it was opened

▶ **9.** In the Tools panel, click the **Free Transform** tool ▦, and then click the **Scale** modifier button 🔲 to select it.

▶ **10.** Drag the lower-right corner handle on the text block to make the text block slightly larger. The Scale step appears in the History panel.

Replaying Steps

TIP

You can select and copy steps taken in one document using the Copy selected steps to the clipboard button, and then apply them using the Paste in Center command in another document.

You can replay one or more selected steps in the History panel. For example, after you create a shape, you can select the steps in the History panel that you took to create the shape, and then replay the steps to create a duplicate of the shape. If you select steps in the History panel that you used to format an object on the Stage, you can replay the steps to apply the same formatting to another object on the Stage. The steps you select in the History panel are applied to the selected object in the order shown in the panel. The replayed steps can be consecutive or nonconsecutive. Steps displayed with an icon that includes a small, red X cannot be replayed.

You will replay the steps you performed previously from the History panel to further modify the sports document.

To replay steps from the History panel:

1. In the History panel, drag to select the **Fill Color** and **Scale** steps. The two consecutive steps are selected. See Figure 2-41.

Figure 2-41   **Steps selected in the History panel**

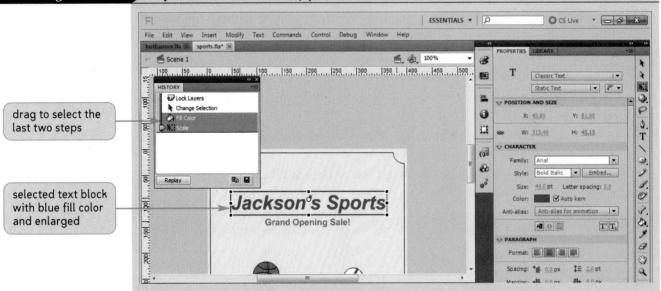

drag to select the last two steps

selected text block with blue fill color and enlarged

Trouble? If the last steps performed are undone, you probably dragged the slider on the left side of the History panel instead of the actual steps. Drag the slider down to the last step you performed, and then repeat Step 1, being careful to select the steps in the History panel and not the slider.

2. In the center of the Stage, click the **Grand Opening Sale!** text block to select it. The new step is added at the end of the History panel.

3. In the History panel, click the **Replay** button. The two selected steps are replayed: The Grand Opening Sale! text block increases in size and its text color changes to blue. The History panel records the Replay Steps step.

4. In the Tools panel, click the **Selection** tool, and then drag the basketball to the top of the Stage. The basketball is repositioned, and the Change Selection and Move steps appear in the History panel.

5. Press and hold the **Ctrl** key, and then, in the History panel, click the **Move** step to select it, click the **Fill Color** step to deselect it, and then release the **Ctrl** key. The nonconsecutive Scale and Move steps are selected in the History panel.

6. On the Stage, click the baseball to select it, and then, in the History panel, click the **Replay** button. The nonconsecutive steps are replayed, and the baseball becomes slightly larger and moves to the top of the Stage. The History panel shows the last two steps you performed. See Figure 2-42.

Figure 2-42   **Steps replayed and applied to baseball**

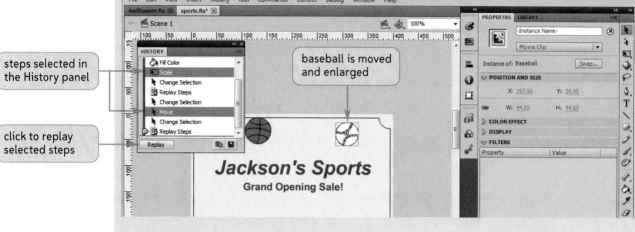

steps selected in the History panel

baseball is moved and enlarged

click to replay selected steps

Undoing Steps

As you create and modify objects, you may want to undo one or more steps within a document. This might occur if you make a mistake and you want to return to the previous step. You can undo one step or as many as 100 steps. This lets you backtrack though a series of steps until the document returns to the particular state at which you want to start over. You can change the default maximum number of steps that can be undone in the Preferences dialog box.

Flash provides two types of undo. In **document-level undo**, the steps you undo affect the entire document. In **object-level undo**, you can undo steps performed on individual objects without affecting the steps performed on other objects. You change from one type of undo to another in the Preferences dialog box. When you change the type of undo, the steps currently recorded in the History panel are deleted. In this tutorial, you work with the default mode, document-level undo.

You can use the History panel to change the document back to how it was before you performed a series of steps. The slider in the History panel initially points to the last step performed. As you drag the slider to a previous step, any subsequent step is undone and is reflected in the document on the Stage. Undone steps appear dimmed in the History panel.

You will use the History panel to undo some of the steps you have performed.

To undo steps in the sports.fla document:

1. In the History panel, drag the slider up to the Scale step. The steps below the Scale step are dimmed, indicating that they have been undone. The objects on the Stage also change to reflect that the steps were undone. See Figure 2-43.

TIP

You can also undo one step at a time by pressing the Ctrl+Z keys.

Figure 2-43 | **Steps undone in the History panel**

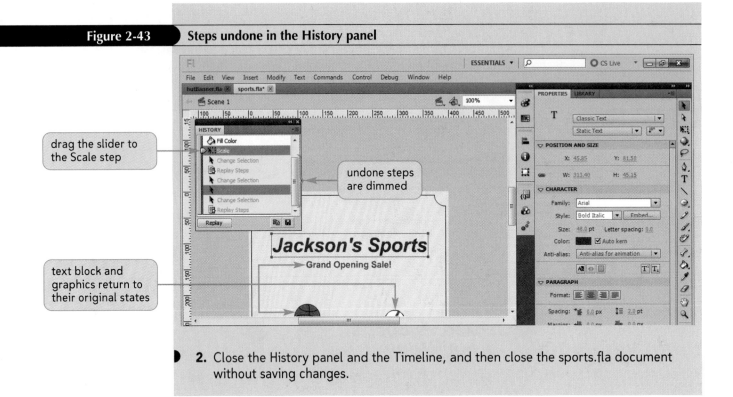

drag the slider to the Scale step

undone steps are dimmed

text block and graphics return to their original states

Jackson's Sports

Grand Opening Sale!

  2. Close the History panel and the Timeline, and then close the sports.fla document without saving changes.

Working with Symbols

You can create a symbol from an existing object or you can create a new symbol. You can also use symbols from other Flash documents in the current document.

Comparing Symbol Behavior Types

Symbols can have one of three behavior types: movie clip, graphic, or button. A movie clip operates independently of the movie in which it appears. For example, a movie clip that contains an animation sequence spanning 10 frames within its own Timeline occupies only one frame within the document's Timeline, yet it still plays its own 10-frame animation. Most of the symbols you create will be movie clips. A graphic symbol operates in sync with the Timeline of the movie in which it appears; for example, a Flash document's Timeline. A button symbol has its own four-frame Timeline so you can create an interactive button. You will learn more about buttons in Tutorial 5.

Creating Symbols

To create a symbol, you can either convert an existing graphic into a symbol or create a new symbol. For each symbol you create, you specify its name and its type. When converting an existing graphic into a symbol, you can also specify its registration point, which can be used to control how the symbol is animated.

Creating a Symbol

- Select an existing graphic, click Modify on the Application bar, and then click Convert to Symbol.
- Type a symbol name in the Name box, click the Type button and select a symbol type, and then click the OK button.

or

- On the Application bar, click Insert, and then click New Symbol.
- Type a symbol name in the Name box, click the Type button and select a symbol type, and then click the OK button.
- In symbol-editing mode, create the graphic(s) for the symbol.
- On the Application bar, click Insert, and then click Edit Document.

You will convert the fish graphic you created for the banner for Jenny's Oyster Hut Web site into a symbol.

To create a symbol from the fish:

1. In the Tools panel, click the **Selection** tool , if necessary, and then click the larger fish on the center of the Stage. The larger fish graphic is selected. You will ungroup the graphic before converting it to a symbol.

   Trouble? If the ocean graphic is selected instead of the fish graphic, you probably didn't click the fish graphic. Click the top part of the fish again to select the fish.

2. On the Application bar, click **Modify**, and then click **Ungroup**. The fish is no longer grouped, but all of its parts are still selected.

3. On the Application bar, click **Modify**, and then click **Convert to Symbol**. The Convert to Symbol dialog box opens. In this dialog box, you can specify a name for the symbol and select a behavior type.

4. In the Name box, type **bigFish**, and then, if necessary, click the **Type** button, and click **Movie Clip**. See Figure 2-44.

| Figure 2-44 | Convert to Symbol dialog box |

type a name for the symbol

select the type of symbol

indicates symbol's registration point

5. Click the **OK** button. The dialog box closes. The symbol is created and added to the library for this document.

Using the Library

You view, organize, and edit symbols stored in the library from the Library panel. When you create a symbol for a document, you assign a name to it, and then specify its properties. These properties are stored with the symbol in the library. Symbols created within a document are saved with that document. However, you can share symbols with other documents by making them part of a shared library. You can modify a symbol's properties using the Library panel. The Library panel displays a list with the names of all the symbols in the library for a document. Each symbol in the Library panel has an icon to the left of its name to show what type of symbol it is.

The Library panel includes information about each symbol, including whether the symbol is shared with other documents (Linkage column), the number of times the symbol is used in the document (Use Count column), the date it was last modified (Date Modified column), and the symbol's type (Type column). You can sort the symbols by clicking a column header; for example, to sort the symbols by date, click the Date Modified header. The dates range from most recent to oldest. This order can be reversed by clicking the Toggle Sorting Order button.

Additional Library panel options can be accessed using the Library panel's menu. This menu includes options to create, rename, edit, delete, or duplicate a symbol.

INSIGHT

Organizing Symbols in the Library

As you work with a document, you will often create many symbols. Some symbols may be related to a particular graphic in the document. For example, you might have multiple symbols that make up a button on the Stage. As the document gets more complex, the number of symbols in the library can increase significantly and become unmanageable. To make it easier to manage and organize the symbols in the Library panel, you can create folders to group and hold related symbols. By default, the Library panel contains a **root folder** that contains all the document's symbols. All new folders are created within the root folder. Any symbols inside a folder are indented under the folder name.

The names you give your folders and symbols can also help keep your work organized. Assign meaningful names to the folders and symbols you create, especially if you plan to have many symbols in a document. Descriptive names, such as bigFish and littleFish, make it easier to find the symbol you want in the Library panel without having to preview each symbol. You can also enter a symbol's name in the Library panel's search box to quickly display the symbol in the panel.

You will explore the hutBanner.fla document's library to see how symbols are stored.

To explore the hutBanner.fla document's library:

TIP

You can also press the Ctrl+L keys to open and close the Library panel.

1. Next to the Property inspector, click the **LIBRARY** tab to bring the Library panel to the front of the panel group. The Library panel displays the symbol for this document. See Figure 2-45.

Figure 2-45 Library panel

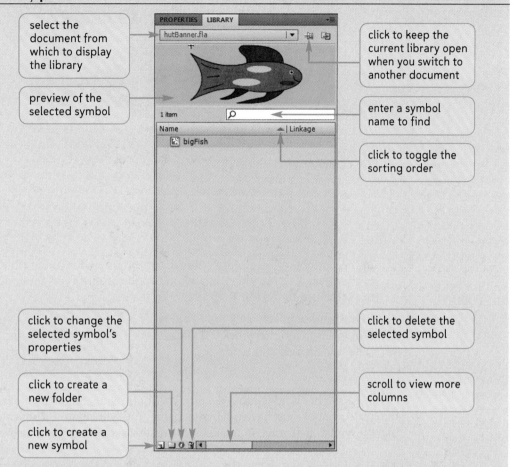

select the document from which to display the library

preview of the selected symbol

click to change the selected symbol's properties

click to create a new folder

click to create a new symbol

click to keep the current library open when you switch to another document

enter a symbol name to find

click to toggle the sorting order

click to delete the selected symbol

scroll to view more columns

▶ **2.** In the Name column of the Library panel, click the **bigFish** symbol, if necessary. A thumbnail of the fish appears in the preview box at the top of the Library panel. The symbol's icon indicates the symbol is a movie clip.

▶ **3.** In the Library panel, click the **Properties** button 🛈. The Symbol Properties dialog box opens for the bigFish symbol. You'll change this symbol's type.

▶ **4.** Click the **Type** button, click **Graphic**, and then click the **OK** button. The Properties dialog box closes, and the bigFish symbol's icon reflects the new type. See Figure 2-46.

Figure 2-46   Changed symbol in the Library panel

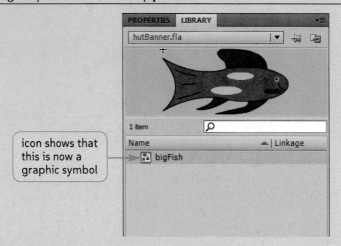

icon shows that
this is now a
graphic symbol

▶ **5.** In the bottom of the Library panel, drag the scroll bar to the right to see the rest of the symbol's properties, including Graphic in the Type column, and then drag the scroll bar to the left to display the Name column.

▶ **6.** In the Library panel, click the **Properties** button ⓘ, click the **Type** button, click **Movie Clip**, and then click the **OK** button. The symbol's icon and type change to reflect the movie clip type.

After a symbol is added to a document's library, you can create a duplicate of it. The duplicate symbol must have a different name. You will create a duplicate symbol of the bigFish symbol that you can then edit to create a second, different fish symbol.

To create a duplicate of the bigFish symbol:

▶ **1.** In the Library panel, click the **panel menu** button ▾≡ to open the panel menu, and then click **Duplicate**. The Duplicate Symbol dialog box opens.

▶ **2.** In the Name box, type **smallFish**. This is the name for the duplicated movie clip symbol. The movie clip type is already selected.

▶ **3.** Click the **OK** button. The smallFish symbol is added to the library.

Editing a Symbol

You can modify a symbol by placing it in symbol-editing mode. A symbol can be edited by itself in symbol-editing mode or it can be edited in place with the rest of the graphics on the Stage dimmed. When a symbol is in symbol-editing mode, the name of the symbol appears on the Edit bar next to the scene name. Flash documents can be divided into multiple scenes, but every document has at least one scene.

REFERENCE

Editing a Symbol

- Select a symbol instance on the Stage, click Edit on the Application bar, and then click Edit Symbols, Edit Selected, or Edit in Place (or double-click a symbol instance on the Stage or select the symbol in the Library panel, click the Library panel menu button, and then click Edit).
- Modify the symbol in symbol-editing mode.
- On the Edit bar, click the Scene 1 link (or double-click an empty area of the Stage or on the Application bar, click Edit, and then click Edit Document).

Aly wants the smallFish symbol to be unique from the bigFish symbol. You will edit the smallFish symbol by changing the fish's body color and resizing the graphic.

To edit the smallFish symbol:

1. In the Library panel, click the **smallFish** symbol to select it, if necessary.

2. In the Library panel, click the **panel menu** button ▼≣, and then click **Edit**. The symbol opens in symbol-editing mode, and smallFish appears on the Edit bar.

3. Click an empty area of the Stage to deselect the fish.

4. In the Tools panel, click the **Paint Bucket** tool 🪣 to select it, click the **Fill Color** control 🎨, and then click the **orange** swatch (#FF9900) in the third column from the right, seventh row of the color palette.

5. On the Stage, click the red body of the fish to change it to orange.

6. On the Application bar, click **Edit**, and then click **Select All**. All of the fish is selected.

7. On the Application bar, click **Window**, and then click **Transform**. The Transform panel opens.

8. In the Transform panel, click the **Constrain** icon 🔗 to change it to 🔗, if necessary. Constrain keeps the width and height proportional when either one is changed.

9. In the Transform panel, drag the **Scale Width** value to the left to change the value to 50%. The height value also changes to 50%, and the fish becomes smaller.

10. On the Edit bar, click the **Scene 1** link to exit symbol editing mode. The banner appears on the Stage.

TIP

You can also press the Ctrl+A keys to select all of the objects on the Stage at one time.

Creating and Editing Instances of Symbols

Every symbol you create is automatically stored in the document's library. To use the symbols in the document, you create instances. Each time you drag a symbol from the Library panel onto the Stage, you create an instance of the symbol in the document. No matter how many instances of a symbol you create, the symbol is stored in the document only once.

Using Instances of Symbols

If you want to use a graphic multiple times in a document, you should convert it into a symbol. Then you can insert instances of the symbol wherever that graphic is needed in the document instead of creating the same graphic multiple times. Using instances of a symbol also makes it easier to modify all instances at the same time by just modifying the symbol. In addition, any graphic you convert into a symbol can be copied from one document's library to another. Finally, using instances of a symbol minimizes the document's size, which in turn reduces the download time of the published SWF file.

Each instance in a document can be edited without changing the symbol in the document's library. For example, consider a document that includes several instances of the same symbol. You can make one instance smaller than the others. You can rotate each instance to a different angle. Any changes you make to one instance do not affect the other instances or the symbol. If you modify the symbol, however, all the instances of that symbol are also changed.

You will place an instance of the smallFish symbol on the banner, and then convert the rightmost fish to a movie clip symbol.

To create a smallFish symbol instance and convert a graphic to a symbol:

▶ **1.** In the Tools panel, click the **Selection** tool .

▶ **2.** Drag the **smallFish** symbol from the Library panel to the Stage to create an instance of the symbol.

▶ **3.** On the Stage, place the **smallFish** instance on the water to the left side of the bigFish instance. See Figure 2-47.

Figure 2-47   **The smallFish symbol instance added to the Stage**

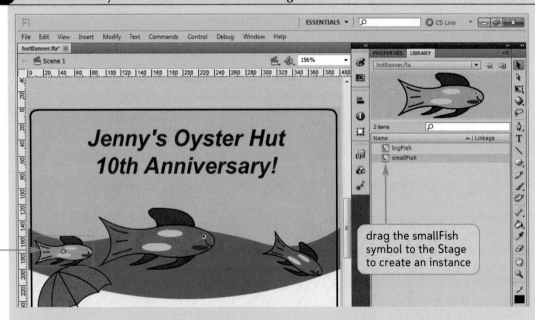

smallFish instance positioned on the banner

drag the smallFish symbol to the Stage to create an instance

▶ **4.** Click the grouped fish graphic on the right side of the Stage to select it.

▶ **5.** On the Application bar, click **Modify**, and then click **Convert to Symbol**. The Convert to Symbol dialog box opens.

6. Type **mediumFish** in the Name box, make sure the type is **Movie Clip**, and then click the **OK** button. The grouped fish graphic is converted to a symbol.

Applying Filters

A **filter** is a special graphic effect, such as a drop shadow, that you can apply to movie clips, buttons, and text. Filters are applied using the Filters section of the Property inspector, which includes preset filters such as drop shadow, blur, glow, and bevel. Multiple filters can be applied to one object, and each filter has properties you can set to adjust the filter's effect on the object. In the Property inspector, you can enable or disable a filter, reset a filter's properties, and delete a filter. You can also copy the filters and properties that have been applied to one object and apply them to another object. Or, you can save a set of filters and properties as a new preset filter, and then apply the saved preset filter to objects in other Flash documents.

You will apply a drop shadow effect to the movie clip symbols and text on the banner.

To apply a filter to objects in the banner:

1. Next to the Library panel, click the **PROPERTIES** tab to bring the Property inspector to the front of the panel group.

2. In the Filters section of the Property inspector, click the **Add filter** button to open a menu of preset filters. See Figure 2-48.

Figure 2-48	Menu of preset filters

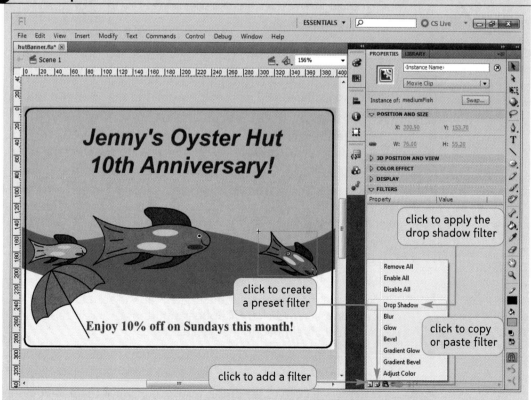

3. Click **Drop Shadow**. A drop shadow effect is applied to the mediumFish instance on the Stage.

4. In the Filters section of the Property inspector, drag the Strength value to the left to set the filter strength to 80%, and then drag the **Distance** value to the right to increase the filter distance to 10px. The drop shadow strength is reduced and its distance from the instance increased. See Figure 2-49.

Figure 2-49	Drop shadow applied to a fish graphic instance

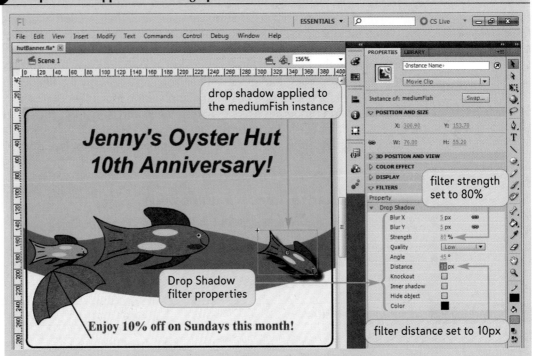

Trouble? If you cannot see the distance value, the pointer is probably covering it. Type 10 in the Distance box, and then press the Enter key.

You will apply the same filter and properties to the other two fish instances on the Stage.

5. In the Filters section of the Property inspector, click the **Clipboard** button 🔖, and then click **Copy All**. The filter effects are stored in the computer's temporary memory.

6. On the Stage, click the **smallFish** instance to select it, and then, in the Property inspector, click the **Clipboard** button 🔖, and click **Paste**. The drop shadow effect is applied to the smallFish instance.

7. On the Stage, click the **bigFish** instance to select it, and then, in the Property inspector, click the **Clipboard** button 🔖, and click **Paste**. The drop shadow effect is applied to the bigFish instance.

8. Click the text block at the bottom of the Stage to select it, and then, in the Property inspector, click the **Clipboard** button 🔖 and click **Paste**. The drop shadow effect is applied to the selected text.

9. In the Property inspector, click **PARAGRAPH** to collapse the Paragraph section. You can now more easily access the Filters section and reset the filter's properties.

10. In the Filters section of the Property inspector, click **Drop Shadow** in the Property column, and then click the **Reset Filter** button 🔄. The filter's properties return to their default values. See Figure 2-50.

Figure 2-50 **Drop shadow effect applied to text**

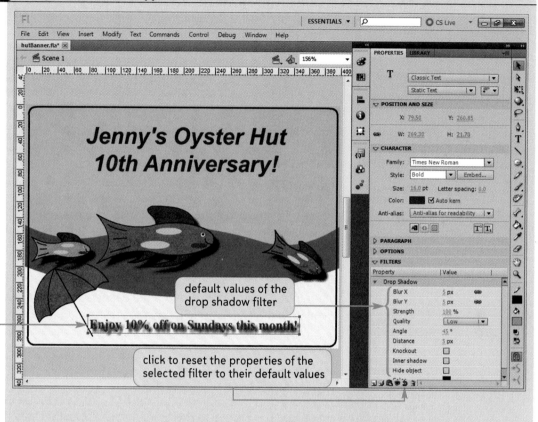

drop shadow filter applied to the text block

default values of the drop shadow filter

click to reset the properties of the selected filter to their default values

11. Save the document, and then close it.

The 10th Anniversary banner is complete. In this session, you added text blocks to the banner for Jenny's Oyster Hut, set the properties for the text, and checked for spelling errors. You exported the banner as a JPG file and previewed it in a Web page. You used the History panel to review, undo, and replay steps. Then, you used the Library panel to work with symbols in the hutBanner.fla document's library. You also applied special graphic effects to movie clips and text. In the next tutorial, you will learn how to create animations with the symbols in Jenny's Oyster Hut banner.

Session 2.2 Quick Check

REVIEW

1. What is the difference between a static text block and a dynamic text field?
2. Why is it important to check the spelling in your document?
3. What does the History panel record?
4. What are the three behavior types for symbols?
5. What is the purpose of the Library panel?
6. Why should you convert a graphic you want to use multiple times in a document into a symbol?
7. What is the difference between a symbol and an instance of a symbol?
8. True or False. When you modify a symbol, the instances created from that symbol are not affected.
9. What is a filter?

Practice the skills you learned in the tutorial using the same case scenario.

PRACTICE

Review Assignments

Data File needed for the Review Assignments: banner.fla

Aly is pleased with the banner you created for Jenny's Oyster Hut Web site. She asks you to modify another version of the banner by changing the color of the umbrella, adding a second umbrella, finishing a fish graphic, adding an instance of the fish to the banner, and adding a text block. She also wants you to change the color and style of the rectangle, add drop shadow effects to the fish, and draw lines as underlines for text.

1. Open the **banner.fla** file located in the Flash2\Review folder, save the document as **newBanner.fla** in the same folder, reset the workspace to the Essentials layout, and then close the Timeline.

2. Edit the umbrella symbol in the Library panel by opening it in symbol-editing mode. Use the Paint Bucket tool to change the color of the two maroon panels in the umbrella to red (#FF0000) so that the panels alternate between yellow and red. Use the Transform panel to decrease the width and height of the symbol to 75%. Exit symbol-editing mode.

3. Place one instance of the umbrella symbol in the lower-left corner of the banner, and then rotate it so that the umbrella leans to the left. Place another instance of the umbrella symbol in the lower-right corner of the banner and lean it to the right.

4. Edit the fish symbol in the Library panel. Use the Oval tool to draw a circle that has a white (#FFFFFF) fill color and no stroke color for the fish's eye on the right part of the fish graphic.

5. Change the fill color to black (#000000) and draw a small circle inside the white circle to represent the eye's pupil.

6. Use the Pencil tool to draw a small line that has a black (#000000) stroke color and a stroke height of 1 below the eye to represent the fish's mouth. Draw three short horizontal line segments on the tail of the fish.

7. Create a color band on the fish by drawing a vertical line inside the fish body starting at the top stroke of the fish near the right side of the top fin and ending at the bottom stroke of the fish near the bottom fin. Draw another vertical line to the left of the first line on the fish from the top stroke to the bottom stroke of the fish. Make sure the vertical lines connect to the strokes representing the fish's body.

8. Use the Paint Bucket tool to apply a yellow-orange color (#FFCC33) to the middle band on the fish created by the vertical lines and to apply a green color (#669966) to the areas inside the top and bottom fins. Exit symbol-editing mode.

9. Place an instance of the fish symbol on the water in the center of the banner.

10. Place another instance of the fish symbol to the right of the first instance, and then rotate the second instance so that it appears to be swimming in the water in a downward direction.

11. Apply a drop shadow filter effect to each fish instance on the Stage. Use a filter distance of 7 px and a filter strength of 90%.

12. Add a new single-line text block as Classic Text that reads **Free Drink with a Dinner Entree!**. Use Verdana for the font family, 16 pt for the point size, Regular for the style, and dark red (#990000) for the text color. Center the new text block on the beach at the bottom of the banner.

13. Use the Line tool to draw horizontal lines under each of the two lines of text on the top of the banner. The lines should be maroon (#660000), have a height of 2, a stroke style of solid, and appear as underlines for the text.

14. Add a drop shadow filter to the top text block. Use default settings for the drop shadow, and change its color to gray (#666666).

15. Edit the rectangle that is framing the banner. Change its color to maroon (#660000), set the stroke height to 3, and choose a stroke style other than Solid.

16. Export the image to the Flash2\Review folder with the name **newBanner.jpg** and in the JPG file format, using the default settings in the Export JPEG dialog box.

17. Submit the finished files to your instructor.

Use shapes, text, and symbols to create a grand opening banner.

APPLY

Case Problem 1

There are no Data Files needed for this Case Problem.

Katie's Pet Resort   Katie's Pet Resort is preparing for its grand opening celebration and sale. Katie meets with John to discuss the development of the store's Web site. John suggests first developing a banner that will set the tone for the rest of the Web site. The banner will help promote the grand opening celebration and sale by including graphics that depict a celebration and text about the grand opening. You will create the banner shown in Figure 2-51.

Figure 2-51

1. Create a new document. Change the document properties so that the width is 500 pixels and the height is 250 pixels. Change the background color to light yellow (#FFFF99).

2. Save the document as **petBanner.fla** in the Flash2\Case1 folder included with your Data Files.

3. Create a square with sides of about 45 pixels in length. Use yellow-orange (#FFCC33) for the fill color and a solid black stroke of 1 pixel in height. Place the square near the upper-left side of the stage.

4. Add a text block centered inside the square with the uppercase letter **K**. Use Classic Text, a font family such as Comic Sans MS, a point size of 32, bold style, and black text. (*Hint*: Use the arrow keys to nudge the text block within the square as needed.)

5. Group the square and the text, being sure to select both the fill and the stroke for the square.

6. Make a copy of the group and edit the copy to change the letter to **A** and the fill color of the square to the color of your choice. Move the copy to the right of the square with the letter K.

7. Repeat Step 6 to make four more copies of the group. Change the letters in the copies to **T**, **I**, **E**, and **'S**, respectively, and use a different color for each square's fill. Move the copies so that the text blocks and squares spell KATIE'S.

8. Use the Free Transform tool to rotate and position each letter block, as shown in Figure 2-51.

9. Convert each of the letter blocks into a movie clip symbol, naming each symbol according to the letter in the text block: **K, A, T, I, E,** and **'S,** respectively. Apply a drop shadow filter effect to each of the letter block instances on the Stage. Use the default settings for the filter.

10. Add a text block in the center of the Stage. Use Classic Text and the same font family as in Step 4 with a point size of 60, black (#000000) text, center align the text, and use bold style. Type **Pet Resort** in the text block.

11. Add a second text block with a point size of 18, green (#003300) text, center align the text, and use Regular style. Type **Grand Opening this Saturday!**, and then on a separate line in the same text block type **Bring your pets for a tour!**.

12. Draw two balloons on the left side of the Stage using the Oval tool with different colors for each balloon. Do not include a stroke for the balloons. Draw a string for each balloon using the Pencil tool with a light gray (#999999) color for the stroke.

13. Repeat Step 12 to draw two more balloons on the right side of the Stage with different colors.

14. Use the Brush tool to draw multicolored confetti on the Stage. Select a small brush size from the Brush Size modifier in the Tools panel. Select a brush color of your choice using the Fill Color control in the Tools panel, and then click dots with the tool on the banner to create the confetti. Repeat to create different colored dots throughout the Stage using at least three different colors.

15. Create a rectangle as a border around all of the objects on the Stage. The rectangle should have slightly rounded corners, a maroon (#660000) stroke, no fill, a stroke height of 3, and a solid style. Draw the rectangle so that it is just inside the edges of the Stage.

16. Export the image to the Flash2\Case1 folder with the name **petBanner.jpg** and in the JPG file format, using Full Document Size and the rest of the default settings in the Export JPEG dialog box.

17. Submit the finished files to your instructor.

Use text, shapes, and symbols to create a banner advertising a zoo.

APPLY

Case Problem 2

There are no Data Files needed for this Case Problem.

Alamo City Zoo   Janet asks Alex to develop a new banner for the Alamo City Zoo's Web site. The new banner will advertise an open house celebration event promoting a new bear exhibit. The banner will contain text with the zoo's name and event information as well as graphic elements depicting bear paws. You'll create the banner shown in Figure 2-52.

Figure 2-52

1. Create a new document. Change the document properties so that the width is 300 pixels and the height is 200 pixels. Change the background color to orange-yellow (#CC9933).

2. Save the document as **zooBanner.fla** in the Flash2\Case2 folder included with your Data Files.

3. Create a single-line text block on the top part of the Stage for the name of the zoo. Use Classic Text, Times New Roman or a font family of your choice, a point size of 36, black (#000000) text color, center aligned, and bold italic style. Type **Alamo City Zoo** in the text block.

4. Create a fixed-width text block of about 200 pixels wide on the lower part of the Stage. Use Classic Text, the Monotype Corsiva font family, a point size of 30, maroon (#660000) text color, and center alignment. Type **New BEAR Exhibit Now Open!** in the text block.

5. Create a single-line text block on the center of the Stage. Use Classic Text, Times New Roman font family, a point size of 18, light yellow text color (#FFFF99), regular style, and center alignment. Type **Special Open House!** in the text block.

6. Use the Free Transform tool to rotate the text block so that it is in a vertical position on the left side of the Stage, as shown in Figure 2-52.

7. Create a new movie clip symbol named **bearPaw**. (*Hint*: On the Application bar, click Insert, and then click New Symbol.) In symbol-editing mode, on the center of the Stage, draw a small circle about 40 pixels wide and 40 pixels high. Use brown (#663300) for the fill color, black (#000000) for the stroke color, solid for the stroke style, and 1 for the stroke height.

8. Zoom in on the circle and use the Selection tool to move the top part of the circle's stroke down to give the circle a slightly flattened appearance. Using the same stroke and fill colors as the circle, draw four small ovals equally spaced above the flattened part of the circle as shown in Figure 2-52.

9. Use the PolyStar tool with the same stroke and fill colors as the circle to draw a small triangle above one of the small ovals. Use polygon for the style and 3 for the number of sides. Draw similar triangles above each of the other ovals. Use the Selection tool to move the left and right sides of each triangle slightly towards its center as shown in Figure 2-52. Exit symbol-editing mode.

10. Drag four instances of the bearPaw symbol from the Library panel to the Stage. Place two instances below the top text block, place one instance to the left of the bottom text block, and place one instance to the right of the bottom text block.

11. Use the Free Transform tool to resize two of the bearPaw instances to make them slightly smaller. Also, rotate the two left instances on the Stage slightly to the left, and then rotate the two right instances on the Stage slightly to the right.

12. Apply a bevel effect to one of the bearPaw instances on the Stage. Change the filter strength to 80% and change the highlight color to a light peach (#FFCC99). Copy all of the filter's properties, and then apply the copied filter effect to each of the other bearPaw instances on the Stage.

13. Draw a rectangle along the inside edges of the Stage as a border around all of the objects on the Stage. Use a dark green (#003300) stroke, a stroke height of 3, the Dashed stroke style, square corners, and no fill color. Use the Selection tool to move the sides of the rectangle slightly towards the center of the Stage.

14. Export the image to the Flash2\Case2 folder with the name **zooBanner.jpg** and in the JPG file format, using Full Document Size and the rest of the default settings in the Export JPEG dialog box.

15. Submit the finished files to your instructor.

Extend your skills by using gradients, filters, and the Oval Primitive tool to create a logo for a nursery.

CHALLENGE

Case Problem 3

There are no Data Files needed for this Case Problem.

Westcreek Nursery   Alice meets with Amanda, who was contracted to update the Westcreek Nursery Web site. Alice requests that a new logo be developed for her business. The logo should contain the business name, phone number, and an appropriate slogan, along with some graphics. You'll create the completed logo shown in Figure 2-53.

Figure 2-53

⊕ **EXPLORE**

1. Create a new document. Change the document properties so that the width is 300 pixels and the height is 150 pixels. Change the background color to light green by typing **#9ACC9A** in the color palette's hexadecimal box.

2. Save the document as **wcLogo.fla** in the Flash2\Case3 folder included with your Data Files.

3. Draw a rectangle about 280 pixels wide and 50 pixels high across the top of the Stage. Use the Rectangle tool and the Merge Drawing model with a dark green (#006600) stroke, a height of 1, a solid style, no fill color, and a rectangle corner radius of –5 for every corner. Place the rectangle about 10 pixels from the left of the Stage and 10 pixels from the top.

4. Create a single-line text block inside the rectangle. Use Classic Text, Verdana or a similar font family of your choice, a point size of 22, white text, left alignment, and bold style. Type **Westcreek** in the text block, and then position the text block on the left side of the rectangle.

5. Draw a straight vertical line to the right of the text block to split the rectangle into two sections. One end of the line should snap to the top of the rectangle and the other end should snap to the bottom of the rectangle. Use a dark green (#006600) stroke, a stroke height of 1, and a solid style.

⊕ **EXPLORE**

6. Use the Paint Bucket tool to apply the green radial gradient fill (fourth gradient from the left on the color palette) to the center of the left section of the rectangle.

7. Create a single-line text block on the right side of the rectangle. Use Classic Text, Verdana or a similar font family of your choice, a point size of 22, black text, left alignment, and bold style. Type **Nursery** in the text block, and, if necessary, position the text block in the center of the right side of the rectangle.

8. Create a single-line text block centered at the bottom of the Stage. Use Classic Text, the same font family as in Step 7, a point size of 10, white text, center alignment, and bold style. Type **We Deliver! Call 555-4444!** in the text block. Apply a drop shadow to the text block.

9. Create a single-line text block in the center of the Stage. Use the same font family as Step 7, a point size of 42, purple (#660099) text, left alignment, and bold style. Type **FLOWERS** in the text block. Using the Free Transform tool, skew the text block so that the letters are slanted to the right.

EXPLORE   10. Apply a gradient glow filter effect to the FLOWERS text block. In the Gradient Glow properties, click the Gradient box, double-click the right gradient marker (small triangle in lower-right corner of gradient), and select an orange color (#FF3300) in the color palette.

11. Draw four straight horizontal lines, each about 40 pixels in length, to the left of the letter F in the center text block. Use black for the stroke color, solid for the style, and 1 for the line height. Position the lines equally spaced and approximately the same distance from the letter F.

12. Use the Oval Primitive tool to draw a circle with a black fill and no stroke about 25 pixels in diameter on the Stage. If necessary, reset the values for the controls in the Property inspector before drawing the circle.

EXPLORE   13. Change the Inner radius value for the circle to 40 to create the image of a car tire.

14. Convert the circle to a movie clip symbol named **tire**. Add a second instance of the tire symbol from the Library panel to the Stage. Move the two tire instances right below the FLOWERS text block. Place one tire right below the L in the FLOWERS text, and place the other tire right below the R.

15. Export the image to the Flash2\Case3 folder with the name **wcLogo.jpg** and in JPG file format, using Full Document Size and the rest of the default settings in the Export JPEG dialog box.

16. Submit the finished files to your instructor.

Use symbols and text blocks to create a banner for an association.

CREATE

Case Problem 4

There are no Data Files needed for this Case Problem.

Missions Support Association   Brittany meets with Anissa to discuss improving the Missions Support Association's Web site. They decide to start by developing a new banner for the site's home page, which will include the association's name as well as keywords highlighting the services available to the association's members. You'll create a banner of your design to do this. Figure 2-54 shows one possible solution.

Figure 2-54

1. Create a new document with the dimensions and background color of your choice.

2. Save the document as **msaBanner.fla** in the Flash2\Case4 folder included with your Data Files.

3. Draw two or more small shapes using the fill and stroke colors of your choice on the Stage, and then set the X and Y coordinates in the Property inspector as needed to position the shapes.

4. Draw a large rectangle shape and then use guides as needed to modify the shape, such as by dragging anchor points to convert the shape to another shape. For example, you could convert the rectangle to a polygon with unequal sides. (*Hint*: You can use the Snap to Objects modifier to make the shape snap to the guides.)

5. Draw a rectangle to frame the banner. Use no fill color but select an appropriate stroke color and stroke height.

6. Modify the frame as needed. For example, you can use the Selection tool to select the bottom frame rectangle that overlaps another shape you drew, and then delete the selected portion.

7. Convert the frame rectangle to a movie clip symbol named **frame**.

8. Apply a filter to the frame instance, changing the filter properties appropriately. For example, you can apply a bevel filter, change the quality to high, and change shadow color to a light gray.

9. Create the text block using the font family, style, size, color, and alignment of your choice, and then type **Helping Preserve History** in the text block. Position the text block attractively on the banner.

10. Create another text block, using the font family, style, size, color, and alignment of your choice (for example, you can use a different font family, different style, larger point size, and different color), and then type **Missions Support Association** in the text block. Apply a filter of your choice such as a drop shadow. Position the text block attractively on the banner.

⊕ **EXPLORE**   11. Create a new movie clip symbol named **star**. In symbol-editing mode, use the PolyStar tool to draw a star shape on the Stage that is about 50 pixels wide and 50 pixels high. Use colors of your choice for the fill and the stroke. In the Tool Settings, set the style to star, the number of sides to 5, and the star point size to 0.50. Exit symbol-editing mode.

12. Place at least two instances of the star symbol on the banner in attractive positions.

13. Apply a drop shadow effect to each star instance on the Stage, using the settings of your choice for the filter.

14. Export the image to the Flash2\Case4 folder with the name **msaBanner.jpg** and in JPG file format, using Full Document Size and the rest of the default settings in the Export JPEG dialog box.

15. Submit the finished files to your instructor.

ENDING DATA FILES

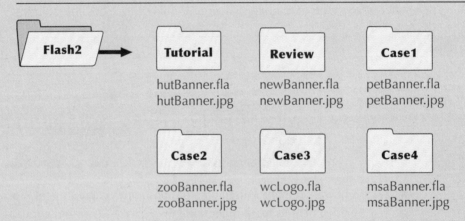

Flash2 →	Tutorial	Review	Case1
	hutBanner.fla	newBanner.fla	petBanner.fla
	hutBanner.jpg	newBanner.jpg	petBanner.jpg

Case2	Case3	Case4
zooBanner.fla	wcLogo.fla	msaBanner.fla
zooBanner.jpg	wcLogo.jpg	msaBanner.jpg

Creating Animations

Developing Tween and Frame-by-Frame Animations

Case | *Admiral Web Design*

Jenny is interested in incorporating animation into the new Jenny's Oyster Hut banner to attract more attention to the anniversary specials being promoted. Aly revised the Jenny's Oyster Hut banner to use as the basis for the animated banner. The new banner will have an initial animation of a fish pulling a shrimp specials sign while the words "Fried Shrimp" and "Shrimp Scampi" are displayed one after the other. The banner will also include an animated fish swimming as well as a sea plant with moving leaves. Before you complete the animation for the Jenny's Oyster Hut banner, Aly wants you to review and modify a document she created for another client, Jackson's Sports.

In this tutorial, you will learn the basics of creating Flash animations and how to coordinate these animations in the Timeline using frames and layers. You will learn how to extend a document using scenes. You will learn how to create motion tweens, classic tweens, frame-by-frame animations, and shape tweens. Finally, you will learn how to create animations using graphic symbols.

STARTING DATA FILES

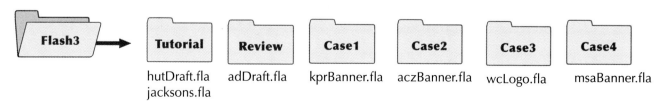

Flash3 → Tutorial   Review   Case1   Case2   Case3   Case4

hutDraft.fla   adDraft.fla   kprBanner.fla   aczBanner.fla   wcLogo.fla   msaBanner.fla
jacksons.fla

SESSION 3.1 VISUAL OVERVIEW

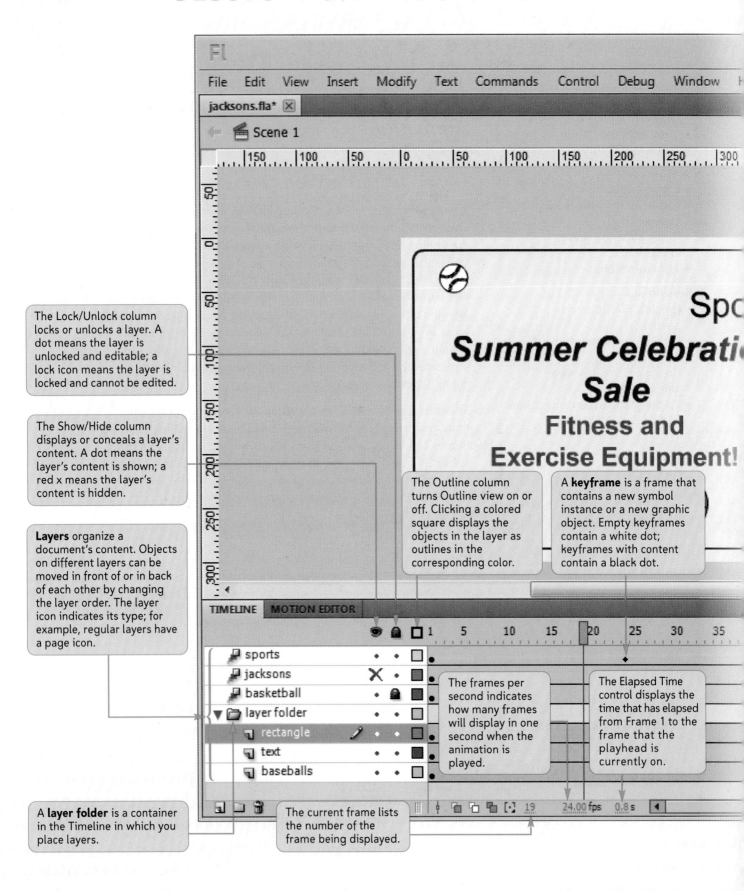

The Lock/Unlock column locks or unlocks a layer. A dot means the layer is unlocked and editable; a lock icon means the layer is locked and cannot be edited.

The Show/Hide column displays or conceals a layer's content. A dot means the layer's content is shown; a red x means the layer's content is hidden.

Layers organize a document's content. Objects on different layers can be moved in front of or in back of each other by changing the layer order. The layer icon indicates its type; for example, regular layers have a page icon.

The Outline column turns Outline view on or off. Clicking a colored square displays the objects in the layer as outlines in the corresponding color.

A **keyframe** is a frame that contains a new symbol instance or a new graphic object. Empty keyframes contain a white dot; keyframes with content contain a black dot.

The frames per second indicates how many frames will display in one second when the animation is played.

The Elapsed Time control displays the time that has elapsed from Frame 1 to the frame that the playhead is currently on.

A **layer folder** is a container in the Timeline in which you place layers.

The current frame lists the number of the frame being displayed.

TIMELINE AND SCENES PANELS

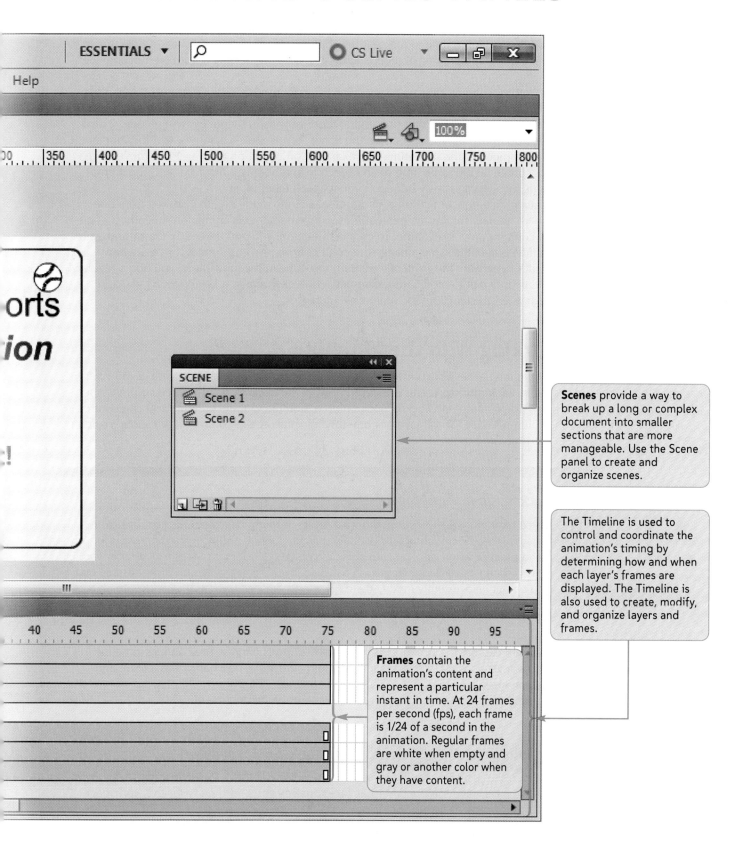

Scenes provide a way to break up a long or complex document into smaller sections that are more manageable. Use the Scene panel to create and organize scenes.

The Timeline is used to control and coordinate the animation's timing by determining how and when each layer's frames are displayed. The Timeline is also used to create, modify, and organize layers and frames.

Frames contain the animation's content and represent a particular instant in time. At 24 frames per second (fps), each frame is 1/24 of a second in the animation. Regular frames are white when empty and gray or another color when they have content.

Elements of Animation

One of the most powerful features of Flash is its ability to create animation. Animation creates the perception of movement by changing the location or appearance of an object from one moment in time to the next. To do this in Flash, you coordinate the document's layers, frames, and graphic objects (such as symbols on the Stage) from the document's Timeline.

A Flash document starts with one layer. You can insert additional layers and then place graphic objects on different layers. This prevents objects that are drawn or moved on top of other objects from splitting or merging those objects in Merge Drawing mode. It also allows you to overlap the objects on the Stage. Layers are especially useful for animating multiple objects at the same time. For example, an object on one layer can move across the document at the same time as an object on another layer moves down. The animations occur simultaneously but don't impact each other in any way.

Placing different content on each frame or slightly modifying the content from one frame to the next creates the perception of movement that is animation. Initially, a document contains only a keyframe. To create animation, you add frames to a layer and then keep the content the same, change the content from previous frames, or create new content. If you want the content to remain the same in the new frame, you add a regular frame. If you want to modify or create new content, you add a keyframe. As you add more frames, the length of the animation increases.

Working with the Timeline

TIP

When working with a complex animation, turn on Outline view to see how the objects from the various layers overlap.

The Timeline header contains the frame numbers and the playhead, as well as the layer controls. Each row represents one layer. Next to the layer names are three columns: the Show/Hide column, the Lock/Unlock column, and the Outline column. You can control the column settings for all layers at one time by clicking the column's corresponding icon in the Timeline header.

INSIGHT

Locking Completed Layers

If you have multiple objects on different layers, it might become difficult to select an object on one layer without accidentally selecting another object on a different layer. A good practice when working with objects on multiple layers is to lock a layer after you finish editing its contents. Objects in a locked layer are not selectable. This ensures that you do not inadvertently modify the objects on a finished layer as you work with objects on another layer.

You will explore the Timeline of the Jackson's Sports banner. The banner's Timeline contains several layers. The layers include animations of a baseball, a basketball, and text. Each layer has a descriptive name and contains 75 frames. You'll play the animation and watch the Timeline as it displays the elements of the document.

To explore the Timeline of the Jackson's Sports banner:

1. Open the **jacksons.fla** file located in the Flash3\Tutorial folder included with your Data Files, save the document as **jacksonsRev.fla**, and then reset the workspace to the Essentials layout. See Figure 3-1.

Figure 3-1   Jackson's Sports banner

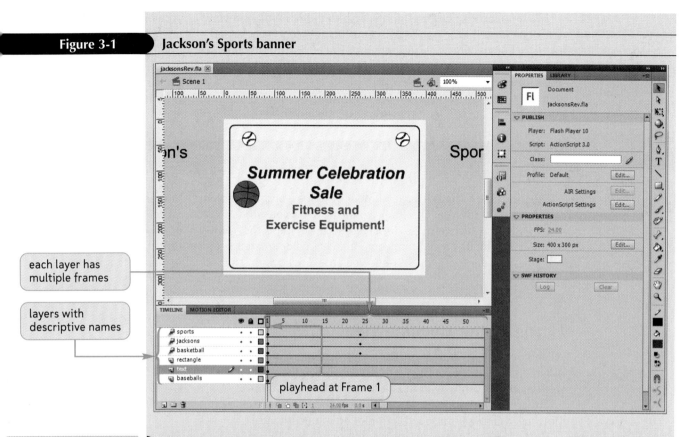

each layer has multiple frames

layers with descriptive names

2. On the Application bar, click **Control**, and then click **Play**. As the playhead moves from Frame 1 to Frame 24 in the Timeline, the basketball moves across the Stage, and the text moves in from the sides of the Stage. After Frame 24, the contents on the Stage remain stationary through Frame 75.

3. Locate the playhead, and then review the current frame (75), frame rate (24.00 fps), and elapsed time (3.1 s) at the bottom of the Timeline. See Figure 3-2.

Figure 3-2   Playhead on Frame 75

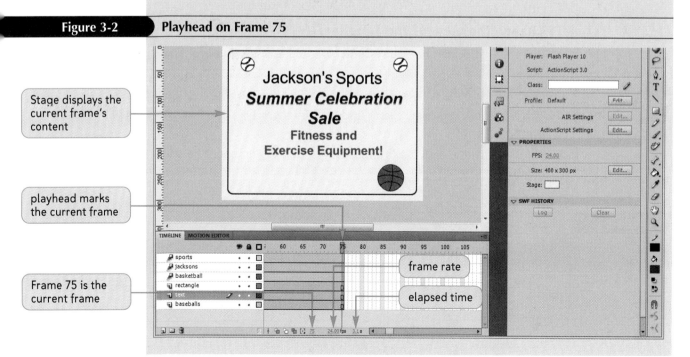

Stage displays the current frame's content

playhead marks the current frame

Frame 75 is the current frame

The Timeline displays useful information that you might review as you test an animation. The Elapsed Time control displays the time that has elapsed from Frame 1 to the frame that the playhead is currently on. The elapsed time depends on the frame rate. By default, the frame rate is 24 frames per second, which means that an animation that spans 24 frames takes one second to play. The length of the Jackson's Sports banner animation you just viewed can be determined by looking at the elapsed time when the playhead is in the last frame. In this case, the length of the animation is 3.1 seconds.

INSIGHT

Checking the Frame Number Before Modifying Content

A document can have a large number of frames, and the contents of the frames often look very similar from one frame to the next. As you work with content on the Stage, be aware of which frame is displayed because that is the frame whose content you are working with. Be careful that you don't change or create the content for the wrong frame. To determine which frame you are working with, check the location of the playhead in the Timeline header or look at the number listed for the current frame.

Changing the Timeline View

As you develop an animation, the number of frames can grow very rapidly, as can the number of layers. At some point, you might need to change the view of the Timeline to work more efficiently with the elements in the animation.

You can also modify the dimensions of the frames to see more frames within the Timeline window or to see more of the frame's contents.

By default, the frames are tinted different colors based on the type of content they contain, such as a blue tint for a motion tween. You will learn about motion tweens later in this tutorial. You can deselect the Tinted Frames option to remove the color tints on the frames.

Because you will be working extensively with the Timeline, you will practice changing the view of its frames and layers.

To change the view of the Timeline:

1. On the Application bar, click **Control**, and then click **Rewind**. The playhead moves to Frame 1.

2. Press the **F4** key. The panels disappear. You'll display the Timeline next.

3. On the Application bar, click **Window**, and then click **Timeline**. The Timeline appears.

4. In the Timeline, click the **Frame View** button to open the panel's menu, and then click **Preview**. The frames increase in size, and the content in Frame 1 is displayed. See Figure 3-3.

Figure 3-3 **Frames in Preview view**

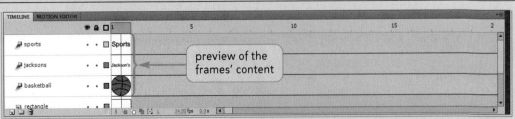

preview of the frames' content

5. In the Timeline, click the **Frame View** button, and then click **Small**. The frames decrease in size.

6. In the Timeline, click the **Frame View** button, and then click **Short**. The height of the layers decreases. See Figure 3-4.

Figure 3-4   Frames in Short view

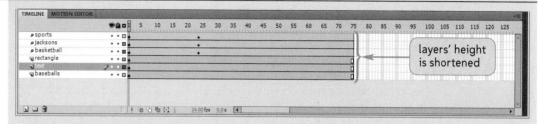

layers' height is shortened

7. In the Timeline, click the **Frame View** button, and then click **Short** to turn off Short view.

8. In the Timeline, click the **Frame View** button, and then click **Normal**. The frames return to their default, or Normal, view.

9. Reset the workspace to the Essentials layout.

Organizing Layers Using the Timeline

TIP

To see all of a layer's selected properties, double-click its layer icon in the Timeline to open the Layer Properties dialog box.

A new document in Flash contains one layer and one frame within that layer. As you create an animation, you add more layers to the document. A lengthy or complex animation could have many layers, which can become difficult to manage. The Timeline is a useful tool for working with the different layers and frames in your document most efficiently.

You select a layer to edit its content. The selected layer is highlighted and a pencil icon appears to the right of the layer's name. You can also delete layers and add new layers as needed. As you add more layers to the Timeline, it's a good idea to name each one according to the content it contains. This helps keep the content organized as the complexity of the animation increases. Layers can also be renamed as needed.

Written Communication: Using Layers to Organize Content

As you add more content or animation to a Flash document, use layers to help organize the document's contents. However, this practice can lead to a large number of layers, creating another challenge of finding what you want to work on. So be sure to plan a logical layer structure for each document.

Another good practice is to assign each layer a meaningful name that corresponds to its content. Then you or someone else who needs to edit the document can easily locate a layer based on its name. Although layer names can include spaces and punctuation marks, these are often omitted for simplicity. Keep in mind that when a document has many layers, you can hide some layers as you work with the content of other layers.

Additional layers don't add to the overall size of the finished file, so you can create an organized structure for the document's content while keeping the size of the final published SWF file as small as possible. This way, the SWF file downloads quickly from the Web server to the viewer's computer.

PROSKILLS

Adding Layer Folders

When you have multiple layers in the document's Timeline, you can create layer folders to help you work more efficiently. The names of layers in a layer folder are indented under the layer folder in the Timeline.

Using a layer folder is similar to how you use a folder on your computer's hard drive—you place related files into the folder to make the files easier to find and manage. You can use a layer folder to keep related layers together. For example, you can create a folder in which to place all of the layers that contain text. Then you can quickly find the text layers when you need to edit them. You can name a layer folder with a descriptive name the same way you name a layer, making it easier to know what each folder contains. You can collapse the layer folders so that the layers in the folders are not visible. This makes the Timeline less cluttered and makes it easier to work with the other layers in the document. Collapsing the folder's layers doesn't affect the view of the layers' content on the Stage.

You'll add a layer folder in the Jackson's Sports document, and then move the related layers into it.

To insert a layer folder in the Jackson's Sports banner:

1. In the Timeline, click the **sports** layer. The layer is selected.

2. In the Timeline, click the **New Folder** button 🗀. A layer folder named Folder 1 is inserted above the sports layer.

3. Double-click **Folder 1** to select the folder name, type **text layers** as the new name, and then press the **Enter** key. The name of the folder changes.

4. Drag the **sports** layer to the text layers folder but do not release the mouse. A black line appears below the text layers folder. See Figure 3-5.

Figure 3-5   **Layer being moved to the layer folder**

new text layers folder

black line indicates that the layer will be moved to the folder

5. Release the mouse button. The sports layer moves into the text layers folder and is indented in the Timeline.

6. Drag the **jacksons** and **text** layers into the text layers folder. Each layer containing text is indented underneath the text layers folder. The order of the text layers is not important because the text blocks do not overlap one another. See Figure 3-6.

Figure 3-6   **Layers moved into the text layers folder**

new text layers folder

layers indented beneath the text layers folder

TIP

To expand the folder's contents and display the layers, click the folder's Expand arrow.

7. Click the text layers folder's **Collapse** arrow ▼. The folder's icon changes to a closed folder and the text layers are no longer visible.

Selecting, Copying, and Moving Frames

A document's frames can be copied or moved within the same layer or from one layer to another. To copy or move frames, you must first select them. You can select individual or multiple frames in the Timeline. You can select frames within one layer or across multiple layers.

You'll select and copy frames in the Jackson's Sports banner.

To select, copy, and paste frames:

1. In the Timeline, click the **baseballs** layer. The layer is selected.

2. In the Timeline, click the **New Layer** button ⬜. A new layer is inserted above the baseballs layer.

3. Double-click the new layer's name, type **new baseballs**, and then press the **Enter** key. The layer is renamed.

4. Click the name of the **baseballs** layer. All of the frames for the baseballs layer are selected. You'll copy these selected frames to the new baseballs layer.

5. Right-click the selected frames to open the context menu, and then click **Copy Frames**.

6. Click the name of the **new baseballs** layer to select all of its frames.

7. Right-click the selected frames to open the context menu, and then click **Paste Frames**. The layer's frames are replaced with the copied frames from the baseballs layer.

8. In the Tools panel, click the **Selection** tool ▶, if necessary. The two copied baseball instances remain selected.

9. Drag the left baseball instance to the lower-left corner of the Stage. Both instances move at the same time. See Figure 3-7.

| Figure 3-7 | Copied instances moved on the Stage |

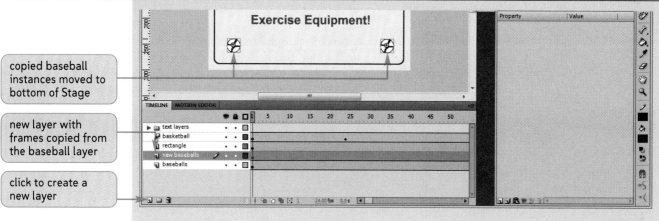

copied baseball instances moved to bottom of Stage

new layer with frames copied from the baseball layer

click to create a new layer

Using Scenes and Multiple Timelines

Every Flash document starts with one scene that contains a Timeline. For more complex animations, a document can have more than one scene, and each scene has its own Timeline, as shown in Figure 3-8. A document's scenes are similar to those of a motion picture. In the same way that the scenes in a motion picture are played in order, the scenes in a Flash document are played one after the other. The content of all layers is displayed one frame at a time within a scene's Timeline. When you add new scenes to a document, you are essentially adding new Timelines that contain their own frames with new content.

Figure 3-8	Multiple scenes in one document

 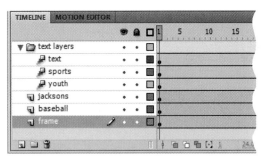

content of Scene 1   content of Scene 2

After a document with multiple scenes is published, the SWF file plays in a Web page using the Flash Player. The player treats all the scenes in a SWF file as one long Timeline. So, if a Flash document has two scenes and each scene has 30 frames, the Flash Player treats this as one long Timeline with 60 consecutive frames and plays them according to the order of the scenes in the Scene panel.

Using the Scene Panel

The Scene panel lists the scenes in the current document in the order in which they will play. From the Scene panel, you can change the order the scenes will play as well as duplicate, add, and delete scenes. A duplicate scene has the same name as the original with the word "copy" added to its name, and it has the same contents as the original. Any new scene you add has the name "Scene," followed by a number that is one higher than the previous scene.

Naming Scenes

When a document has only a few scenes, using the default scene names such as "Scene 1," "Scene 2," and "Scene 3" might be okay. When a document has many scenes, it is better to assign more meaningful names to each scene to make it simpler to manage the document. If you have 10 scenes, for example, you might not remember the content of each scene, and someone else working on the document has no idea of what each scene includes. To locate specific content to work with would require searching through all the scenes. By giving each scene a meaningful name, you and others can easily determine what each scene contains. Scene names can include spaces, symbols, and punctuation marks.

When you add a new scene or create a duplicate of a scene, the Stage automatically displays the new scene. You can tell which scene is currently displayed by the scene number in the upper-left corner of the Stage window or by looking at the Scene panel to see which scene is currently selected. You can switch between scenes at any time.

You will rename and reorder the scenes in the Jackson's Sports document.

To rename and play scenes in the Jackson's Sports banner:

TIP

You can also press the Shift+F2 keys to open and close the Scene panel.

▶ 1. On the Application bar, click **Window**, point to **Other Panels**, and then click **Scene**. The Scene panel opens, showing two scenes named Scene 1 and Scene 2. You will rename these scenes with more meaningful names.

▶ 2. In the Scene panel, double-click **Scene 1** to select the name, type **Fitness and Exercise** as the new name, and then press the **Enter** key to rename the scene.

▶ 3. In the Scene panel, double-click **Scene 2**. The Scene 2 scene name appears on the Edit bar, the contents of the Timeline change to that scene, and the view of the Stage switches to the first frame of that scene.

▶ 4. Type **Celebration**, and then press the **Enter** key. The scene is renamed and the Celebration scene name appears on the Edit bar. See Figure 3-9.

Figure 3-9   **Renamed scenes displayed in the Scene panel**

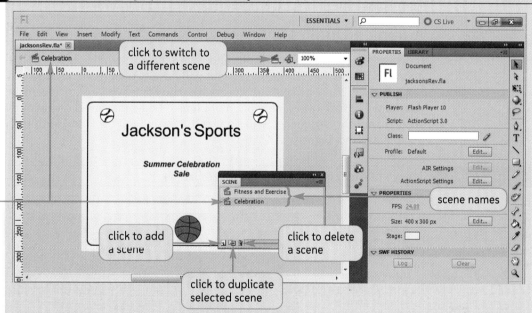

Celebration scene is the active scene and its content appears on the Stage

click to switch to a different scene

scene names

click to add a scene

click to delete a scene

click to duplicate selected scene

▶ 5. Drag the **Scene** panel to the right of the Stage, and then, on the Application bar, click **Control** and click **Play**. The animation for the Celebration scene plays, showing the center text block increasing in size and the baseballs moving.

You'll test the animation to see how both scenes play one after the other.

▶ 6. On the Application bar, click **Control**, point to **Test Movie**, and then click **in Flash Professional**. A new window opens, showing the SWF file as it plays the animation of the Fitness and Exercise scene followed by the animation of the Celebration scene.

▶ 7. On the Flash Player menu bar, click **File**, and then click **Close**. The Flash Player window closes and you return to the document.

You can use the Scene panel to reorder the scenes in a document.

To reorder scenes in the Jackson's Sports banner:

1. In the Scene panel, click and drag the **Celebration** scene so that it is before the Fitness and Exercise scene.

2. On the Application bar, click **Control**, point to **Test Movie**, and then click **in Flash Professional**. The movie plays, but the sequence of the animations changes based on the order of the scenes in the Scene panel. The Celebration scene's increasing text and baseballs animation play first, followed by the animation in the Fitness and Exercise scene.

3. On the Flash Player menu bar, click **File**, and then click **Close** to return to the document.

4. On the Edit bar, click the **Edit Scene** button 🖿 to open a menu that lists all the scenes in the document, and then click **Fitness and Exercise**. The Timeline and Stage for the Fitness and Exercise scene appear.

5. On the Edit bar, click the **Edit Scene** button 🖿, and then click **Celebration** to return to the Celebration scene.

6. Save and close the jacksonsRev.fla document.

Adding a Duplicate Scene

Based on the planning instructions and Aly's sketch shown in Figure 3-10, the new animated banner for Jenny's Oyster Hut will have two animation sequences. The first sequence will show a fish swimming across the Stage with a sign advertising shrimp specials. It will also show an animation of phrases being displayed one after the other. The second animation sequence will show a fish swimming back and forth in the ocean and plant leaves moving.

Figure 3-10   **Jenny's Oyster Hut partially completed banner**

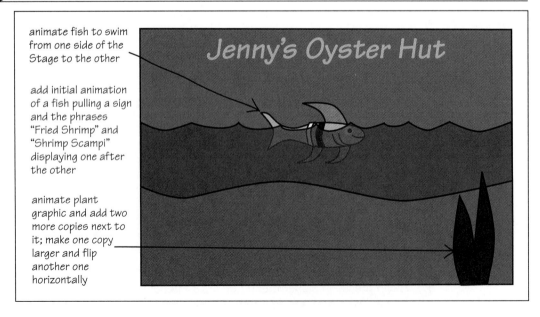

animate fish to swim from one side of the Stage to the other

add initial animation of a fish pulling a sign and the phrases "Fried Shrimp" and "Shrimp Scampi" displaying one after the other

animate plant graphic and add two more copies next to it; make one copy larger and flip another one horizontally

Jenny's Oyster Hut

To make it easier to manage the two animation sequences, you will create each in a separate scene. You'll add a new scene to the banner by duplicating the initial scene, and then renaming both scenes with more meaningful names.

To duplicate and rename scenes in the Jenny's Oyster Hut banner:

▶ **1.** Open the **hutDraft.fla** file located in the Flash3\Tutorial folder included with your Data Files, and then save the document as **hutBanner** in the same folder.

▶ **2.** In the Scene panel, click the **Duplicate Scene** button ⊞. The duplicate scene appears in the Scene panel with the name "Scene 1 copy."

▶ **3.** In the Scene panel, double-click **Scene 1**, type **Shrimp Specials** as the new name, and then press the **Enter** key to rename the scene.

▶ **4.** In the Scene panel, double-click **Scene 1 copy**, type **Fish and Plant**, and then press the **Enter** key. The new scene name appears in the Scene panel.

▶ **5.** Close the Scene panel, and then save the document.

In this session, you learned about the basic elements of Flash that are used in creating animations—layers and frames. You worked with these elements using the Timeline. You also learned how scenes can help you manage a longer or more complex document. In the next session, you will create animations.

Session 3.1 Quick Check

REVIEW

1. What is the purpose of the Timeline?

2. How can you tell which is the current frame in the Timeline?

3. What is the default frame rate for a Flash document?

4. What is the difference between frames and layers?

5. What is a layer folder and what is its purpose?

6. What is a scene?

7. When you have more than one scene, how can you tell in what order the scenes will play?

8. Why would you rename a scene from its default name?

SESSION 3.2 VISUAL OVERVIEW

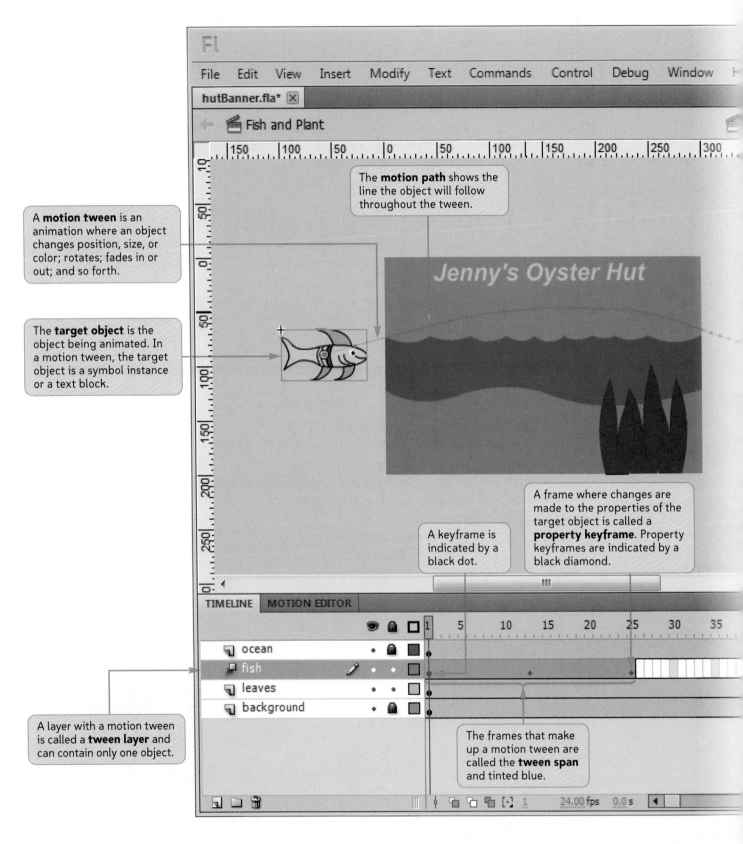

A **motion tween** is an animation where an object changes position, size, or color; rotates; fades in or out; and so forth.

The **target object** is the object being animated. In a motion tween, the target object is a symbol instance or a text block.

The **motion path** shows the line the object will follow throughout the tween.

A frame where changes are made to the properties of the target object is called a **property keyframe**. Property keyframes are indicated by a black diamond.

A keyframe is indicated by a black dot.

A layer with a motion tween is called a **tween layer** and can contain only one object.

The frames that make up a motion tween are called the **tween span** and tinted blue.

MOTION TWEENS

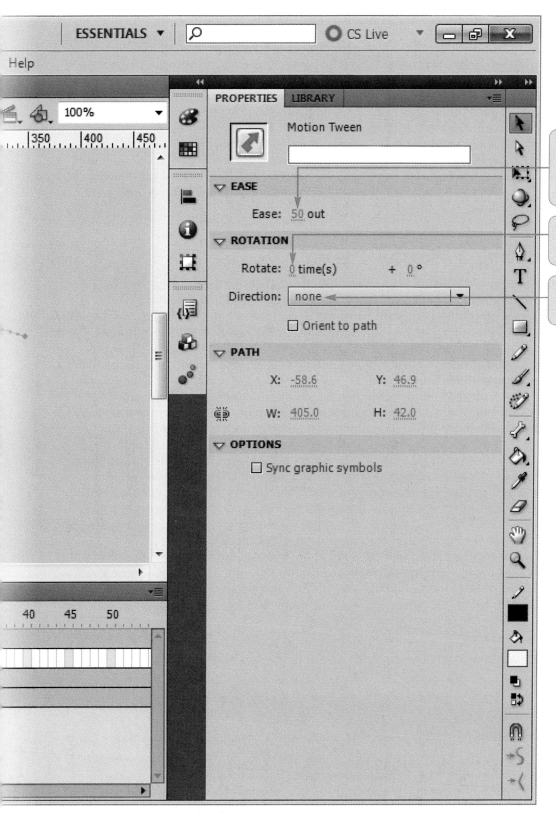

The Ease value makes an object accelerate or decelerate to create a more natural appearance of movement.

The Rotate value sets how many times the object rotates during the motion tween.

The rotation direction can be CW (clockwise) or CCW (counterclockwise).

Creating Animation

Animation is accomplished by displaying the content of different frames one after another. Each frame contains some graphic element that is displayed for a short instant in time. As the content of each frame is displayed in succession, the graphic elements appear to be moving. You can create several types of animations in Flash: motion tweens, classic tweens, shape tweens, and frame-by-frame animations. A **tween** is an animation where you create the beginning content and the ending content, and Flash creates the in-between frames, varying the content evenly in each frame to achieve the animation. The word "tween" comes from the words "in-between." In a frame-by-frame animation, you create or modify the content in each frame of the animation.

The animations of the fish in the new animated banner for Jenny's Oyster Hut will be created with motion tweens. In the second scene, the plant leaves will be animated so that the leaves' tips appear to be moving. This movement will be created with a frame-by-frame animation because you need to specify the positions of the leaves at different moments in time.

Creating a Motion Tween

Motion tweens in Flash are **object-based animations** because after you create a motion tween, you can easily modify the tween as one entity, similar to the way you would modify any other object. You can change the motion tween's duration, change the target object's direction, or move the motion tween within the Timeline. When you make changes to the motion tween, Flash adjusts the contents of all the frames in the tween span. A target object in a tween can be replaced by a different instance without having to re-create the tween.

The process for creating a motion tween animation is relatively simple. You add a symbol instance or a text block in one frame at the start of the animation and then apply a motion tween to the object. Flash creates a tween span in the Timeline that extends for one second, which is 24 frames when the frame rate is set to its default value. At any point in the tween span, you can modify the object by moving it to a different position or changing its properties, such as its size, color tint, or color brightness. A property keyframe is created at each point where you modify the object's properties. Flash varies the content in each intermediate frame to change the object's position or properties slightly from one frame to the next. You can also adjust the settings for the motion tween such as by adding rotation to the target object in the Property inspector.

The Fish and Plant scene will use two motion tweens to create an animation of a fish swimming from one side of the banner to the other. One motion tween will move the fish across the Stage from left to right, and the other motion tween will move the fish from right to left.

To create a motion tween with an instance of the fish symbol:

1. If you took a break after the previous session, make sure the hutBanner.fla file is open, the workspace is reset to the Essentials layout, and the Fish and Plant scene is displayed.

2. In the Timeline, in the Show/Hide column of the ocean layer, click the **dot** ● to hide the layer's contents.

3. In the Timeline, click the **fish** layer to select it, and then convert the fish graphic to a movie clip symbol named **fish**. The fish symbol is created.

4. On the Stage, drag the **fish** instance to the pasteboard to the left of the Stage, keeping the instance in the same relative vertical position. The fish will swim in from the left of the Stage.

5. Right-click the **fish** instance, and then click **Create Motion Tween**. A tween span is created from Frame 1 through Frame 24 in the Timeline and the playhead moves to Frame 24. See Figure 3-11.

Figure 3-11   **Motion tween created**

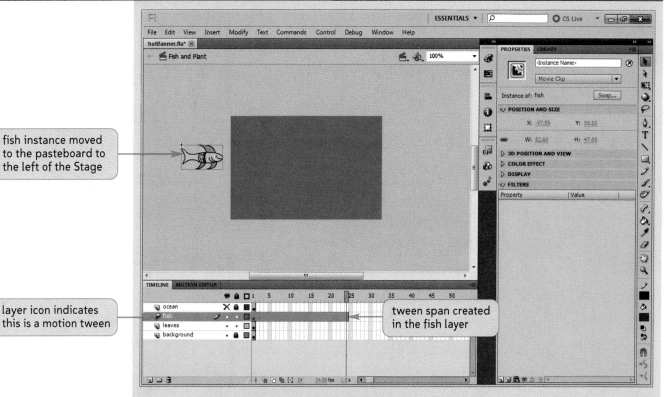

fish instance moved to the pasteboard to the left of the Stage

layer icon indicates this is a motion tween

tween span created in the fish layer

6. In the Timeline, drag the right edge of the tween span in the fish layer to the right, and then release the mouse button at Frame 50. The motion tween extends through Frame 50. See Figure 3-12.

Figure 3-12   **Tween span extended in the Timeline**

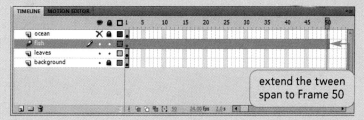

extend the tween span to Frame 50

The plant and background graphics disappeared when you added the motion tween because these graphics exist only in Frame 1. For these graphics to exist through Frame 50, you need to add frames to their respective layers.

7. In the Timeline, click **Frame 50** of the ocean layer, and then, on the Application bar, click **Insert**, point to **Timeline**, and click **Frame**. A regular frame is added at Frame 50. Regular frames are also automatically added between Frames 1 and 50 to fill the empty intervening frames.

8. Repeat Step 7 for the leaves and background layers to insert a regular frame to extend each layer to Frame 50.

Next you'll create a motion path for the motion tween.

9. Drag the **fish** instance from the left side of the Stage to the right side of the Stage, placing it on the pasteboard in the same relative vertical position. A motion path is created and displayed on the Stage. See Figure 3-13.

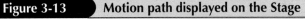

Figure 3-13 | Motion path displayed on the Stage

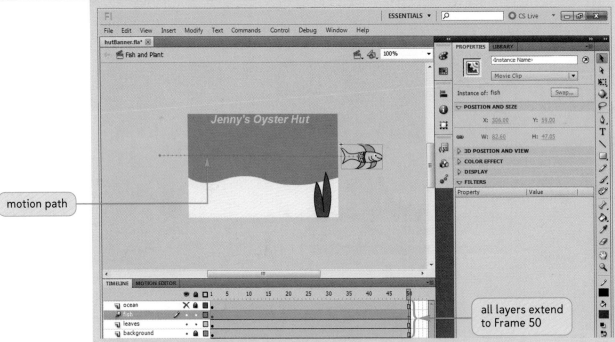

motion path

all layers extend to Frame 50

10. Press the **Enter** key to play the motion tween. The fish moves across the Stage from left to right following the motion path.

The fish is animated to move across the Stage. The fish also needs to move from the right side of the banner to the left. To do this, you will create another motion tween of a fish moving from right to left in a new layer. You will use another instance of the fish symbol and flip the instance so that it faces to the left.

To create a motion tween for a second fish instance:

1. In the Timeline, in the Show/Hide column of the fish layer, click the **dot** to hide its contents temporarily.

2. In the Timeline, click the **New Layer** button . A new layer is inserted in the Timeline above the fish layer.

3. Double-click the name of the new layer to select it, type **second fish**, and then press the **Enter** key to rename the layer.

4. Click the **LIBRARY** tab to display the Library panel, and then drag an instance of the **fish** symbol from the Library panel to the pasteboard on the right side of the Stage at the same relative location as the fish instance in the fish layer.

5. On the Application bar, click **Modify**, point to **Transform**, and then click **Flip Horizontal**. The fish flips so that it faces to the left.

6. Right-click the **fish** instance, and then click **Create Motion Tween**. A tween span is created from Frame 1 through Frame 50 in the Timeline.

7. Drag the **fish** instance from the right side of the Stage to the left side of the Stage, placing it on the pasteboard in the same relative vertical position. A motion path is created. See Figure 3-14.

Figure 3-14	Second motion tween with motion path

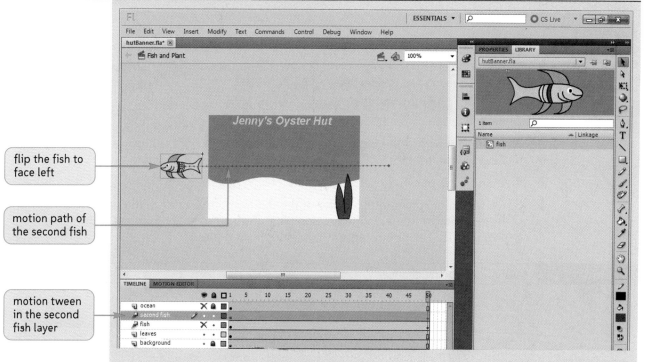

flip the fish to face left

motion path of the second fish

motion tween in the second fish layer

8. In the Timeline, in the Show/Hide column, click the **red X** ☒ for the ocean layer to show that layer, and then click the **red X** ☒ for the fish layer to unhide that layer.

9. On the Application bar, click **Control**, and then click **Play**. The first fish instance moves across the Stage from left to right while the second fish instance moves from right to left.

Modifying a Motion Tween

You can modify a motion tween by changing the properties of the target object anywhere within the tween span or by changing the curve of the motion path. When you make changes to the target object or to the motion path, Flash automatically adjusts the rest of the motion tween. If the target object's properties change, Flash adds property keyframes where the change is made.

Controlling an Object's Speed in an Animation

Objects don't usually move at a constant rate of speed. They might start slowly and then accelerate, or they might start quickly and then decelerate. For example, a kicked ball starts moving quickly but then slows toward the end of its movement. To simulate this natural movement, you can adjust a motion tween's Ease value in the Property inspector. A negative value causes the object to begin slowly and accelerate toward the end of the animation. A positive value causes the object to begin rapidly and decelerate toward the end of the animation. For more control over a motion tween, you can use the Custom Ease In/Ease Out dialog box, which displays an adjustable graph representing an object's degree of motion over time.

You'll modify the properties of the motion tweens.

To modify the properties of the motion tweens:

1. In the Timeline, hide the second fish layer, and then click the **fish** layer to select it. The tween span is selected.

2. Click the **PROPERTIES** tab to display the Property inspector. You will change the motion tween's properties.

3. In the Property inspector, drag the **Ease** value to the right to change the value to **50**. The fish instance will slow down toward the end of the motion tween.

4. In the Tools panel, click the **Selection** tool, if necessary.

5. On the Stage, point to the center of the motion path to change the pointer to , and then drag the pointer up slightly to curve the motion path, as shown in Figure 3-15. The fish instance will follow a curved path.

Figure 3-15   **Motion path being changed**

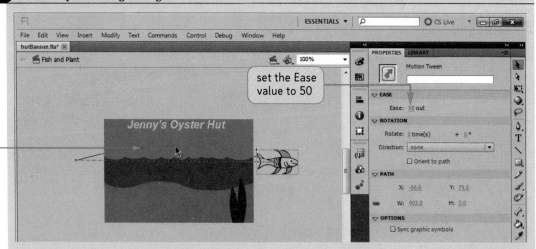

6. In the Timeline, hide the contents of the fish layer, display the contents of the second fish layer, and then click the second fish layer's name to select it.

7. In the Property inspector, drag the **Ease** value to the left to change it to **–50**. The fish instance will move faster toward the end of the motion tween.

8. Point to the center of the motion path on the Stage and drag it up slightly to curve it. The fish instance will follow a curved path.

Because you don't want both fish animations to occur at the same time, you'll move the tween span for the second fish so that its animation occurs after the first fish animation.

To move the tween span for the second fish:

1. In the Timeline, point to **Frame 1** of the tween span in the second fish layer, and then drag the span to the right so that its first frame starts on Frame 51. See Figure 3-16.

Figure 3-16   Tween span moved

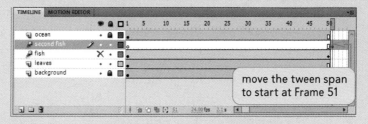

move the tween span to start at Frame 51

2. In the Timeline, move the playhead to the right to Frame 100.

3. In the Timeline, add regular frames at Frame 100 to the ocean, leaves, and background layers. Do not add regular frames to the fish layer. The entire movie now occupies 100 frames.

4. In the Timeline, in the Show/Hide column for the fish layer, click the **red X** X to display the contents of the fish layer.

5. On the Application bar, click **Control**, and then click **Play**. The first fish moves across the Stage from left to right, moving slightly above the water at the center of its path, and then the second fish moves across the Stage from right to left. It also moves slightly above the water at the center of its path.

6. Save the banner.

Using Motion Presets

The simplest and quickest way to create a motion tween is to apply a motion preset to an object selected on the Stage and let Flash create the necessary elements for the animation. A **motion preset** is a prebuilt motion tween animation. Each motion preset you apply is created on its own layer, and the new frames added to the Timeline are based on that motion preset. Figure 3-17 describes some of the default motion preset animations available in the Motion Presets panel. After you select a motion preset, the preview window in the Motion Presets panel displays a preview of the effect.

Figure 3-17   **Default motion presets**

Motion Preset	Description
bounce-smoosh	Animates an object to simulate bouncing on a surface
fly-in-blur-bottom	Animates an object to fly in from the bottom up; a blurring effect is applied to the object to simulate a rate of speed
fly-in-left	Animates an object to fade in and move from the left to the right
med-bounce	Animates an object to bounce across the Stage
pulse	Animates an object to create a pulsating effect

When you apply a motion preset to an object, Flash converts the layer on which the object resides into a motion tween layer and creates frames with the appropriate content for the animation. If the selected object is not a symbol, Flash prompts you to create a new symbol before applying the motion preset animation.

Applying a Motion Preset Animation

One of the animation sequences for the Jenny's Oyster Hut banner is of a fish moving across the Stage while pulling a shrimp specials sign. You will create this animation in the Shrimps special scene using the fly-in-left motion preset. Before you apply the motion preset, you'll draw the sign graphic.

To draw the sign graphic for the animation:

1. On the Edit bar, click the **Edit Scene** button, and then click **Shrimp Specials** to make it the current scene. The plant leaves will not be used in this scene, so you'll delete the leaves layer.

2. In the Timeline, click the **leaves** layer to select it, and then click the **Delete** button. The leaves layer is deleted.

3. In the Timeline, in the Show/Hide column for the ocean layer, click the **dot** to hide the layer. Hiding the ocean layer hidden makes it easier to focus on the sign.

4. On the Edit bar, click the **Zoom control arrow**, and then click **200%**. The contents of the Stage are magnified, making it easier to draw the sign.

5. Display the rulers, and then create horizontal guides approximately **140 pixels** and **180 pixels** from the top of the Stage and create vertical guides approximately **100 pixels** and **170 pixels** from the left of the Stage.

6. In the Tools panel, click the **Rectangle** tool, click the **Black and white** button to change the stroke color to black and the fill color to white, and then, if necessary, click the **Object Drawing** button to deselect it.

7. In the Property inspector, if necessary, set the Rectangle corner radius to **0**, the stroke height to **1**, and the stroke style to **Solid**.

8. In the Timeline, select the **fish** layer, and then, on the Stage, draw a rectangle that is approximately **70 pixels** wide and **40 pixels** high below the fish inside the rectangular area formed by the guides. The rectangle will be the sign the fish pulls across the banner. You'll add the words to the sign next.

9. In the Tools panel, click the **Text** tool, and then, in the Property inspector, if necessary, change the Text engine to **Classic Text**, the Text type to **Static Text**, the font family to **Arial**, the font style to **Bold**, the point size to **14**, the text (fill) color to **black** (#000000), and the format to **Align center**.

10. Create a text block inside the rectangle you drew in Step 8, type **Shrimp** in the text block, press the **Enter** key, and then type **Specials!**.

11. In the Tools panel, click the **Selection** tool ![selection tool], reposition the text block on the Stage so that it is centered within the rectangle, and then click an empty area of the Stage to deselect the text block. See Figure 3-18.

Figure 3-18   **Sign with text**

Shrimp Specials scene is the current scene

rectangle and text for the sign

ocean layer is hidden

fish layer is selected

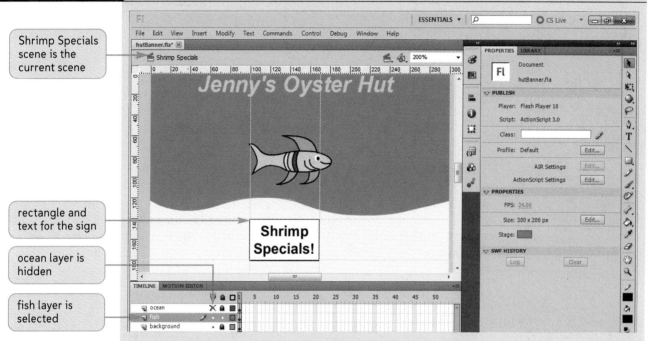

12. On the Application bar, click **View**, point to **Guides**, and then click **Clear Guides**. The guides are cleared from the Stage.

Be sure to select both the rectangle and the text block so they are skewed together.

13. In the Tools panel, click the **Free Transform** tool ![free transform], and then draw a marquee around the rectangle. Both the rectangle and the text block are selected. You'll skew the selected rectangle.

Trouble? If the fish is selected, the marquee you drew probably encompassed the fish. Click the pasteboard, and then draw the marquee again, being sure to select only the rectangle and the text block.

TIP

You can also press the Q key to select the Free Transform tool.

14. In the Tools panel, click the **Rotate and Skew** button ![rotate skew], move the pointer over the bottom side of the rectangle until it changes to ![arrow], and then drag the bottom side of the rectangle slightly to the left to skew the rectangle.

15. In the Tools panel, click the **Line** tool ![line tool], and then, if necessary, click the **Snap to Objects** button ![snap to objects] to select it.

16. In the Property inspector, set the stroke color to **black** (#000000), the stroke height to **1**, and the stroke style to **Solid**, if necessary.

17. On the Stage, draw a line from the fish's lower-left fin to the top of the rectangle, and then draw a line from the fish's lower-right fin to the top of the rectangle. The two lines connect the sign to the fish. See Figure 3-19.

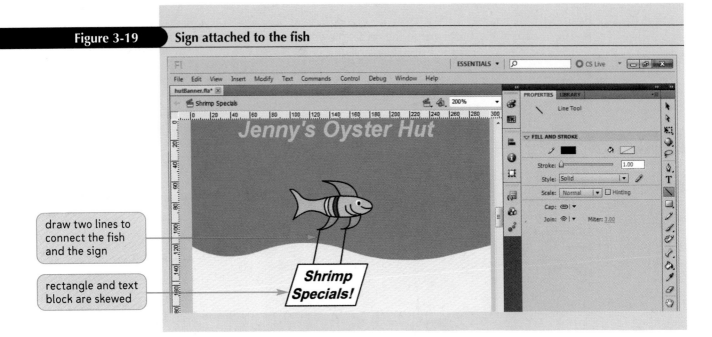

Figure 3-19	Sign attached to the fish

draw two lines to connect the fish and the sign

rectangle and text block are skewed

The graphic of the fish pulling the sign is complete. You are ready to animate the graphic using the fly-in-left motion preset. The animation of the fish and sign will start on the pasteboard to the left of the Stage, move across the Stage, and end near the center of the Stage. Before you can apply the motion preset, you must convert the sign, lines, and fish to a symbol.

To add the fly-in-left motion preset to the Jenny's Oyster Hut banner:

1. In the Tools panel, click the **Selection** tool , and then draw a marquee around the sign, lines, and fish graphic to select all the objects.

2. Convert the selected objects to a movie clip symbol with the name **fish sign**.

3. On the Edit bar, click the **Zoom control arrow**, and then click **100%**. The magnification level of the Stage is reduced.

4. Using the Selection pointer , move the **fish** instance to the left of the Stage and place it on the pasteboard. The fish will start off the Stage and then will move in to the center of the Stage.

5. In the docked panel group, click the **Motion Presets** button . The Motion Presets panel opens.

   Trouble? If the preset folders are not visible, drag the bottom edge of the preview pane up to reduce the size of the pane and display the preset folders.

6. To the left of the Default Presets folder, click the **Expand** arrow , if necessary, to expand the list of motion presets, scroll down, and then click **fly-in-left**. The fly-in-left motion preset is selected, and a preview of the animation is displayed in the preview pane of the Motion Presets panel.

7. In the Motion Presets panel, click the **Apply** button. The motion preset is applied to the selected fish sign instance on the Stage. The fish layer's icon in the Timeline changes to indicate that a motion tween has been created, new frames are added to the layer, and the fish sign instance becomes transparent. See Figure 3-20.

Figure 3-20 Motion tween created from a motion preset

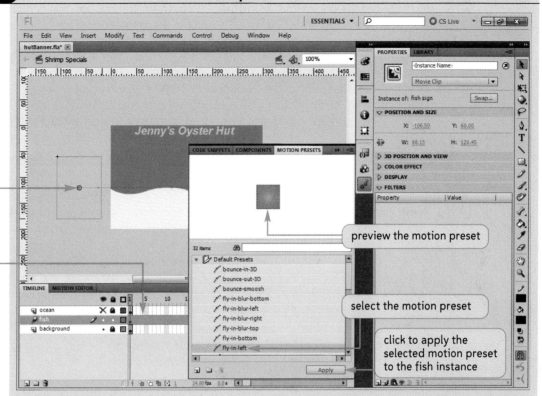

motion preset
applied to the fish
sign instance

tween span for
the motion preset

preview the motion preset

select the motion preset

click to apply the
selected motion preset
to the fish instance

▶ **8.** Click an empty area of the pasteboard to close the Motion Presets panel. You'll complete the animation.

▶ **9.** In the Timeline, point to the end of the tween span and drag it to the right to extend the tween span to Frame 40.

▶ **10.** In the Timeline, in the Show/Hide column for the ocean layer, click the **red X** ⊠. The contents of the ocean layer will be visible again.

TIP

You can also press the F5 key to insert a regular frame in the selected location.

▶ **11.** In the Timeline, click **Frame 60** of the ocean layer to select it, click **Insert** on the Application bar, point to **Timeline**, and then click **Frame** to insert a regular frame. The graphics in the ocean layer are displayed through Frame 60.

▶ **12.** Repeat Step 11 for the fish and background layers to display their graphics through Frame 60. All the layers exist for 60 frames, and the contents of all the layers will display 20 frames after the end of the tween span.

▶ **13.** On the Application bar, click **Control**, and then click **Play**. The fish and sign move across the Stage from the left to the right, starting quickly and slowing down slightly when they reach the end of the animation.

▶ **14.** Save the banner.

Testing an Animation

After you create a document with animation, you need to test it to make sure it works correctly. To test the document's animation, you have several options. You can play the full animation on the Stage. You can test some or all of the animation by scrubbing the playhead back and forth through the frames, which is useful for testing a short animation sequence. Another way to test a document's animation is to create a SWF file from the document, and then play the file using the Flash Player plug-in. Finally, you can test an animation in a Web page. Flash publishes the document as a SWF file and also creates a Web page. The Web page with the SWF file is displayed in your computer's default browser. The SWF files created when testing the animation are saved in the same folder as the FLA file.

PROSKILLS

Problem Solving: Testing Your Animations

When you complete an animation, be sure to take that final step of testing the animation. You can use this final step to check for any problems with the animation. First make sure that the animation effectively conveys the intended message. Check that you haven't overused or underused animation effects, as too much action in one animation can turn off the viewer just as much as not enough action. Then confirm that the animation runs smoothly from the first frame through the final frame. You might also ask peers or an intended viewer to review the finished animation so you can get their feedback on the content and presentation. During this testing process, you may need to modify the animation to correct problems you or others notice. Each time you make a correction, be sure to test the entire animation again. Thorough testing helps to ensure that the animation provides viewers with the experience you intended.

When you test a document's animation on the Stage, Flash plays only the current scene. To see how all of the scenes work together, you need to test the movie in the Flash Player window. Each scene then plays in sequence with the animation repeating until you close the Flash Player window.

REFERENCE

Testing a Document's Animation

- To test an animation on the Stage, on the Application bar, click Control, and then click Play (or press the Enter key).
- To test a few frames of animation, scrub the playhead along the Timeline header.
- To test the animation in a Flash Player window, on the Application bar, click Control, point to Test Movie and then click in Flash Professional.
- To test the animation in a Web page, on the Application bar, click File, point to Publish Preview, and click Default - (HTML).

You will test the banner document in a Flash Player window so you can see the animations in both scenes.

To test the document's animation in a Flash Player window:

1. On the Application bar, click **Control**, point to **Test Movie**, and then click **in Flash Professional**. The movie plays in a Flash Player window, starting with the Shrimp Specials scene. You can control how the animation plays.

TIP

You can also press the Ctrl+Enter keys to test the movie.

▶ **2.** On the Flash Player Application bar, click **Control**, and then click **Loop** to turn off the loop feature and stop the animation from repeating. The animation stops at the current scene.

Trouble? If the Loop command is not active, continue with Step 3.

▶ **3.** On the Flash Player menu bar, click **File**, and then click **Close**. The Flash Player window closes.

The fish animations for both scenes of the banner are complete. In the next session, you will add animation to the plant leaves using a frame-by-frame animation. You will also animate text blocks using classic tween animations.

REVIEW

Session 3.2 Quick Check

1. What is a motion preset?
2. True or False. Each motion preset is created in its own layer.
3. After you create a motion tween in your document, how can you change its properties?
4. Briefly describe the difference between a frame-by-frame animation and a motion tween.
5. How many objects can you have on a layer with a motion tween?
6. What type of tweened animation would you create to have an object move from one side of the Stage to the other?
7. Why is it important to test an animation after you create it?

SESSION 3.3 VISUAL OVERVIEW

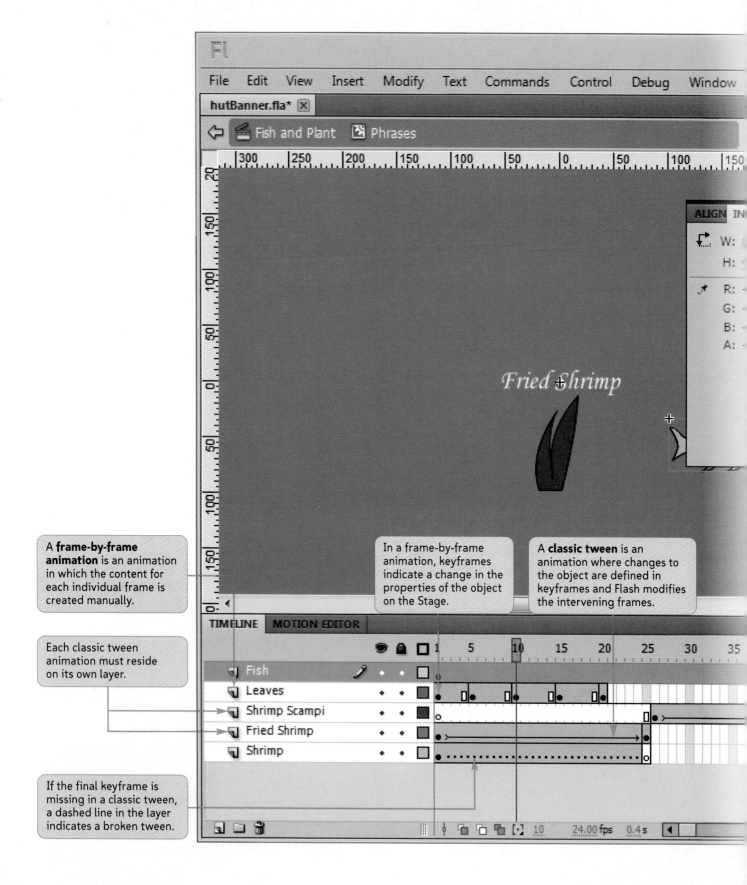

A **frame-by-frame animation** is an animation in which the content for each individual frame is created manually.

In a frame-by-frame animation, keyframes indicate a change in the properties of the object on the Stage.

A **classic tween** is an animation where changes to the object are defined in keyframes and Flash modifies the intervening frames.

Each classic tween animation must reside on its own layer.

If the final keyframe is missing in a classic tween, a dashed line in the layer indicates a broken tween.

CLASSIC TWEEN AND ANIMATION

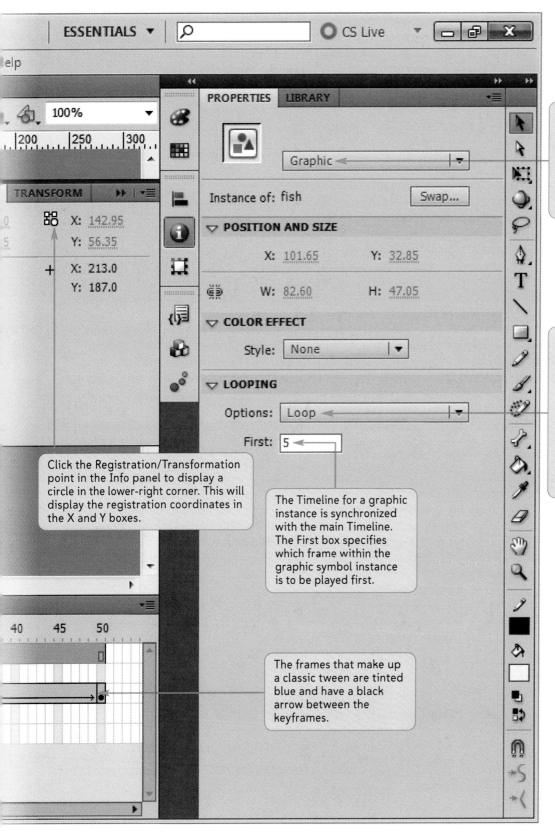

The behavior of a movie clip instance can be changed to Graphic. The graphic instance can be animated so that its Timeline operates in sync with the document's Timeline.

You can specify how you want a graphic instance's animation to play in the Options drop-down list. The Loop option plays the animation continuously. The Play Once option plays the animation only one time. The Single Frame option plays only the frame specified in the First frame box.

Click the Registration/Transformation point in the Info panel to display a circle in the lower-right corner. This will display the registration coordinates in the X and Y boxes.

The Timeline for a graphic instance is synchronized with the main Timeline. The First box specifies which frame within the graphic symbol instance is to be played first.

The frames that make up a classic tween are tinted blue and have a black arrow between the keyframes.

Creating a Classic Tween

Another way to create motion in a document is with a classic tween. A classic tween has a beginning keyframe and an ending keyframe, and each keyframe has an instance of a symbol. The instance's properties are changed in the ending keyframe, and Flash gradually changes the instance's properties in the frames between the beginning and ending keyframes. You can only modify the instance in the keyframes and not in the intermediate frames. A classic tween can have only one symbol instance on a layer.

REFERENCE

Creating a Classic Tween Animation

- In the Timeline, select a frame, and then, on the Application bar, click Insert, point to Timeline, and then click Keyframe.
- Insert an instance of a symbol in the keyframe.
- On the same layer, select another frame, and then, on the Application bar, click Insert, point to Timeline, and click Keyframe.
- In the ending keyframe, modify the instance's properties.
- Select the beginning keyframe, and then, on the Application bar, click Insert, and click Classic Tween (or right-click a frame between the keyframes, and then click Create Classic Tween).

The Jenny's Oyster Hut Web site banner should contain an animation that displays the phrases "Fried Shrimp" and "Shrimp Scampi" on the Stage. These phrases will appear one at a time and continuously change from one phrase to another. The animation will be placed in several places in the document. You will create the animation only once, as a symbol, and then create several instances of this symbol in the Shrimp Specials scene.

INSIGHT

Using Registration Points

The registration point of a symbol is usually at the center of the symbol, and it can be used to control how the symbol is animated. To align several symbols in an animation, make each symbol's registration point the same. You can set the registration point when you create the symbol in symbol-editing mode by setting the symbol's X and Y coordinates. You can set the symbol's coordinates in the Info panel, which displays the registration point coordinates when the Registration/Transformation button displays a small circle in its lower-right corner. When the X and Y coordinates are set to 0, the symbol appears on the center of the Stage.

You will create the animation with the phrases.

To create the Phrases symbol:

1. If you took a break after the previous session, make sure that the hutBanner.fla file is open, the workspace is reset to the Essentials layout, the magnification level is set to 100%, and the Shrimp Specials scene is displayed on the Stage.

2. Create a new movie clip symbol named **Phrases**. The Phrases symbol appears in symbol-editing mode.

3. In the Tools panel, click the **Text** tool [T], and then, in the Property inspector, set the font family to **Monotype Corsiva**, the point size to **24**, the text (fill) color to **white** (#FFFFFF), the Font Rendering method to **Anti-alias for animation**, and the format to **Align center**.

4. On the center of the Stage, create a single-line text block, and then type **Fried Shrimp**.

5. In the Tools panel, click the **Selection** tool [▶] to select the text block.

6. In the docked panel group, click the **Info** button [🛈] to open the Info panel.

7. In the Info panel, click the **Registration/Transformation point** button [⊞] so that it displays a small circle in its lower-right corner [⊞], if necessary. You can now set the X and Y coordinates for the symbol.

8. Type **0** in the X box, type **0** in the Y box, and then press the **Enter** key. The text block is centered on the Stage. See Figure 3-21.

| Figure 3-21 | Settings in the Info panel |

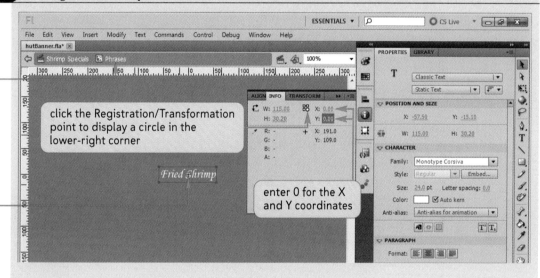

Phrases symbol is in symbol-editing mode

registration point is at the center of the text block

click the Registration/Transformation point to display a circle in the lower-right corner

enter 0 for the X and Y coordinates

Next, you will convert the text block to a movie clip and duplicate it. To animate the text block using a classic tween, the text block must be a symbol.

To convert the text block to a movie clip and duplicate it:

1. With the text block still selected, convert the text block to a movie clip symbol named **Fried Shrimp text**, clicking the center registration point in the Convert to Symbol dialog box. The movie clip symbol is created inside the Phrases symbol.

2. Open the Library panel, and then duplicate the **Fried Shrimp text** symbol, creating a movie clip symbol named **Shrimp Scampi text**.

3. On the Edit bar, click the **Edit Symbols** button [⬀], and then click **Shrimp Scampi text**. The symbol opens in symbol-editing mode so you can change the text in this duplicate symbol.

4. In the Tools panel, if necessary, click the **Selection** tool [▶], double-click the text block, change the text to **Shrimp Scampi**, and then click the **Selection** tool [▶] again.

5. Expand the Info panel, and then set the X and Y values to **0**, if necessary. See Figure 3-22.

Figure 3-22   **Edited Shrimp Scampi text symbol**

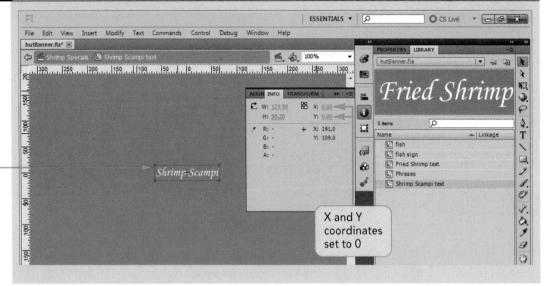

text block is changed

You will create the Fried Shrimp text animation.

To create the Fried Shrimp text animation:

1. On the Edit bar, click the **Edit Symbols** button 🔳, and then click **Phrases**. The Phrases symbol opens in symbol-editing mode.

2. In the Timeline, rename Layer 1 to **Fried Shrimp**, and then click **Frame 25**.

3. On the Application bar, click **Insert**, point to **Timeline**, and then click **Keyframe**. A keyframe is inserted in Frame 25, and regular frames are added in Frames 2 through 24.

4. In the Tools panel, click the **Selection** tool 🔳, if necessary, and then select the **Fried Shrimp text** instance.

5. In the Property inspector, expand the Color Effect section, click the **Style** button, click **Alpha**, and then, if necessary, type **0** in the Alpha amount box and press the **Enter** key. The Fried Shrimp text disappears because an alpha amount of 0% makes an object completely transparent.

6. In the Timeline, right-click **Frame 1** to open the context menu, and then click **Create Classic Tween**. The classic tween is created between Frames 1 and 25. See Figure 3-23.

Figure 3-23 | **Classic tween created**

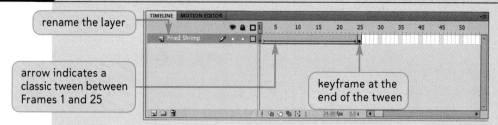

rename the layer

arrow indicates a
classic tween between
Frames 1 and 25

keyframe at the
end of the tween

> **7.** Press the **Enter** key to test the animation. The Fried Shrimp text instance fades
> out throughout the animation.

You need to create a similar animation for the next phrase. Instead of repeating all of
these steps in a new layer, you can copy the frames on the Fried Shrimp layer and paste
them onto a new layer. Then, you can swap the instances of the Fried Shrimp text symbol
with instances of the Shrimp Scampi text symbol. When swapping symbol instances in a
classic tween, you must swap the instances in both the beginning and ending keyframes.
Finally, you will reposition the frames that contain the classic tween so that the animation for the second phrase starts later than the animation for the first phrase.

To create the classic tween animation for the Shrimp Scampi text symbol:

> **1.** In the Timeline, click the **Fried Shrimp** layer name to select all of its frames.

> **2.** Right-click the selected frames, and then click **Copy Frames**. The frames are cop-
> ied to the Windows Clipboard.

> **3.** In the Timeline, click the **New Layer** button 🖪 to insert a new layer.

> **4.** In the Timeline, rename Layer 2 to **Shrimp Scampi**, and then click the **Shrimp
> Scampi** layer name to select all of its frames.

> **5.** Right-click the selected frames, and then click **Paste Frames**. The frames contain-
> ing the Fried Shrimp text animation are pasted into the Shrimp Scampi layer. See
> Figure 3-24.

Figure 3-24 | **Frames pasted in the layer**

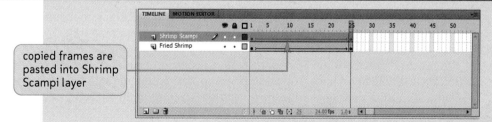

copied frames are
pasted into Shrimp
Scampi layer

You need to swap the Fried Shrimp text symbol with the Shrimp Scampi text symbol.

TIP

You can use the Duplicate Symbol button in the Swap Symbol dialog box to make a copy of a symbol that is stored in the document's library.

6. In the Timeline, click **Frame 1** of the Shrimp Scampi layer, and then click the instance of the **Fried Shrimp text** symbol at the center of the Stage. You can tell the instance is selected because the Property inspector shows "Instance of: Fried Shrimp text."

7. In the Property inspector, click the **Swap** button to open the Swap Symbol dialog box, and then click **Shrimp Scampi text**. See Figure 3-25.

Figure 3-25 **Swap Symbol dialog box**

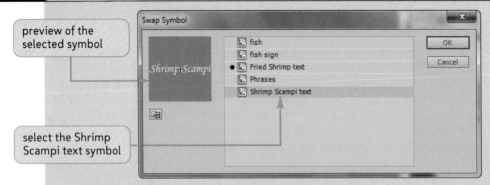

preview of the selected symbol

select the Shrimp Scampi text symbol

8. Click the **OK** button. The Fried Shrimp text instance is replaced with the Shrimp Scampi text instance. The text blocks for the two layers overlap on the Stage, so one word appears on top of the other. You will fix this in the next set of steps.

Next, you'll swap the instance in the ending keyframe.

9. In the Timeline, click **Frame 25** of the Shrimp Scampi layer, and then click the blue outline of the **Fried Shrimp text** instance at the center of the Stage. The words are not visible because you set the alpha amount to 0% at this keyframe.

10. In the Property inspector, click the **Swap** button to open the Swap Symbol dialog box, click **Shrimp Scampi text**, and then click the **OK** button. The Fried Shrimp text instance is replaced with the Shrimp Scampi text instance.

The animation in the Shrimp Scampi layer works the same as the one in the Fried Shrimp layer, except that the symbol being animated is the Shrimp Scampi text symbol and not the Fried Shrimp text symbol.

Now that both animations are complete, you need to reposition the Shrimp Scampi text animation so that the two animations do not occur at the same time. You want the Fried Shrimp text animation to start first, followed by the Shrimp Scampi text animation. This means that the Shrimp Scampi text animation will begin at Frame 26 after the Fried Shrimp text animation ends. The Shrimp Scampi text animation's 25 frames will end at Frame 50. You can easily change the location of frames within a layer.

To reposition the frames within the Shrimp Scampi layer:

1. In the Timeline, click the **Shrimp Scampi** layer name to select all the frames that make up the Shrimp Scampi text animation.

2. Drag the selected frames to the right so that the beginning keyframe starts on Frame 26 of the Shrimp Scampi layer, as shown in Figure 3-26.

Figure 3-26   Selected frames being moved

3. Release the mouse button. The selected frames start on Frame 26 and end on Frame 50.

4. On the Application bar, click **Control**, and then click **Rewind** to move the playhead to Frame 1.

TIP

You can also press the Shift+, keys to rewind the movie to Frame 1.

5. Press the **Enter** key. The phrases appear and fade out in turn as the animation plays.

6. On the Edit bar, click the **Shrimp Specials** scene to exit symbol-editing mode and return to the Shrimp Specials scene.

The Phrases symbol is complete. You will insert two instances of the Phrases symbol onto the Stage for the Shrimp Specials scene.

To insert the Phrases symbol instances and test the scene:

1. In the Timeline of the Shrimp Specials scene, insert a new layer above the ocean layer, name the layer **phrases**, and then click **Frame 1** of the phrases layer.

2. Drag two instances of the **Phrases** symbol from the Library panel to the bottom part of the Stage. See Figure 3-27.

Figure 3-27   **Instances of the Phrases symbol**

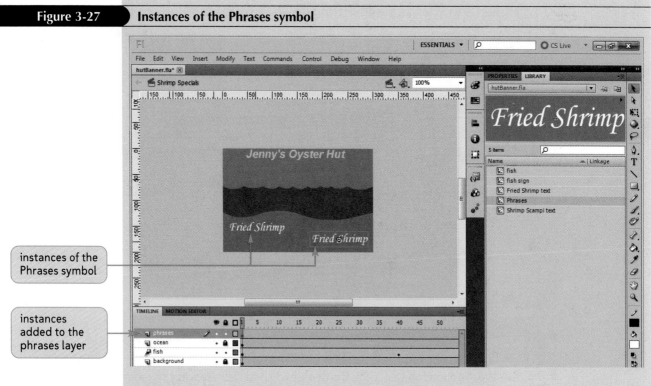

instances of the
Phrases symbol

instances
added to the
phrases layer

3. On the Application bar, click **Control**, and then click **Play**. The Phrases instances do not display their animations on the Stage. You will test the scene's animation in a Flash Player window.

4. On the Application bar, click **Control**, and then click **Test Scene**. The scene opens in a Flash Player window, and the fish move across the Stage as the Phrases instances display the two text blocks in turn.

5. On the Flash Player menu bar, click **File**, and then click **Close**. The Flash Player window closes.

The two instances of the Phrases symbol display their respective text blocks at the same time. Aly wants you to change one of the instances so that its animation starts at a different frame and is not in sync with the other instance. You cannot change the starting frame of a movie clip instance, so you will need to convert it to a graphic instance.

Using Graphic Symbols in Animations

Movie clip instances always start playing from their first frame. With a graphic instance, however, you can specify which of its frames to play first. As a result, if you create an animation with a graphic symbol and then create several instances of the symbol, each instance can have a different starting frame. For example, one instance can start playing at Frame 1 of its Timeline, while another instance can start playing at Frame 20. Using this technique, you can create multiple instances of one graphic symbol in the same scene and have each instance exhibit a different behavior.

Both movie clip and graphic symbols have their own Timelines. With a movie clip symbol, the frames in its Timeline play independently of the document's main Timeline. However, with a graphic symbol, the frames in its Timeline are synchronized with the document's main Timeline. Suppose, for instance, you insert a movie clip instance that contains an animation with 10 frames into a document whose main Timeline has only one frame. Even though the main Timeline contains only one frame, the movie clip's 10 frames still play in their entirety. However, if you insert a graphic instance that contains an animation with 10 frames into a document whose main Timeline has only one frame, then only one frame of the graphic instance will play. If you want all 10 frames of the graphic instance to play, you must extend the length of the document's main Timeline to at least 10 frames. Graphic symbols are useful when you want to synchronize the animations in the symbol to that of the main Timeline.

Unlike movie clip symbol instances, graphic symbol instances display their animation when you scrub the playhead in the document's main Timeline or play the main Timeline's animation on the Stage. You don't need to test the document in the Flash Player to see the animations contained in instances of graphic symbols as you do with animations contained in instances of movie clips, which appear as static objects when played on the Stage.

You will change one of the Phrases movie clip instances on the Stage to a graphic instance and then change its starting frame.

To change a Phrases symbol instance to a graphic instance:

1. On the right side of the Stage, select the **Phrases** symbol instance, if necessary.

2. In the Property inspector, click the **Instance behavior** button, and then point to **Graphic**. See Figure 3-28. You want to change the Phrases instance behavior to the graphic type.

Figure 3-28   Instance behavior being changed

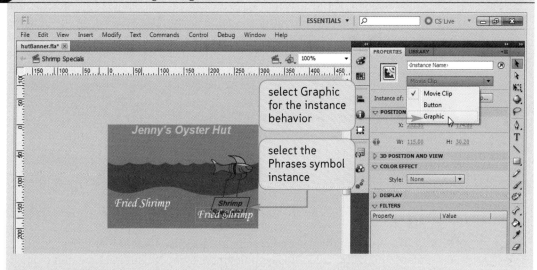

3. Click **Graphic**. The Phrases instance behavior changes to graphic.

4. Expand the Looping section of the Property inspector, type **20** in the First box, and then press the **Enter** key. This instance will start after the first classic tween begins, but before the second classic tween begins in the Phrases animation.

5. In the Property inspector, make sure **Loop** is selected in the Options list. The animation will play continuously. The Shrimp Scampi text is displayed.

6. On the Application bar, click **Control**, and then click **Test Scene**. The scene opens in a Flash Player window, and the Phrases instances each start at a different frame as they fade in and out.

▸ **7.** On the Flash Player menu bar, click **File**, and then click **Close**. The Flash Player window closes.

▸ **8.** Save the banner.

Creating Frame-by-Frame Animations

A frame-by-frame animation requires that the graphic elements of the animation be created for each of its individual frames. If, for example, the animation will have 15 frames, you need to create the content for each of the 15 frames. Some of the content can be the same from one frame to the next, and other content can be slightly modified. As the frames are displayed one after another, the perception of movement is achieved.

To create a frame-by-frame animation, you start with a graphic object in the initial frame. Then, for each place in the animation where the object changes, you add a keyframe. As you add keyframes, you change the position or properties of the graphic object. Depending on the animation, every frame can have a keyframe, or only some frames can have keyframes while the graphic object does not change in the intervening frames. After you have created all of the keyframes, you test the animation.

PROSKILLS

Decision Making: Choosing an Animation Type

As you create animations, keep in mind that the file size affects the viewer's experience with the animation. You want to use the smallest possible file size to create an animation that effectively conveys your message. In animations, each keyframe indicates a change in action. Because Flash stores the contents of every keyframe, the number of keyframes in an animation affects the document's file size. As you decide which type of animation to create, consider the following information.

* Frame-by-frame animations produce larger file sizes because they tend to have many keyframes.
* Classic tweens produce smaller files because they usually have only beginning and ending keyframes.
* Motion tweens also have smaller file sizes because Flash stores only the contents of the target object and the property keyframes.

So, to keep file sizes small, choose frame-by-frame animations only when you cannot achieve the same results with classic and motion tweens.

The Fish and Plant scene contains a graphic element that looks like the leaves of a plant. You will convert this graphic into a symbol with a movie clip behavior, and then create a frame-by-frame animation so that the plant's leaves appear to be moving in the ocean. The leaves will be animated within the Timeline of the plant symbol and not in the main Timeline of the document. Recall that a movie clip symbol has its own Timeline that is independent of the document's Timeline. By adding the animation in the symbol's Timeline, every instance of the symbol automatically includes the animation. This means that each plant instance you create on the Stage will have the same animation built in as part of the instance.

Before you can create the frame-by-frame animation of the leaves, you need to convert the plant object to a symbol.

To convert the leaves graphic in the Fish and Plant scene to a symbol:

▶ **1.** On the Edit bar, click the **Edit Scene** button 🎬, and then click the **Fish and Plant** scene to make it the current scene. You will create a symbol of the leaves graphic.

▶ **2.** In the Timeline, in the Show/Hide column for the ocean layer, click the **dot** ● to hide the layer.

▶ **3.** In the Tools panel, click the **Selection** tool ▶, if necessary, and then, on the Stage, select the **leaves** graphic, including both its stroke and its fill.

▶ **4.** Convert the leaves graphic to a movie clip symbol named **leaves**.

You are ready to animate the leaves symbol. You first need to select the symbol from the Library panel so you can edit it to create an animation within its Timeline.

To create a frame-by-frame animation of the leaves symbol:

▶ **1.** In the Library panel, double-click the **leaves** symbol icon. The symbol opens in symbol-editing mode.

▶ **2.** In the symbol's Timeline, click **Frame 5**. This is the frame where you want to change the animation. See Figure 3-29.

| Figure 3-29 | Leaves symbol in symbol-editing mode |

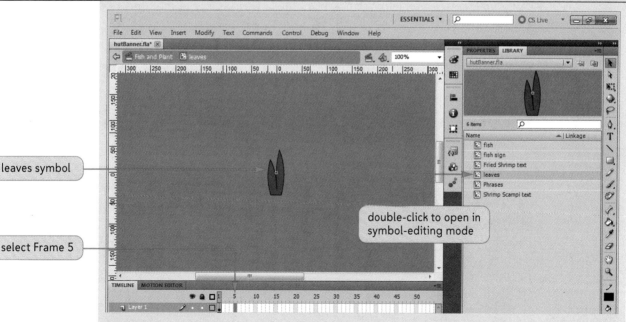

leaves symbol

select Frame 5

double-click to open in symbol-editing mode

TIP

You can also press the F6 key to insert a keyframe at the selected location.

▶ **3.** On the Application bar, click **Insert**, point to **Timeline**, and then click **Keyframe**. A keyframe is inserted in Frame 5 and regular frames are added to Frames 2, 3, and 4 to fill the empty intervening frames. The leaves graphic is automatically copied to all the new frames. See Figure 3-30.

Figure 3-30   Keyframe added in the Timeline of the leaves symbol

keyframe inserted in Frame 5

regular frames added

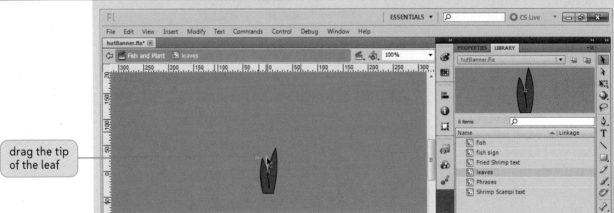

In Frame 5, you'll move the tips of the leaves slightly to the right.

4. In the Tools panel, click the **Selection** tool ▶ if necessary, and then click the **Snap to Objects** button 🧲, if necessary, to deselect it.

5. Click another area of the Stage to deselect the plant, move the pointer over the tip of the right leaf until it changes to ▶⌟, and then click and drag the tip of the leaf slightly to the right.

6. Repeat Step 5 to reposition the other leaf's tip slightly to the right. See Figure 3-31.

Figure 3-31   Tips of the plant leaves modified

drag the tip of the leaf

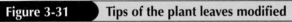

You will repeat this process to add a keyframe every fifth frame and reposition the leaves' tips farther right, then back left, and finally back to their starting positions.

7. Click **Frame 10**, insert a keyframe, and then repeat Steps 5 and 6 to reposition both of the leaves' tips slightly more to the right.

8. Click **Frame 15**, insert a keyframe, and then repeat Steps 5 and 6 to reposition the leaves' tips back slightly to the left.

9. Click **Frame 20**, insert a keyframe, and then repeat Steps 5 and 6 to move the leaves' tips slightly more to the left to almost the same positions where they started in Frame 1.

10. Scrub the playhead through these frames to get a sense of what the animation looks like. This frame-by-frame animation is complete.

11. On the Edit bar, click the **Edit Scene** button 📇, and then click **Fish and Plant** to exit symbol-editing mode.

You have created a frame-by-frame animation within the leaves symbol. Because the animation was created within the symbol's Timeline, each instance of the symbol has the same animation. You can, therefore, place several instances of the leaves symbol in the document, and all the instances will be animated.

The banner needs three animated plants in the lower-right corner of the Stage. Because one instance of the animated plant leaves is already on the Stage, you need to add two more instances. The second instance needs to be modified to make it larger than the first, and the third instance needs to be modified so its leaves point to the right.

To create and modify two instances of the animated leaves symbol:

1. On the Edit bar, click the **Zoom control arrow**, and then click **Show All**. All the contents on the Stage and pasteboard are displayed.

2. In the Timeline, select the **leaves** layer, if necessary, and then drag an instance of the **leaves** symbol from the Library panel to the Stage and place it to the left of the existing instance.

3. In the Tools panel, click the **Free Transform** tool 📐, and then click the **Scale** button 🔲.

4. On the Stage, drag one corner of the bounding box around the plant outward to make this leaves instance slightly larger than the other instance. See Figure 3-32.

Figure 3-32   **Enlarged leaves instance**

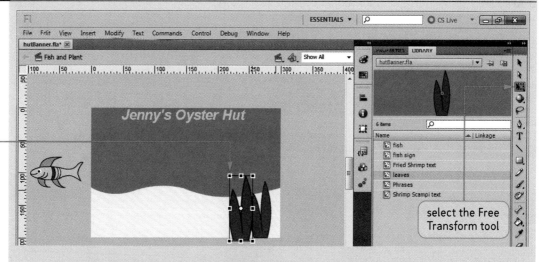

drag a corner to enlarge the instance

select the Free Transform tool

---

5. In the Tools panel, click the **Selection** tool ▶ to select it, and then reposition this instance as needed to align it with the bottom edge of the other leaves instance.

6. Drag another instance of the **leaves** symbol from the Library panel to the Stage and place it to the left of the larger leaves instance.

7. With the third leaves instance still selected on the Stage, on the Application bar, click **Modify**, point to **Transform**, and then click **Flip Horizontal**. The leaves of the instance now face to the right.

8. If necessary, line up the bottoms of the leaves with the bottom part of the Stage. See Figure 3-33.

Figure 3-33   **Three leaves instances arranged on the Stage**

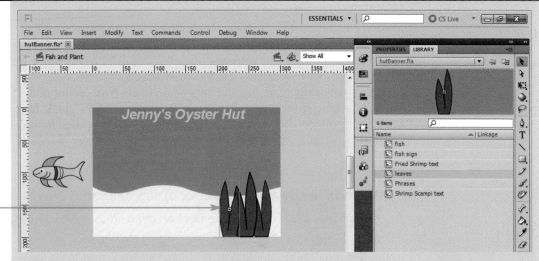

flip the third plant instance horizontally so its leaves face right

9. In the Timeline, in the Show/Hide column of the ocean layer, click the **red X** ⊠. The contents of the ocean layer reappear on the Stage.

10. Save the banner.

Because the leaves symbol's animation is within its own Timeline, you need to test the animation as a SWF file. The movie will appear in a Flash Player window. If you test the animation on the Stage, the leaves symbol's animation will not play. You can also test the animation in a Web page.

To test the animation in a Flash Player window and a Web page:

1. On the Application bar, click **Control**, point to **Test Movie**, and then click **in Flash Professional**. The movie plays in a Flash Player window, starting with the Shrimp specials scene. The leaves display their animation, as shown in Figure 3-34.

Figure 3-34   **Flash Player window with the leaves animation**

leaves animation

TIP

You can also press the F12 key to preview the animation in a Web page in your computer's default browser.

2. On the Flash Player menu bar, click **File**, and then click **Close**. The Flash Player window closes.

3. On the Application bar, click **File**, point to **Publish Preview**, and then click **Default - (HTML)**. Your computer's default browser opens, and the animation plays in a Web page.

Trouble? If the Runtime Shared Library Preloading Warning dialog box opens, click the OK button to continue.

4. Close the browser window when you are finished viewing the animation.

5. Save and close the banner.

Creating a Shape Tween

Shape tweens are created similarly to motion tween animations. A **shape tween** is an animation that takes one shape and transforms it into another shape. To create a shape tween, you create the graphic content in the beginning and ending frames of the animation, and Flash creates the tweened frames to complete the animation. The object in a shape tween must *not* be a symbol or a grouped object. This is different from a motion or classic tween where the object must be a symbol. A shape tween is indicated in the Timeline by a black arrow and a light green color for the frames. You can also control the shape tween's acceleration and deceleration by changing the Ease value in the Property inspector. The Jenny's Oyster Hut banner does not require a shape tween.

In this session, you created animations using frame-by-frame and classic tween animations, and you learned how to create shape tweens. You also learned how to create animations using graphic symbols. Aly is pleased with the completed banner for Jenny's Oyster Hut Web site and is looking forward to showing it to Jenny.

REVIEW

Session 3.3 Quick Check

1. How can you animate a movie clip symbol so that each of its instances automatically contains the animation?
2. List two differences between a movie clip symbol and a graphic symbol.
3. Why do animations within graphic symbols play in a document's main Timeline without the document having to be tested in the Flash Player?
4. In a frame-by-frame animation, what kind of frame do you need to have in the Timeline when the content changes on the Stage?
5. True or False. To create a frame-by-frame animation, the object being animated does not need to be converted to a symbol.
6. Can you include regular frames in a frame-by-frame animation? Why or why not?
7. True or False. To create a shape tween, the object being animated must first be converted to a symbol.

Review Assignments

Data File needed for the Review Assignments: adDraft.fla

Aly wants you to modify the animated ad banner so that a text animation in the first scene includes the words "Lunch", "Dinner", and "Anytime!" displayed one after the other. She also wants you to animate the fish and sign so that they move across the Stage, and she wants the title text block in the first scene to fade in as the fish pulls the sign. Finally, she wants you to add two instances of an animated fish that swim in opposite directions in the second scene.

1. Open the **adDraft.fla** file located in the Flash3\Review folder included with your Data Files, save the file as **jennysAd.fla** in the same folder, and then reset the workspace to its Essentials layout.

2. In the Daily specials scene, select the entire fish and sign graphics on the Stage, and then convert them to a movie clip symbol named **fish and sign**.

3. Move the fish and sign instance to the pasteboard in the lower-left side of the Stage. Create a motion tween so that the fish and sign instance moves into the lower-left corner of the Stage, moves diagonally upward across the Stage, and stops in the middle-right part of the Stage. Extend the motion tween so that it spans 70 frames. Insert a regular frame in Frame 70 of the background layer to extend it.

4. In the Library panel, make two duplicates of the lunch text symbol, and name one duplicate **dinner text** and the other **anytime text**. Edit the dinner text symbol by changing the Lunch text to **Dinner**. Edit the anytime text symbol by changing the Lunch text to **Anytime!**.

5. Create a new graphic symbol named **text animation**. In symbol-editing mode, change the Layer 1 name to **lunch**. Drag an instance of the lunch text symbol from the Library panel to the center of the Stage. In the Info panel, change its X and Y coordinates to 0.

6. Right-click the lunch text instance and create a motion tween. With the playhead on Frame 24 and the lunch text instance selected on the Stage, set the alpha amount to 0% in the Color Effect section of the Property inspector to make the instance transparent. Hide the contents of the lunch layer.

7. In the Timeline, insert a new layer and name it **dinner**, and then drag an instance of the dinner text symbol from the Library panel to the center of the Stage. In the Info panel, change its X and Y coordinates to 0.

8. Right-click the dinner text instance and create a motion tween. Move the playhead to Frame 24, if necessary, and then select the dinner text instance on the Stage. Set its alpha amount to 0% to make it transparent. Hide the contents of the dinner layer.

9. In the Timeline, insert a new layer and name it **anytime**, and then drag an instance of the anytime text symbol from the Library panel to the center of the Stage. In the Info panel, change its X and Y coordinates to 0.

10. Right-click the anytime text instance and create a motion tween. Move the playhead to Frame 24, if necessary, and then select the anytime text instance on the Stage. Set its alpha amount to 0% to make it transparent.

11. Drag the tween span in the dinner layer so that it starts in Frame 24 of the same layer. Drag the tween span in the anytime layer so that it starts in Frame 47 of the same layer. Unhide the lunch and dinner layers and test the text animation. The words appear and fade out in turn. Exit symbol-editing mode.

12. In the Daily specials scene, insert a new layer above the background layer and name it **text**, and then add two instances of the text animation symbol to the Stage. Place one on the lower-left side of the Stage. Place the other on the lower-right side of the Stage and start its animation in Frame 35.

13. In the Library panel, make a duplicate of the small fish symbol and name it **second small fish**, and then edit the second small fish symbol by changing the color of each of its fins to dark green (#339966) and the color of its body to light yellow (#FFFF99). Change the color of the yellow bands on the fish body to dark red (#993300). Exit symbol-editing mode.

14. In the fish layer of the Swimming fish scene, drag an instance of the small fish symbol to the pasteboard next to the lower-left corner of the Stage. Insert a keyframe in Frame 40, and then create a classic tween between Frames 1 and 40. At Frame 40, move the small fish instance to the pasteboard next to the lower-right corner of the Stage. The small fish will move across the Stage from left to right.

15. Insert a keyframe at Frame 41 of the fish layer, change the small fish instance so that it faces to the left, and then insert another keyframe at Frame 80. Create a classic tween between Frames 41 and 80 to have the small fish instance move right to left across the Stage.

16. In the Swimming fish scene, insert a new layer above the fish layer and name it **second fish**. In this layer, drag an instance of the second small fish symbol to the pasteboard next to the middle-right side of the Stage. Create two classic tweens for this second fish instance similar to the classic tweens in the fish layer. You want the second small fish instance to start from the pasteboard on the right side of the Stage, swim left across the Stage to the pasteboard, and then turn around and swim back to its starting point.

17. Insert a regular frame at Frame 80 of the background layer to extend it.

18. Test the animation. The fish and sign move across the banner while the text animation plays, and then the small fish swim back and forth across the banner.

19. Submit the finished file to your instructor.

Add motion tweens, a motion preset, and a frame-by-frame animation to a Web site banner.

APPLY

Case Problem 1

Data File needed for this Case Problem: kprBanner.fla

Katie's Pet Resort   Planning is well underway at Katie's Pet Resort for the grand opening celebration. Katie asks John to make the banner for the new Web site more festive by adding animation to it. John started developing the revised banner shown in Figure 3-35 and wants you to add animations for block graphics and balloon graphics. The balloons will float up as the block graphics rotate. You will also add a fly-in animation to the "Grand Opening!" text.

| Figure 3-35 | Animated banner for Katie's Pet Resort |

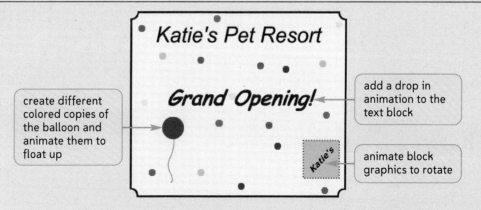

1. Open the **kprBanner.fla** file located in the Flash3\Case1 folder included with your Data Files, and then save the banner as **petBanner.fla** in the same folder.

2. Select the grouped object in the lower-right corner of the Stage with the green square and the word "Katie's." Convert the object to a graphic symbol named **square**. Delete the square instance from the Stage.

3. Convert the balloon into a movie clip symbol named **balloon1**. Be sure to include both the balloon and the string.

4. Create a duplicate of the balloon1 symbol and name it **balloon2**. Edit the balloon2 symbol to change the color of the balloon to red (#FF0000). Create another duplicate of the balloon1 symbol and name it **balloon3**. Edit the balloon3 symbol to change its color to green (#00FF00).

5. Create a motion tween with the balloon1 instance on the Stage. Extend the tween span to Frame 60. At Frame 60, move the balloon1 instance to the pasteboard above the Stage. The balloon1 instance will move from the bottom of the Stage to the pasteboard right above the Stage.

6. Rename the graphics layer to **balloon1**. Insert a new layer above the balloon1 layer and name it **balloon2**. On this layer, select Frame 1, and then drag an instance of the balloon2 symbol to the lower-middle part of the Stage. Create a motion tween so that the balloon moves up to the pasteboard above the Stage. Make sure the tween span extends through Frame 60.

7. Insert a new layer above the balloon2 layer and name it **balloon3**. On this layer, select Frame 1, and then drag an instance of the balloon3 symbol to the lower-right corner of the Stage. Create a motion tween so that the balloon moves up to the pasteboard above the Stage. Make sure the tween span extends through Frame 60.

8. Add a regular frame to Frame 60 of the background layer and to Frame 60 of the title layer.

9. Select Frame 1 of the grand opening layer, convert the "Grand Opening!" text on the Stage to a movie clip symbol named **grand opening**, and then move the instance to the pasteboard above the Stage.

10. From the Motion Presets panel, apply the fly-in-top motion preset found in the Default Presets folder to the grand opening instance so that the "Grand Opening!" text drops in from above the Stage to the center of the Stage. Extend the tween span to Frame 40 of the grand opening layer. At Frame 40, reposition the grand opening instance to the center of the Stage, if necessary. Add a regular frame to Frame 60 of the same layer.

11. Double-click the square symbol in the Library panel to open it in symbol-editing mode. In the square's Timeline, insert a keyframe in Frame 5. Use the Transform tool with the Rotate and Skew modifier to rotate the square and text graphic to the right so that the "Katie's" text is horizontal.

12. Insert a keyframe at Frame 10 and rotate the square and text graphic to the left to its original position. Insert a keyframe at Frame 15 and rotate the square and text graphic to the right so that the text is horizontal. Insert a keyframe at Frame 20 and rotate the square and text graphic to the left to its original position. Insert a regular frame at Frame 25. Return to Scene 1.

13. Insert a new layer above the grand opening layer and name it **squares**. Insert an instance of the square symbol and place it in the lower-left corner of the Stage. Insert another instance of the square symbol and place it in the lower-right corner of the Stage. Have the second instance start its animation in Frame 10 of its Timeline.

14. Test the animation. The "Grand Opening!" text drops in as the balloons float up and out of sight and the squares at the bottom shift back and forth.

15. Submit the finished files to your instructor.

Add animation to a banner.

APPLY

Case Problem 2

Data File needed for this Case Problem: aczBanner.fla

Alamo City Zoo   Janet wants to add animation to the banner that Alex developed promoting the new bear exhibit, as shown in Figure 3-36. You will add two text blocks that will be animated and animate the bear paw graphic.

Figure 3-36   Animated banner for Alamo City Zoo

duplicate paw print and animate duplicates

add a text block here and animate it to increase in size

animate bear to move and fade in

add a text block here and animate it to fade in

1. Open the **aczBanner.fla** file located in the Flash3\Case2 folder included with your Data Files, and then save the banner as **bearBanner.fla** in the same folder. The document contains some of the graphic elements that will be used to create the animated banner.

2. Delete the bear and bear paw instances from the Stage, rename Layer 1 as **background**, and then lock the layer.

3. Create a new movie clip symbol named **bear tracks**. In symbol-editing mode, add a horizontal guide at the center of the Stage that aligns with the 0 mark on the left vertical ruler. Add another horizontal guide approximately 40 pixels above the first guide.

4. Drag an instance of the bear paw symbol from the Library panel to the center of the Stage. If necessary, select the instance and set both the X and Y values in the Position and Size section of the Property inspector to 0 so that the center of the instance is exactly centered on the Stage.

5. Insert a keyframe at Frame 10, and then drag another instance of the bear paw symbol so that its center is on the top guide and approximately 30 pixels to the right of the first instance. Insert a keyframe at Frame 20, and then drag an instance of the bear paw symbol so that its center is on the bottom guide and approximately 30 pixels to the right of the second bear paw instance.

6. Insert a keyframe at Frame 30, and then drag an instance of the bear paw symbol so that its center is on the top guide and approximately 30 pixels to the right of the third instance. Insert a keyframe at Frame 40, and then drag an instance of the bear paw symbol so that its center is on the bottom guide and approximately 30 pixels to the right of the fourth bear paw instance. Insert a keyframe at Frame 50, and then drag an instance of the bear paw symbol so that it is positioned on the top guide approximately 30 pixels from the fifth bear paw.

7. Insert a regular frame at Frame 70 of Layer 1 in the Timeline to extend the end of the animation, and then test the animation. The bear paws should be displayed one at a time.

8. In the main Timeline, insert a new layer and name it **tracks**. Drag an instance of the bear tracks symbol from the Library panel to the Stage. Position the instance so that it is on the left side of the Stage in the bear paw instance's original position.

9. Insert regular frames at Frame 70 of the tracks layer and background layer.

10. Insert a new layer above the tracks layer and name it **bear**. Drag an instance of the bear symbol to the lower-right corner of the Stage. In the Motions Preset panel, select the fly-in-bottom preset from the Default Presets, and then apply the preset to the bear instance. Extend the tween span in the bear layer to Frame 40, and then add a regular frame at Frame 70.

11. Select Frame 40 of the bear layer, and then move the bear instance down so that it aligns with the bear tracks instance at the end of the motion tween.

12. Insert a new layer above the bear layer and name it **title**. In Frame 1 of this layer, create a classic text block with the text **Alamo City Zoo**. Use a fancy font such as Monotype Corsiva and use a point size such as 24. Select maroon (#660000) for the font color and select Align center for the paragraph format. Center the text block on the banner above the bear tracks and bear.

13. Select the text block and convert it to a movie clip symbol named **title text**. Right-click the title text instance and create a motion tween. Select Frame 30 of the title layer, and then select the title text instance on the Stage. In the Position and Size section of the Property inspector, change the width of the instance to 250. Make sure the height value changes proportionally.

14. Insert a new layer and name it **exhibit**. Create a classic text block in Frame 1 of the exhibit layer with the text **Visit the Bear Exhibit!** using the same font family and size as the title text. Use brown (#663300) for the font color. Center the text block below the bear tracks and bear.

15. Select this text block and convert it to a movie clip symbol named **exhibit text**. Right-click the text instance and create a motion tween. Select Frame 1 of the exhibit layer, and then select the exhibit text instance on the Stage. In the Color Effect section of the Property inspector, select the Alpha style and change the alpha amount to 0%.

16. Select Frame 35 of the exhibit layer, and then select the exhibit text instance. In the Color Effect section of the Property inspector, change the alpha amount to 100%.

17. Test the animation. The title text expands, the bear tracks are displayed one after the other, the bear moves and fades in from the bottom of the banner, and the exhibit text fades in.

18. Submit the finished files to your instructor.

Create a logo with shape tweens, motion tweens, and a frame-by-frame animation using a graphic symbol.

Case Problem 3

Data File needed for this Case Problem: wcLogo.fla

Westcreek Nursery   Amanda and Alice agree that the logo for the Westcreek Nursery Web site could be enhanced by adding some animation. Amanda wants you to revise the logo by adding shape tweens to the Westcreek Nursery company name and applying a motion tween to the word "FLOWERS." The banner will look similar to the one shown in Figure 3-37.

Figure 3-37   Animated banner for Westcreek Nursery

1. Open the **wcLogo.fla** file located in the Flash3\Case3 folder included with your Data Files, and then save the file as **nurseryLogo.fla** in the same folder.

2. Rename Layer 1 to **background**, and then insert regular frames so that the layer extends to Frame 60.

3. Insert three layers and name them **westcreek**, **nursery**, and **flowers**, respectively.

4. Select the Westcreek text block. Use the Cut command on the Edit menu to cut the text block. Then, on Frame 1 of the westcreek layer, use the Paste in Place command on the Edit menu to place the text in the same relative position as it was in the background layer.

5. Select the Nursery text block. Use the Cut command to cut the text. Insert a keyframe on Frame 30 of the nursery layer. In this frame, use the Paste in Place command to place the text in the same relative position as it was in the background layer.

6. Select the FLOWERS text block in the center of the Stage. Make sure you don't select any other graphics besides the text. Use the Cut command to cut the text block. Then, on Frame 1 of the flowers layer, use the Paste in Place command to place the text in the same relative position as it was on the background layer.

7. Use the Scene panel to create a duplicate of Scene 1. Rename Scene 1 copy **wheel animation** and rename Scene 1 **flowers animation**.

⊕ **EXPLORE** 8. In the flowers animation scene, select the "Westcreek" text and use the Break Apart command to break the text apart into individual letters. Use the command a second time to break the letters into filled shapes.

⊕ **EXPLORE** 9. Insert a keyframe in Frame 30 of the westcreek layer. In Frame 1, draw a rectangle over the Westcreek text block. Use green (#009900) for the rectangle's fill and do not include a stroke. If necessary, turn off Snap to Objects to make it easier to draw the rectangle. The size of the rectangle should be just slightly larger than the text block itself.

⊕ **EXPLORE** 10. Insert a shape tween between Frames 1 and 30 of the westcreek layer. Test the animation. The rectangle should transform into the text "Westcreek."

11. In Frame 30 of the nursery layer, select the "Nursery" text and apply the Break Apart command twice to break the text into filled shapes. Insert a keyframe in Frame 50 of the nursery layer.

12. In Frame 30 of the nursery layer, draw a rectangle with a green (#009900) fill and no stroke over the Nursery text block. The rectangle should be slightly larger than the text block. Insert a shape tween between Frames 30 and 50. Test the animation. The rectangle should transform into the text "Nursery."

13. In the same scene, select the "FLOWERS" text in Frame 1 of the flowers layer and convert the text block into a movie clip symbol named **flowers text**. Right-click the symbol instance and create a motion tween. Select Frame 1 of the flowers layer, and then, if necessary, select the flowers text instance on the Stage. In the Property inspector, select Alpha for the Style and change the alpha amount to 0%.

14. Select Frame 30 of the flowers layer, and then, if necessary, select the flowers text instance. Change the alpha amount to 100%.

⊕ EXPLORE 15. Select Frame 45 of the flowers layer, and then, if necessary, select the flowers text instance. Press the Left Arrow key four times to move the instance four pixels to the left.

16. Preview the motion tween to see the text block fade in gradually and then move slightly to the left.

17. Switch to the wheel animation scene. Select the left oval representing a wheel below the "FLOWERS" text and convert it to a graphic symbol named **wheel**. Open the wheel symbol in symbol-editing mode.

18. Zoom in on the wheel graphic, and then draw a short horizontal line across the middle of the white area of the wheel graphic to represent a wheel spoke. Use black as the color and 2 for the stroke height. Draw a short vertical line across the middle of the white area of the wheel graphic to represent another wheel spoke.

⊕ EXPLORE 19. Create a frame-by-frame animation to rotate the wheel, as follows: Insert a keyframe in Frame 2. Select the wheel graphic, if necessary, and in the Transform panel enter a value of 30 for the number of degrees to rotate the wheel. (Be sure to press the Enter key to apply the Rotate value.) Insert another keyframe at Frame 3 and enter 30 for the rotate value in the Transform panel to rotate the wheel again. Repeat inserting keyframes and entering 30 for the rotate value in the Transform panel for Frames 4, 5, and 6. Exit symbol-editing mode and return to the wheel animation scene.

20. Delete the original wheel under the "R" of "FLOWERS" on the Stage and add an instance of the wheel graphic symbol in the same position. In the Looping section of the Property inspector, change the First frame of the instance to 3.

21. Switch to the flowers animation scene and replace the two wheel graphics with instances of the wheel symbol. In the Looping section of the Property inspector, set the Looping for each instance to Single Frame and make sure the First frame of each instance is set to 1.

22. Test the animation. Two rectangles transform into the Westcreek Nursery company name, the "FLOWERS" text shifts left, and then the wheels rotate.

23. Submit the finished files to your instructor.

Create tween animations, shape animations, and a frame-by-frame animation.

C R E A T E

Case Problem 4

Data File needed for this Case Problem: msaBanner.fla

Missions Support Association   Brittany and Anissa decide that adding animation to the new banner for the Missions Support Association's Web site will enhance its appearance. Anissa started to develop the banner shown in Figure 3-38, and you will complete it by adding animation using the shapes she created. You will also create an animation of the key phrases "Preserve History", "Volunteer Opportunities", "Special Events", "School Tours", and "Join Now!" on the banner.

Figure 3-38	Animated banner for Missions Support Association

use a preset motion to animate the text in Scene 1 and use a classic tween to animate the text in Scene 2

animate the shapes

Missions Support Association

add a frame-by-frame animation that displays key phrases

1. Open the **msaBanner.fla** file located in the Flash3\Case4 folder included with your Data Files, and then save the file as **missionsBanner.fla** in the same folder. The document contains some of the graphic elements that will be used to create the animated banner.

2. Animate the circle and shapes on the Stage using motion or shape tweens to provide interest. For example, the shapes could move from corner to corner around the banner, or the circle and square could change into triangles. The Timeline should extend to at least 45 frames. (*Hint*: You'll need to create each animation in its own layer.)

3. Use a preset motion to animate the "Missions Support Association" text.

4. Create a duplicate of Scene 1 in which to create animation for the key phrases. Delete the circle and square layers from Scene 2, and then rename both scenes appropriately.

5. In the second scene, remove the motion tween and use a classic tween to animate the Missions Support Association text block to move near the top of the Stage.

6. Insert a new layer in which to create a frame-by-frame animation that changes the text block to a different phrase periodically, and then rename the layer with a descriptive name.

7. In Frame 6, create a text block with the words **Preserve History** on the center of the Stage, using the font family, color, and size of your choice. Convert the text block to a graphic symbol.

8. Edit the graphic symbol to create a frame-by-frame animation that changes the text block to a different phrase periodically between Frames 1 and 45. Use the Info panel to set X and Y coordinates to 0. (For example, in symbol-editing mode, you can insert a keyframe every tenth frame, edit the text block at each keyframe to change the key phrase, and then insert a regular frame at Frame 45 to extend the symbol's timeline.) Exit symbol-editing mode.

9. Test the animation.

10. Submit the finished files to your instructor.

ENDING DATA FILES

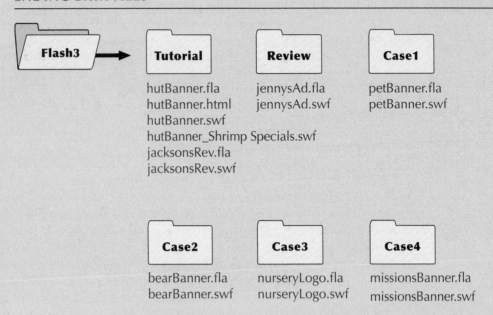

Flash3 → Tutorial

hutBanner.fla
hutBanner.html
hutBanner.swf
hutBanner_Shrimp Specials.swf
jacksonsRev.fla
jacksonsRev.swf

Review

jennysAd.fla
jennysAd.swf

Case1

petBanner.fla
petBanner.swf

Case2

bearBanner.fla
bearBanner.swf

Case3

nurseryLogo.fla
nurseryLogo.swf

Case4

missionsBanner.fla
missionsBanner.swf

Creating Complex Animations

Animating with Masks, Text Blocks, Onion Skinning, 3D Rotations, and Inverse Kinematics

OBJECTIVES

Session 4.1
- Modify an animation's motion path
- Modify motion tweens using the Motion Editor
- Create an animation using a mask layer

Session 4.2
- Animate text blocks
- Animate individual letters within a text block
- Apply 3D rotation effects to movie clips

Session 4.3
- Create nested movie clips
- Test animations using onion skinning
- Create an inverse kinematic animation
- Use the Movie Explorer

Case | *Admiral Web Design*

Aly wants to develop a second banner for the Jenny's Oyster Hut Web site to provide Jenny a choice of banners. The second banner will consist of two scenes. Aly started the first scene, which will have a fish swimming across the banner. You need to make the fish swim along a curved path rather than in a straight line. You will create a second animated fish that exhibits more natural movements of its fins and tail, and you will create an animation showing a spotlight effect on the Jenny's Oyster Hut name. The second scene will include an animation of the company name. In this complex animation, the individual letters of the Jenny's name will rotate in three-dimensional (3D) space one after another on the screen. As each letter rotates, it will increase and decrease in size. The scene will also contain several text blocks promoting the restaurant's anniversary.

In this tutorial, you will create an animation using a mask layer and you will modify motion paths using the Selection tool and the Motion Editor. You will create complex animations using text blocks, individual letters, and nested movie clips. You will apply a 3D animation to text, and you will create an animation using inverse kinematics with the Bone tool. You will also test an animation using onion skinning. Finally, you will use the Movie Explorer to review all of the document's elements.

STARTING DATA FILES

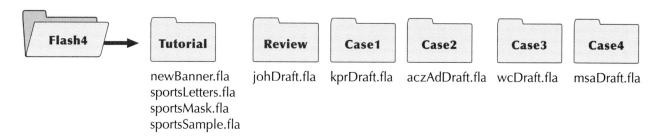

Flash4 → Tutorial

newBanner.fla
sportsLetters.fla
sportsMask.fla
sportsSample.fla

Review

johDraft.fla

Case1

kprDraft.fla

Case2

aczAdDraft.fla

Case3

wcDraft.fla

Case4

msaDraft.fla

SESSION 4.1 VISUAL OVERVIEW

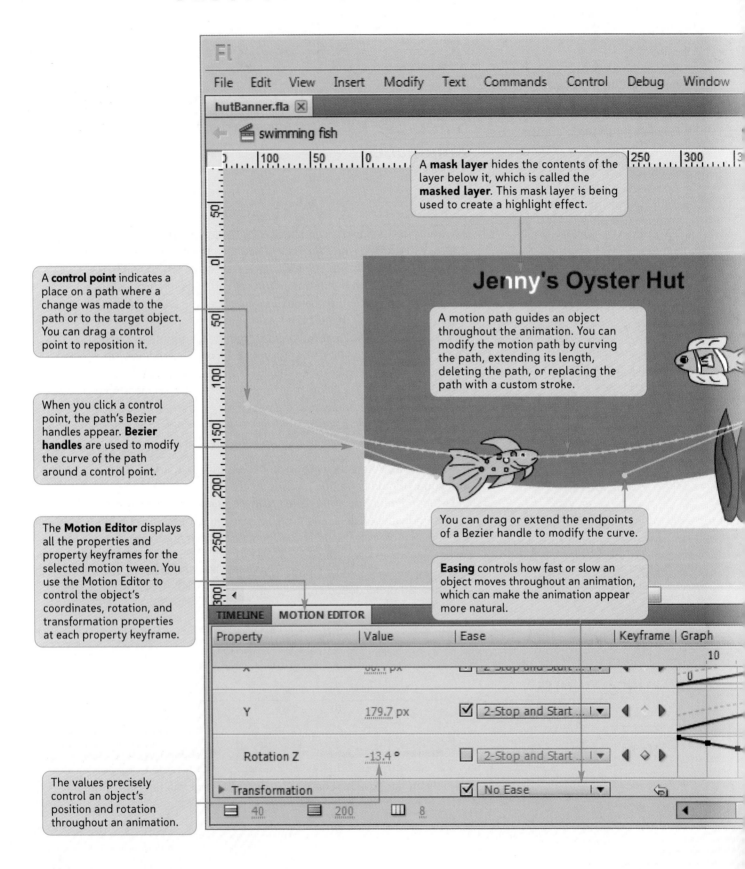

A **control point** indicates a place on a path where a change was made to the path or to the target object. You can drag a control point to reposition it.

When you click a control point, the path's Bezier handles appear. **Bezier handles** are used to modify the curve of the path around a control point.

The **Motion Editor** displays all the properties and property keyframes for the selected motion tween. You use the Motion Editor to control the object's coordinates, rotation, and transformation properties at each property keyframe.

The values precisely control an object's position and rotation throughout an animation.

A **mask layer** hides the contents of the layer below it, which is called the **masked layer**. This mask layer is being used to create a highlight effect.

A motion path guides an object throughout the animation. You can modify the motion path by curving the path, extending its length, deleting the path, or replacing the path with a custom stroke.

You can drag or extend the endpoints of a Bezier handle to modify the curve.

Easing controls how fast or slow an object moves throughout an animation, which can make the animation appear more natural.

MOTION TWEENS AND MASK LAYERS

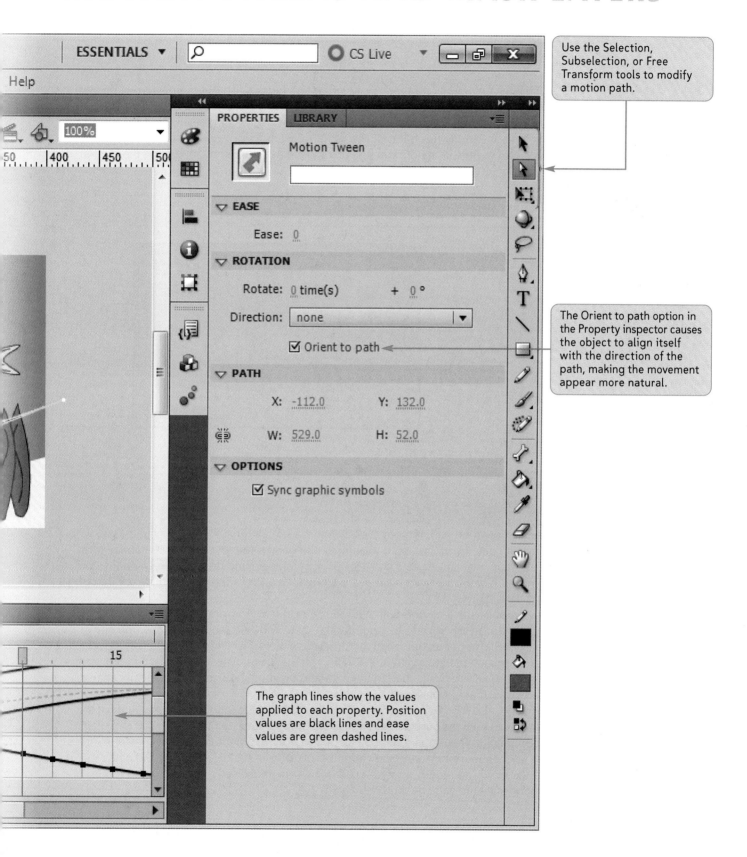

Use the Selection, Subselection, or Free Transform tools to modify a motion path.

The Orient to path option in the Property inspector causes the object to align itself with the direction of the path, making the movement appear more natural.

The graph lines show the values applied to each property. Position values are black lines and ease values are green dashed lines.

Modifying Motion Tweens

A motion tween animates an object to move from one part of the Stage to another, following along a motion path. The default motion path is a straight line, although you can modify the motion path and change the object's orientation to the motion path to create a more natural movement. You can also use the Motion Editor to control an object's position, rotation, and speed throughout the animation.

The alternate banner for Jenny's Oyster Hut includes a fish swimming across the banner in a straight line. Aly's notes, shown in Figure 4-1, indicate that the fish needs to swim along a curved path. You will change the existing motion tweens by modifying the motion paths that the fish follows. The fish also needs to move more slowly during the middle part of the animation. You will change the fish's speed by modifying the motion tween's properties.

Figure 4-1	Animation plan for the alternate banner

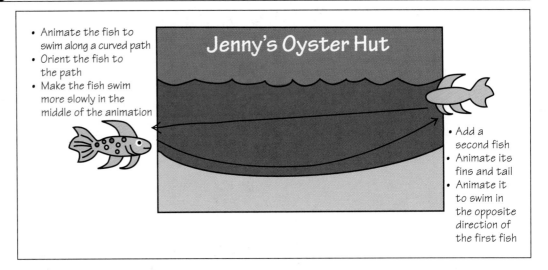

- Animate the fish to swim along a curved path
- Orient the fish to the path
- Make the fish swim more slowly in the middle of the animation

Jenny's Oyster Hut

- Add a second fish
- Animate its fins and tail
- Animate it to swim in the opposite direction of the first fish

Modifying a Motion Path

The default motion path for a motion tween is a straight line. For many objects, you will want to modify the motion path to animate the objects to move in a more natural way. For example, you can make a ball appear to bounce up and down while gradually coming to a stop, you can make a car move along a curved road, or you can make a bird fly in a circular pattern.

You can modify a motion path with the Selection tool by dragging any segment of the path using the Selection tool pointer the same way you modify a stroke. You can also extend a motion path's length by dragging either of its endpoints. You can move a selected motion path to a different location on the Stage. As you adjust the motion path, the target object stays attached to the path and the motion tween automatically changes based on your adjustments.

You can also modify the motion path with the Subselection tool. When you click the motion path with the Subselection tool pointer, its control points appear. You can drag a control point to reposition it or you can click a control point to display its Bezier handles. You can then move or extend the endpoints of a Bezier handle to modify the path's curve.

Another way to modify a motion path is by using the Free Transform tool to rotate, skew, or scale the path, as shown in Figure 4-2.

Figure 4-2   Motion path modified with the Free Transform tool

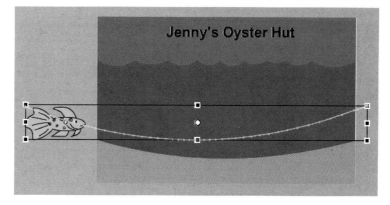

Finally, you can modify a motion path by selecting it and then making changes to its properties in the Property inspector or in the Transform panel.

REFERENCE

Modifying a Tween's Motion Path

- In the Tools panel, click the Selection tool, and then drag a segment of the motion path to curve it or drag one of its endpoints to extend the path.
- In the Tools panel, click the Subselection tool, click the motion path to select it, and then drag one of its control points to reposition it or click a control point and then drag a Bezier handle to adjust the path's curve around the control point.
- In the Tools panel, click the Free Transform tool, click the motion path to select it, click the Rotate and Skew modifier or the Scale modifier, and then drag the handles on the path to adjust it.
- Select the motion path on the Stage, and then, in the Property inspector, change its X and Y coordinates or its width and height values.
- Select the motion path on the Stage, and then, in the Transform panel, change the path's dimensions, rotate properties, or skew properties.
- Select the motion path on the Stage, and then, in the Motion Editor, change the path's dimensions, rotate properties, or skew properties.

You will modify the motion paths of the fish in the banner so that the fish will swim along a curved path. Each motion path guides the fish across the Stage.

To modify fish's motion paths:

1. Open the **newBanner.fla** file located in the Flash4\Tutorial folder included with your Data Files, save the file as **hutBanner.fla** in the same folder, and then reset the workspace to the Essentials layout.

2. In the Timeline, hide the ocean layer, and then select the **fish1** layer. The motion path followed by the fish is displayed on the Stage.

3. In the Tools panel, make sure the **Selection** tool is selected, and then, on the Stage, drag the center of the motion path downward to curve it. See Figure 4-3.

Figure 4-3	Motion path being curved

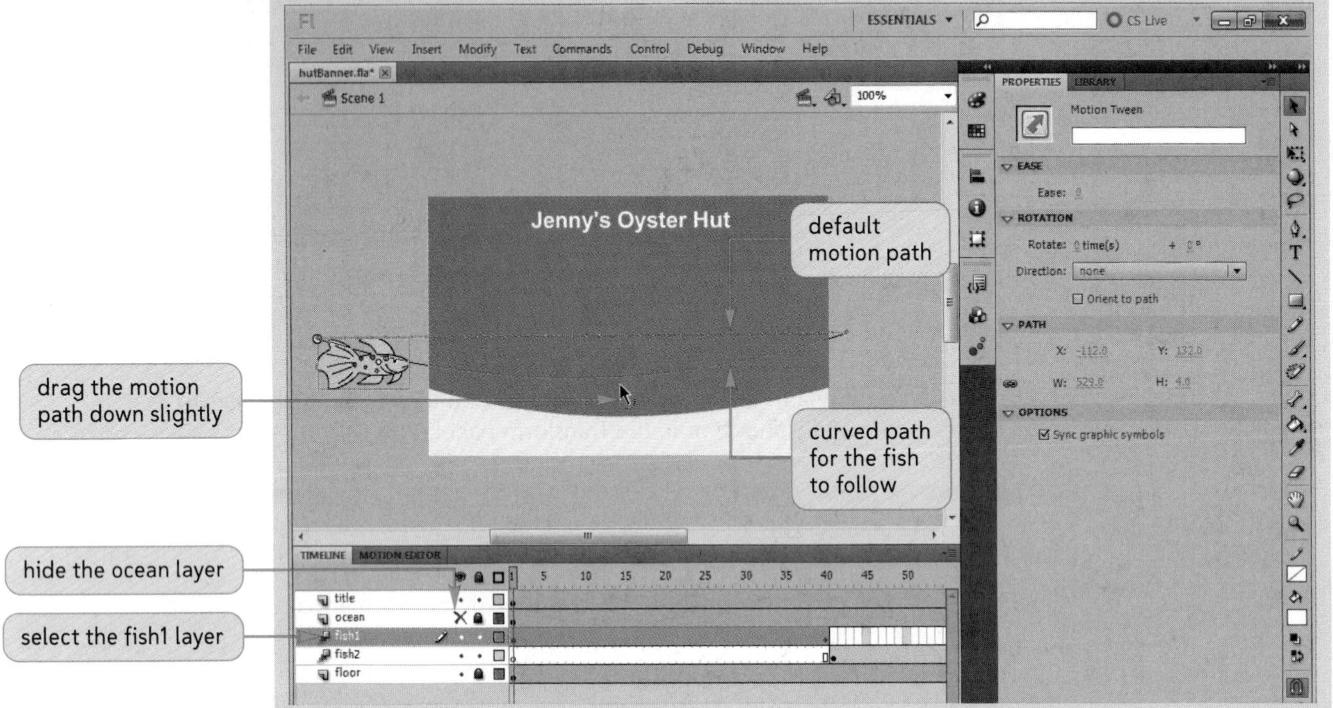

4. Release the mouse button. The motion path is curved.

5. In the Timeline, select the **fish2** layer, and then drag the playhead to **Frame 41**. The motion path for the tween is displayed on the Stage.

6. On the Stage, drag the center of the tween span's motion path downward to curve it similarly to the first tween span's motion path.

7. In the Timeline, drag the playhead to **Frame 1**, and then press the **Enter** key to play the animation. The fish follows the curved motion paths.

When you animate an object to follow a curved path, the object stays in a horizontal position as it moves along the path. You'll usually want the object to move in a more natural way, which you can do by selecting the Orient to path option in the Property inspector. The Orient to path option works best with curves that have gentle slopes. You'll orient the fish to follow the slope of the path.

To orient the fish to the curved paths:

1. In the Timeline, click **Frame 1** of the fish1 layer.

2. In the Property inspector, in the Rotation section, click the **Orient to path** check box to check it. Property keyframes are added in Frames 2 through 40, representing how the fish is slightly rotated in each frame of the tween span. The fish will have a more natural movement during the animation. See Figure 4-4.

Figure 4-4 **Orient to path applied to motion tween**

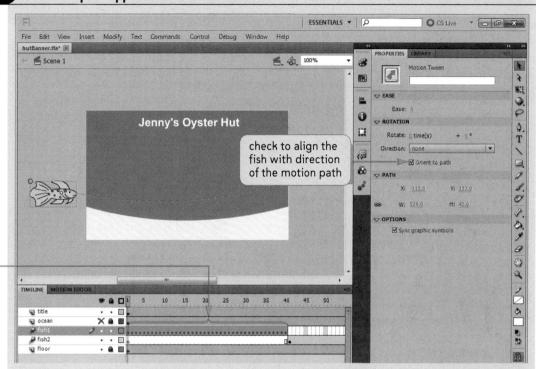

property keyframes added to Frames 2 through 40

check to align the fish with direction of the motion path

3. In the Timeline, click **Frame 41** of the fish2 layer, and then, in the Property inspector, click the **Orient to path** check box to check it. Property keyframes are added to the tween span.

4. In the Timeline, move the playhead to **Frame 1**, and then press the **Enter** key to play the animation again. The fish orients itself to the slope of the motion paths.

5. Save the banner.

Changing Tween Properties in the Motion Editor

The Motion Editor is based on a feature of Adobe After Effects program, an industry-standard tool used to create motion graphics and visual effects for video. Using the Motion Editor in Flash, you can control individual tween properties within their own Timeline and modify a motion tween more precisely by setting the values of individual property keyframes, adding or removing property keyframes, and adding or removing filters or color effects. The Motion Editor displays the values of a motion tween's properties both numerically and graphically to make it simpler to change the properties and create complex animations. In addition to controlling an object's position and rotation throughout a motion tween, you can use the Motion Editor to change the object's ease value, which makes the object move faster or slower throughout the animation. You can also add preset eases to a motion tween to modify its properties.

PROSKILLS

Decision Making: Deciding When to Use the Motion Editor

Decision making is the process of choosing between alternative courses of action. When creating a tween, you need to decide the best way create and modify the animation. This requires determining the level of complexity you want to use for the animation, and then determining the best method for creating it. For most standard or simple tweens such as animating a fish to move across the Stage, you can create and modify the animation using the Timeline and tools from the Tools panel. For more complex animations in which you modify various properties of the animated object at different points in the tween span, consider using the Motion Editor.

With the Motion Editor, you can change the position, scale, color, or ease attributes of the animated object at multiple frames within the tween span. For example, you should use the Motion Editor if you need to animate a fish to increase in size throughout part of the tween span as its transparency changes, and exhibit a filter effect during certain frames. You can also use the Motion Editor to precisely control how an animated object starts and stops by selecting a preset ease and then modifying the ease effect before you apply it to the tweened object. After you test the animation, you can make additional adjustments to the ease effect in the Motion Editor to obtain the desired animation effect. As you modify a tweened object's properties in the Motion Editor, you can test the effect of the changes by playing the animation in both Timeline and the Motion Editor.

Careful review of end results you want to achieve with an animation will help you decide on the best way to accomplish those goals.

You'll use the Motion Editor to explore and modify a sample animation that Aly created for another client, Jackson's Sports.

To view a motion tween's properties using the Motion Editor:

1. Open the **sportsSample.fla** file located in the Flash4\Tutorial folder included with your Data Files, and then save it as **sportsModified.fla** in the same folder.

2. Press the **Enter** key to play the animation. The Jackson's text block moves into the Stage and the Annual Sale text fades in.

3. In the Timeline, move the playhead to **Frame 1**, and then select the **jacksons** layer.

4. Click the **MOTION EDITOR** tab to open the panel. You want to resize the Motion Editor to see more of the panel.

5. Point to the top edge of the Timeline and Motion Editor panel group until the pointer changes to ↕, and then drag up to increase the size of the panel group, as shown in Figure 4-5.

| Figure 4-5 | Timeline and Motion Editor panel group being resized |

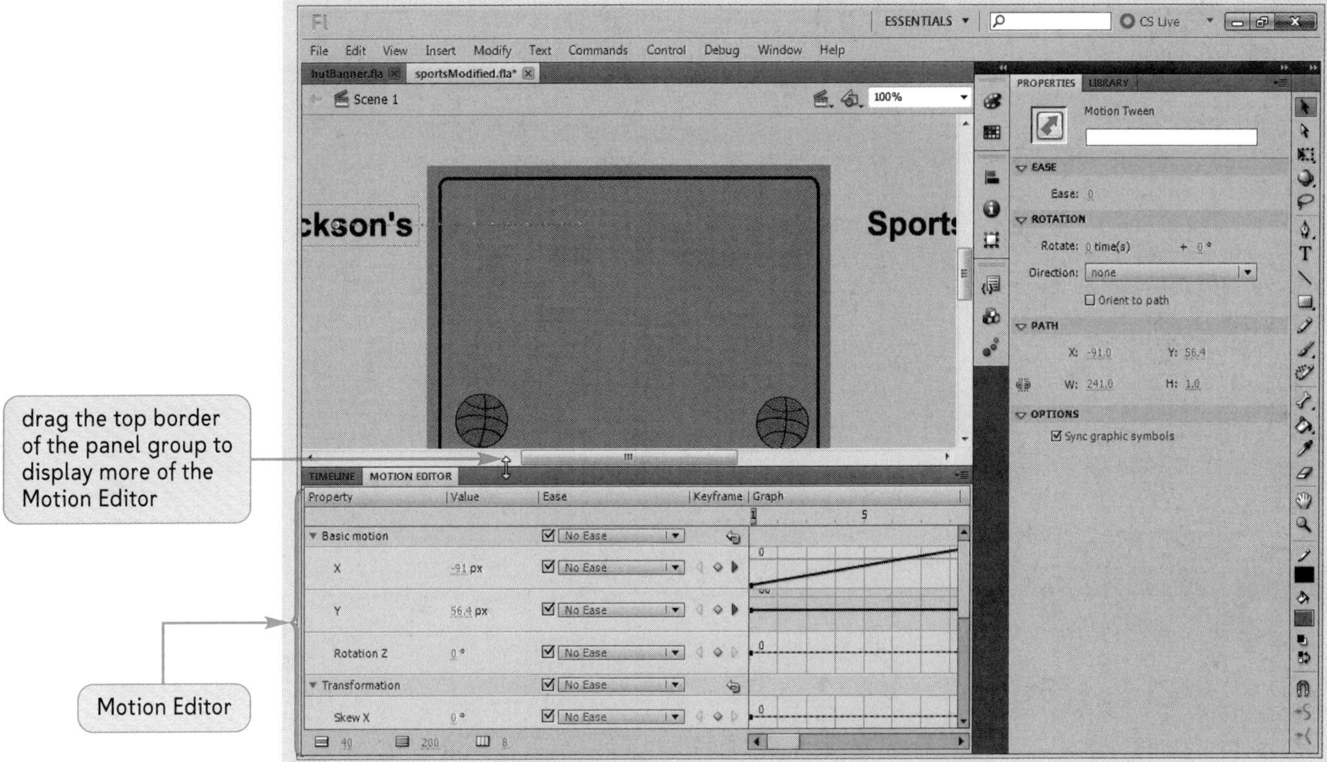

drag the top border of the panel group to display more of the Motion Editor

Motion Editor

6. In the Motion Editor, scroll up to the Basic motion category, if necessary, and then in the Property column, click the expand arrow ▶ next to the Basic motion category to expand the category, if necessary. The Motion Editor displays the X, Y, and Rotation Z properties for the motion tween, along with their associated values in the Value column. At Frame 1, the X property value is –91 px, which places the Jackson's text block to the left of the Stage.

7. In the Motion Editor, move the playhead to **Frame 15**. The Jackson's text block moves to the center of the Stage, and the X property value in the Motion Editor changes to 150 px. See Figure 4-6.

| Figure 4-6 | X property value in the Motion Editor |

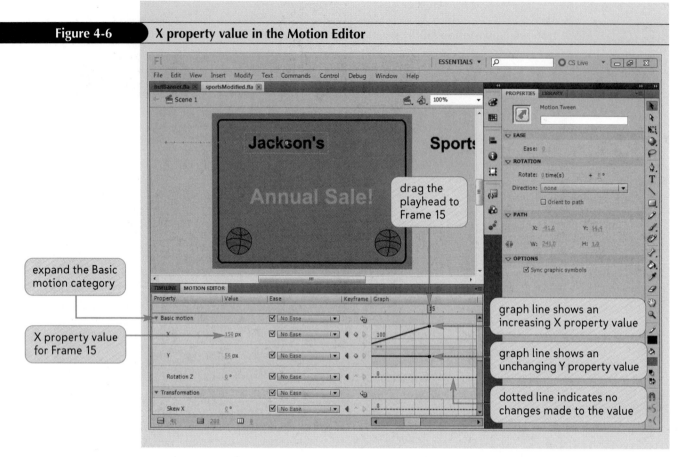

expand the Basic motion category

X property value for Frame 15

drag the playhead to Frame 15

graph line shows an increasing X property value

graph line shows an unchanging Y property value

dotted line indicates no changes made to the value

As you can see in Figure 4-6, in the Graph column of the Motion Editor, the X property curve is a straight line with an upward slope because the X property value increases from –91 pixels in Frame 1 to 150 pixels in Frame 15. The Y property curve is a flat line because the text block doesn't change vertical position. The Rotation Z property contains a dashed line because no changes have been made to the rotation value.

You'll create a new motion tween and modify it using the Motion Editor.

To create and modify a motion tween:

1. On the Stage, right-click the **Sports** text block, and then click **Create Motion Tween** on the context menu. The Graph column of the Motion Editor displays dashed lines because no motion paths have been created yet.

2. Make sure the playhead is on **Frame 15**, and then, in the Graph column, scroll to the left to center Frame 15.

3. In the Motion Editor, in the Keyframe column of the X property, click the **Add or Remove keyframe** icon ◇ to add a property keyframe. Flat lines appear in the Graph column for the X and Y property curves. See Figure 4-7.

TIP

You can change the Expanded Graph Size value at the bottom of the Motion Editor to increase or decrease the size of the Graph column.

Figure 4-7   Property curves added in the Graph column

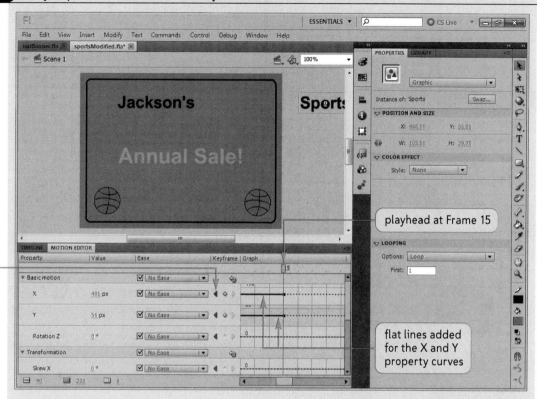

click to add a property keyframe at the current frame

playhead at Frame 15

flat lines added for the X and Y property curves

4. In the Value column, drag the X position value to the left to change the value to **285**. A downward slope is added to the property curve in the Graph column, reflecting the new X property value. The Sports text block moves to the center of the Stage.

   Trouble? If you reach the left side of the screen before reaching 285, release the mouse button, and then repeat Step 3 to continue to reduce the X position value.

5. Move the playhead to **Frame 1**, and then press the **Enter** key to play the animation. The Sports text block moves from the right of the Stage as the Jackson's text block moves in from the left of the Stage.

6. Save and close the sportsModified.fla file.

   Next, you will use the Motion Editor to modify the motion tweens for the fish in the banner for Jenny's Oyster Hut. Based on Aly's notes, you need to add easing to the motion tweens to make the fish slow down in the middle of the animation. You'll add a preset ease to the motion tweens for both fish instances.

To add an easing effect to a motion tween:

1. In the hutBanner.fla document, click the **TIMELINE** tab to display the Timeline, and then click **Frame 1** of the fish1 layer to select its motion tween.

2. Click the **MOTION EDITOR** tab to display the Motion Editor, and then scroll down as needed to view the Eases category.

3. In the Eases category, click the **Add Color, Filter or Ease** button 🔄, and then click **Stop and Start (Slow)** in the pop-up menu The preset ease is available and can be added to the motion tween.

4. In the Motion Editor, scroll down to see the preset ease property, value and graph displayed in the Eases category. See Figure 4-8.

| Figure 4-8 | Stop and Start (Slow) ease available in the Eases category |

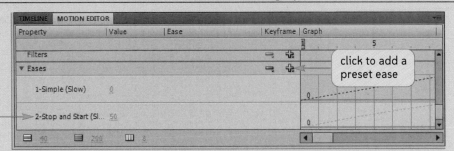

add this preset ease to the motion tween

5. In the Motion Editor, scroll up, if necessary, to the Basic motion category.

6. In the Basic motion category, click the **Selected Ease** button, and then click **2-Stop and Start (Slow)** to add the preset ease to the motion tween's X and Y properties. The ease appears as a green dashed curve next to the X and Y property curves in the Graph column. See Figure 4-9.

| Figure 4-9 | Ease curves in the Graph column |

click to add a preset ease to the motion tween's X and Y properties

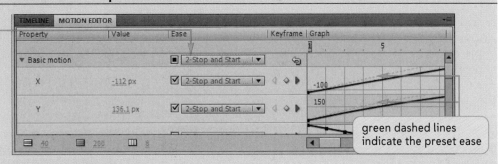

green dashed lines indicate the preset ease

7. Click the **TIMELINE** tab to display the Timeline, and then click **Frame 41** of the fish2 layer to select its motion tween.

8. Click the **MOTION EDITOR** tab to display the Motion Editor, and then scroll down to view the Eases category.

9. In the Eases category, click the **Add Color, Filter or Ease** button 🔄, and then click **Stop and Start (Slow)**. The preset ease is now available.

10. In the Motion Editor, scroll up to view the Basic motion category.

11. In the Basic motion category, click the **Selected Ease** button, and then click **2-Stop and Start (Slow)** to add the ease preset to the motion tween's X and Y properties. The Stop and Start (Slow) ease has been added to both motion tweens.

12. Click the **TIMELINE** tab to display the Timeline, move the playhead to **Frame 1**, and then press the **Enter** key to play the animation. The fish swims across the Stage as before, but now it slows down in the middle of the motion tweens.

13. Save the banner.

Using a Mask Layer in an Animation

You can create animations that incorporate a mask layer to create special effects. A mask layer can also be used with motion tweens and frame-by-frame animations. For example, you can create an animation in a mask layer to show different areas of a masked layer throughout the animation.

Creating an Animated Picture Masked with Text

You can create an interesting effect with mask layers by using text for the mask object and having another object such as a picture show through the text. With this technique, the text acts like a window for the content behind it. For example, if you animate a picture on the masked layer, as the picture moves, only the parts of the picture that are behind the text will be visible.

To create an animation using a mask layer, you create the object to be masked on one layer and add a new layer above it that will contain the mask. When you change the top layer to a mask layer, the bottom layer becomes the masked layer. The masked layer is indented below the mask layer in the Timeline.

The object on the mask layer can be a filled shape, such as an oval or a rectangle. It can also be text or an instance of a symbol. The fill of the shape on the mask layer will reveal the content in the underlying masked layer. This shape determines what part of the masked layer's content is visible. The color of the shape is irrelevant because its color is not displayed. You can animate either the object on the mask layer or the object on the masked layer. For example, you can animate an oval shape on the mask layer so that it moves over some stationary text on the masked layer. This technique creates a spotlight effect, as shown in Figure 4-10.

Figure 4-10 **Masked layer example**

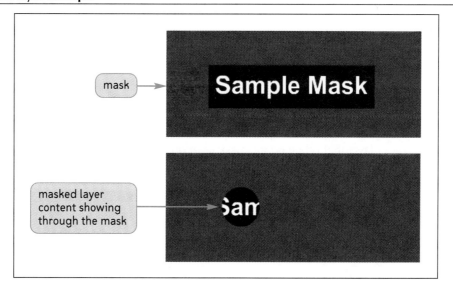

If you animate the object on the masked layer while the object on the mask layer remains stationary, you can create a different type of effect. For example, you can create a scrolling text effect by drawing a rectangle on the mask layer and then animating a block of text on the masked layer. As the text block moves across the mask, only the portion of the text behind the rectangle is visible, as shown in Figure 4-11.

Figure 4-11   **Masked layer with scrolling text effect**

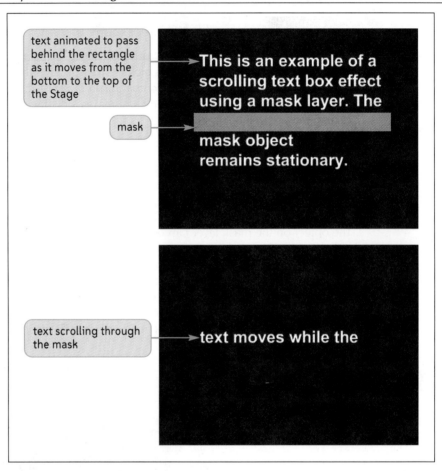

When you first create a mask layer, Flash locks both the mask and the masked layers. These layers must be locked to preview the effects of the mask on the Stage. When the layers are locked, the mask layer object is not visible, and only the content in the masked layer that is behind the mask layer object becomes visible. You need to unlock the layers to work with the objects on both layers, and then lock the layers again to test the animation.

REFERENCE

Creating a Mask Layer Animation

- Select the layer whose content will be masked.
- In the Timeline, click the New Layer button.
- Add content to the new layer that will be used as the mask.
- Right-click the new layer's name, and then click Mask.
- Unlock the layers and create an animation in either the mask layer or the masked layer.
- Lock the layers, and then test the animation.

You'll explore a mask layer animation Aly created for Jackson's Sports.

To explore the mask layer animation in the Jackson's Sports banner:

▶ 1. Open the **sportsMask.fla** file located in the Flash4\Tutorial folder included with your Data Files, and then reset the workspace to the Essentials layout. The sports-Mask.fla document opens, but the mask layer content is not visible because the layer is locked.

▶ 2. In the Timeline, unlock the mask layer. The layer is unlocked, and you can see the contents of the mask layer.

▶ 3. In the Timeline, hide the light text layer. The content of the mask layer is just a motion tween animation of a circle shape. As the circle moves across the Stage, different parts of the underlying white Annual Sale text become visible. See Figure 4-12.

Figure 4-12	Mask layer animation

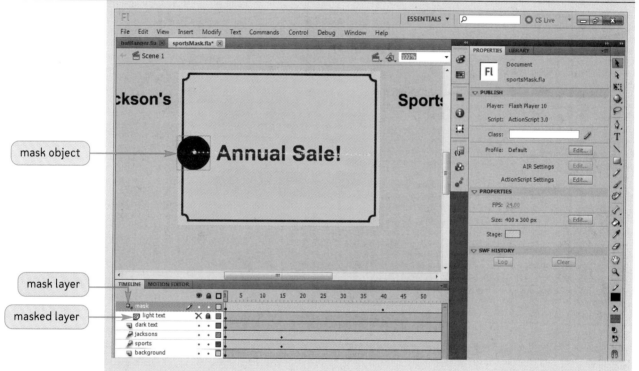

▶ 4. In the Timeline, show the light text layer.

▶ 5. In the Timeline, lock the mask layer. When a mask layer is locked, the masking effect is visible on the Stage.

▶ 6. Press the **Enter** key to play the animation. The part of the light text layer under the circle becomes visible as the circle moves across the Stage.

▶ 7. Close the sportsMask.fla document without saving any changes.

Creating an Animation Using a Mask Layer

Aly's notes for the Jenny's Oyster Hut banner indicate that the Jenny's Oyster Hut text block should have a spotlight effect, as shown in Figure 4-13. You will create a spotlight effect where the spotlight moves across the Jenny's Oyster Hut text block.

Figure 4-13	Animation plan for the spotlight effect

add a spotlight effect so that the spotlight moves back and forth across the title text

You need to create the mask layer animation. You will start by creating a duplicate of the title text block.

To add layers for the mask animation:

1. On the Stage, click the **Jenny's Oyster Hut** text block to select it. You will create a duplicate of this text block.

2. On the Application bar, click **Edit**, and then click **Copy**. The text is copied to the Clipboard.

3. In the Timeline, insert a new layer above the ocean layer, and then rename the new layer **gray text**.

4. On the Application bar, click **Edit**, and then click **Paste in Place** to paste the text block in the new gray text layer in the same relative position as it is in the title layer.

5. In the Timeline, hide the title layer. The layer's content is no longer visible.

6. On the Stage, make sure the text block is selected, and then, in the Property inspector, change its text (fill) color to **dark gray** (#333333).

7. In the Timeline, lock the gray text layer, and then show the title layer. The text in the title layer will provide the white text in the spotlight effect.

8. In the Timeline, insert a new layer above the title layer, and then rename the new layer **title mask**. The title mask layer will be the mask layer and will contain a motion tween of a circle.

9. In the Timeline, right-click the **title mask** layer name, and then click **Mask** on the context menu. The layer changes to a mask layer and the title layer changes to a masked layer indented below the title mask layer. Both layers are locked. See Figure 4-14.

Figure 4-14   Locked mask and masked layers

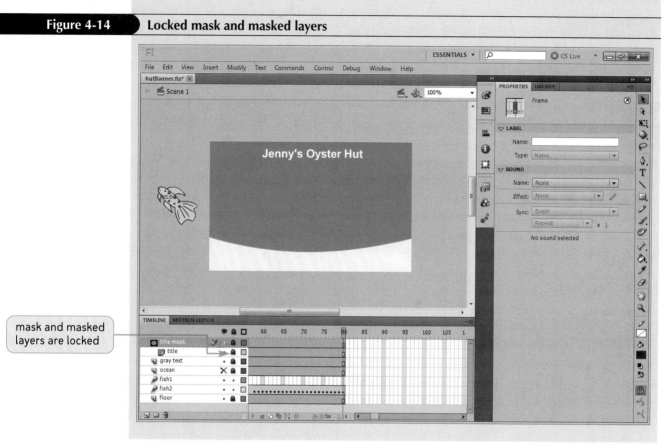

mask and masked layers are locked

Now you need to create a motion tween of a circle and have it move across the text. You will draw the circle shape, convert it to a symbol, and then create a motion tween.

To create the mask layer animation:

1. In the Timeline, unlock the title mask layer, and then click **Frame 1** of the title mask layer. You will draw a circle on the title mask layer to represent the spotlight.

2. In the Tools panel, select the **Oval** tool, and then set the fill color to **white** (#FFFFFF) and the stroke color to **no color**.

3. On the Stage, draw a small circle to the left of the letter J in the Jenny's Oyster Hut text block. See Figure 4-15.

Figure 4-15   **Circle drawn in the title mask layer**

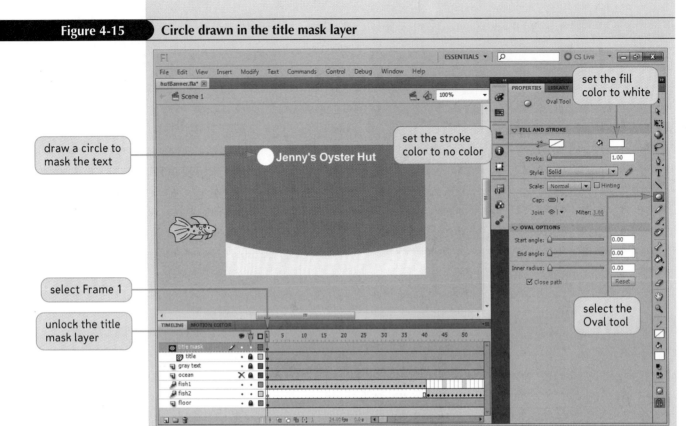

- draw a circle to mask the text
- set the stroke color to no color
- set the fill color to white
- select Frame 1
- unlock the title mask layer
- select the Oval tool

Jenny's Oyster Hut

4. In the Tools panel, click the **Selection** tool, and then, on the Stage, select the circle.

5. Convert the circle to a movie clip symbol named **circle**. You'll create a motion tween for the circle instance.

6. On the Stage, right-click the **circle** instance, and then click **Create Motion Tween** on the context menu. A motion tween is created in the title mask layer.

   You'll create a highlight effect by moving the circle to the right of the title text block and then back to its starting point.

7. Click **Frame 40** of the title mask layer, and then drag the **circle** instance to the right of the last letter of the text block.

8. Select **Frame 80** of the title mask layer, and then drag the **circle** instance back to the left of the first letter in the text block. Frame 80 represents the end of the motion tween where the circle moves back to its starting point.

9. In the Timeline, lock the title mask layer so that you can play the animation.

10. Move the playhead to **Frame 1**, and then press the **Enter** key to play the animation. The circle creates a spotlight effect as it moves across and back over the title text.

11. Save the document.

TIP

You can move the play-head forward or back one frame at a time by pressing the period or comma key, respectively.

In this session, you modified a motion path to make the fish instance swim along a curved path and then changed the tween's properties in the Motion Editor. You also created a mask layer animation to create a spotlight effect. In the next session, you will create text animations on the Jenny's Oyster Hut banner.

REVIEW

Session 4.1 Quick Check

1. List three ways you can modify a motion path.
2. What are Bezier handles, and how can you use them to modify a motion path?
3. What is the purpose of the Orient to path option in the Property inspector?
4. Name three motion tween properties you can modify in the Motion Editor.
5. How can you see the effect that a mask layer has on a masked layer when testing an animation within the Flash workspace?
6. True or False. Text can be used as a mask in a mask layer.
7. True or False. In a mask layer animation, the contents of the mask layer are revealed when the object in the masked layer moves over it.

SESSION 4.2 VISUAL OVERVIEW

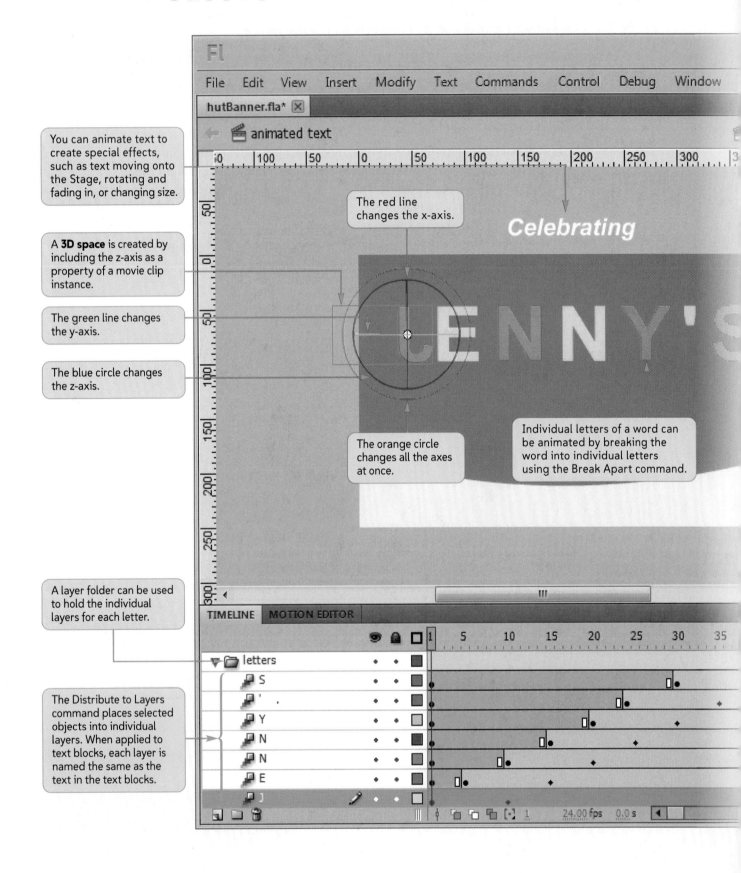

You can animate text to create special effects, such as text moving onto the Stage, rotating and fading in, or changing size.

A **3D space** is created by including the z-axis as a property of a movie clip instance.

The green line changes the y-axis.

The blue circle changes the z-axis.

A layer folder can be used to hold the individual layers for each letter.

The Distribute to Layers command places selected objects into individual layers. When applied to text blocks, each layer is named the same as the text in the text blocks.

The red line changes the x-axis.

The orange circle changes all the axes at once.

Individual letters of a word can be animated by breaking the word into individual letters using the Break Apart command.

File Edit View Insert Modify Text Commands Control Debug Window

hutBanner.fla*

animated text

Celebrating

LENNY'S

TIMELINE   MOTION EDITOR

letters

S
' .
Y
N
N
E
J

TEXT ANIMATIONS AND 3D EFFECTS

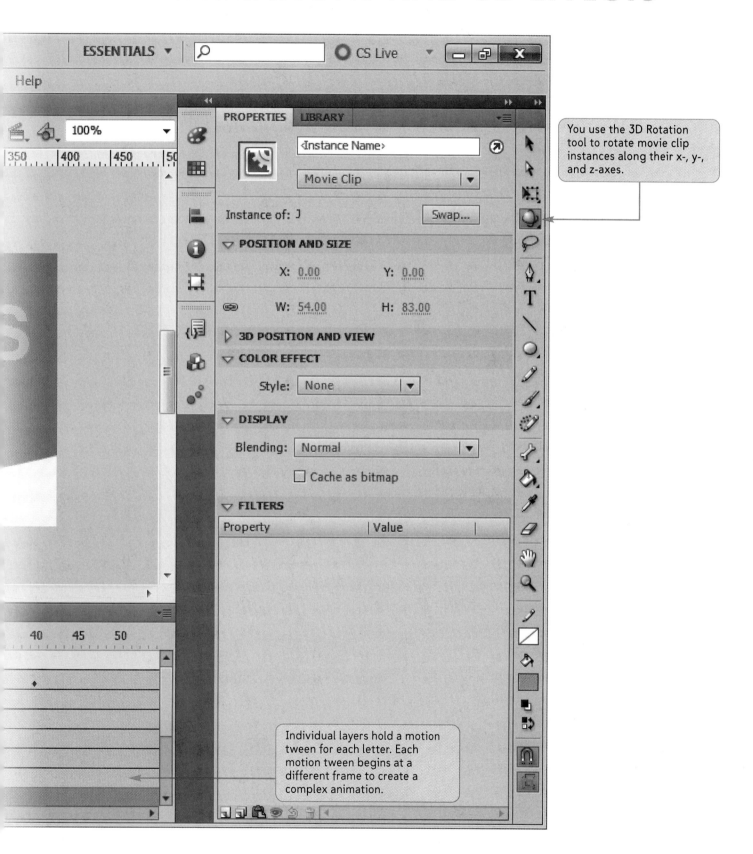

You use the 3D Rotation tool to rotate movie clip instances along their x-, y-, and z-axes.

Individual layers hold a motion tween for each letter. Each motion tween begins at a different frame to create a complex animation.

Animating Text Blocks

You can animate text to create special effects. For example, you can have text move onto the Stage in a fly-in effect. Or, in a more complex animation, you can make the individual letters of a text block rotate and fade in as they appear one at a time to form a word or phrase on the Stage. You can also animate text so that it increases and decreases in size to create a pulsating effect.

You can animate text blocks using motion tweens or frame-by-frame animations. For example, you can have a text block move from one side of the Stage to the other using a frame-by-frame animation by changing the location of the text in each keyframe. Using a motion tween, you can animate a text block so that it rotates or changes in size as the animation is played. If you convert the text block to a symbol and then apply a motion tween, you can have the text block exhibit other changes throughout an animation such as fading in or changing color.

You can also apply a shape tween to text. However, you must first convert the text to fills by using the Break Apart command. When you apply the Break Apart command to a text block, each character in the text block becomes an individual text block. You can apply the command again to the individual letters to convert them to fills. After the text blocks are converted to fills, you can apply a shape tween to them. For example, you can make the letters change into a rectangle shape, as shown in Figure 4-16. Be aware that after you convert the text to fills, you can no longer edit the fills as text.

Figure 4-16   **Sample shape tween**

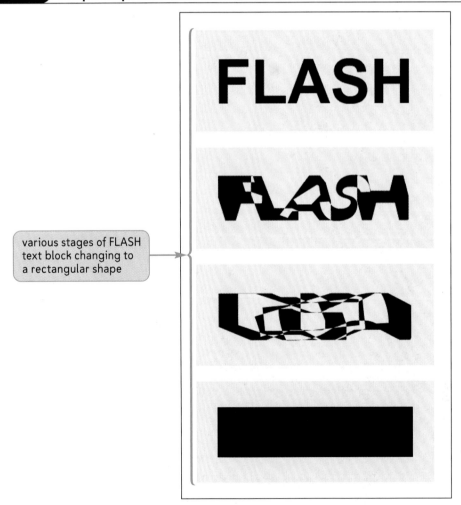

various stages of FLASH text block changing to a rectangular shape

REFERENCE

Creating Text Animations

- For a shape tween, select the text block in the first frame of the animation.
- On the Application bar, click Modify, and then click Break Apart to break the text into individual letters.
- On the Application bar, click Modify, and then click Break Apart a second time to convert the text to fills.
- Create a keyframe in the last frame of the animation and change the shape of the text fills or create a new shape.
- Right-click between the first and last keyframe, and then click Create Shape Tween on the context menu.

or

- For a motion tween, select the text block in the first frame of the animation, and then, optionally, convert the text block into a symbol.
- Right-click the text block, and then click Create Motion Tween on the context menu.
- On the last frame of the animation, change the text block's position, size, or orientation or change the symbol instance's tint or transparency.

Adding Animated Text

Based on Aly's notes for completing the banner, shown in Figure 4-17, you need to add three text blocks to the banner for the second scene. The Celebrating text block will drop down along a curved path from the pasteboard above the Stage to the center of the Stage. The our text block will appear below the Celebrating text block and rotate once. The 10th Anniversary! text block will fade in after the first two text blocks and will increase in size. Each text block will be on its own layer so you can animate it individually.

| Figure 4-17 | Animation plan for text blocks |

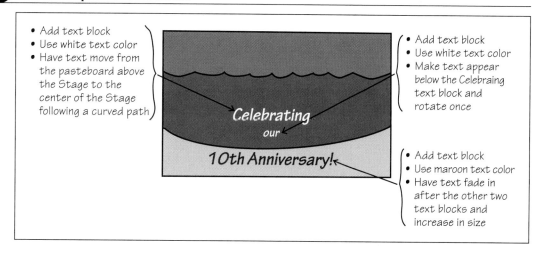

You will start by adding a new scene named "animated text" that will contain the text animations. In this scene you will add three new layers, one for each text block.

To add a new scene and the layers for the text animations:

▶ 1. If you took a break after the previous session, make sure the hutBanner.fla file is open and the workspace is reset to the Essentials layout.

▶ 2. Open the **Scene** panel.

TIP

You can press the Shift+F2 keys to open and close the Scene panel.

▶ 3. In the Scene panel, click the **Duplicate Scene** button ⬚. A copy of Scene 1 is added to the document. You'll rename both scenes.

▶ 4. In the Scene panel, double-click **Scene 1**, type **swimming fish**, and then press the **Enter** key to rename the scene.

▶ 5. In the Scene panel, double-click **Scene 1 copy**, type **animated text**, and then press the **Enter** key to rename the scene. The animated text scene is the current scene.

▶ 6. Close the **Scene** panel. The current scene is animated text.

▶ 7. In the Timeline, select the **fish1** layer, and then click the **Delete** button ⬚. The fish1 layer is deleted.

▶ 8. Delete the **fish2**, **title mask**, **title**, and **gray text** layers. The unneeded layers in the animated text scene are deleted.

▶ 9. In the Timeline, select the **ocean** layer of the animated text scene, if necessary, and then insert three new layers and rename them **celebrating text**, **our text**, and **anniversary text**. The new layers appear above the ocean layer. See Figure 4-18.

Figure 4-18   **New layers added to the Timeline**

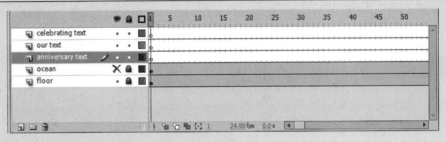

Next, you will add a new text block with the word "Celebrating." Then, you will animate the text block so that it moves from the top of the Stage to the center of the Stage and follow a curved path throughout the animation.

To create the Celebrating text block:

▶ 1. If necessary, display the rulers, and then drag a horizontal guide to approximately **170 pixels** from the top of the Stage and drag a vertical guide to approximately **200 pixels** from the left of the Stage. The guides will help you align the text.

▶ 2. In the Tools panel, click the **Text** tool ⟨T⟩, and then, in the Property inspector, select the **Classic Text** text engine, set the font family to **Arial**, set the font style to **Bold Italic**, set the point size to **22**, set the text fill color to **white** (#FFFFFF), set the font rendering method to **Anti-alias for animation**, and set the paragraph format to **Align center**. You will use these text properties for the text block you will create in Frame 1 of the celebrating text layer.

3. In the Timeline, click **Frame 1** of the celebrating text layer, and then, on the Stage, click the intersection of the two guides to create a text block and type **Celebrating**. The formatted text is entered in the text block.

4. In the Tools panel, click the **Selection** tool ▶, and then reposition the text block on the horizontal guide, if necessary. This is the final position for the text block. See Figure 4-19.

Figure 4-19   **Ending position for the Celebrating text block**

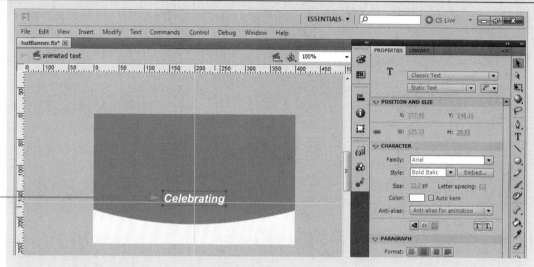

center the text block on the Stage

You'll create a motion tween next from Frame 1 through Frame 24 so that the text moves in from the top of the Stage following a curved path to its current position. First, you'll insert a keyframe at Frame 25 so that the text block is in the current position after the motion tween.

To animate the Celebrating text block:

1. In the Timeline, click **Frame 25** of the celebrating text layer, and then insert a keyframe. This indicates the final frame of the motion tween.

2. In the Timeline, click **Frame 1** of the celebrating text layer, and then, on the Stage, right-click the **Celebrating** text block and click **Create Motion Tween** on the context menu. A tween span is created from Frame 1 through Frame 24.

3. On the Stage, drag the **Celebrating** text block to the pasteboard above the Stage, keeping the text aligned with the vertical guide. This is the text block's starting position. See Figure 4-20.

Figure 4-20   **Starting position for the Celebrating text block**

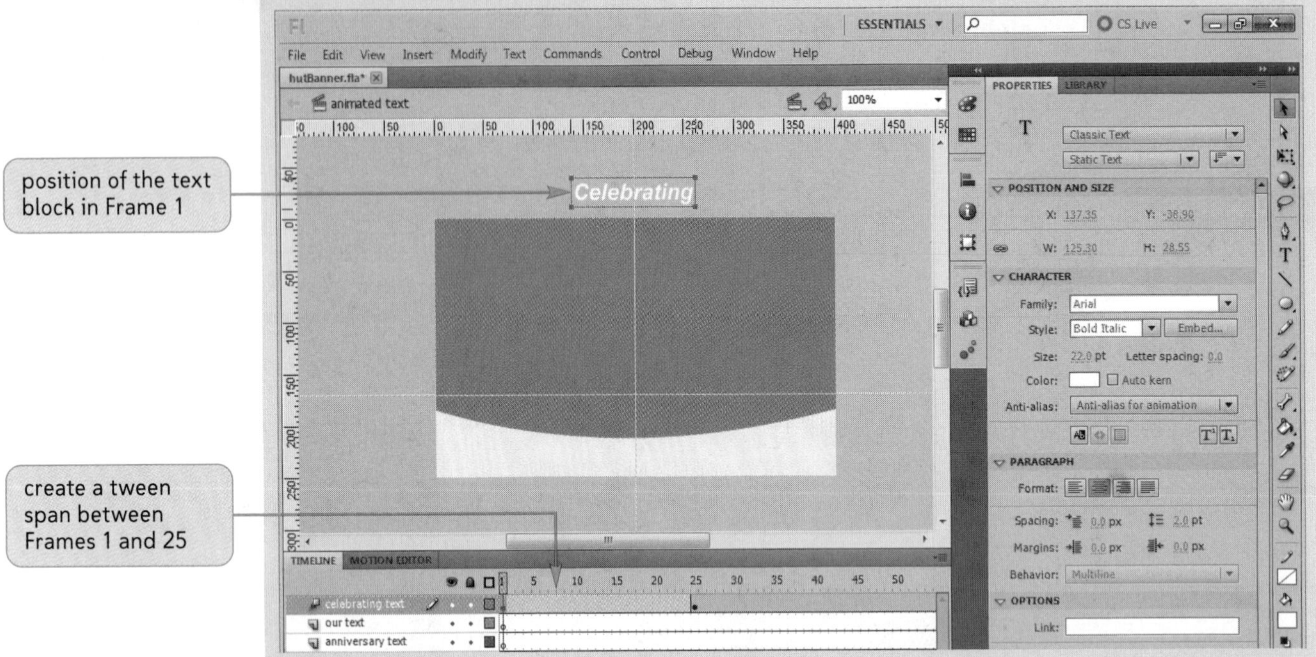

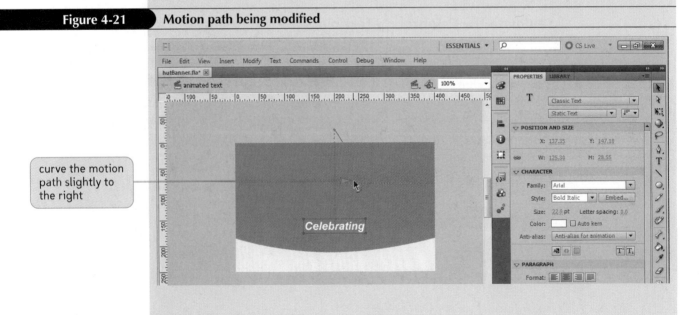

position of the text block in Frame 1

create a tween span between Frames 1 and 25

4. In the Timeline, select **Frame 24** of the celebrating text layer, and then move the text block back to the center of the Stage in its original position. This is the text block's position at the end of the motion tween.

5. On the Application bar, click **View**, point to **Guides**, and then click **Show Guides**. The guides are hidden, making it easier to view and modify the motion path.

6. On the Stage, use the Selection pointer ↖ to curve the motion path to the right, as shown in Figure 4-21.

Figure 4-21   **Motion path being modified**

curve the motion path slightly to the right

7. Scrub the playhead from Frame 1 through Frame 24. The text block moves from the top of the Stage to the center of the Stage, following a curved path. The motion tween for the Celebrating text block is complete.

8. On the Application bar, click **View**, point to **Guides**, and then click **Show Guides**. The guides are displayed.

The text block for the our text layer will not display from Frame 1 through Frame 29, but instead will only appear starting with Frame 30. At Frame 30, a motion tween will make the text rotate once in place, and then, starting at Frame 40, the text block will be stationary through Frame 80.

To add the our text block:

1. In the Timeline, click **Frame 30** of the our text layer, and then insert a keyframe. The our text block will appear in Frame 30.

2. In the Tools panel, click the **Text** tool ⊤, and then, in the Property inspector, change the point size to **18**. The other properties of the our text block are the same as the Celebrating text block.

3. On the Stage, create a text block on the vertical guide below the Celebrating text block, and then type **our**. The formatted text is entered in the text block.

4. In the Tools panel, click the **Selection** tool ▶, and then drag the text block so that it is centered on the Stage, as shown in Figure 4-22.

| Figure 4-22 | The our text block centered on the Stage |

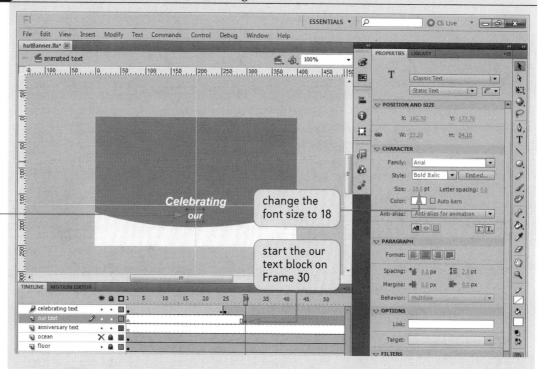

center the text block below the Celebrating text block

change the font size to 18

start the our text block on Frame 30

5. In the Timeline, click **Frame 40** of the our text layer, and then insert a keyframe. This frame represents the initial frame after the motion tween.

6. In the Timeline, click **Frame 30** of the our text layer, and then, on the Stage, right-click the **our** text block and click **Create Motion Tween** on the context menu. A tween span is created from Frame 30 through Frame 39.

7. In the Timeline, click **Frame 30** of the our text layer, and then in the Rotation section of the Property inspector, set the rotate value to **1** and make sure the rotation direction is set to **CW** (clockwise). See Figure 4-23.

Figure 4-23 **Rotation value set for the our text block**

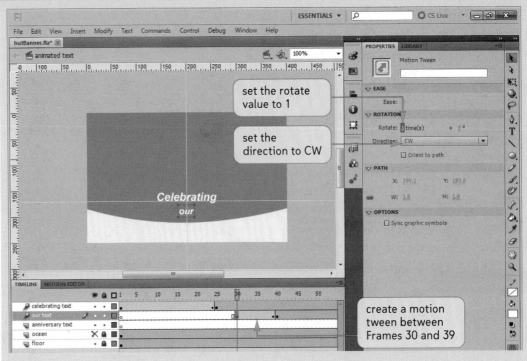

The 10th Anniversary! text block will be animated with a motion tween. Although the text block will not move, it will change in size and fade in throughout the animation. Recall that to change a text block's transparency or color, it must first be converted to a symbol. To create the fade-in effect, you need to convert the 10th Anniversary! text block to a movie clip symbol. The text block will not be visible until Frame 30, at which point the motion tween will start.

To create and animate the 10th Anniversary! text block:

1. In the Timeline, click **Frame 30** of the anniversary text layer, and then insert a keyframe. The motion tween for the 10th Anniversary! text will begin at Frame 30.

2. In the Tools panel, click the **Text** tool T, and then, in the Property inspector, change the point size to **12** and change the font color to **maroon** (#660000).

3. On the Stage, click the vertical guide below the our text block, and then type **10th Anniversary!**. The formatted text is entered in the text block.

4. In the Tools panel, click the **Selection** tool, and then, on the Stage, drag the **10th Anniversary!** text block so that it is centered about 230 pixels from the top of the Stage. See Figure 4-24.

Figure 4-24   The 10th Anniversary! text centered on the Stage

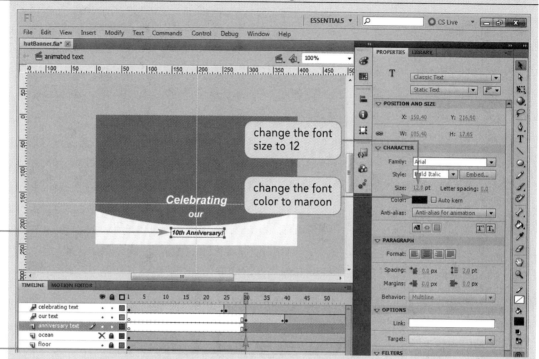

center the text block 230 pixels from the top of the Stage

change the font size to 12

change the font color to maroon

start the text block on Frame 30

5. Convert the text block to a movie clip symbol named **anniversary text**.

6. On the Stage, right-click the **anniversary text** instance, and then click **Create Motion Tween** on the context menu. A tween span is added between Frame 30 and Frame 80.

7. In the Timeline, click **Frame 45** of the anniversary text layer. The text block will fade in and reach its maximum size at this frame.

8. On the docked panel group, click the **Transform** button to open the Transform panel.

TIP

You can also press the Ctrl+T keys to open and close the Transform panel.

9. In the Transform panel, click the **Constrain** button, if necessary, to change it to.

10. In the Transform panel, click the **Scale Width** value, type **230** in the Scale Width box, and then press the **Enter** key. The size of the text in the 10th Anniversary! text block increases. See Figure 4-25.

Figure 4-25   **Size of the 10th Anniversary! text scaled**

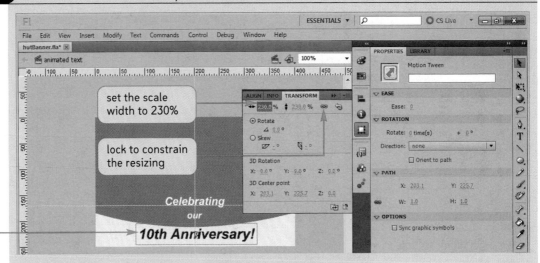

> **11.** Scrub the playhead between Frame 30 and Frame 45 to see the text block increase in size throughout the motion tween animation.

Aly's notes indicate that in addition to increasing in size, the 10th Anniversary! text block should fade in throughout the animation. You will change the alpha amount of the text block at the beginning and end of the motion tween to create the fade-in effect.

To apply a fade-in effect to the 10th Anniversary! text block:

> **1.** In the Timeline, click **Frame 30** of the anniversary text layer.

> **2.** On the Stage, select the **10th Anniversary!** text block.

> **3.** In the Color Effect section of the Property inspector, click the **Color styles** button, and then click **Alpha**. The Alpha amount slider and box appear.

> **4.** Drag the **Alpha** slider to the left to set the alpha amount to **0**. The text block becomes transparent.

> **5.** In the Timeline, click **Frame 45** of the anniversary text layer, and then, on the Stage, select the **10th Anniversary!** text block, indicated by the blue outline.

> **6.** In the Property inspector, drag the **Alpha** slider to the right to set the alpha amount to **100**. The text block becomes opaque at Frame 45.

> **7.** Scrub the playhead between Frame 30 and Frame 45 to see the 10th Anniversary! text block increase in size and fade in throughout the animation.

> **8.** In the Timeline, drag the playhead to **Frame 1**, and then press the **Enter** key to play the animation. The Celebrating text block moves in from the top of the Stage to the middle of the Stage, the our text block appears and rotates once, and then the 10th Anniversary! text block fades in below the our text block and increases in size.

> **9.** On the Application bar, click **View**, point to **Guides**, and then click **Clear Guides**. The guides are cleared.

Animating Individual Letters

You can animate individual letters in a word or phrase to create interesting text effects. For example, you can animate the letters of a word to fall into place on the Stage one at a time. Or you can have a word explode with the individual letters flying off the Stage in different directions. Another example is to have the individual letters of a word increase and decrease in size to create a pulsating effect. To create most of these text effects, you first need to break a word into its individual letters and then animate each letter separately. The simplest way to animate each letter is to create motion tweens. This means that each letter must reside on its own layer.

INSIGHT

Creating Symbols when Animating Text Blocks

When animating text blocks, it's a good idea to create a symbol for each text block even though converting text to symbols is not required in certain types of animations. Converting text blocks to symbols enables you to use the text block instances more than once in a document without increasing the file size. You can also add color or transparency changes as part of an existing animation without having to create new duplicate text blocks. And, with text blocks as symbols, advanced users of Flash can manipulate the text block instances through programming code to create more complex animations.

Aly has been working on a banner for Jackson's Sports that includes individual letter text animation. In this banner, each letter has the same motion tween applied to it to create a pulsating effect. The text blocks in this animation did not have to be converted to symbols because the motion tweens only include changes to the text blocks' dimensions.

To explore the Jackson's Sports banner with individual letters text effect:

▶ 1. Open the **sportsLetters.fla** file located in the Flash4\Tutorial folder included with your Data Files.

▶ 2. Press the **Enter** key to play the animation. Each letter increases and decreases in size one after the other. Notice that each letter resides on its own layer.

▶ 3. In the Timeline, click **Frame 1** of the J layer, and then look at the size of the letter J on the Stage.

▶ 4. In the Timeline, click **Frame 5** of the J layer, and then look at how the letter J increases in size on the Stage. The property keyframe in this frame represents the change in the text block's dimensions.

▶ 5. In the Timeline, click **Frame 10** of the J layer, and then look at the letters J and A on the Stage. In this frame, the letter J returns to its original size. At the same time, the next letter, A, increases in size. A property keyframe in this frame represents the change in dimensions for the J text block. See Figure 4-26.

Figure 4-26   **Sample letters animation**

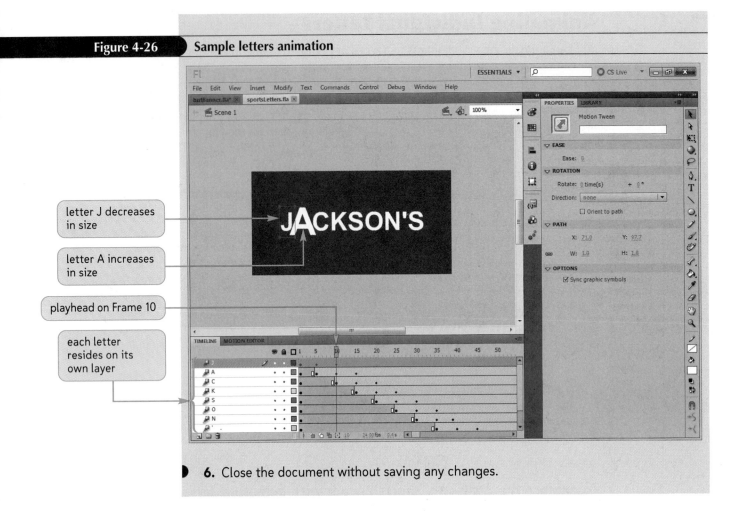

letter J decreases in size

letter A increases in size

playhead on Frame 10

each letter resides on its own layer

6. Close the document without saving any changes.

Creating a Complex Text Animation

The next animation you will create for the Jenny's Oyster Hut banner consists of individual letters rotating one after the other, as described in Aly's notes shown in Figure 4-27. Each letter will rotate around an imaginary axis in three-dimensional space. Three-dimensional graphics are discussed later in this session. Each letter will also increase and decrease in size as it rotates. This effect involves animating the individual letters of the word in a similar way to the animated text in the banner Aly created for Jackson's Sports.

Figure 4-27   Animation plan for the title text

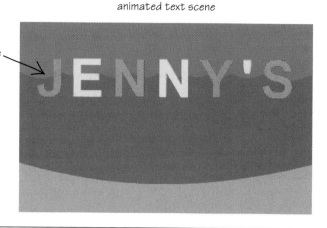

- Use alternating colors of orange and yellow
- Make the individual letters rotate one after another into place to form the word JENNY'S
- Make each letter increase and decrease in size as it rotates

animated text scene

To create the animations for the individual letters, you will first create the Jenny's text block, convert each letter in that text block into its own individual text block, and then distribute these individual letter text blocks onto their own layers.

REFERENCE

Animating Individual Letters

- On the Stage, select the text block containing the letters to be animated.
- On the Application bar, click Modify, and then click Break Apart.
- On the Application bar, click Modify, point to Timeline, and then click Distribute to Layers.
- Delete the original layer, which is now empty.
- If necessary, convert each letter that will be animated to a symbol with an appropriate name.
- Create a motion tween for each letter.

Before animating the letters, you will change the colors of the letters in the JENNY'S text block to alternate between yellow and orange to enhance the special effect. You will initially create the Jenny's text block in a new layer folder. Then, when you distribute the letters to individual layers, all of the new layers will be inside the folder. This new animation will reside in the animated text scene, which will play after the swimming fish scene in the document. You'll create a new layer folder for the new text block.

To create the JENNY'S text block in the animated text scene:

1. In the Timeline, click **Frame 1** of the celebrating text layer, insert a new layer, and then rename the new layer as **title**. The title layer is created above the celebrating text layer.

2. In the Timeline, click the **New Folder** button to create a new layer folder, and then rename the new layer folder as **letters**. The letters layer folder is created above the title layer.

3. In the Timeline, drag the **title** layer into the letters folder, and then click **Frame 1** of the title layer.

4. In the Tools panel, click the **Text** tool T , and then, in the Property inspector, set the font family to **Arial**, set the font style to **Bold**, set the point size to **70**, set the letter spacing to **10**, set the text fill color to **yellow** (#FFFF00), set the font rendering method to **Anti-alias for animation**, and set the paragraph format to **Align center**.

5. On the Stage, create a text block, and then type **JENNY'S**.

6. In the Tools panel, click the **Selection** tool ▲ , and then, on the Stage, drag the **JENNY'S** text block to center it about 100 pixels from the top of the Stage. See Figure 4-28.

Figure 4-28 | **JENNY'S text block**

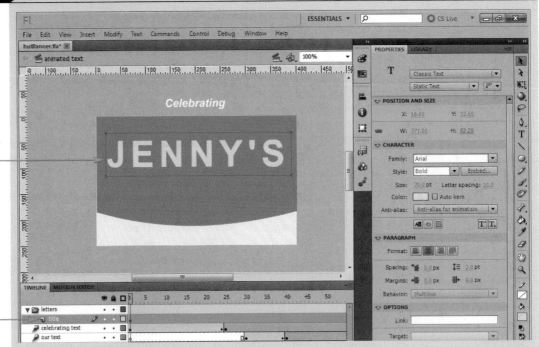

text block centered 100 pixels from the top of the Stage

title layer in the letters folder

7. On the Stage, double-click the **JENNY'S** text block, click and drag in the text block to select the letter **J**, and then change the letter's text fill color to **light orange** (#FF9900).

8. Repeat Step 7 to change the color of the first letter **N**, the letter **Y**, and the letter **S** to the same light orange color. The letters in the word JENNY'S alternate between light orange and yellow.

9. In the Tools panel, click the **Selection** tool ▲ . The JENNY'S text block remains selected.

Distributing Objects to Individual Layers

Animating a word's individual letters as in the Jackson's Sports banner requires each letter to be placed on its own layer. A quick way to place each letter into its own layer is to use the Distribute to Layers command. This command takes a group of selected objects and places each individual object onto its own layer. Each new layer is named based on its content. For example, if the objects distributed are text blocks, the names of the new layers are the same as the text in the text blocks. If the objects are symbols, the names of the new layers are the same as the names of the symbols. Other layers are named "Layer" followed by a number. This helps you to identify to which layers the selected objects have been distributed. The layer that originally contained the grouped objects will be empty after you apply the Distribute to Layers command and can be deleted. Before you apply the Distribute to Layers command, be sure to select all of the objects you want distributed.

PROSKILLS

Written Communication: Organizing Distributed Layers in a Layer Folder

File organization is critical to keeping track of and working effectively with the documents you create. The same is true for layer organization within a Flash document. As a Flash document becomes more intricate and includes complex animations, the number of layers and objects expands and can quickly become unmanageable. To help keep layers organized and logical, use layer folders to combine layers into logical groups. Although you can create layer folders at any time and move existing layers into them, it can be easier to create the layer folder first. A clear naming convention makes it simpler and faster to locate layers and objects.

For example, when you animate individual letters in a text block, each letter needs to be in a separate layer. Before distributing a group of objects to layers, you can create a new layer folder and move the layer containing the objects into the layer folder. After the objects are distributed to layers, all of the new layers will reside within the layer folder. You can then collapse the layer folder to hide the individual layers when you aren't working with them. This makes it easier to work with the document's Timeline and other layers in the document.

A well planned organization and clear, descriptive naming convention makes it easier to work with a Flash document. It also ensures that someone else can quickly determine how you structured the objects and layers in the document if you need to collaborate on an animation.

To convert the JENNY'S text block into individual letters so they can be distributed to individual layers, you need to break the text block into separate text blocks, one for each letter, using the Break Apart command. When you apply the Distribute to Layers command to the selected text blocks, each letter is placed on its own layer. You then can create the necessary motion tween animations for each of the letters.

You will start by separating the letters into individual text blocks and distributing the text blocks into individual layers.

To create the individual letters from the word JENNY'S:

1. On the Application bar, click **Modify**, and then click **Break Apart**. Each letter is placed in its own text block, and all the text blocks are selected. See Figure 4-29.

Figure 4-29   **Individual letter text blocks**

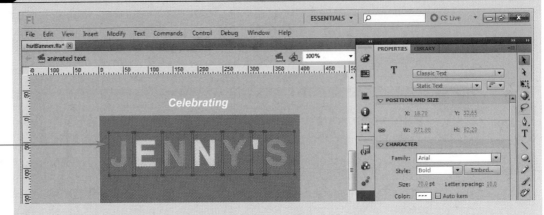

each letter in the title layer is a text block

2. With all of the letters still selected, on the Application bar, click **Modify**, point to **Timeline**, and then click **Distribute to Layers**. Each letter is placed on its own layer that is named with the letter it contains. The title layer is empty and is no longer needed.

3. In the Timeline, delete the **title** layer. The empty title layer is deleted from the Timeline.

Now that the letters in the JENNY'S text have been split into individual text blocks and on separate layers, you can animate each letter to create the animation. You will convert each letter into a movie clip symbol and then create a motion tween for each letter instance. The motion tween for letter J, the first letter, will start in Frame 1. The other motion tweens will start every fifth frame.

To convert each letter to a symbol and create motion tweens:

1. On the Stage, select the letter **J**, and then convert the letter to a movie clip symbol named **J**. The symbol is added to the document's library.

2. Repeat Step 1 for each of the remaining letters, naming each symbol for the letter it represents, using **N1** as the symbol name for the first letter N, **N2** as the symbol name for the second letter N, and **Apostrophe** as the symbol name for the apostrophe. All the letters are converted to symbols.

3. In the Timeline, insert a keyframe at **Frame 5** of the E layer. The animation for the letter E will start in the fifth frame of the layer. You didn't insert a keyframe for the letter J because it will start in the first frame of the layer.

4. Repeat Step 3 to insert a keyframe in the first layer N at **Frame 10**, in the second layer N at **Frame 15**, in layer Y at **Frame 20**, in layer ' (apostrophe) at **Frame 25**, and in layer S at **Frame 30**. See Figure 4-30. The order of your layers may be different.

Figure 4-30 | **Keyframes inserted in each layer**

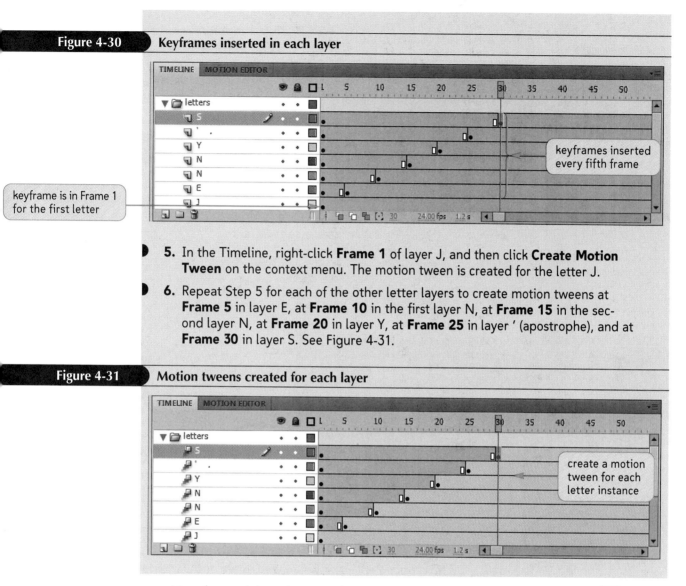

keyframes inserted every fifth frame

keyframe is in Frame 1 for the first letter

5. In the Timeline, right-click **Frame 1** of layer J, and then click **Create Motion Tween** on the context menu. The motion tween is created for the letter J.

6. Repeat Step 5 for each of the other letter layers to create motion tweens at **Frame 5** in layer E, at **Frame 10** in the first layer N, at **Frame 15** in the second layer N, at **Frame 20** in layer Y, at **Frame 25** in layer ' (apostrophe), and at **Frame 30** in layer S. See Figure 4-31.

Figure 4-31 | **Motion tweens created for each layer**

create a motion tween for each letter instance

Now that each layer has a motion tween, you need to change the properties of each instance at the starting frame for its tween span.

Creating 3D Graphic Effects

Every object in Flash has x and y properties, which represent the object's horizontal and vertical coordinates relative to the Stage. By adding a third property, the z property, you can create an illusion of depth, where an object appears to be closer or farther away than other objects. You can also manipulate an object in three dimensions along its x-, y-, or z-axis. To create this illusion in Flash, you create three-dimensional (3D) effects by moving and rotating movie clips in 3D space. You can only apply 3D properties to movie clip instances. These instances can be moved along their z-axis using the 3D Translation tool or rotated along their x- or y-axis with the 3D Rotation tool.

You will use the 3D Rotation tool to rotate each letter along its y-axis.

To rotate each letter instance in 3D space:

1. In the Timeline, click **Frame 1** of the J layer.

2. In the Tools panel, click the **3D Rotation** tool 🔵 to select it. The J instance is overlaid with 3D axes. You change the 3D properties of an instance by dragging one of its axes.

3. On the Stage, drag the green line on the right of the J movie clip instance to its left to rotate the letter so that it faces to its left. The J movie clip instance rotates along its y-axis in 3D space. See Figure 4-32.

Figure 4-32 | **J instance being rotated**

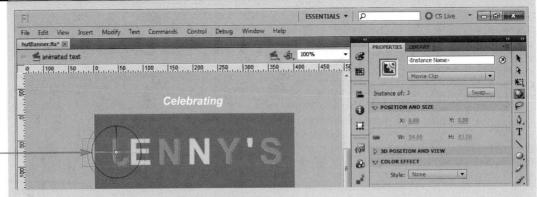

drag the green line left to rotate the letter along its y-axis

4. In the Timeline, click **Frame 10** of the J layer.

5. On the Stage, drag the green line on the left of the J movie clip instance to its right to rotate the letter so that it faces to its right. The J instance rotates back to its original orientation in Frame 10.

6. Scrub the playhead from Frames 1 through 10 to see the 3D rotation effect on the letter J. Because the letter instance was rotated with the 3D Rotation tool, Flash converts the movie clip into a 3D movie clip.

7. Repeat Steps 3 from 6 for each letter instance to rotate each letter left in the starting keyframe of its tween span and rotate the letter back to its original orientation 10 frames later. Make sure you select the starting frame for each letter and that you select only one letter at a time.

8. Drag the playhead to **Frame 1**, and then press the **Enter** key to play the animation. Each letter in JENNY'S rotates in 3D space one after the other. See Figure 4-33.

TIP

To prevent selecting more than one letter at one time, lock layers you aren't working with and then unlock the layers as needed to modify them.

Figure 4-33 **Completed JENNY'S text animation**

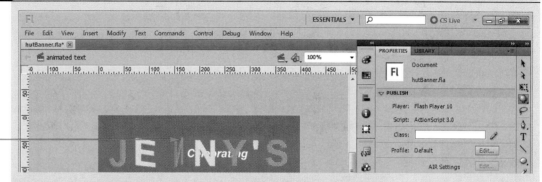

letters rotating in 3D space one after the other

9. Save the document.

In this session, you animated text blocks in the second scene of the banner. You also created an animation of the individual letters of the Jenny's name and applied a 3D rotation effect to each letter. In the next session, you will complete the banner by adding a complex animation to the first scene.

Session 4.2 Quick Check

REVIEW

1. List two examples of how text can be animated.
2. To apply a shape tween to a text block, what must you do first to the text?
3. If you apply the Distribute to Layers command to a group of selected text blocks, how will the new layers be named in the Timeline?
4. Why must each letter to be animated be on its own layer?
5. Why is it a good idea to place all of the individual letter layers in a layer folder?
6. True or False. A layer whose contents are distributed to separate layers with the Distribute to Layers command retains a copy of its original contents.
7. True or False. A 3D space is created by including the z-axis as a property of a movie clip instance.

SESSION 4.3 VISUAL OVERVIEW

Inverse kinematics is an animation method used to create bone structures. When one bone moves, the other bones move in relation to it.

A **bone** is a link from one symbol instance to another or from one interior part of a shape to another.

A chain of bones is called an **armature**.

When you add bones to a symbol instance or to a shape, the instance or shape and its armature are moved to a new layer called a **pose layer**.

Onion skinning displays more than one frame at a time on the Stage. The Onion Skin button toggles feature on and off.

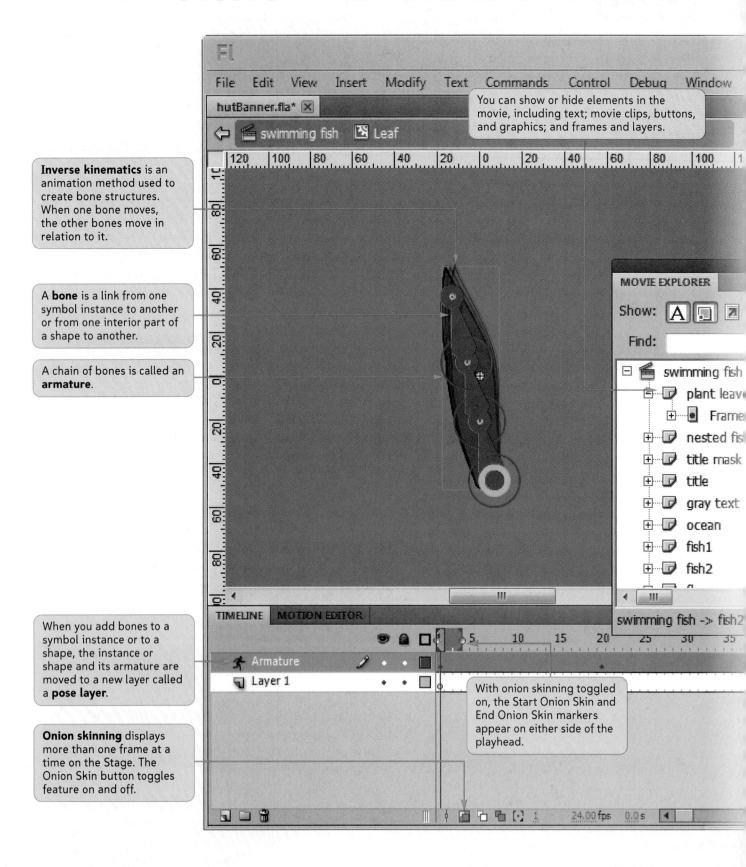

You can show or hide elements in the movie, including text; movie clips, buttons, and graphics; and frames and layers.

With onion skinning toggled on, the Start Onion Skin and End Onion Skin markers appear on either side of the playhead.

File   Edit   View   Insert   Modify   Text   Commands   Control   Debug   Window

hutBanner.fla*

swimming fish   Leaf

MOVIE EXPLORER

Show:

Find:

swimming fish
  plant leave
    Frame
  nested fish
  title mask
  title
  gray text
  ocean
  fish1
  fish2

swimming fish -> fish2

TIMELINE   MOTION EDITOR

Armature
Layer 1

24.00 fps   0.0 s

NESTED SYMBOLS AND INVERSE KINEMATICS

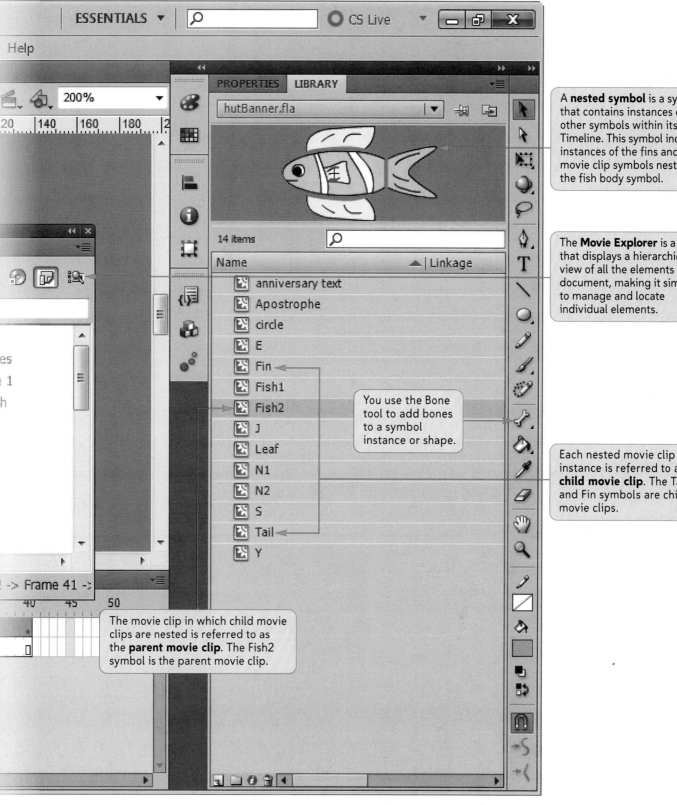

A **nested symbol** is a symbol that contains instances of other symbols within its Timeline. This symbol includes instances of the fins and tails movie clip symbols nested in the fish body symbol.

The **Movie Explorer** is a panel that displays a hierarchical view of all the elements in a document, making it simpler to manage and locate individual elements.

You use the Bone tool to add bones to a symbol instance or shape.

Each nested movie clip instance is referred to as a **child movie clip**. The Tail and Fin symbols are child movie clips.

The movie clip in which child movie clips are nested is referred to as the **parent movie clip**. The Fish2 symbol is the parent movie clip.

Animating Nested Symbols

As you have seen, complex animations can be created by animating objects on separate layers. For example, you can animate one object to move across the Stage on one layer while at the same time another object on another layer rotates and increases in size. So, by adding more layers to the document's main Timeline, you can create complex animation effects.

You cannot always achieve a desired special effect by just adding layers with more animations. For example, the Jenny's Oyster Hut banner has a fish swimming across the Stage, but the fish's fins and tail remain stationary in relation to the fish. A better design creates animations for the fins and the tail so that the fish moves more realistically. You could separate the fins and the tail from the body of the fish, convert them to movie clip symbols, and then create animations for each one on separate layers. Then you could animate the fish body, fins, and tail to move across the Stage at the same time as one object, which creates a more natural look. This is difficult to do, however, because all the animations must be synchronized to work together. A simpler way to achieve this same result is to create a nested symbol.

Creating Complex Animations with Nested Symbols

A nested symbol contains instances of other symbols within its Timeline. So, the Timeline of a movie clip symbol can include instances of other symbols that in turn can contain their own animations within their own Timelines. Instances of the parent movie clip can then be inserted into the document's main Timeline, and modified and animated just like any other symbol instance. When you modify or animate the parent movie clip, the child movie clips are also affected.

In the case of the fish, the parent movie clip can consist of the fish body plus nested instances of the fins and the tail, as shown in Figure 4-34. The fins and tail movie clip instances can contain their own animations to make them change slightly to simulate the movement of a real fish. These animations are independent of the fish body. The whole fish, which is the parent movie clip, can then be inserted in the document's main Timeline and animated to move across the Stage. When you apply a motion tween to the whole fish to make it move across the Stage, the motion tween is also applied to its nested instances. As a result, the fish body, fins, and tail all move across the Stage as one object while the fins and tail exhibit their own animations.

Figure 4-34	Example of a nested movie clip symbol

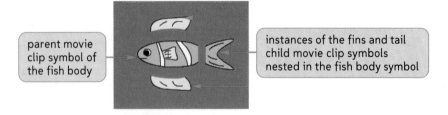

Creating a Nested Movie Clip Symbol

The first scene of the banner requires a fish that has its fins and tail animated to appear more natural. To do this, you will create a fish using separate fin and tail symbols that contain their own animations. Aly already created movie clip symbols for the fish body, fin, and tail. You will use these to create frame-by-frame animations for the fin and the tail. Then you will add two instances of the fin movie clip and one instance of the tail movie clip to the fish body. You will then insert the resulting nested movie clip symbol into the swimming fish scene of the restaurant's banner and animate it to move across the Stage.

You will start by creating a frame-by-frame animation for the fin. To create the animation for the fin, you'll add keyframes at every other frame of the fin Timeline starting at Frame 3. You will then change the shape of the fin slightly at each keyframe for a total of nine frames.

To insert frames for the fin frame-by-frame animation:

▶ **1.** If you took a break after the previous session, make sure the hutBanner.fla file is open and the workspace is reset to the Essentials layout.

▶ **2.** On the Edit bar, click the **Edit Symbols** button 🔯, and then click **Fin**. The Fin symbol opens in symbol-editing mode.

▶ **3.** Change the zoom magnification to **200%**. The magnification of the Stage increases, making it easier to see the Fin symbol on the Stage.

▶ **4.** In the Timeline, insert keyframes in the Layer 1 layer at **Frame 3**, **Frame 5**, **Frame 7**, and **Frame 9**. The fin is copied to each of the new frames.

Using Onion Skinning with Complex Animations

When working with complex animations, it is often helpful to use onion skinning. Onion skinning shows the current frame plus two or more frames on the Stage at once. The contents of the frames within the onion skin markers are displayed on the Stage. The content of the current frame, indicated by the position of the playhead, appears in full color as usual. The contents of the frames before and after the current frame appear dimmed. Onion skinning can be especially helpful when creating a frame-by-frame animation where you need to compare the current frame's contents to the previous frame's contents.

You can also click the Onion Skin Outlines button to display only the outlines of the content on the Stage, which can be helpful when working with complex animations. The Edit Multiple Frames button makes the content of all the frames in a frame-by-frame animation that are within the onion skin markers available for editing.

INSIGHT

Locking Layers While Onion Skinning

When using onion skinning with a complex document, a confusing array of images might be displayed on the Stage. Because the content of locked layers is not affected when onion skinning is turned on, lock any layers you are not editing. You can then focus on the contents of the layers you are editing. Remember to toggle off onion skinning when you are finished so that you again see only one frame at one time.

You will toggle on onion skinning to help you as you create the fin frame-by-frame animation.

TIP
You can also drag the onion skin markers on the Timeline header to increase or decrease the number of frames displayed on the Stage.

To create the fin frame-by-frame animation:

▶ **1.** In the Timeline, click the **Onion Skin** button 🔲. The onion skin markers appear in the Timeline header.

▶ **2.** In the Timeline, click the **Modify Onion Markers** button 🔲, and then click **Onion 2**. The two frames before and after the current frame appear on the Stage.

3. In the Timeline, click **Frame 3** of the Layer 1 layer. This is the frame where you will first modify the fin.

4. In the Tools panel, click the **Selection** tool.

5. Click an empty area of the Stage to deselect the fin, and then drag the right side of the fin slightly to the left. The onion skinned frames provide a reference of the changed fin. See Figure 4-35.

Figure 4-35   Fin movie clip modified in Frame 3

location of the fin in the current frame

onion skin markers indicate how many frames appear on the Stage

click to modify the onion skin markers

click to toggle onion skinning on and off

location of the fin in the other frames

In Frame 5 and Frame 7, you'll repeat this process to modify other parts of the fin. In Frame 9, the fin returns to its original state, so you won't make any changes in this frame.

6. In the Timeline, click **Frame 5**, deselect the fin on the Stage, and then drag the top edge of the fin slightly up. See Figure 4-36.

Figure 4-36   Fin movie clip modified in Frame 5

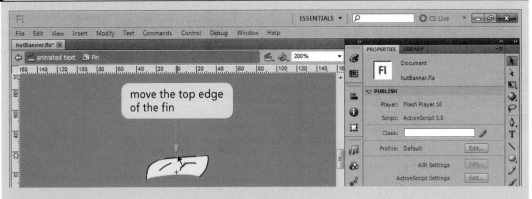

move the top edge of the fin

7. In the Timeline, click **Frame 7**, deselect the fin on the Stage, and then drag the upper-right tip of the fin slightly to the right. The fin animation is complete.

8. Drag the playhead to **Frame 1**, and then press the **Enter** key to play the frame-by-frame animation. The fin changes slightly at each keyframe throughout the animation.

The frame-by-frame animation for the fin is complete. You will create a similar frame-by-frame animation for the Tail symbol. You'll use the same number of keyframes for the Tail symbol as you did for the Fin symbol and change the shape of the tail slightly at each keyframe.

To create the tail frame-by-frame animation:

1. On the Edit bar, click the **Edit Symbols** button 🔄., and then click **Tail**. The Tail symbol opens in symbol-editing mode.

2. In the Timeline, insert keyframes in the Layer 1 layer at **Frame 3**, **Frame 5**, **Frame 7**, and **Frame 9**. The tail is copied to each of the new frames. Onion skinning is still on and will remain that way until you click the Onion Skin button.

3. In the Timeline, click **Frame 3** of the Layer 1 layer, and then click an empty area of the Stage to deselect the tail.

4. On the Stage, drag the two tips on the right side of the tail slightly inward. The dimmed tail from the previous frame provides a reference as you change the shape of the tail. See Figure 4-37.

Figure 4-37   Tail movie clip modified in Frame 3

5. In the Timeline, click **Frame 5**, deselect the tail on the Stage, and then drag the tail's top edge near the left side of the tail slightly down. See Figure 4-38.

Figure 4-38   Tail movie clip symbol modified in Frame 5

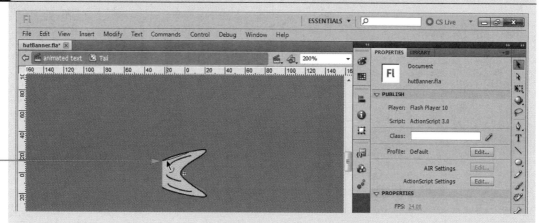

6. In Frame 5, drag the tail's bottom edge near the left side of the tail slightly up. The midsection of the tail is narrower.

7. In the Timeline, click **Frame 7**, deselect the tail on the Stage, and then drag the two tips on the right side of the tail slightly inward as you did in Step 4. In Frame 9, the tail returns to its original state, so no changes are needed in this frame.

8. In the Timeline, click the **Onion Skin** button 🔲. Onion skinning toggles off.

9. In the Timeline, click **Frame 1**, and then press the **Enter** key to play the frame-by-frame animation. The tail changes slightly at each keyframe throughout the animation.

Now that you have created the animations for the Fin movie clip symbol and the Tail movie clip symbol, you are ready to insert instances of these symbols in the Fish2 symbol, which contains the fish body. The instances will be nested inside the Fish2 symbol.

To create the Fish2 nested movie clip symbol:

1. On the Edit bar, click the **Edit Symbols** button 🔷, and then click **Fish2**. The Fish2 symbol opens in symbol-editing mode.

2. Click the **LIBRARY** tab, and then drag an instance of the **Fin symbol** from the Library panel and place it directly above the fish body on the Stage. See Figure 4-39.

Figure 4-39　**Fin instance placed on top of the fish**

position the fin directly above the fish body

drag an instance of the fin symbol onto the Stage

3. If necessary, press the arrow keys to nudge the fin into place.

4. Drag another instance of the **Fin symbol** from the Library panel and place it below the fish body.

5. On the Application bar, click **Modify**, point to **Transform**, and then click **Flip Vertical**. The fin will now fit below the fish body.

6. Position the **Fin** instance right below the fish body, pressing the arrow keys as needed to nudge the fin into place.

7. Drag an instance of the **Tail symbol** from the Library panel and place it to the right side of the fish, positioning the tail precisely against the fish body.

8. Click an empty area of the Stage to deselect the fish. The fish is now complete. See Figure 4-40.

Figure 4-40   **Completed nested symbol**

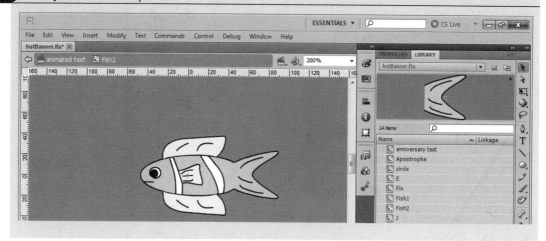

The Fish2 symbol is complete with its nested movie clip symbols. You will place the complete fish in the swimming fish scene and apply a motion tween to make the fish swim across the Stage. The fins and tail will move together with the fish.

To insert and animate the Fish2 symbol in the swimming fish scene:

1. On the Edit bar, click the **Edit Scene** button, and then click **swimming fish**. The swimming fish scene appears.

2. Change the zoom magnification to **100%**.

3. In the Timeline, insert a new layer above the title mask layer and rename it **nested fish**. The nested fish layer is selected in the Timeline.

4. Drag an instance of the **Fish2** symbol from the Library panel and place it on the pasteboard to the right of the Stage about 130 pixels from the top of the Stage.

5. In the Tools panel, click the **Free Transform** tool, and then click the **Scale** button.

6. On the pasteboard, drag a corner handle of the Fish2 symbol to reduce the size of the instance so that it is about the same size as the Fish1 instance. See Figure 4-41.

Figure 4-41   **Nested movie clip instance in the swimming fish scene**

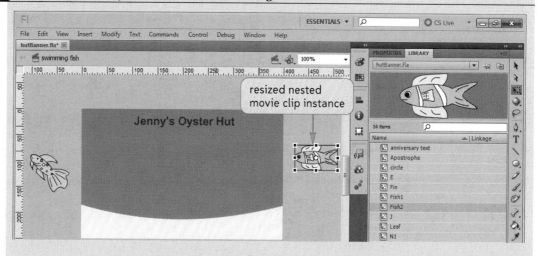

▶ 7. In the Tools panel, click the **Selection** tool ▍.

▶ 8. On the pasteboard, right-click the **Fish2** instance, and then click **Create Motion Tween**. A tween span is added to the nested fish layer.

▶ 9. In the Timeline, click **Frame 50** of the nested fish layer, and then move the **Fish2** instance to the pasteboard on the left side of the Stage. The fish will move across the Stage as the frames play.

The motion tween animation is complete for the Fish2 instance. You'll test the animation next. Because the Fin and Tail symbols are movie clip symbols and their Timelines are independent of the main document's Timeline, their animations will not play when you test the animation of the fish within the Document window. To see their animations, you will play the current scene as a SWF file in the Flash Player.

To test the nested movie clip animation:

▶ 1. In the Timeline, click **Frame 1** of the nested fish layer, and then press the **Enter** key to play the motion tween animation. The Fish2 instance moves across the Stage, but the nested fin and tail animations do not play.

TIP

You can also press the Ctrl+Alt+Enter keys to test the current scene in the Flash Player.

▶ 2. On the Application bar, click **Control**, and then click **Test Scene**. The swimming fish scene plays in a Flash Player window. As the Fish2 instance moves across the Stage, its fins and tail exhibit their animations.

You will stop the main document's Timeline from playing to see only the animations for the Fin and Tail instances.

▶ 3. When the Fish2 instance moves across the Stage, press the **Enter** key. The fish stops swimming. The fins and tail of the Fish2 instance continue their animations because they are on independent Timelines.

▶ 4. Press the **Enter** key. The fish starts swimming again.

▶ 5. Close the Flash Player window, and then save the banner.

Using Inverse Kinematics

In Flash, inverse kinematics let you animate one or more objects in relation to each other. With inverse kinematics, you can easily create complex animations and natural movement. For example, you can create character animation in which the arms and legs of a body are connected to each other with bones. When a bone in one part of the character moves, the other bones move accordingly without you defining every single movement. You specify only the start and end positions of an object by positioning its bones, and the other bones shift into a different pose.

Bones can be added to connect one symbol instance to another, or they can be added to the interior of a shape object so that you can move or animate parts of the shape without having to draw the shape multiple times. When you add bones to a symbol instance or shape, the instance or shape and its armature are moved to a pose layer named Armature.

The Jenny's Oyster Hut banner requires a plant leaf animation. You will use the Bone tool to add bones to a leaf shape that Aly created. You will then move the bones slightly at different frames in the pose layer to create the animation.

To create a plant leaf animation using inverse kinematics:

1. On the Edit bar, click the **Edit Symbols** button [icon], and then click **Leaf**. The Leaf symbol opens in symbol-editing mode.

2. Increase the zoom magnification to **200%**.

3. In the Tools panel, click the **Bone** tool [icon] to select it. You use the Bone tool to add bones to an instance or to a shape. Each time you click and drag with the Bone tool, a new bone is created.

4. On the Stage, click the base of the plant leaf, and then drag the pointer up to about one-third of the length of the leaf shape. A bone is added to the shape, and a new layer named "Armature" is created. See Figure 4-42.

| Figure 4-42 | Bone added to the plant leaf shape |

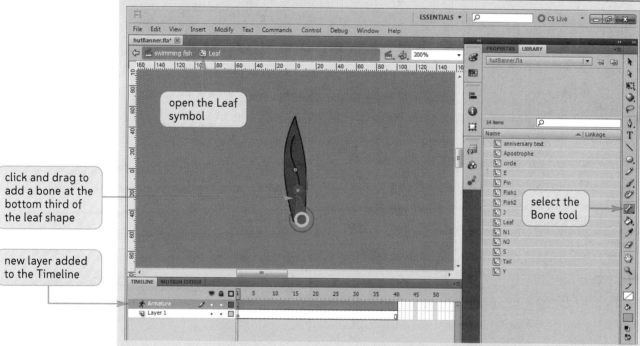

Start the second bone from the end of the first bone to create a chain of bones so the connecting bones will shift when you later move a bone.

5. On the Stage, click the endpoint of the first bone and drag the pointer up to about two-thirds of the length of the leaf shape to create a second bone. See Figure 4-43.

Figure 4-43   Second bone added to the plant leaf shape

click and drag to
add a bone at the
middle third of
the leaf shape

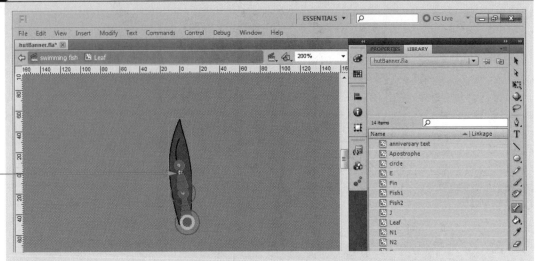

6. On the Stage, click the end point of the second bone and drag the pointer up to right below the tip of the leaf shape to create a third bone. You will move the bones to create an inverse kinematic animation.

7. In the Tools panel, click the **Selection** tool ▶ to select it, and then, in the Timeline, click **Frame 1** of the Armature layer, if necessary.

8. On the Stage, drag the top bone slightly to the left. Moving the bones creates an inverse kinematic animation. See Figure 4-44.

Figure 4-44   Plant leaf starting position

drag the top
bone to the left

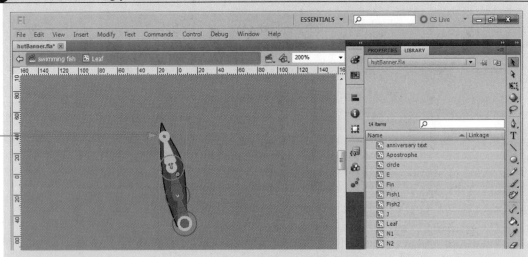

9. In the Timeline, click **Frame 20** of the Armature layer, and then, on the Stage, drag the top bone slightly to the right of the leaf's original position. A new pose is created at Frame 20. See Figure 4-45.

Figure 4-45   New pose created in the plant leaf symbol

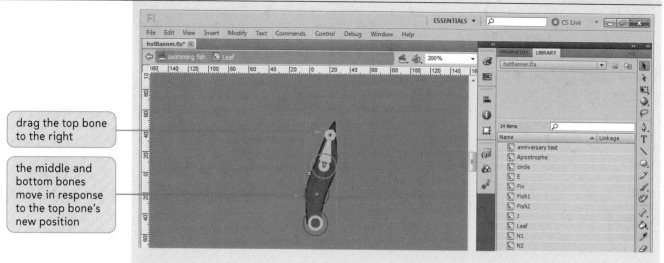

drag the top bone to the right

the middle and bottom bones move in response to the top bone's new position

▶ 10. In the Timeline, click **Frame 40** of the Armature layer, and then, on the Stage, drag the top bone slightly to the left to approximately the leaf's original position. A new pose is created at Frame 40.

▶ 11. Scrub the playhead between Frame 1 and Frame 40 to see the inverse kinematic animation.

The plant leaf animation is complete. Several instances of the plant leaf symbol will be added to the swimming fish scene. One instance will be flipped horizontally so that its animation moves in the opposite direction of the other two instances.

To add the plant leaf animation to the swimming fish scene:

▶ 1. On the Edit bar, click the **swimming fish** link. The swimming fish scene is the current scene.

▶ 2. In the Timeline, move the playhead to **Frame 1**, insert a new layer above the nested fish layer, and then rename the new layer **plant leaves**.

▶ 3. Drag an instance of the **Leaf** symbol from the Library panel and place it in the lower-right corner of the Stage, and then drag two more instances of the **Leaf** symbol and place them next to the first instance. See Figure 4-46.

Figure 4-46   **Leaf instances arranged on the Stage**

make swimming fish the current scene

drag three instances of the Leaf symbol onto the Stage

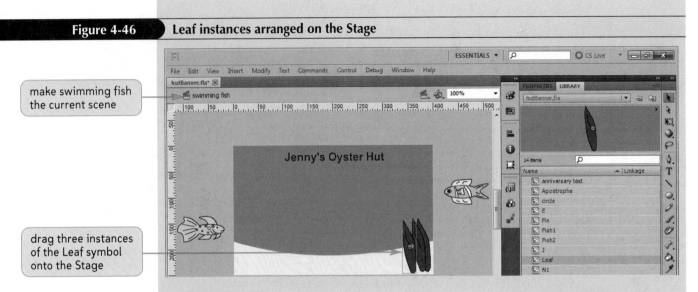

▶ **4.** Click the middle **Leaf** instance to select it, and then, on the Application bar, click **Modify**, point to **Transform**, and click **Flip Horizontal**. The middle leaf instance faces the other direction.

▶ **5.** On the Application bar, click **Control**, point to **Test Movie**, and then click **in Flash Professional**. The movie plays in a Flash Player window. The Leaf instances exhibit their animation.

▶ **6.** Close the Flash Player window, and then save the banner.

Using the Movie Explorer

As a Flash document gets more complex with many symbols, text blocks, layers, and scenes, it can become difficult to manage all the elements or to find a specific element. The Movie Explorer can help you view each of the document's elements, to search for a specific element, to find all instances of a particular symbol, or even to print a list of the document's elements as listed in the Movie Explorer.

You can choose which elements to display in the Movie Explorer panel. For example, you can display only the text blocks used in the document, and then each text block appears in the Movie Explorer with information about the font and point size used in the text block. Likewise, you can choose to display each instance of the symbols used in the document. When you select an instance in the Movie Explorer, information about where the instance is located in the document appears at the bottom of the panel. The Movie Explorer's panel menu button provides access to additional options, including:

- Go to Symbol Definition, which selects the symbol definition for the symbol selected in the Movie Explorer.
- Show in Library, which displays the selected symbol in the Library panel.
- Show Movie Elements, which displays the document's elements such as its layers, frames, and symbol instances.
- Show Symbol Definitions, which displays all elements associated with a symbol.
- Show All Scenes, which displays the elements and symbols for all scenes in the document, not just the current scene.

PROSKILLS

Teamwork: Using the Movie Explorer to Troubleshoot Problems

Creating a Flash document is often a collaborative process that could involve clients, designers, artists, and others. If you're working with a team of people to create a new Flash document, then you'll already be familiar with how the document is organized. If you're working with a Flash document developed by someone else, the organization may not be as clear. In that case, you can use the Movie Explorer to become familiar with the way the scenes, symbols, and other elements are organized. You can explore how and where each of the document's symbols is used as well as how the symbol is constructed. You can then more easily modify the document.

You can also use the Movie Explorer to troubleshoot problems that arise, which might occur when you are working with complex animations. For example, if an animation is not working correctly, you can check the symbol instances that are part of the animation and determine whether they are in the correct scene, layer, and frame.

Teams commonly work together to create Flash documents. The Movie Explorer provides a good tool to help you evaluate the document if you didn't create it, saving you time and energy when you try to locate specific elements or determine specifics about the element.

Because the banner you created for the Jenny's Oyster Hut Web site has multiple scenes, layers, and symbols, you can use the Movie Explorer to review all of its elements and view how all the various symbol instances throughout the document are organized.

To use the Movie Explorer to examine the banner's elements:

1. On the Application bar, click **Window**, and then click **Movie Explorer**. The Movie Explorer opens.

2. If necessary, click the **Show text** button A to select it and click the other Show buttons to deselect them.

3. Click the **Movie Explorer panel menu** button ▾≣, and then click **Show Movie Elements** to select it, if necessary.

4. Repeat Step 3 to select **Show Symbol Definitions** and **Show All Scenes**. The panel displays the scenes that contain text blocks as well as the symbols that contain text. This will make it easier to locate text blocks within the document.

5. Drag the bottom edge of the Movie Explorer window down to increase its size so you can see more of the elements in the window.

6. If necessary, click the **plus sign** next to the animated text scene name to expand its contents. The Movie Explorer displays all of the text blocks for the scene, including the text properties. You can compare the text properties of all the text blocks in the scene. This information can be useful if you need to maintain consistency across all of the text blocks within a scene. See Figure 4-47.

TIP

If a text block does not reside in a locked layer, you can double-click the text block in the Movie Explorer to change its contents.

Figure 4-47	Movie Explorer displaying text blocks

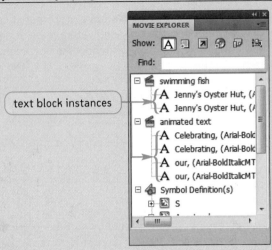

text block instances

7. In the Movie Explorer, click the **Show frames and layers** button to select it, and then click the **plus sign** next to the swimming fish scene to expand its display, if necessary. Each layer of the swimming fish scene is displayed in the panel. Selecting a layer name in the panel also selects the layer in the document, enabling you to find specific layers in a complex document.

TIP

Selecting a keyframe in the Movie Explorer also selects that keyframe in the Timeline.

8. In the Movie Explorer, scroll down the panel, click the **fish2** layer name under the swimming fish scene, and then, if necessary, click the **plus sign** next to it. Each keyframe within the fish2 layer is displayed. See Figure 4-48.

Figure 4-48	Movie Explorer displaying the fish2 layer and its keyframes

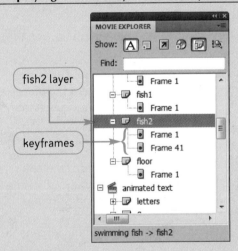

fish2 layer

keyframes

9. In the Movie Explorer, click the **Show movie clips, buttons, and graphics** button to select it, and then click the **Fish1** instance in Frame 41 of the fish2 layer. The path of the instance at the bottom of the panel indicates where the instance is located within the document. See Figure 4-49.

Figure 4-49   **Fish1 instance in Frame 41 of the fish2 layer**

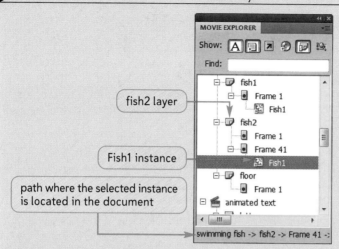

fish2 layer

Fish1 instance

path where the selected instance is located in the document

10. In the Movie Explorer, click the **Movie Explorer panel menu** button ⬛, and then click **Go to Symbol Definition**. The Movie Explorer shows the Fish1 symbol under the Symbol Definitions area. The Symbol Definitions area shows all the elements associated with the selected symbol.

11. Close the Movie Explorer, and then close the hutBanner.fla file.

TIP

You can also press the Alt+F3 keys to open and close the Movie Explorer.

Aly is pleased with the document elements and is ready to show the banner to Jenny. In this session, you used onion skinning to display the contents of multiple frames on the Stage. You also created nested movie clips, which contain instances of other movie clips within their Timelines. You also created an inverse kinematic animation using bones. Finally, you used the Movie Explorer to review the elements of a complex document.

Session 4.3 Quick Check

REVIEW

1. How can you change the position of the onion skin markers in the Timeline header?
2. How can onion skinning help you when working with a complex animation?
3. What is a nested movie clip?
4. What is a movie clip that has other movie clips nested within it called?
5. Why will the animations of movie clips embedded in a nested movie clip not play when you test them within the Flash Player window?
6. True or False. Inverse kinematics uses bones to create complex animations and natural movement.
7. How can you use the Movie Explorer to find the definition of a particular symbol?

Review Assignments

Data File needed for the Review Assignments: johDraft.fla

Based on Jenny's feedback, Aly wants you to create a third banner for the Jenny's Oyster Hut Web site. This banner will have two fish swimming along curved paths. The same scene will include a mask effect on the Jenny's Oyster Hut title that makes the text block appear gradually from left to right. The banner also requires a new animation of a small circular sign that contains rotating text inside. Two instances of the sign will be animated to move in the scene.

1. Open the **johDraft.fla** document located in the Flash4\Review folder included with your Data Files, and then save the file as **johBanner.fla** in the same folder.

2. In Frame 1 of the Fish1 layer, add an instance of the Fish1 symbol to the pasteboard on the left side of the Stage so its center is about 170 pixels from the top of the Stage.

3. Insert a keyframe in Frame 36 of the Fish1 layer, and then create a motion tween at Frame 1 of the Fish1 layer.

4. At Frame 35, move the Fish1 instance to the pasteboard on the right side of the Stage. Curve the center of the motion path up. Orient the fish to the path.

5. At Frame 36 of the Fish1 layer, move the Fish1 instance to the right side of the pasteboard, and then flip the Fish1 instance to face to the left. Create a motion tween at Frame 36 of the Fish1 layer.

6. At Frame 70, move the Fish1 instance to the pasteboard on the left side of the Stage. Curve the center of the motion path up. Orient the fish to the path.

7. Insert a new layer above the Fish1 layer and rename it **Fish2**. Add an instance of the Fish2 symbol to the right side of the Stage slightly below the top edge of the ocean.

8. Insert a keyframe at Frame 36 of the Fish2 layer, and then create a motion tween at Frame 1 of the Fish2 layer.

9. At Frame 35, move the Fish2 instance to the pasteboard on the left side of the Stage. Curve the center of the motion path down. Orient the fish to the path.

10. At Frame 36 of the Fish2 layer, move the Fish2 instance to the pasteboard on the left side of the Stage, and then flip the Fish2 instance to face to the right. Create a motion tween at Frame 36 of the Fish2 layer.

11. At Frame 70, move the Fish2 instance to the pasteboard on the right side of the Stage. Curve the center of the motion path down. Orient the fish to the path.

12. Insert a new layer above the Title layer, rename it **Mask**, and then change its type to Mask. Make sure the Title layer's type is changed to Masked and that it is indented below the Mask layer.

13. Unlock the Mask layer. Draw a rectangle with no stroke and a fill color of your choice that covers the entire Jenny's Oyster Hut text block. The rectangle's width should be the same width as the text block and its height should be only as high as the text block. Convert this rectangle to a movie clip symbol named **Rectangle**.

14. Insert a keyframe at Frame 35 of the Mask layer. At Frame 1, move the rectangle to the left of the text block to reveal the entire text block. Create a motion tween from Frame 1 to Frame 34 so that the rectangle moves from left to right to gradually cover the text block. Lock the Mask layer and test the mask animation effect. The text block should appear gradually from left to right.

15. Create a new movie clip symbol named **Rotating text**. In symbol-editing mode, add a Classic text block to the center of the symbol's Stage. Use Arial for the font family, bold for the font style, 12 for the point size, 0 for the letter spacing, white for the text color, and align center for the paragraph format. Type **Shrimp** in the text block. In the Property inspector, set the text block's X and Y coordinates to 0.

16. Insert a keyframe at Frame 15, create a motion tween between Frames 1 and 15, and then, in the Property inspector, set the text to rotate clockwise one time.

17. Insert a keyframe at Frame 20 and replace the Shrimp text with the word **Catfish**. Insert another keyframe at Frame 35 and create a motion tween between Frames 20 and 35. Set the Catfish text block to rotate counterclockwise one time.

18. Insert a keyframe at Frame 40 and replace the Catfish text with the word **Oysters**. Insert another keyframe at Frame 55 and create a motion tween between Frames 40 and 55. Set the Oysters text block to rotate clockwise one time. Insert a regular frame at Frame 60. Exit symbol-editing mode.

19. Create a new movie clip symbol named **Rotating sign**. In symbol-editing mode, add a small circle with a dark blue (#003366) fill color and no stroke to the center of the symbol's Stage. Use the Property inspector to make the circle 60 pixels wide and 60 pixels high, and to set its X and Y coordinates to 0. Drag an instance of the Rotating text symbol to the center of the circle. Exit symbol-editing mode.

20. Insert a new layer above the Mask layer and name it **Rotating sign**. On this layer, drag an instance of the Rotating sign symbol to the pasteboard at the lower-left of the Stage. Insert a keyframe at Frame 35, and then create a motion tween between Frames 1 and 35 so that the Rotating sign instance moves from the pasteboard to the center of the beach graphic at the bottom of the Stage.

21. Test the new animations for the document using the Test Movie command.

22. Submit the finished files to your instructor.

Animate letters, add motion tweens, and create motion guide layers.

APPLY

Case Problem 1

Data File needed for this Case Problem: kprDraft.fla

Katie's Pet Resort   Katie asks John about creating a new Flash document to use on the Katie's Pet Resort Web site to promote the resort's services. You will create the advertisement based on a document John has developed. You'll add new text messages promoting the grand opening sale and the services provided by the resort. The resort's name will be animated so that it is displayed one letter at a time. After the resort's name appears, the next text message will fade in. Another text message will appear and will increase in size and change in color. Also, you'll add several instances of the balloon symbol. The finished advertisement is shown in Figure 4-50.

Figure 4-50   **Finished advertisement for Katie's Pet Resort**

1. Open the **kprDraft.fla** file located in the Flash4\Case1 folder included with your Data Files, and then save the document as **kprBanner.fla** in the same folder.

2. Create a new layer folder named **letters** above the resort layer and move the resort layer inside the folder. Convert the text block in the resort layer to individual text blocks, one for each character. Distribute the characters to individual layers inside the letters layer folder, and then delete the empty resort layer.

3. Move the keyframes in Frame 1 of each letter layer so that each starts one frame after the previous character. The first letter, K, starts in Frame 1. The second letter, a, starts in Frame 2. The third letter, n, starts in Frame 3, and so on. The characters will appear one at a time to form the complete resort name. Collapse the letters layer folder.

4. Insert a new layer above the background layer and rename it **sale**. At Frame 25 of the sale layer, insert a keyframe, and then drag an instance of the Sale symbol from the Library panel to the center of the Stage. Animate the text block instance to fade in over the next 15 frames. (*Hint*: Insert a keyframe at Frame 40 of the sale layer. At Frame 25, create a motion tween and change the alpha amount of the Sale instance to 0%. At Frame 39, change the alpha amount to 100%.)

5. Animate the text of the Sale text block instance to change from red to blue. At Frame 55, insert a keyframe. At Frame 40, create a motion tween. At Frame 54, change the tint of the Sale text instance to 100% blue (#0000FF). At Frame 55, change the tint to 100% blue (#0000FF) to match the text block's tint at the end of the motion tween.

6. Change the tint of the Sale text block back to red. At Frame 55, create a motion tween. At Frame 70, change the text block's tint to 100% red (#FF0000). Lock the sale layer.

7. Insert a new layer above the sale layer and rename it **services**. At Frame 40, insert a keyframe, drag an instance of the Services symbol to the lower part of the Stage, and then create a motion tween.

8. At Frame 40, use the Transform panel to reduce the size of the Services instance to 50% of its original size and change the alpha amount to 0%. At Frame 55, change the size of the instance back to 100% and change its alpha amount to 100%. The text block will fade in as it increases in size from Frame 40 to Frame 55.

9. At Frame 60 of the services layer, reduce the size of the Services instance to 80% of its original size. At Frame 65, increase the size of the text block to 100%. The text block will decrease in size slightly and increase back to its original size. Lock the services layer.

10. Insert a new layer above the background layer and rename it **balloon1**. Drag an instance of the Balloon symbol to the lower-left side of the Stage. At Frame 1 of the balloon1 layer, create a motion tween. At Frame 50, move the Balloon instance to the upper-right corner of the Stage. Use the Selection tool to curve the motion path down slightly.

11. Insert a new layer above the balloon1 layer and rename it **balloon2**. At Frame 20, insert a keyframe, drag an instance of the Balloon symbol to the lower-right side of the Stage, and then create a motion tween. At Frame 70, move the Balloon instance to the upper-left corner of the Stage. Use the Selection tool to curve the motion path down slightly.

12. Test the animation in Flash and in the Flash Player. Submit the finished files to your instructor.

Add a mask layer effect, and animate letters and text blocks.

APPLY

Case Problem 2

Data File needed for this Case Problem: aczAdDraft.fla

Alamo City Zoo   Janet asks Alex to develop a new advertising banner for the Alamo City Zoo Web site. The banner should include new animations that highlight the Alamo City Zoo name. It should also display several text messages on the banner that promote the zoo's attractions, including the new bear exhibit. You will create the new advertisement based on a banner that Alex started. You'll add a spotlight effect where the spotlight starts small at the center of the banner and increases to reveal the banner. You'll also develop a special text effect for the zoo's name where the letters increase in size one after the other to give it a pulsating effect. Finally, you will add the text messages promoting the zoo. The finished banner is shown in Figure 4-51.

| Figure 4-51 | Finished advertising banner for Alamo City Zoo |

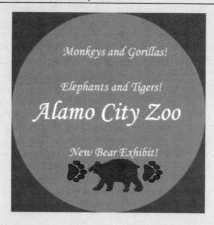

1. Open the **aczAdDraft.fla** file located in the Flash4\Case2 folder included with your Data Files, and then save the document as **aczAd.fla** in the same folder.

2. Create a new movie clip symbol named **circle**. In symbol-editing mode, draw a circle with a white fill and no stroke at the center of the Stage. Select the circle and in the Info panel, set its dimensions to 40 pixels wide and 40 pixels high, and set the X and Y registration point coordinates to 0. Exit symbol-editing mode.

3. Insert a regular frame at Frame 20 of the zoo name layer. Insert a new layer above this layer and rename it **mask**. At Frame 1 of the mask layer, drag an instance of the circle symbol from the Library panel to the center of the Stage. In the Property inspector, set the instance's X and Y coordinates to 150 each to center it on the Stage.

4. Select the circle instance and create a motion tween. At Frame 20 of the mask layer, change the size of the circle instance to 300 pixels wide by 300 pixels high.

5. Copy all the frames on the mask layer to the Clipboard. Insert a new layer above the mask layer, select all of its frames, and then paste the copied frames to the new layer. Rename the layer **circle**.

6. Temporarily hide the contents of the mask layer to work with the contents of the circle layer. At Frame 1 of the circle layer, change the alpha amount of the circle instance on the Stage to 40%. Move the circle layer below the zoo name layer.

7. Show the mask layer, right-click the layer, and then change its type to Mask. Make sure the zoo name layer is masked. Test the animation. The mask gradually reveals the company name. The motion tween on the circle layer displays the dimmed circle to coincide with the circle on the mask layer to create the special effect.

8. Hide the mask layer temporarily, unlock the zoo name layer, and then copy the text block on the Stage. Insert a new layer above the mask layer and rename it **name**. Use the Paste in Place command to paste the text block in the name layer in the same relative position as in the zoo name layer.

9. Insert a layer folder above the name layer, name it **letters**, and then move the name layer inside the letters folder.

10. Select the text block in the name layer, convert the text to individual letters, and then distribute the letters to individual layers. Delete the empty name layer. Move all the letter keyframes to Frame 20 by selecting all the Frame 1s of the individual letter layers and dragging them all to start in Frame 20. This is where the individual letters' animation will begin.

11. Extend all of the layers except the mask and zoo name layers by inserting regular frames at Frame 130 of each layer.

12. To make each letter change in size for a moment, insert two keyframes in each layer where the size of the letter is increased slightly in the first of the two new keyframes and where the second keyframe is inserted three frames after the first. So for the A layer, add keyframes at Frames 22 and 25, and then use the Transform panel to change the size of the instance in Frame 22 to 130% larger. For the next letter in layer 1, insert keyframes at Frames 26 and 29, and then increase the size of the instance in Frame 26 to 130%. For the letter a in layer a, insert keyframes at Frames 30 and 33, and then increase the size of the letter in Frame 30 to 130%.

13. Repeat Step 12 for each letter, starting one frame after the last keyframe of the previous letter. The last layer (for the second o in Zoo) will have keyframes at Frames 66 and 69. Show the mask layer, lock the zoo name layer, and then test the animation. The individual letters should increase in size one at a time after the mask effect. Collapse the letters folder.

14. Place horizontal guides about 50 pixels, 100 pixels, and 200 pixels from the top of the Stage.

15. Insert three new layers above the mask layer and rename them **text1**, **text2**, and **text3**. At Frame 60 of the text1 layer, insert a keyframe, and then create a Classic text block centered just below the guide 50 pixels from the top of the Stage. Use the Monotype Corsiva font family, a 20 point size, and light yellow (#FFFFCC) text fill color. Type **Monkeys and Gorillas!** in the text block.

16. Create a motion tween in Frame 60 of the text1 layer. At Frame 60, use the Transform panel to reduce the size of the text block to 50% of its original size. At Frame 65, increase the size of the text back to 100%. The text will increase in size throughout the motion tween.

17. Insert a keyframe of Frame 65 of the text2 layer. Create a new text block in the pasteboard to the left of the Stage just below the guide 100 pixels from the top. Use the same text settings as in Step 15 and type **Elephants and Tigers!** in this text block.

18. Create a motion tween in Frame 65 of the text2 layer. At Frame 70, move the text instance to the Stage about 100 pixels from the top and centered on the banner. The text will fly in from the left of the Stage throughout the motion tween.

19. Create another text motion tween in the text3 layer between Frames 70 and 75. Create a text block with the words **New Bear Exhibit!** in the pasteboard to the right of the Stage just below the guide 200 pixels from the top of the Stage. This text block should fly in from the right of the Stage to the center of the banner about 200 pixels from the top. Clear the guides.

20. Insert a new layer above the text1 layer and rename it **paw1**. Insert a keyframe at Frame 80. Drag an instance of the bear paw symbol to the upper-left corner of the banner, staying within the large circle. Insert a keyframe at Frame 90 and move the bear paw instance toward the bottom so that it is below the letters "Ne" in the New Bear Exhibit! text. Create a motion tween at Frame 80 of the paw1 layer and have the bear paw instance rotate clockwise twice. At Frame 89, move the bear paw instance to the same position as it is in Frame 90.

EXPLORE 21. Use the Motion Editor to apply the Spring ease to the motion tween in the paw1 layer. The paw instance will exhibit a spring effect at the end of its motion tween.

22. Insert a new layer above the paw1 layer and rename it **bear**. Insert a keyframe at Frame 90. Drag an instance of the bear symbol to the right of the bear paw instance below the New Bear Exhibit! text. Create a motion tween at Frame 90 and change the bear instance's alpha amount to 0%. At Frame 100, change the alpha amount to 100% so that the bear instance fades in throughout the tween.

23. Insert a new layer above the bear layer and rename it **paw2**. Insert a keyframe at Frame 100. Drag an instance of the bear paw symbol to the upper-right side of the banner, staying within the large circle. Insert another keyframe at Frame 110 and move the bear paw instance toward the bottom so that it is below the New Bear Exhibit! text and to the right of the bear instance. Create a motion tween at Frame 100 and have the bear paw instance rotate counterclockwise twice. At Frame 109, move the bear paw instance to the same position as it is in Frame 110.

⊕ **EXPLORE**   24. Use the Motion Editor to apply the Spring ease to the motion tween in the paw2 layer. The paw instance will exhibit a spring effect at the end of its motion tween.

25. Test the banner's animation in Flash and the Flash Player to view all the animations.

26. Submit the finished files to your instructor.

Create 3D animations of letters, text block animations, a nested movie clip, and a curved motion path.

CHALLENGE

Case Problem 3

Data File needed for this Case Problem: wcDraft.fla

Westcreek Nursery   Westcreek Nursery is expanding and opening a store at a new location. To advertise the new location and promote her business, Alice started a new marketing campaign. As part of this campaign, she asks Amanda to develop an ad to place on the local newspaper's Web site. To help Amanda, you will create several animations, including one where the letters in the word "Westcreek" fall into place followed by an animation of the word "Nursery" to create the title for the ad. Then several animated text blocks will move into place on the ad, followed by a graphic of the word "Flowers" that will move across the ad banner simulating a truck. The graphic will have animated tires. Figure 4-52 shows the completed advertisement.

Figure 4-52   **Completed advertisement for Westcreek Nursery**

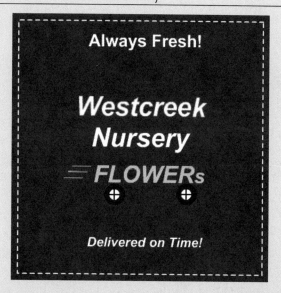

1. Open the **wcDraft.fla** file located in the Flash4\Case3 folder included with your Data Files, and then save the document as **westcreekAd.fla** in the same folder.

2. Create horizontal guides at 50 pixels and at 150 pixels from the top of the Stage.

3. Insert a new layer and rename it **title1**, and then create a text block with the word **Westcreek**. Use white for the text color, Arial for the font family, Bold Italic for the font style, and 40 for the point size. Center the word on the guide 150 pixels from the top of the Stage.

4. Insert a layer folder above the title1 layer and rename it **westcreek text**. Move the title1 layer to the new layer folder. Then select the title1 text block, break it apart, and distribute the individual letters to separate layers. The new layers for the letters should be inside the layer folder. Delete the title1 layer.

⊕ EXPLORE

5. Convert each of the letters into symbols with movie clip behavior. Use the following names for the symbols to match the letters they represent: **W**, **E1**, **S**, **T**, **C**, **R**, **E2**, **E3**, and **K**. Create a new folder in the Library, rename it **Westcreek**, and then move all the letter symbols inside the folder.

6. Each letter will be animated to drop in from the top part of the Stage to its current location 150 pixels from the top. The letters will move one at a time, rotating in 3D space, and fading in as they move to form the word Westcreek. The first letter will start in Frame 1 and the next letters will start every 10 frames. Move each of the letters' keyframes that are in Frame 1 of their respective layers to start every 10 frames. The keyframes should be moved to the following frames: W — Frame 1; e — Frame 10; s — Frame 20; t — Frame 30; c — Frame 40; r — Frame 50; e — Frame 60; e — Frame 70; and k — Frame 80. Be sure to keep each letter on its own layer.

7. Create a motion tween for each letter on its own layer.

⊕ EXPLORE

8. Select Frame 10 of the W layer, open the Motion Editor, and insert a property keyframe for the X property under the Basic Motion category. A property keyframe is automatically added for the Y property. Select Frame 1 and use the 3D Translation tool to move the W instance up so that its center is on the guide 50 pixels from the top of the Stage. Move the instance slightly to its left. In the Motion Editor, at Frame 1, set the Rotation X and the Rotation Y properties to 90 degrees. At Frame 10, insert a property keyframe for the Rotation X and the Rotation Y properties, and then set their values to 0 degrees. At Frame 10, select the Alpha property under the Color Effects category and add a property keyframe. Set the alpha amount in Frame 1 to 0% and in Frame 10 to 100%. The W instance will rotate, fade in, and move into place from Frame 1 to 10.

9. Repeat Step 8 for each letter instance so that it rotates, fades in, and falls into place using the following starting and ending frames: e layer — Frames 10–20; s layer — Frames 20–30; t layer — Frames 30–40; c layer — Frames 40–50; r layer — Frames 50–60; e layer — Frames 60–70; e layer — Frames 70–80; and k layer — Frames 80–90. Test the letter animations. The letters for the word "Westcreek" drop into place one at a time. They fade in and rotate as they fall. Collapse the Westcreek text folder and lock it to make it easier to work with the other layers in the Timeline.

10. Insert a layer above the background layer and rename it **nursery**. Insert a keyframe at Frame 91. Create a text block using the same type settings as in Step 3. Type **Nursery** in the text block. Center this text block on the guide 50 pixels from the top of the Stage.

11. Convert the Nursery text block to a movie clip symbol named **Nursery text**. Create a motion tween for the Nursery text instance. At Frame 91, change the alpha amount of the instance to 0%. At Frame 100, move the instance so that it is centered below the Westcreek text and change its alpha amount to 100%. The Nursery text should move from its initial position to below the Westcreek text and should fade in as it moves into position.

12. Insert a new layer and rename it **text1**. Insert a keyframe at Frame 100 of this layer and then create a text block in this frame. The text should be white, Arial for the font, 26 for the point size, and Bold for the font style. Place the text block on the pasteboard to the left of the Stage about 50 pixels from the top. Type **Always Fresh!** in this text block. Create a motion tween on this text block, and at Frame 105, move the text block to the center of the Stage, keeping it about 50 pixels from the top. The text block moves in from the left of the Stage.

13. Insert a new layer and rename it **text2**. Insert a keyframe at Frame 105 and create a text block using the same settings used in Step 12, but change the font size to 20 and use Bold Italic for the font style. Place the text block in the pasteboard to the right of the

Stage about 350 pixels from the top. Type **Delivered on Time!** in this text block. Create a motion tween on this text block, and at Frame 110, move the text block to the center of the Stage, keeping it about 350 pixels from the top. The text block moves in from the right of the Stage.

14. Create a graphic that will simulate a truck moving across the Stage. Start by creating a rotating wheel symbol that will be embedded in the truck graphic. Create a new movie clip symbol named **Rotating wheel**. In symbol-editing mode, insert an instance of the Wheel symbol from the library to the center of the Stage. In the Property inspector, if necessary, set the X and Y coordinates to 0. Create a motion tween on the Wheel instance and in the Property inspector, set the Wheel instance to rotate clockwise one time. The Rotating wheel symbol is complete. Exit symbol-editing mode.

15. Create a new movie clip symbol named **Truck**. In symbol-editing mode, create a text block at the center of the Stage using Arial for the font, Bold Italic for the style, 36 for the point size, and green (#66FF99) for the font color. Type the word **FLOWERs** in all uppercase, except for the letter s. Reduce the font size of the letter s to 30. Use the Info panel to set the X and Y registration point coordinates to 0 to center the text on the Stage.

16. Use the Line tool to draw a short horizontal line about 30 pixels wide using a stroke color of yellow (#FFFF00), a stroke height of 1, and Solid for the stroke style. Draw the line about 5 pixels to the left of the letter F. Create two copies of this line and place the lines to the left of the letter F. Each line should be a little farther distance from the letter F and equally spaced from each other. The lines will add to the effect of the FLOWERs text moving.

17. Drag an instance of the Rotating wheel symbol to the Stage and place it right below the letter L in FLOWERs. Drag another instance and place it below the letter R. These instances will be the wheels for the truck. The Truck symbol is complete. Exit symbol-editing mode.

18. Insert a new layer above the text2 layer and rename it **truck**. Insert a keyframe at Frame 70 and drag an instance of the Truck symbol in the pasteboard to the upper-left side of the Stage. Create a motion tween at Frame 70 for the Truck instance. At Frame 100, move the Truck instance to the center of the Stage below the Nursery text block.

⊕ **EXPLORE** 19. Use the Selection tool to drag the center of the motion path for the Truck instance down slightly to curve it.

⊕ **EXPLORE** 20. Use the Subselection tool to click an endpoint on the motion path to reveal the curve's Bezier handles. Drag the top endpoint Bezier handle to the left to further curve the top part of the motion path. Drag the bottom endpoint Bezier handle up and to the right to create an upward curve on the bottom part of the motion path.

21. Test the animation in Flash and the Flash Player.

22. Submit the finished files to your instructor.

Create an ad banner with a mask animation, motion tween animations, and individual letters.

CREATE

Case Problem 4

Data File needed for this Case Problem: msaDraft.fla

Missions Support Association   Brittany meets with Anissa to discuss the development of a new advertisement banner that the Missions Support Association can use to promote the association in various Web sites. The ad will contain the association's name, an animation of a star moving across the banner, and several graphics containing text messages. You'll create the new ad, which will be similar to the one shown in Figure 4-53.

Figure 4-53   **Sample advertisement banner for Missions Support Association**

1. Open the **msaDraft.fla** file located in the Flash4\Case4 folder included with your Data Files, and then save the document as **msaAd.fla** in the same folder.

2. In a new layer, create a text block with the text **Missions Support Association** at an appropriate location on the Stage, using the text properties of your choice.

3. Create a spotlight effect for the text using a mask animation.

4. In a new layer, create an animation of an instance of the star symbol that rotates as it moves. For example, the Star instance could move from the lower-left corner of the Stage in a curved path up toward the center of the Stage, move back down to the lower-right corner of the Stage, and then move in a curved path back toward the lower-left corner.

5. At the frame(s) of your choice, in separate layers, create a text block for each word of the text **Preserving History**. The words should appear on the Stage in an appropriate location. Use the text properties of your choice.

6. Create a pulsating effect on the individual letters of the word "History."

7. Make any other changes you feel enhance the advertisement.

8. Test the document's animation in Flash and the Flash Player.

9. Submit the finished files to your instructor.

ENDING DATA FILES

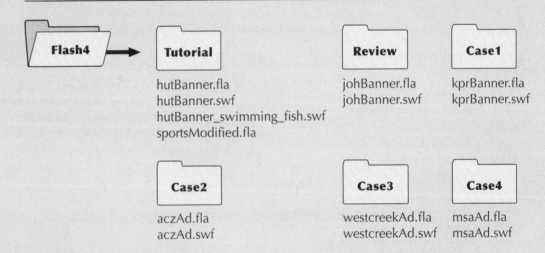

FLASH

Session 5.1
- Explore the different button states
- Add a button from the Buttons library
- Edit a button instance
- Create a custom button
- Align objects on the Stage

Session 5.2
- Learn about actions
- Use the Actions panel to add actions to buttons and to frames
- Compare different types of sound effects
- Import sounds from a file or the Sounds library
- Add sound to buttons and as a background sound
- Change sound settings and add sound effects

Making a Document Interactive

Adding Buttons, Actions, and Sounds

Case | *Admiral Web Design*

Admiral Web Design is designing a lunch specials page for the Jenny's Oyster Hut Web site. Jenny Emerson wants the new banner design for the lunch specials page to be similar to the site's other banners and to include a background sound as well as animation. Aly suggests providing the option to turn off the animation and the background sound, which some users might find distracting while they view the page. She suggests adding several buttons to the banner to control the animation and to mute the sound. She also suggests that the buttons include their own sound effects to help the user know when the button has been clicked. Jenny agrees with Aly's suggestions and approves the development of the new banner.

In this tutorial, you will create buttons, including buttons that change in response to the pointer. You will add buttons to a document, and then add actions to the buttons so they can be used to control the animation. You will also learn how to change the way the animation plays by using frame actions. Finally, you will add sound effects to the buttons and a background sound to the animation.

STARTING DATA FILES

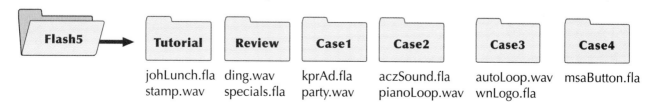

Flash5 →	Tutorial	Review	Case1	Case2	Case3	Case4
	johLunch.fla	ding.wav	kprAd.fla	aczSound.fla	autoLoop.wav	msaButton.fla
	stamp.wav	specials.fla	party.wav	pianoLoop.wav	wnLogo.fla	

SESSION 5.1 VISUAL OVERVIEW

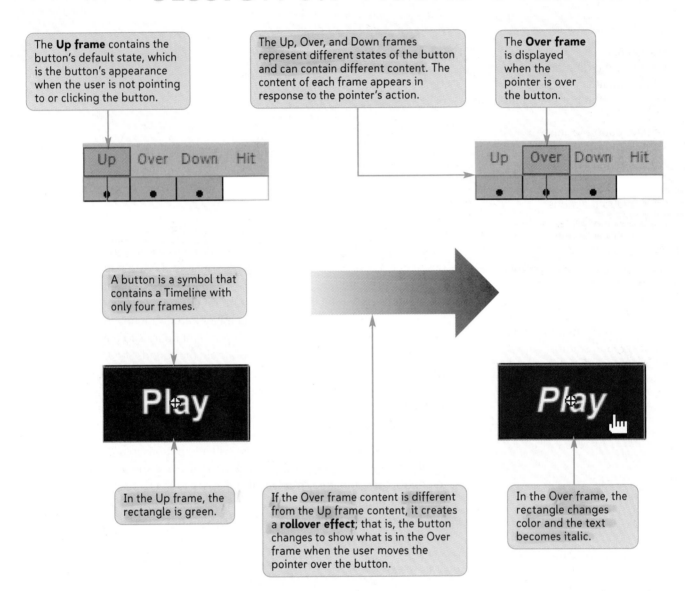

The **Up frame** contains the button's default state, which is the button's appearance when the user is not pointing to or clicking the button.

The Up, Over, and Down frames represent different states of the button and can contain different content. The content of each frame appears in response to the pointer's action.

The **Over frame** is displayed when the pointer is over the button.

A button is a symbol that contains a Timeline with only four frames.

In the Up frame, the rectangle is green.

If the Over frame content is different from the Up frame content, it creates a **rollover effect**; that is, the button changes to show what is in the Over frame when the user moves the pointer over the button.

In the Over frame, the rectangle changes color and the text becomes italic.

BUTTONS AND BUTTON STATES

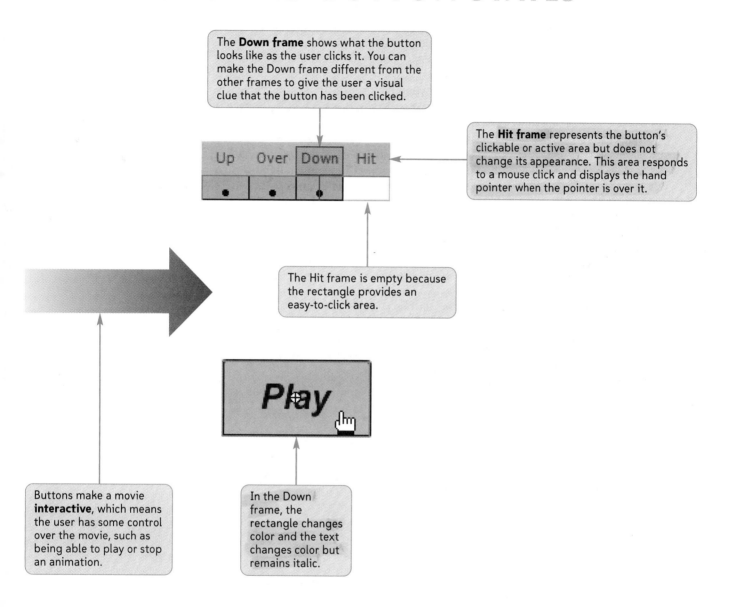

The **Down frame** shows what the button looks like as the user clicks it. You can make the Down frame different from the other frames to give the user a visual clue that the button has been clicked.

The **Hit frame** represents the button's clickable or active area but does not change its appearance. This area responds to a mouse click and displays the hand pointer when the pointer is over it.

The Hit frame is empty because the rectangle provides an easy-to-click area.

Buttons make a movie **interactive**, which means the user has some control over the movie, such as being able to play or stop an animation.

In the Down frame, the rectangle changes color and the text changes color but remains italic.

Adding a Button from the Buttons Library

Published Flash SWF files, also called movies, can include interactive elements. Adding interaction to a movie draws the viewer in because the viewer is able to do more than passively watch the animation. One of the simplest ways to include interactivity is to add buttons that perform an action, such as stopping and starting an animation or muting sound. A button can take many forms, can include sound effects, and can even change appearance or behavior when the user positions the pointer over it or clicks it.

The Buttons library has a variety of predesigned buttons you can use to quickly add a button to a document. The Buttons library is one of the Common Libraries, which store symbols that install with Flash and can be copied to your documents. The library's button symbols can be copied to a document's library and used within that document.

Aly included a background sound in the new banner design, which is shown in Figure 5-1. You will add a button from the Buttons library that allows the user to mute the background sound that you will add later. This way, users can decide whether they want to listen to background sounds when visiting the Web site.

Figure 5-1	Initial banner design

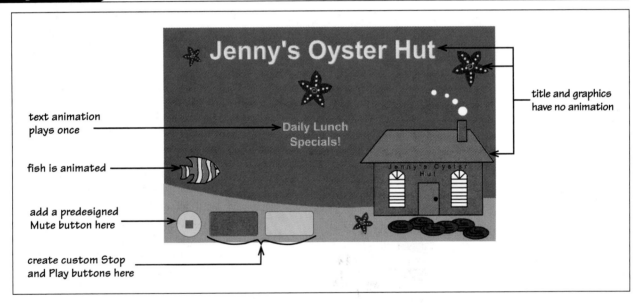

You will add the Mute button to the banner design that Aly started.

To add the flat blue stop button from the Buttons library:

1. Open the **johLunch.fla** file located in the Flash5\Tutorial folder included with your Data Files, and then save the file as **johLunchSpecials.fla** in the same folder.

2. Reset the workspace to the **Essentials** layout, move the playhead to **Frame 1**, and then display the rulers, if necessary. All of the banner contents are visible.

3. In the Timeline, add a new layer above the title layer, and then rename the new layer **buttons**. You will place all the buttons for the banner on the buttons layer.

4. On the Application bar, click **Window**, point to **Common Libraries**, and then click **Buttons**. The Buttons Library panel opens in the middle of the program window. The library contains 277 items organized into folders by categories such as "buttons oval" and "classic buttons."

5. In the Buttons Library panel, scroll down and then double-click the **playback flat** folder icon. The folder expands, displaying a list of buttons.

6. In the playback flat folder, click the **flat blue stop** button to select it. A preview of the button appears at the top of the panel. See Figure 5-2. You want to copy the flat blue stop button into the buttons layer of the document.

Figure 5-2 ▶ Buttons Library panel

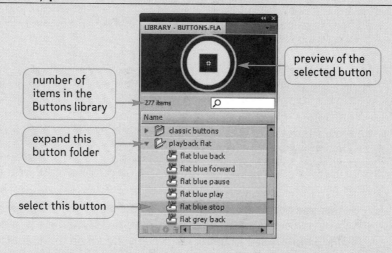

7. In the Timeline, make sure that the buttons layer is still selected, and then drag the **flat blue stop** button from the Buttons Library panel to the lower-left corner of the Stage to create an instance of the button. The flat blue stop button is added to the document's library as a symbol with a button behavior.

8. On the Stage, drag the **flat blue stop** button instance approximately 10 pixels from the left edge of the Stage and approximately 210 pixels from the top of the Stage.

9. On the Buttons Library panel tab, click the **Close** button ⊠. The Buttons library closes.

10. Click the **LIBRARY** tab to open the Library panel, and then expand the **playback flat** folder. The library contains six items, including the flat blue stop button you just added. See Figure 5-3.

Figure 5-3 **Button symbol added to the banner**

flat blue stop button instance positioned on the Stage

new button symbol added to the library

buttons layer added to the Timeline

After you add a button instance to a document, you should test it to be sure that it works as expected. You can do this within the Flash program window by turning on the Enable Simple Buttons command. When you turn on this command, the button exhibits its behavior on the Stage. When you move the pointer over the button, the pointer changes to a hand pointer and the button displays any rollover effects that are part of the button. After you review the button's behavior, you must turn off the Enable Simple Buttons command to select the button instance on the Stage and continue to modify it. You cannot select a button with the hand pointer.

You'll use the Enable Simple Buttons command to test the new button instance.

To view the flat blue stop button's behaviors:

1. On the Application bar, click **Control**, and then click **Enable Simple Buttons**. The command is toggled on so you can test the button.

2. On the Stage, click an empty area away from the button to deselect the button.

3. On the Stage, position the pointer over the flat blue stop button instance. The pointer changes to 🖑, indicating that an action will occur after the button is clicked.

4. Click the **flat blue stop** button. The button changes color to indicate that it was clicked.

Editing a Button Instance

You can edit any button you add from the Buttons library. For example, you can change the contents of the Over frame to change the button's rollover effect, or you can change the contents of the Down frame to change the effect that occurs when the button is clicked. You can also change the colors or graphics in a predesigned button to match the design of the document and to make it look less like a predesigned button. You can even delete the contents in one of the button's frames if you don't want the button to exhibit a certain behavior such as a rollover effect.

PROSKILLS

Decision Making: Including a Button's Hit Frame

Creating a button requires a certain amount of decision making. You first need to evaluate how the button should look and function in all states. The button's appearance in the Up, Over, and Down frames should fit with the design on the movie and be placed in an accessible area of the movie.

You also need to decide whether to use the Hit frame, which is the area of the button the user can roll over or click to perform an action. When a button is a solid shape, such as a rectangle or oval, the button area is easy to click and you can leave the Hit frame empty. When a button consists of text, the user must click the letters in the text to activate the button. This can be difficult, especially if the text is small. To make it easier to click the button, draw a filled shape such as a rectangle to cover the text in the Hit frame. The shape is not visible in the published movie, but it represents the area the user can click to activate the button.

Each button you create should be simple to use. Adding a shape to the Hit frame can help make a button easy to click. Doing so will enhance the user's experience and avoid the frustration that can occur when the button doesn't work as expected.

You will modify the flat blue stop button so that it uses a different color for its Down frame. This frame is displayed when the button is clicked, giving the user visual feedback that the button has been clicked. Because the button is a symbol, you must be in symbol-editing mode to modify it.

To edit the Down frame of the flat blue stop button:

1. In the Library panel, double-click the **flat blue stop** button icon 🔲. The button opens in symbol-editing mode, and its four-frame Timeline appears.

Trouble? If the button does not open in symbol-editing mode, you might be clicking the button instance on the Stage and not the button icon in the library. Try double-clicking the button icon in the library. If the button still doesn't open in symbol-editing mode, on the Application bar, click Control, and then click Enable Simple Buttons to toggle off the command, complete Steps 1 through 6, toggle on the Enable Simple Buttons command, and then continue with Step 7.

2. Increase the magnification level to **400%** to get a better view of the button. See Figure 5-4.

Figure 5-4   **Flat blue stop button in symbol-editing mode**

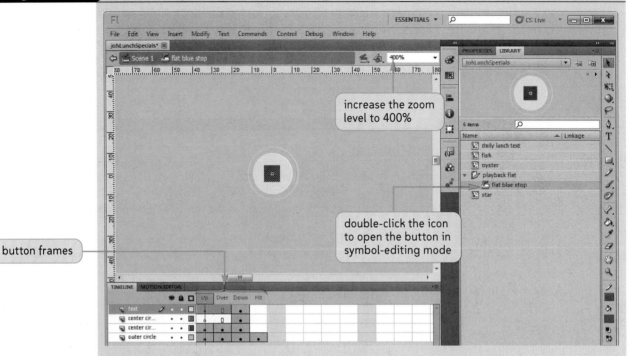

button frames

increase the zoom
level to 400%

double-click the icon
to open the button in
symbol-editing mode

TIP

You can also press the
comma or period key
to move the playhead
backward or forward,
respectively, one frame
at a time.

3. In the Timeline, drag the playhead back and forth between the Up frame and the Down frame to see how the button changes.

4. In the Timeline, click the **Down** frame of the text layer. The small white square in the center of the button is selected, which is indicated by the dot pattern.

5. In the Tools panel, change the fill color of the square to **blue** (#0000FF). See Figure 5-5.

Figure 5-5   **Color changed in the button's Down frame**

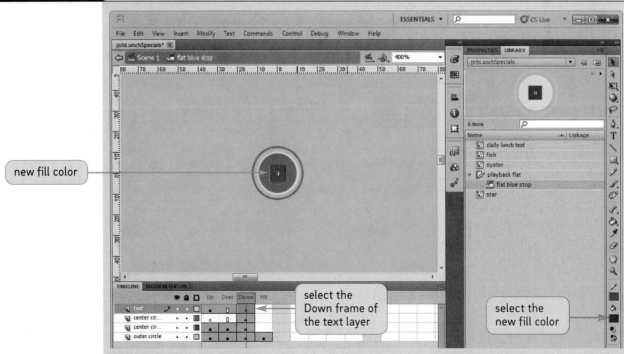

new fill color

select the
Down frame of
the text layer

select the
new fill color

6. On the Edit bar, click the **Scene 1** link to exit symbol-editing mode and return to the document.

7. On the Stage, click the **flat blue stop** button instance. The small gray square in the center of the button turns blue when you click the button instance.

8. On the Application bar, click **Control**, and then click **Enable Simple Buttons**. The Enable Simple Buttons command is toggled off, so you can select the button instance on the Stage.

INSIGHT

Anti-Aliasing Text

To improve readability, Flash uses a rendering engine that provides high-quality, clear text in Flash documents. Anti-aliasing, which is part of the rendering process, smooths the edges of text displayed on the computer screen. Anti-aliasing is especially effective when using small font sizes. When text is selected on the Stage, you can choose a font-rendering method in the Property inspector. Two of the methods available are Anti-alias for animation and Anti-alias for readability. Select Anti-alias for animation when the text will be animated, such as when you apply a motion tween to a text object. This results in a smoother animation. If the text will not be animated, select Anti-alias for readability. This improves the legibility of the text.

Labels often identify the purpose of each button so that it is clear to the user what will happen when a button is clicked. You should add a label either within the button's frames or to an instance of a button on the Stage. You will add text below the flat blue stop button instance on the Stage to label it as the Mute button. This tells the user what happens when the button is clicked. Otherwise, the user may not know what purpose the button serves.

To add text to identify the Mute button instance:

1. Increase the magnification level to **200%**.

2. In the Tools panel, click the **Hand** tool 🖐, and then drag the document to center the button instance on the Stage.

3. In the Tools panel, click the **Text** tool Ｔ. You will set the text properties and add a text block below the button.

4. In the Property inspector, set the font family to **Arial**, set the font style to **Bold**, set the point size to **10**, and then set the text fill color to **black** (#000000).

5. In the Property inspector, if necessary, click the **Anti-alias** button, and then click **Anti-alias for readability**. This anti-aliasing option improves the legibility of the text.

6. On the Stage, add a text block below the button and then type **Mute** in the text block.

7. In the Tools panel, click the **Selection** tool ▶.

8. On the Stage, reposition the text block as shown in Figure 5-6, and then deselect the text block.

TIP

You can also hold down the spacebar to change the pointer to a hand pointer, drag the document on the Stage, and then release the spacebar to return to the previous pointer.

Figure 5-6   Mute label added below the button

add the text block below the button

9. Save the document.

Creating a Custom Button

The buttons in the Buttons library provide many choices to use in documents. For a more professional look, you will often want to create unique buttons that match your project's design. Flash has the tools to create almost any kind of button you need. Buttons can be any shape, such as rectangles and ovals, or even text.

You can convert an existing object on the Stage, such as a rectangle, into a button symbol and then edit the button in symbol-editing mode, creating or modifying the contents for each of the button's four frames as needed. The object on the Stage becomes an instance of the button symbol, and the symbol is added to the library. You can also create a new symbol with a button behavior and then draw the button shape in symbol-editing mode as well as create or modify the contents for each of the button's four frames. The button you created is stored in the document's library, available for you to create instances of the button on the Stage.

REFERENCE

Creating a Custom Button

- On the Stage, create the button's shape, and then select the shape.
- On the Application bar, click Modify, and then click Convert to Symbol.
- Type a name in the Name box, click the Type button, click Button, and then click the OK button.
- Switch to symbol-editing mode, and then modify the contents for each of the button's four frames as needed.

or

- On the Application bar, click Insert, and then click New Symbol.
- Type a name in the Name box, click the Type button, click Button, and then click the OK button.
- Create the button's shape on the Stage.
- Switch to symbol-editing mode, and then modify the contents for each of the button's four frames as needed.

Based on Aly's instructions, you need to create two buttons for the banner. Both buttons are rectangles with rounded corners. However, one button is a Stop button, which the user clicks to stop the animation while it is playing. The second button is a Play button, which the user clicks to start the animation playing at any time. Because the buttons have a similar appearance, you can create the Stop button, and then modify a copy of the Stop button to create the Play button.

To create the Stop button:

TIP

In the Property inspector, click the Reset button to set the corner radius values to zero and lock the values.

1. In the Tools panel, click the **Rectangle** tool ▢ to select it.

2. In the Property inspector, lock the corner radius controls and enter **10** as the Rectangle corner radius. Each corner radius is set to 10.

3. In the Property inspector, set the stroke color to **black** (#000000), set the fill color to **red** (#FF0000), set the stroke height to **2**, and then set the stroke style to **Solid**.

4. In the Timeline, select the **buttons** layer, if necessary.

5. On the Stage to the right of the Mute button, draw a rectangle that is approximately **60** pixels wide and **20** pixels high. See Figure 5-7.

Figure 5-7   **Rectangle button shape**

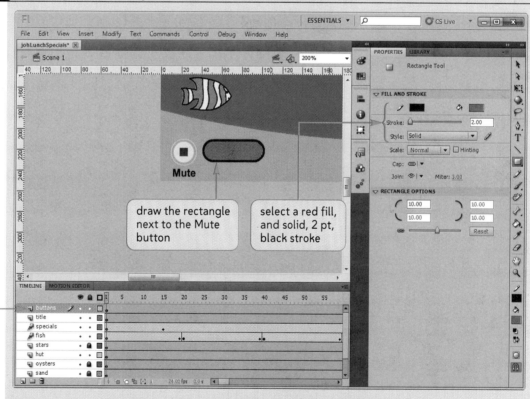

make sure the buttons layer is selected

draw the rectangle next to the Mute button

select a red fill, and solid, 2 pt, black stroke

6. In the Tools panel, click the **Selection** tool ▸ to select it.

7. Select the rectangle, and then convert it to a button symbol named **Stop button**. The new button is added to the document's library, and the selected button instance remains on the Stage.

You will edit the Stop button to add a text label and to create the different states of the button. The Stop button will have a rollover effect so that when the pointer moves over the button, the button's fill color changes from red to a red radial gradient. This provides a visual clue to the user that something will happen if the button is clicked. The button will also move when it is clicked, providing visual feedback that reinforces the user's action. The button's Timeline contains the four frames. The Up frame has a keyframe and contains the rectangle you created for the default state of the button. You will add text to the Up frame and then add keyframes to the Over and Down frames to create the different states of the button. You don't need to add anything to the Hit frame because the rectangle shape provides the clickable, or active, area for the button.

To add text to the Stop button and create the different states of the button:

1. In the Library panel, double-click the **Stop button** icon to open the button in symbol-editing mode, and then increase the magnification level to **200%**. See Figure 5-8.

| Figure 5-8 | Stop button in symbol-editing mode |

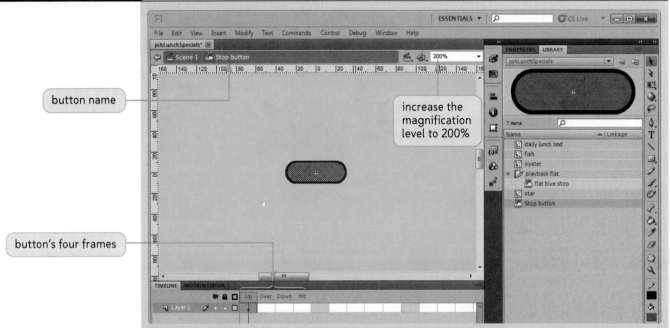

button name

increase the magnification level to 200%

button's four frames

2. In the Tools panel, click the **Text** tool T to select it, and then, if necessary, in the Property inspector, set the font family to **Arial**, set the font style to **Bold**, set the point size to **10**, and set the text fill color to **white** (#FFFFFF).

3. Inside the rectangle, create a text block, and then type **Stop**. You want the text block to be centered inside the rectangle.

4. In the Tools panel, click the **Selection** tool to select it, and then click the **Snap to Objects** button to deselect it.

5. On the Stage, drag the text block so that it is centered inside the rectangle. See Figure 5-9.

Figure 5-9   **Label added to the Stop button**

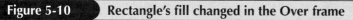

center the text
block within the
rectangle

6. In the Timeline, click the **Over** frame to select it, and then insert a keyframe. The contents of the Up frame are automatically copied to the Over frame. You will change the button's fill color in the Over frame so that the button's color changes when the user moves the pointer over the Stop button.

7. In the Tools panel, change the fill color to the **red radial gradient**, which is the third swatch in the bottom row of the color palette. The red radial gradient replaces the rectangle's red fill. See Figure 5-10.

Figure 5-10   **Rectangle's fill changed in the Over frame**

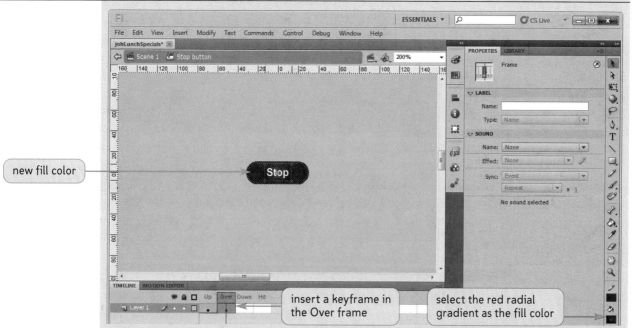

new fill color

insert a keyframe in
the Over frame

select the red radial
gradient as the fill color

8. In the Timeline, click the **Down** frame, and then insert a keyframe. The contents of the Over frame are copied to the Down frame. You need to change the button's position in the Down frame so that when the user clicks the Stop button, the button appears as if it has been pressed and released.

9. With the rectangle and text box still selected, press the ↓ key three times, and then press the → key three times. The rectangle moves three pixels down and three pixels to the right, which will make the button appear to shift when the user clicks it.

▶ **10.** On the Edit bar, click the **Scene 1** link to exit symbol-editing mode and return to the document.

The Stop button and its different states are complete. You'll preview the button instance's behavior on the Stage to make sure the different effects you created appear correctly. You use the Enable Simple Buttons command to preview the effects.

To test the Stop button instance's rollover effects:

▶ **1.** On the Application bar, click **Control**, and then click **Enable Simple Buttons**. The command is toggled on and you can test the button.

▶ **2.** On the Stage, click a blank area to deselect the button, and then move the pointer over the **Stop button** instance. Because of the rollover effect, the button changes color. See Figure 5-11.

| Figure 5-11 | Stop button's rollover effect |

rollover effect changes the button's color

▶ **3.** Click the **Stop button** instance. The button shifts down and right, providing a visual cue that the button was clicked. You are done testing the visual effects of the Stop button.

▶ **4.** On the Application bar, click **Control**, and then click **Enable Simple Buttons**. The command is toggled off, and you can again select the button instances on the Stage.

Copying and Editing a Custom Button

Many times, a Flash document requires two or more buttons that are similar. Rather than creating each button individually, you can create the first button and then copy and modify the button for each of the remaining buttons. This method is faster and helps to ensure consistency in the design of the buttons.

The lunch specials banner requires a Play button, which looks very similar to the Stop button. Instead of creating a new button, you will make a copy of the Stop button, and then modify it to create the Play button.

To create a copy of the Stop button:

1. In the Library panel, right-click the **Stop** button, and then click **Duplicate** on the context menu. The Duplicate Symbol dialog box opens with the duplicate button's name, "Stop button copy," selected. You will rename the button.

2. In the Name box, type **Play button**. The symbol type remains set to Button and the folder in which the Play button symbol is stored remains the root folder of the library.

3. Click the **OK** button. The Duplicate Symbol dialog box closes, and the Play button symbol is added to the document's library. See Figure 5-12.

Figure 5-12 Play button symbol in the library

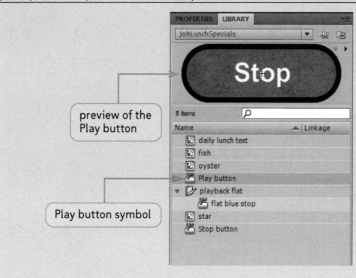

You need to modify the Play button so it is not an exact copy of the Stop button. The Play button will be dark green in its default state and change to a green radial gradient color when the user positions the pointer over the button. As you change the button's colors, check that you have selected the appropriate frame. Also, make sure that you don't change the text block. For example, in the Up frame, you want to change the rectangle's fill color to dark green. So the Up frame must be selected and the text block must be deselected. After you modify the Play button in the document's library, you need to create an instance of the button symbol in the document.

To edit the Play button and add an instance to the Stage:

1. In the Library panel, double-click the **Play button** icon [icon]. The button opens in symbol-editing mode.

2. Increase the magnification level to **200%**. The close-up view of the button makes the button easier to edit.

   For the Up frame, you want to change the rectangle's fill color to dark green, so you need to select the Up frame and deselect the text block.

3. In the Timeline, click the **Up** frame.

4. On the Stage, click a blank area to deselect the rectangle and the text block, and then click the rectangle's fill to select it. Only the rectangle's fill in the Up frame is selected. You will apply a different color to the button.

5. In the Tools panel, set the fill color to **dark green** (#006600). The Play button's fill color changes to dark green, replacing the red color. See Figure 5-13.

Figure 5-13 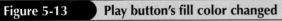 **Play button's fill color changed**

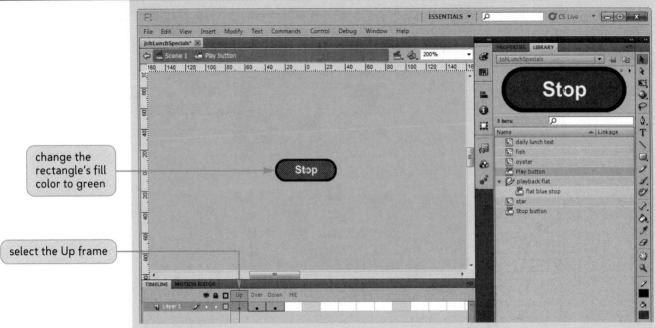

change the rectangle's fill color to green

select the Up frame

6. In the Tools panel, click the **Text** tool T to select it, and then make sure the font family is **Arial**, the font style is **Bold**, the point size is **10**, and the text fill color is **white** (#FFFFFF).

7. On the Stage, click the **Stop** text block to select it, and then change the text to **Play**. The button text changes to reflect the button's purpose.

So far, you changed the color and text of the Up frame. The Over and Down frames still contain the red fill and the Stop text. You will modify those frames next.

8. In the Timeline, click the **Over** frame to select the button.

9. In the Tools panel, click the **Selection** tool ▶ to select it.

10. On the Stage, deselect the button, and then select the rectangle's fill.

11. In the Tools panel, set the fill color to the **green radial gradient**, the fourth gradient swatch in the bottom row of the color palette. The button's fill color changes color. You will change the button's text next.

12. In the Tools panel, click the **Text** tool T to select it, and then, on the Stage, click the **Stop** text block and change the text to **Play**. The Over frame is edited for the Play button.

13. In the Tools panel, click the **Selection** tool ⬚ to select it. See Figure 5-14.

Figure 5-14   Over frame modified

change the text block to "Play"

change the rectangle's fill color to green radial gradient

select the Over frame

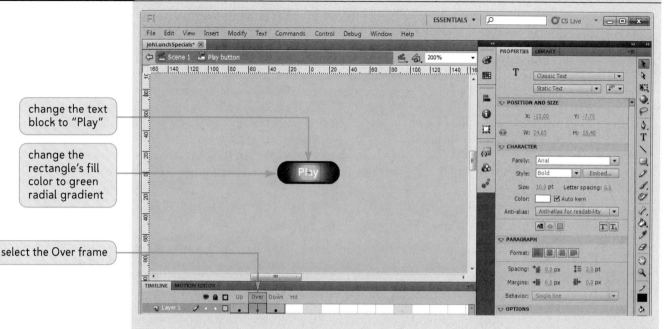

14. In the Timeline, click the **Down** frame, and then repeat Steps 10 through 13. The button changes in the Down frame to the green radial gradient fill and the button text is updated to "Play."

15. On the Edit bar, click the **Scene 1** link to exit symbol-editing mode. The Play button is complete.

16. Drag the **Play** button from the Library panel to the Stage, placing the instance to the right of the Stop button instance. See Figure 5-15.

Figure 5-15   Play button instance added to the document

drag a Play button instance next to the Stop button

finished Play button symbol

Aligning Objects on the Stage

When a document includes multiple objects similar in design, you should align them with each other. If several objects are placed vertically, you should align them by their left or right edges. If the objects are placed horizontally, you should align them by their top or bottom edges. Also, be sure to make the space between the objects the same. Taking the time to align and space objects evenly gives a document a more polished and professional appearance.

The Align panel includes different options to arrange a group of selected objects on the Stage. You can line up selected objects by their edges or centers, and you can also distribute them so that they are evenly spaced. Objects will align with the far left or far right selected object when aligned by their left edges or right edges, respectively. They will align with the highest or lowest selected object when aligned by their top edges or bottom edges, respectively.

The Mute, Stop, and Play buttons should be aligned by their bottom edges. You also need to make sure that they are positioned with an equal amount of space between them.

To align the Mute, Stop, and Play buttons:

1. In the Tools panel, click the **Hand** tool to select it, drag the Stage until the buttons appear in the lower-left corner of the Stage, and then click the **Selection** tool to select it.

2. On the Stage, click the **Mute** button instance, press and hold the **Shift** key, click the **Stop** button instance, click the **Play** button instance, and then release the **Shift** key. All three button instances are selected on the Stage.

3. In the docked panel group, click the **Align** button. The Align panel opens. See Figure 5-16.

> **TIP**
>
> You can also press the Ctrl+K keys to open and close the Align panel.

Figure 5-16   Align panel

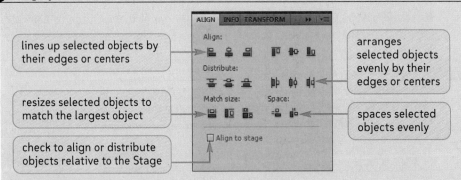

- lines up selected objects by their edges or centers
- arranges selected objects evenly by their edges or centers
- resizes selected objects to match the largest object
- spaces selected objects evenly
- check to align or distribute objects relative to the Stage

4. In the Align panel, click the **Align to stage** check box to remove the check mark, if necessary. The selected objects will align relative to each other and not relative to the Stage.

5. In the Align group, click the **Align bottom edge** button. The three button instances align along their bottom edges.

6. In the Space group, click the **Space evenly horizontally** button. The button instances now have an equal amount of space between them. See Figure 5-17.

Figure 5-17   **Three buttons aligned and evenly spaced**

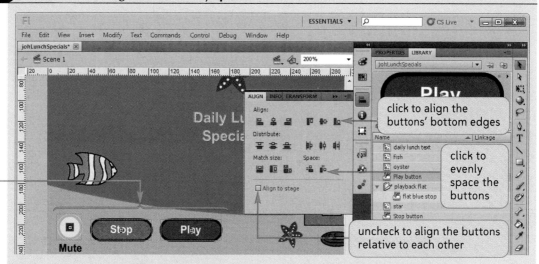

buttons aligned and evenly spaced

click to align the buttons' bottom edges

click to evenly space the buttons

uncheck to align the buttons relative to each other

7. Close the Align panel, click a blank area of the Stage to deselect the buttons, and then save the document.

In this session, you created buttons to mute, stop, and play animation. You added a button from the Buttons library to the banner, and then modified it to create a Mute button. You also created custom buttons for the Stop and Play buttons. You then aligned the buttons along their bottom edges and spaced the buttons evenly. The buttons, though attractive and professional looking, do not control anything yet. You will modify them in the next session to control the banner's animation.

Session 5.1 Quick Check

REVIEW

1. What is a button?
2. Why would you add buttons to a document?
3. How can you add a button from the Buttons library to your document's library?
4. What are the four frames in a button's Timeline?
5. How do you create a rollover effect for a button?
6. How can you test a button in Flash?
7. How can you align several objects on the Stage?

SESSION 5.2 VISUAL OVERVIEW

The Actions toolbox organizes the available actions into categories and subcategories. For example, the Global Functions category contains the Timeline Control category, which contains a list of actions that control the timeline.

You use **ActionScript**, the programming language used in Flash, to create scripts that tell Flash what action to take when a certain event occurs. You work with ActionScript 2.0 in this tutorial.

A **frame label** is a name you assign to a keyframe that appears in the Timeline.

A **loop** is a special animation effect in which a group of frames plays repeatedly by having the playhead return to an earlier frame.

When you select an action, the appropriate statements are added to the script.

In Script Assist mode, you select actions from the Actions toolbox.

An **event handler** tells Flash how to respond to an event.

An **event** is a situation where the user interacts with a button, such as clicking a button with the mouse and then releasing it.

An **action** is an instruction that is used to control a document while its animation is playing.

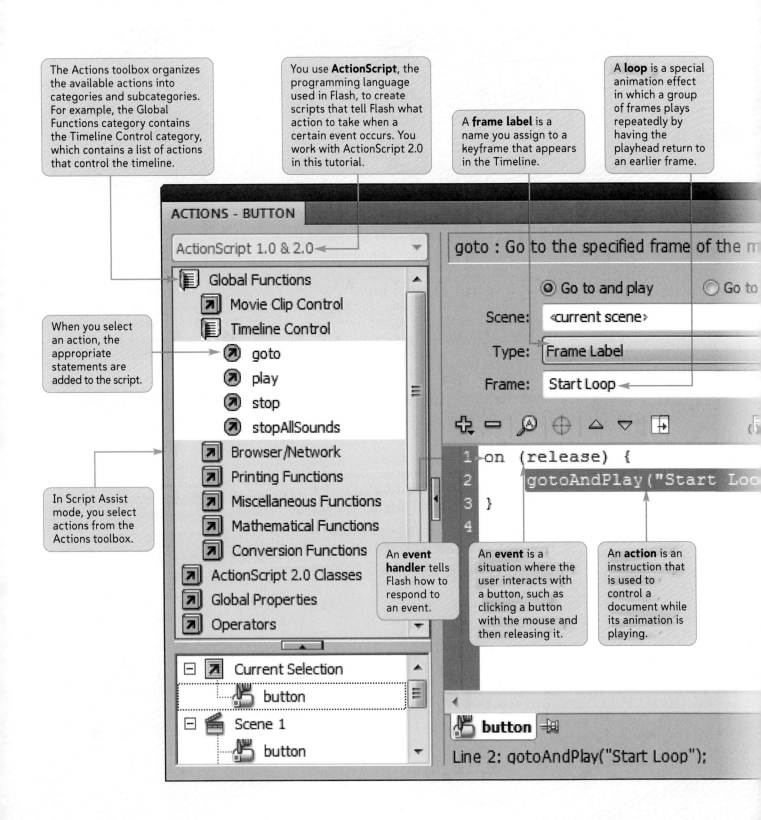

ACTIONS AND SOUNDS

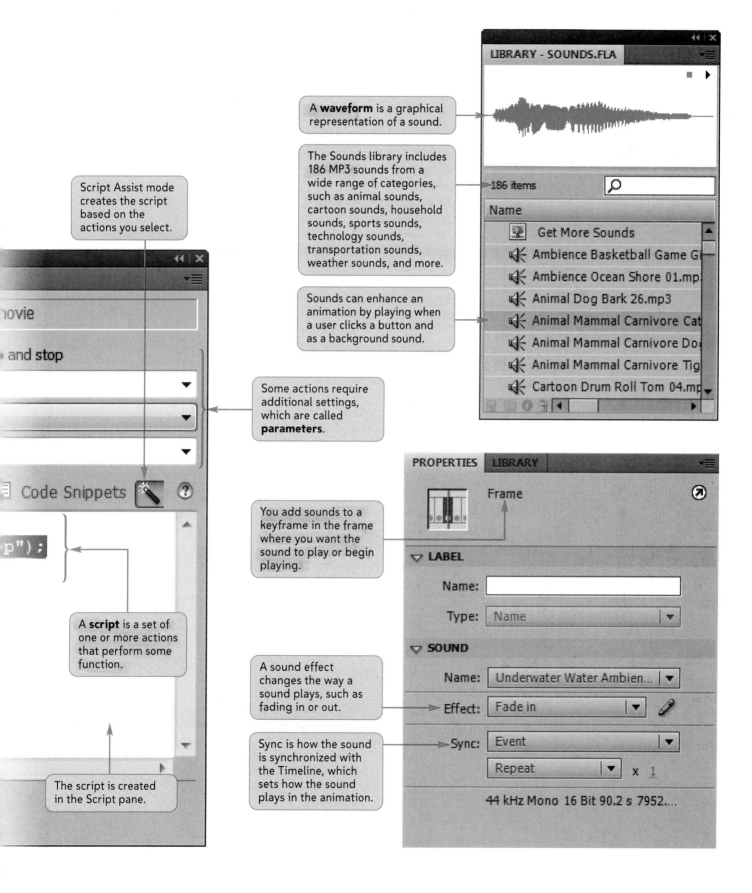

A **waveform** is a graphical representation of a sound.

The Sounds library includes 186 MP3 sounds from a wide range of categories, such as animal sounds, cartoon sounds, household sounds, sports sounds, technology sounds, transportation sounds, weather sounds, and more.

Sounds can enhance an animation by playing when a user clicks a button and as a background sound.

Script Assist mode creates the script based on the actions you select.

Some actions require additional settings, which are called **parameters**.

A **script** is a set of one or more actions that perform some function.

The script is created in the Script pane.

You add sounds to a keyframe in the frame where you want the sound to play or begin playing.

A sound effect changes the way a sound plays, such as fading in or out.

Sync is how the sound is synchronized with the Timeline, which sets how the sound plays in the animation.

LIBRARY - SOUNDS.FLA

186 items

Name

Get More Sounds
Ambience Basketball Game G
Ambience Ocean Shore 01.mp
Animal Dog Bark 26.mp3
Animal Mammal Carnivore Cat
Animal Mammal Carnivore Do
Animal Mammal Carnivore Tig
Cartoon Drum Roll Tom 04.mp

PROPERTIES   LIBRARY

Frame

LABEL

Name:

Type: Name

SOUND

Name: Underwater Water Ambien...

Effect: Fade in

Sync: Event

Repeat   x 1

44 kHz Mono 16 Bit 90.2 s 7952....

Code Snippets

movie

and stop

p")

Understanding Actions

The buttons you added to the banner do not yet allow the user to control the document's animation. When the button is clicked, the animation does not change. The document still plays sequentially, one frame after another, until it reaches the end of the animation. According to Aly's instructions, the buttons should allow the user to stop and play the animation.

TIP

The ActionScript language is very similar to the Web language **JavaScript**, which is used to add interactive elements to Web pages.

To make a button fully functional and interactive, you need to add an action. Actions are part of ActionScript, the programming language used in Flash. Many of the actions in ActionScript are simple and can be used to create basic navigation controls to manage a document's animation. For example, you can add actions that stop or play an animation. You use ActionScript to create scripts that tell Flash what action to take when a certain event occurs. The Flash Player listens for these events, which can be used to trigger, or start, the actions in a script.

The sample script shown in Figure 5-18 contains three lines of code. The first line has the mouse event handler `on`, which tells Flash how to respond to an event. The event handler is followed by the event `release` in parentheses; `release` is an event that occurs when the user clicks and then releases the mouse button. The second line has the action. In this script, the event handler is triggered when the user clicks and then releases the button, causing the stop action to execute. The movie then stops playing. You will add this script to the Stop button instance in the banner.

Figure 5-18   **Sample script**

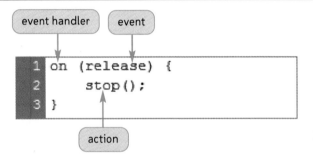

Using the Actions Panel

You do not need to fully understand ActionScript to use its basic actions. Also, you don't need to write scripts from scratch. Instead, you can select actions in the Actions panel and have Flash create the scripts needed for these actions to work in your document.

There are several versions of ActionScript. ActionScript 3.0 is conceptually different from ActionScript 1.0 and 2.0 and supports more complex programming structures. You will work with ActionScript 3.0 in Tutorial 8. In Tutorials 5 through 7, you will use ActionScript 2.0, which is simpler to use when adding basic navigation actions to buttons. Because ActionScript 2.0 is still used on many Web sites, it's beneficial to have a working knowledge of the basic elements of this version.

With ActionScript 2.0, you can use the Actions panel in normal mode or Script Assist mode. In normal mode, you write the scripts yourself, which requires a more in-depth understanding of the ActionScript language. In Script Assist mode, you select an action from the Actions toolbox, and Flash adds the appropriate statements to the script, depending on the action and the object to which the action is applied. Some actions require additional settings, called parameters, which can be selected or entered in the parameters area of the Actions panel.

ActionScript Versions

ActionScript 3.0, the latest version of the Flash programming language, is compliant with industry standards and is based on an international standardized programming language known as ECMAScript. Programs written in ActionScript 3.0 can run up to 10 times faster than those written in previous versions and require Flash Player 9 or higher to run. Using ActionScript 3.0 also makes developing highly complex applications easier. For a novice, learning ActionScript 3.0 can be challenging. However, if you only need to add simple actions to a document, you can still use previous versions of the language such as ActionScript 2.0. ActionScript 2.0 is still in use on many Web sites and is supported by the latest versions of Flash Player. At some point, this version of ActionScript may be deprecated.

During the planning phase, when you determine how and where the user needs to interact with a document, you also need to plan what interactions will be part of the document and where these interactions will be placed. You can add actions to buttons or to frames in the Timeline.

Using the Actions Panel in Script Assist Mode

- In the Actions panel, click the Script Assist button to turn on Script Assist mode.
- If necessary, click the Show/Hide Toolbox button to show the Actions toolbox.
- In the Actions toolbox, click a category to display additional categories or actions.
- Double-click or drag an action to add it to the Script pane.
- To delete an action from the Script pane, select it and then click the Delete (–) button.
- Select or enter values in the parameters section.

Adding Actions to Buttons

Buttons are one way to give the user control over the animation. If you want to use buttons, you need to plan what actions are required to make the buttons functional. You then add the appropriate actions to the button instances on the Stage and not to the button symbol in the library. A button symbol cannot have actions applied to it, only instances of the button. Different instances of the same button symbol can have different actions.

You will add the stop action to the Stop button.

To add the stop action to the Stop button:

1. If you took a break after the previous session, make sure the johLunchSpecials.fla file is open, the workspace is reset to the Essentials layout, the magnification level is 200%, and no elements are selected on the banner.

2. On the Stage, click the **Stop** button instance to select it. You will add the stop action to this button instance.

3. On the Application bar, click **Window**, and then click **Actions**. The Actions panel opens.

4. In the Actions panel, click the **Filter items shown in the Actions toolbox** button, and then click **ActionScript 1.0 & 2.0**, if necessary.

5. In the Actions panel, click the **Build scripts by selecting items from the Actions toolbox** button to select it, if necessary. The parameters area appears in the upper-right corner of the Actions panel and the Action toolbox displays a list of action categories.

6. In the Actions toolbox, click **Global Functions** to display its subcategories, if necessary. The stop action controls the Timeline, so it is located in the Timeline Control category.

7. Click **Timeline Control** to display its actions, if necessary. A list of the available Timeline Control actions appears.

8. Double-click **stop**. The stop action is added to the Stop button instance, and the action and its script are visible in the Script pane. See Figure 5-19.

Figure 5-19   **Stop script created in the Script pane**

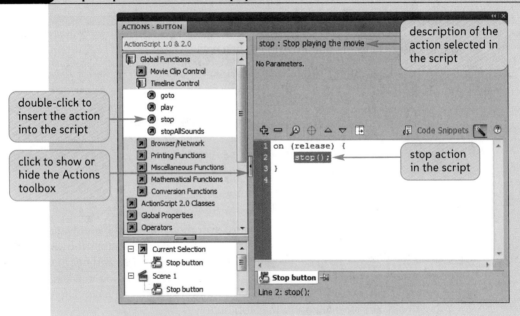

Next, you will add the play action to the Play button. The process is similar, though you first need to select the button instance.

To add the play action to the Play button:

1. In the Actions panel title bar, click the **Collapse to Icons** button to collapse the panel so that you can see the Stage.

2. On the Stage, click the **Play** button instance to select it.

3. On the Actions panel title bar, click the **Expand Panels** button to expand the Actions panel.

4. In the Timeline Control category of the Actions toolbox, double-click **play**. The play action and its script are added to the Play button instance.

5. On the Actions panel title bar, click the **Collapse to Icons** button ◀◀ to collapse the Actions panel.

You have added the appropriate actions to the Stop and Play buttons. Next, you will test them to make sure they work correctly.

To test the Stop and Play button actions:

1. On the Application bar, click **Control**, point to **Test Movie**, and then click **in Flash Professional**. The animation plays in the Flash Player, and the fish swims across the banner.

2. In the Flash Player, click the **Stop** button to stop the animation.

3. Click the **Play** button to restart the animation. The buttons work in Flash Player.

4. Close the Flash Player window, and then save the document.

Adding Actions to Frames

Actions that have been added to buttons are executed when certain events occur, such as when the user clicks the button. Another place where you can add actions is in individual frames. Actions in a frame execute when that particular frame is played. Scripts created for frame actions do not require an event handler. For example, if you add a stop action to a frame, the script contains only one line: `stop();`. Frame actions do not depend on an event to occur. Instead, they execute as soon as the frame they are in is played.

Frame actions can be used to change the sequence in which the frames are played in the Timeline. A movie usually plays sequentially, starting with Frame 1, continuing through the last frame, and then repeating again at Frame 1. However, you can create a special animation effect by playing the frames in a different order. For example, you can create an animation in which a group of frames plays repeatedly by having the playhead return to an earlier frame. This is called a loop. To create a loop, you place an action in the last frame of the group, which causes the animation to go back to the specified frame, as shown in Figure 5-20. The frame action is indicated by a small "a" in the frame—in this case, Frame 50. Every time the last frame is played, the playhead in the Timeline jumps back to Frame 25.

| Figure 5-20 | Loop created with a frame action |

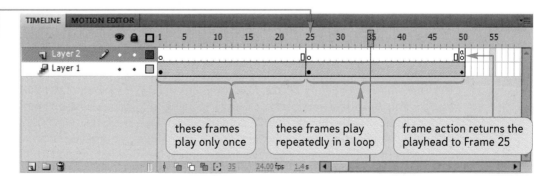

loop starts at Frame 25

these frames play only once

these frames play repeatedly in a loop

frame action returns the playhead to Frame 25

When you need to refer to specific frames in an action, you should use frame labels instead of the frame numbers. A frame label is a name you assign to a keyframe that appears in the Timeline, as shown in Figure 5-21. Remember, a keyframe must be inserted anytime a change occurs in a frame, including the addition of a label. You refer to the frame label in an action the same way you refer to a frame number.

Figure 5-21	Frame label

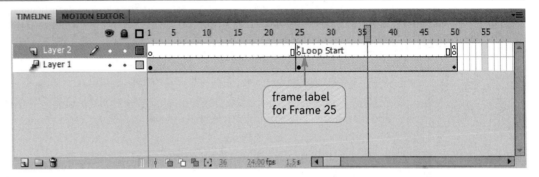

If you use frame numbers in an action and then later add or delete frames from the Timeline, the action might reference the wrong frames. This is because adding or deleting frames causes the subsequent frames to be renumbered. You would then have to update each action that refers to the renumbered frame. However, if you use frame labels, adding or deleting frames does not affect the labels. For example, if you add a frame label to Frame 25 and then delete Frame 14, the label stills exists, but it now exists in Frame 24. The renumbered frames still have the appropriate labels attached to them. Any actions that refer to the frames by their labels work correctly and, therefore, do not have to be changed.

INSIGHT

Organizing Actions Using Layers

To keep documents you create in Flash organized, place frame actions and frame labels on separate layers. Although not required, the separate layers make it easier to keep track of the actions and frames, especially when a document contains more than one action. If you later need to modify other parts of the document, the actions and frame labels are not affected. As a Flash document gets more complex, placing the different elements on separate layers makes it easier to keep track of them.

The lunch specials banner contains three motion tweens to make the fish swim back and forth. It also contains a motion tween that animates the Daily Lunch Specials text block. When the banner is published, the text and fish motion tweens repeat continuously because the movie plays from Frame 1 to Frame 80 and then restarts again at Frame 1.

You need to change the animation sequence so that the text animation plays only once and then remains stationary as the fish continues to swim. This means that the text motion tween should not be repeated. To accomplish this, you need to change the animation sequence so that the animation returns to Frame 25 where the text animation ends instead of Frame 1, and then continues to loop from Frame 25 to Frame 80.

You will add a frame action to the last frame in the document that moves the playhead to Frame 25. The playhead then continues from Frame 25 to Frame 80. As a result, the playhead does not replay the text block's animation, but instead continues with the last two fish motion tweens. Because frames might be added or deleted from the banner at a later date, the frame action in the last frame should refer to a frame label and not to a frame number. At Frame 25, you'll add a frame label that can be referred to by the frame action in Frame 80.

To add a frame label and an action to the banner:

1. In the Timeline, insert a new layer above the buttons layer and name it **actions**, and then insert a new layer above the actions layer and name it **labels**. The labels layer is the current layer.

2. In labels layer, insert a keyframe in Frame 25. Without this keyframe in Frame 25, the label would be added to Frame 1.

3. Make sure the keyframe in Frame 25 of the labels layer is selected.

4. In the Label section of the Property inspector, type **Start Loop** in the Name box, and then press the **Enter** key. The frame label is added to Frame 25 of the labels layer. See Figure 5-22.

Figure 5-22 Keyframe with the frame label

frame label added to the keyframe in Frame 25

5. In the Timeline, insert a keyframe in Frame 80 of the actions layer. You'll add the frame action to this last frame of the actions layer to direct the animation to go back to the Start Loop frame.

6. On the Actions panel title bar, click the **Expand Panels** button to expand the Actions panel.

7. In the Actions toolbox, under the Global Functions category and Timeline Control subcategory, double-click the **goto** action. The action is added to the Script pane.

   The script in the Script pane reads `gotoAndPlay(1);`. This means that the action causes the playhead to go back to Frame 1. You want to change the action so that the playhead goes back to Frame 25 instead of Frame 1, which is where the text block motion tween ends. Rather than referring to a frame number in the script, you will refer to the frame label you added to Frame 25.

8. In the parameters area of the Actions panel, click the **Type** button to display the available types, and then click **Frame Label**.

TIP

You can also click the Add a new item to the script button above the Script pane, point to an action category, and then click an action to add it to the Script pane.

▶ **9.** Click the **Frame** arrow to display the available labels, and then click **Start Loop** to insert it into the script. The Script pane displays `gotoAndPlay("Start Loop");`. The frame action is indicated by a small "a" in Frame 80 of the actions layer in the Timeline. See Figure 5-23.

Figure 5-23   Action added to the frame

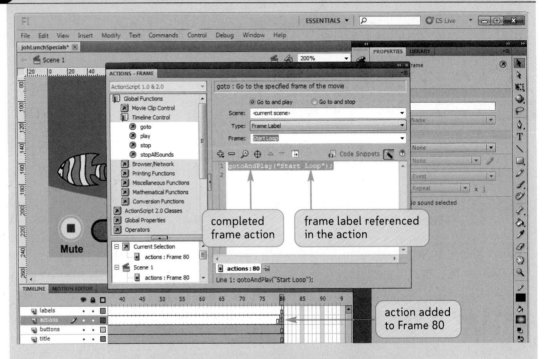

completed frame action

frame label referenced in the action

action added to Frame 80

▶ **10.** On the Actions panel title bar, click the **Close** button ✖ to close the Actions panel.

You should test the frame action you added to make sure the animation plays properly. You can do this within the Flash program window by toggling on the Enable Simple Frame Actions command. When you toggle this command on, frame actions will play when you press the Enter key or use the Play command to test the movie. Testing the frame actions within the Flash program window is another way to test the movie in the Flash Player.

To test the frame action:

▶ **1.** On the Application bar, click **Control**, and then click **Enable Simple Frame Actions**. The command is toggled on and the frame action will play.

▶ **2.** On the Application bar, click **Control**, and then click **Play**. The animation plays on the Stage. When the playhead reaches Frame 80, it goes back and starts again at the frame labeled Start Loop, which is Frame 25. This makes the fish swim back and forth continuously while the text remains stationary.

▶ **3.** On the Application bar, click **Control**, and then click **Stop**. The animation stops.

▶ **4.** On the Application bar, click **Control**, and then click **Enable Simple Frame Actions**. The command is toggled off.

▶ **5.** Save the document.

Using Sounds in a Flash Animation

Flash offers a variety of ways to use sounds. You can add sound effects to instances of buttons to make them more interactive. For example, you can add a sound that plays when a user clicks a button. You can add a sound to a document that plays continuously and that is independent of the Timeline, such as a background sound. You can add a sound that is synchronized with the animation, such as a sound simulating a clap of thunder that coincides with an animation of a lightning bolt. You can also add a sound in the form of a voice narration to supplement the information being displayed in the Web page as text or graphics.

PROSKILLS

Aa

Verbal Communication: Enhancing an Animation with Audio

Adding sound to an animation can have a very powerful effect, bringing another level of interest to a well-designed document. The sound you use can be subtle or loud. It can be lengthy or short, playing throughout the animation, for a short time, or when the user clicks a button. The sound can use special effects, such as fading in and repeating.

Use sound to enhance the animation, keeping in mind that too much sound can overwhelm an animation. You can use sound to add a mood to an animation, such as adding a bubbling background sound to animation showing fish swimming. You can use sound to highlight an element in an animation. For example, a drumroll sound could play when each sale item appears in an animation about an upcoming sale. You can also use sound to draw attention to or provide an audio cue. For instance, a doorbell ding could play when a user clicks a button. However, keep in mind that using the same sound repeatedly will get old really fast.

If you're in doubt about whether the sound or effect will enhance what you have to say, consider leaving it out. Your final animations will be more effective and enjoyable to others.

Finding Sounds for Animations

You can create sounds with a separate sound-editing program and then import the sounds into Flash. Or, you can acquire prerecorded sounds from other sources. Most vendors offer a wide variety of sound effects and music that can be purchased on disk. Sounds are also available for purchase on the Web. You can even download sounds for free from Web sites such as Flash Kit (*www.flashkit.com*). Flash Kit provides a wealth of resources for Flash developers. At its site, shown in Figure 5-24, you can find sounds under Sound FX and under Sound Loops. You can search for sounds using keywords or browse for sounds by category. Sounds listed at the site can also be previewed before being downloaded. Note that the Flash Kit Web site may have been updated or modified since this tutorial was published. Other sites that have free sounds available for download include ccMixter (*ccmixter.org*), The Free Sound Project (*www.freesound.org*), and Incompetech Creative Industries (*www.incompetech.com*).

Figure 5-24 | **Flash Kit Web site**

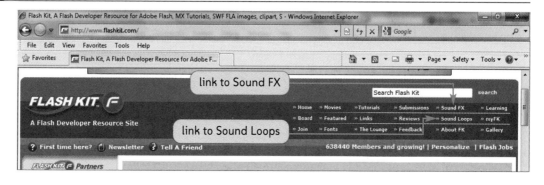

Other Web sites offer sounds for purchase. These Web sites have preproduced sounds from which you can select. They will even create customized sounds for a fee. Two examples of such sites are Royalty Free Music (*www.royaltyfreemusic.com*) and SoundShopper (*www.soundshopper.com*). These sites also have a few sounds that you can download for free to use in personal projects such as a family or hobby Web site.

Licensing Issues When Using Sounds

When acquiring sound files, carefully examine the license agreement that determines how you can use the sounds. Even though a sound file can be downloaded for free, restrictions may apply on how you can use it, especially if you plan to distribute the sound with a document. Look for sounds that are **royalty-free**, which means that no additional usage fees apply when you distribute the sounds with your projects. An alternative to downloading free sounds or purchasing sounds is to record your own. This is not always possible, but if you record a sound file yourself, you don't have to worry about licensing issues.

Adding Sounds to a Document

TIP

A good sound format to use in Flash movies is MP3, which produces small sound files, retains very good sound quality, and is compatible with Windows and Macintosh computers.

You cannot create sounds in Flash. As a result, the sound files you use in documents must first be imported into Flash. To be imported, sounds must be in a file format that is compatible with Flash, such as Windows Waveform (WAV), Audio Interchange File Format (AIFF) used with Macintosh computers, MPEG-3 (MP3) used with both Windows and Macintosh operating systems, and Adobe Soundbooth (ASND) used with both Windows and Macintosh operating systems. The WAV and AIFF formats are not compressed and tend to be larger than MP3 files, which are compressed.

Compressed files are smaller because the parts of the sound data that listeners are not likely to notice have been removed. Compressing a sound file basically means that its size has been reduced without sacrificing too much of the sound quality. You need to pay attention to the size of sound files you add to a Flash document, because they can significantly increase the overall size of the published file, affecting its download time. You can import a WAV file into a document and then compress it to MP3 format within Flash.

Sound files you import are placed in the document's library along with any symbols and buttons already in the library. In the library, a sound is preceded by a sound icon. Also, when you select a sound in the library, its waveform appears in the Library panel's preview box. After you have a sound file in the document's library, you can use it as many times as you need in the document. The additional uses do not further increase the document's file size, because only one copy of the sound is stored in the file.

Before you add a sound to a document, you should create a separate layer for each and name the layer for the sound it contains. This makes the sound easier to identify in the Timeline. Also, sounds can be added only to keyframes in the main Timeline or a button's Timeline. After you add a sound to a keyframe, it plays when the playhead reaches the keyframe.

To import the stamp.wav sound to the library:

1. On the Application bar, click **File**, point to **Import**, and then click **Import to Library**. The Import to Library dialog box opens.

2. Navigate to the **Flash5\Tutorial** folder included with your Data Files, click the **stamp.wav** sound file, and then click the **Open** button. The stamp.wav file is added to the document's library.

3. In the Library panel, click the **stamp.wav** sound. The preview box shows the sound's waveform. See Figure 5-25.

Figure 5-25 **The stamp.wav sound in the Library panel**

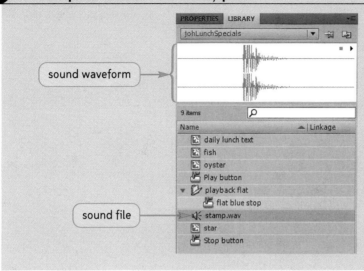

sound waveform

sound file

Adding Sound to a Button

You can add sounds to buttons to make a button more interactive, such as a sound that plays when the user clicks the button or even when the user moves the pointer over the button. You add a sound to a button's Over frame or to its Down frame. A sound added to the Over frame plays when the pointer is moved over the button. A sound placed in the Down frame plays when the button is clicked.

REFERENCE

Adding a Sound to a Button

- Open the button in symbol-editing mode.
- In the button's Timeline, create a new layer for the sound.
- In the frame where the sound will be placed, create a keyframe and then select it.
- In the Sound section of the Property inspector, click the Name button, and then click the sound (or drag the sound from the Library panel to the Stage).

Based on the banner plan, Aly wants you to add a sound effect to the Stop and Play buttons. You'll add a stamp sound to the Down frame, so that it plays when the user clicks the button, providing an audio cue that the button was clicked.

To add the stamp.wav sound effect to the Stop button:

1. On the Stage, double-click the **Stop button** instance. The Stop button opens in symbol-editing mode.

2. In the Timeline, insert a new layer and name the layer **sound**. You will add the stamp.wav sound to the sound layer.

TIP

You can also add a sound to a document by selecting the keyframe where the sound starts and dragging the sound from the Library panel to the Stage.

3. On the sound layer in the Timeline, click the **Down** frame to select it, and then insert a keyframe. You will add the stamp.wav sound to this keyframe.

4. In the Property inspector in the Sound section, click the **Name** button to display the available sounds, and then click **stamp.wav**. The sound is added to the Down frame. See Figure 5-26.

Figure 5-26   **Sound added to the Down frame**

insert a layer for the sound

select the stamp.wav sound

stamp.wav sound waveform appears with the keyframe in the Down frame

5. On the Edit bar, click the **Scene 1** link to return to the document and exit symbol-editing mode.

You should test sounds you add to make sure they work correctly. You can test sounds within the Flash program window after you toggle on the Enable Simple Buttons command. In this case, when clicked, the Stop button should exhibit its rollover effect and play the stamp.wav sound.

To test the sound effect added to the Stop button:

1. On the Application bar, click **Control**, and then click **Enable Simple Buttons**. The command is selected, so clicking the Stop button tests the button rather than selects it.

2. On the Stage, click the **Stop** button. The stamp.wav sound plays.

Trouble? If you don't hear a sound when you click the Stop button, your computer's speakers might be off or at a soft volume. Make sure that the speakers are turned on and the volume is turned up.

3. On the Application bar, click **Control**, and then click **Enable Simple Buttons**. The command is toggled off.

The Play button uses the same stamp.wav sound effect. Because the stamp.wav sound file is already part of the document's library, you don't need to import another copy to the library. You'll use another method to add the sound to the Play button.

To add the stamp.wav sound effect to the Play button:

1. In the Library panel, double-click the **Play button** icon 🖼. The button opens in symbol-editing mode.

2. In the Timeline, insert a new layer and name it **sound**. You will add the sound to this new layer.

3. On the sound layer, click the **Down** frame, and then insert a keyframe.

4. Drag the **stamp.wav** sound from the Library panel onto the Stage. The sound is added to the Down frame.

5. On the Edit bar, click the **Scene 1** link to return to the document.

6. On the Application bar, click **Control**, and then click **Enable Simple Buttons**. You can now test the button by clicking it.

7. On the Stage, click the **Play** button to hear the sound.

8. On the Application bar, click **Control**, and then click **Enable Simple Buttons**. The command is toggled off, and you can again select the button on the Stage.

Adding a Background Sound

The user's experience with a Flash movie can be enhanced by playing a background sound. You add a background sound in a separate layer and in the keyframe where you want the sound to start playing. Again, you can import into Flash a sound you have purchased or recorded yourself. Another option is to use a sound from the Sounds library that comes with Flash. The Sounds library includes 186 MP3 sounds from a wide range of categories, such as animal sounds, cartoon sounds, household sounds, sports sounds, technology sounds, transportation sounds, weather sounds, and more.

Aly wants you to use a bubbling sound as the background sound for the banner. You will import a sound from the Sounds library into your document's library, and then add it as a background sound.

To import a bubbling background sound to the banner:

1. On the Application bar, click **Window**, point to **Common Libraries**, and then click **Sounds**. The Sounds Library panel opens.

2. Scroll about halfway down the alphabetical list of sounds, and then click **Liquid Water Bubble Surfacing And Popping Multiple 02.mp3**. The sound's waveform appears in the preview box along with a Stop button ■ and a Play button ▶. See Figure 5-27.

Figure 5-27   Sounds library

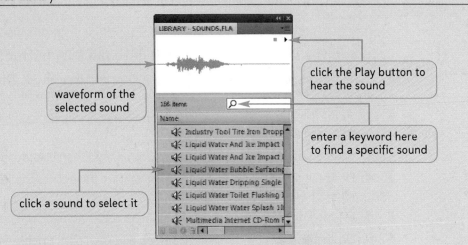

waveform of the selected sound

click the Play button to hear the sound

enter a keyword here to find a specific sound

click a sound to select it

3. In the preview box, click the **Play** button ▶ to play the sound.

4. Click in the search box, type **un** to scroll the alphabetical list of sounds.

5. Click **Underwater Water Ambience Fish Aquarium Filter Bubbles 01.mp3**, and then click the **Play** button ▶. The bubbling sound starts to play and will continue for 90 seconds.

6. In the preview box, click the **Stop** button ■ to end the sound. You'll use this bubbling sound in the animation.

7. Drag **Underwater Water Ambience Fish Aquarium Filter Bubbles 01.mp3** from the Sounds library to the document's library. The sound file is added to the document's library.

8. Close the Sounds Library panel.

9. In the Timeline, insert a new layer above the labels layer, and then name the new layer **sound**. You will add the sound to this layer.

10. In the Timeline, click **Frame 1** of the sound layer.

11. In the Property inspector, click the **Name** button to view the available sounds, and then click **Underwater Water Ambience Fish Aquarium Filter Bubbles 01.mp3**. The sound is added to the sound layer. See Figure 5-28.

Figure 5-28   Bubbling sound waveform in the sound layer

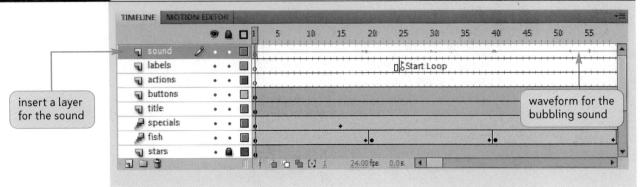

insert a layer for the sound

waveform for the bubbling sound

Changing the Sound Sync Settings

After you have added a sound to a document, you can control the way the sound plays by using the sound settings in the Property inspector. The Sync setting lets you set the sound as an event sound or as a stream sound, which are the two main types of sounds used in Flash. An **event sound** does not play until the entire sound has downloaded completely. Event sounds are not synchronized with the Timeline, which means that after an event sound is started, it continues to play regardless of the Timeline until the entire sound is played or the user takes an action to stop it. A **stream sound** is synchronized with the Timeline and begins playing as soon as enough data has downloaded. Stream sounds are useful when you want the animation in a movie to coincide with the sound.

After an event sound starts, the sound continues to play until it is stopped by the user or finishes. As a result, several instances of the same sound might play at one time. Because event sounds play independently of the Timeline, an event sound starts to play when the playhead reaches the sound's keyframe and continues to play until it is completely finished. If the playhead returns to the keyframe with the sound before the sound has finished playing, another instance of the sound starts playing at the same time. This means that one sound instance overlaps the other.

To prevent sounds from overlapping, you can change the Sync setting of the sound to Start instead of Event. With the Start Sync setting, a new instance of the sound does not start if the first instance of the sound is still playing, preventing the overlap of multiple instances of the same sound. To end a sound that is playing, you can change the Sync setting to Stop. For example, you might want a sound that starts playing in Frame 1 to stop playing in Frame 10. You add the same sound in Frame 1 to Frame 10 but use the Stop Sync setting. Then, when the playhead reaches Frame 10, the sound stops playing.

The Loop and Repeat sound settings let you set how many times a sound replays. If you want a sound to play continuously for a period of time, select Repeat and then specify how many times the sound should play. For example, if you want a sound to play for 2 minutes and the sound is 10 seconds long, enter 12 as the number of times to repeat; the sound will play 12 times for a total of 120 seconds, or 2 minutes. If you want the sound to repeat continuously, select Loop.

The banner's background sound should be an event sound. You'll make this change now.

To change the Sync setting for the background sound:

1. In the Property inspector, in the Sound section, click the **Sync** button, and then click **Event**, if necessary. Event is the default setting and is used when you don't need the sound synchronized with the Timeline.

2. Below the Sync button, click the **Sound loop** button, and then click **Repeat**, if necessary. You will set how many times the sound should repeat.

3. Change the number of times to loop setting to **2**. The information below the Sync settings indicates that the sound is 90.2 seconds long. If the Repeat setting is 0, the sound ends if the user views the animation for more than 90.2 seconds. By changing the Repeat setting to 2, the sound continues playing for 180.4 seconds—approximately 3 minutes. See Figure 5-29.

Figure 5-29	Sound settings in the Property inspector

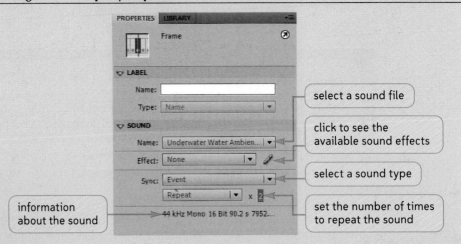

- select a sound file
- click to see the available sound effects
- select a sound type
- information about the sound
- set the number of times to repeat the sound

TIP
You can also test a sound by playing the movie in a Web page.

4. On the Application bar, click **Control**, point to **Test Movie**, and then click **in Flash Professional**. The movie opens in a Flash Player window. The bubbling background sound plays.

5. Close the Flash Player window to return to the document.

Adding Sound Effects

The sound effect setting changes the way a sound plays. The Left channel effect plays the sound only in the left speaker, whereas the Right channel effect plays the sound only in the right speaker. The Fade to right effect starts the sound in the left speaker and gradually moves the sound to the right speaker. The Fade to left effect starts the sound in the right speaker and gradually moves the sound to the left speaker. The Fade in effect gradually increases the sound, whereas the Fade out effect gradually decreases the sound. Finally, the Custom setting allows you to create your own sound effects by adjusting the sound's starting point and controlling its volume.

You will explore the sound effect settings to see how they impact the banner's background sound.

To explore the sound effect settings with the background sound:

1. In the Timeline, click **Frame 1** of the sound layer to select it, if necessary. You will try different sound effects for the sound in this layer.

2. In the Property inspector, click the **Effect** button to display the list of effects, and then click **Fade to right**. The effect is applied to the bubbling background sound.

3. On the Application bar, click **Control**, point to **Test Movie**, and then click **in Flash Professional** to play the movie and hear the background sound.

4. Close the Flash Player window to return to the document.

5. Repeat Steps 2 through 4 to apply and test at least three other sound effect settings.

6. In the Property inspector, click the **Effect** button, and then click **Fade in**. The effect is applied to the background sound and fits well with the overall design and purpose of the banner. Even though the background sound is set to repeat twice, the fade-in effect will not be repeated. The sound effect is applied only when the sound first starts playing.

Although some users may enjoy the background sound, other users may not want to hear it. You want to give the user the option to turn off the sound. You already added a Mute button for this purpose, but you still need to add an action to the button instance to turn off the sound. Using the Actions panel, you will add an action to the Mute button instance that will stop all sounds that are playing when the button is clicked. Subsequent sounds that are played, such as the sound effects you added to the Stop and Play buttons, are not affected because they will not be playing when the Mute button is clicked.

To add an action to mute the background sound:

Be sure to select the button and not the Mute text block.

1. On the Stage, click the **Mute** button to select it.

2. Right-click the selected **Mute** button, and then click **Actions** on the context menu. The Actions panel opens. You'll display the basic Timeline control actions.

3. If necessary, in the Actions toolbox, click **Global Functions**, and then click **Timeline Control**. The action to stop the background sound is in this list.

4. Double-click **stopAllSounds**. The action is selected, and its script is added to the button instance and appears in the Script pane. See Figure 5-30.

Figure 5-30	Stop all sounds script

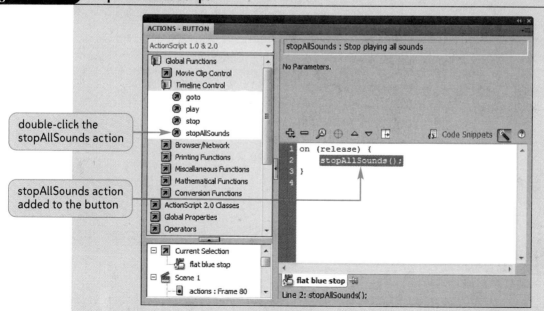

5. Close the Actions panel, and then save the document.

6. On the Application bar, click **Control**, point to **Test Movie**, and then click **in Flash Professional**. The animation and the background sound play in the Flash Player.

> **7.** In the Flash Player window, click the **Mute** button. The sound stops, but the animation continues to play.
>
> **8.** Close the Flash Player window, and then close the document.

You have completed the banner by adding buttons, actions, and sounds. Jenny is pleased with the progress you made on the banner. In this session, you added actions—which are part of ActionScript language—to button instances and to frames on the banner to control the animation, and then you tested those actions. Next, you learned how to acquire sounds, the types of sounds Flash uses, and the different sound file formats that can be imported into documents. You imported sounds to the document's library, added the sounds to buttons and as a background sound, and also changed the sound effect settings. Finally, you added an action to a button to stop all sounds from playing.

Session 5.2 Quick Check

REVIEW

1. What is ActionScript?
2. What are actions?
3. True or False. Actions are added to a button symbol and not to an instance of the symbol.
4. What is an example of an event that triggers an action on a button to execute?
5. Why is it better to refer to a frame label in an action instead of a frame number?
6. Where is sound that you import into a document stored?
7. True or False. Sounds can only be added to keyframes.
8. Describe the two main types of sounds used in a Flash document.

PRACTICE

Review Assignments

Data Files needed for the Review Assignments: specials.fla, ding.wav

Aly asks you to make some changes to another interactive banner she has started for a fish and shrimp specials page. You will modify the Mute button and add an action to stop all sounds when the button is clicked. You will add actions to the Play and Stop buttons to control the animation of the fish and to change the animation for the Fish and Shrimp Specials text block to only play one time. Finally, you will select a different sound effect for the Stop and Play buttons and change the text on the Play button to "Start."

1. Open the **specials.fla** file located in the Flash5\Review folder included with your Data Files, save the document as **fishSpecials.fla** in the same folder, and then reset the workspace to the Essentials layout.
2. Open the Mute button symbol in symbol-editing mode, select the Down frame in Layer 2, change the color of the small black square in the middle of the button to green (#00FF00), and then exit symbol-editing mode.
3. Use the Actions panel in Script Assist mode to add a stopAllSounds action to the Mute button instance.
4. Use the Actions panel in Script Assist mode to add an action to the Play button instance to play the animation when the button is clicked, and then add an action to the Stop button instance to stop the animation when the button is clicked.
5. In the Timeline, insert a new layer above the buttons layer and name it **actions**, and then insert a new layer above the actions layer and name it **labels**.
6. Create a frame label in Frame 20 of the labels layer with the name **Loop**.
7. Use the Actions panel in Script Assist mode to add a gotoAndPlay action to Frame 60 of the actions layer. In the parameters area, set the type to Frame Label and select Loop as the frame.
8. Import the **ding.wav** file located in the Flash5\Review folder to the document's library.
9. Open the Stop button symbol in symbol-editing mode, insert a new layer and name it **sound**, and then add the ding.wav sound to the Down frame so that the sound plays when the button is clicked.
10. Open the Play button symbol in symbol-editing mode, insert a new layer and name it **sound**, and then add the ding.wav sound to the Down frame.
11. Change the text block in the Play button to from Play to **Start**. (*Hint*: Be sure to change the text in each of the button's frames.)
12. Test the banner in the Flash Player to make sure the buttons work and the Fish and Shrimp Specials text block animation plays only one time.
13. Submit the finished files to your instructor.

APPLY

Case Problem 1

Data Files needed for this Case Problem: kprAd.fla, party.wav

Katie's Pet Resort   Katie asks John to create a variation of the advertisement being used on the Katie's Pet Resort Web site. The banner contains text animations that display text blocks with the resort's name, a grand opening sale announcement, and a list of services provided by the resort. John wants you to add sound and two buttons from the Buttons library to the advertisement. The Repeat and Play Song buttons should be similar in design, appear after the first set of animations is finished, and have a short sound effect that plays when the buttons are clicked. Then, you'll add an action to the Repeat button so that it plays the first set of animations, and you'll add an action to the Play Song button so that it plays the second set of animations plus a background sound. Finally, you will add a frame action to the last frame that moves the playhead to the start of the second set of animations. The finished advertisement is shown in Figure 5-31.

Figure 5-31   Completed advertisement for Katie's Pet Resort

1. Open the **kprAd.fla** file located in the Flash5\Case1 folder included with your Data Files, and then save the document as **kprAdWithSound.fla** in the same folder.

2. Insert a new layer above the letters layer folder, name it **buttons**, and then insert a keyframe at Frame 40 of the buttons layer.

3. In the Buttons library, expand the classic buttons folder, and then expand the Circle Buttons folder. Make sure the buttons layer is selected, drag the circle button – previous button to the lower-left corner of the Stage, and then drag the circle button – next button to the right of the first button.

4. Open the circle button – previous button in symbol-editing mode, insert a new layer and name it **sound**, import the **Impact Wood Drop 04.mp3** sound from the Sounds library to the document's library, and then add the sound to the Down frame of the sound layer.

5. Open the circle button – next button in symbol-editing mode, insert a new layer and name it **sound**, add the Impact Wood Drop 04.mp3 sound to this button in its Down frame of the sound layer, and then exit symbol-editing mode.

6. Insert a new layer and name it **labels**, add a frame label in Frame 1 with the text **Start**, and then add a frame label in Frame 40 with the text **Part2**.

7. Insert a new layer and name it **actions**, and then add a stop action at Frame 40 of the actions layer.

8. Add the gotoAndPlay action to the circle button – previous button instance and set the parameters so that the playhead moves to the Start frame, repeating the first set of animations.

9. Add the play action to the circle button – next button instance. This causes the second set of animations to play.

EXPLORE   10. Add a gotoAndStop action at Frame 100 of the actions layer and then set the parameters so that the playhead moves to the Part2 frame. (*Hint*: Double-click the goto action in the Timeline Control category within the Global Functions category in the Actions panel, and then click the Go to and stop option button in the parameters.)

11. Insert a new layer and name it **background sound**.

12. Import the **party.wav** sound file located in the Flash5\Case1 folder included with your Data Files to the document's library, add the party.wav sound to start at Frame 41 of the background sound layer, make its Sync setting Start, and then set the number of times to repeat to 1.

13. Test the revisions to the advertisement. Make sure the buttons work and the sounds play.

14. Submit the finished files to your instructor.

Add sound and interactivity to an animated banner for a zoo.

CHALLENGE

Case Problem 2

Data Files needed for this Case Problem: aczSound.fla, pianoLoop.wav

Alamo City Zoo   Janet asks Alex to develop a new banner for the Alamo City Zoo Web site. She wants the banner to include sound and Alex suggests using buttons to make the banner interactive. You will complete the banner Alex created by adding an action that repeats the movement of the bear and bear paws without repeating the text animations. You will add a button that resembles a bear paw that users can click to start the animation from the beginning. You will also add a background sound to the banner and a sound effect to the button. The finished banner is shown in Figure 5-32.

Figure 5-32   Completed banner for Alamo City Zoo

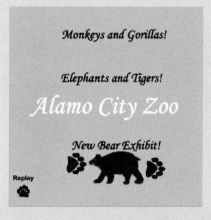

1. Open the **aczSound.fla** file located in the Flash5\Case2 folder included with your Data Files, and then save the document as **aczSoundButtons.fla** in the same folder.

2. In the Timeline, insert a new layer above the paw2 layer and name it **labels**, and then insert a new layer above the labels layer and name it **actions**.

3. In Frame 1 of the labels layer, add the label name **Start**, and then, in Frame 16, add the label name **Loop**. The motion tweens for the bear paws begin in Frame 16.

4. In Frame 60 of the actions layer, add a gotoAndPlay action and set the parameters to make the playhead go to the Loop frame to repeat the last group of frames that keeps the animated bear and bear paws moving.

5. In the Timeline, insert a new layer and name it **music**, and then import the **pianoLoop.wav** sound located in the Flash5\Case2 folder included with your Data Files into the document's library.

6. Add the pianoLoop.wav sound to Frame 10 of the music layer, and then change its Sync setting to Start and have it play one time.

⊕ **EXPLORE**

7. Create a duplicate of the bear paw symbol in the library, name the copy **bear paw button**, and set its type to Button.

8. Open the bear paw button in symbol-editing mode, and then use the Transform panel to set the bear paw's Rotate value to -90 and its width and height to 60%.

9. Add a keyframe in the Over frame, and then change the color of the bear paw's fill to the green color of your choice.

⊕ EXPLORE

⊕ EXPLORE

10. Add a keyframe in the Down frame, and then use the arrow keys to move the bear paw three pixels up and three pixels to the right.

11. Add a keyframe in the Hit frame, and then draw a rectangle that covers the bear paw for the clickable area of the button. (*Hint*: The stroke and fill colors of the rectangle do not show in the animation.)

12. Insert a new layer into the button's Timeline and name it **sound**, import a sound of your choice from the Sounds library, add the sound to the Down frame of the sound layer, and then exit symbol-editing mode. (*Hint*: Play the sound in the Sounds library before importing it to be sure the sound is short and complements the banner.)

13. In the Timeline, insert a new layer and name it **button**. Add an instance of the bear paw button symbol to the banner in the button layer, and then place the instance in an appropriate location on the banner.

14. On the Stage, select the bear paw button instance, if necessary, and then, in the Actions panel, add the gotoAndPlay action and set the parameters so that the action refers to the Start frame. When the button is clicked, the playhead goes to the Start frame and repeats all of the animation.

15. Add a text block above the bear paw button with the text **Replay**. Use a small font size and black text.

16. Test the animation to make sure the background music plays and the button works.

17. Submit the finished files to your instructor.

Add sounds and interactive components to an animated logo for a nursery.

APPLY

Case Problem 3

Data Files needed for this Case Problem: wnLogo.fla, autoLoop.wav

Westcreek Nursery   Alice and her employees have suggested including sound and interactive components to a new animated logo for the Westcreek Nursery Web site. Amanda asks you to add a background sound to the logo as well as adding a Stop button and a Go button, each with a sound effect. You will also add a frame action to control how the animation plays. The wheels should continue to rotate after the Westcreek text shape animation has finished. The Stop button will stop the wheel animations, and the Go button will start the wheel animations. The finished logo is shown in Figure 5-33.

Figure 5-33	**Completed logo for Westcreek Nursery**

1. Open the **wnLogo.fla** file located in the Flash5\Case3 folder included with your Data Files, and then save the file as **wnLogoAnimated.fla** in the same folder.

2. Insert three layers above the flowers layer, and then name the layers **action**, **stopLabel**, and **loopLabel**, respectively.

3. In Frame 19 of the stopLabel layer, add the frame label **Stop**, and then, in Frame 20 of the loopLabel layer, add the frame label **Loop**.

4. In the last frame of the action layer, add an action that makes the playhead go to the frame with the Loop label and continues playing the animation from that frame. The shape tween animation plays one time and the tire animations play repeatedly.

5. Import the **autoLoop.wav** sound located in the Flash5\Case3 folder included with your Data Files to the document's library, insert a new layer and name it **sound**, add the autoLoop.wav sound to Frame 20 of the sound layer, and set it to play three times without overlapping itself.

⊕ **EXPLORE**

6. In Frame 55 of the sound layer, add a keyframe, add the autoLoop.wav sound, and then change the Sync sound setting to Stop.

7. Insert a new button symbol named **Stop button**, and then make the button shape a circle about 20 pixels in diameter with a red fill and black stroke to represent a red stop light.

8. Import a car horn sound of your choice from the Sounds library, and then add the sound to the Stop button's Down frame. (*Hint*: Look in the Transportation sounds, and play the sound before importing it.)

9. Duplicate the Stop button, name the duplicate **Go button**, and then change its fill to green.

10. Insert a new layer in Scene 1 and name it **buttons**.

11. In Frame 19 of the buttons layer, add an instance of the Go button in the lower-right corner of the Stage, and then add an instance of the Stop button above the Go button instance. Align the buttons as needed.

12. Add an action to the Stop button instance that causes the playhead to go to the frame with the Stop label, at which point the animation should stop.

13. Add an action to the Go button instance that causes the playhead to go to the frame with the Loop label and continue to play the animation.

14. Test the logo animation, making sure the sounds play and that the buttons work properly.

15. Submit the finished files to your instructor.

Find sounds, add actions, and create a button to replay an animation.

CREATE

Case Problem 4

Data File needed for this Case Problem: msaButton.fla

Missions Support Association   Brittany wants Anissa to add some interaction with appropriate sounds to enhance the impact of the advertisement banner that Missions Support Association will use to promote the association. You will modify the advertisement banner so that the animation stops when it reaches the last frame. You will also add a button that complements the design to repeat the animation. You will search the Web to find a background sound for the advertisement banner and a sound effect to add to the button. The starting banner is shown in Figure 5-34.

Figure 5-34   Initial banner for Missions Support Association

1. Open the **msaButton.fla** file located in the Flash5\Case4 folder included with your Data Files, and then save the document as **msaButtonSounds.fla** in the same folder.

2. Go to the Flash Kit Web site (*www.flashkit.com*) or another site of your choice that has sound files you can download and use for free. Find two sound files appropriate

for the advertisement. One sound should be short to use as a sound effect on a button. The other should be a sound loop to use as a background sound. Download the sounds to the Flash5\Case4 folder.

3. Import the sound loop you downloaded into the document's library, and then add the sound to the first frame of a sounds layer that you create above the letters layer folder. Add appropriate sound effect, sync, and loop settings.

4. In the last frame of a new actions layer, add a stop action that stops the animation and keeps it from repeating.

5. Duplicate a symbol in the library or create a new symbol using the Button behavior type and the name **repeat button**. (*Hint*: If you duplicate the star shape, you can create an interesting effect by placing the button instance over the star symbol in the last frame of the animation. The button instance will look the same as the star symbol until the pointer is moved over it and the rollover effect changes the way it looks.)

6. In the Over frame of the button, change the button in some way to provide a visual clue that the pointer is over the button.

7. In the Down frame, shift the button so that it is offset by a few pixels, and then add the sound effect you imported.

8. In the last frame of a new buttons layer that you insert in Scene 1, add a repeat button instance in an attractive place on the advertisement banner.

9. Add a play action to the button instance so that the animation will start to play.

10. Test the banner animation, making sure the sounds play and that the button works properly.

11. Submit the finished files to your instructor.

ENDING DATA FILES

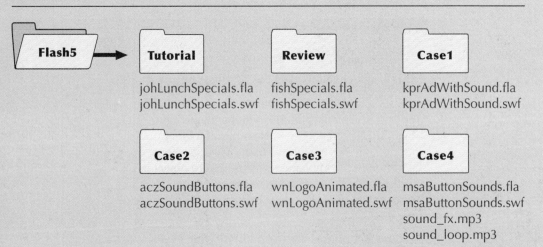

Flash5 →

Tutorial
johLunchSpecials.fla
johLunchSpecials.swf

Review
fishSpecials.fla
fishSpecials.swf

Case1
kprAdWithSound.fla
kprAdWithSound.swf

Case2
aczSoundButtons.fla
aczSoundButtons.swf

Case3
wnLogoAnimated.fla
wnLogoAnimated.swf

Case4
msaButtonSounds.fla
msaButtonSounds.swf
sound_fx.mp3
sound_loop.mp3

OBJECTIVES

Session 6.1
- Import a bitmap graphic
- Change a bitmap graphic's properties
- Create a fade effect animation using bitmaps
- Convert a bitmap graphic to a vector graphic

Session 6.2
- Create, save, and transform a gradient
- Publish a Flash movie
- Create a publish profile
- Export a Flash graphic
- Insert a Flash movie into a Web page

Creating Special Effects and Publishing Files

Working with Bitmaps and Gradients, and Publishing Flash Files

Case | *Admiral Web Design*

Jenny wants to update the Jenny's Oyster Hut Web site with a new banner for the home page and a new logo throughout the Web site. During the planning meeting, Aly suggests using photos of sample seafood items as part of an animation. Chris suggests using a gradient for the banner's background. The banner will include an animation where two photos of seafood dishes fade in and out within a mask. The banner's background will be a radial gradient that is a blend of a light blue color that transitions into a dark gray color. The gradient's light blue center will be positioned behind the seafood animation, giving the photos a highlighted effect. The logo will show the restaurant name over a picture of a lobster in the background.

As you complete the banner and create the logo, you will add bitmaps and create gradients. Then, you will prepare the final movies for use on the restaurant's Web site. You will explore the various export and publish options available with Flash, and then incorporate the banner and logo into an existing Web page.

STARTING DATA FILES

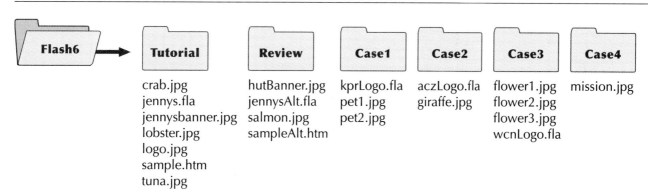

Flash6 →	Tutorial	Review	Case1	Case2	Case3	Case4
	crab.jpg	hutBanner.jpg	kprLogo.fla	aczLogo.fla	flower1.jpg	mission.jpg
	jennys.fla	jennysAlt.fla	pet1.jpg	giraffe.jpg	flower2.jpg	
	jennysbanner.jpg	salmon.jpg	pet2.jpg		flower3.jpg	
	lobster.jpg	sampleAlt.htm			wcnLogo.fla	
	logo.jpg					
	sample.htm					
	tuna.jpg					

SESSION 6.1 VISUAL OVERVIEW

The contents of the masked layer that are covered by the filled shape in the mask layer appear when the movie is played.

A bitmap in the document's library is not a symbol, although the copies you drag onto the Stage are called instances.

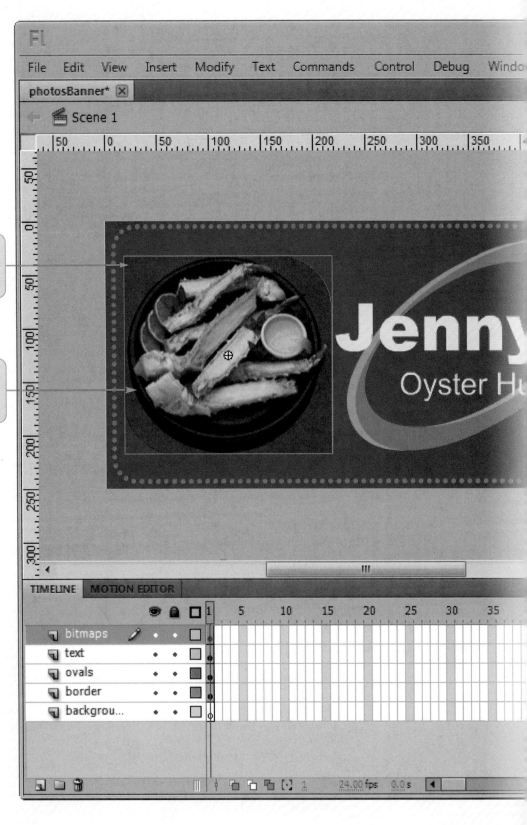

BITMAP GRAPHICS

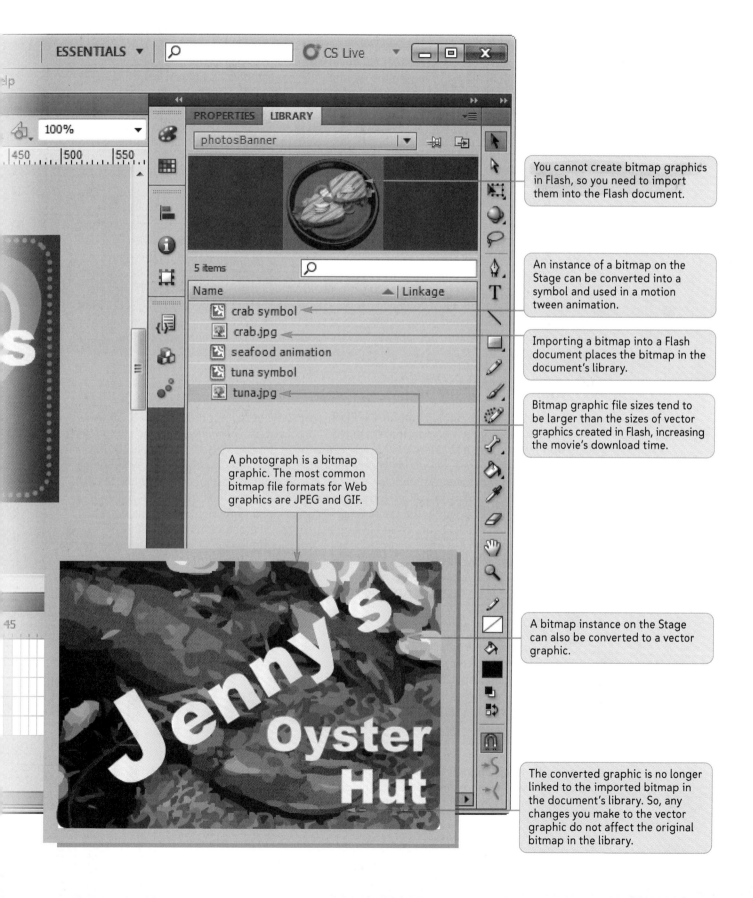

You cannot create bitmap graphics in Flash, so you need to import them into the Flash document.

An instance of a bitmap on the Stage can be converted into a symbol and used in a motion tween animation.

Importing a bitmap into a Flash document places the bitmap in the document's library.

Bitmap graphic file sizes tend to be larger than the sizes of vector graphics created in Flash, increasing the movie's download time.

A photograph is a bitmap graphic. The most common bitmap file formats for Web graphics are JPEG and GIF.

A bitmap instance on the Stage can also be converted to a vector graphic.

The converted graphic is no longer linked to the imported bitmap in the document's library. So, any changes you make to the vector graphic do not affect the original bitmap in the library.

Working with Bitmaps

The Jenny's Oyster Hut banner and logo that you will create will use photographs. A photograph is a bitmap graphic. Recall that a bitmap graphic is stored as a row-by-row list of every pixel in the graphic, along with each pixel's color. The most common bitmap file formats for Web graphics are JPEG and GIF. Bitmap graphics are different from vector graphics, which are stored as mathematical instructions that describe the color, outline, and position of all the shapes in the graphic. Bitmap graphics do not resize well, and their file sizes tend to be larger than the vector graphics created in Flash. As a result, using bitmaps in a Flash movie increases the movie's download time. However, file size and download time alone should not keep you from using bitmap graphics in Flash documents. Just make sure that the graphic really is needed in the document's design.

INSIGHT

Using Bitmaps in Flash

You cannot easily edit bitmap graphics within Flash, so you should use an image editing program such as Adobe Photoshop or Adobe Fireworks to edit and resize the bitmaps before importing them into a Flash document. Before using a bitmap graphic in Flash, optimize it by reducing its size while maintaining its quality. Reducing the file size of the bitmap minimizes its impact on the download time of the Flash document. If possible, also consider the target audience and the types of Internet connections they have. Flash documents targeted at users with slower connections should include few, if any, bitmap graphics, even if the bitmap graphics can greatly enhance a document's design.

Importing Bitmaps

You cannot create bitmap graphics in Flash, so you need to import them into Flash. After you have imported a bitmap into Flash, you can change its properties such as compression settings, use it in animations, and even convert it into a vector graphic. Importing a bitmap into a Flash document places the bitmap in the document's library. After the bitmap is in the document's library, you can create multiple instances of it on the Stage. No matter how many instances you create, only one copy of the bitmap is stored with the Flash file. A bitmap in the document's library is not a symbol, although the copies you drag onto the Stage are called instances. An instance of a bitmap on the Stage can be converted into a symbol that can be used in a motion tween animation. This symbol is stored in the document's library separately from the original bitmap.

REFERENCE

Importing a Bitmap

- On the Application bar, click File, point to Import, and then click Import to Stage or Import to Library.
- In the Import or Import to Library dialog box, navigate to the location of the bitmap file, and then click the bitmap file in the file list.
- Click the Open button.

The new Jenny's Oyster Hut banner, shown in the sketch provided by Aly in Figure 6-1, uses an animation that includes two photos of seafood. You need to import these photos into the library of the partially completed banner that Aly has created.

Figure 6-1	Sketch for the new Jenny's Oyster Hut banner

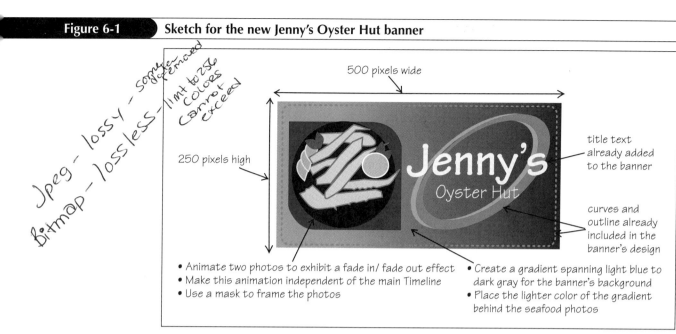

Jpeg - lossy - some detail removed
Bitmap - lossless - limit to 256 colors cannot exceed

500 pixels wide

250 pixels high

title text already added to the banner

curves and outline already included in the banner's design

• Animate two photos to exhibit a fade in/ fade out effect
• Make this animation independent of the main Timeline
• Use a mask to frame the photos

• Create a gradient spanning light blue to dark gray for the banner's background
• Place the lighter color of the gradient behind the seafood photos

You'll import the photos into the banner's library.

To import the seafood bitmap images into the banner document:

1. Open the **jennys.fla** file located in the Flash6\Tutorial folder included with your Data Files, save the file as **photosBanner.fla** in the same folder, reset the workspace to the **Essentials** layout, and then display the rulers, if necessary.

2. On the Application bar, click **File**, point to **Import**, and then click **Import to Library**. The Import to Library dialog box opens.

3. Click the **All Formats** button, and then click **All Image Formats**.

4. Navigate to the **Flash6\Tutorial** folder, click the **crab.jpg** file, press and hold the **Ctrl** key, click the **tuna.jpg** file, and then release the **Ctrl** key.

5. Click the **Open** button. The two bitmap files are imported into the document's library and appear in the Library panel.

6. In the Library panel, click the **crab.jpg** bitmap. The crab.jpg picture appears in the preview area. See Figure 6-2.

Figure 6-2	Bitmaps in the Library panel

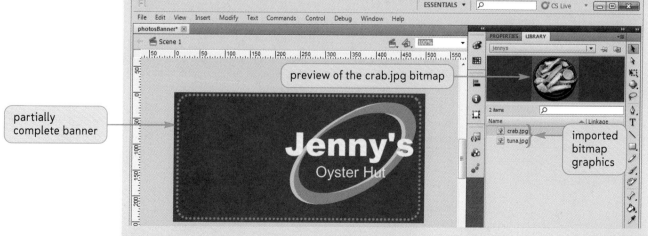

preview of the crab.jpg bitmap

imported bitmap graphics

partially complete banner

▶ **7.** In the Library panel, click the **tuna.jpg** bitmap. The tuna.jpg picture appears in the preview area.

Setting a Bitmap's Properties

You can modify a bitmap's properties by changing the bitmap's name, updating the bitmap if the original file has been modified, and even changing its compression settings. **Compression** takes away some of a file's data to reduce its size. You can compress a bitmap yet maintain its quality. **Lossy compression**, used by the JPEG format, removes some of the original data in the image to achieve a smaller file size. **Lossless compression**, used by the GIF format, retains all the original data in the image but is limited to 256 colors. JPEG uses a compression method designed for compressing full-color images such as photographs. Although JPEG removes some of the image data, it stores full-color information, resulting in very good image quality. The GIF and PNG formats are better for images with solid areas of color such as logos and drawn shapes. The PNG format is not as widely used as the GIF format, but is supported by most current Web browsers.

PROSKILLS

Problem Solving: Finding the Right Compression

A bitmap file in the JPEG file format is already compressed. Compressing it further in Flash can degrade the quality of the picture, so you need to balance how much compression to apply to a bitmap with the picture's quality. This requires some problem solving.

First, think about how you plan to use the bitmap. Keep in mind that pictures in a Flash movie don't always have to be of the highest quality, especially if they are small and are used as part of a larger graphic. Applying additional compression to bitmaps in Flash reduces the overall size of the final movie.

Trial and error is a good way to find the right compression for a particular bitmap. Experiment with several quality values and compare how the picture quality is affected. Select the value that maintains the picture quality needed for the particular design while still compressing the bitmap as much as possible.

The bitmap properties available depend on the bitmap's file type. Figure 6-3 describes the different properties, which are available in the Bitmap Properties dialog box.

Figure 6-3   **Bitmap properties**

Property	Description
Name	Specifies the name of the bitmap in the document's library.
Smoothing	Offers the option to smooth the edges of the bitmap so they do not appear jagged.
Compression	Specifies the type of compression: Lossless (PNG/GIF) is for bitmaps in the PNG or GIF file formats or that have large areas of single colors. Photo (JPEG) is for bitmaps with many colors or many color transitions, such as photographs.
Quality	Specifies the amount of compression to apply to the bitmap, ranging from 0 (most compression) to 100 (least compression). The more compression that is applied, the more data that is lost. You can also keep the quality setting of the original bitmap for JPEGs, or use the quality value set for the whole document for PNGs or GIFs.

Before placing the bitmaps in the banner, Aly wants you to minimize the size of the final movie by changing the compression settings for each bitmap. You will reduce the JPEG quality to decrease the overall size of the final movie, and then check what effect the new JPEG quality value will have on the pictures.

To change the crab.jpg and tuna.jpg bitmap properties:

1. In the Library panel, click the **crab.jpg** bitmap, and then click the **Properties** button ⓘ at the bottom of the panel. The Bitmap Properties dialog box opens.

TIP

Drag the preview image in the Bitmap Properties dialog box to see other areas of the bitmap.

2. Right-click the **bitmap preview** in the upper-left corner, and then click **Zoom In** on the context menu. The preview image is larger, so you can more easily see the effects of changes to the bitmap's properties.

3. In the Quality section, click the **Custom** option button. You want to adjust the bitmap's compression rather than use its imported compression data. The Custom box shows the default value of 50.

4. In the Custom box, double-click **50**, and then type **20**.

5. Click the **Test** button. The preview shows the bitmap with the new compression settings. With the lower quality value, the picture quality is poor. Some colors have changed significantly, and the picture has less detail, as evidenced by the small blocks that appear throughout the picture. See Figure 6-4.

Figure 6-4 **Bitmap Properties dialog box**

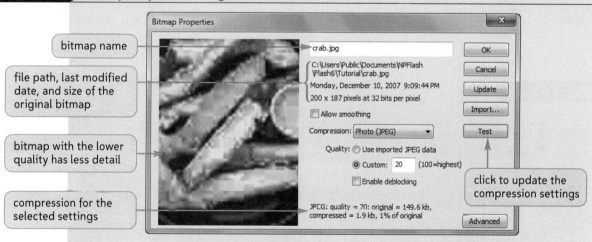

bitmap name

file path, last modified date, and size of the original bitmap

bitmap with the lower quality has less detail

compression for the selected settings

click to update the compression settings

6. In the Custom box, type **80** and then click the **Test** button. The compressed bitmap is smaller than the original file while maintaining the picture quality.

7. Click the **OK** button to accept the compression value.

8. In the Library panel, click the **tuna.jpg** bitmap, and then click the **Properties** button ⓘ. The Bitmap Properties dialog box opens.

9. In the Quality section, click the **Custom** option button, type **80** in the Custom box, and then click the **Test** button. The preview of the tuna.jpg picture looks fine with this setting.

10. Click the **OK** button to accept the compression value.

Animating Bitmaps

You animate an imported bitmap the same way you animate any other object. For instance, you can create a motion tween that causes the bitmap to move, rotate, change in size (scale), or fade in or out. To animate a bitmap in a motion tween, you first need to convert the bitmap instance on the Stage to a symbol.

Aly's instructions for the banner indicate that the crab.jpg and tuna.jpg bitmaps are part of an animation where one bitmap appears and then fades away, while the second bitmap fades in over the first. To accomplish the fade effect, you change the alpha amount for each instance. The **alpha amount** controls the transparency of an image. The alpha amount is a percentage from 0 to 100. An alpha amount of 0% makes the object completely transparent; an alpha amount of 100% makes the object completely opaque, which means it has no transparency. A motion tween that starts the object at an alpha amount of 100% and changes it at the end of the tween to 0% makes the object appear to fade out of view. You reverse the amounts to make the object appear to fade into view. Because this animation should be independent of any other animation that may be added to the banner, you will create a movie clip symbol that contains the seafood pictures animation within its own Timeline, independent of the main document's Timeline.

To create the movie clip symbol with the seafood pictures:

1. Create a new movie clip symbol named **seafood animation**. The new movie clip symbol opens in symbol-editing mode.

2. Drag an instance of the **crab.jpg** bitmap from the Library panel to the Stage.

3. Open the Info panel, click the **Registration/Transformation point** button 🔲 to select it, if necessary, and then change the X and Y coordinates to **0**. The selected bitmap instance is centered within the editing window. See Figure 6-5.

Figure 6-5	The crag.jpg bitmap instance centered

select the center point of the Registration icon

centered bitmap

set the X and Y coordinates to 0

4. Convert the **crab.jpg** bitmap instance on the Stage to a movie clip symbol named **crab symbol**, and then click the center registration point in the Registration icon 🔳. The registration point specifies what part of the symbol is used for alignment. Because the crab.jpg and the tuna.jpg images need to be in the same position on the Stage, you specify a point in the crab image to use for alignment when you position the tuna image. See Figure 6-6.

Figure 6-6 **Convert to Symbol dialog box**

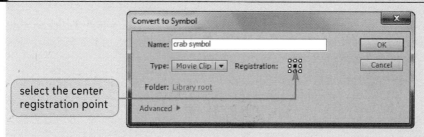

select the center registration point

5. Click the **OK** button. The crab symbol is created, and you can use it in a motion tween animation.

6. Close the Info panel, if necessary.

In the animation, the crab.jpg bitmap fades out of view after a period of time, and then the tuna.jpg bitmap fades in. Aly provides the sketch, shown in Figure 6-7, that outlines how the animation should occur. Based on the sketch, the animation of the pictures takes place over six seconds. During the first two seconds, the crab.jpg picture is displayed. During the third second, the crab.jpg picture fades out as the tuna.jpg picture fades in. Then, during the next two seconds, the tuna.jpg picture is displayed. Finally, during the last second, the tuna.jpg picture fades out and the crab.jpg picture fades back in. Because the frame rate is 24 frames per second, each second requires 24 frames. Converting these time specifications to frame numbers means that you need keyframes at Frames 1, 48, 72, 120, and 144. These are the frames where a change occurs from the previous frames.

Figure 6-7 **Fade animation plan**

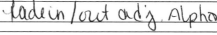

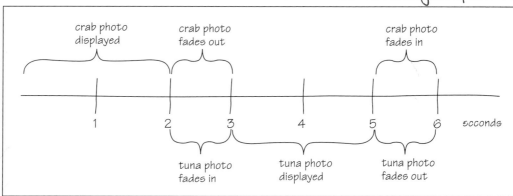

You'll insert keyframes for the crab animation, create a motion tween, and then set the alpha amounts for the crab instance to control the transparency, which creates the fade-in and fade-out effects.

To create the crab animation:

1. In the Timeline, rename Layer 1 as **crab**, select **Frame 1** of the crab layer, and then select the **crab symbol** instance on the Stage.

2. In the Color Effect section of the Property inspector, click the **Style** button, and then click **Alpha**. The Alpha setting appears in the Property inspector.

3. If necessary, drag the **Alpha** slider to the right until **100** appears in the % box. The crab symbol instance is fully opaque with the alpha amount set to 100%.

 4. In the crab layer, insert a keyframe at **Frame 48**, select the **crab symbol** instance on the Stage, and then, in the Color Effect section of the Property inspector, make sure the alpha amount remains set to 100%.

 5. In the Timeline, insert a keyframe at **Frame 72**, select the **crab symbol** instance on the Stage, and then, in the Property inspector, set the alpha amount to **0%**.

 6. In the Timeline, create a ~~motion~~ *Classic* tween between Frame 48 and Frame 72.

 7. In the Timeline, right-click **Frame 71**, point to **Insert Keyframe**, and then click **Color**. A property keyframe is added to the motion tween, so you can set the ending alpha amount for the motion tween.

 8. Select the **crab symbol** instance on the Stage, and then, in the Color Effect section of the Property inspector, set the alpha amount to **0%**. The crab symbol instance is transparent. See Figure 6-8.

Figure 6-8   **Transparent crab symbol instance**

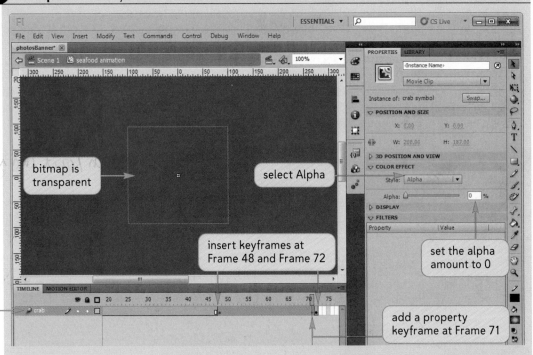

9. Move the playhead to **Frame 1**, and then play the animation. As the motion tween plays, the crab symbol instance is displayed and then fades out. See Figure 6-9.

Figure 6-9 Crab bitmap animation

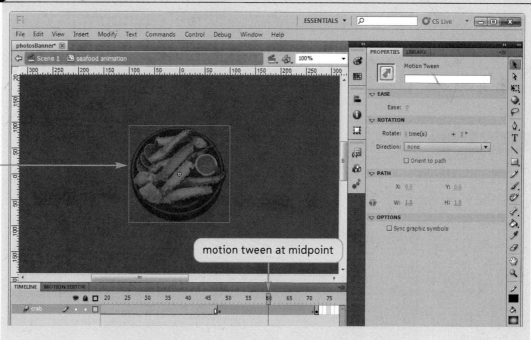

crab bitmap fades out during the motion tween

motion tween at midpoint

The crab photo is supposed to fade out and then fade back into view at the end of the animation. You will create another motion tween to fade in the crab.

To create a motion tween to fade in the crab symbol instance:

1. In the Timeline, insert keyframes at **Frame 120** and **Frame 144**, and then create a motion tween between Frame 120 and Frame 144.

2. In the Timeline, right-click **Frame 143**, point to **Insert Keyframe**, and then click **Color**. A property keyframe is added to the motion tween, so you can set the ending alpha amount for the motion tween.

3. Select the **crab symbol** instance on the Stage, and then, in the Property inspector, set the alpha amount to **100%**. The motion tween is created to fade in the crab symbol instance.

4. In the Timeline, click **Frame 144**, select the **crab symbol** instance on the Stage, and then, in the Property inspector, set the alpha amount to **100%**. The crab symbol instance becomes fully visible for the last frame of the animation.

5. Move the playhead to **Frame 1**, and then play the animation. The crab symbol instance is displayed, fades out, and then fades back in at the end of the animation.

You will follow a similar process to make the tuna.jpg bitmap fade in as the crab.jpg bitmap fades out. The tuna.jpg bitmap will then fade out as the crab.jpg bitmap fades back in. You'll place the tuna animation on a separate layer.

To add the tuna.jpg bitmap to the animation:

1. In the Timeline, insert a new layer, name the layer **tuna**, and then insert a keyframe at **Frame 48**.

2. Drag an instance of the **tuna.jpg** bitmap from the Library panel to the center of the Stage.

3. Open the Info panel, set the X and Y values to **0**, and then close the Info panel. The tuna.jpg bitmap instance is centered on the Stage. See Figure 6-10.

Figure 6-10 The tuna.jpg bitmap added to the tuna layer

center the tuna bitmap on the Stage

add a keyframe in Frame 48

insert the tuna layer

4. Convert the tuna.jpg bitmap on the Stage to a movie clip symbol named **tuna symbol** with the center registration point selected in the Registration icon.

5. In the Timeline, insert a keyframe at **Frame 72** of the tuna layer, select the **tuna symbol** instance on the Stage, and then set the alpha amount to **100%**. The tuna symbol instance becomes fully visible in this frame.

6. In the Timeline, click **Frame 48** of the tuna layer, select the **tuna symbol** instance on the Stage, and then, in the Property inspector, set the alpha amount to **0%**. The tuna symbol instance is transparent, allowing the crab symbol instance to show through.

7. In the Timeline, create a motion tween at **Frame 48** of the tuna layer.

8. In the Timeline, right-click **Frame 71** of the tuna layer, point to **Insert Keyframe**, and then click **Color**. A property keyframe is added to the motion tween, so you can set the ending alpha amount for the motion tween.

9. Select the **tuna symbol** instance on the Stage, and then, in the Property inspector, set the alpha amount to **100%**. The motion tween is created to fade in the tuna symbol instance.

10. In the Timeline, scrub the playhead between Frame 48 and Frame 72 to preview how the tuna picture fades in while the crab picture fades out. See Figure 6-11.

Figure 6-11 **Motion tweens fade the pictures**

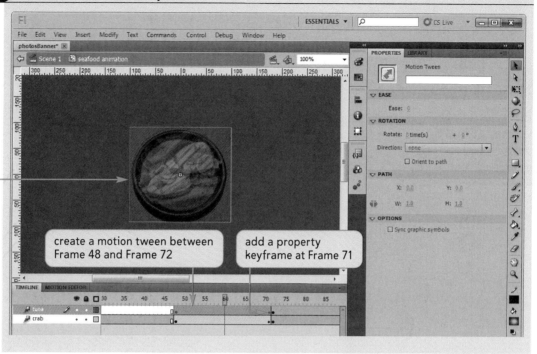

one bitmap fades out while the other fades in

create a motion tween between Frame 48 and Frame 72

add a property keyframe at Frame 71

You'll create the motion tween for the tuna symbol instance to fade out of view and the crab symbol instance to fade back into view.

To create the motion tween to fade out the tuna symbol instance:

1. In the Timeline, insert keyframes at **Frame 120** and **Frame 144** of the tuna layer, and then create a motion tween.

2. In the Timeline, click **Frame 120** of the tuna layer, click the **tuna symbol** instance on the Stage to select it, and then, in the Property inspector, set the alpha amount to **100%**, if necessary.

3. In the Timeline, click **Frame 144** of the tuna layer, click the **tuna symbol** instance on the Stage, and then, in the Property inspector, set the alpha amount to **0%**.

4. In the Timeline, insert a Color property keyframe at **Frame 143** of the tuna layer, select the **tuna symbol** instance on the Stage, and then, in the Property inspector, set the alpha amount to **0%**. The motion tween fades out the tuna symbol instance.

5. In the Timeline, move the playhead to **Frame 1**, and then play the animation. The crab picture appears and then fades out when the tuna picture fades in. Then the crab picture fades back in while the tuna picture fades out. The seafood animation is complete.

Based on Aly's instructions, you need to add a mask. Recall that a mask is created on a separate mask layer. The layer below the mask layer becomes the masked layer. The contents of the masked layer that are covered by the filled shape in the mask layer appear when the movie is played. In this case, you need to create a mask layer, draw a filled shape that covers the seafood animation, and then make both the crab layer and the tuna layer masked layers. The filled shape determines how much of the seafood animation shows through.

To create the mask layer for the seafood animation:

1. In the Timeline, select the **tuna** layer, if necessary, and then insert a new layer and name it **mask**. This new layer will be the mask layer.

2. Right-click the **mask** layer, and then click **Mask** on the context menu. The mask layer's icon changes to represent the layer's property. The tuna layer is indented, and its icon changes to indicate it is a masked layer.

TIP

You can also double-click a layer's icon to open its Properties dialog box.

3. Right-click the **crab** layer, and then click **Properties** on the context menu. The Layer Properties dialog box opens so you can change the crab layer's properties to Masked. See Figure 6-12.

Figure 6-12	Layer Properties dialog box

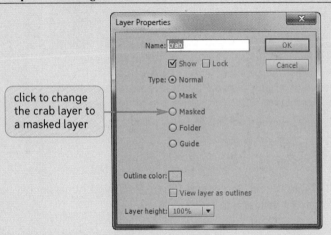

click to change the crab layer to a masked layer

4. Click the **Masked** option button, and then click the **OK** button. The dialog box closes. The crab layer in the Timeline is indented, and its icon changes to indicate that it is a masked layer. The mask layer starts out locked to display its effect. See Figure 6-13.

Figure 6-13	Layers converted to masked layers

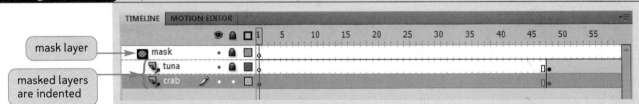

mask layer

masked layers are indented

5. In the Timeline, click the **mask** layer, and then click the **lock** icon 🔒 to unlock the layer. With the layer unlocked, you can draw the shape for the mask, which can be any shape that contains a fill. The area covered by the shape's fill determines which part of the masked layer's contents is displayed.

6. In the Tools panel, click and hold the **Rectangle** tool ▢, click the **Rectangle Primitive** tool ▢, and then set the fill color to **yellow** (#FFFF00). Although you set the fill to yellow, the shape's fill can be any color because it is not displayed.

7. On the Stage, drag the crosshair pointer ┼ from the upper-left corner of the crab symbol instance to its lower-right corner. The yellow rectangle covers the entire picture.

8. Open the Info panel, set the rectangle's width to **200**, its height to **185**, and its X and Y coordinates to **0**, and then close the Info panel. The rectangle frames the seafood animation.

9. In the Property inspector, click the **lock** icon ⊜ for the corner radius boxes to unlock the values, enter **50** in the lower-left corner radius value box, and then enter **50** in the upper-right corner radius value box. The rectangle shape has two rounded corners. See Figure 6-14.

Figure 6-14 ▶ **Mask covers the bitmaps**

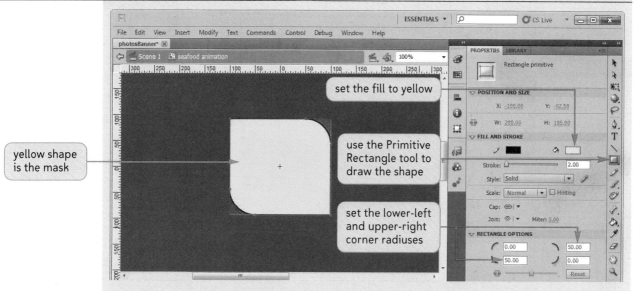

yellow shape
is the mask

set the fill to yellow

use the Primitive
Rectangle tool to
draw the shape

set the lower-left
and upper-right
corner radiuses

10. In the Timeline, click the **Lock or Unlock All Layers** icon 🔒 to lock all of the layers and display the result of the mask. The crab picture shows through the mask. The mask for the seafood animation is complete. See Figure 6-15.

Figure 6-15 ▶ **Bitmaps show through the mask**

bitmaps are visible
through the mask

11. Click the **Scene 1** link on the Edit bar to exit symbol-editing mode and return to the document's main Timeline.

12. In the Tools panel, click the **Selection** tool ▶.

You need to add the completed seafood animation movie clip to the left side of the banner based on the specifications that Aly provided.

To add the seafood animation to the banner:

▶ **1.** In the Timeline, insert a new layer above the text layer and name it **bitmaps**. You'll add the seafood animation to the banner in this layer.

▶ **2.** Drag the **seafood animation** symbol from the Library panel to the left side of the Stage. The animation is added to the banner.

▶ **3.** In the Position and Size section of the Property inspector, enter **118** for the X coordinate and **125** for the Y coordinate. The animation is positioned on the left side of the banner. See Figure 6-16.

| **Figure 6-16** | **Seafood animation in the banner** |

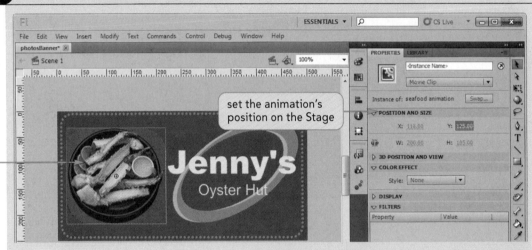

▶ **4.** Save the banner.

Because the animation was created inside the movie clip's Timeline, you cannot preview it within the main document's Timeline. To preview the seafood animation with the banner, you need to create a SWF file and play it in a separate window or in a Web page.

To preview the animation in the banner:

▶ **1.** On the Application bar, click **Control**, point to **Test Movie**, and then click **in Flash Professional**. A Flash Player window opens with the banner and the seafood animation.

▶ **2.** View the animation in the banner, and then close the Flash Player window.

Converting a Bitmap to a Vector Graphic

A bitmap instance on the Stage can also be converted to a vector graphic. You can modify the converted graphic just like any other vector graphic created in Flash. The converted graphic is no longer linked to the imported bitmap in the document's library.

So, any changes you make to the vector graphic do not affect the original bitmap in the library, which can still be used to create instances of the bitmap on the Stage.

Converting a bitmap to a vector graphic has several benefits. If the imported bitmap is geometric, converting it to a vector graphic enables you to use the Flash editing tools to edit the graphic. You might also want to convert a bitmap to a vector graphic so you can create a visual effect with the image. Finally, converting a bitmap instance to a vector graphic can reduce the file size of the final movie.

The Trace Bitmap command converts a bitmap instance on the Stage into a vector graphic by comparing each pixel in the graphic and assigning each a specific color. Pixels with similar colors are converted into areas of one color, essentially reducing the number of colors in the picture. Also, areas of contrasting color are converted to lines and curves. You specify how Flash should do this conversion through the settings in the Trace Bitmap dialog box, which are described in Figure 6-17.

Figure 6-17   **Trace Bitmap dialog box settings**

Setting	Description
Color threshold	Determines how pixels are compared to assign colors to them. The value ranges from 1 to 500. Higher values create fewer distinct colors because adjacent pixels must vary more before they are considered a different color. Smaller values result in more distinct colors.
Minimum area	Specifies the number of surrounding pixels to average when assigning a color to each pixel. The value ranges from 1 to 1000. A smaller minimum area compares fewer surrounding pixels, creating more colors. A larger area compares more surrounding pixels, creating fewer colors.
Corner threshold	Specifies whether sharp edges are retained or smoothed out. The Many Corners setting results in more detail, whereas the Few Corners setting results in less detail.
Curve fit	Specifies how smoothly the outlines are drawn. The value ranges from Pixels, which results in more detail, to Very Smooth, which results in less detail.

Selecting different values for the settings in the Trace Bitmap dialog box creates different effects in the converted graphic. For example, a bitmap that is converted to a vector graphic using a color threshold of 50, a minimum area of 50, a normal curve fit, and a normal corner threshold creates the special effect shown in Figure 6-18.

Figure 6-18   **Bitmap converted to a vector**

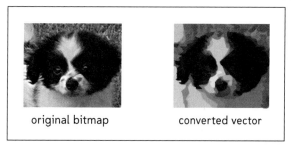

original bitmap   converted vector

Jenny wants the new company logo to include a photo of a lobster, as shown in the sketch of the logo in Figure 6-19. Aly provides a lobster photo to use as the logo's background. You will convert the bitmap to a vector graphic in order to create a special effect using the Trace Bitmap command.

Figure 6-19   **Sketch for the new Jenny's Oyster Hut logo**

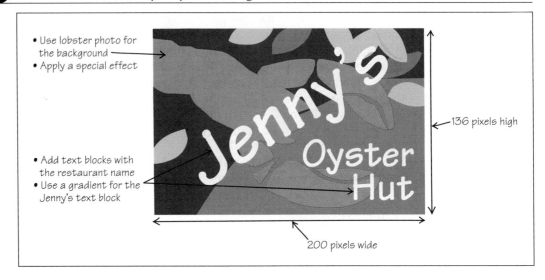

- Use lobster photo for the background
- Apply a special effect

- Add text blocks with the restaurant name
- Use a gradient for the Jenny's text block

136 pixels high

200 pixels wide

You'll convert the bitmap to a vector graphic.

To convert the lobster bitmap to a vector graphic:

1. Create a new **ActionScript 3.0** document, and then set the document properties so that the width is **200** pixels and the height is **136** pixels. The document's dimensions match the logo dimensions in Aly's sketch in Figure 6-19.

2. Save the file as **jennysLogo.fla** in the Flash6\Tutorial folder included with your Data Files, reset the workspace to the **Essentials** layout, and then set the zoom magnification to **200%**.

3. Import the **lobster.jpg** bitmap file located in the Flash6\Tutorial folder included with your Data Files to the document's library.

4. Drag a copy of the **lobster.jpg** bitmap from the Library panel to the Stage, and then, in the Position and Size section of the Property inspector, set the X and Y coordinates to **0**. The lobster bitmap instance is centered on the Stage and remains selected.

5. On the Application bar, click **Modify**, point to **Bitmap**, and then click **Trace Bitmap**. The Trace Bitmap dialog box opens. See Figure 6-20.

Figure 6-20   **Trace Bitmap dialog box**

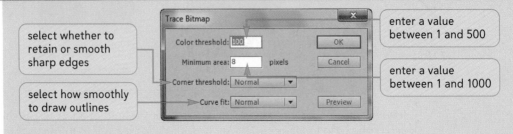

select whether to retain or smooth sharp edges

select how smoothly to draw outlines

enter a value between 1 and 500

enter a value between 1 and 1000

6. In the Color threshold box, type **60**. The color threshold setting determines how pixels are compared when assigning colors to them.

7. In the Minimum area box, type **10**. The minimum area setting specifies how many surrounding pixels to average when assigning a color to each pixel.

8. Click the **Corner threshold** button, and then click **Many Corners**. This setting determines whether sharp edges are retained or smoothed out. Many corners results in more detail.

9. Click the **Curve fit** button, and then click **Very Smooth**. This setting affects how the outlines are drawn. Very Smooth results in less detail.

10. Click the **OK** button. The lobster bitmap converts to a vector graphic based on the settings you entered in the Trace Bitmap dialog box. The lobster vector graphic contains less detail, larger areas of solid color, and smoother outlines than the original bitmap.

11. In the Tools panel, click the **Selection** tool , and then click the pasteboard to deselect the graphic. The changes to the graphic are visible.

12. In the Timeline, rename Layer 1 as **graphic**, and then lock the graphic layer to prevent accidentally changing its contents. See Figure 6-21.

| Figure 6-21 | The lobster.jpg picture converted to a vector graphic |

vector graphic

lock the layer

You will complete the logo by adding text on top of the graphic, as shown in Aly's planning sketch. The graphic is the background for the logo. You will add the text on a separate layer.

To add text to the logo:

1. In the Timeline, insert a new layer and name it **jennys**. You will create the text for the logo in this layer.

2. In the Tools panel, click the **Text** tool T, and then, in the Property inspector, change the font family to **Arial**, change the font style to **Black**, change the point size to **38**, change the text color to **green** (#00FF00), and change the paragraph format to **Align left**.

3. Click the left-center area of the lobster, type **Jenny's**, select the letter **J**, and then, in the Property inspector, change the point size to **58**. The first letter is larger than the rest of the word.

4. In the Tools panel, click the **Free Transform** tool, and then click the **Rotate and Skew** button. A bounding box appears around the text block.

5. Drag a corner handle on the bounding box around the text to rotate the text block counterclockwise, and then reposition the text block as needed to center it on the picture. See Figure 6-22.

Figure 6-22 Rotated and centered text block

6. Click the pasteboard to deselect the Jenny's text block. You need to create two more text blocks for the other words in the restaurant name.

7. In the Tools panel, click the **Text** tool T, and then, in the Property inspector, change the point size to **24** and change the text color to **light yellow** (#FFFF99).

8. On the lower-right corner of the Stage, create a text block, type **Oyster**, and then click the pasteboard to deselect the text block.

9. In the Property inspector, change the text color to **lighter yellow** (#FFFFCC), and then, on the Stage, create another text block below the Oyster text and type **Hut**.

Trouble? If the lighter yellow (#FFFFCC) color is not available on the color palette, then you need to enter the code manually. Point to the hexadecimal code in the color palette, click the code, type the new code, and then press the Enter key.

10. In the Tools panel, click the **Selection** tool, and then reposition the two text blocks so that they are in the lower-right corner of the Stage and their right edges are aligned. See Figure 6-23.

Figure 6-23 Logo with text

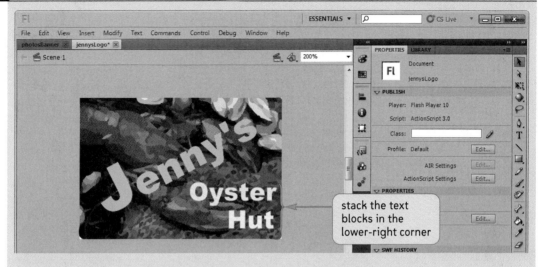

stack the text blocks in the lower-right corner

11. Save the logo.

In this session, you added bitmaps to the lunch specials banner. You imported the bitmaps into the document's library and then created instances on the Stage. You created an animation with two bitmaps, changing the alpha amount to create a fade effect. You also converted a bitmap to a vector graphic to create the new logo. In the next session, you'll modify the logo with gradients. Then you will publish the banner file.

REVIEW

Session 6.1 Quick Check

1. What is a bitmap?
2. What is the difference between the Import to Stage and the Import to Library commands?
3. How do you access a bitmap's properties within Flash?
4. For what type of bitmaps should you use the Photo (JPEG) compression setting?
5. What alpha amount makes an object transparent?
6. What command do you use to convert a bitmap to a vector graphic?
7. When converting a bitmap to a vector graphic, how does the color threshold value affect the resulting graphic?

SESSION 6.2 VISUAL OVERVIEW

A **gradient** is a gradual blend or transition from one color to another. This background is a gradient.

You can move a gradient's center, change its size, or change its direction.

You can apply gradients as fills in shapes such as circles, rectangles, and triangles, as well as backgrounds and text. The text "Jenny's" is filled with a gradient.

Before you can apply a gradient to text, you must first convert the text to a fill with the Break Apart command.

GRADIENT FILLS

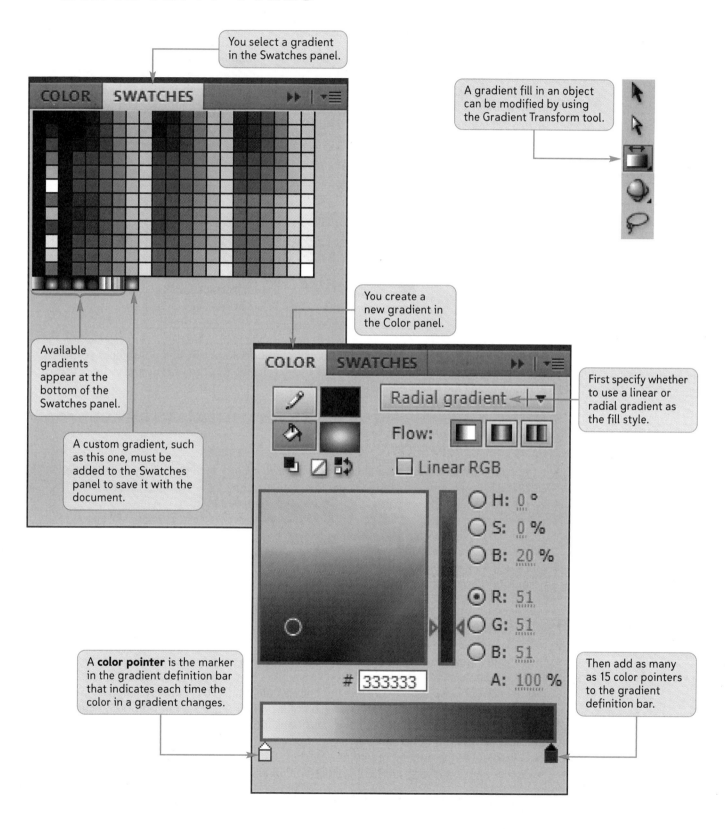

You select a gradient in the Swatches panel.

A gradient fill in an object can be modified by using the Gradient Transform tool.

You create a new gradient in the Color panel.

Available gradients appear at the bottom of the Swatches panel.

A custom gradient, such as this one, must be added to the Swatches panel to save it with the document.

First specify whether to use a linear or radial gradient as the fill style.

A **color pointer** is the marker in the gradient definition bar that indicates each time the color in a gradient changes.

Then add as many as 15 color pointers to the gradient definition bar.

COLOR   SWATCHES

Radial gradient

Flow:

Linear RGB

H: 0 °
S: 0 %
B: 20 %

R: 51
G: 51
B: 51

333333   A: 100 %

Using Gradients

A gradient is a gradual blend or transition from one color to another. Gradients can create special effects and can add a professional touch to documents. For example, you can use a gradient for a banner's background, create a gradient to simulate a sunset or a rainbow, or use a gradient as part of an animation. Gradients can be added as fills to any object the same way you add solid color fills.

The two types of gradients you can create in Flash are linear and radial. A **linear gradient** blends the colors from one point to another in a straight line. A **radial gradient** blends the colors from one point outward in a circular pattern. Figure 6-24 shows examples of linear and radial gradients.

| Figure 6-24 | Gradient examples |

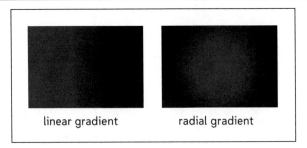

linear gradient   radial gradient

Flash includes several preset gradients in the color palette and in the Swatches panel. You can use these gradients as fills for any closed shape. You can also create custom gradients using the Color panel.

INSIGHT

Gradients Impact Performance

Although gradients are easy to create and add to a Flash document, they increase the processing requirements of the computer displaying the SWF movie. Because of the greater number of colors in a gradient, a computer's processor might have to work harder to display a gradient compared to displaying solid colors. If you have concerns about a movie's performance when displayed on a user's computer, you can reduce the number of gradients used in the movie or omit them altogether if the SWF movie contains complex graphics or animations. You should always test the movie to ensure its quality is acceptable.

Creating and Saving a Custom Gradient

You create a new gradient in the Color panel. First, you specify whether to use a linear or radial gradient as the fill style, and then you add a color pointer to the gradient definition bar at each spot you want to change the color in the gradient. A gradient can have anywhere from two to 15 color pointers. Each color pointer creates a **fall-off point**, which is the spot where the gradient shifts or transitions from one color to another. A gradient's colors are displayed in the color space at the bottom of the Color panel. You can add a new gradient to the document's color swatches that appear in the color palette and in the Swatches panel. The new gradient is stored only with the current document.

Creating, Editing, and Saving a Gradient

- To create a gradient, open the Color panel, click the Color type button, and then click Linear gradient or Radial gradient.

  or

  Click a preset gradient in the color palette or the Swatches panel.
- To edit a gradient, add or delete a color pointer.
- To specify a color for a color pointer, select the color pointer, and then enter the color's RGB values, hexadecimal value, or click the color picker in the Color panel.
- To add a color pointer, click a spot on the gradient definition bar.
- To remove a color pointer, drag it down, away from the gradient definition bar.
- To reposition a color pointer, drag it to the left or right on the gradient definition bar.
- To save a gradient with the current document, click the Color panel options menu, and then click Add Swatch.

The background of the new banner for Jenny's Oyster Hut should be a radial gradient using a blend of a light blue color that transitions into a dark gray color. You will create the radial gradient to use as the fill for the banner's background.

To create a custom radial gradient for the banner:

1. If you took a break after the previous session, make sure the photosBanner.fla and the jennysLogo.fla files are open and the workspace is reset to the Essentials layout.

2. Click the **photosBanner.fla** tab to make the document active, and then click the **Swatches** button ⊞ on the docked panel group to open the Swatches panel. The preset gradients appear at the bottom of the Swatches panel.

3. In the Swatches panel, click the **gray radial** gradient (the second gradient from the left) with the eyedropper pointer 🖋. You'll modify this gradient to create the custom gradient. See Figure 6-25.

Figure 6-25   Swatches panel

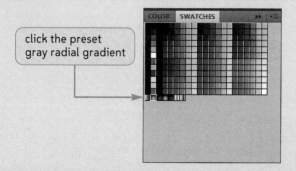

click the preset gray radial gradient

4. Switch to the **Color** panel. The Color panel displays the preset gray radial gradient and its two color pointers. You'll change these color pointers to create the new gradient based on the colors specified in the planning sketch.

5. In the Color panel, click the **left color** pointer below the gradient definition bar to select it. The small triangle for the color pointer changes to black to indicate it is selected.

6. In the Hex box, type **99FFFF**, and then press the **Enter** key. The left color pointer for the gradient changes to a light blue color.

7. Click the **right color** pointer below the gradient definition bar, type **333333** in the Hex box, and then press the **Enter** key. The right color pointer is set to a dark gray color, and the color preview shows the new gradient. See Figure 6-26.

Figure 6-26	Color panel with the custom gradient

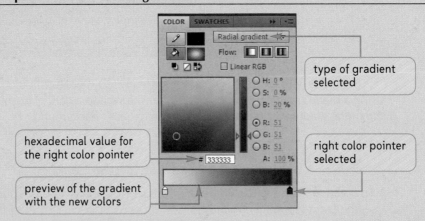

type of gradient selected

hexadecimal value for the right color pointer

right color pointer selected

preview of the gradient with the new colors

You'll add this gradient as a swatch to the Swatches panel for the document. If you don't, the gradient is discarded when you close the document.

8. In the Color panel, click the **panel menu** button ▼≡, and then click **Add Swatch**. The gradient is saved with the document, and the custom gradient appears at the end of the preset gradients in the Swatches panel.

9. Display the Swatches panel. See Figure 6-27.

Figure 6-27	New gradient in the Swatches panel

TIP

To delete a swatch, click the Swatches panel menu button, and then click Delete Swatch.

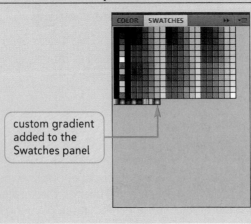

custom gradient added to the Swatches panel

Applying a Gradient Fill

Gradient fills can be applied to shapes such as circles, rectangles, and triangles as well as to text. You apply a gradient fill to an object the same way you apply a solid fill. You can select the gradient fill color before you draw a shape such as a rectangle, or you can use the Paint Bucket tool to apply a gradient to an existing shape. When using the Paint Bucket tool to apply a radial gradient, you specify the gradient's center point, which is where the first color begins. The point you click becomes the gradient's center point, as shown in Figure 6-28. When using the Paint Bucket tool to apply a linear gradient, you draw a straight line with the Paint Bucket pointer ⬧. The line you draw determines the direction of the gradient.

| Figure 6-28 | Radial gradient being applied with the Paint Bucket tool |

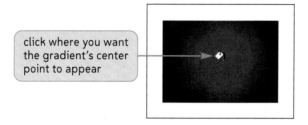

click where you want the gradient's center point to appear

You can also use the Paint Bucket tool's Lock Fill modifier when applying gradients. With the Lock Fill modifier selected, the Paint Bucket tool paints one gradient across several objects on the Stage rather than one gradient for each object, as shown in Figure 6-29.

| Figure 6-29 | Effect of the Lock Fill modifier on gradients |

gradients applied to each shape without the Lock Fill modifier

gradients applied to each shape with the Lock Fill modifier; the gradient spreads across all objects

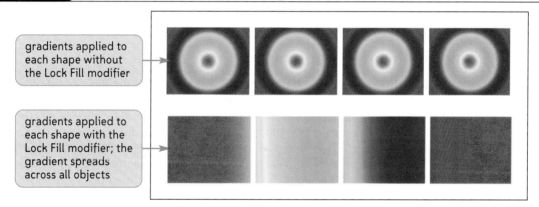

You will use the custom gradient as the fill for a rectangle that will be the banner's background.

To add a rectangle with the custom gradient to the background layer:

1. In the Timeline, select the **background** layer. You'll draw the rectangle for the banner's background in this layer.

2. In the Tools panel, click and hold the **Rectangle Primitive** tool ▣, and then click the **Rectangle** tool ▢ to select it.

3. In the Tools panel, set the fill color to the gradient you created, which appears in the bottom row of the color palette. The rectangle will use the gradient you created as its fill.

4. In the Property inspector, set the stroke color to **no color**, and then set the rectangle corner radius to **0**. The rectangle you draw will not have a visible stroke and will have square corners.

5. On the Stage, draw a large rectangle the size of the Stage. The rectangle covers the entire Stage but does not obscure the text and images because the rectangle is in the bottom layer. See Figure 6-30.

Figure 6-30 | **Gradient background added to the banner**

rectangle with the custom gradient

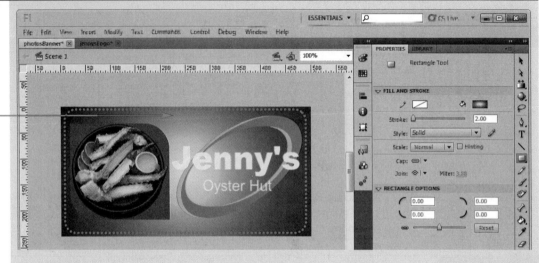

6. Save the photosBanner.fla banner.

Filling Text with a Gradient

You can also apply a gradient fill to text. Before you can apply a gradient to text, you must first convert the text to a fill with the Break Apart command. If the text block has multiple letters, the first time you apply the Break Apart command to a text block, the text block is broken into smaller text blocks consisting of the individual letters. When you apply the Break Apart command a second time, the letter text blocks are converted into fills. Then, you can apply a gradient to the individual letters the same way you do any other shape. If the text block only has one letter, the Break Apart command needs to be applied only once to convert the letter into a fill.

The Jenny's text block in the logo should have a gradient fill applied to it. You will convert the text block to fills, apply a preset gradient, and then modify the colors to create a custom gradient.

To apply a gradient fill to the Jenny's text block:

1. Click the **jennysLogo.fla** tab to make the logo document active.

2. In the Tools panel, click the **Selection** tool , and then select the **Jenny's** text block on the Stage.

3. On the Application bar, click **Modify**, and then click **Break Apart**. The text block breaks into individual blocks for each letter. See Figure 6-31.

Figure 6-31   **Jenny's text block broken apart**

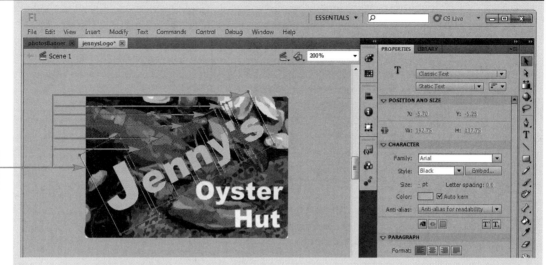

individual text blocks created for each letter

4. On the Application bar, click **Modify**, and then click **Break Apart**. The individual text blocks are converted to fills. The text fills are selected and ready for you to apply a gradient fill.

5. Open the Color panel, click the **Color type** button, and then click **Linear gradient**. A linear gradient is applied to the text fills.

   You will modify the gradient used in the selected text fills.

6. In the Color panel, click the **left color** pointer below the gradient definition bar to select it, type **FFFFFF** in the Hex box, and then press the **Enter** key. The starting color for the linear gradient is set.

7. In the Color panel, click the **right color** pointer to select it, type **FFFF00** in the Hex box, and then press the **Enter** key. The ending color for the linear gradient is set, and the text gradient fill color changes.

8. Click the pasteboard to deselect the text. See Figure 6-32.

Figure 6-32   **Gradient applied to text fills**

Jenny's text with modified linear gradient fill

9. Save the jennysLogo.fla banner.

Transforming Gradient Fills

A gradient fill in an object can be modified by using the Gradient Transform tool. You can move a gradient's center, change its size, or change its direction. When you select a linear gradient with the Gradient Transform tool, a bounding box surrounds it. When you select a radial gradient, a bounding circle surrounds it. The gradient's center point also appears along with editing handles, as shown in Figure 6-33. You drag these handles to transform the gradient.

Figure 6-33	Editing handles

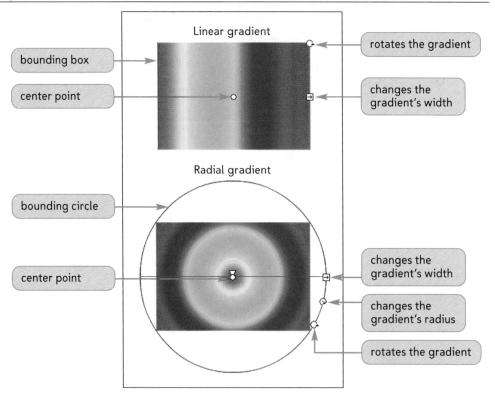

You drag a gradient's center point to reposition it. The linear gradient has a circular handle to rotate the gradient and a square handle to change the gradient's width. The radial gradient has two circular handles. The middle circular handle changes the gradient's radius, and the bottom circular handle rotates the gradient. It also has a square handle, which changes the gradient's width. A radial gradient also has a focal point, indicated by a small triangle, which is initially in the same position as the center point. You can drag the small triangle to change the gradient's focal point.

Aly wants you to modify the gradient in the banner background so that the lighter color of the gradient is behind the animation of the seafood pictures. To do this, you will move the gradient's center point to the left side of the banner over the seafood animation and increase its radius slightly to spread more of the lighter color to the rest of the banner.

To modify the gradient in the banner background:

1. Click the **photosBanner.fla** tab to make the document active. The banner appears on the Stage.

2. In the Tools panel, click and hold the **Free Transform** tool ⬚, and then click the **Gradient Transform** tool ⬚, if necessary. The Gradient Transform tool is selected.

3. Click the rectangle with the gradient fill. The gradient's bounding circle and editing handles appear.

4. Set the zoom magnification to **50%**. The entire bounding circle is visible, making the rectangle easier to work with. See Figure 6-34.

Figure 6-34   **Gradient selected for transformation**

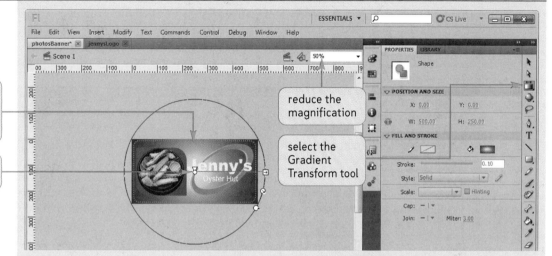

click the background rectangle to display the bounding circle and editing handles

center point of the gradient

reduce the magnification

select the Gradient Transform tool

5. Position the pointer over the center point of the gradient until the pointer changes to ✛ to indicate it is over the center point, and then drag the center point of the gradient to the left until it is positioned over the center of the seafood animation instance. The entire bounding circle moves as you reposition the center point of the gradient.

6. Drag the **radius handle** outward until the right side of the bounding circle touches the right of the letter "s" in the "Jenny's" text. See Figure 6-35. The gradient's radius increases so that the light blue color extends more than halfway across the banner.

Figure 6-35   **Gradient's radius increased**

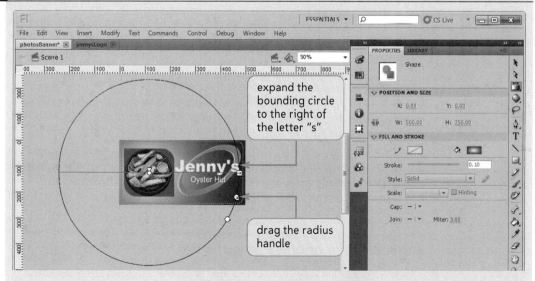

expand the bounding circle to the right of the letter "s"

drag the radius handle

7. Save the photosBanner.fla banner.

Comparing Publishing Options

FLA documents created in Flash are usually made available for use on the Web. To do so, the document must be published or exported into a format readable by a Web browser. You have done this when you published FLA documents as SWF movie files in previous tutorials to test or preview the movie. You have used the Test Movie command to create a SWF file that plays in a separate Flash Player window. You have also used the Default – (HTML) command, which creates both a SWF file and an HTML file to play the movie. The browser uses the Flash Player plug-in to play the movie. In most cases, when you create movies for the Web, you want to publish a SWF file. However, sometimes you need to publish or export the document in a different file format. Flash allows you to publish Flash documents in such file formats as JPEG, GIF, and PNG.

You can also save the publishing settings as a profile to use with other documents.

INSIGHT

Creating a Projector File

A Flash file can be published as a projector file, which is a stand-alone application with the .exe extension. A projector file has the Flash Player incorporated into it and plays the movie in its own window rather than in a Web browser. This is a useful option if you want to distribute a Flash movie on a platform other than the Web. The advantage to distributing a Flash projector file is that it can be viewed on a computer that does not have the Flash Player plug-in installed. The disadvantage is that its file size will be larger than the corresponding SWF file because the Flash Player is embedded in the projector file.

Selecting a Document's Publish Settings

You specify how you want an FLA document published in the Publish Settings dialog box. The Formats tab lists the file formats in which you can publish a Flash document. Most of the time, you will use only the Flash (.swf) and HTML (.html) file types because the documents you create are meant to be played in a Web page. However, you can choose to publish a document in a different format such as the JPEG Image (.jpg) file format. Each file format selected on the Formats tab has a corresponding tab in the Publish Settings dialog box with additional options and settings for that file type.

The banner you just completed will be added to the home page of the Jenny's Oyster Hut Web site. Because the Web page already exists, you need to publish the banner only as a SWF file. When publishing in the Flash (.swf) format, the Flash tab in the Publish Settings dialog box contains options to specify the player and the script versions as well as other settings. Player specifies the oldest version of the Flash Player in which the published movie will play. The published banner SWF file should be compatible with all Flash Player plug-ins starting with version 7. Script specifies which version of the Flash programming language ActionScript the published movie will use. In this case, the banner does not use ActionScript, so you don't need to change the default setting. The JPEG quality and audio settings can also be changed in this dialog box. However, the bitmap properties you set as you worked with the photos override these JPEG settings. This movie includes no sounds, so the audio settings are not used. Aly wants you to generate a size report, which shows the size of the different parts of the movie. The report is created as a text file using the FLA file's name plus the word "Report," followed by the extension .txt. The report also appears in the Output panel after the file is published.

TIP

A file published with the compressed movie option only plays in Flash Player 6 or later. Compression is especially useful for a text-intensive Flash document.

To publish the photosBanner.fla file in the SWF file format:

▶ 1. On the Application bar, click **File**, and then click **Publish Settings**. The Publish Settings dialog box opens to the Formats tab. See Figure 6-36.

| Figure 6-36 | Formats tab in the Publish Settings dialog box |

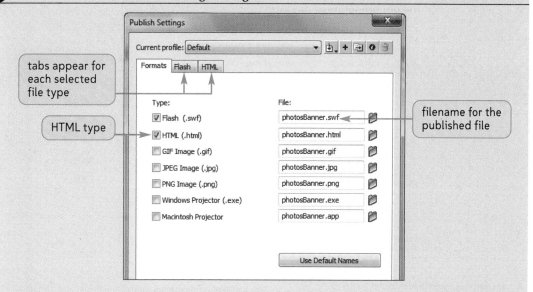

2. On the Formats tab, click the **HTML (.html)** check box to remove the check mark and its corresponding tab, if necessary, and then make sure that the **Flash (.swf)** check box is checked. You want to publish the banner only in the Flash format.

3. In the File box to the right of Flash (.swf), type **banner.swf** to specify the name for the published SWF file.

4. To the right of the Flash (.swf) File box, click the **Select Publish Destination** button ⬚. The Select Publish Destination dialog box opens.

5. Navigate to the **Flash6\Tutorial** folder included with your Data Files, if necessary, and then click the **Save** button to specify the folder in which to save the published SWF file.

6. In the Publish Settings dialog box, click the **Flash** tab to display the settings for this format. You will set the publishing options for the published movie on this tab.

7. Click the **Player** button, and then click **Flash Player 7**. You selected the earlier version so that the movie can be played on all computers with Flash Player 7 or later. You'll leave ActionScript 2.0 as the script version because the banner does not use ActionScript.

8. In the SWF Settings section, click the **Compress movie** check box to remove the check mark. You don't need to compress the movie because it is not a large file.

9. In the SWF Settings section, click the **Include hidden layers** check box to remove the check mark. The movie doesn't have any hidden layers.

10. In the SWF Settings section, click the **Include XMP metadata** check box to remove the check mark.

11. In the Advanced section, click the **Generate size report** check box to insert a check mark. The report will specify how big each part of the movie is. See Figure 6-37.

Figure 6-37   **Flash publish settings**

select Flash Player version 7

uncheck these options

check this option to create a
text file with information
about the size of the published
file and its components

```
Publish Settings                                        X

Current profile: Default              ▼  ⬆ + ⊞ ❶ ⸛

 Formats │ Flash

                      Player:  [Flash Player 7    ▼]   [ Info... ]
                      Script:  [ActionScript 2.0  ▼]   [ Settings... ]

Images and Sounds
                JPEG quality:  [━━━━━━━━●━━]   [ 80 ]
                               ☐ Enable JPEG deblocking
                Audio stream:  MP3, 16 kbps, Mono      [ Set... ]
                 Audio event:  MP3, 16 kbps, Mono      [ Set... ]
                               ☐ Override sound settings
                               ☐ Export device sounds

SWF Settings
                               ☐ Compress movie
                               ☐ Include hidden layers
                               ☐ Include XMP metadata   [ File Info... ]
                               ☐ Export SWC

Advanced
               Trace and debug: ☑ Generate size report
                                ☐ Protect from import
                                ☐ Omit trace actions
                                ☐ Permit debugging
                    Password:  [                    ]
        Local playback security: [Access local files only  ▼]
        Hardware Acceleration:  [None                     ▼]
             Script time limit:  [ 15 ]  seconds

                    [ Publish ]   [ OK ]   [ Cancel ]
```

▶ **12.** Click the **Publish** button. The Publish Settings dialog box remains open, and the SWF file and the size report file are created in the same folder as the FLA file. The report also appears in the Output panel.

▶ **13.** Click the **OK** button to close the Publish Settings dialog box.

You'll review the size report text file generated by Flash when you published the banner. The file opens in the Output panel, but you can also open it in Notepad, which is an application included with Windows. The report file shows information about the movie, including its number of frames, the total size of the movie in bytes, a list of the symbols in the movie, and a list of the bitmaps. This information can be useful when optimizing a larger, more complex movie to find ways to reduce its size. You will view the report in the Output panel.

To view the size report file in the Output panel:

TIP

You can also press the
F2 key to open or close the
Output panel.

▶ **1.** Drag the **Output** panel to the center of the Stage.

   Trouble? If the Output panel is not open, you need to open it manually. On the Application bar, click Window, and then click Output.

▶ **2.** Drag the lower edge of the Output panel to enlarge the panel as needed, and then scroll to the top of the panel to view the report. The report shows that the movie is 31324 bytes in size (yours might differ), has three symbols with a total size of 66 bytes, and has two bitmaps, each of which is compressed. See Figure 6-38.

Figure 6-38   Output panel with the movie report

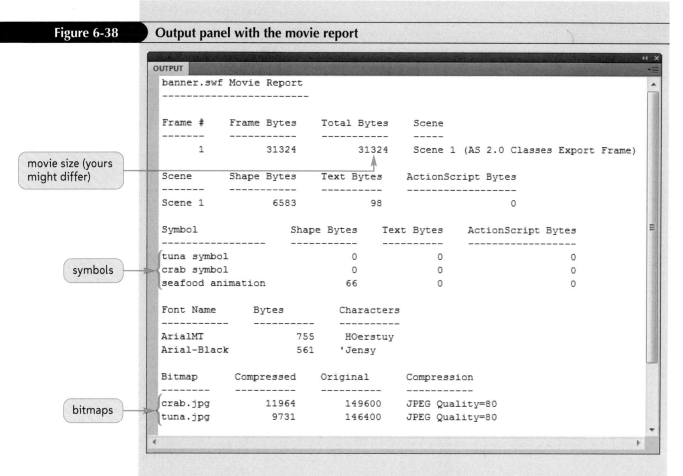

movie size (yours might differ)

symbols

bitmaps

▶ **3.** On the Output panel, click the **Close** button ✕ to close the panel.

You can save your preferred publish settings for a document, including the Flash and HTML settings, as a **publish profile**. The settings in the publish profile are available to any document you create in Flash on the same computer. After you save a publish profile, the Publish command publishes the files according to the settings saved in the profile. A profile can be deleted in the Publish Settings dialog box. Also, if you remove HTML (.html) as a format for a file, the Publish Preview command will default to the first format selected in the Formats tab of the Publish Settings dialog box.

You'll create a publish profile for all the Jenny's Oyster Hut documents.

To create a publish profile for the Jenny's Oyster Hut documents:

▶ **1.** On the Application bar, click **File**, and then click **Publish Settings**. The Publish Settings dialog box opens.

▶ **2.** Click the **Create new profile** button ➕. The Create New Profile dialog box opens.

▶ **3.** In the Profile name box, type **Oyster Hut**, and then click the **OK** button. The Oyster Hut profile is created and appears as the current profile in the Publish Settings dialog box. All the settings revert to the defaults. See Figure 6-39.

Figure 6-39   **Publish Settings dialog box with a publish profile**

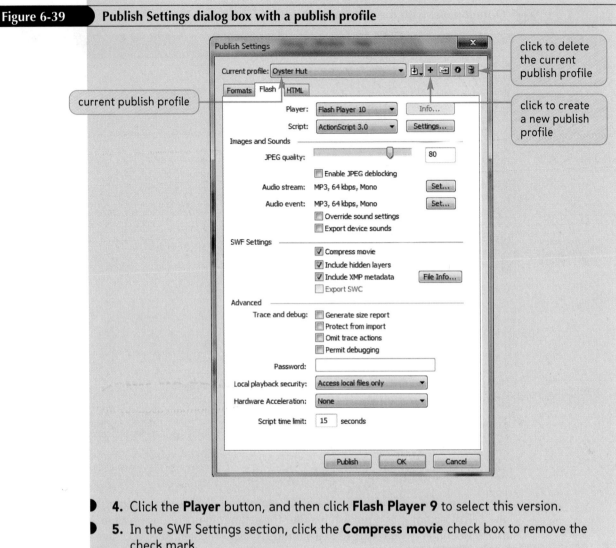

4. Click the **Player** button, and then click **Flash Player 9** to select this version.

5. In the SWF Settings section, click the **Compress movie** check box to remove the check mark.

6. Click the **Publish** button to publish the SWF and HTML files.

Aly wants to check some statistics about the target users and the version of Flash they might have on their computers before creating a final profile. So you will delete this publish profile.

To delete the Oyster Hut publish profile:

1. In the Publish Settings dialog box, click the **Delete profile** button ⬛. A dialog box opens to confirm that you want to delete the profile.

2. Click the **OK** button. The Oyster Hut profile is deleted.

3. Click the **OK** button to close the Publish Settings dialog box.

4. Save and close the photosBanner.fla document.

Decision Making: Choosing a Flash Player Version

Making a good decision requires selecting the best possible alternative for the specific situation. When publishing Flash movies, you can specify on which version of the Flash Player they run. The means you must obtain very specific information about the target audience, including which player is likely installed on their computers. The information will direct your decision making.

If you are certain that everyone in the target audience has the latest player installed on their computers, then publishing to the latest format is not a problem. Publishing to the latest format ensures that all features of the Flash CS5 program work in the Flash Player.

If you are unsure which version of Flash Player the target audience has, it's a good idea to publish to a player that is two or three versions earlier. For example, if the current version of the Flash Player is version 10, you can set the version in the Publish Settings dialog box to version 7 or 8 to ensure that most of your target audience can see the Flash movies. If you publish to version 7 of the Flash Player, for example, then anyone with Flash Player 7 or later can see the Flash movie. Publishing the Flash movie to the latest version might limit the number of people who can see the movie, especially in a workplace or an organization where polices may prevent users from upgrading to the latest player.

Carefully consider the target audience and select an appropriate Flash Player version to ensure that the movie plays for the largest group of people.

Exporting a Flash Document as an Image

The JPEG and GIF file types are the most common file formats used for images in Web pages. JPEG is best for images that include many colors, such as the original photograph of the lobster. GIF is best for images with fewer colors, such as the lobster bitmap you converted to a vector for the logo. You can use the Publish Settings dialog box to select JPEG or GIF as the format in which to publish. You can also use the Export Image command, which allows you to specify the type of format you want to export to and then displays settings you can change based on the selected file format. Some of the formats you can export to include JPEG Image (*.jpg), GIF Image (*.gif), and PNG (*.png).

Because the logo you created is static, includes only a picture and some text, and contains mostly solid areas of color, you can export it as a GIF image. The GIF settings include the dimensions and resolution of the exported GIF image, the image area to export, and the number of colors to export. If the document has empty space, the Minimum Image Area setting will not export the empty space. The standard number of colors in a GIF image is 256, but if an image uses fewer colors, you can decrease the number of colors to export, reducing the file size.

TIP

The Publish command saves the export settings you select with the document; the Export Image command does not store these settings.

To export the logo as a GIF image:

1. On the Application bar, click **File**, point to **Export**, and then click **Export Image**. The Export Image dialog box opens.

2. If necessary, navigate to the **Flash6\Tutorial** folder included with your Data Files, type **jennysLogo** in the File name box, click the **Save as type** button, and then click **GIF Image (*.gif)**.

3. Click the **Save** button. The Export GIF dialog box opens.

4. If necessary, click the **Include** button, and then click **Full Document Size**.

5. Click the **Match Screen** button to ensure that the dimensions are set to 200 by 136 pixels and the resolution is set to 72 dpi.

6. If necessary, click the **Colors** button, and then click **Standard colors**.

7. Make sure the **Smooth** check box is checked and the **Transparent**, **Interlace**, and **Dither solid colors** check boxes are unchecked. See Figure 6-40.

Figure 6-40   ▶   Export GIF dialog box

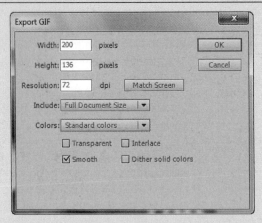

8. Click the **OK** button. The dialog box closes, and the logo is saved as a GIF image.

9. Close the jennysLogo.fla document.

Adding Flash Graphics to a Web Page

The final output of creating movies with Flash is a Web page that displays the movies along with text, hyperlinks, and other graphics. After you complete a Flash graphic, such as a banner or a logo, you need to incorporate its file information into the Web page's HTML. When you publish a movie with the HTML format option, Flash creates a simple Web page to display the movie. More often, you'll want to add the SWF file to an existing Web page, which requires you to edit the actual Web page. You can do this with a Web page editing program such as Adobe Dreamweaver. You can also edit the HTML in a text editor such as Notepad.

The published banner and exported logo are ready to be placed in a Web page that Chris has already created. The Web page includes a simple banner and logo that you will replace. You will edit the Web page using Notepad.

To add the banner and logo to a sample Web page:

1. On the taskbar, click the **Start** button, click **All Programs**, click **Accessories**, and then click **Notepad**. The Notepad program starts.

2. On the Notepad menu bar, click **File**, and then click **Open**. The Open File dialog box opens.

3. Navigate to the **Flash6\Tutorial** folder included with your Data Files, set the file type to **All Files**, click **sample.htm** in the file list, and then click the **Open** button. The HTML for the sample Web page opens in the Notepad window.

4. On the title bar, click the **Maximize** button ▣ to maximize the Notepad program window. See Figure 6-41.

Figure 6-41	Sample Web page HTML

The tenth line contains the following image tag, which places the current banner at the top of the Web page:

```
<img src= "jennysbanner.jpg" alt="Jenny's Oyster Hut" width="600"
height="150">
```

You need to replace this tag with a special EMBED tag for the SWF file. EMBED is used to load external media such as a SWF movie that requires the use of a plug-in.

To add the banner and logo to a sample Web page:

1. In line 10, replace the image tag, including the two angle brackets, with the following code: `<embed src="banner.swf" width="500" height="250">`

   You need to replace the reference for the current logo with a reference for the new logo file, jennysLogo.gif, and then update the logo's dimensions.

2. On line 17, replace `logo.jpg` with `jennysLogo.gif`. The code references the logo you created.

3. On line 17, replace `width="180" height="150"` with `width="200" height="136"`. The code includes the correct dimensions for the logo.

4. Save and close the file, and then exit Notepad. The Web page is updated with the new banner and logo.

TIP

When possible, insert Flash graphics in a Web page with an HTML editor such as Adobe Dreamweaver, which inserts code as well as the EMBED tag so that Flash movies display properly in most browsers.

You changed the HTML of the sample Web page so that the page will display the animated banner and logo that you created for Jenny's Oyster Hut. You will test the Web page by opening the page in your browser.

To preview the sample.htm Web page:

1. Start your Web browser, and then, if necessary, click the **Tools** button, point to **Toolbars**, and then click **Menu Bar** to display the menu bar.

2. On the menu bar, click **File**, and then click **Open**. The Open dialog box opens.

3. Click the **Browse** button, navigate to the **Flash6\Tutorial** folder included with your Data Files, click **sample.htm** in the file list, and then click the **Open** button. The file path to the sample Web page appears in the Open box.

4. Click the **OK** button.

5. Click the **Tools** button, and then click **Menu Bar** to hide the menu bar. The sample Web page opens in the browser window. The banner at the top of the page plays the animation, and the logo appears below the banner. See Figure 6-42.

Figure 6-42   **Sample Web page with Flash graphics**

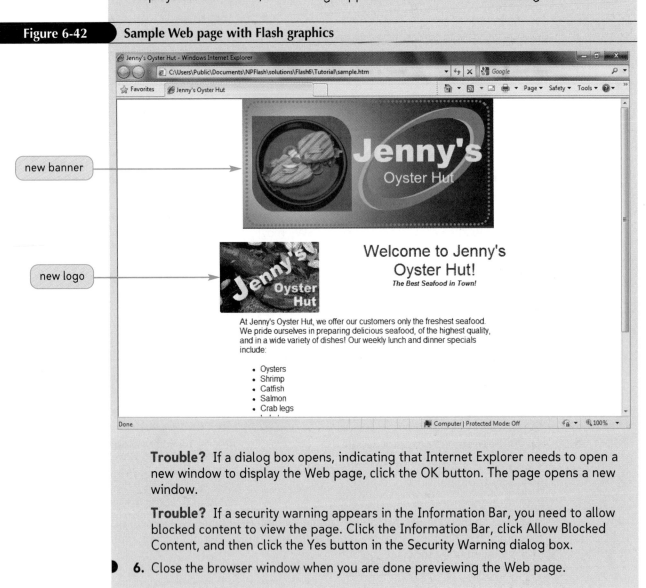

Trouble? If a dialog box opens, indicating that Internet Explorer needs to open a new window to display the Web page, click the OK button. The page opens a new window.

Trouble? If a security warning appears in the Information Bar, you need to allow blocked content to view the page. Click the Information Bar, click Allow Blocked Content, and then click the Yes button in the Security Warning dialog box.

6. Close the browser window when you are done previewing the Web page.

Aly likes the look of the new banner and logo in the Web page and will present the finished pieces to Jenny at their next meeting.

Session 6.2 Quick Check

REVIEW

1. What is a gradient?
2. Describe two different kinds of gradients available in Flash.
3. True or False. A gradient is saved only within the current document.
4. When using the Paint Bucket tool to apply a linear gradient, how do you specify the direction of the gradient?
5. What is the purpose of the Player setting in the Flash tab of the Publish Settings dialog box?
6. How can you use the information generated by a size report when publishing a file?
7. Why would you save a document's publish settings in a publish profile?
8. True or False. To add a SWF file to an existing Web page, you must use Notepad.

Practice the skills you learned in the tutorial using the same case scenario.

PRACTICE

Review Assignments

Data Files needed for the Review Assignments: jennysAlt.fla, salmon.jpg, sampleAlt.htm, hutBanner.jpg

Aly wants you to make some changes to an alternate version of the Jenny's Oyster Hut banner before she shows it to Jenny. She wants you to add a salmon bitmap in the sea-food animation. The salmon bitmap will appear after the fish bitmap, be displayed for two seconds, and then fade out while the salmon bitmap fades in. This will extend the animation by three seconds. She also asks you to change the letters in the Jenny's text block to a gradient fill.

1. Open the **jennysAlt.fla** file located in the Flash6\Review folder included with your Data Files, and then save the banner as **jennysAlternate.fla** in the same folder.

2. Import the **salmon.jpg** bitmap located in the Flash6\Review folder included with your Data Files into the document's library. Modify the salmon bitmap's properties so that the quality value is 80.

3. Open the seafood animation movie clip in symbol-editing mode, and then add a new layer above the shrimp layer and name it **salmon**. Make sure the salmon layer is indented under the mask layer. Temporarily hide the contents of the fish layer, the shrimp layer, and the mask layer while you work with the salmon layer.

4. At Frame 120 of the salmon layer, insert a keyframe, and then drag a copy of the salmon bitmap to the Stage. In the Info panel, set the X and Y coordinates to 0 and make sure the center registration point is selected. Convert the salmon.jpg bitmap into a movie clip symbol named **salmon symbol** with the center registration point selected.

5. At Frame 144 of the salmon layer, insert a keyframe. At Frame 120, change the alpha amount of the salmon symbol to 0%. At Frame 144, make sure the alpha amount is 100%. Create a motion tween at Frame 120. Insert a color property keyframe at Frame 143 and set the alpha amount to 100%.

6. At Frame 216 of all the layers, add regular frames to extend the layers.

7. In the salmon layer, insert a keyframe at Frame 192 and at Frame 216. At Frame 216, change the alpha amount of the salmon symbol to 0%. Create a motion tween at Frame 192. Insert a color property keyframe at Frame 215 and set the alpha amount to 0%.

8. Temporarily hide the contents of the salmon layer and show the contents of the fish layer. Select Frame 120 through Frame 144 of the fish layer, and then drag the selected frames to the right, placing them in Frame 192 through Frame 216 of the fish layer.

9. Show all the layers, lock all the layers, test the animation, and then exit symbol-editing mode.

10. On the Stage, select the Jenny's text block, and then apply the Break Apart command twice to convert the text to fills.

11. With the text still selected, use the Color panel to select the white-to-black linear gradient, change the color of the left color pointer to #FF6600, and leave the right color pointer at #000000.

12. Publish the banner as a SWF file with the name **altBanner.swf**, and then change the Flash publish settings to uncheck the SWF Settings options and do not generate a size report.

13. In your text editor, open the **sampleAlt.htm** Web page located in the Flash6\Review folder included with your Data Files, replace the image tag that has the hutBanner.jpg reference to an EMBED tag with the altBanner.swf reference using the code **<embed src="altBanner.swf" width="500" height="250">** so that the Web page will display the new banner.

14. Save and close the sampleAlt.htm file, and then preview sampleAlt.htm in a Web browser.

15. Submit the finished files to your instructor.

Create and export a logo with a bitmap fade animation and a gradient fill.

APPLY

Case Problem 1

Data Files needed for this Case Problem: kprLogo.fla, pet1.jpg, pet2.jpg

Katie's Pet Resort   Katie asks John to develop a new logo for the resort's Web site. She wants the logo to include two pictures that are each displayed for a few seconds at a time. John asks you to create an animation of the pictures where one fades out while the other fades in to use as the background for the logo. He also wants you to create a gradient to use as the fill for the letters in the logo. Figure 6-43 shows the completed logo.

Figure 6-43   Katie's Pet Resort logo

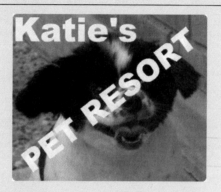

1. Open the **kprLogo.fla** file located in the Flash6\Case1 folder included with your Data Files, and then save the document as **katieLogo.fla** in the same folder.

2. Import the **pet1.jpg** and **pet2.jpg** bitmaps located in the Flash6\Case1 folder included with your Data Files directly into the document's library. Modify each bitmap's properties by changing the compression quality to 80%.

3. Create a new movie clip symbol named **resort animation**. In symbol-editing mode, drag an instance of the pet1.jpg bitmap to the center of the Stage, and then, in the Info panel, set its X and Y coordinates to 0, and, if necessary, select the center registration point. Convert the bitmap instance to a movie clip symbol named **pet1 symbol**. Rename Layer 1 to **pet1**.

4. In the pet1 layer, insert keyframes at Frame 36 and Frame 48. At Frame 36, set the alpha amount for the pet1 symbol instance to 100%. At Frame 48, change the alpha amount for the pet1 symbol instance to 0%. Create a motion tween at Frame 36, add a color property keyframe at Frame 47, and then set the alpha amount for the pet1 symbol instance to 0% so that the pet1 symbol instance fades out between Frame 36 and Frame 48.

5. In the pet1 layer, insert a keyframe at Frame 84, create a motion tween at Frame 84, extend the motion tween to Frame 96, add a color property keyframe at Frame 96, and then set the alpha amount for the pet1 symbol instance to 100% so that the pet1 symbol instance fades in between Frame 84 and Frame 96.

6. In the Timeline, add a new layer and name it **pet2**. In Frame 36, insert a keyframe, and then add an instance of the pet2.jpg bitmap to the Stage. In the Info panel, center the bitmap on the Stage and select its center registration point. Convert the pet2.jpg bitmap instance to a movie clip symbol named **pet2 symbol**.

7. In the pet2 layer, insert a keyframe at Frame 48. In Frame 36, change the alpha amount of the pet2 symbol to 0%. Create a motion tween at Frame 36, and then add a color property keyframe at Frame 47, and set the alpha amount for the pet2 symbol instance to 100% so that the pet2 symbol instance fades in between Frame 36 and Frame 48.

8. In the pet2 layer, insert a keyframe at Frame 84, set the alpha amount for the pet2 symbol instance to 100%, create a motion tween, insert a color property keyframe at Frame 96, and then set the alpha amount to 0% so that the pet2 symbol instance fades out between Frame 84 and Frame 96. Exit symbol-editing mode.

9. In the Timeline, select the background layer, and then drag a copy of the resort animation from the library to the center of the Stage. In the Align panel, align the bitmap to the left edge and the top edge of the Stage. Lock the background layer.

10. In the pet resort layer, change the text to fills by applying the Break Apart command twice.

11. In the Swatches panel, select the gray radial gradient. In the Color panel, change the color of the right color pointer to #FFFF33. The text now has a white-to-yellow gradient. Deselect the text, and then lock the pet resort layer.

12. Publish the logo in the SWF, HTML, and JPEG file formats. Use the default names and settings for the published files.

13. Preview the logo in a Web browser using the HTML file created by Flash.

14. Submit the finished files to your instructor.

Create and then publish a logo with a bitmap and a custom gradient.

APPLY

Case Problem 2

Data Files needed for this Case Problem: aczLogo.fla, giraffe.jpg

Alamo City Zoo   Janet asks Alex to create a new logo that can be used as an advertisement on other Web sites to promote the Alamo City Zoo's new giraffe exhibit. Alex suggests that the logo should include a picture of a giraffe and use a gradient in the background. To complete the logo, you need to import a bitmap of a giraffe and then add the bitmap as a background for the logo. You will also add a rectangle with a radial gradient that is partially transparent over the bitmap to enhance the logo. Figure 6-44 shows the completed logo.

| Figure 6-44 | Alamo City Zoo logo |

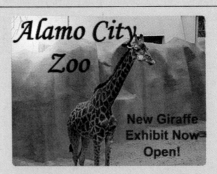

1. Open the **aczLogo.fla** file located in the Flash6\Case2 folder included with your Data Files, and then save the document as **zooLogo.fla** in the same folder.

2. Import the **giraffe.jpg** bitmap located in the Flash6\Case2 folder included with your Data Files to the document's library, and then change the bitmap's compression quality to 80%.

3. In the background layer, drag a copy of the giraffe bitmap from the library to the center of the Stage. In the Position and Size section of the Property inspector, set the X and Y coordinates to 0. Lock the background layer.

4. In the Timeline, insert a new layer above the background layer and name it **gradient**. In the Swatches panel, select the gray radial gradient. In the Color panel, change the Hex value of the right color pointer to #FFFF99.

5. In the Color panel, set the alpha amount to 10% to make the gradient partially transparent.

6. In the gradient layer, draw a rectangle with no stroke and the new gradient as its fill that covers the entire Stage. If necessary, in the Property inspector, set the X and Y coordinates to 0, set the width to 300, and set the height to 225.

7. With the rectangle still selected, use the Gradient Transform tool to display the gradient's bounding circle. Drag the middle editing handle on the lower-right side of the bounding circle to reduce the gradient's radius to about half its original size.

8. Drag the gradient's center point to the upper-left corner of the Stage between the letters "A" and "l" in the "Alamo" text.

9. In the Publish Settings dialog box, create a new profile and name it **zooProfile**. Set the zooProfile to publish a Flash file, an HTML file, and a JPEG image file using the default names.

10. In the Flash publish settings, change the player version to Flash Player 8 and do not include hidden layers. In the HTML publish settings, in the Playback section, do not display the menu and do not loop. In the JPEG publish settings, change the quality value to 90. Publish the files.

11. Preview the logo in a browser using the HTML file created by Flash.

12. Submit the finished files to your instructor.

Create and publish an animated logo with bitmaps in a mask and an animated gradient.

CHALLENGE

Case Problem 3

Data Files needed for this Case Problem: wcnLogo.fla, flower1.jpg, flower2.jpg, flower3.jpg

Westcreek Nursery   Alice and her staff like the interactive logo developed for the Westcreek Nursery Web site, but think that pictures of flowers in an animation could enhance the logo even more. Amanda agrees and wants you to add some sample pictures of flowers to the logo. Amanda also suggests changing the logo's title to make it more dynamic. You'll help Amanda revise the logo by creating an animation with the flower bitmaps and adding a new, more dynamic title. Figure 6-45 shows the completed logo.

Figure 6-45   Westcreek Nursery logo

1. Open the **wcnLogo.fla** file located in the Flash6\Case3 folder included with your Data Files, and then save the document as **flowerLogo.fla** in the same folder.

2. Import the **flower1.jpg**, **flower2.jpg**, and **flower3.jpg** bitmaps located in the Flash6\Case3 folder included with your Data Files to the document's library. Modify the properties of each bitmap to have a compression quality of 80%.

3. Create a new movie clip symbol named **flower animation**. In symbol-editing mode, extend Layer 1 to Frame 90, rename Layer 1 to **flower1**, drag an instance of the flower1 bitmap to the center of the Stage, and then use the Info panel to center it on the Stage.

4. Convert the flower1 bitmap instance to a movie clip symbol named **flower1 symbol**. Create a motion tween between Frame 10 and Frame 20 to fade out the flower1 symbol instance (the alpha amount should be 100% at Frame 10 and 0% at Frame 20). Create a motion tween between Frame 80 and Frame 90 to fade in the flower1 symbol (the alpha amount should be 0% at Frame 80 and 100% at Frame 90).

5. Insert a new layer and name it **flower2**. In Frame 20, insert a keyframe and then drag an instance of the flower2 bitmap to the center of the Stage, using the Info panel to center it.

6. Convert the flower2 bitmap instance to a movie clip symbol named **flower2 symbol**. Create a motion tween between Frame 20 and Frame 30 to fade in the flower2 symbol. Create a motion tween between Frame 40 and Frame 50 to fade out the flower2 symbol.

7. Insert a new layer and name it **flower3**. In Frame 50, insert a keyframe, and then drag an instance of the flower3 bitmap to the center of the Stage, using the Info panel to center it on the Stage.

8. Convert the flower3 bitmap instance to a movie clip symbol named **flower3 symbol**. Create a motion tween between Frame 50 and Frame 60 to fade in the flower3 symbol. Create a motion tween between Frame 70 and Frame 80 to fade out the flower3 symbol.

9. Insert a new layer above the flower3 layer and name it **mask**. Change it to a mask layer, and then change all of the flower layers into masked layers. The flower layers should all be indented under the mask layer.

⊕ EXPLORE 10. In the mask layer, draw a five-sided star shape with a point size of 0.50, no stroke, and a fill color of your choice. In the Info panel, set the star shape's width to 200, its height to 195, and its X and Y coordinates to 0. Lock all of the layers. Exit symbol-editing mode. (*Hint*: To draw a star shape, select the PolyStar tool in the Tools panel, click the Options button in the Tools Settings section of the Property inspector, and then set the appropriate options in the Tool Settings dialog box.)

11. Insert a new layer and name it **star**. Move the star layer below the content layer. In the star layer, add an instance of the flower animation symbol to the center of the Stage.

12. Open the title symbol in symbol-editing mode. Copy the text block in the title text layer. Add a new layer and name it **title mask**. In this layer, use the Paste in Place command to paste a copy of the text in the same relative position as in the title text layer. If necessary, deselect the text.

⊕ EXPLORE 13. Create a new linear gradient. Select the gray linear gradient from the Swatches panel as a starting point. In the Color panel, add two more color pointers close together in the center of the gradient definition bar. Make these two new gradient colors white (#FFFFFF). Make the far left gradient color black (#000000). The middle of the gradient has a narrow white band. (*Hint*: Click the color definition bar to place a new color pointer.)

14. Insert a new layer above the title text layer and name it **gradient**. In the gradient layer, draw a rectangle with the gradient you created as the fill and with no stroke that covers "West" in "Westcreek" and is 150 pixels wide and 55 pixels high.

15. Convert the rectangle to a movie clip symbol name **gradient symbol**. Extend all the layers to Frame 20. Insert keyframes in the gradient layer at Frame 10 and Frame 20. In Frame 10 of the gradient layer, move the gradient instance to the right so that it covers the last four letters ("reek") of "Westcreek." Create motion tweens at Frame 1 and Frame 10.

16. Change the title mask layer to a mask layer, and make sure the gradient layer becomes the masked layer. The letters mask the gradient, giving the text a moving highlight effect. Exit symbol-editing mode.

17. In the Publish Settings dialog box, create a new profile and name it **wcnProfile**. Set the profile to publish a Flash file, an HTML file, a GIF file, and a PNG file using the default filenames.

18. In the Flash publish settings, change the Player to Flash Player 9, and then check the Compress movie, Include hidden layers, Include XMP metadata, and Protect from import options. In the HTML publish settings, use the default settings. In the GIF publish settings, check the Optimize colors, Interlace, Smooth, and Dither solids options. In the PNG publish settings, set the Bit depth to 24-bit. Publish the files.

⊕ **EXPLORE** 19. Export the new profile and save it with its default name in the Flash6\Case3 folder included with your Data Files. (*Hint*: Click the Import/export profile button in the Publish Settings dialog box, and then click Export.)

20. Preview the logo in a browser using the HTML file created by Flash. Make sure the flowers within the star fade in and out and the "Westcreek" text has the gradient moving through its letters.

21. Submit the finished files to your instructor.

Create and publish a banner with a bitmap background and custom gradients.

CREATE

Case Problem 4

Data File needed for this Case Problem: mission.jpg

Missions Support Association   Brittany asks Anissa to create a new banner that can be used on the Missions Support Association Web site to promote the association to its members. The banner should include the mission.jpg bitmap (which has the dimensions of 300 pixels × 300 pixels), motion tweens that create a fade effect for a symbol instance, and gradients. You will design and create the new banner. Figure 6-46 shows one possible banner.

Figure 6-46 **Sample Missions Support Association banner**

1. Create a new document, and then save it as **msaPromotion.fla** in the Flash6\Case4 folder included with your Data Files. Edit the document properties to set the dimensions and Stage color appropriately.

2. Import the **mission.jpg** bitmap located in the Flash6\Case4 folder included with your Data Files into the document's library. Modify the properties of the bitmap to allow smoothing and to have a quality setting of 80%.

3. Create a fade effect somewhere in the banner design using the mission.jpg bitmap. For example, you could create a movie clip symbol of the bitmap and have the image fade in as the banner's background.

4. Add the association's name, **Missions Support Association**, to the banner, using the properties of your choice. For example, you can create a movie clip symbol that includes the text block on a background shape with a custom gradient that fades in or moves onto the banner.

5. Add the key points about the association to the banner, using the text properties of your choice. You can use the text **Special events**, **Volunteer opportunities**, and **Educational tours**, or make up your own. For example, you could make the text fade in and then fade out of the banner.

6. Use at least one gradient fill color in the banner. Customize the fill color to match your banner design. Transform the gradient appropriately.

7. Publish the banner as a Flash file and an HTML file using the default filenames. In the Flash publish settings, check the Compress movie, Include hidden layers, Include XMP metadata, and Protect from import options. In the HTML publish settings, use the default options.

8. Preview the logo in a browser using the HTML file created by Flash.

9. Submit the finished files to your instructor.

ENDING DATA FILES

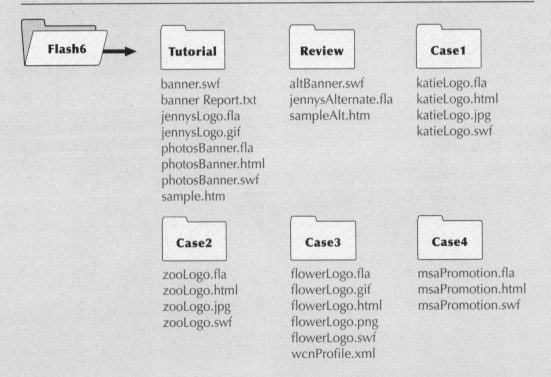

Flash6 →

Tutorial
banner.swf
banner Report.txt
jennysLogo.fla
jennysLogo.gif
photosBanner.fla
photosBanner.html
photosBanner.swf
sample.htm

Review
altBanner.swf
jennysAlternate.fla
sampleAlt.htm

Case1
katieLogo.fla
katieLogo.html
katieLogo.jpg
katieLogo.swf

Case2
zooLogo.fla
zooLogo.html
zooLogo.jpg
zooLogo.swf

Case3
flowerLogo.fla
flowerLogo.gif
flowerLogo.html
flowerLogo.png
flowerLogo.swf
wcnProfile.xml

Case4
msaPromotion.fla
msaPromotion.html
msaPromotion.swf

TUTORIAL **7**

OBJECTIVES

Session 7.1
- Review the structure of a Flash Web site
- Plan and create a Flash Web site
- Review Web site accessibility

Session 7.2
- Create a Flash template and use the template to create Flash documents
- Make a Flash Web site accessible
- Work with external libraries
- Create a navigation bar with complex buttons

Session 7.3
- Learn basic ActionScript 2.0 commands
- Load external SWF files into the Flash Player using levels
- Use the Actions panel
- Load external image files into the Flash Player using a movie clip
- Use the Behaviors panel

FLASH

Planning and Creating a Flash Web Site

Building a Site with a Template, a Navigation Bar, and ActionScript

Case | *Admiral Web Design*

Jackson's Sports, a local sports equipment and supply company, provides discounted equipment, team uniforms, and player trophies to youth basketball, baseball, softball, volleyball, and soccer teams. Dan Jackson, owner of the company, wants Admiral Web Design to develop a new Jackson's Youth Sports Web site that is accessible through links provided on the existing site and that focuses on services the company provides to local youth sports. The Web site will have a home page with appropriate graphic elements and a navigation scheme that will lead to the other key areas of the site. Chris, as site developer, suggests using Flash to develop the entire site—not just the graphic elements of the site. With Flash, the site can be more visually interesting and include multimedia elements such as team photos that change regularly to showcase different teams and players.

In this tutorial, you will plan and create the Flash Web site based on the client's requirements.

STARTING DATA FILES

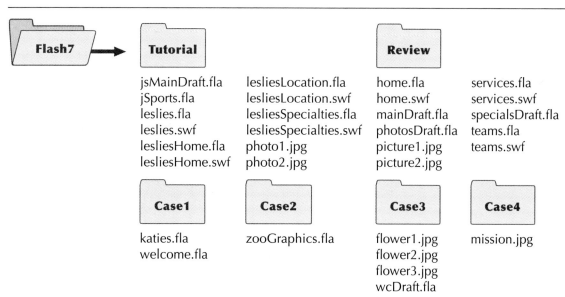

Flash7 → **Tutorial**

jsMainDraft.fla   lesliesLocation.fla
jSports.fla   lesliesLocation.swf
leslies.fla   lesliesSpecialties.fla
leslies.swf   lesliesSpecialties.swf
lesliesHome.fla   photo1.jpg
lesliesHome.swf   photo2.jpg

Review

home.fla   services.fla
home.swf   services.swf
mainDraft.fla   specialsDraft.fla
photosDraft.fla   teams.fla
picture1.jpg   teams.swf
picture2.jpg

Case1

katies.fla
welcome.fla

Case2

zooGraphics.fla

Case3

flower1.jpg
flower2.jpg
flower3.jpg
wcDraft.fla

Case4

mission.jpg

SESSION 7.1 VISUAL OVERVIEW

Buttons load a different SWF file using **levels**, which are like different planes where the Flash Player can load SWF files or other content such as images.

The main SWF file is loaded at level 0 in the Flash Player.

The **navigation system** for a Flash Web site is a set of buttons or graphic elements that users click to navigate to the various parts of one or more SWF files.

Welcome to

Visit our newes
Choose from a va
fruits, fruit bas
smoothies, and
Sample some of o
Always F

The navigation system can be a **navigation bar**, which is a set of buttons arranged vertically (as shown here) or horizontally.

You can set content to load when the Web site is initially displayed and when a button is clicked, such as this welcome text.

Leslie's Fruit Shop

Home
Location
Specialties

Fresh Fruit
Daily!

Welcome to Leslie's!

Visit our newest location!
Choose from a variety of fresh
fruits, fruit baskets, fruit
smoothies, and fruit pies.
Sample some of our fruit cups!
Always Fresh!

Leslie's Fruit S

Home
Location
Specialties

Leslie's

Conveniently Lo
Leslie's now has 5 f.
to serve you

Come Visit Us

Fresh Fruit
Daily!

The content loaded at level 1 appears on top of the main SWF file at level 0.

Clicking a button loads a new page at level 1 in the Flash Player.

NAVIGATION FOR A FLASH WEB SITE

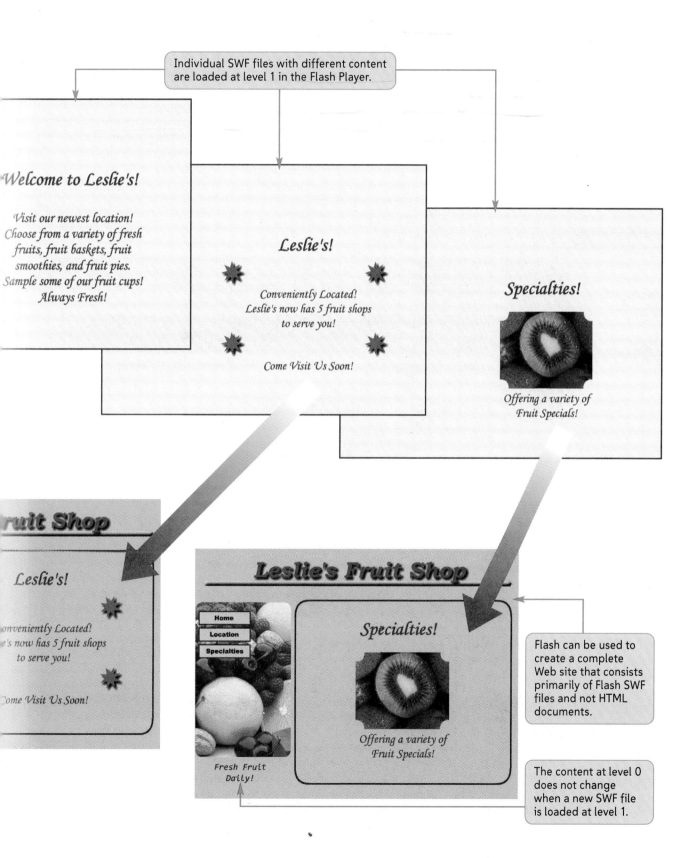

Individual SWF files with different content are loaded at level 1 in the Flash Player.

Flash can be used to create a complete Web site that consists primarily of Flash SWF files and not HTML documents.

The content at level 0 does not change when a new SWF file is loaded at level 1.

Understanding the Structure of a Flash Web Site

Many of the Web sites you see on the Internet consist mainly of HTML. These documents, often called **Web pages**, can contain text, graphics, hyperlinks, and multimedia elements such as those created with Flash. The animations and graphic elements you have created so far with Flash are all meant to be part of an HTML document. However, Flash can also be used to create a complete Web site that consists primarily of Flash SWF files and not HTML documents.

A Flash Web site includes a navigation system that allows users to move between the various SWF files. In some cases, a Web site is built in two versions, one using mostly HTML and one using mostly Flash. An organization might build an HTML version of the Web site in addition to the Flash version to accommodate users who don't have a fast Internet connection, who don't have the latest version of the Flash Player installed on their computers, or who don't use a computer or device that supports Flash. An example of a Flash Web site is shown in Figure 7-1.

Figure 7-1	Ford F-Series truck Flash Web site

The SWF files that make up the Web site are referenced from an HTML document. The HTML document is usually created by the site developer using a program such as Adobe Dreamweaver. It can also be created in Flash by selecting the HTML format in the publish settings for the document. Notice that the URL of the Flash site shown does not reference a SWF file. Instead, the URL shows the path that leads to the site's default home page, which is an HTML document. The HTML document appears in the Web browser and then calls or references the SWF file that activates the Flash Player plug-in, which, in turn, enables the Web browser to play SWF files. Within the HTML document, the Flash Player plays the SWF file and initially displays the home or main page of the Web site. In the Web site shown in Figure 7-1, when the user clicks the Diesel Radiator button on the Ford F-Series page, another SWF file containing the cooling system information page loads into the Flash Player using the same HTML document, as shown in Figure 7-2.

Figure 7-2   **Ford F-Series diesel radiator page**

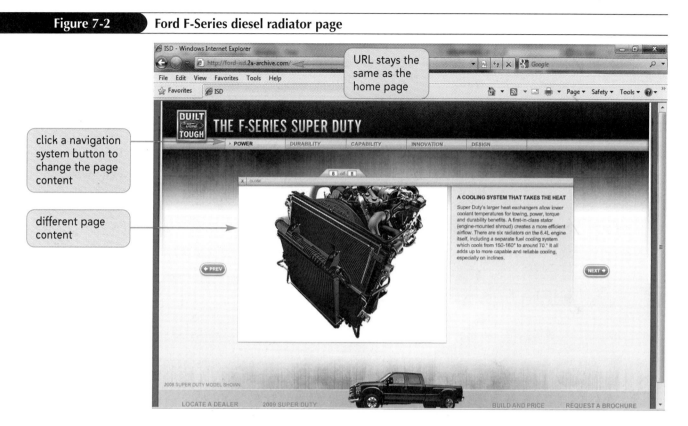

click a navigation system button to change the page content

different page content

URL stays the same as the home page

Creating a Navigation System

A navigation system can work two ways. In one system, the buttons cause the playhead to go to different frames in the same Timeline. The content for each part of the Web site is placed in separate frames, and actions are added to the frames to control the playhead. In the other system, the buttons load different SWF files using levels. You can load a SWF file into the Flash Player so that it replaces the currently playing SWF file or so that it loads on top of the currently playing SWF file. The first SWF file is usually loaded into the Flash Player at level 0 and is considered the home or main page of the Flash Web site. Other SWF files can then be loaded at higher levels. For example, a SWF file specified to load at level 1 plays on top of the SWF file that is already playing at level 0, and the content of the SWF file at level 0 shows through any empty areas of the SWF file at level 1, as shown in the Session 7.1 Visual Overview.

When a SWF file loads at a level already occupied by another SWF file, the newly loaded SWF file replaces the file currently playing. However, the properties of the SWF file at level 0 take precedence over those of the SWF files loaded at higher levels. For example, if the SWF file at level 0 has a green background and a SWF file with a blue background is loaded at level 1, then the level 1 SWF file also has a green background. The same applies to the Stage dimensions. The dimensions of the SWF file at level 0 take precedence over the dimensions of the SWF files that load at higher levels.

TIP

It is important to make certain that the contents of the loaded SWF files do not interfere with those of the SWF file loaded at level 0.

Exploring a Sample Flash Web Site

The Jackson's Youth Sports Web site will use levels in its navigation system. To get a better idea of how a Flash Web site that uses levels works, you will explore a sample site for Leslie's Fruit Shop. The site is organized with a home page, a location page, and a specialties page. The SWF file that contains the title, background picture, large rectangle, and buttons is loaded at level 0 of the Flash Player. Each button, when clicked, will load a different SWF file at level 1 to replace the content within the rectangle.

To explore the Leslie's Fruit Shop Flash Web site:

1. Open the **leslies.fla** file located in the Flash7\Tutorial folder included with your Data Files, and then reset the workspace to the Essentials layout.

2. On the Application bar, click **File**, point to **Publish Preview**, and then click **Default – (HTML)**. Your browser opens and displays the leslies.html file with the leslies.swf file playing in the Flash Player.

   Trouble? If the file doesn't appear in your Web browser, the browser might have restricted the Web page from running. Click the Information Bar, click Allow Blocked Content, and then click the Yes button in the Security Warning dialog box to confirm that you want to open the file.

3. Click the **Location** button. The location information appears in the Flash Player window, although the URL in the Address bar still shows leslies.html as the last part of the URL. See Figure 7-3.

Figure 7-3	Leslie's Fruit Shop Flash Web site

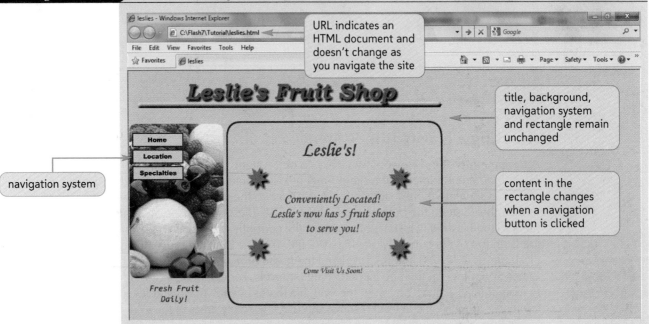

4. Click the **Specialties** button. The specialties information appears, although, again, the URL does not change.

5. Click the **Home** button to return to the home page. The home page appears, although the URL remains unchanged.

6. Close the browser to return to Flash.

7. Open the **lesliesSpecialties.fla** file located in the Flash7\Tutorial folder included with your Data Files. This document contains only the information about the specialty items. It does not contain the navigation buttons or any of the graphic elements of the Web site, such as the background and title banner. Those elements are contained only in the leslies.fla file.

TIP
You can also press the Ctrl+Alt+W keys to close all open documents at once.

8. On the Application bar, click **File**, and then click **Close All** to close the leslies.fla and lesliesSpecialties.fla files without saving any changes.

Comparing Navigation Systems for Flash and HTML Web Sites

Because a Flash Web site uses only one HTML document rather than a series of HTML documents, the Back and Forward buttons on the Web browser toolbar do *not* provide the same functionality as they do for an HTML Web site. With a traditional HTML Web site, each time you navigate to a different Web page within the Web site, the browser tracks a history of which Web pages you visited, and the URL in the Address bar changes based on the filename of the current Web page. In a Flash Web site, however, only one HTML document might be displayed, so the URL doesn't change, even though the frames or SWF files being displayed in the Flash Player within the HTML document change. The HTML document displayed in the Web browser acts only as a container for the Flash content. After a user has navigated to several parts of the Flash Web site, the browser's Back button does not display the most recently visited SWF file. Instead, it returns to the most recently visited URL. As a result, it's essential to provide a clear and intuitive navigational system within the Flash Web site so that users can easily understand how to navigate within the site without using the browser navigation buttons.

Planning a Flash Web Site

The first and most crucial task in creating a Flash Web site is to plan the content and structure for the site. As discussed, a Flash Web site might consist of a series of Flash SWF files that work together to present the desired information. The basic process for developing a Web site requires the following steps. First, identify the goals and objectives for the Web site based on the needs of the client. Based on the goals and objectives, develop the content of the site. The content then leads to the design of the Web pages including the navigation system. Finally, build the site and test it to make sure all parts of the site work as designed.

Developing a Flash Web Site ⭐

- Identify the site goals and objectives.
- Determine the target audience.
- Develop the site content.
- Create a storyboard, and design the navigation system and the site pages.
- Build the site.
- Test the site.

Identifying the Site Goals and Objectives

The first step in the development process is to identify the goals of the site. **Site goals** represent what the Web site is intended to accomplish. A Web site can have one goal or many goals, but initially you should define only three to five goals to ensure that the developed site can effectively accomplish these goals. The goals must be clearly defined; otherwise, the developed site might not meet the needs of the client. You start defining the site goals by discussing with the client what he or she wants the site to accomplish.

Consider these examples. The client might want the site to help the company sell a product or to provide information about the services offered by the company. The client might want the site to increase brand awareness for the company's products or to provide information for the company's employees, such as company policies and procedures. Or the client might want to disseminate information to customers about how to use certain products. Each of these goals requires a different approach and results in a different type of Web site. The success of the site depends on how well it meets the goals that have been developed and agreed to by the client. The goals identified for a Web site impact the overall design of the Web site and determine how the site is developed.

To develop goals for the Jackson's Youth Sports Flash Web site:

1. Write down three goals for the Jackson's Youth Sports Web site.

2. Review the list of goals to make sure they are clearly defined.

3. Compare your goals to those identified by Aly and Chris after their meeting with Dan Jackson. See Figure 7-4.

| Figure 7-4 | Jackson's Youth Sports Web site goals |

Goals for Jackson's Youth Sports Web Site
- Promote the Jackson's Sports name.
- Increase sales to local youth sports teams.
- Provide a site dedicated to serving local youth sports.

Based on the site goals, develop a list of objectives. The **site objectives** more clearly define the information the Web site will contain, the types of media that are required, and the number of Web pages necessary to provide the information and fulfill the needs of the client. The objectives also help determine how the Web site pages are organized and what types of pages to develop. For example, one type of site might require pages with many pictures and little text, whereas another type of site might require pages with a lot of text and only a few pictures. Other sites might require pages that display animations or even videos.

The objectives must be clear and measurable so that after the site is complete, you can determine whether each objective has been met. For example, if one site goal is to enhance a company's brand awareness, one objective might be to include a list of the benefits of using the company's products, and another objective might be to highlight the company logo that appears on all of its products. These objectives are focused and quantifiable. You can easily develop a page that has a list of the benefits of using the company's products. You can also include the company logo on all the pages of the Web site, increasing the company's brand awareness.

To develop objectives for the Jackson's Youth Sports Flash Web site:

1. Review the Jackson's Youth Sports Web site goals.

2. Determine four objectives based on the site's goals.

3. Compare your objectives to those developed by Aly. See Figure 7-5.

| Figure 7-5 | Jackson's Youth Sports Web site objectives |

Objectives for Jackson's Youth Sports Web Site
- Include the message that Jackson's Sports supports local youth sports.
- Provide a list of products and services offered by Jackson's Sports.
- Provide the names of local teams doing business with Jackson's Sports.
- Include pictures of the teams; these pictures will change every few weeks.

Determining the Target Audience

As part of the planning process, you must consider the **target audience**, which is the group of people intended to use the site. The characteristics of the people who will be using the site impact how the information is presented on the Web site. The characteristics could be based on demographic information such as the age group, education level, or economic level of the audience. A young audience might indicate that more engaging animations need to be included, whereas a more mature audience might indicate that the site include less animation and perhaps a more conservative color scheme. You can also try to determine the expectations of the target audience. Do they expect to be entertained, or do they expect to obtain detailed information about a product? This determines whether to include interactive games and graphics or detailed information in the form of text. The target audience for the Jackson's Youth Sports Web site consists of team coaches, players, and players' parents. The site, therefore, should appeal to both young sports participants and the adults involved with the teams.

Making a Web Site Accessible

The **World Wide Web Consortium (W3C)** is an international consortium whose mission is to develop Web standards. The W3C has established the **Web Content Accessibility Guidelines (WCAG) 2.0**, which is a standard to help Web designers and developers create Web sites with the needs of users with disabilities in mind. The guidelines cover a wide range of recommendations for making Web content more accessible to users with disabilities such as impaired vision, blindness, hearing loss, or deafness.

One method used to apply these recommendations is to make Web content accessible via a **screen reader**, which is software that visually-impaired users can run to read a Web site's text content aloud. A screen reader can read descriptions you provide for the SWF file or for the movie clips, images, or other graphical content within the file. You make an object accessible to a screen reader by assigning a name and description to the object. You can also specify whether to make a movie clip's child objects accessible. A **child object** is an object inside the movie clip. In addition to making objects accessible to a screen reader, you can also make objects that present no inaccessible content so as not to confuse the user.

Design your Web site with the assumption that your audience will include people with disabilities by making your Web site content accessible. The target audience for the Jackson's Youth Sports Web site might include users with impaired vision. The site, therefore, should be made accessible to screen readers.

The rest of the Web site planning process is guided by the site's goals, objectives, target audience, and accessibility needs. They determine which Flash documents need to be developed, what information each document should contain, and how the documents should be organized.

Developing the Web Site Content

The next step is to determine what content the site's pages will contain. The content is determined in large part by what the client wants the site to accomplish and partly by the target audience. The site goals and objectives identified in the first step help determine the pages and media that the Web site must include. Each objective for the Jackson's Youth Sport site will result in one or more separate Web pages designed to meet that specific objective. For example, one page will display pictures that need to change regularly, so that capability has to be designed as part of the page.

One way to determine the site's content is to develop an outline with categories and subcategories. Each category might correspond to one objective, or a stated objective may have more than one category. The categories in the outline can correspond to the pages that will be developed for the site and also help determine the navigation system. You'll develop an outline for the Jackson's Youth Sports Web site.

To develop an outline for the Jackson's Youth Sports Web site content:

1. Review the Jackson's Youth Sports Web site objectives.

2. Develop an outline with categories that correspond to the objectives.

3. Compare your outline with the one developed by Aly and Chris, which has one page for each objective. See Figure 7-6.

Figure 7-6	Jackson's Youth Sports Web site outline

Outline for Jackson's Youth Sports Web Site
1. Home page
    a. Banner
    b. Message about Jackson's Sports' support of local youth sports
    c. Navigation bar with buttons exhibiting rollover effects and animation
2. Services
    a. List of products and services
3. Teams
    a. Names of local teams
4. Photos
    a. Pictures of local teams

After the outline is complete, you can start to gather and organize the required information, bitmaps, videos, and other graphics to include on the site. The client usually provides much of the information for a site, such as the products and services available. Graphic elements, such as bitmap files of pictures or video files, often need to be prepared by the site developer or the graphic designer.

Developing a Storyboard and Designing the Navigation System and Site Pages

After the Web site's main areas of content are outlined, you create a **storyboard**, which is a diagram that shows how all of the site's pages are organized. The storyboard shows a sketch of each page with lines indicating how the page links to the other pages. The way the pages link to each other determines the navigation system for the site. As you develop the navigation system, you should keep in mind the characteristics of the target audience. For example, if a large segment of the target audience has limited Internet skills, you should keep the navigation simple and easy to understand.

Based on the content outline for the Jackson's Youth Sports Web site, Aly and Chris have developed a storyboard for the site, as shown in Figure 7-7. The storyboard shows the site's main page as well as the other pages that will be developed and the basic design of each page. The main page will be loaded at level 0 in the Flash Player. The other pages, which will be loaded at level 1, include the Teams page, the Services page, and the Photos page. In addition, the Welcome page will appear when the main page is first displayed. The Welcome page will be replaced when another page is loaded at level 1. When the site visitor clicks the Home button, the Welcome page will load again, replacing the page currently at level 1.

Figure 7-7   **Storyboard for Jackson's Youth Sports Web site**

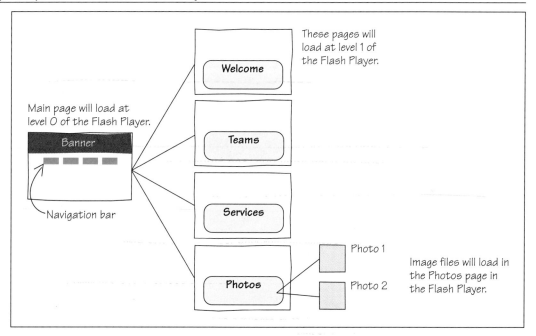

Written Communication: Documenting Web Site Specifications

After you develop the goals, objectives, outline, and storyboard for a Web site, you should compile all of this information in a written report. An effective report is clearly organized, contains detailed summaries of decisions and specifications for the Web site, and has no spelling, grammar, or punctuation errors. The client should review and sign the report to indicate that he or she is in agreement. It's very important to have the client sign off on the Web site specifications before you start creating the Flash files for the Web site. Otherwise, the client might request changes during the development of the Flash files, forcing you to revise or re-create files you have already completed. After you start creating the Web site files, any changes requested by the client should also be in writing. When the Web site is complete, the documentation is proof that the developed site meets the agreed-upon specifications.

During the planning of the Jackson's Youth Sports Web site, you determined the site's goals and objectives, developed an outline of the site's contents, assessed the accessibility needs, and created a storyboard to show the site's pages and navigation system. In the next session, you will create the site's pages and the navigation bar.

Session 7.1 Quick Check

1. The SWF files of a Flash Web site are referenced from a(n) __HTML__ file.
2. (True) or False. The first SWF file in a Flash Web site is usually loaded into the Flash Player at level 0 and is considered the home or main page.
3. The Flash Player uses _____ to load multiple SWF files at once.
4. True or False. When a SWF file is loaded at the same level already occupied by another SWF file, the new SWF file is automatically loaded at a higher level.
5. List the steps in the planning process for developing a Web site.
6. How can you start to define the goals of the site?
7. What is a storyboard?

SESSION 7.2 VISUAL OVERVIEW

An **external library** contains the symbols for a stored document, making these symbols available to the active document.

An external library opens in a Library panel separate from the current document's Library panel.

You can copy symbols from the external library into the active document.

The Accessibility panel provides options for making a movie accessible to users with disabilities such as impaired vision or hearing.

An object must have an instance name assigned to it in the Property inspector to have accessibility options applied to it. This is the movie name, not the instance name.

A screen reader can read the description entered for the selected object.

Templates are organized in categories.

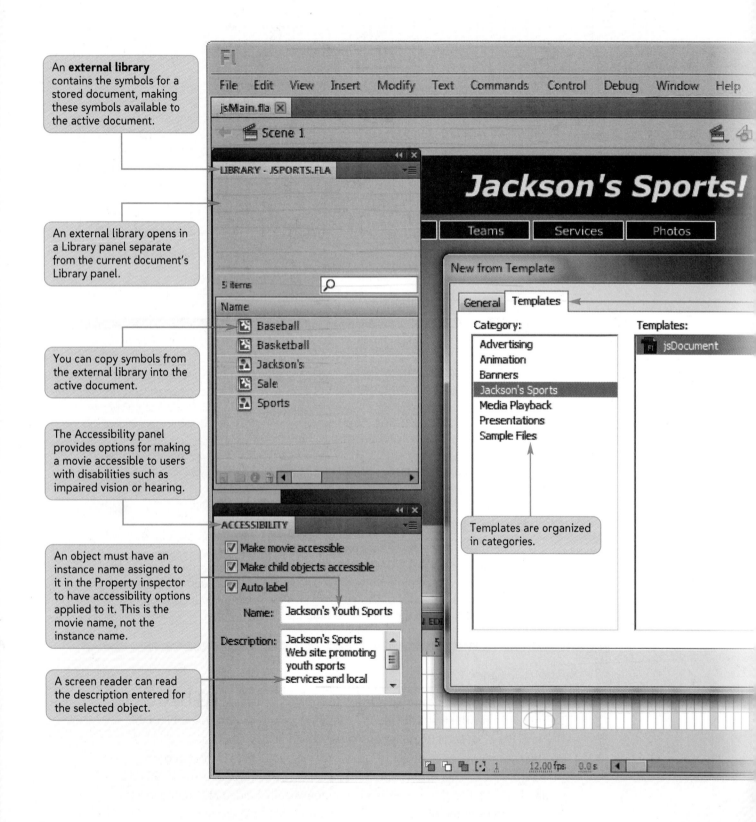

TEMPLATES AND EXTERNAL LIBRAR

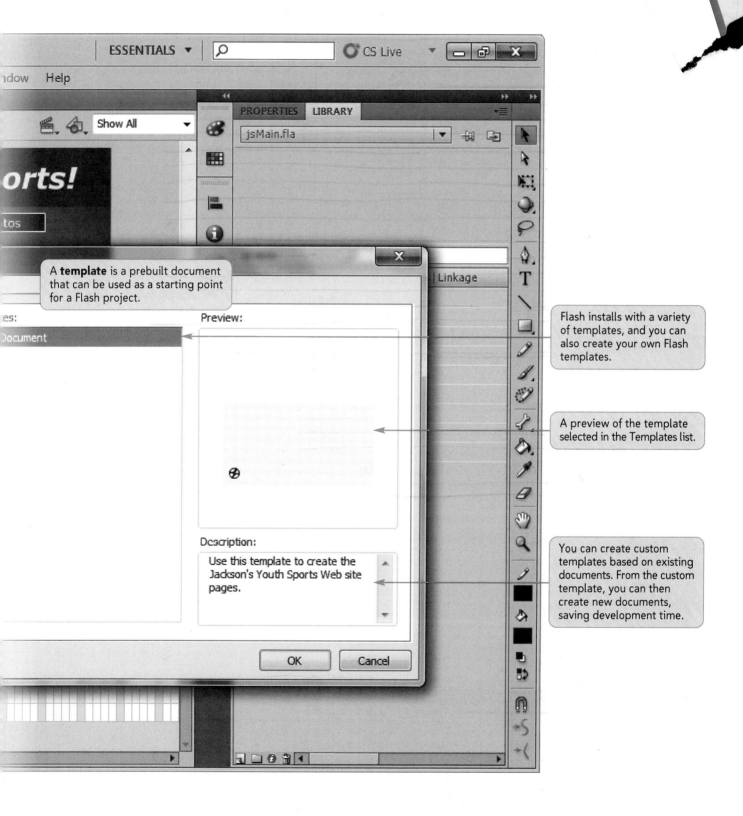

ESSENTIALS ▾ | 🔍 | CS Live ▾

ndow   Help

Show All ▾

PROPERTIES   LIBRARY

jsMain.fla

orts!

tos

A **template** is a prebuilt document that can be used as a starting point for a Flash project.

Linkage

es: Preview:

Document

Description:

Use this template to create the Jackson's Youth Sports Web site pages.

OK   Cancel

Flash installs with a variety of templates, and you can also create your own Flash templates.

A preview of the template selected in the Templates list.

You can create custom templates based on existing documents. From the custom template, you can then create new documents, saving development time.

FL 334

Creating Content for a Web Site

To create a site's contents, you start by creating a Flash document that will be the main page displayed when the user first enters the Web site. You create this document in the same way you have created other Flash documents, but you also include a navigation system that works with other Flash documents. Because you want the site's documents to work together and to provide a consistent viewing experience, all the documents should be the same size and have the same background.

As in the Leslie's Fruit Shop Web site, the main document of the Jackson's Youth Sports Web site will contain the background, banner, and navigation system. The other documents in the Web site will contain only the elements specific to a particular component of the Web site. These documents can have any number of graphic elements, including animations. Because these documents will play on top of the main document, you need to make certain that the elements on one document do not hide or overlap the elements of the main document.

Creating the Main Document's Content

The main document is the part of the Web site that doesn't change as other levels are loaded and displayed. Based on Aly's instructions, the main document of the Jackson's Youth Sports Web site will have a banner with an animation of the store's name and a background picture. It will also contain a navigation bar consisting of a set of buttons. The page needs to be accessible to screen readers. You'll start by making the Web site accessible, and then you'll create the banner in the Web site's main document provided by Aly. Because you will use ActionScript 2.0 for the actions in this document, the Flash file has been created with the ActionScript 2.0 profile.

You can make a Flash document or an individual object accessible to a screen reader from the Accessibility panel by assigning a name and description to it and specifying whether to make child objects accessible. If you select an object on the Stage, such as a movie clip, you can make that object accessible. If no objects are selected on the Stage, you can use the Accessibility panel to make the entire Flash document accessible. The panel also has options to make a document's child objects accessible or to have labels automatically assigned to objects. An individual object must have an instance name assigned to it in the Property inspector to have accessibility options applied to it. Note that Flash movies made accessible to screen readers must be viewed in Internet Explorer on Windows.

To make the Jackson's Youth Sports main page accessible to screen readers, you will use the Accessibility panel to assign a name and description.

To open the Jackson's Youth Sports Web site's main page and make the site accessible:

1. Open the **jsMainDraft.fla** file located in the Flash7\Tutorial folder included with your Data Files, and then save the file as **jsMain.fla** in the same folder.

2. Reset the workspace to the Essentials layout, and then change the Stage magnification to **Show Frame**. The Stage resizes to fill the Document window.

3. On the Application bar, click **Window**, point to **Other Panels**, and then click **Accessibility**. The Accessibility panel opens.

4. In the Accessibility panel, click the **Make movie accessible** check box to select it.

5. In the Name box, type **Jackson's Youth Sports**. This is the movie name.

6. In the Description box, type **Jackson's Sports Web site promoting youth sports services and local teams**. This description will be read by a screen reader.

7. Make sure the **Make child objects accessible** and **Auto label** check boxes are checked. See Figure 7-8.

Figure 7-8	Accessibility panel

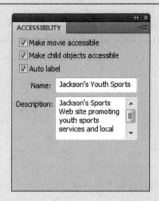

8. Close the Accessibility panel.

The banner in the main document has been created as a symbol. You will complete the banner by adding a bitmap and a text animation.

To add a bitmap and text to the banner:

1. On the Edit bar, click the **Edit Symbols** button ⬡, and then click **jsBanner**. The jsBanner symbol opens in symbol-editing mode.

2. In the Timeline, select the background layer. The soccer.jpg bitmap will be placed in this layer.

3. Go to the **Library** panel, and then drag an instance of the **soccer.jpg** bitmap from the Library panel to the left edge of the rectangle on the Stage. The bitmap picture is included as part of the banner.

4. Select both the bitmap and the rectangle.

5. On the panel shortcut bar, click the **Align** button to open the Align panel.

6. On the Align panel, click the **Align to stage** check box to deselect it if necessary, click the **Align left edge** button, and then click the **Align top edge** button.

7. Click an empty area of the Stage to deselect the objects. The left and top sides of the two objects on the Stage are aligned. See Figure 7-9.

TIP

Press the Ctrl+Alt+1 keys to align the left edges of selected objects; press the Ctrl+Alt+4 keys to align their top edges.

Figure 7-9   **Bitmap and rectangle aligned**

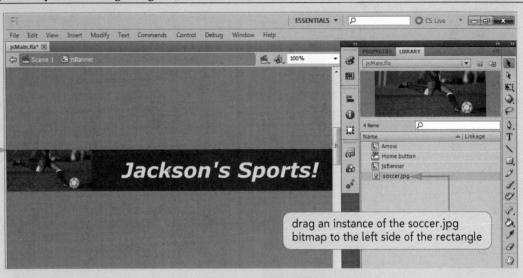

align the bitmap and rectangle along their left and top edges

drag an instance of the soccer.jpg bitmap to the left side of the rectangle

8. In the Timeline, insert regular frames at **Frame 30** of the background and JSports layers to extend their content through Frame 30, and then lock both layers to prevent their objects from being moved accidentally.

9. In the Timeline, insert a new layer and name it **Youth**. You'll add text to the banner in this layer.

10. In the Tools panel, select the **Text** tool [T], and then, in the Property inspector, set the font family to **Verdana**, set the font style to **Bold Italic**, set the point size to **24**, set the text color to **white** (#FFFFFF), set the font rendering method to **Anti-alias for animation**, and then set the paragraph format to **Align left**.

11. On the Stage, click the left side of the picture to create a text block, type **Supporting**, and then change the point size of the letter "S" to **34**.

12. Create a text block below the Supporting text using the same attributes you set in Step 10, and type **Our Youth**.

13. In the Tools panel, click the **Selection** tool [↖], position the two text blocks over the picture as shown in Figure 7-10, and then deselect the text blocks.

Figure 7-10 | **Text blocks added to the banner**

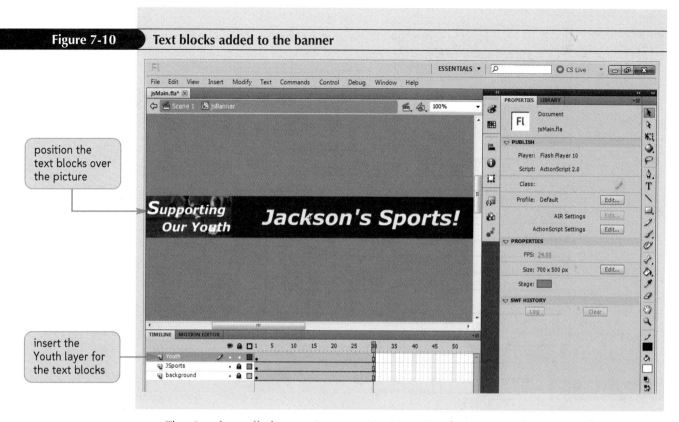

position the text blocks over the picture

insert the Youth layer for the text blocks

The site plan calls for creating an animation using the text over the picture. The text will be animated to increase in size over a short period of time and then decrease. Aly wants the animation to span 30 frames. You will create a motion tween in which the text starts out 50% smaller than its original size and then increases to slightly larger than its original size. After a short pause, the text will decrease back to its original size.

To animate the Supporting Our Youth text:

1. On the Stage, select the **Supporting** text block, press and hold the **Shift** key, select the **Our Youth** text block, and then release the **Shift** key. Both text blocks are selected.

2. Convert the selected text blocks to a movie clip symbol named **Support text**.

3. On the Stage, right-click the **Support text** instance, and then click **Create Motion Tween** on the context menu. A motion tween is created in the Youth layer.

4. In the Timeline, select **Frame 1** of the Youth layer, open the Transform panel, click the **Constrain** button to lock it if necessary, and then set the scale width to **50%**. The Support text instance decreases to half its size in Frame 1.

5. In the Timeline, select **Frame 15** of the Youth layer, and then, in the Transform panel, set the scale width to **110%**. The Support text instance increases to a slightly larger than original size at Frame 15.

6. In the Timeline, select **Frame 20** of the Youth layer, and then, in the Transform panel, set the scale width to **100%**. The Support text instance decreases at Frame 20 to its original size.

7. In the Timeline, drag the playhead to **Frame 1**, and then press the **Enter** key to play the animation. The Support text instance starts small, increases in size, and then decreases to its original size. The text animation is complete.

8. On the Edit bar, click the **Scene 1** link to exit symbol-editing mode and return to the main document.

The banner is complete and an instance of the banner can now be added on the Stage. The banner will be aligned along the left and top edges of the Stage.

To add an instance of the banner to the Stage:

1. In the Timeline, insert a new layer and name it **banner**.

2. Drag an instance of the **jsBanner** symbol from the Library panel to the top of the Stage.

3. Open the Align panel, click the **Align to stage** check box to select it, click the **Align left edge** button ⬛, click the **Align top edge** button ⬛, click an empty area of the Stage to deselect the objects, and then close the Align panel. The banner aligns with the left and top sides of the Stage. See Figure 7-11.

Figure 7-11   jsBanner instance added to Stage

jsBanner instance aligned with the left and top edges of the Stage

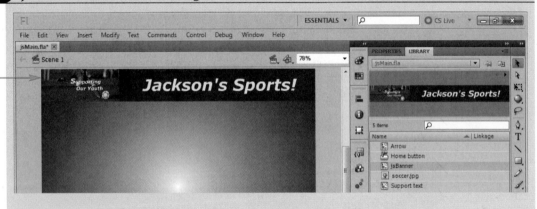

4. Lock the banner layer. The banner instance now cannot be repositioned.

5. Save the jsMain.fla document.

The graphics for the main page are complete. The only item missing is the navigation bar with the buttons to control how the Web site pages are loaded. Before creating the navigation bar, you will create the additional pages for the Web site using a Flash template.

Using a Flash Template to Create Additional Web Pages

The additional documents for the Web site will load on top of the main document. The main document will be at level 0, and its contents will remain visible on the Stage as other documents are loaded at higher levels. These additional documents, therefore, don't need to include the banner or background rectangle contained in the main document. They should include only the content to be displayed. These documents will have the same dimensions as the main page to ensure that the additional text appears consistently in the correct location. The background color of the loaded documents does not matter because the documents automatically default to the gray background of the main document. To ensure that all the additional documents have the same dimensions as the main document and to make it simpler to create new documents for this Web site, you can create a Flash template.

Finding Templates on the Flash Exchange

The preinstalled templates available in Flash enable you to quickly create professional documents such as advertisements, photo slideshows, or documents that play on mobile devices. You can then customize the templates to produce a document with the look and feel you want. Additional templates are available through the Flash Exchange, which is accessible from the Help menu or the Welcome screen. The **Flash Exchange** is an Adobe Web site with many templates created by the Flash developer community. If the preinstalled templates don't meet your needs, explore the ones available on the Flash Exchange.

You can create custom templates based on existing documents. From the custom template, you can then create new documents, saving development time. For example, you can create a template that contains the basic graphic elements, background, and animations you want to include in other documents. Then, each time you create a new document based on the template, the graphic elements, background, and animations are already included with the new document. You can save any Flash document as a template within an existing template category or a new category. You can also include a description of the template that appears when the template is selected in the New from Template dialog box.

Creating a Flash Template

- Create a Flash document.
- On the Application bar, click File, and then click Save as Template.
- Type a name for the template.
- Select an existing template category or create a new category.
- Type a description for the template.
- Click the Save button.

Because you need to create several documents for the Jackson's Youth Sports Web site and because each document will have the same dimensions as well as other similar elements, Aly wants you to create a template. First, you will create the document with the basic graphic elements. Then you will save the document as a template, which you will use to create the other documents.

The banner occupies the top 80 pixels of the main document. The navigation bar, consisting of buttons arranged horizontally, will be placed just below the banner. Therefore, the content of the new documents must be placed below the navigation bar so it will not interfere with the content on the main document. You will place a horizontal guide 150 pixels from the top edge of the Stage, and then add the new content below the horizontal guide.

TIP

You can create a new document by clicking ActionScript 2.0 in the Create New section of the Welcome screen.

To create a Flash document for the Jackson's Youth Sports Web pages:

1. Create a new **ActionScript 2.0** document.
2. In the Properties section of the Property inspector, click the **Edit** button to open the Document Settings dialog box, set the dimensions to **700 px × 500 px**, and then click the **OK** button.
3. Change the Stage magnification to **Show Frame** to display the entire Stage.
4. Show the rulers, and then drag a horizontal guide to **150** pixels from the top edge of the Stage. The content for each document based on this template will be added below the horizontal guide.
5. In the Tools panel, click the **Rectangle** tool, and then, if necessary, click the **Object Drawing** button to deselect it.
6. In the Property inspector, set the fill color to **light yellow** (#FFFFCC), set the stroke color to **no color**, and then set the rectangle corner radius to **10** for all corners. The rectangle you draw will be light yellow with rounded corners.
7. On the Stage, draw a rectangle with its top edge aligned with the horizontal guide.
8. In the Tools panel, click the **Selection** tool, and then select the rectangle on the Stage.
9. In the Property inspector, set the rectangle's width to **600** pixels, set its height to **320** pixels, and then center the rectangle horizontally on the Stage. See Figure 7-12.

Figure 7-12 Rectangle aligned with the horizontal guide

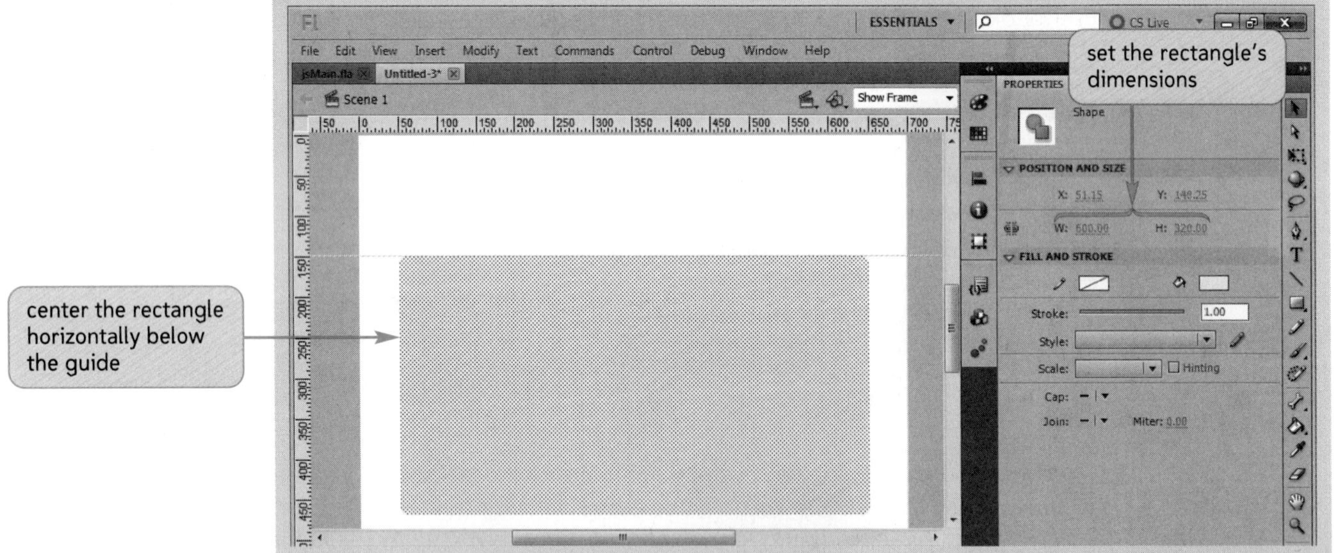

10. In the Timeline, change the name of Layer 1 to **rectangle** and then insert a new layer and name it **contents**. Insert another layer and name it **graphic**. The contents layer will remain empty in the template, but will be used to create the content of each new Web site document.

With the standard structure and content in place, you can save the Flash file as a template. In the Save as Template dialog box, you enter a name for the template, select an existing category or create a new category for the template, and provide a description of the template. Organizing templates in categories makes it simpler to locate a template when you need it. A meaningful description is also helpful in ensuring that the template includes the elements you expect. You will save the Flash document you just created as a template for the Jackson's Youth Sports Web pages.

To save the Flash document as a template:

1. On the Application bar, click **File**, and then click **Save as Template**. The Save as Template dialog box opens.

   Trouble? If the Save As Template Warning dialog box opens, click the Save As Template button.

2. Type **jsDocument** in the Name box, type **Jackson's Sports** in the Category box, and then type **Use this template to create the Jackson's Youth Sports Web site pages.** in the Description box. See Figure 7-13.

Figure 7-13   Save as Template dialog box

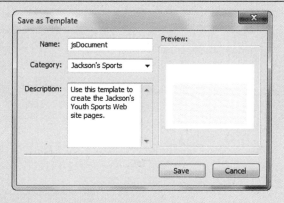

3. Click the **Save** button to save the template.

Using External Libraries

The template will contain animations of a baseball and a basketball. Rather than creating a new graphic object of each ball, you can copy them from existing symbols in another Flash document to the template document. Both symbols will then be available to every document created from the template. To copy symbols from an existing document, you open the document's library as an external library. You can drag instances of the symbols from the external library's Library panel to the current document's Library panel or to the Stage.

REFERENCE

Copying Symbols from an External Library

- On the Application bar, click File, point to Import, and then click Open External Library.
- Select the file with the symbols you want to copy, and then click the Open button.
- Drag an instance of a symbol from the external library's Library panel to the current document's Library panel or to the Stage.
- Close the external library.

Aly created a sample document for Jackson's Youth Sports that contains a basketball symbol and a baseball symbol. You will copy these symbols to the template document.

To copy symbols from an external library:

1. Display the Library panel.

2. On the Application bar, click **File**, point to **Import**, and then click **Open External Library**. The Open as Library dialog box opens.

3. Click the **jSports.fla** document located in the Flash7\Tutorial folder included with your Data Files, and then click the **Open** button. The jSports.fla Library panel opens as an external library.

4. Drag the **Baseball** symbol from the jSports.fla Library panel to the jsDocument.fla Library panel.

5. Drag the **Basketball** symbol from the jSports.fla Library panel to the jsDocument.fla Library panel. Both symbols are copied to the current document's library. See Figure 7-14.

Figure 7-14	External Library panel for jsSports.fla

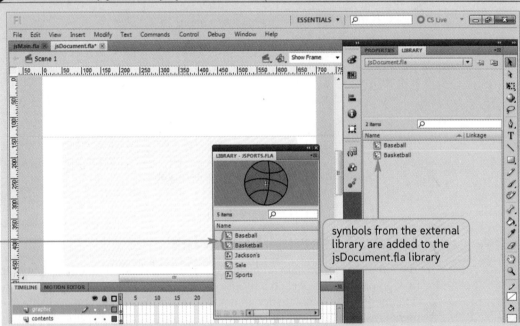

drag these symbols to the jsDocument.fla Library panel

symbols from the external library are added to the jsDocument.fla library

Trouble? If the symbols do not copy to the jsDocument.fla Library panel, you are probably dragging the symbol to the preview area. Drag the symbol from the jSports.fla Library panel to the lower pane of the jsDocument.fla Library panel.

6. Close the jSports.fla Library panel. The external library closes.

Both the basketball and the baseball symbols are stored in the current document's library. You will use the baseball in an animation that you will create next as part of the jsDocument template. You will use the basketball symbol in an animation you create later in this tutorial.

To create an animation with the baseball symbol:

1. Create a new movie clip symbol and name it **Baseball animation**.

2. Drag an instance of the **Baseball** symbol from the Library panel to the center of the Stage.

3. In the Position and Size section of the Property inspector, set the X and Y values to **0**. The Baseball instance is centered on the Stage.

4. On the Stage, right-click the **Baseball** instance, and then click **Create Motion Tween**. A motion tween is created in Frame 1 through Frame 24.

5. In the Timeline, select **Frame 1**, and then, in the Property inspector, set the rotation count to **1** and set the direction to **CW**. The baseball will rotate clockwise once. The animation is complete. Exit symbol-editing mode and return to Scene 1.

6. In the Timeline, select the **graphic** layer, if necessary, and then drag an instance of the Baseball animation symbol from the Library panel to the lower-left corner of the yellow rectangle on the Stage.

7. Save and close the jsDocument.fla file. The jsMain.fla document remains open.

The template for the Jackson's Youth Sports Web site is complete. You are ready to create the additional pages according to Aly's instructions. The first page you will create will load initially with the main document. This page's content will be displayed the first time the Web site is visited and each time the Home button is clicked. You will create the Home button later in this session.

To create the home page from the jsDocument.fla template:

1. On the Application bar, click **File**, click **New** to open the New Document dialog box, and then click the **Templates** tab. The template you created is added to the category you specified—Jackson's Sports.

2. Click **Jackson's Sports** in the Category box, and then, if necessary, click **jsDocument** in the Templates box. The template is selected. See Figure 7-15.

Figure 7-15   New from Template dialog box

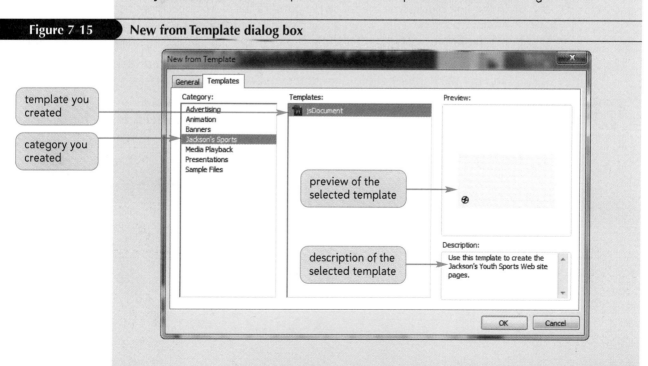

template you created

category you created

preview of the selected template

description of the selected template

3. Click the **OK** button. A new untitled document based on the jsDocument template opens.

4. Save the document as **home.fla** in the Flash7\Tutorial folder included with your Data Files.

5. Change the Stage magnification to **Show All** to display all the contents on the Stage.

The home page includes all of the contents contained in the jsDocument template. You'll add the specific content needed for the home page.

To add content to the home page:

1. In the Timeline, select the **contents** layer.

2. In the Tools panel, click the **Text** tool T, and then, in the Property inspector, set the font family to **Arial**, set the font style to **Bold**, set the point size to **24**, set the Letter spacing to **0**, set the text color to **black** (#000000), and set the paragraph format to **Align left**.

3. On the Stage, create a text block at the top of the yellow rectangle approximately **150 pixels** from the left edge of the Stage and **175 pixels** from the top of the Stage, type **Welcome to Jackson's Youth Sports!** as the page title, and then deselect the title text block.

4. In the Property inspector, set the point size to **14**, and then set the font style to **Regular**.

5. On the Stage, create a text block approximately **150 pixels** from the left edge of the Stage and **230 pixels** from the top of the Stage, and then drag to the right to approximately **550 pixels** from the left edge of the Stage. A fixed-width text block with an approximate width of 400 pixels appears on the Stage. The text you type will wrap onto separate lines within the text block, as opposed to appearing on one long line.

6. In the text block, type the following paragraphs of text, allowing the text to wrap around to the next line when it reaches the right side of the text block, and pressing the **Enter** key twice after the first paragraph:

   At Jackson's Sports, we value your business and we'll do our best to provide you the best sports equipment and supplies at the best prices.

   We are proud to support our local youth sports teams. We have been supplying equipment and sports supplies to many of the local teams for over 15 years.

7. Check the spelling in the document, making any corrections needed. See Figure 7-16.

Figure 7-16	Text for the home page

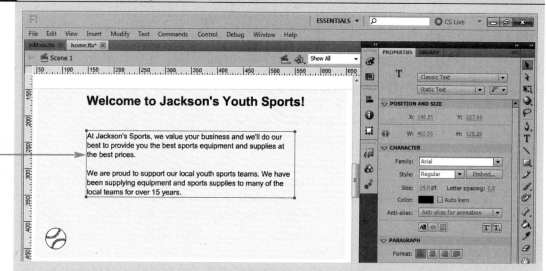

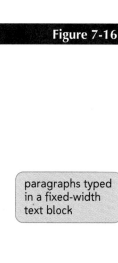

paragraphs typed in a fixed-width text block

Trouble? If a dialog box opens indicating that, based on your settings, there is nothing to check, you need to set up the spelling options. On the Application bar, click Text, and then click Spelling Setup to open the Spelling Setup dialog box. In the Document options section, click the Check text fields content check box. In the Checking options section, click the Suggest typographical matches check box. Click the OK button, and then repeat Step 7.

TIP

You can also press the Ctrl+S keys to save the active document.

8. Save the document.

The home page that appears on top of the main document when the main document is first displayed is complete. You need to create three other pages. One contains the names of local sports teams that have done business with Jackson's Sports. The second is a list of services offered by the store. The third contains pictures of local teams and players. You will create each of these pages using the jsDocument template as a starting point.

To create the Teams page:

1. Create a new document based on the **jsDocument** template, save the document as **teams.fla** in the Flash7\Tutorial folder included with your Data Files, and then change the Stage magnification to **Show All**. The entire contents of the Stage appear.

2. In the Timeline, if necessary, select the **contents** layer.

3. On the Stage, create a text block centered at the top of the yellow rectangle approximately **240 pixels** from the left edge of the Stage and **175 pixels** from the top of the Stage, set the font family to **Arial**, set the font style to **Bold**, set the point size to **24**, set the text color to **black** (#000000), set the paragraph format to **Align left**, and then type **Local Sports Teams** in the text block. The title text block is complete.

4. Deselect the title text block, set the point size to **14**, set the font style to **Regular**, and then create a fixed-width text block approximately **150 pixels** from the left edge of the Stage, **230 pixels** from the top of the Stage, and **400 pixels** wide.

5. Type the following paragraphs of text in the text block, pressing the **Enter** key twice after the first paragraph and once between the other paragraphs:

Jackson's Sports is proud to support the following youth sports teams. For more information about these teams, contact our staff.

The Stars Basketball Team
The Sting Volleyball Team
The Tigers Softball Team
The Angels Baseball Team

6. Check the spelling of the document, correcting any misspelled words.

7. In the Tools panel, click the **Selection** tool, select the **rectangle** on the Stage, and then, in the Property inspector, change the rectangle's fill color to **peach** (#FFCC99). The changed color of the background rectangle will provide a visual cue to the user that a different page has loaded. See Figure 7-17.

Figure 7-17   **Text for the Teams page**

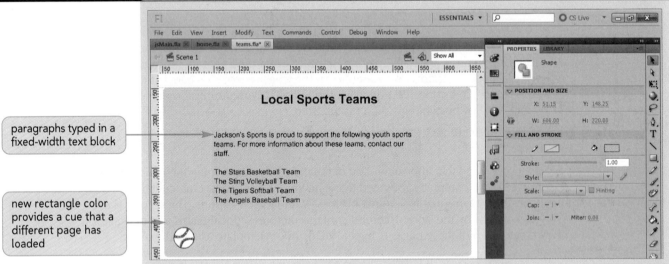

paragraphs typed in a fixed-width text block

new rectangle color provides a cue that a different page has loaded

8. Save the document.

The Services page contains a list of the main services offered by Jackson's Sports. The document has a format similar to the Home and Teams documents, but will use the basketball graphic in the animation instead of the baseball.

To create the Services page:

1. Create a new document based on the **jsDocument** template, save the file as **services.fla** in the Flash7\Tutorial folder included with your Data Files, and change the zoom to **Show All**. The entire contents of the Stage appear.

2. In the **contents** layer, create a text block centered at the top of the yellow rectangle approximately **160 pixels** from the left edge of the Stage and **175 pixels** from the top of the Stage, set the font family to **Arial**, set the font style to **Bold**, set the point size to **24**, set the text color to **black** (#000000), set the paragraph format to **Align left**, and then type **Jackson's Youth Sports Services** in the text block.

3. Deselect the title text block, set the point size to **14**, set the font style to **Regular**, and then create a fixed-width text block approximately **150 pixels** from the left edge of the Stage, **230 pixels** from the top of the Stage, and **400 pixels** wide.

4. Type the following paragraphs of text in the text block, pressing the **Enter** key twice between paragraphs, and then check the spelling, correcting any misspelled words.

   - **Sale of equipment and supplies at a discount**

   - **Team and individual trophies, including engraving of players' names**

   - **Sponsorship of tournaments**

   - **Team and player pictures**

5. In the Tools panel, click the **Selection** tool [▶], select the **rectangle** on the Stage, change the rectangle's fill color to **light green** (#99FFCC) in the Property inspector, and then deselect the rectangle. The color of the rectangle provides a visual cue that a different page is loaded. See Figure 7-18.

Figure 7-18 **Text for the Services page**

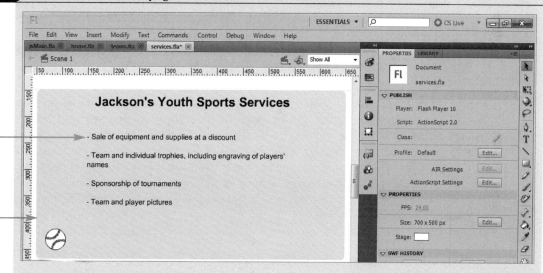

paragraphs typed in a fixed-width text block

new rectangle color provides a cue that a different page has loaded

Next, you will change the animated graphic to the basketball symbol you copied from the external library earlier.

6. In the Library panel, create a duplicate of the Baseball animation symbol, name it **Basketball animation**, and then open the Basketball animation symbol in symbol-editing mode.

7. Right-click the **Baseball** instance on the Stage, and then click **Swap Symbol**. The Swap Symbol dialog box opens.

8. Click the **Basketball** symbol, and then click the **OK** button. The Baseball instance changes to a Basketball instance on the Stage. Exit symbol-editing mode and return to Scene 1.

9. Delete the Baseball animation instance on the Stage.

10. Add an instance of the Basketball animation to the upper-left corner of the green rectangle, and then add another instance of the Basketball animation instance to the upper-right corner of the green rectangle.

11. Save the document.

The Photos page contains buttons that load pictures of local teams or players. This document will be similar in format to the previous documents, but it will not include the animation.

To create the Photos page:

1. Create a new document based on the **jsDocument** template, save the file as **photos.fla** in the Flash7\Tutorial folder included with your Data Files, and then change the zoom to **Show All**. The entire contents of the Stage are visible.

2. In the Timeline, select the **graphic** layer, and then click the **Delete** button 🗑. The layer is deleted, removing the animation from the page because it is not used with this page.

3. In the **contents** layer, create a text block centered at the top of the yellow rectangle approximately **230 pixels** from the left edge of the Stage and **175 pixels** from the top of the Stage, set the font family to **Arial**, set the font style to **Bold**, set the point size to **24**, set the text color to black (#000000), set the paragraph format to **Align left**, type **Team and Player Photos** in the text block, and then deselect the text block.

4. Save the document. You will complete the Photos page later in this tutorial.

PROSKILLS

Written Communication: Organizing Web Pages Consistently

When you create a Web site, the pages should have a consistent look and feel. The banner and navigation system should appear in the same place on each page, and the changing content should be in the same location on each page. One way to ensure that all pages in a Web site use the same organization is to create a template that you use to develop each page in the Web site. A template helps to ensure that all the pages have the same layout, whether you create them all at once or add pages periodically. Having a consistent organization for a Web site enhances the user's ability to navigate the site and locate the information being presented.

Creating a Navigation Bar

A Web site needs a way for users to navigate from one Web page to another. In an HTML-based Web site, hyperlinks load another HTML document into the Web browser when clicked. In a Flash Web site, the hyperlinks are replaced with a navigation system that moves the playhead to other frames or loads other SWF files into the Flash Player. In most Web sites, this is a navigation bar. You create the buttons for a navigation bar the same way you created the buttons to control animations. When using levels to load SWF files, the buttons have ActionScript programming code that instructs the Flash Player which SWF file to load and how to load it. You will add this programming code in the next session. The buttons must include obvious visual clues that indicate how the buttons can be used to navigate the site. It is also helpful if some sort of animated effect occurs when the pointer is over the button, indicating that something will happen when you click the button.

The buttons in a navigation bar often look the same but have different text to indicate what action will occur when the button is clicked. For the Jackson's Youth Sports Web site, the navigation bar will appear below the banner of the main document and include four buttons arranged horizontally. Each button will load a different SWF file when clicked. To make it easier to create and place on the Stage, you will create the navigation bar as a symbol and add an instance of it to the main document. The navigation bar will always appear as long as the main document is played in the Flash Player.

Adding an Animation to a Button Frame

A simple rollover effect reinforces the fact that clicking the button causes something to happen. You can also add animations to any of the Up, Over, or Down frames of the button's Timeline to provide visual cues. One common effect is an animation in the Over frame that appears only when the pointer is over the button. When the pointer is not over the button, the animation does not appear. To create this effect, you need to create a separate movie clip symbol with an animation in its Timeline and then place an instance of the symbol in the Over frame. The animation of the movie clip appears only when the Over frame is active, which is when the pointer is over the button. This effect is similar to the nested movie clip animations you created that included an instance of a movie clip inside the Timeline of another symbol. In the case of buttons, you will place an instance of another symbol inside the button's Timeline.

Aly wants you to add an animation to the Home button that appears only when the pointer is over the button. You will create the animation in a movie clip symbol. This animation will be a simple motion tween of a small arrow shape moving back and forth.

To create the small arrow animation:

1. Click the **jsMain.fla** page tab to make the document active.

2. In the Tools panel, click the **Selection** tool ▸ to select it.

3. Create a new movie clip symbol named **Button animation**. The Button animation symbol opens in symbol-editing mode. You will add an instance of the Arrow symbol and animate it with a motion tween.

4. Drag an instance of the **Arrow** symbol from the Library panel to the center of the editing window, and then, in the Property inspector, set its X and Y properties to **0** to center it.

5. Set the zoom to **200%** to enlarge the view.

6. Right-click the **Arrow** instance, and then click **Create Motion Tween** on the context menu. A tween span is created in Layer 1.

7. In the Timeline, click **Frame 1** of Layer 1 to select it, and then click the **Arrow** instance on the Stage, if necessary, to select it. You'll change the horizontal position of the Arrow instance at various points in the tween span.

8. Open the **Motion Editor**, and then, in the Basic motion section, change the X position to **0**.

9. In the Motion Editor, select **Frame 10**, and then, in the Basic motion section, change the X position to **15**. The Arrow instance moves to the right. See Figure 7-19.

Figure 7-19   **Arrow instance repositioned in Frame 10**

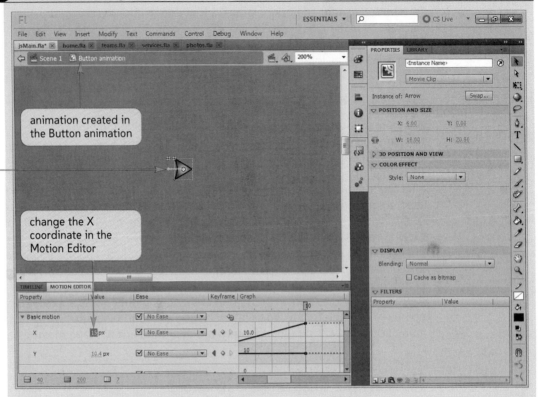

▶ **10.** In the Motion Editor, click **Frame 15** of Layer 1 to select it, and then, in the Basic motion section of the Motion Editor, change the X position to **0**. The Arrow moves back to its starting position.

▶ **11.** In the Timeline, move the playhead to **Frame 1**, and then play the animation. As the animation plays, the Arrow instance moves to the right and then returns to its starting position.

The Button animation is complete. Next, you'll add the animation to the Over frame of the Home button symbol so that the animation plays only when the pointer is over the button.

To add the Button animation to the Over frame:

▶ **1.** Open the **Home button** in symbol-editing mode.

▶ **2.** In the Timeline, insert a new layer above the text layer and name it **animation**. You'll add the movie clip animation on this layer.

▶ **3.** In the Over frame of the animation layer, insert a keyframe. You'll add the movie clip animation to this frame.

▶ **4.** Drag an instance of the **Button animation** symbol from the Library panel to the left side of the button in the editing window. See Figure 7-20.

Figure 7-20   **Button animation instance added to the button's Over frame**

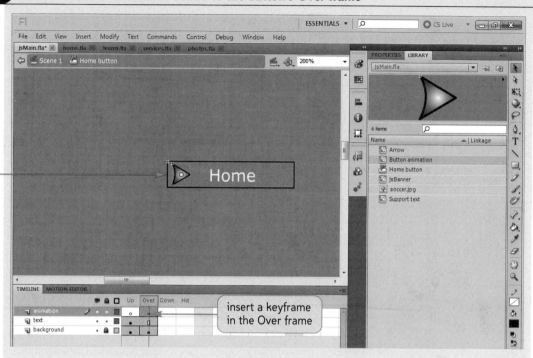

drag the Button animation instance to the button

insert a keyframe in the Over frame

The Home button symbol is complete. The other three buttons for the navigation bar are similar to this button. The only difference will be the text that appears on the buttons. Rather than creating the other buttons from scratch, you will make duplicates of the Home button symbol and then change the text for the other buttons.

To create three additional buttons for the navigation bar:

1. In the Library panel, right-click the **Home button**, and then click **Duplicate** on the context menu. The Duplicate Symbol dialog box opens.

2. Type **Teams button** in the Name box, and then click the **OK** button. The Teams button is added to the library.

3. Repeat Steps 1 and 2 to create a duplicate of the Home button named **Services button** and a duplicate of the Home button named **Photos button**. The four buttons are exactly the same. You'll change the text of the buttons next.

4. Open the **Teams button** symbol in symbol-editing mode.

5. In the Timeline, select the **Up frame** of the text layer, click the **Text** tool T in the Tools panel, click the **Home** text block, select **Home**, and then type **Teams**.

6. Repeat Steps 4 and 5 to open the **Services button** in symbol-editing mode and change the Home text to **Services**.

7. Repeat Steps 4 and 5 to open the **Photos button** in symbol-editing mode and change the Home text to **Photos**, and then exit symbol-editing mode.

The additional buttons are complete. You will combine button instances in a movie clip symbol to create the navigation bar. The navigation bar will contain the Home, Teams, Services, and Photos buttons arranged horizontally. After you place the button instances in the symbol, you will add an instance of the navigation bar to the Stage of the main document.

To create the navigation bar:

▶ 1. Set the zoom to **100%**. Create a new movie clip symbol named **Navbar**. You will add instances of the buttons in symbol-editing mode.

▶ 2. Drag an instance of the **Home button** symbol from the Library panel to the left side of the editing window.

▶ 3. Drag an instance of the **Teams button** symbol from the Library panel to the right of the Home button instance.

▶ 4. Drag an instance of the **Services button** symbol from the Library panel to the right of the Teams button instance.

▶ 5. Drag an instance of the **Photos button** symbol from the Library panel to the right of the Services button instance.

▶ 6. On the Application bar, click **Edit**, and then click **Select All** to select all of the button instances at one time.

▶ 7. On the docked panel group, click the **Align** button 🔲 to open the Align panel.

▶ 8. On the Align panel, click the **Align to stage** check box to deselect it if necessary, click the **Align vertical center** button 🔳 to align the buttons, and then click the **Space evenly horizontally** button 🔳 to space the buttons evenly.

▶ 9. Center the group of button instances in the editing window. See Figure 7-21.

Figure 7-21 **Completed navigation bar**

click the Align button to open the Align panel

buttons are aligned, spaced evenly, and centered

The navigation bar is complete. You will add an instance of the navigation bar below the banner in the main document.

To add the navigation bar to the main document:

▶ 1. On the Edit bar, click the **Scene 1** link to return to the main document's Timeline, and then set the zoom to **Show All** to display all the contents on the Stage.

▶ 2. In the Timeline, insert a new layer above the background layer and name it **navbar**.

▶ 3. Drag an instance of the **Navbar** symbol from the library to the Stage below the banner, and then center the navigation bar horizontally. See Figure 7-22.

Figure 7-22 **Navigation bar on the jsMain.fla document**

place the Navbar symbol below the banner

4. Save the main document, click **Control** on the Application bar, point to **Test Movie**, and then click **in Flash Professional**. The SWF file opens in a separate window.

5. Move the pointer over each of the four buttons to test how the button changes color and plays the Arrow animation while the pointer is over it.

6. Close the Flash Player to return to the main document.

In this session, you created the documents that make up the Jackson's Youth Sports Web site. You created the site's main document and then created a Flash template that you used to create the additional documents for the site. You also created the navigation bar with a set of buttons to navigate from one document to another in the Web site. The buttons include a movie clip animation that is displayed when the pointer is over the buttons. Although the navigation bar and its buttons are complete, they do not yet control anything. In the next session, you will add the ActionScript code to these buttons.

Session 7.2 Quick Check

REVIEW

1. What is a Flash template?
2. What is the purpose of opening a document's library as an external library in another document?
3. A(n) _____ effect reinforces the fact that clicking a button causes something to happen.
4. True or False. An external library opens in a Library panel separate from the Library panel for the current document.
5. In a Flash Web site, _____ are replaced with buttons that move the playhead to other frames or load other SWF files into the Flash Player when clicked.
6. Briefly explain how you add an animation to a button that is displayed when the pointer is over the button.

SESSION 7.3 VISUAL OVERVIEW

ActionScript, which is the programming language used within Flash, allows you to add actions to objects or frames in a document.

ActionScript code is arranged in categories. You click a category to display its contents.

Buttons use the on event handler, which has been added to the Home button of the navigation bar.

You can add actions to frames. Because frame actions are not part of a button, they are not enclosed within an event handler.

The Actions panel tab indicates if a button or frame is currently selected.

The event handler determines the action to take when a specific event occurs.

The event handler is followed by the statement to be executed within curly braces.

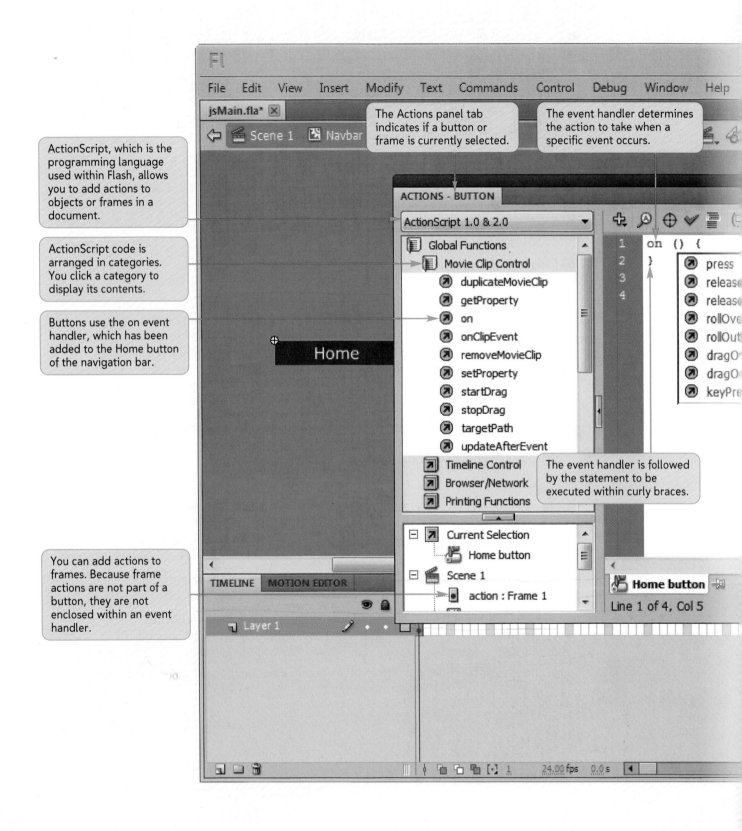

ACTIONSCRIPT AND THE ACTIONS PANEL

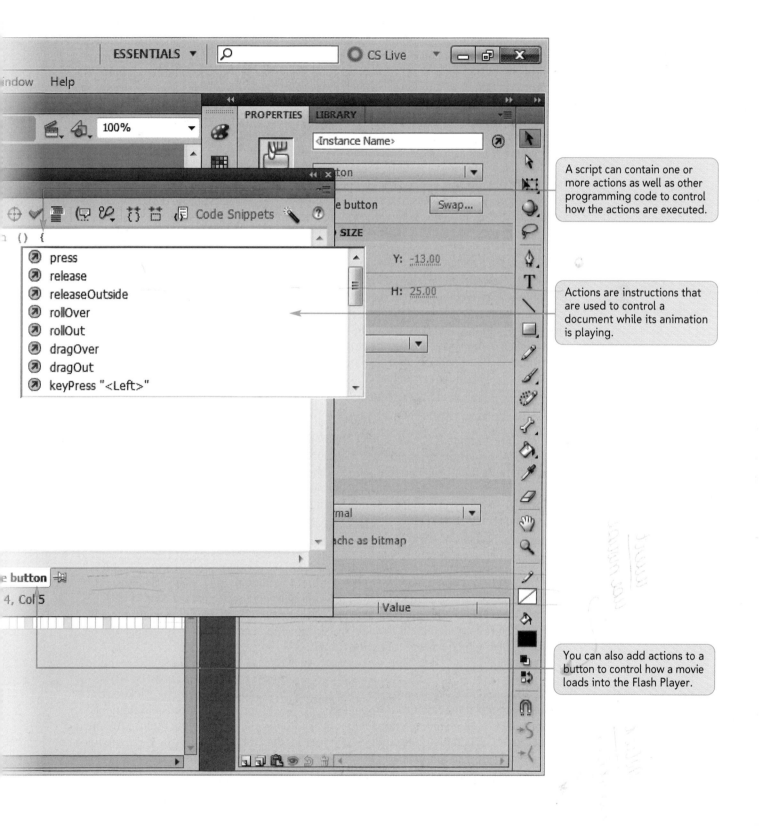

A script can contain one or more actions as well as other programming code to control how the actions are executed.

Actions are instructions that are used to control a document while its animation is playing.

You can also add actions to a button to control how a movie loads into the Flash Player.

Using ActionScript

A Flash Web site's navigation system consists of a set of buttons. When you click a button, the Flash Player loads a different SWF file at the specified level. The navigation bar you created for the Jackson's Youth Sports Web site has buttons that don't yet control anything. To make the buttons operational, you need to add ActionScript instructions to them.

ActionScript, the programming language used within Flash, allows you to add actions to objects or frames in a document. Actions are instructions that are used to control a document while its animation is playing. You have added actions to buttons to make the buttons control an animation. You can also add actions to buttons to control how a movie loads into the Flash Player.

You will use the Actions panel to add actions in the form of scripts, which can contain one or more actions as well as other programming code to control how the actions are executed. The actions will be added to the button instances on the Navbar symbol. The two latest versions of ActionScript are versions 2.0 and 3.0, and you can use either version, depending on the complexity of the animation. Because you need to add only simple scripts to the buttons to control how the Web site's pages are loaded, you will use ActionScript 2.0. You will work with ActionScript 3.0 in Tutorial 8.

Using the loadMovieNum Action

In a Flash Web site, the main document loads into the Flash Player at level 0 and other SWF files can then be loaded at different levels. A SWF file loaded at a higher level will be on top of the SWF file at level 0. Using this method, you can load the Web site's main document with the banner, background, and navigation bar at level 0, and then load the other pages of the Web site at level 1 or higher. For example, you will load the Services page at level 1 so it will be displayed on top of the main document loaded at level 0.

To load a SWF file into the Flash Player at a specific level, you need to create an ActionScript script with the `loadMovieNum` action. This action has the following format:

```
loadMovieNum("filename.swf", level)
```

Within the parentheses, you specify the parameters of the action. The parameters give the action the information it needs to execute properly. In the case of the `loadMovieNum` action, the two parameters are the name of the SWF file to be loaded and the level number at which the file will be loaded. The name of the SWF file must be enclosed in quotation marks and a comma must separate the filename and the level number. For example, the following action loads the Services page at level 1:

```
loadMovieNum("services.swf", 1)
```

The `loadMovieNum` action is executed only when the button instance to which it is attached is clicked and released. For the action to work with the button, you must add an event handler that determines when to execute the action. Flash uses event handlers to check for events, such as when a button is clicked or when it is released. The event handler determines the action to take when a specific event occurs. Buttons use the on event handler, which has the following format:

```
on (mouseEvent)
```

The `mouseEvent` can be press or release. Press refers to a button being clicked. The event handler is followed by a pair of curly braces within which you place statements such as the `loadMovieNum` action. When the button is clicked with the mouse, the press event occurs. When the mouse button is released, the release event occurs. So, the following on event handler executes an action after the button is released:

```
on (release)
```

The event handler is then followed by the statement to be executed within curly braces. The complete script to load the Services page is as follows:

```
on (release) {
    loadMovieNum("services.swf", 1);
}
```

The curly braces can be placed on the same lines as other statements or on separate lines. The preceding format is recommended to make the script easier to read. It is also recommended practice to end ActionScript statements with a semicolon.

PROSKILLS

Problem Solving: Finding and Fixing Errors in Scripts

Scripts must be error free to run as expected. Even something as small as a missing quotation mark or a misplaced comma can cause a script to return an error. After you create a script, be sure to test it to ensure that the script works as intended. If it doesn't, you need to locate and resolve the problem. The Check syntax button in the Actions panel provides a quick way to find which lines of the code have incorrect syntax. After locating the line with a problem, check the code carefully to ensure that there are no spelling errors, missing punctuation, or misplaced punctuation. If the syntax is correct but the script still doesn't run correctly, check the script to ensure that you entered the right actions, event handlers, filenames, levels, and so forth. Continue problem solving until the code runs without error.

Using the Actions Panel

You can use the Actions panel in either Script Assist mode or normal mode. In Script Assist mode, Flash helps you create the scripts when you select actions from the Actions toolbox. In normal mode, you write all or part of the scripts yourself. You will use normal mode to write the scripts so you gain a better understanding of ActionScript.

REFERENCE

Adding ActionScript Code to a Button

- Select the button instance on the Stage.
- In the Actions panel, select a category from the Actions toolbox, and then double-click an action to add its code to the Script pane.
- If necessary, type required code such as parameters that reference filenames.
- Click the Check syntax button to check the script for errors.

Because the navigation bar for the Jackson's Youth Sports Web site has buttons that are designed to load a SWF file when clicked, you will add the on event handler with the release parameter. So, when the button is clicked and then released, the event handler executes the loadMovieNum action to load the specified movie at a particular level. This script will be added to each button instance with the corresponding name of the SWF file.

To add ActionScript to the Home button:

1. If you took a break after the previous session, make sure the jsMain.fla, home.fla, teams.fla, services.fla, and photos.fla documents are open; the jsMain.fla document is active; the workspace is reset to the Essentials layout; and the zoom magnification is set to Show All.

2. Open the **Navbar** symbol in symbol-editing mode.

3. Deselect the button instances, and then select only the **Home button** instance. This is the first button to which you will add ActionScript.

4. Open the Actions panel, and then click the **Script Assist** button 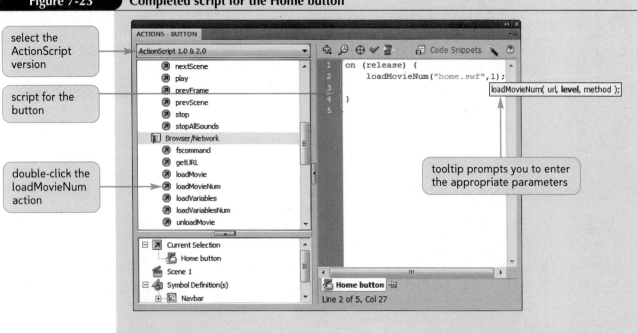 to deselect it, if necessary.

TIP

You can press the F9 key to open and close the Actions panel.

5. If necessary, click the **ActionScript** button (its tooltip is "Filter items shown in the Actions toolbox"), and then click **ActionScript 1.0 & 2.0**. The Actions panel is set to write code for ActionScript 1.0 and 2.0.

6. In the Actions toolbox, click **Global Functions** to expand the category, click **Movie Clip Control** to expand the category, and then double-click the **on** event handler. The on event handler is added to the Script pane along with parentheses and curly braces. Also, a code hints list of events opens so that you can quickly add the appropriate event to the script.

7. Double-click the **release** event. The word "release" is added between the parentheses. The loadMovieNum action must now be added between the two curly braces.

Trouble? If the list of events does not open, type **release** within the parentheses.

8. Press the → key until the insertion point is at the end of the first line after the opening curly brace in the Script pane, and then press the **Enter** key to add a new line between the curly braces.

9. In the Actions toolbox, scroll down as needed, and then click **Browser/Network** to expand this category. A list of actions opens.

10. Scroll down as needed, and then double-click the loadMovieNum action to add it to the script. A tooltip appears, prompting you to type the parameters for the filename and the level number within the parentheses.

Type the parameters exactly as shown so that the correct file opens when you test the Web site.

11. In the Script pane, within the parentheses of the loadMovieNum action, type **"home.swf",1** to complete the script. See Figure 7-23.

Figure 7-23   **Completed script for the Home button**

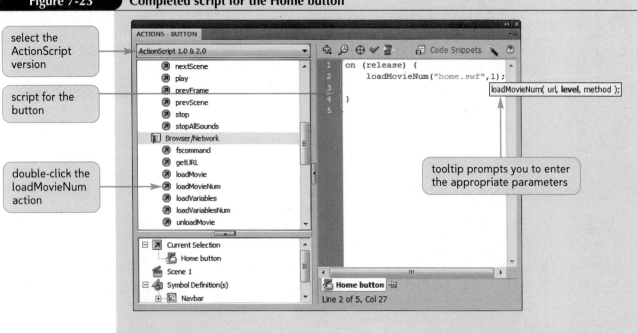

The Actions panel includes an option to check the script for errors. You will use this option to ensure the script does not contain errors.

▶ **12.** In the Actions panel, click the **Check syntax** button ☑. The script is checked. If no errors are displayed in the Compiler Errors panel, the script is correct.

   Trouble? If your script contains errors, the errors are listed in the Compiler Errors Panel at the bottom of the screen. Compare your script to the script shown in Figure 7-23, make any necessary corrections, and then repeat Step 12 until no errors are found.

The Home button is operational. When clicked, the button loads the home.swf file into the Flash Player at level 1. The same script must be added to the rest of the buttons. The only difference is the name of the SWF file within the parentheses of the `loadMovieNum` action. You will add the scripts to the remaining buttons.

To add ActionScript to the remaining buttons:

▶ **1.** At the top of the Actions panel, click the **Collapse to Icons** button ◀◀ to collapse the panel, select the **Teams button** instance on the Stage, and then click the **Expand Panels** button ▶▶ to expand the Actions panel.

▶ **2.** In the Actions toolbox, double-click the **on** event handler in the Movie Clip Control category to add it to the Script pane, and then double-click the **release** event from the list of events. The event handler and event are added to the Script pane.

▶ **3.** Press the → key until the insertion point in the Script pane is at the end of the first line after the opening curly brace, and then press the **Enter** key to add a new line.

▶ **4.** In the Actions toolbox, double-click the `loadMovieNum` action in the Browser/Network category to add it to the script.

▶ **5.** In the Script pane, within the parentheses of the `loadMovieNum` action, type **"teams.swf", 1** to add the parameters for the filename and the level number, completing the script.

▶ **6.** In the Actions panel, click the **Check syntax** button ☑ to check the script for errors.

   Trouble? If your script contains errors, make the necessary corrections, and then repeat Step 6 until no errors are found.

   Next, you'll create the script for the Services and Photos button.

▶ **7.** Collapse the Actions panel, select the **Services button** instance on the Stage, expand the Actions panel, and then repeat Steps 2 through 6, typing **"services.swf"** for the filename parameter in the `loadMovieNum` action in Step 5 to create the script for this button.

▶ **8.** Collapse the Actions panel, select the **Photos button** instance on the Stage, expand the Actions panel, and then repeat Steps 2 through 6, typing **"photos.swf"** for the filename parameter in the `loadMovieNum` action in Step 5 to create the script for this button.

▶ **9.** Close the Actions panel, and then, on the Edit bar, click the **Scene 1** link to return to the main document.

The scripts for the buttons are complete. You want to ensure that the buttons work as expected. To test the buttons, you must first publish each of the site's documents as SWF files. Remember, the `loadMovieNum` action will load the SWF files named in the parameter portion of the ActionScript code. You will publish the Flash documents you created and saved as FLA files using the Publish Settings command. After the documents have been published, you will use the Test Movie command for the main document to test the buttons in the navigation bar.

TIP

You can also press the Crtl+Shift+F12 keys to open the Publish Settings dialog box.

To test the buttons in the navigation bar:

1. Click the **home.fla** page tab to make the home document active.

2. On the Application bar, click **File**, and then click **Publish Settings**. The Publish Settings dialog box opens. This file needs to be published only as a SWF file.

3. Deselect the **HTML (.html)** check box so that only the Flash (.swf) check box is checked.

4. Click the **Publish** button to publish the SWF file. The home.swf file is created and saved to the same folder as the home.fla file.

5. Click the **OK** button to close the Publish Settings dialog box.

6. Switch to the **teams.fla** document, and then repeat Steps 2 through 5 to publish the teams.swf file.

7. Switch to the **services.fla** document, and then repeat Steps 2 through 5 to publish the services.swf file.

8. Switch to the **photos.fla** document, and then repeat Steps 2 through 5 to publish the photos.swf file.

9. Switch to the **jsMain.fla** document. You'll open the main document in the Flash Player, and then test the buttons.

10. On the Application bar, click **Control**, point to **Test Movie**, and click **in Flash Professional**. Flash creates the SWF file for the jsMain.fla document and displays the jsMain.swf file in a separate window.

11. Click the **Home** button on the navigation bar to display the home.swf file. See Figure 7-24.

Figure 7-24	Home page of the Jackson's Youth Sports Web site

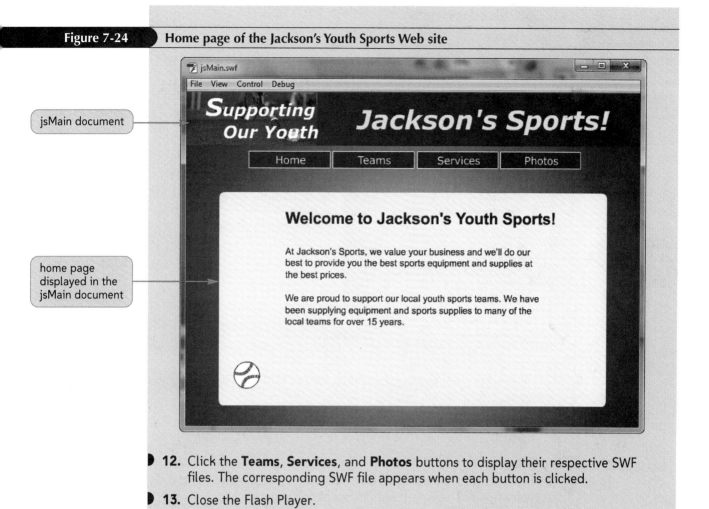

jsMain document

home page displayed in the jsMain document

▶ **12.** Click the **Teams**, **Services**, and **Photos** buttons to display their respective SWF files. The corresponding SWF file appears when each button is clicked.

▶ **13.** Close the Flash Player.

When the jsMain.swf file was first displayed, the contents of the home.swf file did not appear until you clicked the Home button. When someone visits the Jackson's Youth Sports Web site, you want the home.swf file to load right away without requiring the site visitor to click the Home button. This requires another `loadMovieNum` action to tell the Flash Player to load the home.swf file as soon as the jsMain.swf file is loaded. Because this action is not part of a button, it is not enclosed within an event handler. Instead, the action is added to Frame 1 of the jsMain.fla document's Timeline. Then, when the jsMain.swf file is loaded into the Flash Player and Frame 1 plays, the `loadMovieNum` action causes the home.swf file to load right away. You will add this action next.

To add the loadMovieNum action to Frame 1 of the jsMain.fla document:

▶ **1.** In the Timeline of the main document, insert a new layer above the banner layer, name it **action**, and then select **Frame 1** of the action layer. You'll add the action to this frame.

▶ **2.** Open the Actions panel, and then, in the Actions toolbox, double-click the `loadMovieNum` action in the Browser/Network category to add it to the Script pane.

▶ **3.** In the Script pane, within the parentheses of the `loadMovieNum` action, type **"home.swf",1** to enter the parameters for the filename and the level number and complete the action. See Figure 7-25.

| Figure 7-25 | Script in Frame 1 |

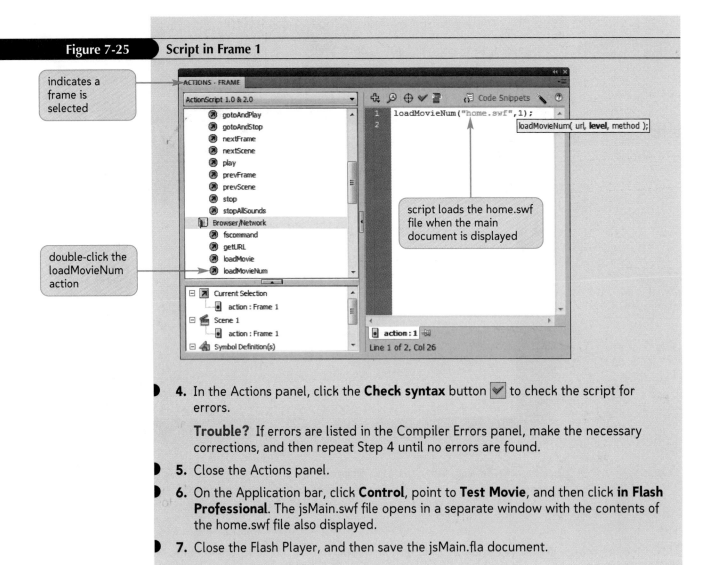

indicates a frame is selected

double-click the loadMovieNum action

script loads the home.swf file when the main document is displayed

4. In the Actions panel, click the **Check syntax** button ✅ to check the script for errors.

   Trouble? If errors are listed in the Compiler Errors panel, make the necessary corrections, and then repeat Step 4 until no errors are found.

5. Close the Actions panel.

6. On the Application bar, click **Control**, point to **Test Movie**, and then click **in Flash Professional**. The jsMain.swf file opens in a separate window with the contents of the home.swf file also displayed.

7. Close the Flash Player, and then save the jsMain.fla document.

The ActionScript scripts you added make the navigation bar buttons operational and will load the home.swf file when the jsMain.swf file is first loaded into the Flash Player. The site is almost complete. You only need to complete the Photos page so that it displays several pictures of local youth sports teams and events.

Loading External Image Files

The Photos page will display bitmap pictures of sports teams and individual players. The pictures will change as different teams submit pictures to Jackson's Sports. Usually, a picture displayed in a Flash document is imported and becomes part of the document. However, because the pictures on the Photos page will change regularly, you would need to modify the document each time a different set of pictures is to be displayed. A better option is to leave the pictures as separate files and bring them into the Flash Player only when they are to be displayed. These external image files should reside in the same folder as the photos.swf file, which will make it easier to reference the files from within the Photos page. All the pictures will be displayed in the same area of the page, so they should be no larger than the display area. The images should be assigned nonspecific filenames such as photo1.jpg so that the replacement picture can be assigned the same name of photo1.jpg and saved to the same folder. When the photos.swf file loads the photo1.jpg file, the new picture appears. The Flash document doesn't have to be modi-fied each time the pictures are replaced.

Preparing Pictures for Flash Documents

When using pictures in a Flash document, determine the dimensions of the area in the Flash document where the pictures will be displayed. Then size the pictures in an image-editing program such as Adobe Photoshop so that the pictures fit within the specified dimensions. You should also optimize each picture by reducing its file size while main-taining its quality. This will help minimize the download time.

Using the loadMovie Action

Loading external image files into a SWF file in the Flash Player can be accomplished by using the loadMovie action. The loadMovie action is similar to the loadMovieNum action but can be used to load image files into a movie clip instance instead of a level. You create an empty movie clip symbol in a document, add an instance of the symbol to the Stage, and then use the loadMovie action to load a picture into the movie clip instance. The format of the loadMovie action is:

```
movieclip.loadMovie("filename")
```

In this action, movieclip represents the name of the movie clip instance. To use this action, you must assign a name to the movie clip instance on the Stage in addition to the name of the symbol in the library. If you have a movie clip instance named picture_mc, the following action loads the picture file photo1.jpg into the instance:

```
picture_mc.loadMovie("photo1.jpg")
```

You can create this loadMovie action along with the event handler code using the Actions panel similarly to how you created the loadMovieNum action. However, you can also add this action to a button using the Behaviors panel, which is simpler than using the Actions panel.

When using the loadMovie action, the image files for the pictures need to be in the standard JPEG file format and not in the progressive JPEG format. The **progressive JPEG** format causes a picture that is downloading to a Web browser to appear to fade in by displaying the picture as the browser is gradually downloading the data that makes up the picture.

Aly has prepared two pictures for the Jackson's Youth Sports Web site. You will use the Behaviors panel to add the loadMovie action to a new set of buttons you will create on the Photos page. You will add the movie clip, buttons, and behaviors to complete the Photos page. There will be two buttons, one for each picture. The buttons will be created as part of a navigation bar that will be placed on the left side of the rectangle in the pho-tos page. Instead of creating the buttons from scratch, you will copy the Home button from the jsMain.fla file and modify it to create the new buttons.

To create the buttons for the navigation bar in the Photos page:

▶ 1. Click the **photos.fla** page tab to make the document active, and then change the zoom to **Show All**.

▶ 2. In the Library panel, click the library button above the symbol preview pane, and then click **jsMain.fla** to display its symbols. See Figure 7-26.

Figure 7-26   jsMain.fla library displayed in photos.fla document

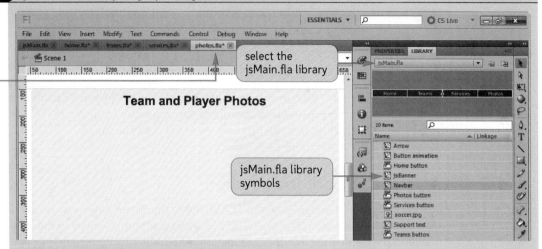

photos.fla is the active document

select the jsMain.fla library

jsMain.fla library symbols

3. Drag an instance of the **Home button** from the Library to the Stage to make it part of the photos.fla document, and then delete the Home button instance on the Stage. The symbol will remain in the document's library.

4. In the Library panel, click the library button above the symbol preview pane, and then click **photos.fla**. The Home button is displayed in the photos.fla library.

   You will rename and edit the button.

5. In the Library panel, double-click the Home button name, type **Photo1 button** and then press the **Enter** key to rename the button.

6. Open the **Photo1 button** in symbol-editing mode.

7. In the Timeline, insert a new layer above the background layer, name it **rectangle** and then delete the background layer. You will add a new rectangle as a background for the button.

8. In the Tools panel, click the **Rectangle Primitive** tool, and then, in the Property inspector, set the stroke color to **black** (#FFFFFF), set the stroke height to **1**, set the stroke style to **Solid**, and then set the fill color to **medium blue** (#6699CC).

9. Click the **Lock corner radius controls to one control** button to unlock it, set the upper-left rectangle corner radius to **10**, and then set the lower-right rectangle corner radius to **10**.

10. Draw a small rectangle in the center of the editing window.

11. In the Property inspector, click the **Lock width and height values together** button to unlock it if necessary, set the width to **125**, set the height to **25**, and then set its X and Y coordinates to **0** to center the rectangle in the editing window.

12. In the Timeline, lock the rectangle layer to prevent its content from changing.

13. In the Tools panel, click the **Text** tool, change the Home text on the Stage to **Photo 1** and then deselect the button. The button label is changed and the button is complete. See Figure 7-27.

Figure 7-27 **Photo1 button symbol**

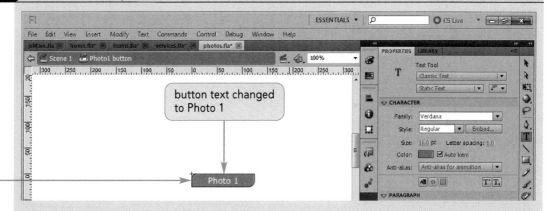

new rectangle for
button background

button text changed
to Photo 1

14. In the Library panel, create a duplicate of the Photo1 button symbol named **Photo2 button**. The new symbol is an exact copy of the Photo1 button symbol.

15. Open the **Photo2 button** in symbol-editing mode, double-click the text block, and then change the text to **Photo 2**. The button label is changed and the second button is complete.

You have created the two buttons for the navigation bar. Next, you will create the navigation bar as a movie clip symbol and add instances of the buttons.

To create the navigation bar for the Photos page:

1. Create a new movie clip symbol named **Photos navbar**. The symbol opens in symbol-editing mode.

2. Drag an instance of the **Photo1 button** symbol from the library to the center of the editing window, and then drag an instance of the **Photo2 button** symbol and place it below the Photo1 button instance.

3. On the Application bar, click **Edit**, and then click **Select All** to select both button instances at the same time.

4. On the Application bar, click **Modify**, point to **Align**, and then click **Horizontal Center** to align the buttons with each other.

5. In the Property inspector, set the X and Y values to **0** to center the buttons.

6. On the Edit bar, click the **Scene 1** link to return to the document's main Timeline.

7. In the Timeline, click the **contents** layer to select it, and then drag an instance of the **Photos navbar** from the Library panel to the left side of the rectangle on the Stage, as shown in Figure 7-28.

Figure 7-28   **Navigation bar added to the Photos page**

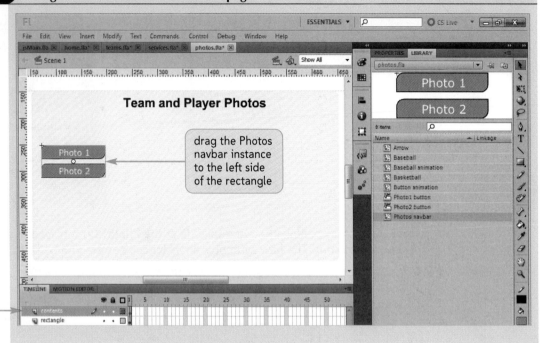

select the
contents layer

drag the Photos
navbar instance
to the left side
of the rectangle

The buttons for the Photos page's navigation bar are complete. To make them operational, however, you need to add the `loadMovie` action to each button instance. Before you add the action, you will create an empty movie clip symbol and place an instance of it on the Stage. The instance will be indicated by a small circle on the Stage, which is the symbol's registration point. When a picture is loaded into the movie clip instance, the upper-left corner of the picture will be aligned with the registration point of the instance. Also, the instance must be named so that the `loadMovie` action can refer to it when it loads the pictures to the instance on the Stage.

To create the Picture holder movie clip:

1. Create a new movie clip symbol named **Picture holder**. The Picture holder symbol opens in symbol-editing mode. Because the movie clip will be empty, you will exit symbol-editing mode.

2. On the Edit bar, click the **Scene 1** link to return to the document's main Timeline.

3. Drag an instance of the **Picture holder** symbol from the Library panel to the Stage below the title, and then place the instance approximately **220 pixels** from the top of the Stage and **300 pixels** from the left of the Stage. The instance is indicated by a small circle.

4. In the Property inspector, type **picture_mc** in the Instance name box, and then press the **Enter** key. The instance is named. See Figure 7-29.

Figure 7-29   The picture_mc movie clip instance

Figure 7-29   The picture_mc movie clip instance

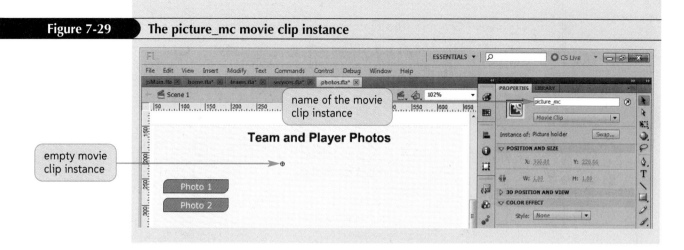

Using the Behaviors Panel

Instead of writing actions with the Actions panel, you can use pre-coded actions called behaviors. A **behavior** is an action with a prewritten ActionScript script that assigns controls and transitions to an object on the Stage. You can use behaviors to control an object in a document without writing any ActionScript coding yourself. Various behaviors are available for Flash objects, including movie clips, video, and sound files. Behaviors are only available with ActionScript 1.0 and 2.0.

You'll use the Behaviors panel to add actions to the Photo1 button and the Photo2 button.

To add actions to the buttons using the Behaviors panel:

1. Open the **Photos navbar** symbol in symbol-editing mode.

2. Select the **Photo1 button** instance by itself in the editing window.

3. On the Application bar, click **Window**, and then click **Behaviors**. The Behaviors panel opens.

TIP

You can also press the Shift+F3 keys to open and close the Behaviors panel.

4. In the Behaviors panel, click the **Add Behavior** button ⊞, point to **Movieclip**, and then point to **Load Graphic**. See Figure 7-30.

Figure 7-30   Behaviors panel

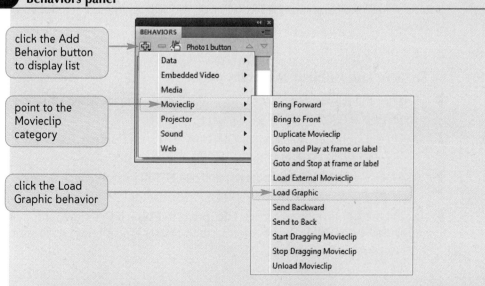

▶ **5.** Click **Load Graphic**. The Load Graphic dialog box opens.

▶ **6.** In the Enter the URL to the .JPG to load box, type **photo1.jpg**, click **picture_mc** in the Select the movie clip into which to load the graphic box, and then click the **Relative** option button, if necessary. See Figure 7-31.

Figure 7-31	Load Graphic dialog box

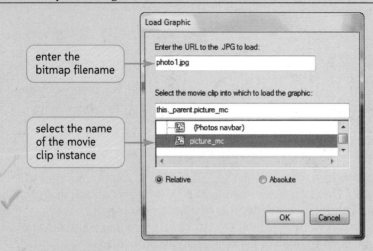

enter the bitmap filename

select the name of the movie clip instance

▶ **7.** Click the **OK** button to create the behavior and close the Load Graphic dialog box.

▶ **8.** Select the **Photo2 button** instance on the Stage, and repeat Steps 4 through 7, typing **photo2.jpg** in the Enter the URL to the .JPG to load box in Step 6 to add the behavior to the other button.

▶ **9.** Close the Behaviors panel, and then, on the Edit bar, click the **Scene 1** link to return to the photos.fla document's main Timeline.

The photos.fla document needs to be saved and published as a SWF file so that it will work with the main document.

▶ **10.** Save the photos.fla document, click **File** on the Application bar, and then click **Publish** to create the photos.swf file.

TIP

You can also press the Shift+F12 keys to publish a document.

The photo buttons and the Photos page are complete. When the Photos page is loaded into the Flash Player, the buttons appear. The site visitor can click one of the photo buttons to load a picture into the Flash Player. You will test the completed Web site in a browser.

To save and publish the main page:

▶ **1.** Click the **jsMain.fla** page tab to make that document active. You need to set the publish settings.

▶ **2.** On the Application bar, click **File**, and then click **Publish Settings**. The Publish Settings dialog box opens.

▶ **3.** Make sure that the **Flash (.swf)** and the **HTML (.html)** check boxes are checked, and then click the **OK** button to close the dialog box.

▶ **4.** On the Application bar, click **File**, point to **Publish Preview**, and then click **Default - (HTML)**. The Jackson's Youth Sports Web site opens in your Web browser.

5. Click the **Photos** button to display the Photos page, and then click the **Photo 1** button to display the first picture. See Figure 7-32.

Figure 7-32   **Photos page previewed in a Web browser**

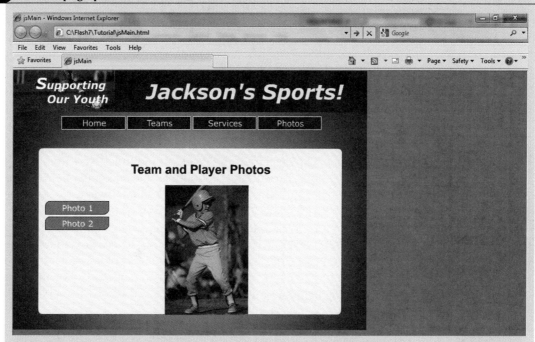

6. Click the **Photo 2** button to display the second picture.

7. Close the browser, and then save and close all the documents.

In this session, you used the Actions panel to add ActionScript scripts to the buttons in the navigation bar to make them operational. You also used the Behaviors panel to add actions to buttons on the photos page to load external image files into the Flash Player. The site is ready to show to Dan and Gloria.

Session 7.3 Quick Check

REVIEW

1. What is ActionScript?

2. Write the ActionScript statement to load the staff.swf file to level 1 of the Flash Player.

3. What is the purpose of the on event handler?

4. What option in the Actions panel can be used to check for errors in your script?

5. What action can be used to load external image files into a movie clip instance?

6. When you use the Load Graphic behavior, you must assign a(n) _____ to the movie clip instance where the picture will be loaded.

Practice the skills
you learned in
the tutorial using
the same case
scenario.

PRACTICE

Review Assignments

Data Files needed for the Review Assignments: specialsDraft.fla, mainDraft.fla, photosDraft.fla, picture1.jpg, picture2.jpg, home.fla, home.swf, services.fla, services.swf, teams.fla, teams.swf

Aly developed an alternative Web site for Jackson's Sports. She wants you to add a new Specials page that includes information about the weekly sales promotion offered by Jackson's Sports and to complete the main document's navigation bar by adding buttons to load the Web site's pages. You will also complete the Player photos page to display two photos.

1. Open the **specialsDraft.fla** file located in the Flash7\Review folder included with your Data Files, and then save the file as **specials.fla** in the same folder.

2. Select the contents layer, and then add a text block near the top of the yellow rectangle with the text **Specials of the Week!**, using Times New Roman for the font family, 24 for the point size, black (#000000) for the text color, bold for the font style, and align center for the paragraph format. Position the text block on the rectangle approximately 170 pixels from the top and 310 pixels from the left.

3. Add another text block in the center of the rectangle (approximately 270 pixels from the top and 280 pixels from the left), using Times New Roman for the font family, 16 for the point size, black (#000000) for the text color, regular for the font style, and align center for the paragraph format, and then enter the following text:

   The following items are on sale this week:

   Softball bats—as low as $89

   Softballs—$3.99 each

   Batting gloves—$12.99

4. Save and publish the document to create the specials.swf file.

5. Open the **mainDraft.fla** file located in the Flash7\Review folder included with your Data Files, and then save the file as **main.fla** in the same folder.

6. In the Library panel, make a duplicate of the Home button symbol named **Teams**, and then edit the Teams button symbol by changing the text in the Up and Over frames of the text layer to **Teams**.

7. Repeat Step 6 to create three more duplicates of the Home button symbol named **Services**, **Photos**, and **Specials**, and then edit each symbol to change the text in the Up and Over frames of the text layer to **Services**, **Photos**, and **Specials**, respectively.

8. Edit the jsNavbar symbol and add instances of the Teams, Services, Photos, and Specials symbols below the Home button instance and within the blue rectangle. Select all of the buttons on the Stage simultaneously, and then use the Align panel to align the buttons vertically by their left edges and to space the buttons evenly.

9. Add the `loadMovieNum` action to the Teams, Services, Photos, and Specials button instances, using the on event handler so that the action executes when the button is released after being clicked. The `loadMovieNum` action should load the respective SWF file (teams.swf, services.swf, photos.swf, specials.swf) into level 1 of the Flash Player. Return to Scene 1.

10. Add a new layer above the banner layer and name it **navbar**. Drag an instance of the jsNavbar to the Stage approximately 50 pixels below the banner and align it to the left side of the Stage.

11. Save and publish the main.fla file to create the main.swf file.

12. Open the **photosDraft.fla** file located in the Flash7\Review folder included with your Data Files, and then save the file as **photos.fla** in the same folder.

13. Make a duplicate of the Pic_button1 symbol named **Pic_button2**, and then edit the Pic_button2 symbol by changing the text to **Picture 2**. Return to Scene 1.

14. Add an instance of the Pic_button2 symbol to the Stage below the Pic_button1 instance in the content layer, and then align the horizontal centers of the two instances.

15. Create a new movie clip symbol named **Picture holder**. The symbol should be empty and will be used to load the pictures onto the Stage.

16. Add an instance of the Picture holder symbol to the Stage, place it approximately 200 pixels from the top of the Stage and 350 pixels from the left of the Stage, and then assign the name **picture_mc** to the instance.

17. Add the Load Graphic behavior to the Pic_button1 instance so that it loads the **picture1.jpg** file located in the Flash7\Review folder included with your Data Files. The picture should be loaded to the picture_mc movie clip instance.

18. Repeat Step 16 to add the Load Graphic behavior to the Pic_button2 instance so that it loads the **picture2.jpg** file into the picture_mc movie clip instance.

19. Save and publish the photos.fla file to create the photos.swf file.

20. Test the Web site to make sure the Teams, Services, Photos, and Specials buttons load the respective pages and the Photos page displays photos using the buttons.

21. Submit the finished files to your instructor.

Create a new template-based Flash Web site for a pet resort.

APPLY

Case Problem 1

Data Files needed for this Case Problem: katies.fla, welcome.fla

Katie's Pet Resort   Katie asks John to create a new Web site for Katie's Pet Resort that will include information to promote some of the resort's special services. She wants the site to be visually appealing and easy to use for anyone who owns pets. Based on John's meeting with Katie, John developed the following list of goals for the Web site:

- Promote the Katie's Pet Resort name.
- Increase awareness of its services.

Based on these goals, John put together the following list of objectives:

- Provide a list of services.
- Highlight the pet training classes available.
- Highlight the monthly pet adoption service.

John then prepares the outline for the site, which includes a home page with a banner at the top with the name of the store and a navigation bar on the left side. The navigation bar will have buttons that link to a Services page, a Training page, and an Adoptions page.

John asks you to create the Web site that will include the Main, Welcome, Services, Training, and Adoptions pages. You will create the Services, Training, and Adoptions pages based on the Welcome page that John has prepared. The banner and the navigation for the site will be in the site's main page. John also created a document with several symbols that you will use in the site, including a button for the navigation bar, a picture and graphic for the banner, and an animation for some of the pages. Figure 7-33 shows the completed home page.

Figure 7-33   Katie's Pet Resort home page

1. Create a new document 600 pixels wide by 400 pixels high based on ActionScript 2.0. Use light yellow (#FFFFCC) for the background color. In the Accessibility panel, enter **Katie's Pet Resort** as the name, and enter **Pet Services Web Site** for the description. Save the document as **main.fla** in the Flash7\Case1 folder included with your Data Files.

2. Create a new movie clip symbol named **petBanner**. In the petBanner symbol, create a rectangle 600 pixels wide by 100 pixels high. Use light green (#CCCC99) for the fill and do not include a stroke. Center the rectangle on the editing window. Rename Layer 1 as **background**.

3. Insert a new layer and name it **graphics**. Open the **katies.fla** file located in the Flash7\Case1 folder included with your Data Files as an external library. On the graphics layer, add an instance of the masked dog symbol from the external library to the left side of the banner. Also, add two instances of the star symbol, placing one instance to the right of the masked dog instance and the other instance on the right side of the rectangle.

4. Insert a new layer above the graphics layer and name it **text**. On the text layer, add a text block in the center of the rectangle. Use Times New Roman for the font family, bold italic for the font style, 42 for the point size, and black (#000000) for the text color. Type **Katie's Pet Resort** in the text block. If necessary, center the text block within the banner. The banner is complete.

5. In Scene 1, insert an instance of the petBanner symbol at the top of the Stage. Align the petBanner instance with the top and left sides of the Stage. Rename Layer 1 as **background**.

6. Create a new movie clip symbol named **petNavbar**. In the petNavbar symbol, create a rectangle 100 pixels wide by 300 pixels high. Use light orange (#FFCC99) for the fill and do not include a stroke. Center the rectangle on the editing window. Rename Layer 1 as **background** and lock it.

7. Insert a new layer and name it **buttons**. On the buttons layer, drag an instance of the button symbol from the external library to about 20 pixels from the top of the rectangle. Rename the button symbol to **Home button**.

8. Edit the Home button symbol. In the button's Timeline, change the fill color of the Up frame to light green (#339966). Rename Layer 1 as **background** and lock it.

9. Insert a new layer and name it **text**. On the text layer, add a text block with the word **Home**. Use Times New Roman for the font family, bold for the font style, 18 for the point size, white (#FFFFFF) for the text color, and align center for the paragraph format. Place the text block at the center of the button shape.

10. On the text layer, insert a keyframe in the Over frame and then change the text color to black (#000000).

11. Make three duplicates of the Home button, and then rename the duplicate buttons as **Services button**, **Training button**, and **Adoptions button**, respectively. Change the text in the Services button to **Services**. Change the text in the Training button to **Training**. Change the text in the Adoptions button to **Adoptions**.

12. Edit the petNavbar symbol. Add an instance of the Services button about 10 pixels below the Home button instance. Add an instance of the Training button, placing it about 10 pixels below the Services button instance. Add an instance of the Adoptions button, placing it about 10 pixels below the Training button instance. Align the four button instances by their left edges.

13. Select the Home button in the petNavbar symbol, open the Actions panel, and add a loadMovieNum action so that when the button is clicked and then released, the welcome.swf file loads at level 1 of the Flash Player. Add loadMovieNum actions to the other button instances to load SWF files at level 1. The Services button should load the services.swf file. The Training button should load the training.swf file. The Adoptions button should load the adoptions.swf file.

14. Return to Scene 1, insert a new layer, and name it **navbar**. On the navbar layer, add an instance of the petNavbar symbol to the left side of the Stage below the banner. Align the petNavbar instance with the left and bottom edges of the Stage.

15. Insert a new layer and name it **action**. In Frame 1 of the action layer, add a loadMovieNum action that loads the welcome.swf file at level 1 as soon as Frame 1 is played. This displays the welcome.swf file as soon as the main.swf page plays in the Flash Player. Save the main.fla file.

16. Open the **welcome.fla** file located in the Flash7\Case1 folder included with your Data Files. Rename Layer 1 to **content**, and then insert a new layer and name it **animation**. In the animation layer, add an instance of the animated dog symbol from the external library so that it's in the lower-right corner of the Stage.

17. Save the welcome.fla file as a template named **kprTemplate** in a new template category called **Pet Resort** with **Template for the Katie's Pet Resort Web site pages** as the description. Close the kprTemplate.fla file. The welcome.fla document remains unchanged.

18. Create a new document based on the kprTemplate, and then save this document as **services.fla** in the Flash7\Case1 folder included with your Data Files. Change the top text block to **Katie's Pet Resort Services!** and then center the text block above the second text block. Change the second text block to the following text, and then check the spelling of the text and make the necessary corrections:

Katie's offers many of the services you need to keep your pet happy, including boarding, grooming, and training. We also have a variety of pet supplies including pet food, pet toys, and pet accessories to keep your pet safe and healthy. Check back regularly for sales and special promotions.

19. Create a new document based on the kprTemplate, and then save this document as **training.fla** in the Flash7\Case1 folder included with your Data Files. Change the top text block to **Pet Training Classes are Fun!**, center it above the second text block, and then change the text color to blue (#0000FF). Change the second text block to

the following text, check the spelling of the text and make the necessary corrections, and then change the text color to maroon (#660000):

Here at Katie's, we can teach your pet new tricks. We can train your dog how to use the pet door, come when you call, or even to give you a high-five! We can even train your cat to stay off your kitchen counters. Training classes are scheduled each month and are affordably priced. Make your reservations early as our classes fill up fast.

 20. Create a new document based on the kprTemplate, and then save this document as **adoptions.fla** in the Flash7\Case1 folder included with your Data Files. Change the top text block to **Katie's Adoption Events!**, center the text block above the second text block, and change the text color to dark green (#006600). Change the second text block to the following text, check the spelling of the text and make the necessary corrections, and then change the text color to maroon (#660000):

Ask about our regular adoption events. Every third Saturday of each month, we hold an adoption event at Katie's Pet Resort in conjunction with the local pet shelter. During each adoption event, you'll have an opportunity to see a variety of pets ready for adoption. Light snacks are served. Ask one of our staff members for more details.

 21. Save and publish each of the documents to create the services.swf, training.swf, and adoptions.swf files. Open the **welcome.fla** file located in the Flash7\Case1 folder included with your Data Files, and then publish it to create the welcome.swf file. Return to the main.fla document and test the Web site by using the Test Movie command. Test each of the buttons and make certain the individual pages are loaded. Make any necessary corrections.

22. Submit the finished files to your instructor.

Create a new template-based Flash Web site for a zoo.

APPLY

Case Problem 2

Data File needed for this Case Problem: zooGraphics.fla

Alamo City Zoo   Janet meets with Alex to discuss the development of a new Web site to showcase some special exhibits at the Alamo City Zoo. They agree on the following goal for the Web site: Promote some of the unique exhibits available at Alamo City Zoo.

Based on this goal, Alex puts together the following list of objectives:

- Highlight the zoo's special animal exhibits.
- Highlight the zoo's educational resources.
- Promote the kids' summer camps.

You will help Alex create the new Web site based on these goals and objectives. Alex designed a background picture for the Web site as well as some of the graphics you will use. He provided these graphics in a Flash document. You'll develop the main page, shown in Figure 7-34, and then create a template for the remaining pages. The navigation system will use a bear paw graphic that appears on a button when the user moves the pointer over the button.

Figure 7-34   Alamo City Zoo Home page

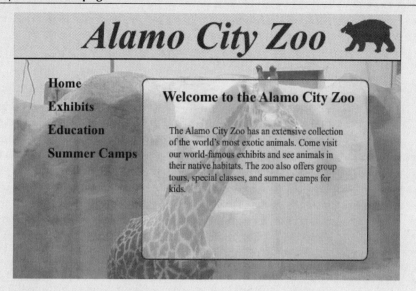

1. Create a new document that is 600 pixels wide by 400 pixels high based on ActionScript 2.0 with white for the background color, and then save the document as **aczMain.fla** in the Flash7\Case2 folder included with your Data Files.

2. Open the **zooGraphics.fla** document located in the Flash7\Case2 folder included with your Data Files as an external library, drag an instance of the zooBack.jpg bitmap onto the Stage, align the picture with the left and bottom edges of the Stage, and then rename Layer 1 as **background**.

3. Create a new movie clip symbol named **zooBanner**. In the zooBanner symbol, create a rectangle 600 pixels wide by 70 pixels high with light tan (#FFCC99) for the fill, black (#000000) for the stroke, and a stroke height of 2. Center the rectangle on the editing window, and then rename Layer 1 as **background**.

4. Drag an instance of the bear symbol from the external library to the right side of the rectangle.

5. Insert a new layer and name it **text**. Add a text block in the center of the rectangle. Use Times New Roman for the font family, bold italic for the font style, 58 for the point size, maroon (#660000) for the text color, and align center for the paragraph format. Type **Alamo City Zoo** in the text block, and then center the text inside the rectangle. If necessary, set the font rendering method to anti-alias for readability. The banner is complete.

6. Return to Scene 1, add an instance of the zooBanner symbol to the top of the Stage, and then align the instance with the top and left edges of the Stage. Lock the background layer.

7. Create a new button symbol named **Home button**. In symbol-editing mode, rename Layer 1 to **text**. Add a text block at the center of the editing window. Use Times New Roman for the font family, bold for the font style, 20 for the point size, black (#000000) for the text color, and align left for the paragraph format. Type **Home** in the text block. Insert a regular frame in the Over frame to have the text be displayed when the pointer is over the button.

8. Insert a new layer and name it **graphic**. In the graphic layer, insert a keyframe in the Over frame and then drag an instance of the bear paw symbol from the external library to the left of the Home text. The bear paw instance will be present only in the Over frame of the button's Timeline.

⊕ **EXPLORE**

9. Insert a blank keyframe in the Hit frame of the text layer. Turn on onion skinning and extend the onion skin markers to cover all four frames of the Timeline. In the Hit frame of the text layer, draw a small rectangle to cover the area for both the bear paw and the text. The Home button is complete.

10. Make three duplicates of the Home button, and then name the duplicate buttons **Exhibits button**, **Education button**, and **Camps button**, respectively.

11. Change the text in the Up frame of the Exhibits button to **Exhibits**, and then resize the rectangle in the Hit frame of the text layer to cover all the text. Change the text in the Up frame of the Education button to **Education**, and then resize the rectangle in the Hit frame to cover all the text. Change the text in the Up frame of the Camps button to **Summer Camps**, and then resize the rectangle in the Hit frame to cover all the text.

12. Create a new movie clip symbol named **Navbar**. In the Navbar symbol, drag an instance of the Home button to the center of the editing window, and then drag an instance of the Exhibits button, the Education button, and the Camps button below the previous button instance. Align the instances along their left edges and space them evenly using the Align panel.

13. Select the Home button in the Navbar, open the Actions panel, and add a `loadMovieNum` action so that when the button is clicked and then released, the home.swf file loads at level 1 of the Flash Player. Add `loadMovieNum` actions to the other button instances to load SWF files at level 1. The Exhibits button should load the exhibits.swf file. The Education button should load the education.swf file. The Camps button should load the camps.swf file. The Navbar is complete.

14. Return to Scene 1, insert a new layer and name it **navbar**, and then drag an instance of the Navbar symbol to the left side of the Stage. Place the instance below the banner approximately 50 pixels from the left side of the Stage.

15. Insert a new layer and name it **action**. In Frame 1 of the action layer, add a `loadMovieNum` action that loads the home.swf file at level 1 as soon as Frame 1 is played. This displays the home.swf file as soon as the aczMain.swf page plays in the Flash Player. Save the aczMain.fla file.

16. Create a new ActionScript 2.0 document to save as the Home page and as a template that is 600 pixels wide by 400 pixels high. Drag a horizontal guide to 100 pixels from the top edge of the Stage and drag a vertical guide to 200 pixels from the left of the Stage.

17. Draw a rectangle below and to the right of the guides to frame the contents of each page. Use maroon (#660000) for the stroke, white (#FFFFFF) for the fill, a stroke height of 2, and 10 pixels for the corner radius to round each corner. Make the rectangle 350 pixels wide by 270 pixels high. Align the upper-left corner of the rectangle with the intersection of the guides.

18. Select the white fill of the rectangle and convert it to a movie clip symbol named **rectangle fill**. Change the alpha value of the instance to 50% to make it slightly transparent. Rename Layer 1 as **rectangle**, and then lock it.

19. Insert a new layer and name it **text**. Add a text block inside the rectangle. Place it close to the top of the rectangle. Use Times New Roman for the font family, 22 for the point size, black (#000000) for the text color, bold for the font style, and align left for the paragraph format. Type **Welcome to the Alamo City Zoo** in the text block. Center the text block within the rectangle.

20. Add a fixed-width text block below the first text block. Use Times New Roman for the font family, regular for the font style, 14 for the point size, black (#000000) for the text color, and align left for the paragraph format. Type the following in this text block:
The Alamo City Zoo has an extensive collection of the world's most exotic animals. Come visit our world-famous exhibits and see animals in their native habitats. The zoo also offers group tours, special classes, and summer camps for kids.

21. Center the two text blocks within the rectangle. Insert a new layer and name it **graphic**. Change the publish settings to publish only the SWF file. Save this page as **home.fla** in the Flash7\Case2 folder included with your Data Files, and then publish the home.swf file.

22. Save this same document as a template named **aczTemplate** in a new template category called **Alamo** with the description **Template for the Alamo City Zoo Web site pages**. Close the azcTemplate.fla file.

23. Create a new document based on the azcTemplate, and save the document as **exhibits.fla** in the Flash7\Cases2 folder included with your Data Files. Change the top text block to **Alamo City Zoo Exhibits**, and then center the text block within the rectangle. Change the second text block to the following text:

    Alamo City Zoo has one of the largest collections of exotic animals from all over the world. We have bears, elephants, giraffes, and rhinoceros to name a few. Come visit our zoo and plan to spend the day enjoying the many animal exhibits with the animals shown in their natural habitats.

24. Select the graphic layer, and then drag an instance of the elephant.jpg bitmap from the external library to the lower-left corner of the Stage. Flip the bitmap horizontally so that the elephant faces to the right. Save the exhibits.fla file.

25. Create a new document based on the aczTemplate, and then save the document as **education.fla** in the Flash7\Case2 folder included with your Data Files. Change the top text block to **Zoo Educational Classes**, and then center the text block within the rectangle and change the text color to dark orange (#CC3300). Change the second text block to the following text:

    Alamo City Zoo has an exciting schedule of educational and fun classes. These classes are available for the general public, with some special classes available to zoo members only. Local schoolteachers can bring their students to visit the zoo and get special discounts on educational tours.

26. Select the graphics layer, and then drag an instance of the rhino.jpg bitmap from the external library to the lower-left corner of the Stage. Save the education.fla file.

27. Create a new document based on the aczTemplate, and then save the document as **camps.fla** in the Flash7\Case2 folder included with your Data Files. Change the top text block to **Summer Camps**, center the text block within the rectangle, and change the text color to dark green (#006600). Change the second text block to the following text:

    Alamo City Zoo offers a full schedule of summer camps for kids 8–14. Kids get to visit up close with many of the zoo animals and will learn more about how zoo staff feed and care for the animals. Be sure to ask about our overnight camps.

28. Select the graphic layer and drag an instance of the bear.jpg bitmap from the external library to the lower-left corner of the Stage. Save the camps.fla file.

29. Publish each of the documents to create the exhibits.swf, education.swf, and camps.swf files. Return to the azcMain.fla document, and then test the Web site. Test each of the buttons and make sure the individual pages are loaded. Make any necessary corrections.

30. Submit the finished files to your instructor.

Create a new template-based Flash Web site for a nursery.

Case Problem 3

Data Files needed for this Case Problem: wcDraft.fla, flower1.jpg, flower2.jpg, flower3.jpg

Westcreek Nursery   Alice asks Amanda about creating a new Web site to showcase Westcreek Nursery's weekly specials. This Web site will be separate from the current Web site. After meeting with Alice, Amanda develops the following goals for the new Web site:

- Promote the Westcreek Nursery name.
- Showcase weekly specials available for delivery.

Based on these goals, Amanda develops the following objectives:

- Provide a welcome message with contact information.
- Showcase flowers and plants available for delivery.
- Display photos of flowers and plants.

You will help Amanda create the Web site. The outline Amanda prepared for the site includes a Home page with a banner at the top consisting of the Westcreek Nursery name with an animation. The navigation bar will have buttons in the shape of a car wheel which rotate when the pointer is over them. She wants a link to the Photos page, with buttons to display each of three pictures. You will start with a document Amanda has created and use the graphics and photos she has provided. Figure 7-35 shows the completed home page.

| **Figure 7-35** | **Westcreek Nursery Home page** |

1. Open the **wcDraft.fla** file located in the Flash7\Case3 folder included with your Data Files and then save the document as **wcMain.fla** in the same folder.
2. Create a new movie clip symbol named **wcBanner**. In the wcBanner symbol, create a text block in the center of the editing window. Use Verdana for the font family, bold italic for the font style, 46 for the point size, black (#000000) for the text color, and align center for the paragraph format. Type **Westcreek Nursery** in the text block. Center the text block and then change the name of Layer 1 to **wcText**.

⊕ EXPLORE

3. Insert a new layer and name it **wcText copy**. Copy the text block on the wcText layer, and then use the Paste in Place command to paste the copy on the wcText copy layer in the same position as the original text block.

4. Insert a new layer between the wcText and wcText copy layers and name it **gradient**. Drag an instance of the Gradient symbol to Frame 1 of the gradient layer, placing the instance on the right side of the text block so that the rectangle's left side covers the letter y. Create a motion tween in Frame 1 of the gradient layer. Insert regular frames at Frame 24 of both the wcText and wcText copy layers to extend them.

5. At Frame 24 of the gradient layer, move the Gradient instance to the left side of the text block so that the rectangle's right side covers only the letter "W." The Gradient instance will move across the text from the right to the left side.

6. Change the wcText copy layer to a mask layer and make certain that the gradient layer becomes a masked layer. The banner is complete.

7. Return to Scene 1, insert a new layer and name it **banner**. On the banner layer, add an instance of the wcBanner symbol to the top of the Stage. Center the instance right below the top edge of the box created by the rectangle on the Stage.

8. Create a new button symbol named **Home button**. Drag an instance of the Wheel symbol from the library to the center of the editing window. Add a text block to the right of the Wheel instance in the editing window. Use Verdana for the font family, regular for the font style, 16 for the point size, align left for the paragraph format, and black (#000000) for the text color. Type **Home** in the text block.

9. Insert a keyframe in the Over frame, swap the Wheel instance with an instance of the Rotating Wheel symbol, and then change the text color to white (#FFFFFF).

⊕ EXPLORE 10. Add a blank keyframe in the Hit frame of Layer 1. Turn on onion skinning and extend the onion skin markers to cover all four frames of the Timeline. In the Hit frame of Layer 1, draw a small rectangle to cover the area for both the wheel and the text. The Home button is complete.

11. Make a duplicate of the Home button named **Photos button**. Change the text in both the Up and Over frames of the Photos button to **Photos**, and then resize the rectangle in the Hit frame of the Photos button to cover all of the text.

12. Create a new movie clip symbol named **Navbar**. In the Navbar symbol, drag an instance of the Home button to the left side of the crosshair on the editing window. Drag an instance of the Photos button to the right of the Home button. Align both symbol instances along their top edges.

13. Select the Home button in the Navbar, open the Actions panel, and add a `loadMovieNum` action so that when the button is clicked and then released, the nursery.swf file loads at level 1 of the Flash Player. Add a `loadMovieNum` action to the Photos button instance to load the photos.swf file at level 1. The Navbar is complete.

14. Return to Scene 1, insert a new layer, and name it **navigation**. Drag a horizontal guide to 100 pixels from the top edge of the Stage. On the navigation layer, drag an instance of the Navbar symbol to the Stage and center it below the banner and above the horizontal guide.

15. Insert a new layer and name it **action**. Add a `loadMovieNum` action at Frame 1 of the Action layer that loads the nursery.swf file at level 1 as soon as Frame 1 is played. This file is displayed as soon as the wcMain.swf page plays in the Flash Player.

16. Create a new document 600 pixels wide by 400 pixels high. Drag a horizontal guide to 100 pixels from the top edge of the Stage. The content for the page will be below this guide.

17. Add a text block below the guide, 150 pixels from the top edge of the Stage. Use Verdana for the font family, bold for the font style, 16 for the point size, black (#000000) for the text color, and align left for the paragraph format. Type **Westcreek Specials of the Week!** in the text block. Add a fixed-width text block below the first text block. Change the font style to regular and change the point size to 14. Type the following in this text block:

Welcome to Westcreek's specials of the week. Here, you'll find information about some of our great deals on flowers, plants, shrubs, and trees. Each week, we'll

highlight several items available for quick delivery to your home or business. Please call our friendly staff for more information.

18. Center the two text blocks on the Stage, and then save the page as **nursery.fla** in the Flash7\Case3 folder included with your Data Files.

19. Create a new document 600 pixels wide by 400 pixels high. Drag a horizontal guide to 100 pixels from the top edge of the Stage. The content for the page will be below this guide.

20. Create a new movie clip symbol named **Photo holder**. Exit the movie clip's symbol-editing mode and return to Scene 1. Drag an instance of the Photo holder symbol to the Stage. Use the Property inspector to place the movie clip instance at the X coordinate of 200 and the Y coordinate of 100. Also, assign the name **photo_mc** to the movie clip instance.

21. Create a new movie clip symbol named **Photos navbar**. In symbol editing mode, draw a star shape with a dark green (#006600) fill and a black stroke. Set the star's width and height to 45 pixels each. Convert the star shape to a button symbol named **Photo button**. Edit the Photo button symbol, add a keyframe in the Over frame, and then, in the Over frame, change the color of the star's fill to light yellow (#FFFF99).

22. Return to the Photos navbar symbol, add two more instances of the Photo button to the Stage, and then arrange the instances vertically below the first instance. Add a text block above the buttons. Use Verdana as the font family, regular for the font style, 12 for the point size, and black (#000000) for the text color. Type **Click a star to see a picture:** in the text block.

⊕ EXPLORE   23. Select the top button instance, open the Behaviors panel, and add a Load Graphic behavior to the button instance. The behavior should load the flower1.jpg file into the photo_mc movie clip instance. The Behavior text box should display this._parent.photo_mc, indicating the graphic will load into the photo_mc instance on the Scene 1 Timeline. Also, add the Load Graphic behavior to the other two button instances on the Stage. One should load the flower2.jpg file, and the other should load the flower3.jpg file. Both photos should load in the photo_mc movie clip instance.

24. Return to Scene 1, and then drag an instance of the Photos navbar symbol to the left side of the Stage just below the guide and 20 pixels from the left of the Stage. Save the page as **photos.fla** in the Flash7\Case3 folder included with your Data Files.

25. Publish each of the documents to create the **nursery.swf** and **photos.swf** files. Return to the wcMain.fla document and test the Web site in the Flash Player. Test each of the buttons and verify that the individual pages and photos are loaded. Make any necessary corrections.

26. Submit the finished files to your instructor.

Create a Flash Web site based on a template for an association.

CREATE

Case Problem 4

Data File needed for this Case Problem: mission.jpg

Missions Support Association   Anissa is developing a preliminary version of a new Web site for Missions Support Association that will highlight special services available to the association's members. Based on discussions with Brittany, president of the association, the following goals are developed:

* Promote the association's main services.
* Promote the association's name.

Based on these goals, Anissa and Brittany develop the following objectives for the Web site:

- Provide information about special events.
- Provide information about volunteer opportunities.
- Provide information about tours available for schools.
- Use a picture for the background of the content and allow for the picture to be changed periodically.

You will develop the Web site for Anissa. The Web site will be a preliminary version and the content for each page is under development. Figure 7-36 shows one possible design for the Web site.

Figure 7-36   **Sample Missions Support Association Home page**

1. Plan the Flash Web site, including a main page with the organization's name, navigation bar, and a content area for the level 1 pages, as well as the level 1 pages for the different informational areas. Also, plan how you will use the **mission.jpg** file included in the Flash7\Case4 folder with your Data Files in the Web site.
2. Create a new document for the main page, save it as **msaMain.fla** in the Flash7\Case4 folder included with your Data Files, and use the dimensions and background color of your choice.
3. In a new layer, create a text block, using the text properties and location of your choice, with the organization's name, **Missions Support Association**.
4. Create the buttons for the navigation bar to load the different level 1 pages in the main page. Be sure to include some distinguishing characteristic in each frame to provide visual cues for the user. Include an animation in one frame (for example, you can create motion tweens to increase the width of the button's shape to 120% between Frame 1 and Frame 5, and then decrease to its original size in Frame 10). Label each button appropriately. Add a clickable shape in the Hit frame, if necessary. You can use onion skinning to see all the contents of the frames as you draw a rectangle that covers any shapes and text in the button. (*Hint:* You can create one button, and then edit duplicates of the button to create the other buttons you need.)

5. Create a navigation bar for the main page that includes each button you created. Add a `loadMovieNum` action to each button so that when the button is clicked and then released, the corresponding file loads at level 1 of the Flash Player. Place the navigation bar on the main page.

6. Add an action to Frame 1 of the main page that loads one of the files at level 1 as soon as Frame 1 is played.

7. Create a new document with the same document dimensions and background color as the main page, and then save it as a template named **msaTemplate** in a new template category using an appropriate description. You will use this template to create the level 1 pages. Follow your design plan to complete the template, adding images, shapes, text, actions, and guides as needed.

8. Create a new document based on the template for each level 1 page you need to create for the site, saving each document with an appropriate filename (such as **main.fla**, **events.fla**, **tours.fla**, **volunteer.fla**, and so on) in the Flash7\Case4 folder included with your Data Files. Add appropriate content to the page in the location specified by the guides.

9. Save and publish each of the documents to create the SWF files.

10. Return to the main document, and then test the movie, verifying that when you click each button, the corresponding page loads. Make any necessary corrections.

11. Submit the finished files to your instructor.

ENDING DATA FILES

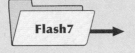

Flash7 →   **Tutorial**

home.fla
home.swf
jsDocument.fla
jsMain.fla
jsMain.html
jsMain.swf
photo1.jpg
photo2.jpg
photos.fla
photos.swf
services.fla
services.swf
teams.fla
teams.swf

Review

home.swf
main.fla
main.swf
photos.fla
photos.swf
picture1.jpg
picture2.jpg
services.swf
specials.fla
specials.swf
teams.swf

Case1

adoptions.fla
adoptions.swf
kprTemplate.fla
main.fla
main.swf
services.fla
services.swf
training.fla
training.swf
welcome.fla
welcome.swf

Case2

aczMain.fla
aczMain.swf
aczTemplate.fla
camps.fla
camps.swf
education.fla
education.swf
exhibits.fla
exhibits.swf
home.fla
home.swf

Case3

flower1.jpg
flower2.jpg
flower3.jpg
nursery.fla
nursery.swf
photos.fla
photos.swf
wcMain.fla
wcMain.swf

Case4

events.fla
events.swf
msaMain.fla
msaMain.swf
msaTemplate.fla
tours.fla
tours.swf
volunteer.fla
volunteer.swf
welcome.fla
welcome.swf

OBJECTIVES

Session 8.1
- Review the basics of ActionScript programming
- Compare ActionScript 2.0 and ActionScript 3.0
- Learn ActionScript 3.0 syntax
- Create ActionScript 3.0 code using the Code Snippets panel
- Modify ActionScript code to create functions and handle events

Session 8.2
- Create links to external Web sites
- Create and test a Flash preloader

Session 8.3
- Create input and dynamic text fields
- Create an input form

Programming with ActionScript 3.0

Adding Interactive Elements to a Flash Web Site

FLASH

Case | *Admiral Web Design*

Dan Jackson, owner of Jackson's Sports, meets with Aly and Chris and requests additional pages for the Jackson's Sports Web site. He wants a Resources page that will contain hyperlinks to other sports-related Web sites. He also wants a page that team coaches can use to calculate the cost of team jerseys by entering the number of jerseys needed and choosing from various options to calculate and display the total cost. Aly and Chris revise the design of the Jackson's Sports Web site. You will add the requested pages as well as a simple animation that will provide visual feedback while the site contents load into the Flash Player.

In this tutorial, you will learn how to use ActionScript 3.0 to add interactive elements to Flash documents. You will also learn about the structure and syntax of the ActionScript programming language. Finally, you will use the Code Snippets panel to write ActionScript code to control the navigation for the Web site, to create links to other Web sites, to input values, and to perform calculations.

STARTING DATA FILES

Flash8 → Tutorial   Review   Case1   Case2   Case3   Case4

Tutorial	Review	Case1	Case2	Case3	Case4
sportsWeb.fla	softballSite.fla	kprDraft.fla	aczDraft.fla bear.jpg giraffe.jpg rhino.jpg	flower1.jpg flower2.jpg flower3.jpg preloaderScript.as wcDraft.fla	msaDraft.fla

SESSION 8.1 VISUAL OVERVIEW

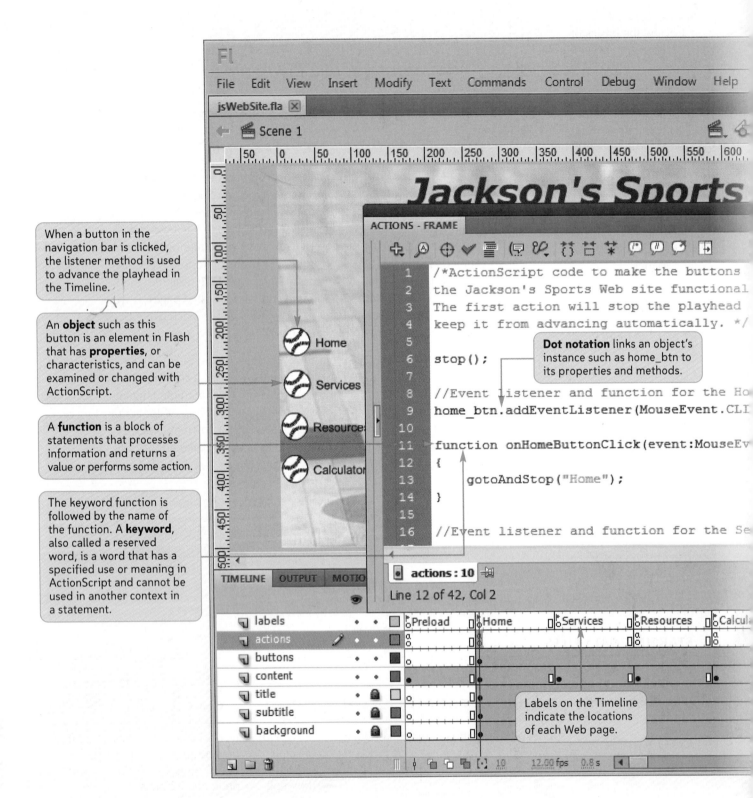

When a button in the navigation bar is clicked, the listener method is used to advance the playhead in the Timeline.

An **object** such as this button is an element in Flash that has **properties**, or characteristics, and can be examined or changed with ActionScript.

A **function** is a block of statements that processes information and returns a value or performs some action.

The keyword function is followed by the name of the function. A **keyword**, also called a reserved word, is a word that has a specified use or meaning in ActionScript and cannot be used in another context in a statement.

Dot notation links an object's instance such as home_btn to its properties and methods.

Labels on the Timeline indicate the locations of each Web page.

```
1   /*ActionScript code to make the buttons
2   the Jackson's Sports Web site functional
3   The first action will stop the playhead
4   keep it from advancing automatically. */
5
6   stop();
7
8   //Event listener and function for the Ho
9   home_btn.addEventListener(MouseEvent.CLI
10
11  function onHomeButtonClick(event:MouseEv
12  {
13      gotoAndStop("Home");
14  }
15
16  //Event listener and function for the Se
```

ACTIONSCRIPT 3.0

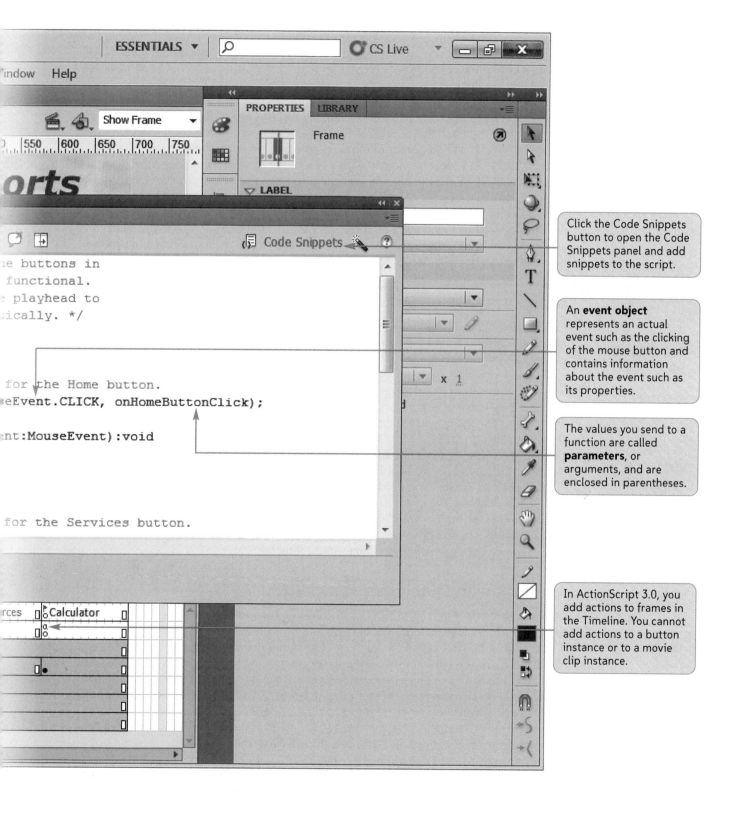

Click the Code Snippets button to open the Code Snippets panel and add snippets to the script.

An **event object** represents an actual event such as the clicking of the mouse button and contains information about the event such as its properties.

The values you send to a function are called **parameters**, or arguments, and are enclosed in parentheses.

In ActionScript 3.0, you add actions to frames in the Timeline. You cannot add actions to a button instance or to a movie clip instance.

Programming with ActionScript 3.0

ActionScript is a robust programming language that gives Flash developers a virtually unlimited number of ways to make a Flash document interactive. ActionScript can be used to create actions that control multimedia elements such as buttons, and to control the way the different parts of a movie are played. ActionScript programming requires writing scripts that consist of actions, event handlers, and other programming statements to control how the actions are executed. In previous tutorials, you added actions to buttons that controlled animations in movies and controlled when and how SWF files were loaded into the Flash Player.

In addition to controlling the order in which frames play in a document's Timeline or making buttons operational, ActionScript can be used to enable the viewer to input data and have the Flash Player process that data to return a result. ActionScript can also be used to change the properties of movie clips while they play in the Flash Player. For example, you can have a movie clip with a graphic of a car that changes color when a button is clicked. With ActionScript, you can also test a condition and then execute different actions based on the test results. For example, you can create a script that compares an input value with a set value to determine what actions to execute.

In this tutorial, you will write ActionScript code to control multimedia elements, access external Web pages, and provide the user with a means of entering and processing information in the Jackson's Sports Web site.

Comparing ActionScript 3.0 and ActionScript 2.0

ActionScript 3.0 is the latest version of the ActionScript programming language and is conceptually different from the previous version, ActionScript 2.0, which you used in earlier tutorials. ActionScript 3.0 has many more capabilities than ActionScript 2.0 and is designed to enable Flash developers to create highly complex applications. Versions 9 and later of the Flash Player plug-in use the **ActionScript Virtual Machine 2 (AVM2)**, which is the Flash Player built-in code that plays Flash movies. Previous versions of the Flash Player use the original ActionScript Virtual Machine (AVM1). Improvements in the AVM2 enable current versions of the Flash Player to run faster and more efficiently than previous versions. ActionScript 3.0 code doesn't run on the AVM1, so Flash movies using ActionScript 3.0 run only on Flash Player 9 or later.

TIP

You can run SWF files that contain ActionScript 2.0 in versions 9 and 10 of the Flash Player.

In a previous tutorial, you used ActionScript 2.0 to create an event handler assigned to a button instance. The event handler carried out an action such as stopping or playing a movie when the button was clicked and then released. In ActionScript 3.0, you cannot add actions to a button instance or to a movie clip instance. Instead, you add actions that reference button instances to frames in the Timeline.

Working with Objects and Properties

ActionScript is used to control and modify objects. The multimedia elements you work with in Flash, such as buttons, movie clips, and text blocks, are considered objects. For example, a button has properties such as width, height, and location on the Stage. An instance of a movie clip symbol has similar properties. ActionScript code can be written to read or change these properties in response to certain events, such as a mouse click, a key press, or a certain frame in the Timeline being played. The properties for an object include alpha (which controls the movie clip's transparency), rotation (which controls the movie clip's orientation), and visible (which controls the movie clip's visibility). These properties can be examined and modified using ActionScript.

Any object you want to reference in ActionScript requires a name. Recall that you can have multiple instances of one movie clip symbol, which means that multiple objects are based on the same symbol. When using ActionScript to refer to a specific instance, you must refer to its instance name.

After you assign a name to an instance, you can refer to it in the action using dot notation. For example, if a movie clip instance is named circle_mc, the following code changes the alpha property of the instance to 30%:

```
circle_mc.alpha = .30
```

The values for an object's alpha property range from 0 to 1, where 1 represents 100%. The dot (.) links the property to the particular instance or object.

Aly and Chris sketched the storyboard with the design of the Jackson's Sports Web site, as shown in Figure 8-1. The sketch shows the new pages to be completed as well as the site navigation.

Figure 8-1   Jackson's Sports Web site storyboard

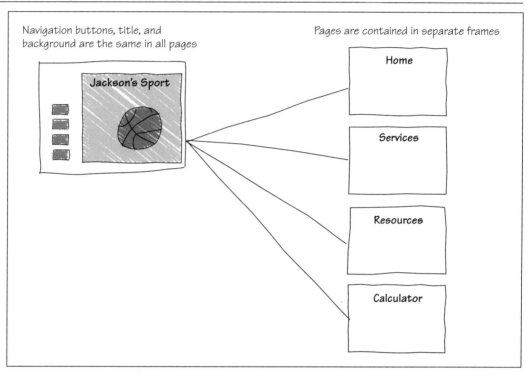

You'll review the new Jackson's Sports Web site that Aly and Chris created, assign names to the objects representing the buttons for the site's navigation, and then extend the Timeline of the document to add the Resources and Calculator pages.

To name button objects and extend the Timeline in the Jackson's Sports Web site:

1. Open the **sportsWeb.fla** file located in the Flash8\Tutorial folder included with your Data Files, save the file as **jsWebSite.fla** in the same folder, reset the workspace to the **Essentials** layout, and then change the Stage magnification to **Show Frame**.

2. In the Timeline, move the playhead to **Frame 10**, if necessary, to display the Home page for the Web site on the Stage, and then move the playhead to **Frame 20** to display the Services page. Each Web page in the site will be in a separate frame.

3. In the Tools panel, click the **Selection** tool, and then, on the Stage, click the **Home** button to select it. The name of the Home button instance, home_btn, appears in the Instance name box in the Property inspector. See Figure 8-2.

Figure 8-2 **Home button instance name**

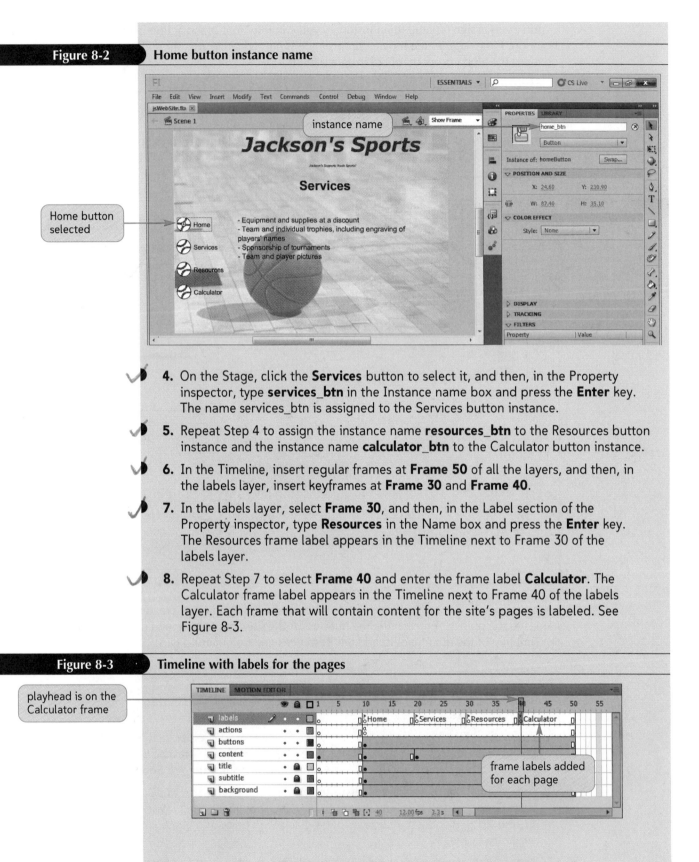

Home button selected

instance name

4. On the Stage, click the **Services** button to select it, and then, in the Property inspector, type **services_btn** in the Instance name box and press the **Enter** key. The name services_btn is assigned to the Services button instance.

5. Repeat Step 4 to assign the instance name **resources_btn** to the Resources button instance and the instance name **calculator_btn** to the Calculator button instance.

6. In the Timeline, insert regular frames at **Frame 50** of all the layers, and then, in the labels layer, insert keyframes at **Frame 30** and **Frame 40**.

7. In the labels layer, select **Frame 30**, and then, in the Label section of the Property inspector, type **Resources** in the Name box and press the **Enter** key. The Resources frame label appears in the Timeline next to Frame 30 of the labels layer.

8. Repeat Step 7 to select **Frame 40** and enter the frame label **Calculator**. The Calculator frame label appears in the Timeline next to Frame 40 of the labels layer. Each frame that will contain content for the site's pages is labeled. See Figure 8-3.

Figure 8-3 **Timeline with labels for the pages**

playhead is on the Calculator frame

frame labels added for each page

9. In the content layer, insert a keyframe at **Frame 30**, and then, on the Stage, replace the "Services" text with **Sports Web Site Resources** and delete the large text block in the center of the Stage. You will add the page content later in this tutorial.

10. In the content layer, insert a keyframe at **Frame 40**, and then, in this frame, replace the "Sports Web Site Resources" text with **Team Jersey Calculator**. See Figure 8-4.

Figure 8-4 | **Content for the Calculator page**

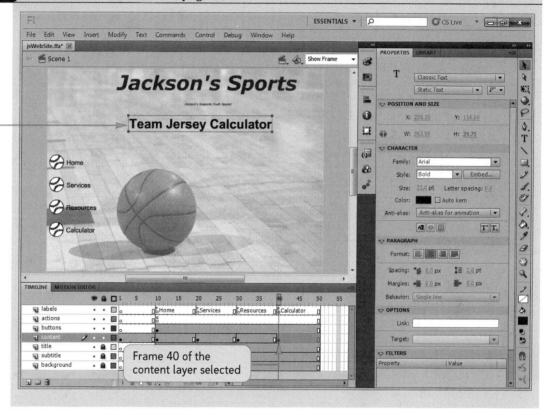

Calculator page content added in Frame 40

Frame 40 of the content layer selected

Using Actions, Methods, and Functions

An action is a statement, such as `gotoAndStop()`, that instructs the SWF file to do something. The terms *action* and *statement* are often interchangeable.

Flash includes a number of prebuilt functions, such as the `trace()` function, which displays values in the Output panel, and the `math.Random()` function, which returns a random number. You can also create your own functions. For example, you can create a function that accepts the temperature value in Fahrenheit degrees and returns the value in Celsius degrees. Then you can **call**, or execute, the function from different parts of the script in which it is defined. To use a function, you need to know what value or values to send to it and what value or values to expect in return. For example, the text "You are here" in the function `trace("You are here")` is a parameter of the function. Not all functions require parameters. For example, the math.Random() function requires no parameters, so nothing is enclosed in the parentheses.

A **method** is a function specific to a particular object. It is a built-in capability of the object that performs a certain action or responds to a certain event. Methods are similar to other functions and actions, but they're part of an object and can be used to control the object. For example, if you have a movie clip instance named circle_mc in the document's main Timeline that has 20 frames in its own Timeline, you can control which of the 20 frames will play. You do this with the `gotoAndPlay()` method for the movie clip. Using dot notation, you code the object name followed by a dot followed by the method's name. The following code sets the movie clip instance to start playing at Frame 10 of its Timeline:

```
circle_mc.gotoAndPlay(10);
```

The parameter value of 10 in the parentheses specifies to which frame the playhead will go. Because `gotoAndPlay()` is a method of the movie clip object, the movie clip knows how to respond when the method is executed. The `gotoAndPlay()` method is also considered an action in the main Timeline because the main document is considered an object. When using the `gotoAndPlay()` method for the document's main Timeline, it isn't necessary to specify an object name.

The Jackson's Sports Web site will use functions to move the playhead to specific frames in the Timeline by referring to frame labels. For example, the `gotoAndStop("Home")` action will move the playhead to the frame labeled Home, Frame 10 of the labels layer, which contains the home page for the site. The content of each page of the Jackson's Sports Web site is in a separate frame that will be referred to by its label.

Writing ActionScript Code

When writing ActionScript code, you must follow certain rules, which are known as the **syntax** of the language. As shown in previous examples, actions and functions are often written in mixed uppercase and lowercase letters. For example, the `gotoAndPlay()` function uses the uppercase letters "A" and "P," but lowercase for the remainder of the letters. Because ActionScript is case sensitive, writing this function as `gotoandplay()` with all lowercase letters will generate an error message. Also, even though most statements work without an ending semicolon, it's good programming practice to include it. Ending the statements with a semicolon follows the format of other programming languages. Other required syntactical elements are parentheses, which are used to group arguments in methods and functions, and curly braces, which group a block of related statements. Figure 8-5 shows a sample of ActionScript syntax.

| Figure 8-5 | Sample ActionScript syntax |

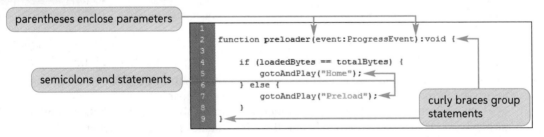

You'll review the actions in Frame 10 of the actions layer of the Jackson's Sports Web site.

To review the actions in Frame 10 of the actions layer:

1. In the Timeline, click **Frame 10** of the actions layer. The "a" at the top of the frame indicates that the frame contains an action.

TIP

You can also double-click the vertical bar between the Actions toolbox and the Script pane to collapse or expand the Actions toolbox.

2. On the Application bar, click **Window**, and then click **Actions**. The Actions panel opens and displays a script.

3. If necessary, click the **collapse** button ▌ in the vertical bar between the Actions toolbox and the Script pane. The Actions toolbox collapses and the Script pane expands.

4. If necessary, click the **Script Assist** button 🪄 to deselect it. The Script Assist area collapses. See Figure 8-6.

Figure 8-6   Script for Frame 10 of the actions layer

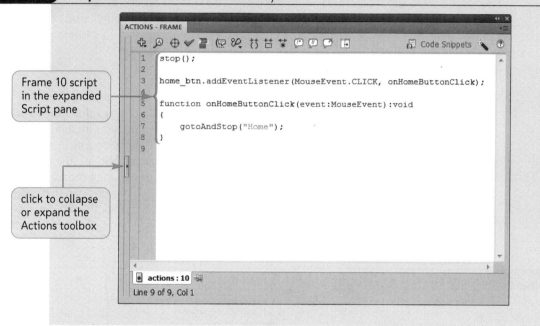

Frame 10 script in the expanded Script pane

click to collapse or expand the Actions toolbox

```
1  stop();
2
3  home_btn.addEventListener(MouseEvent.CLICK, onHomeButtonClick);
4
5  function onHomeButtonClick(event:MouseEvent):void
6  {
7      gotoAndStop("Home");
8  }
9
```

actions : 10

Line 9 of 9, Col 1

The first line of the Actions panel contains stop();, which will stop the playhead on Frame 10 and prevent the movie from playing continuously. The third line contains an event listener, which is discussed later in this session. The fifth line contains the function onHomeButtonClick(event:MouseEvent):void, which defines the onHomeButtonClick function.

To define a function, you use the function keyword followed by the function name. The function name is a user-defined name and should be unique. The name should not start with a number, but it can include letters, numbers, the underscore character, and the dollar sign character. Within the parentheses following the function name, you specify the parameter of the function, which in this case is an event object with the user-defined name of event. The event object must be assigned an event type—in this case, MouseEvent. Object types are coded with a colon followed by the type identifier. The event type, MouseEvent, distinguishes the event parameter from other types of events.

Written Communication: Using a Standard Naming Convention

When assigning names to objects such as functions, variables, movie clips, and buttons, use a mixed case format where the first letter of the name is lowercase and the first letter of each word that is part of the name is capitalized, such as onHomeButtonClick. This naming convention makes it easier to read names within the ActionScript code and is similar to naming conventions used with other programming languages such as Java. One benefit of using a consistent naming convention is that programs written by one programmer are easier to understand by other programmers within a team or organization. Also, previously written code is simpler to read when it needs to be reused at a later time. This naming convention also makes it easier to write more meaningful names by enabling the programmer to use names consisting of several words joined together without spaces that are easy to read as opposed to being limited to using single word names. This naming convention is sometimes called *camel case* because the uppercase letters form humps in the name.

A function can return a value, such as the result of a calculation, based on the actions in the function. The result of the function, such as a return value, must also be assigned a data type. If the function does not return a value, you include the `void` keyword after the colon to indicate no value is returned. The statements in a function must be enclosed in curly braces. In this case, the curly braces enclose the statement `gotoAndStop("Home");`, which is the action to be performed when the function is called. Although this function requires only one statement, functions can include multiple statements. When the onHomeButtonClick function is called, the playhead will move to the frame labeled Home, and the movie will stop playing. The function structure is shown in Figure 8-7.

Figure 8-7   **Structure of onHomeButtonClick function**

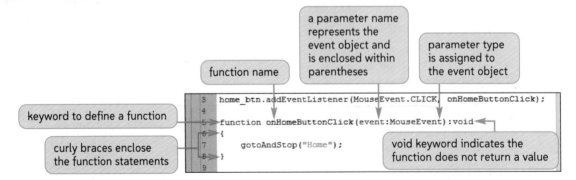

Using the Code Snippets Panel

Writing ActionScript code from scratch can be a challenging task for a beginning programmer. Fortunately, the Code Snippets panel provides snippets of prewritten ActionScript 3.0 code that can be added to a Flash document. The panel includes code snippets you can add to affect the behavior of objects on the Stage, to enable navigation within the Timeline, to load and unload images and other SWF files, to control audio and video elements, or to handle events such as mouse clicks. (Events are covered later in this session.) When code snippets are applied to a Flash document, the ActionScript code is added to the current frame on the Timeline and in an Actions layer, if one exists.

If no Actions layer exists, one is added above all other layers. The code snippets also contain instructions on how to customize the code to achieve the desired results. After you insert the code, you can modify it using the Actions Panel.

INSIGHT

Learning to Write ActionScript

Adding prebuilt code using the Code Snippets panel is a good way to learn ActionScript 3.0 because the panel doesn't require knowledge of the ActionScript language. The code snippets contain the lines of code needed to add interactivity to a Flash document, they are error-free, and they contain instructions about the purpose of the code and about which lines can be customized. By reviewing the code snippets, you can begin to understand the structure of ActionScript code and how the various elements of the language are used to control objects in Flash. This makes it easier to write similar lines of code from scratch.

You will use the Code Snippets panel to add functions to move the playhead to each frame representing a Web page.

To add a new function for the Jackson's Sports Web site:

1. On the Stage, click the **Services** button to select it. You will add ActionScript code to control what happens when the Services button is clicked.

2. On the Actions panel menu bar, click the **Code Snippets** button to open the Code Snippets panel.

3. In the Code Snippets panel, click the small arrow ▶ to the left of the Timeline Navigation folder, if necessary, to expand the list of snippets. See Figure 8-8.

Figure 8-8 Code Snippets panel

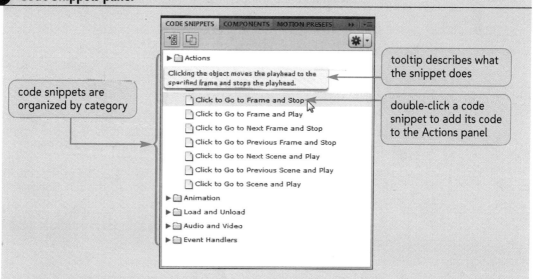

4. Double-click the **Click to Go to Frame and Stop** snippet to add its code to the Actions panel. The code snippet containing a function is added after the existing code in the Actions Panel.

5. In the Actions panel, click an empty area after the last selected line to deselect the code. The code contains an event listener statement and a function with a `gotoAndStop()` action. See Figure 8-9.

Figure 8-9   **Code added to the Script pane**

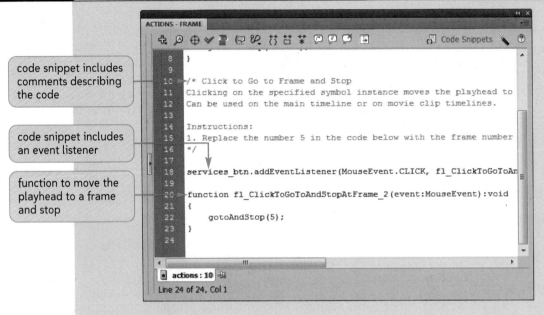

code snippet includes comments describing the code

code snippet includes an event listener

function to move the playhead to a frame and stop

```
 8    }
 9
10    /* Click to Go to Frame and Stop
11    Clicking on the specified symbol instance moves the playhead to
12    Can be used on the main timeline or on movie clip timelines.
13
14    Instructions:
15    1. Replace the number 5 in the code below with the frame number
16    */
17
18    services_btn.addEventListener(MouseEvent.CLICK, fl_ClickToGoToAn
19
20    function fl_ClickToGoToAndStopAtFrame_2(event:MouseEvent):void
21    {
22         gotoAndStop(5);
23    }
24
```

The gray lines at the beginning of the code snippet are comments. A **comment** is a note within the ActionScript code that explains what is happening but doesn't cause any action to be performed. The comments added with the code snippet explain the purpose of the code and provide instructions on how to modify the code.

Next, you will add code snippets for the Resources and Calculator button instances.

To add functions for the other buttons:

1. On the Stage, click the **Resources** button to select it. You will add ActionScript code to control what happens when the Resources button is clicked.

2. In the Actions panel, click the **Code Snippets** button and then double-click the **Click to Go to Frame and Stop** snippet to add its code to the Actions panel. The code snippet is added after the existing code in the Actions Panel.

   The name of the function is similar to the function name added for the Services button. Each time you add the same code snippet, the function name is changed by adding a number at the end of its name.

3. Repeat Steps 1 and 2 to add the same code snippet for the Calculator button instance.

Using Events and Event Listeners

Events are things that happen when a movie is playing, such as when the user clicks a button or presses a key. ActionScript can respond to or handle an event by carrying out instructions based on the event. The code to respond to or handle events consists of three elements: the event source, the event, and the response. The **event source**, also known as the event target, is the object to which the event will happen, such as a button instance. The event is the thing that will happen to the object, such as a button click or a key press. The **response** is the steps that are performed when the event occurs. The ActionScript code to handle events must include these three elements. The code snippets added in the previous steps contain all three elements.

Creating an Event Listener

In the Jackson's Sports Web site, clicking a button with the mouse is the event that will control which function is called. If the Home button is clicked, for example, then the onHomeButtonClick function should be called to move the playhead to the Home frame. To call a function when a button is clicked, you need an event listener. An **event listener** is a method that the Flash Player executes in response to a specific event. Every object that has an event has an event listener.

The event listener method, `addEventListener()`, establishes a connection between the function, such as onHomeButtonClick, and the event source, such as the home_btn instance. The `addEventListener()` method registers the function to be called with the event source to listen for a specified event. When the event occurs, the Flash Player can respond by calling the associated function. The `addEventListener()` method has two parameters: the event to listen for and the function to call when the event happens. The code for the event listener for the home_btn is:

```
home_btn.addEventListener(MouseEvent.CLICK,
onHomeButtonClick);
```

This code contains the three elements required to respond to an event. The event source is the home_btn, which is the instance name of the Home button. The event is CLICK, which is a property of the MouseEvent object and represents the clicking of the mouse. And the response is the call to the onHomeButtonClick function. The `addEventListener()` method is called to register the onHomeButtonClick function with the button instance. The code structure is shown in Figure 8-10.

Figure 8-10   **Format of an event listener**

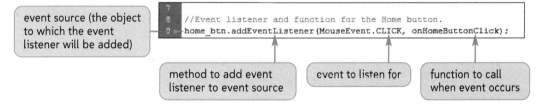

The code snippets added in the previous steps use predefined names for the functions, such as fl_ClickToGoToAndStopAtFrame(). When you add the same code snippet more than once, Flash appends a number to the end of the function name to distinguish it from an existing function with the same name. Also, the action within the function references Frame 5, and in the comments you are instructed to change the frame number. You will modify the function names to be more descriptive, and you will change the frame reference to move the playhead to the frame label associated with the button.

To modify the function names and actions:

1. In the Script pane, scroll up to see the `services_btn.addEventListener()` line, and then double-click the function referenced within the parentheses, `fl_ClickToGoToAndStopAtFrame_2`. The function name is selected.

2. Type `onServicesButtonClick` to change the name of the function that is called when the Services button is clicked. The name of the function in the next statement where the function is defined needs to match the function referenced in the `services_btn.addEventListener()` line.

3. In the Script pane, below the `services_btn.addEventListener()` line, select the function name `fl_ClickToGoToAndStopAtFrame_2`, and then type `onServicesButtonClick` to change the name of the function.

Next, you will change the frame referenced in the `gotoAndStop()` function.

4. In the next line located within the curly braces, select the number **5** in the `gotoAndStop(5);` function, and then type `"Services"`. The function will now cause the playhead to move to the frame labeled Services. See Figure 8-11.

| Figure 8-11 | Updated function name and frame reference |

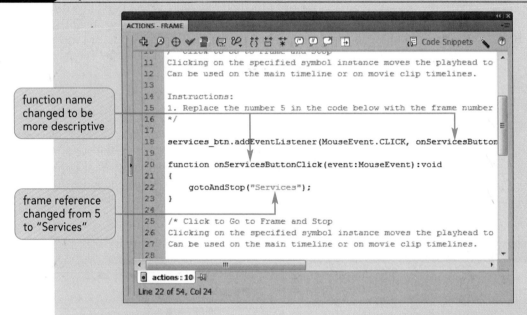

function name changed to be more descriptive

frame reference changed from 5 to "Services"

You also need to change the function names and frame references in the code snippets inserted for the Resources and Calculator buttons.

TIP

You can click the Find icon in the Actions panel to open the Find and Replace dialog box. Use the dialog box to replace multiple instances of text in the Script pane.

5. In the Script pane, scroll down to see the `resources_btn.addEventListener()` line, select the function name within the parentheses, `fl_ClickToGoToAndStopAtFrame_3`, and then type `onResourcesButtonClick` to change the name of the function that is called when the Resources button is clicked.

6. In the Script pane, below the `resources_btn.addEventListener()` line, select the function name `fl_ClickToGoToAndStopAtFrame_3`, and then type `onResourcesButtonClick` to change the name of the function.

7. In the next line located within the curly braces, select the number **5** in the `gotoAndStop(5);` function, and then type `"Resources"` to change the frame referenced within the function. The function will now cause the playhead to move to the frame labeled Resources.

8. In the Script pane, in the `calculator_btn.addEventListener()` line, select the function name within the parentheses, `fl_ClickToGoToAndStopAtFrame_4`, and then type `onCalculatorButtonClick` to change the name of the function that is called when the Calculator button is clicked.

9. In the Script pane, below the `calculator_btn.addEventListener()` line, select the function name `fl_ClickToGoToAndStopAtFrame_4`, and then type `onCalculatorButtonClick` to change the name of the function.

10. In the next line located within the curly braces, select the number **5** in the `gotoAndStop(5);` function, and then type `"Calculator"` to change the frame referenced within the function. The function will now cause the playhead to move to the frame labeled Calculator.

You have modified the code snippets to use more descriptive names for the functions and to reference the frame labels in the gotoAndStop() statements. Because you have made multiple changes to the code, you should check the code to make sure you haven't introduced any syntax errors. You should then test the movie to make sure that when the navigation buttons are clicked, the playhead moves to the associated frame.

To check for the code for errors and test the movie:

1. In the Actions panel, click the **Check syntax** button to check for syntax errors in the code. The script is checked. If no errors are displayed in the Compiler Errors panel, the script is correct.

Trouble? If your code contains errors, the errors are listed in the Compiler Errors panel at the bottom of the screen. Review your script to compare it to the code you modified in the previous steps, make any necessary corrections, and then repeat Step 1 until no errors are encountered.

2. Save the document. You will test the Jackson's Sports Web site.

3. On the Application bar, click **Control**, point to **Test Movie**, and then click **in Flash Professional**. The movie opens in the Flash Player window. The Loading text appears briefly, and then the Home page opens.

4. Click the **Services** button to display the Services page, click the **Resources** button to display the Resources page, click the **Calculator** button to display the Calculator page, and then click the **Home** button to display the Home page.

5. Close the Flash Player window and return to the document.

Trouble? If the Output panel displays a message about embedding fonts, ignore the message and click the Timeline tab to display the Timeline. You will not need to embed fonts in the SWF file.

Adding Comments

The comments added with the code snippets provide instructions on the use of the snippets. After you modify the code snippets, you can delete these comments. However, as scripts get longer and more complex, comments become increasingly helpful. Even though a comment is not necessary for the action to work, they can be very useful to the programmer writing the code and to other programmers who might later modify the code. Single-line comments are indicated by two forward slashes (//). Any text after the slashes in the same line is not interpreted by the Flash Player. Comments that span multiple lines are enclosed with the /* and */ characters.

You will delete existing comments and add new comments to the code in the Jackson's Sports Web site document.

To delete and add comments to the Jackson's Sports Web site script:

▶ **1.** In the Actions panel, place the insertion point to the left of stop(); on the first line, and then type the following code, pressing the **Enter** key after each line to create a multiple-line comment.

```
/* ActionScript code to make the buttons in
the Jackson's Sports Web site functional.
The first action will stop the playhead to
keep it from advancing automatically. */
```

▶ **2.** Press the **Enter** key to add a blank line between the last line of the comments and the stop(); code.

▶ **3.** In the Actions panel, place the insertion point to the left of the word "home_btn" on line 8 (which contains the event listener), type the following code, and then press the **Enter** key to create a single-line comment.

```
// Event listener and function for the Home button.
```

▶ **4.** In the Actions panel, select the multiple-line comment above the event listener for the services_btn, delete the comment, and then type the following code to create a single-line comment. See Figure 8-12.

```
// Event listener and function for the Services button.
```

Figure 8-12   **Multi-line comment replaced**

single-line comment added in place of multi-line comment

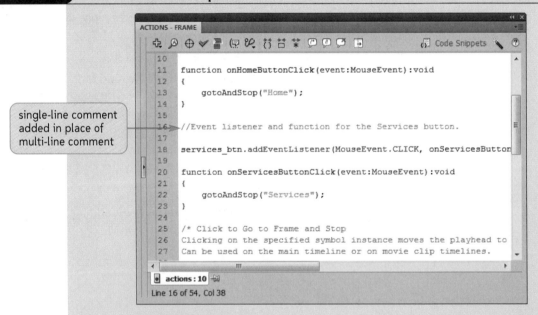

```
10
11    function onHomeButtonClick(event:MouseEvent):void
12    {
13        gotoAndStop("Home");
14    }
15
16    //Event listener and function for the Services button.
17
18    services_btn.addEventListener(MouseEvent.CLICK, onServicesButton
19
20    function onServicesButtonClick(event:MouseEvent):void
21    {
22        gotoAndStop("Services");
23    }
24
25    /* Click to Go to Frame and Stop
26    Clicking on the specified symbol instance moves the playhead to
27    Can be used on the main timeline or on movie clip timelines.
```

actions : 10

Line 16 of 54, Col 38

▶ **5.** In the Actions panel, select the multiple-line comment above the event listener for the resources_btn, delete the comment, and then type the following code to create a single-line comment.

```
// Event listener and function for the Resources button.
```

▶ **6.** In the Actions panel, select the multiple-line comment above the event listener for the calculator_btn, delete the comment, and then type the following code to create a single-line comment.

```
// Event listener and function for the Calculator button.
```

▶ **7.** Save the document and close the Actions panel.

In this session, you learned the basic components and rules for the ActionScript programming language. You learned about actions, functions, methods, and event listeners. You also learned how to use the Code Snippets panel to enter code to make the Jackson's Sports Web site's navigation operational. In the next session, you will write ActionScript code for the two new pages that will be added to the Jackson's Sports Web site.

REVIEW

Session 8.1 Quick Check

1. What is ActionScript?
2. True or False. In ActionScript 3.0, you always add code directly to a button instance to handle mouse events.
3. A(n) _____ is an element in Flash that has properties or characteristics that can be examined or changed with ActionScript.
4. In the Code Snippets panel, the Click to Go to _____ and Stop snippet adds code that will move the playhead to a specified frame and then stop.
5. Write the ActionScript expression to change the alpha property of the car_mc instance to 50.
6. What three programming elements are needed to respond to or handle events?
7. Why should you add comments to ActionScript code?

SESSION 8.2 VISUAL OVERVIEW

When clicked, these buttons will open the associated Web site in the default Web browser.

This event listener calls the onSoccerButtonClick function when soccer button is clicked.

The onSoccerButtonClick function contains actions to perform when the soccer button is clicked.

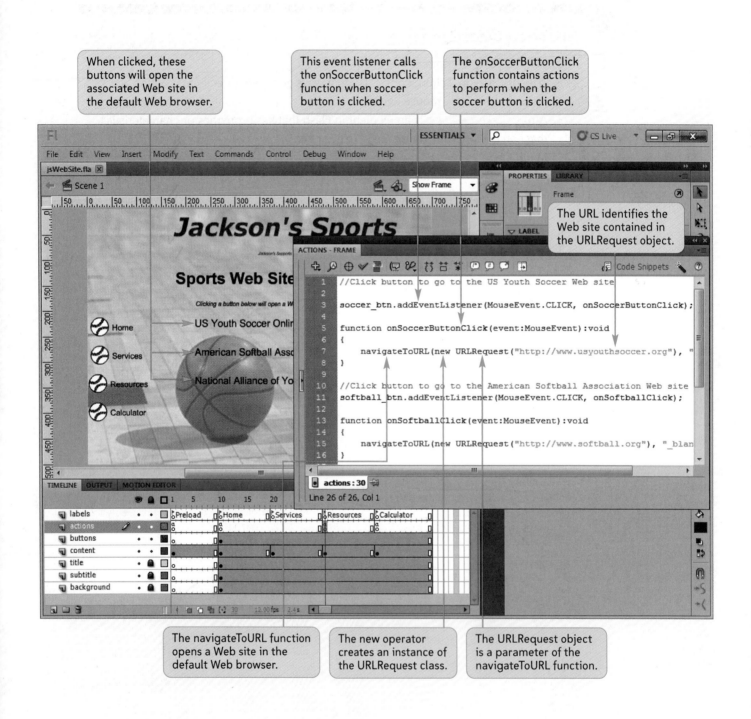

The URL identifies the Web site contained in the URLRequest object.

```
//Click button to go to the US Youth Soccer Web site

soccer_btn.addEventListener(MouseEvent.CLICK, onSoccerButtonClick);

function onSoccerButtonClick(event:MouseEvent):void
{
    navigateToURL(new URLRequest("http://www.usyouthsoccer.org"), "
}

//Click button to go to the American Softball Association Web site
softball_btn.addEventListener(MouseEvent.CLICK, onSoftballClick);

function onSoftballClick(event:MouseEvent):void
{
    navigateToURL(new URLRequest("http://www.softball.org"), "_blan
}
```

The navigateToURL function opens a Web site in the default Web browser.

The new operator creates an instance of the URLRequest class.

The URLRequest object is a parameter of the navigateToURL function.

LINKS AND PRELOADERS

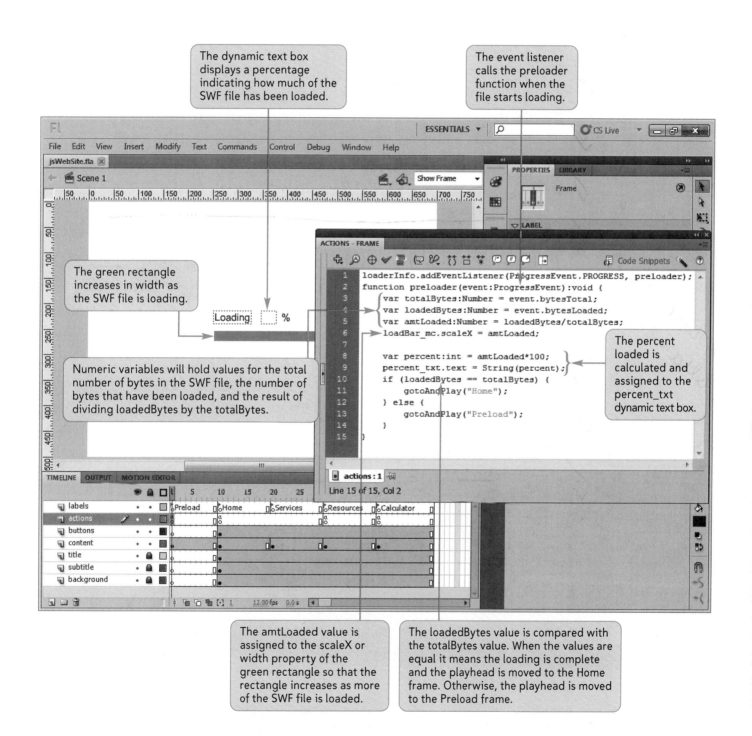

The dynamic text box displays a percentage indicating how much of the SWF file has been loaded.

The event listener calls the preloader function when the file starts loading.

The green rectangle increases in width as the SWF file is loading.

Numeric variables will hold values for the total number of bytes in the SWF file, the number of bytes that have been loaded, and the result of dividing loadedBytes by the totalBytes.

The percent loaded is calculated and assigned to the percent_txt dynamic text box.

```
loaderInfo.addEventListener(ProgressEvent.PROGRESS, preloader);
function preloader(event:ProgressEvent):void {
    var totalBytes:Number = event.bytesTotal;
    var loadedBytes:Number = event.bytesLoaded;
    var amtLoaded:Number = loadedBytes/totalBytes;
    loadBar_mc.scaleX = amtLoaded;

    var percent:int = amtLoaded*100;
    percent_txt.text = String(percent);
    if (loadedBytes == totalBytes) {
        gotoAndPlay("Home");
    } else {
        gotoAndPlay("Preload");
    }
}
```

The amtLoaded value is assigned to the scaleX or width property of the green rectangle so that the rectangle increases as more of the SWF file is loaded.

The loadedBytes value is compared with the totalBytes value. When the values are equal it means the loading is complete and the playhead is moved to the Home frame. Otherwise, the playhead is moved to the Preload frame.

Creating Links to Web Sites

A Flash document can include links in the form of buttons or movie clips that use ActionScript to direct the Flash Player to open a specified Web site. Dan wants the Resources page of the Jackson's Sports Web site to include three links to Internet Web sites that might be of interest to his clients. You will complete the Resources page by creating buttons that represent links to the external Web sites and adding the corresponding ActionScript code. When the viewer clicks a button, a browser window will open, displaying an external Web site.

You will start by creating three buttons and assigning names to the button instances on the Stage.

To add button instances to the Resources page:

1. If you took a break after the previous session, make sure the jsWebSite.fla document is open, the workspace is reset to the Essentials layout, and the Stage magnification is set to Show Frame.

2. In the Timeline, click **Frame 30** of the content layer, and then deselect the title text. The content layer is where you will create the buttons for the Resources page.

3. In the Tools panel, click the **Text** tool 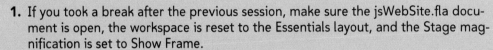, and then, in the Property inspector, set the font family to **Arial**, set the font style to **Regular**, set the point size to **20**, set the text color to **black**, and set the paragraph format to **Align left**.

4. Create a text block at the center of the Stage below the title and type **US Youth Soccer Online** in the text block.

5. In the Tools panel, click the **Selection** tool . The text block remains selected.

6. Convert the text block to a button symbol named **soccerButton** and select the upper-left **Registration point** .

7. On the Edit bar, click the **Edit Symbols** button , and then click **soccerButton**. The symbol opens in symbol-editing mode.

8. In the Timeline, insert a keyframe in the Over frame, select the **US Youth Soccer Online** text on the Stage, and then, in the Property inspector, change the font style to **Bold**. The text is bolded, providing visual feedback when the user moves the pointer over the button.

9. In the Timeline, insert a blank keyframe in the Hit frame, click the **Rectangle** tool in the Tools panel, and then draw a rectangle with a **black** fill that is about **250** pixels wide by **25** pixels high to cover the text block. The rectangle you drew over the text block in the Hit frame makes it easier for the viewer to click the button. Without it, the viewer must move the pointer directly over a letter to activate the button. See Figure 8-13.

Figure 8-13 | **Rectangle in the button's Hit frame**

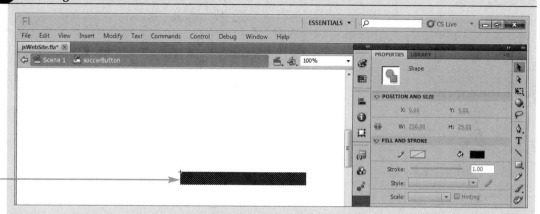

rectangle drawn in the Hit frame covers the text

10. On the Edit bar, click the **Scene 1** link to return to the document's main Timeline.

You'll create duplicates of the soccerButton symbol, and then modify the text in the Up, Over, and Hit frames of each of the duplicate button symbols to create the other two buttons for the Resources page.

To create the other button instances for the Resources page:

1. In the Library panel, duplicate the **soccerButton** symbol twice to create a button symbol named **asaButton** and a button symbol named **naysButton**. Copies of the soccerButton symbol named asaButton and naysButton appear in the library.

2. Open the **asaButton** button in symbol-editing mode, and then, in the Timeline, select the **Up** frame.

3. In the Tools panel, click the **Text** tool T to select it, and then change the button text to **American Softball Association** in both the Up frame and the Over frame.

4. In the Timeline, select the **Hit** frame and then change the width of the rectangle to **290** pixels.

5. Exit symbol-editing mode and return to Scene 1. The button text is updated.

6. Repeat Steps 2 through 5 to open the **naysButton** symbol in symbol-editing mode, change the button text to **National Alliance of Youth Sports** in both the Up and Over frames, change the width of the rectangle in the Hit frame to **320** pixels, and then exit symbol-editing mode.

7. From the Library panel, drag an instance of the **asaButton** symbol to below the soccerButton instance on the Stage, and then drag an instance of the **naysButton** to below the asaButton instance on the Stage.

8. In the Tools panel, click the **Selection** tool ▶ to select it, press and hold the **Shift** key, click each of the three button instances on the Stage, and then release the **Shift** key. All three button instances on the Stage are selected.

9. On the Application bar, click **Modify**, point to **Align**, and then click **Align to Stage**, if necessary, to deselect it. The buttons on the Stage will align relative to each other.

10. On the Application bar, click **Modify**, point to **Align**, and then click **Left** to align the buttons along their left edges.

11. On the Application bar, click **Modify**, point to **Align**, click **Distribute Heights** to space the buttons evenly, and then deselect the button instances. See Figure 8-14.

Figure 8-14	**Text buttons on the Resources page**

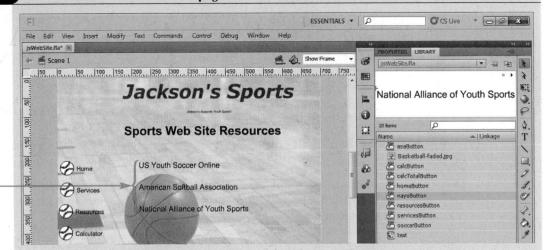

text buttons for the Web links vertically aligned and evenly distributed

Trouble? If the location of the buttons in your document differs from Figure 8-14, you need to reposition the buttons. Use the Selection tool to select all three buttons, and then drag them to the location shown in the figure.

Aly wants you to add a message for site visitors explaining that a browser window will open when one of the buttons is clicked. Also, the three button instances must be assigned names before you can add ActionScript code that references them.

To add instructions and name the button instances to the Resources page:

1. In the Tools panel, click the **Text** tool **T** to select it, and then set the font family to **Arial**, set the font style to **Italic**, set the point size to **12**, set the text color to **black**, set the paragraph format to **Align left**, and set the font rendering method to **Anti-alias for readability**.

2. On the Stage, add a text block above the soccerButton instance, type **Clicking a button below will open the Web site in a new window** in the text block, and then deselect the text. See Figure 8-15.

Figure 8-15 Instructions added to the Resources page

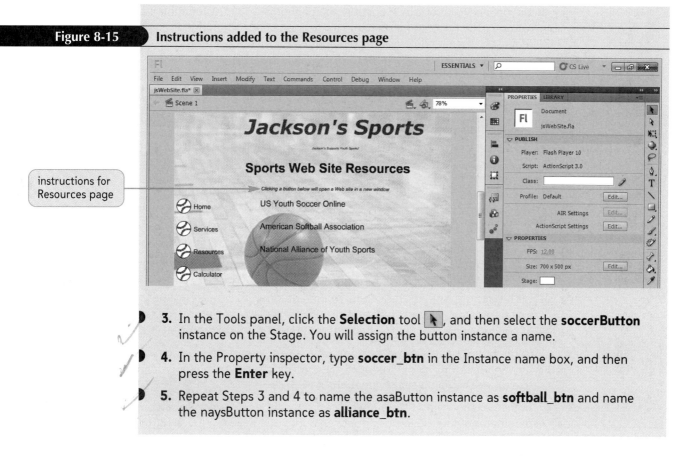

instructions for Resources page

3. In the Tools panel, click the **Selection** tool ▶, and then select the **soccerButton** instance on the Stage. You will assign the button instance a name.

4. In the Property inspector, type **soccer_btn** in the Instance name box, and then press the **Enter** key.

5. Repeat Steps 3 and 4 to name the asaButton instance as **softball_btn** and name the naysButton instance as **alliance_btn**.

Using the URLRequest Class

To create a link to an external Web site, you need to create a function as you did in the previous session. The function will use the URLRequest() class to define an object with the value of the Web address of the site to which you want to link. A **class** is a blueprint for an object that describes the properties, methods, and events for the object. All objects in ActionScript are defined by classes. The ActionScript code for the function to link to a Web site is shown in Figure 8-16.

Figure 8-16 Function to add a link to a Web site

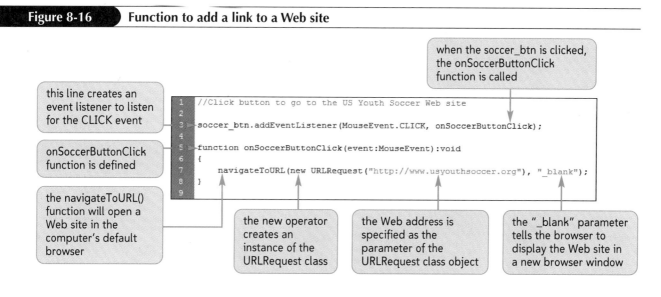

when the soccer_btn is clicked, the onSoccerButtonClick function is called

this line creates an event listener to listen for the CLICK event

onSoccerButtonClick function is defined

the navigateToURL() function will open a Web site in the computer's default browser

the new operator creates an instance of the URLRequest class

the Web address is specified as the parameter of the URLRequest class object

the "_blank" parameter tells the browser to display the Web site in a new browser window

```
//Click button to go to the US Youth Soccer Web site

soccer_btn.addEventListener(MouseEvent.CLICK, onSoccerButtonClick);

function onSoccerButtonClick(event:MouseEvent):void
{
    navigateToURL(new URLRequest("http://www.usyouthsoccer.org"), "_blank");
}
```

In the onSoccerButtonClick function, the `navigateToURL()` function is used to link to a Web site. The first parameter of the `navigateToURL()` function is an instance of the URLRequest class that contains the web address for the Web site. The new operator is a special method used to create instances of objects based on a class.

You will add the code using the Code Snippets panel to create the functions for the Web site links in the Resources page.

To create a script with a function to control the first Resources page button:

1. In the Timeline, in Frame 30, select the **soccer_btn** instance on the Stage, open the **Actions** panel, and then click the **Code Snippets** button to open the Code Snippets panel.

2. In the Code Snippets panel, click the **arrow** ▶ to expand the Actions folder, double-click the **Click to Go To Web Page** snippet to add its code to the Script pane, and then deselect the code.

3. In the Script pane, in the `soccer_btn.addEventListener()` line, select the function name within the parentheses, `fl_ClickToGoToWebPage`, and type `onSoccerButtonClick` to change the name of the function that is called.

4. In the Script pane, below the `soccer_btn.addEventListener()` line, select the function name `fl_ClickToGoToWebPage`, and then type `onSoccerButtonClick` to change the name of the function.

5. In the next line within the curly braces, select **http://www.adobe.com** in the parameter of the URLRequest function and type **http://www.usyouthsoccer.org**. The function will now assign the new URL as the parameter of the navigateToURL function.

6. Delete the multi-line comment above the `soccer_btn.addEventListener()` line and type the following comment in its place. See Figure 8-17.

   `// Click button to go to the US Youth Soccer Web site`

Figure 8-17   Function added to link to the soccer Web site

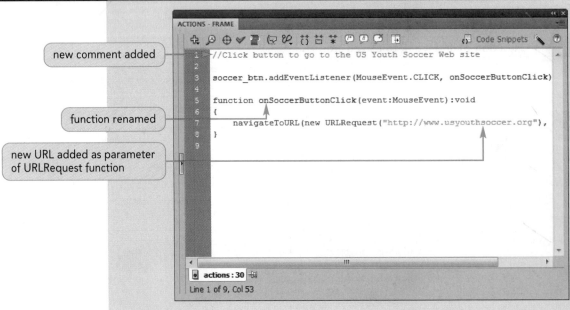

- new comment added
- function renamed
- new URL added as parameter of URLRequest function

7. In the Actions panel, click the **Check syntax** button ☑ to check for syntax errors in the code. The script is checked. If no errors are displayed in the Compiler Errors panel, the script is correct.

Trouble? If your code contains errors, the errors are listed in the Compiler Errors panel at the bottom of the screen. Review your script to compare it to the code you modified in the previous steps, make any necessary corrections, and then repeat Step 7 until no errors are encountered.

You will add the same code snippet and modify its code to make the American Softball Association button and the National Alliance of Youth Sports button operational.

To create the functions for the other buttons in the Resources page:

1. Collapse the Actions panel, click **Frame 30** in the Timeline, and then select the **softball_btn** instance on the Stage.

2. Expand the **Actions** panel, and then click the **Code Snippets** button to open the Codes Snippets panel.

3. In the Code Snippets panel, double-click the **Click to Go To Web Page** snippet to add its code to the Script pane, and then deselect the code.

4. In the Script pane, in the `softball_btn.addEventListener()` line, change the function name within the parentheses to `onSoftballButtonClick` so that the function name is more descriptive.

5. In the Script pane, below the `softball_btn.addEventListener()` line, change the function name to `onSoftballButtonClick`.

6. In the navigateToURL() line within the function, change the URLRequest() parameter to `"http://www.softball.org"`.

7. Delete the multi-line comment above the `softball_btn.addEventListener()` line and type the following comment in its place.

```
// Click button to go to the American Softball Association Web site
```

8. Repeat Steps 1 through 7 to add the code for the alliance_btn instance. Use `onAllianceButtonClick` for the function name and `"http://www.nays.org"` for the URL. Delete the multi-line comment and type the following comment in its place.

```
// Click button to go to the National Alliance of Youth Sports Web site
```

9. In the Actions panel, click the **Check syntax** button ☑ to check for syntax errors in the code. The script is checked. If no errors are displayed in the Compiler Errors panel, the script is correct.

Trouble? If your code contains errors, the errors are listed in the Compiler Errors panel at the bottom of the screen. Review your script to compare it to the code you modified in the previous steps, make any necessary corrections, and then repeat Step 9 until no errors are encountered.

10. Save the jsWebSite.fla document.

The code for the event listeners and functions, necessary to make the buttons operational, is complete. You will test the links in the Resources page.

To test the buttons in the Resources page:

1. On the Application bar, click **File**, point to **Publish Preview**, and then click **Default – (HTML)**. The Jackson's Sports Web site opens in the default browser.

   Trouble? If the Web page doesn't open and the Information Bar appears, indicating that Internet Explorer has restricted this Web page from running scripts, you need to allow the blocked content. Click the Information Bar, click Allow Blocked Content, and then click the Yes button in the dialog box that opens to confirm that you want to allow the blocked content.

2. In the browser window, click the **Resources** button to display the Resources page, and then click the **US Youth Soccer Online** button to open the Web site in a separate window. If necessary, switch to the window displaying the US Youth Soccer Web site.

   Trouble? If an error message appears stating the page cannot be displayed, your computer might not be connected to the Internet. If necessary, connect to the Internet and repeat Step 2. If your computer is connected to the Internet, check the URL in the URLRequest() parameter to make certain it is correct. If you still cannot connect to the Internet, read the rest of the steps in this section.

   Trouble? If an Adobe Flash Player window opens, stating that an ActionScript error has occurred, click the Continue button.

   Trouble? If an Adobe Flash Player Security dialog box opens, stating that the Flash Player stopped a potentially unsafe operation, click the Settings button. A Web page displays the Adobe Flash Player Settings Manager. In the Settings Manager, click the Edit locations button and then click Add location. In the Trust this location box, click the Browse for files button, navigate to the folder containing the jsWebSite.swf file, select the file, and then click the Open button. Close the Web browser, and then repeat Steps 1 and 2.

3. Close the browser window displaying the Web site, switch to the browser window displaying the Jackson's Sports Web site, and then click the **American Softball Association** button to test that it opens the appropriate Web site.

4. Repeat Step 3 to test the **National Alliance of Youth Sports** button.

5. Close the browser window to return to the jsWebSite.fla document. The Resources page is complete. You have added the buttons and ActionScript code to open external Web sites in a browser.

Using a Flash Preloader

SWF files, like HTML files, are downloaded over the Internet from a Web server to the user's computer, known as the **client computer**, where the files will reside. A major factor that affects the amount of time a file takes to download is the size of the file, measured in kilobytes. A **kilobyte** is approximately 1000 bytes, and a **byte** is equivalent to one character of information. Flash Web sites typically contain various multimedia elements, such as graphics, animations, pictures, audio, and video. Each of these elements adds to the overall size of the published file. Even though the SWF files are compressed and contain vector graphics that tend to be small, they might still take some time to download.

PROSKILLS

Problem Solving: Factors Affecting SWF File Download Times

Multimedia elements in a Flash SWF file can increase the time it takes for the file to download to a user's computer. The download time depends on the type of Internet connection used by the client computer. A broadband connection using a cable or DSL modem provides high-speed download capability. A dial-up connection using a telephone modem, however, is much slower. When the SWF file starts to download from a Web server to a client computer, it is loaded into the Flash Player one frame at a time. The first frames start playing in the Flash Player as soon as the frames load, even though other frames of the file are still downloading. This is a result of the **streaming** capability of Flash files in which the initial content can start playing while the rest of the content continues to be downloaded, reducing the wait time for the user. A problem occurs, however, when the client computer plays all of the loaded frames and then has to wait for additional frames to load. This can happen if a particular frame has a large amount of content such as bitmap images. The wait causes the Flash Player to pause the playing of the SWF file while additional frames load. This delay affects the way the SWF file plays and might confuse or frustrate the user. Also, if the wait is more than a few seconds and no visual indication appears that something is still loading, the user may think the Web site is not working and decide to go to another site. To prevent confusion or frustration by the user, reduce the size of the SWF file as much as possible and include a preloader animation that provides the user with feedback about the downloading progress.

To avoid losing site visitors, Flash developers usually add a **preloader**, which is a short animation or message located in the first few frames of the Flash file. The preloader typically contains a short animation and the word "Loading" to indicate that the Web site is still loading. This visual feedback helps assure the site visitor that the Web site is loading while the frames of the SWF file continue to download. After all the content has downloaded, the preloader stops and the rest of the SWF file plays. Several examples of preloaders are shown in Figure 8-18.

Figure 8-18   **Examples of preloaders**

Creating a Preloader

Adding a preloader to a Flash file requires ActionScript code, along with a loading message and/or an animation placed in the first frame of the Timeline. The preloader message and animation are displayed only while the file is being loaded. A script can be added to a later frame in the Timeline to control the preloader and to check if all of the content has downloaded. The basic logic involves knowing how much of the SWF file has loaded and comparing that with the total size of the file. The amount of content that has loaded and the total size of the file can be measured in either number of frames or number of bytes, both of which can be examined using ActionScript. By checking how much content has been loaded and comparing it to the total size of the file, different actions can be performed. For example, if the number of bytes that have loaded into the Flash Player is equal to the total number of bytes for the file, the entire SWF file has loaded. At that point, the SWF file can play as designed. Otherwise, the preloader animation continues to play. If the SWF file contains a large number of frames, you can create a preloader that checks the number of frames loaded.

In the case of the Jackson's Sports Web site, the number of frames is small, so it is best to check the number of bytes loaded. To create the preloader code, the script will need to get the total number of bytes to be loaded and the number of bytes that have been loaded. The number of bytes loaded will increase as more of the file is downloaded into the Flash Player. As long as these two values are not the same, the preloader animation will continue to play. When the two values are the same, the SWF has finished loading. At that point, the preloader animation will stop and the rest of the frames in the movie will be played. The steps for the preloader code are as follows:

> Get the total number of bytes
> Get the number of bytes loaded
> Update the preloader animation
> If the number of bytes loaded equals the total number of bytes
>   play the rest of the SWF file
>
>   Otherwise
>
>   continue playing the preloader animation

These steps will be followed to create the code for the preloader for the Jackson's Sports Web site.

To get the total number of bytes, you will create a function with an instance of the ProgressEvent class as its parameter. The ProgressEvent class has the event type PROGRESS, which includes the properties bytesTotal and bytesLoaded. The bytesTotal property contains the total number of bytes in the SWF file. The bytesLoaded property contains the number of bytes loaded. These numbers will be compared to each other to determine if the SWF file has completed loading into the Flash Player. The numbers can also be used to calculate what percentage of the file has loaded.

You will start creating the script for the preloader in the first frame of the actions layer by creating an event listener, creating a function, and defining two variables. A **variable** is a user-defined object that holds data and whose value can change while the SWF movie plays. You define a variable using the var keyword followed by the variable's name, which must be one word that includes only alphanumeric, underscore, and dollar sign characters. A variable must be **typed**, which means you need to specify what type of data it can contain. The data type of the variable is listed after a colon character.

In previous scripts, the event listeners registered button instances with functions to be performed when a button was clicked. In the preloader script, the event listener will call the preloader function when a specific event occurs. In this case, the event is not when a button is clicked. Instead, the event is when a part of the SWF file has loaded into the Flash Player. The event.PROGRESS event will indicate when a new part of the SWF file has loaded. Because the event is dispatched or generated by a LoaderInfo object of the main Timeline, you need to register the event listener with the object. You can do this using the `addEventListener()` method of the loaderInfo object. You will add the event listener and function code in the Script pane.

To create the first part of the preloader script:

1. Collapse the Actions panel, and then click **Frame 1** of the labels layer in the Timeline.

2. In the Label section of the Property inspector, type **Preload** in the Name box, and then press the **Enter** key. This label will be referred to in the script for the pre-loader. You will add the preloader script in this frame.

3. In the Timeline, click **Frame 1** of the actions layer, expand the **Actions** panel, and then, in the Script pane, type the following lines of code, pressing the **Enter** key after each line.

```
loaderInfo.addEventListener(ProgressEvent.PROGRESS, preloader);
function preloader(event:ProgressEvent):void {
```

Trouble? If an import statement is automatically added to your code, continue typing. The import statement will not affect the results of the script.

The first line defines the event listener. When content is loaded into the Flash Player, the PROGRESS event occurs, and the addEventListener() method calls the preloader function. The second line creates a function named preloader with the object event as its parameter. The event object is set as a ProgressEvent data type.

4. In the Script pane of the Actions panel, type the following lines of code after the `function preloader()` line, pressing the **Enter** key after each line.

```
var totalBytes:Number = event.bytesTotal;
var loadedBytes:Number = event.bytesLoaded;
```

The first var line creates a new variable named totalBytes whose data type is Number. The value of the bytesTotal property of the event object is assigned to the variable. The second var line creates a variable named loadedBytes with a data type of Number. The value of the bytesLoaded property of the event object is assigned to the variable.

Creating the Preloader Animation

The totalBytes and loadedBytes variables can also be used to control the animation used in the preloader. Recall from the previous session that the properties of a movie clip instance can be modified using ActionScript. You can create a movie clip in the shape of a rectangle and then gradually increase the horizontal size of the rectangle to match how much of the file has been loaded. Because the rectangle instance is an object, you can modify the object's scaleX and scaleY properties, which represent the relative size of the object compared to its original size. The scaleX property can be used to scale the object horizontally. The property uses a fractional value such as 0.5 to represent a percentage of the object's original size. For example, a scaleX value of 0.5 changes the object to display 50% of its original size. So by changing the scaleX property of the rectangle from 0 to 1, the rectangle appears to grow horizontally from 0% to 100% of its original size.

You will create an instance of a movie clip in the shape of a rectangle with a registration point on its upper-left corner. The rectangle will grow horizontally, starting from the left side and growing to the right side. When the rectangle is back to its original size, the SWF file has finished loading.

INSIGHT

Calculating the scaleX Property

To determine the value to assign to the scaleX property of the rectangle, divide the loadedBytes value by the totalBytes value, resulting in fractional values ranging from 0 to 1. The result, which represents the percentage of how much of the file has loaded, can be assigned to the scaleX property of the rectangle. It increases gradually until the two values are equal, resulting in a value of 1, which means all of the file's content has loaded and the scaleX property of the rectangle is 100%.

You'll add a preloader animation to the content layer.

To add the graphic and code for the preloader animation:

1. Close the Actions panel to see the Stage, and then, in the Timeline, click **Frame 1** of the content layer.

2. Below the Loading text block on the Stage, draw a rectangle with a **dark green** (#009900) fill and no stroke that is **300** pixels wide and **20** pixels high. See Figure 8-19.

Figure 8-19	Rectangle for the preloader animation

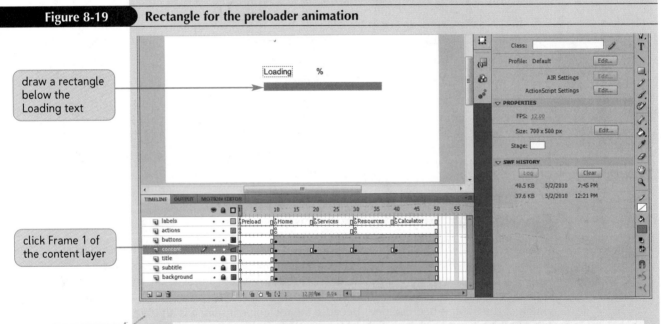

draw a rectangle below the Loading text

click Frame 1 of the content layer

Select the upper-left registration point of the rectangle movie clip so it expands from left to right as the SWF file loads.

3. Convert the rectangle to a movie clip symbol named **rectangle** with the upper-left registration point selected.

4. In the Property inspector, type **loadBar_mc** in the Instance name box, and then press the **Enter** key to name the movie clip instance. The preloader movie clip instance is complete.

You'll add the code to change the loadBar_mc's scaleX property.

5. In the Timeline, click **Frame 1** of the actions layer, open the **Actions** panel, and then, in the Script pane after the second var statement, type the following code, pressing the **Enter** key after each line. See Figure 8-20.

```
var amtLoaded:Number = loadedBytes/totalBytes;
loadBar_mc.scaleX = amtLoaded;
```

| Figure 8-20 | Partial preloader script |

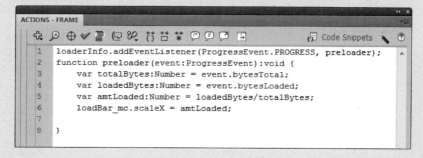

```
1   loaderInfo.addEventListener(ProgressEvent.PROGRESS, preloader);
2   function preloader(event:ProgressEvent):void {
3       var totalBytes:Number = event.bytesTotal;
4       var loadedBytes:Number = event.bytesLoaded;
5       var amtLoaded:Number = loadedBytes/totalBytes;
6       loadBar_mc.scaleX = amtLoaded;
7
8   }
```

The amtLoaded variable will hold the result of dividing loadedBytes by totalBytes. This resulting number is a fractional value that represents the percentage of how much of the SWF file has been loaded. This value is assigned to the scaleX property of the Rectangle movie clip, loadBar_mc, causing it to increase horizontally each time the loadedBytes value changes.

In addition to the loadBar_mc animation, you will add a special type of text box that will display a changing value, from 0% to 100%, indicating how much of the SWF file has loaded. You will add this text box and its associated ActionScript code in Session 8.3.

 Completing the Preloader Code

The next part of the function is a comparison using a conditional statement. A **conditional statement** compares one value to another. Based on the result of the comparison, certain actions are performed. Conditional statements use **comparison operators**, such as ==, which is used to test for equality. This is different from the assignment operator =, which is used to assign a value to a variable. Other comparison operators include >, <, and !=, which are used to test for greater than, less than, and not equal to, respectively. You create a conditional statement using the if keyword, which tests a condition. If the condition is true, the Flash Player performs actions within the curly braces that follow it. You can also include the else keyword, which contains the actions to perform when the condition is false.

The if statement compares the values of loadedBytes and totalBytes. If the values are not equal, the loading has not finished, so the playhead is moved to the Preload frame, which is Frame 1. If the values are equal, then the loading has finished, and the playhead is moved to the first part of the Web site, which is the frame with the Home label. You use the gotoAndPlay() function to direct the playhead to a specific frame, referring to a frame by its label. You will add the if conditional statement to the script next.

To add code to compare the loadedBytes and totalBytes values:

1. In the Script pane of the Actions panel, click after the last statement, and then press the **Enter** key to add a blank line.

2. Type the following code, pressing the **Enter** key after each line. See Figure 8-21.

```
if (loadedBytes == totalBytes) {
 gotoAndPlay("Home");
} else {
 gotoAndPlay("Preload");
}
```

Figure 8-21 Conditional statement in preloader script

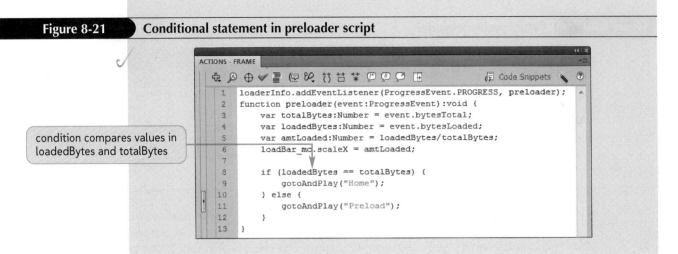

condition compares values in loadedBytes and totalBytes

```
1   loaderInfo.addEventListener(ProgressEvent.PROGRESS, preloader);
2   function preloader(event:ProgressEvent):void {
3       var totalBytes:Number = event.bytesTotal;
4       var loadedBytes:Number = event.bytesLoaded;
5       var amtLoaded:Number = loadedBytes/totalBytes;
6       loadBar_mc.scaleX = amtLoaded;
7
8       if (loadedBytes == totalBytes) {
9           gotoAndPlay("Home");
10      } else {
11          gotoAndPlay("Preload");
12      }
13  }
```

The condition, enclosed in parentheses, compares the values in the loadedBytes and totalBytes variables. If the values are equal, the gotoAndPlay("Home"); statement is executed, causing the playhead to move to the first page of the Web site. If the values are not equal, the gotoAndPlay("Preload"); statement is executed, causing the playhead to move to the frame labeled Preload. This causes the script to run again.

The function for the preloader script is complete. You will test the script next.

To test the preloader script:

1. In the Actions panel, click the **Check syntax** button to check for syntax errors in the code. The script is checked. If no errors are displayed in the Compiler Errors panel, the script is correct.

Trouble? If your code contains errors, the errors are listed in the Compiler Errors panel at the bottom of the screen. Review your script to compare it to the code you modified in the previous steps, make any necessary corrections, and then repeat Step 1 until no errors are encountered.

2. Save the jsWebSite.fla document, and then close the Actions panel.

3. On the Application bar, click **Control**, point to **Test Movie**, and then click **in Flash Professional**. The SWF file plays in the Flash Player; however, the preloader appears for only a fraction of a second.

Because the SWF file is loading from your computer's drive, the file's content loads instantly. As a result, the preloader animation is only visible for a very short time. This will not be the case when the SWF file is downloaded from the Internet, especially using a slower connection. To test the preloader, you can use the Simulate Download command. This command simulates the time it takes to download the SWF file based on the type of Internet connection you select.

4. On the Flash Player menu bar, click **View**, point to **Download Settings**, and then click **56K (4.7 KB/s)** to select it, if necessary.

5. On the Flash Player menu bar, click **View**, and then click **Simulate Download**. After a few seconds, the preloader animation plays. See Figure 8-22.

Figure 8-22   Simulated download process

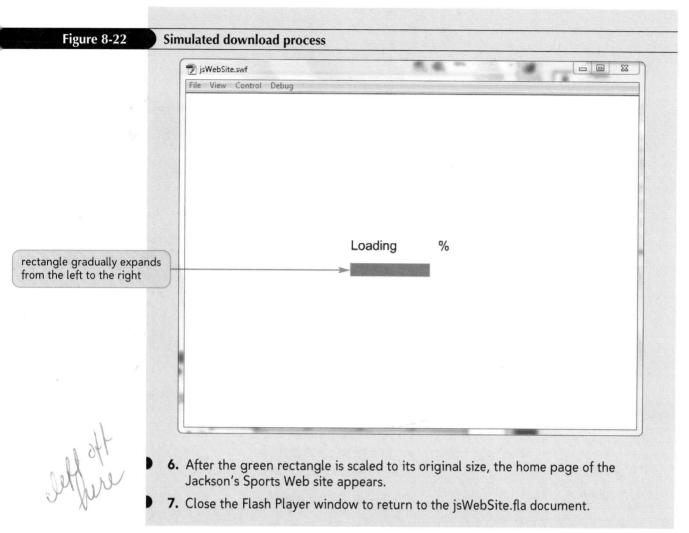

rectangle gradually expands from the left to the right

6. After the green rectangle is scaled to its original size, the home page of the Jackson's Sports Web site appears.

7. Close the Flash Player window to return to the jsWebSite.fla document.

The preloader for the Jackson's Sports Web site is complete. In this session, you used the `URLRequest()` function to create buttons with URL links to Web sites on the Internet. You also created a preloader using ActionScript and tested the preloader by simulating the download speed of a 56K modem Internet connection.

REVIEW

Session 8.2 Quick Check

1. Write the ActionScript code to create a function named `gotoAdobeSite()` that will use the `navigateToURL()` function and the `URLRequest()` class to open the Web site *http://www.adobe.com*.
2. What does it mean that a variable has to be typed?
3. What is streaming?
4. What is the purpose of a preloader?
5. An object's scaleX and scaleY properties represent the relative size of the object compared to its _____ size.
6. Explain how you can simulate the downloading of a SWF file within Flash.

SESSION 8.3 VISUAL OVERVIEW

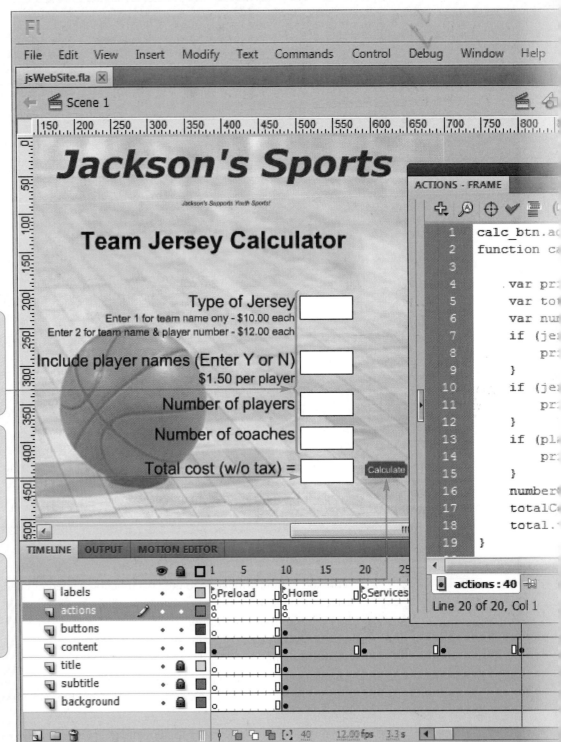

Input text boxes enable the user to enter text that is then stored in a variable and used in an ActionScript script. Input text boxes can be formatted to display with a border around the text.

Characters or numbers from a Web server or from an expression in ActionScript can be displayed in a dynamic text box. In this example, the total cost is calculated and then displayed in this text box.

The user clicks a button to run a script that calculates a value based on the numbers entered in the input text boxes. The result is then displayed in the dynamic text box.

INPUT AND DYNAMIC TEXT FIELDS

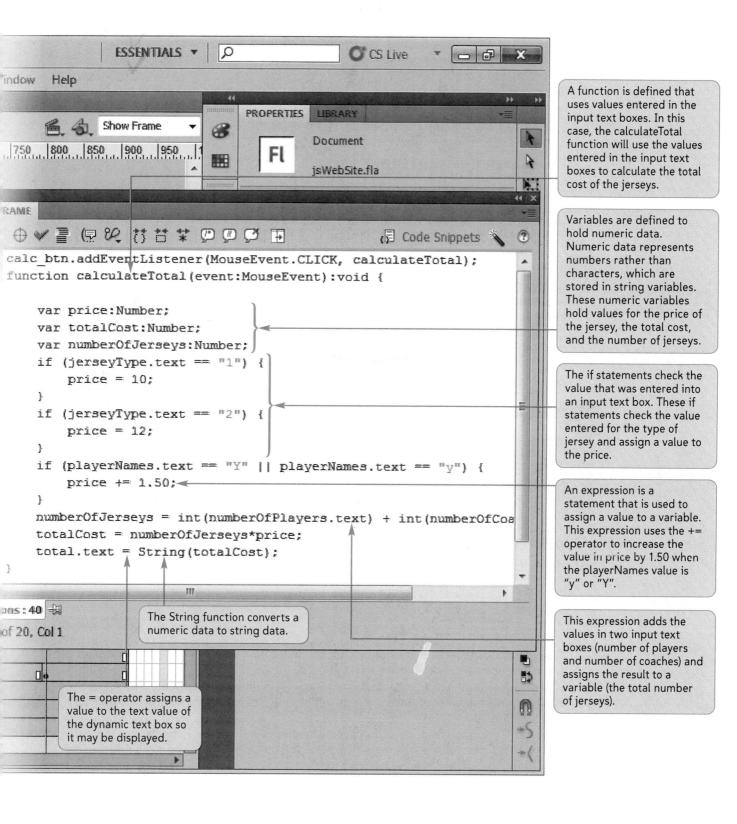

A function is defined that uses values entered in the input text boxes. In this case, the calculateTotal function will use the values entered in the input text boxes to calculate the total cost of the jerseys.

Variables are defined to hold numeric data. Numeric data represents numbers rather than characters, which are stored in string variables. These numeric variables hold values for the price of the jersey, the total cost, and the number of jerseys.

The if statements check the value that was entered into an input text box. These if statements check the value entered for the type of jersey and assign a value to the price.

An expression is a statement that is used to assign a value to a variable. This expression uses the += operator to increase the value in price by 1.50 when the playerNames value is "y" or "Y".

This expression adds the values in two input text boxes (number of players and number of coaches) and assigns the result to a variable (the total number of jerseys).

The String function converts a numeric data to string data.

The = operator assigns a value to the text value of the dynamic text box so it may be displayed.

```
calc_btn.addEventListener(MouseEvent.CLICK, calculateTotal);
function calculateTotal(event:MouseEvent):void {

    var price:Number;
    var totalCost:Number;
    var numberOfJerseys:Number;
    if (jerseyType.text == "1") {
        price = 10;
    }
    if (jerseyType.text == "2") {
        price = 12;
    }
    if (playerNames.text == "Y" || playerNames.text == "y") {
        price += 1.50;
    }
    numberOfJerseys = int(numberOfPlayers.text) + int(numberOfCoa
    totalCost = numberOfJerseys*price;
    total.text = String(totalCost);
}
```

Creating an Input Form

An input form is a common element found on many Web sites. An **input form** allows the user to enter data into text boxes. The data can then be submitted for storage and processing on a Web server. The server software sends results of the processing back to the user's computer to be displayed on the same form or on another Web page. A page developed with Flash can also allow the user to enter data, have the data processed, and return a result directly on the user's computer from the Flash Player. The page developer uses ActionScript to write the underlying functions required to create a form with several input fields coded to accept data from the site visitor, such as the number and type of items to be purchased. Other fields on the form display results based on the site visitor's input, such as a total price. Creating an input form requires the use of dynamic and input text.

Using Dynamic and Input Text

Text is an important element of a Flash document. All of the text you have created so far has been static text. Static text cannot be changed after the document plays in the Flash Player. Recall, however, that there are two other types of text in Flash: dynamic text and input text. Although static text cannot change, dynamic text can. Dynamic text can be received in the form of characters or numbers from a Web server or from an expression in ActionScript. Then it can be displayed on a Web page in the Flash Player. Dynamic text is defined to display the contents of a variable. The variable can be used in ActionScript to change the value displayed. For example, if a dynamic text block is assigned the variable Amount, you can code an expression in ActionScript that assigns the result of a calculation to the variable. The value stored in the variable Amount will then appear in the text block on the Web page. Input text is used to allow the user to enter text into the text block. This text can then be stored in a variable and used in an ActionScript script.

PROSKILLS

Written Communication: Using Descriptive Labels for Input Text Boxes

The goal of using labels with input text boxes is to make it clear exactly what should be entered into the corresponding input text boxes. These text labels prompt the user about what to enter in the text boxes. Text labels that are unclear or difficult to understand will confuse or frustrate the user or will cause him or her to enter incorrect or invalid data in the text boxes. This will lead to invalid results or error messages. Text labels used as prompts for input boxes should be concise, easy to understand, and as descriptive as possible about the value that the user should enter in the text box. Consider what information should be included in each label, and reread each label to ensure that it clearly identifies what data to enter, explains how to enter the data, and uses standard spelling, grammar, and punctuation. The extra time you take to create effective labels will help lead to a positive experience for the user.

Based on Dan's request, you will create a form for the Calculator page for the Jackson's Sports Web site. This page will allow a user such as a team manager to enter several values for the type and number of team jerseys the team needs to buy. The page will contain a button that, when clicked, will use the entered values to calculate a total cost and display the result.

You will complete the Calculator page by creating the input and dynamic text blocks. You will also add a Calculate button and write the ActionScript code to make the button operational so that it calculates the total cost. You will start by adding the static text blocks for the page.

To create the static text boxes for the Calculator page:

1. If you took a break after the previous session, make sure the jsWebSite.fla document is open, the workspace is reset to the Essentials layout, and the Stage magnification is set to Show Frame.

2. In the Timeline, click **Frame 40** of the content layer. The Calculator page appears on the Stage.

3. Display the rulers, and then create a horizontal guide **200** pixels from the top edge of the Stage and a vertical guide **500** pixels from the left edge of the Stage. The guides will be used to place the text blocks.

4. Deselect the title text block, click the **Text** tool ⊤ in the Tools panel, and then, in the Property inspector, set the font family to **Arial**, the font style to **Regular**, the point size to **22**, the text color to **black**, and the paragraph format to **Align right**.

5. On the Stage, click the vertical guide below the horizontal guide to create a text block, type **Type of Jersey**, press the **Enter** key to create a new line, type **Enter 1 for team name ony - $10.00 each**, press the **Enter** key to create a new line, and then type **Enter 2 for team name & player number - $12.00 each**.

6. Select the last two lines of the text block, and then, in the Property inspector, change the point size to **14**. If necessary, reposition the text blocks to match those shown in Figure 8-23.

Figure 8-23   Type of Jersey text block

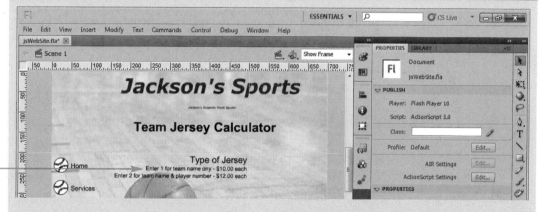

text block added to the Stage

7. Create another text block below the Type of Jersey text block, use the same text attributes as the first text block but change the point size to **22**, type **Include player names (Enter Y or N)**, press the **Enter** key, and then type **$1.50 per player**.

8. Select the second line in the text block, and then, in the Property inspector, change the point size to **18**.

9. Create a text block below the previous text block, use the same text attributes as the previous text block but change the point size to **22**, and then type **Number of players**.

10. Create a text block below the previous text block, use the same text attributes, and then type **Number of coaches**.

11. Create a text block below the previous text block, use the same text attributes, and then type **Total cost (w/o tax) =**.

> **12.** In the Tools panel, click the **Selection** tool 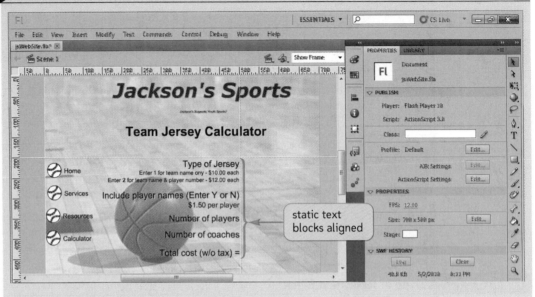, reposition the text blocks on the Stage as needed so that their right edges are aligned, and then deselect the text blocks. See Figure 8-24.

Figure 8-24   **Static text blocks**

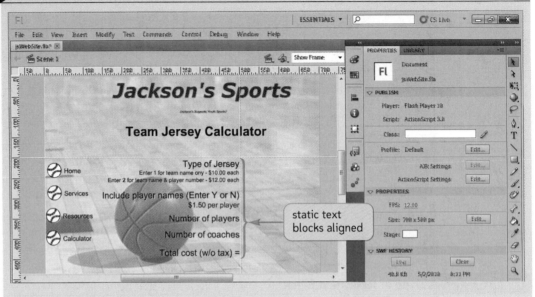

The static text blocks are complete. Each text block provides instructions to the user about the values that can be entered into the input text boxes. You will create the input text boxes next. You will also assign instance names to each input text box so that it can be referenced in the ActionScript code.

To create the input text boxes for the Calculator page:

> **1.** In the Tools panel, click the **Text** tool ⊤, and then, in the Property inspector, click the **Text type** button and click **Input Text**. The next text block you create will be for input text.

> **2.** In the Property inspector, set the font family to **Arial**, set the font style to **Regular**, set the point size to **20**, set the text color to **black**, and then set the paragraph format to **Align right**.

> **3.** On the Stage, click to the right of the Type of Jersey text block to create an input text block, and then, in the Tools panel, click the **Selection** tool ⊢. The input text block remains selected on the Stage.

> **4.** In Property inspector, enter **jerseyType** as the Instance name, and then, in the Position and Size section, set the dimensions to **70** pixels wide and **30** pixels high.

> **5.** In the Character section of the Property inspector, set the font rendering method to **Use device fonts**, and then click the **Show border around text** button 🔳 to select it.

> **6.** In the Paragraph section of the Property inspector, click the **Behavior** button, and then click **Single line** for the line type.

> **7.** In the Options section of the Property inspector, set the Max chars to **1** to allow only one character in the input box. See Figure 8-25.

Figure 8-25 | **Input text block properties**

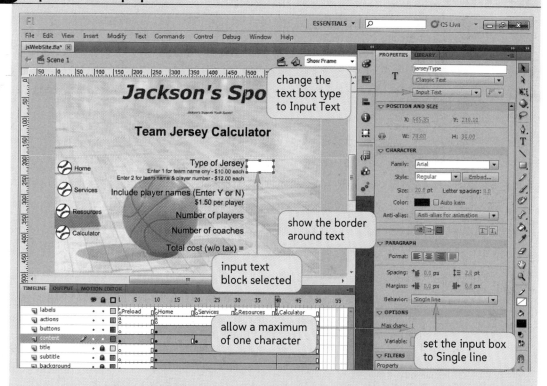

8. Repeat Steps 1 through 7 to create an input text block to the right of the Include player names (Enter Y or N) line, entering **playerNames** as the instance name.

9. Repeat Steps 1 through 7 to create an input text block to the right of the Number of players line, entering **numberOfPlayers** as the instance name and setting the maximum characters to **0**.

10. Repeat Steps 1 through 7 to create an input text block to the right of the Number of coaches line, entering **numberOfCoaches** as the instance name and setting the maximum characters to **0**.

11. In the Tools panel, click the **Selection** tool , reposition the input text boxes as needed so that they are vertically aligned, and then deselect the text boxes. See Figure 8-26.

TIP

Setting the maximum characters to 0 allows the input box to accept an unlimited number of characters, not zero characters.

Figure 8-26   Completed input text boxes

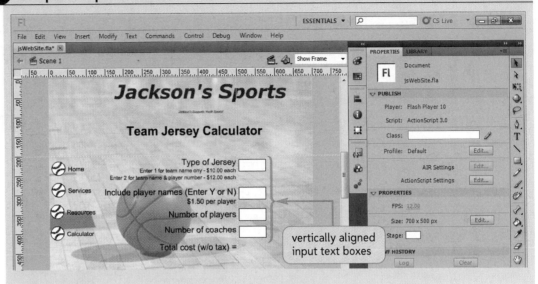

The input text boxes the visitor will use to enter data are complete. You will add a dynamic text block next. This text block instance must also be assigned a name. You will also create an instance of a Calculate button that Aly created.

To add the dynamic text box and button to the Calculator page:

1. In the Tools panel, click the **Text** tool T , and then create a text block to the right of the Total cost (w/o tax) = line.

2. In the Property inspector, set the text type to **Dynamic Text**, set the font family to **Arial**, set the font style to **Regular**, set the point size to **20**, set the text color to **black**, set the font rendering method to **Use device fonts**, and then set the paragraph format to **Align right**.

3. In the Tools panel, click the **Selection** tool , and then, in the Property inspector, enter **total** as the instance name, set the text block dimensions to **70** pixels wide and **30** pixels high, and click the **Selectable** button to deselect it, if necessary. The properties for the dynamic text block are set.

4. Drag an instance of the **calcTotalButton** symbol from the Library panel to the right side of the dynamic text block, and then, in the Property inspector, enter **calc_btn** as the instance name. The button instance is placed on the Stage and assigned a name.

Writing ActionScript Code to Do a Calculation

The calcTotalButton instance requires ActionScript code to make it operational. The user will enter values in the input text boxes you created, and then click the calcTotalButton instance to compute the total cost for the jerseys. As you have done with previous scripts, you need to define a function. The function will process the values entered in the input text boxes and calculate a total cost that will be displayed in the dynamic text box. The first part of the script will create an event listener and a function called `calculateTotal`. After defining the function, you will add several statements to define variables that will be used within the script. These variables do not represent objects on the Stage, but instead hold intermediate values used as part of the calculations.

Each variable is defined with the var keyword, a name, and the Number data type. The Number data type specifies that the variables will contain numbers.

TIP

You can also right-click the frame, and then click Insert Keyframe to add a keyframe.

To define the function and the initial variables for the script:

▶ **1.** In the Timeline, insert a keyframe at **Frame 40** of the actions layer. Actions for the Calculator page will be created in Frame 40.

▶ **2.** Open the **Actions** panel, and then, in the Script pane, type the following lines of code to define the event listener and the function.

```
calc_btn.addEventListener(MouseEvent.CLICK, calculateTotal);
function calculateTotal(event:MouseEvent):void {
```

Trouble? If an import statement is automatically added to your code, continue typing. The import statement will not affect the results of the script.

▶ **3.** Press the **Enter** key twice to insert a blank line, and then type the following lines of code to define the variables, pressing the **Enter** key after each line.

```
var price:Number;
var totalCost:Number;
var numberOfJerseys:Number;
```

The first input text block will contain either a 1 or a 2 for the type of jersey. To determine which price to use for the jersey, you must use an if conditional statement. The condition that needs to be checked is whether the jerseyType value the user entered is 1 or 2. You will create two conditional statements; one to check for the value of 1 and one to check for the value of 2. Based on the results of the conditions, the price variable will be assigned a value of 10 or 12, corresponding to the cost of the selected jersey.

Using Expressions and Operators

An **expression** is a statement that is used to assign a value to a variable. For example, the expression UserName = "Tom" assigns the text "Tom" to the variable UserName. When referring to text in an expression, it is enclosed in quotation marks. The characters within the quotation marks are considered string data, which is handled differently than numeric data. **String data** is a series of characters—such as letters, numbers, and punctuation—and is always enclosed in quotation marks. **Numeric data** is a number or numbers and is not enclosed in quotation marks. So, to assign a numeric value to a variable, you do not enclose the value in quotation marks. For example, the expression Amount = 20 assigns the numeric value 20 to the variable named Amount.

The equal sign in the expression is an example of an operator. Operators are used in expressions to tell Flash how to manipulate the values in the expression. There are several types of operators. For example, the equal sign is an example of an **assignment operator** because it assigns a value to a variable. ActionScript also has **arithmetic operators** such as +, −, *, and / that are used to indicate addition, subtraction, multiplication, and division, respectively. Another type of operator is a comparison operator, which is an operator used in conditional statements, as you learned earlier.

The script to calculate the results will use expressions and operators.

To code the statements to determine the price of the jerseys:

1. In the Script pane of the Actions panel, type the following lines of code after the last var statement, pressing the **Enter** key after each line.

```
if (jerseyType.text == "1") {
 price = 10;
 }
```

In this code, jerseyType is the name assigned to the first input text block and it contains the value entered by the user. The text property of the jerseyType object represents the value contained in the input box. The conditional operator == compares the input box value to the text value of "1". If the values are equal, the next line assigns a value of 10 to the price variable. You'll code a second conditional statement to check for a jerseyType value of "2".

2. Type the following lines of code after the closing curly brace typed in the previous step, pressing the **Enter** key after each line.

```
if (jerseyType.text == "2") {
 price = 12;
 }
```

If the text value of the jerseyType object is "2", a value of 12 is assigned to the Price variable.

After the second if statement is performed, the price variable will contain either a value of 10 or 12 depending on the jerseyType value entered by the user.

The next action to perform is another if statement to determine whether the user entered Y or N. This determines if the player names will be included on the jerseys. If the user entered Y, you will add 1.50 to the price of the jerseys. Because ActionScript is case sensitive, you need to check for both a lowercase y and an uppercase Y. This will ensure that the correct value is calculated, regardless of how the user entered the letter.

There is no need to check for the letter N because if the user entered N, the price will not change. To check for two conditions within the same if statement, you use the logical operator ||, which represents the Or comparison. You will add the ActionScript code for the if statement next.

TIP

You can use shortcuts to combine assignment and arithmetic operators, such as Amount += 5 instead of Amount = Amount + 5 to increment the value in the variable Amount by 5.

To code the statement to check if player names will be included:

1. In the Script pane of the Actions panel, type the following lines of code after the closing curly brace of the lines you typed in the previous steps, pressing the **Enter** key after each line.

```
if (playerNames.text =="Y" || playerNames.text == "y") {
 price += 1.50;
 }
```

In this code, playerNames is the name of the input text box that contains the value the user enters to specify whether the names of the players will be included on the jerseys. The text property represents the value entered by the user. The || operator causes the condition to be true if either one of the comparisons is true. If the condition is true, the variable price is increased by 1.50.

The next two input text blocks contain values that represent how many players and coaches are on the team. These two values will be added together to get the total number of jerseys to be purchased. Before the values can be added, they need to be converted to numbers. Because the number of players and number of coaches are whole numbers, you will use the int() function.

Converting Values to Numeric Data

Values entered into an input text block are considered string data and not numeric data. That is, the values are not treated as numbers, but instead are treated as text characters. Using the + operator to add the two values will not yield the correct result if the values are not first converted to numeric data. The int() function can be applied to the values to convert them to integer numbers, which are whole numbers that do not include decimals.

After you have calculated the number of jerseys, you can multiply the number by the price of each jersey to get a total cost. You will add the statements to determine the total cost next.

To code the statements to determine the total cost of the jerseys:

1. In the Script pane of the Actions panel, after the closing curly brace in the previous lines you added, type the following line of code.

```
numberOfJerseys = int(numberOfPlayers.text) +int(numberOfCoaches
.text);
```

The numberOfPlayers and numberOfCoaches variables were defined in the input text blocks. The text property is used to get the value entered by the user for each text box. These values are converted to integers and then added together. The result is then assigned to the variable numberOfJerseys.

2. Press the **Enter** key twice to insert a blank line, and then type the following line of code.

```
totalCost = numberOfJerseys*price;
```

The value in the numberOfJerseys is multiplied by the value in price, and the result is assigned to the totalCost variable.

The final step is to assign the value in totalCost to the dynamic text block so that it will be displayed for the user. The dynamic text block can contain only string data. Because the totalCost value is a number, it must first be converted to string data before it can be assigned to the dynamic text box named total. To convert the number to a string, you apply the `string()` function to the totalCost value. The results of the `string()` function can then be assigned to the total dynamic text box. You will add this code next.

To code the statement to display the final result:

1. In the Script pane of the Actions panel, after the line you typed in the previous set of steps, type the following line of code.

```
total.text = String(totalCost);
```

The totalCost value is converted to a string and assigned to the text property of the total dynamic text box. The value will then be displayed to the user. See Figure 8-27.

Figure 8-27   Complete script for calculation

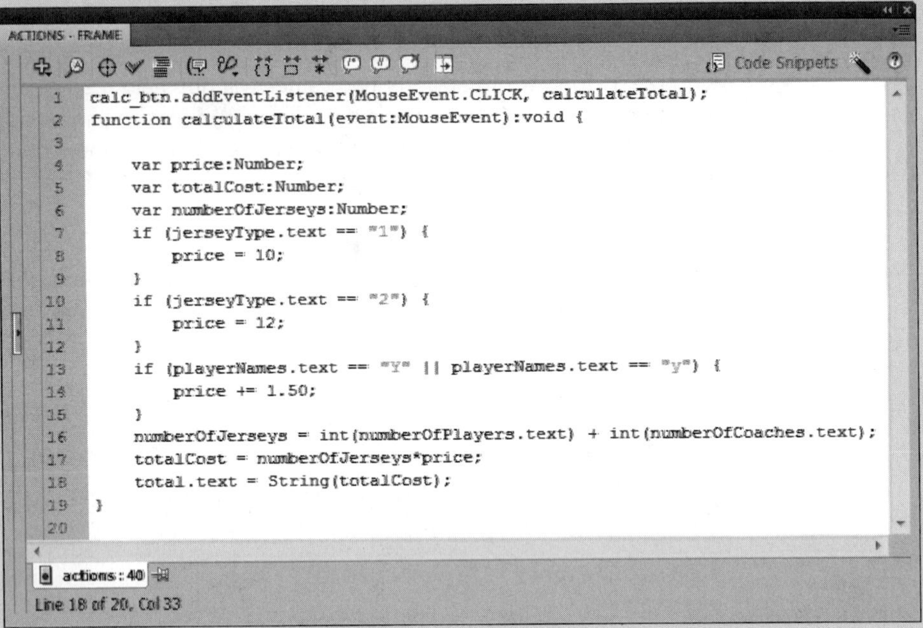

```
ACTIONS - FRAME
                                                              Code Snippets
 1   calc_btn.addEventListener(MouseEvent.CLICK, calculateTotal);
 2   function calculateTotal(event:MouseEvent):void {
 3
 4       var price:Number;
 5       var totalCost:Number;
 6       var numberOfJerseys:Number;
 7       if (jerseyType.text == "1") {
 8           price = 10;
 9       }
10       if (jerseyType.text == "2") {
11           price = 12;
12       }
13       if (playerNames.text == "Y" || playerNames.text == "y") {
14           price += 1.50;
15       }
16       numberOfJerseys = int(numberOfPlayers.text) + int(numberOfCoaches.text);
17       totalCost = numberOfJerseys*price;
18       total.text = String(totalCost);
19   }
20
```
actions : 40

Line 18 of 20, Col 33

The code is complete. Next you need to check the code for syntax errors, and then test it using several input values to make sure you get the correct result. You will test the script next.

To check for errors and test the script:

1. In the Actions panel, click the **Check syntax** button ☑ to check for syntax errors in the code. The script is checked. If no errors are displayed in the Compiler Errors panel, the script is correct.

   Trouble? If your code contains errors, the errors are listed in the Compiler Errors panel at the bottom of the screen. Review your script to compare it to the code you modified in the previous steps, make any necessary corrections, and then repeat Step 1 until no errors are encountered.

2. Save the document. You will test the Jackson's Sports Web site.

3. On the Application bar, click **Control**, point to **Test Movie**, and then click **in Flash Professional**. The movie opens in the Flash Player window. The Loading text appears briefly, and then the Home page opens.

4. Click the **Calculator** button to advance to the Team Jersey Calculator page, and then enter **1** in the Type of Jersey box, **Y** in the Include player names box, **10** in the Number of players box, and **2** in the Number of coaches box.

5. Click the **Calculate** button. The Total cost (w/o tax) field displays 138. See Figure 8-28.

| Figure 8-28 | Calculation results |

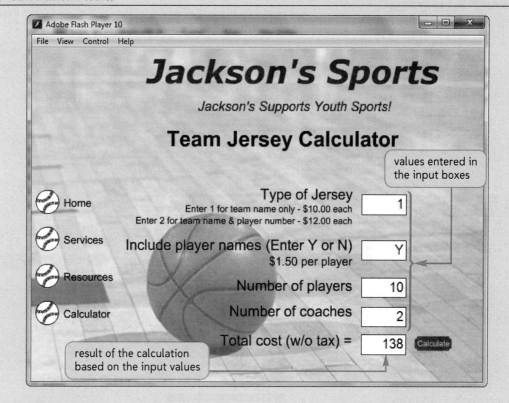

Trouble? If you don't get the correct results, make sure you entered the correct input values and also check the variable names of your input and dynamic text boxes. Remember that ActionScript is case sensitive. If the case of the variable names assigned to the text boxes differs from that used in the code, the result will be incorrect.

6. Enter a set of input values of your choice, click the **Calculate** button to see the total cost, and then repeat with another set of input values.

7. Close the Flash Player window to return to the jsWebSite.fla document.

Adding Numeric Feedback to the Preloader

In the previous session, you created an animation for the preloader to provide visual feedback to the user. In the animation, the scaleX property of a rectangle was changed based on how much of the SWF file had loaded into the Flash Player. In addition to the visual feedback, Flash developers often include numeric feedback showing what percentage of the file has been loaded. The same value used to change the scaleX property of the rectangle can be displayed as a percentage. To display the number, you need to create a dynamic text block similar to the one you created to display the results of the calculation in the Calculator page. You will add a dynamic text block for the preloader and then you will add the code to calculate and display the percentage of the file loaded.

To add a dynamic text block to the preloader:

1. Close the Actions panel to view the Stage, clear the guides, and then in the Timeline, click **Frame 1** of the content layer.

2. On the Stage, create a dynamic text block between the Loading text block and the % text block, set the font family to **Arial**, set the font style to **Regular**, set the point size to **18**, set the text color to **black**, set the font rendering method to **Use device fonts**, set the paragraph format to **Align right**, and then deselect the **Show border around text** button.

3. In the Property inspector, set the text block's dimensions to **30** pixels wide and **26** pixels high, and then enter **percent_txt** as the instance name of the text block instance. See Figure 8-29.

Figure 8-29	Dynamic text block

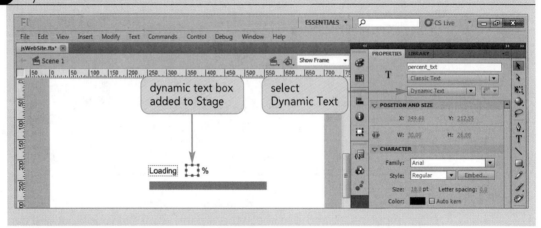

Next, you will add the code to the preloader function to calculate and display the percentage of the file loaded.

To add numeric feedback code, check for errors, and test the script:

1. In the Timeline, click **Frame 1** of the actions layer, and then open the **Actions** panel.

2. In the Script pane of the Actions panel, place the insertion point in front of the line with the if conditional statement, press the **Enter** key to add a blank line, and then in the blank line, type the following line of code.

```
var percent:int = amtLoaded*100;
```

This line creates a new variable named percent with integer as its data type. The value in amtLoaded is multiplied by 100 to change the amtLoaded value to a percentage. This percentage is assigned to the percent variable.

3. Press the **Enter** key to add a new line, and then type the following line of code.

```
percent_txt.text = String(percent);
```

The value in the percent variable is converted to a string using the String() function, and the result is then assigned to the text property of the percent_txt object, which is the dynamic text block instance on the Stage. The result is that the percent value is displayed in the dynamic text box instance.

4. In the Actions panel, click the **Check syntax** button ☑ to check for syntax errors in the code. The script is checked. If no errors are displayed in the Compiler Errors panel, the script is correct.

Trouble? If your code contains errors, the errors are listed in the Compiler Errors panel at the bottom of the screen. Review your script to compare it to the code you modified in the previous steps, make any necessary corrections, and then repeat Step 4 until no errors are encountered.

▶ **5.** Save the document. You will test the Jackson's Sports Web site.

▶ **6.** On the Application bar, click **Control**, point to **Test Movie**, and then click **in Flash Professional**. The movie opens in the Flash Player window. The Loading text appears briefly, and then the Home page opens.

▶ **7.** On the Flash Player Application bar, click **View**, and then click **Simulate Download**. After a few seconds, the preloader animation plays and the percent loaded value is displayed. See Figure 8-30.

Figure 8-30   **Simulated download process**

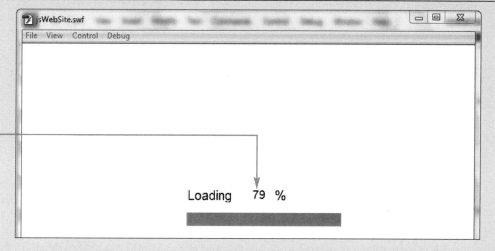

percentage of file loaded into the Flash Player

After the percent loaded value reaches 100%, the home page of the Jackson's Sports Web site appears.

▶ **8.** Close the Flash Player window, and then close the jsWebSite.fla document.

You have completed and tested the input form page that allows the user to enter values in input text blocks, calculates the total cost of the jerseys based on the values entered, and displays the result in a dynamic text block. You also added a dynamic text block to display the percent loaded value with the preloader animation.

Session 8.3 Quick Check

REVIEW

1. What is the purpose of input text?

2. How can you limit the number of characters that can be entered in an input text block?

3. Write a statement to multiply the value in the numeric variable subTotal by 15 and assign the result to the dynamic text block with the instance name of subtotal_txt.

4. Explain the purpose of the || operator in the following conditional statement:
`if (Code == "1" || Code == "2").`

5. What is the purpose of the int() function?

Practice the skills you learned in the tutorial using the same case scenario.

PRACTICE

Review Assignments

Data File needed for the Review Assignments: softballSite.fla

Aly developed a different version of the Jackson's Youth Sports Web site with an emphasis on softball teams. She asks you to complete the Web site by adding links to the Web Links page, adding input and dynamic text boxes to the Player Trophy Cost page, and adding the ActionScript code to make the navigational buttons, the Web Links, and the Trophy cost calculate button operational. You also need to complete the preloader animation and code.

1. Open the **softballSite.fla** file located in the Flash8\Review folder included with your Data Files, and then save the file as **jsSoftball.fla** in the same folder.

2. In the labels layer, insert keyframes at Frame 20, Frame 30, and Frame 40, and then add the label **Preload** at Frame 1, the label **Services** at Frame 20, the label **Weblinks** at Frame 30, and the label **Trophies** at Frame 40.

3. In the Timeline, select Frame 10. On the Stage, select the Services button instance, and then, in the Property inspector, name the instance **services_btn**. Name the Web Links button instance as **weblinks_btn**, and then name the Trophies button instance as **trophies_btn**.

4. In the Timeline, select Frame 10 of the actions layer, and then, in the Actions panel, insert the following comment before the first line.

   `//Keep the playhead from advancing automatically`

5. In the Actions panel, insert the following comment on the line after the `stop();` statement.

   `// Functions to make buttons operational`

6. Select the Services button and then add the Click to Go to Frame and Stop code snippet to make the button operational. Delete the multi-line comment, change the function name to **onServicesClick**, and change the frame reference in the `gotoAndStop(5)` action to `gotoAndStop("Services")`.

7. Select the Web Links button and then add the Click to Go to Frame and Stop code snippet to make the button operational. Delete the multi-line comment, change the function name to **onWeblinksClick**, and change the frame reference in the `gotoAndStop(5)` action to `gotoAndStop("Weblinks")`.

8. Select the Trophies button and then add the Click to Go to Frame and Stop code snippet to make the button operational. Delete the multi-line comment, change the function name to **onTrophiesClick**, and change the frame reference in the `gotoAndStop(5)` action to `gotoAndStop("Trophies")`.

9. Check the code for syntax errors, make any necessary corrections, and then collapse the Actions panel.

10. In the Library panel, make a duplicate of the asaYouth button symbol named **youthSoftball** and then edit the youthSoftball button by changing the text in both its Up frame and Over frame to **Youth Softball**. In the button's Timeline, insert a keyframe in the Hit frame, and then draw a rectangle with a black fill and no stroke to cover the text block.

11. In the Library panel, make a duplicate of the asaYouth button symbol, name the duplicate **USASoftball** and then edit the USASoftball button by changing the text in both its Up frame and Over frame to **USA Softball**. In the button's Timeline, insert a keyframe in the Hit frame, and then draw a rectangle with a black fill and no stroke to cover the text block.

12. Edit the asaYouth button by inserting a keyframe in its Hit frame, and then draw a rectangle with a black fill and no stroke to cover the text block.

13. In the Scene 1 Timeline, select Frame 30 of the content layer, add an instance of the youthSoftball button below the asaYouth button instance, and then add an instance of the USASoftball button below the youthSoftball button instance. Select all three button instances on the center of the Stage, and then, in the Align panel, deselect the To stage button, click the Align left edge button, and click the Space evenly vertically button to align the instances and distribute them evenly.

14. On the Stage, select the youthSoftball button instance and name the instance **youthSoftball _btn**, and then select the USASoftball button instance and name the instance **USASoftball_btn**.

15. On the Stage, select the Youth Softball button, and then add the Click to Go to Web Page code snippet. Delete the multi-line comment, change the function name to `gotoYouthSoftballSite`, and change the URL reference in the `URLRequest()` function to `"http://www.infosports.com/softball"`.

16. On the Stage, select the USA Softball button and then add the Click to Go to Web Page code snippet. Delete the multi-line comment, change the function name to `gotoUSASoftballSite`, and change the URL reference in the `URLRequest()` function to `"http://www.usasoftball.com"`.

17. In the Actions panel, check the code for syntax errors, and make any necessary corrections.

18. Collapse the Actions panel, select Frame 40 of the content layer, create an input text block to the right of the Add individual names (Enter Y or N) text block, select Arial for the font family, Regular for the font style, black for the text color, 20 for the point size, and right align for the paragraph format, make the text block 70 pixels wide and 30 pixels high, set the font rendering method to Use device fonts, set the line type to Single line, show the border around text, set the maximum characters to 1, and then name the input text box instance as **playerNames**.

19. Create an input text block to the right of the Number of players text block using the same dimensions and properties as the playerNames text box, except set the maximum characters to 0, and name the input text box instance as **numberOfPlayers**.

20. Create a dynamic text block to the right of the Total cost (w/o tax) = text block using the same dimensions and properties as the playerNames text box, except name the dynamic text block instance **total**.

21. Align the text boxes vertically by their left edges.

22. In the Timeline, select Frame 40 of the actions layer, and then, in the Actions panel, type the following code after the last line, check the code for syntax errors, and make any necessary corrections.

```
if (trophyType.text == "1") {
    price = 5.95;
    }
if (trophyType.text == "2") {
    price = 8.95;
    }
if (playerNames.text =="Y" || playerNames.text == "y") {
    price += .50;
}
totalCost = int(numberOfPlayers.text)*price;
total.text = String(totalCost);
}
```

23. In the Actions panel, check the code for syntax errors, and make any necessary corrections.

24. Collapse the Actions panel, select Frame 1 of the content layer, deselect all the contents on the Stage, and select the rectangle's green fill but not its stroke. Convert the rectangle's fill to a movie clip symbol named **Rectangle** with the upper-left registration point selected. In the Property inspector, name the Rectangle instance **loadBar_mc**.

25. On the Stage, create a dynamic text block to the left of the % text block, set the font family to Arial, set the font style to regular, set the point size to 20, set the text color to black, set the paragraph format to align right, deselect the Show border around text button, set the font rendering method to Use device fonts, make the dimensions of the text block 70 pixels wide and 40 pixels high, and then name the text block instance **percent_txt**.

26. In the Timeline, select Frame 1 of the actions layer, and then, in the Actions panel, type the following code after the last line, check the code for syntax errors, and make any necessary corrections.

```
loadBar_mc.scaleX = amtLoaded;
var percent:int = amtLoaded*100;
percent_txt.text = String(percent);

if (loadedBytes == totalBytes) {
        gotoAndPlay("Home");
} else {
        gotoAndPlay("Preload");
}
}
```

27. Save the jsSoftball.fla document, and then test it. In the Flash Player, use the Simulate Download command to test the preloader. Click the Web Links button to go to the Web Links page. On the Web Links page, click each link button to open its linked Web site in a browser window. (If an error message appears indicating an error opening the Web pages, the URLs for these Web sites might have changed since the printing of this tutorial. See your instructor or technical support person for assistance.)

28. Click the Trophies button to go to the Player Trophy Cost page. In the Type of Trophy text box, type **1**. In the Add individual names (Enter Y or N) text box, type **Y**. In the Number of players text box, type **11**. Click the Calculate button to display 70.95 for the total cost.

29. Submit the finished files to your instructor.

Add Web links, an input form, and ActionScript code in a Flash Web site.

APPLY

Case Problem 1

Data File needed for this Case Problem: kprDraft.fla

Katie's Pet Resort   Katie meets with John to discuss adding two new elements to the Web site, including a new page with hyperlinks to Web sites with additional pet adoption information. She also wants a page for customers to select from several options for pet boarding. These options include the type of boarding (day or overnight), the number of days if overnight boarding, and whether grooming is included. The page will then display the cost of the boarding based on the selections. You will make the changes to the Web site, including the Boarding page, which is shown Figure 8-31.

Figure 8-31   Boarding page

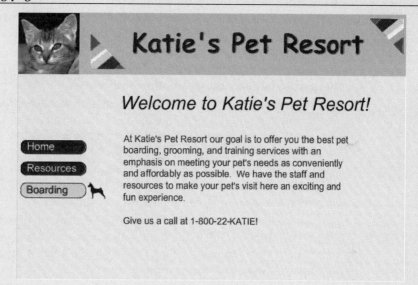

1. Open the **kprDraft.fla** document located in the Flash8\Case1 folder included with your Data Files, and then save the file as **resortWeb.fla** in the same folder.

2. In the Timeline, insert a new layer above the buttons layer and name it **actions**. In the actions layer, insert keyframes at Frame 10 and Frame 20. Insert a layer above the actions layer and name it **labels**. In the labels layer, insert keyframes at Frame 10 and Frame 20, and then add the label **Home** in Frame 1, add the label **Resources** in Frame 10, and add the label **Boarding** in Frame 20.

3. On the Stage, select the Home button instance, and then, in the Property inspector, name the instance as **home_btn**. Name the Resources button instance as **resources_btn**, and name the Boarding button instance as **boarding_btn**.

4. In the Timeline, select Frame 1 of the actions layer, and then in the Actions panel, insert the following code.

```
//Keep the playhead from advancing
stop();
// Functions to make buttons operational
```

5. Select the Home button, and then add the Click to Go to Frame and Stop code snippet to make the button operational. Delete the multi-line comment, change the function name to **onHomeClick** and change the frame reference in the `gotoAndStop(5)` action to `gotoAndStop("Home")`.

6. Select the Resources button, and then add the Click to Go to Frame and Stop code snippet to make the button operational. Delete the multi-line comment, change the function name to **onResourcesClick**, and change the frame reference in the `gotoAndStop(5)` action to `gotoAndStop("Resources")`.

7. Select the Boarding button, and then add the Click to Go to Frame and Stop code snippet to make the button operational. Delete the multi-line comment, change the function name to **onBoardingClick** and change the frame reference in the `gotoAndStop(5)` action to `gotoAndStop("Boarding")`.

8. Check the code for syntax errors and make any necessary corrections.

9. In the Timeline, select Frame 10 of the content layer, and then, on the Stage, create a static text block within the yellow rectangle at about 200 pixels from the left edge of the Stage and 270 pixels from the top edge of the Stage. Use Arial for the font family, regular for the font style, 16 for the point size, black for the text color, and align left for the paragraph format. Type **Adopt a Pet** in the text block.

10. Create another static text block below the first one with the same text properties, and then type **Best Friend Pet Adoption** in the text block. Create another static text block below the second one with the same text properties, and then type **SPCA of Texas** in the text block. Select the three text blocks, and then align them by their left edges and distribute them evenly vertically.

11. Convert each of the three text blocks into a button symbol named **adopt button**, **bestFriend button**, and **spca button**, respectively.

12. Edit the adopt button symbol, insert a keyframe in its Over frame and make the text italic, and then insert a keyframe in the Hit frame and draw a rectangle to make it easier to click the button. Edit the bestFriend button symbol and the spca button symbol in the same way. Exit symbol-editing mode.

13. On the Stage, select the adopt button instance, and then, in the Property inspector, name the instance **adopt_btn**. Name the bestFriend button instance **bestFriend_btn** and then name the spca button instance as **spca_btn**.

14. On the Stage, select the adopt button instance, and then add the Click to Go to Web Page code snippet. Delete the multi-line comment, change the function name to `gotoAdoptAPetSite`, and change the URL reference in the `URLRequest()` function to `"http://www.adoptapet.com/"`.

15. On the Stage, select the bestFriend button instance, and then add the Click to Go to Web Page code snippet. Delete the multi-line comment, change the function name to `gotoBestFriendtSite` and change the URL reference in the `URLRequest()` function to `"http://www.bfpa.org/"`.

16. On the Stage, select the spca button instance, and then add the Click to Go to Web Page code snippet. Delete the multi-line comment, change the function name to `gotoSPCASite` and change the URL reference in the `URLRequest()` function to `"http://www.spca.org/"`.

17. Check the code for syntax errors and make any necessary corrections.

18. Create a new static text block below the spca button. Use Arial for the font family, italic for the font style, 10 for the point size, black for the text color, and align left for the paragraph format. Type **Click a button above to open the Web site in a browser window.** in the text block.

19. In the Timeline, select Frame 20 of the content layer, and create an input text block to the right of the Enter letter for the desired boarding option line. Make the text block 40 pixels wide by 20 pixels high. Use Arial for the font family, 12 for the point size, regular for the font style, black for the text color, and align right for the paragraph format. If necessary, select single line as the line type behavior, show the border around the text, set the font rendering method to Use device fonts, and enter **1** as the maximum characters. Name the text block instance as **boardingType_txt**.

20. Create a second input text block with the same dimensions and properties as the boardingType_txt text block. Place this text block to the right of the How many days? line. Set the maximum characters to 0 and name the text block instance as **days_txt**.

21. Create another input text block with the same dimensions and properties as the boardingType_txt text block, and place it to the right of the Bath and grooming for $24.95 (Y- yes or N- no) line. Set the maximum characters to 1 and name the text block instance as **grooming_txt**.

22. Create a dynamic text block to the right of the Total cost (w/o taxes) line. Use the same dimensions and text properties as the input text blocks. Name the text block instance as **total_txt**.

23. Drag an instance of the calc button from the Library panel to the left side of the Total cost (w/o taxes) line, and then name the text block instance as **calc_btn**.

24. In the Timeline, select Frame 20 of the actions layer, and then, in the Actions panel, type the following code, check the code for syntax errors, and make any necessary corrections.

```
//Calculate cost of retreat
calc_btn.addEventListener(MouseEvent.CLICK, Calculate);
function Calculate(event:MouseEvent):void
{
      var price:Number;
      var totalCost:Number;

      if (boardingType_txt.text == "D" || boardingType_txt.text == "d")
         {
            price = 14.95;
         }
         else
         {
            price = 19.95;
         }
         totalCost = int(days_txt.text) * price;
         if (grooming_txt.text == "Y" || grooming_txt.text == "y")
         {
            totalCost += 24.95;
         }

         total_txt.text = String(totalCost);
}
```

25. Save the resortWeb.fla document, and then test it. Click the Resources button to display the Resources page. Click each link to open its Web site in a browser window. (If an error message appears indicating an error opening the Web pages, the URLs for these Web sites might have changed since the printing of this tutorial. See your instructor or technical support person for assistance.)

26. Click the Boarding button to display the Boarding page. Enter **O** for the type of boarding, **2** for the number of days, and **Y** for bath and grooming. Click the Calculate Total button to display 64.85 for the total cost.

27. Submit the finished files to your instructor.

Create a Flash Web site with buttons to display the previous and next frames.

APPLY

Case 2

Data Files needed for this Case Problem: aczDraft.fla, bear.jpg, giraffe.jpg, rhino.jpg

Alamo City Zoo   Janet meets with Alex to request a new Web site that will display zoo animals. Several pages will display special exhibits and the user will be able to change the display from one exhibit to another. Alex asks you to help him modify a draft page by adding buttons to control the display of each exhibit and by adding each exhibit on a separate frame. Each exhibit will display a picture of a zoo animal and a short message about the exhibit. Alamo City Zoo currently has three special exhibits. Figure 8-32 shows the contents of Frame 1.

Figure 8-32   **Frame 1 of the special exhibits pages**

1. Open the **aczDraft.fla** document located in the Flash8\Case2 folder included with your Data Files, and then save the file as **exhibits.fla** in the same folder.

2. In the Timeline, insert three new layers above the contents layer, and then name the layers **buttons**, **actions**, and **labels**.

3. In the Timeline, select the buttons layer, open the Buttons Common Library, drag an instance of the flat blue back symbol from the playback flat folder to the Stage, place the instance below the text block and rectangle at the center of the Stage, and then name the instance **prev_btn**. Drag an instance of the flat blue forward symbol, place the instance just to the right of the flat blue back instance, and then name the instance **next_btn**. Close the Buttons library panel.

4. Select both of the button instances and then top align the buttons relative to each other.

5. In the Timeline, insert regular frames at Frame 7 of all the layers. Insert a keyframe in Frame 2 of the contents layer, and then delete the bottom and middle text blocks.

6. Import the **bear.jpg**, **giraffe.jpg**, and **rhino.jpg** files located in the Flash8\Case2 folder included with your Data Files to the document's library. Drag an instance of the rhino.jpg bitmap from the document's Library panel to the center of the rectangle and place it below the title text block.

7. In Frame 2 of the contents layer, add a fixed-width static text block to the left of the rhino picture. Make the text block's width about 140 pixels and place it about 180 pixels from the top of the Stage and about 100 pixels from the left of the Stage. Use Arial for the font family, regular for the font style, 14 for the point size, maroon (#660000) for the text color, and align left for the paragraph format. Type **The rhinoceros stands about 60 inches at the shoulder and weighs between 1 to 1½ tons. Rhinos are vegetarians and live up to 40 years.** in the text block.

8. In the Timeline, insert a keyframe at Frame 3 of the contents layer. On the Stage, swap the instance of the rhino.jpg bitmap with an instance of the giraffe.jpg bitmap. Change the text in the text block to the left of the picture to **The giraffe stands at a height of 14 to 18 feet and weighs up to 2 tons. Giraffes are vegetarians and are able to grasp leaves with their tongue.**

9. In the Timeline, insert a keyframe at Frame 4 of the contents layer. On the Stage, swap the instance of the giraffe.jpg bitmap with an instance of the bear.jpg bitmap. Change the text in the text block to the left of the picture to **Bears, such as the grizzly bear, grow from 5 to 7 feet in length and weigh up to 900 pounds. Bears eat plants, insects, fish, and meat and have a lifespan of about 25 years.**

10. In the Timeline, select Frame 1 of the labels layer. In the Property inspector, assign the label **Begin** to this frame. Insert a keyframe at Frame 4 of the labels layer, and assign the label **End** to the frame.

11. In the Timeline, select Frame 1 of the actions layer. In the Actions panel, type the code shown below. (This code stops the playhead at Frame 1; the first function will move the playhead to the previous frame except when the playhead is on Frame 1, in which case the playhead will move to the frame labeled End; the second function will move the playhead to the next frame except when the playhead is on Frame 4, in which case the playhead will move to the frame labeled Begin.)

```
//Keep the playhead from advancing
stop();
//Advance the playhead to the previous frame
prev_btn.addEventListener(MouseEvent.CLICK, onPrevClick);
function onPrevClick(event:MouseEvent):void
{
        if (currentFrame == 1)
        {
                gotoAndStop("End");
        }
        else
        {
                prevFrame();
        }
}
//Advance the playhead to the next frame
next_btn.addEventListener(MouseEvent.CLICK, onNextClick);

function onNextClick(event:MouseEvent):void
{
        if (currentFrame == 4)
        {
                gotoAndStop("Begin");
        }
        else
        {
                nextFrame();
        }
}
```

12. Check the code for syntax errors, and make any necessary corrections.

13. Save the exhibits.fla file, and then test it. Click the buttons to display each exhibit in the frames.

14. Submit the finished files to your instructor.

Add ActionScript code to advance the playhead and add a preloader to a Flash Web site.

CHALLENGE

Case 3

Data Files needed for this Case Problem: wcDraft.fla, flower1.jpg, flower2.jpg, flower3.jpg, preloaderScript.as

Westcreek Nursery   Alice requests a different version of the photos page to display pictures of flowers and plants for sale. Because the number of pictures varies each week, only one button will be used. Each time the button is clicked, a different picture will appear. This will allow more pictures to be added without adding more buttons. You will modify a revised photos page by adding one picture with text per frame and adding a button to advance from one frame to the next. You will also add a preloader, which will display a message and an animation indicating the progress of the loading. Figure 8-33 shows the photos page with the first picture.

Figure 8-33   **Photos page**

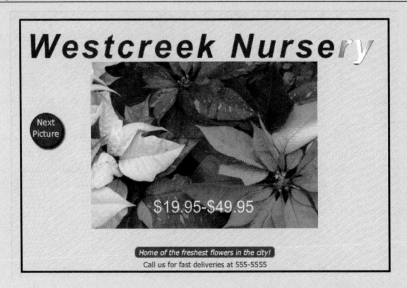

1. Open the **wcDraft.fla** file located in the Flash8\Case3 folder included with your Data Files, and then save the file as **wcPhotos.fla** in the same folder.

2. In the Timeline, insert a new layer above the background layer and name it **pictures**. Insert two layers above the preloader layer, and name them **actions** and **labels**.

3. In the pictures layer, insert a keyframe at Frame 10 and set the magnification level of the Stage to Show Frame.

⊕ EXPLORE   4. Use the Import to Stage command to import the **flower1.jpg** file located in the Flash8\Case3 folder included with your Data Files. Click the Yes button to import all of the images in the sequence, which places each of the three pictures in separate frames positioned at the center of the Stage.

⊕ EXPLORE   5. In the Timeline, insert regular frames at Frame 12 of all the layers except the pictures layer.

6. Select Frame 10 of the pictures layer, and then create a static text block in the lower-center of the picture. Use Arial for the font family, regular for the font style, 24 for the point size, align center for the paragraph format, and white for the text color. Type **$19.95–$49.95** in the text block.

7. Select Frame 11 of the pictures layer, create a static text block in the lower-center of the picture using the same properties as in Step 6, and then type **$24.95–$59.95** in the text block.

8. Select Frame 12 of the pictures layer, create a static text block in the lower-center of the picture using the same properties as in Step 6, and then type to **$9.95–$29.95** in the text block.

9. Insert a keyframe at Frame 10 of the labels layer, and then add the label **preload** in Frame 1 and the label **begin** in Frame 10.

10. On the Stage, name the nextPicture button instance as **next_btn**.

11. Select Frame 1 of the preloader layer, and then, on the Stage, draw a rectangle above the Loading text block. Use orange (#FF9900) for the fill, do not include a stroke, and use 15 for the rectangle corner radius. Set the rectangle's dimensions to 300 pixels wide and 20 pixels high. Convert the rectangle to a movie clip symbol named **loadBar** with the upper-left registration point selected. In the Property inspector, name the instance as **loadBar_mc**.

⊕ EXPLORE   12. Select Frame 1 of the actions layer, open the Actions panel, and import the **preloaderScript.as** file located in the Flash8\Case3 folder included with your Data Files. (*Hint*: Select Import Script in the Options menu of the Actions panel.)

13. Type the following code in the Actions panel before the //Event Listener line to keep the playhead from advancing automatically.

```
//Keep the playhead from advancing
stop();
```

14. Type the following code in the Actions panel before the closing curly brace. The code will compare the bytes loaded with the total bytes. After the document is loaded, the playhead is moved to the frame labeled begin.

```
if (loadedBytes==totalBytes) {
    gotoAndPlay("begin");
} else {
    gotoAndPlay("preload");
}
```

⊕ EXPLORE 15. In the Actions panel, click the Auto format button to apply proper formatting to the code. Check the code for syntax errors and make any necessary corrections.

16. Move the playhead to Frame 10 and select the next_btn instance on the Stage.

⊕ EXPLORE 17. Apply the Mouse Click Event code snippet located in the Event Handlers category. In the Actions panel, change the code snippet function name, fl_MouseClickHandler, to **onNextClick** in the event listener and in the function definition.

18. In the Actions panel, replace the multi-line comments at the beginning of the script with the following code.

```
//Keep the playhead from advancing
stop();

//Advance the playhead to the begin label or to the next frame
```

⊕ EXPLORE 19. In the Actions panel, within the onNextClick function, replace the comments and the trace() statement with the following code. This code will advance the playhead to the next frame each time the button is clicked unless the playhead is on the last frame, in which case the playhead is moved to the frame labeled begin.

```
if (currentFrame == 12) {
    gotoAndStop("begin");
} else {
    nextFrame();
}
```

⊕ EXPLORE 20. In the Actions panel, click the Auto format button to apply proper formatting to the code. Check the code for syntax errors and make any necessary corrections.

21. Save the wcPhotos.fla file, and then test it. Use the Simulate Download command to test the preloader. After the document loads, the first picture is displayed. Click the Next picture button to display the next picture.

22. Submit the finished files to your instructor.

Complete a Flash Web site by adding ActionScript code to compare input values and calculate a result.

CREATE

Case 4

Data File needed for this Case Problem: msaDraft.fla

Missions Support Association   While reviewing the Web site with the association's president, Brittany suggests adding a page that enables the visitor to calculate the cost of a group tour. The group tour calculator will enable the user to enter a type of tour and the number of people in the group. The calculator will determine and display the cost of the tour based on the values entered. The formula to determine the cost of the tour is as follows:

group tour cost = base cost of tour × cost per person × number of people

The base cost of tour is a cost assigned to each type of tour. A guided 30-minute tour of one mission has a base cost of $20. A guided one-hour tour of three missions has a base cost of $30. A two-hour bus tour of all the missions has a base cost of $40. The cost per person depends on the number of people in the group. For a group of fewer than 8 people, the cost is $10 per person. For groups of 8 to 15 people, the cost is $8 per person. For groups with more than 15 people, the cost is $5 per person.

You will develop the new page for the Web site, similar to the one shown in Figure 8-34, based on a document that Anissa has developed from the information Brittany provided.

Figure 8-34　　　Sample Group Tour Calculator page

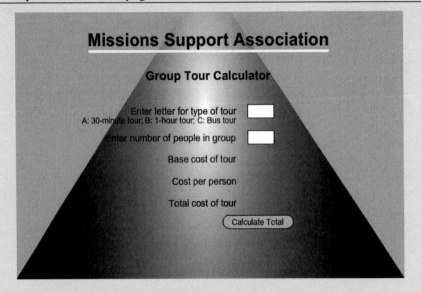

1. Open the **msaDraft.fla** document located in the Flash8\Case4 folder included with your Data Files, and then save the file as **tourCalc.fla** in the same folder.
2. In the Timeline, insert four new layers above the title layer and name them **contents, text fields, button,** and **actions**, respectively.
3. In the Timeline, select the contents layer and create a text block below the title text block. Use a smaller font size than the title text and type **Group Tour Calculator**. Create another text block below the Group Tour Calculator text block, with a smaller font size and type **Enter letter for type of tour**, press the Enter key and type **A: 30-minute tour; B: 1-hour tour; C: Bus tour**. Reduce the font size for the second line. Right-align both lines.
4. In the contents layer, create another text block below the previous text block using the same font size as the Enter letter for type of tour text block and type **Enter number of people in group**. Create three more text blocks right-aligned and arranged vertically below the previous one with the following contents: **Base cost of tour**, **Cost per person**, **Total Cost of Tour**.
5. In the text fields layer, create an input text block to the right of the Enter letter for type of tour text. Create another input text block to the right of the Enter number of people in group text block. Assign instance names to each input text block and show the border around each input text block.
6. In the text fields layer, create a dynamic text block to the right of the Base cost of tour text block. Create another dynamic text block to the right of the Cost per person text block. Create one more dynamic text block to the right of the Total Cost of Tour text block. Assign instance names to each dynamic text block.

7. Create a new button symbol that will be used to calculate the results. In the Timeline, add an instance of the button symbol in the button layer. Assign an instance name to the button.

8. Select Frame 1 of the actions layer, and then, in the Actions panel, type the following code to create a function that will calculate the cost of the tour.

```
// Event listener for the Calculate Total button
calcTotal_btn.addEventListener(MouseEvent.CLICK,
calculateTourCost);
// Function to calculate total tour cost
function calculateTourCost(event:MouseEvent):void
{
```

⊕ EXPLORE 9. In the Actions panel, use a switch statement to determine the base cost of the tour, which is different for each type of tour a user can select. The user will enter a letter into an input text box that represents the type of tour. The switch statement will check the value in the input text block and then compare the value to the values in the case statements. If the value entered matches a value in the case statement, the statement following the case statement is executed. For example, if the value entered into the input text box is either A or a, the value 20 should be assigned to the base cost. A break statement is used to exit each case statement. The first part of the switch statement code is as follows. The var statement defines a variable used to store the base cost assigned.

```
// Define the base_cost variable
var base_cost:Number;
// Use the switch statement to assign the tour's base cost
switch (tourType_txt.text)
{
    case "A" :
    case "a" :
        base_cost = 20;
        break;
```

⊕ EXPLORE 10. Type additional case statements to check for B or b and for C or c and to assign the appropriate value to the base_cost.

⊕ EXPLORE 11. End the switch statement with a default statement as follows. If the letter entered does not match any of the case statements, the base cost will be 40.

```
    default :
        base_cost = 40;
}
```

12. Type the following lines of code to create two variables. One variable will hold the value of the number of people entered in the input text box. The input value needs to be converted into an Integer number as shown below. The other variable will hold the cost per person.

```
// Convert input value into Integer number
var people:Number = int(numberOfPeople_txt.text);
// Determine cost per person based on number of people in group
var cost_per_person:Number;
```

13. Type the following if statement to check when the number of people in the group is less than eight. The cost per person is $10 based on the value entered into the input text block for the number of people.

```
if (people < 8)
{
    cost_per_person = 10;
}
```

14. Type another if statement to check when the number of people in the group is more than seven and less than 16 in which case the cost per person is $8. (*Hint*: Use two conditions in the if statement with the && operator to check that both conditions are true.)

15. Type another if statement to check when the number of people in the group is more than 15 in which case the cost per person is $5.

16. Type a line of code to calculate the total cost. The total cost is the base cost plus the number of people times the cost per person. Include a comment that identifies the code you entered.

17. Type lines of code to display the base cost, cost per person and total cost in the corresponding dynamic text blocks. End the function. Remember to convert the values into strings before assigning them to the dynamic text blocks. Also, include a comment that identifies the code you entered.

18. Check for syntax errors and make any necessary corrections.

19. Save the file and test it. Enter **B** for the type of tour and **11** for the number of people. Click the Calculate Total button. The base cost is 30, the cost per person is 8, and the total cost of the tour is 118.

20. Submit the finished files to your instructor.

ENDING DATA FILES

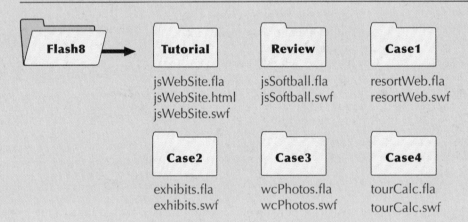

Flash8 → Tutorial
jsWebSite.fla
jsWebSite.html
jsWebSite.swf

Review
jsSoftball.fla
jsSoftball.swf

Case1
resortWeb.fla
resortWeb.swf

Case2
exhibits.fla
exhibits.swf

Case3
wcPhotos.fla
wcPhotos.swf

Case4
tourCalc.fla
tourCalc.swf

FLASH

Using Components and Video, and Creating Printable and Mobile Content

Adding Web Links, Photos, and Video to a Flash Web Site and Creating Mobile Content

Case | *Admiral Web Design*

Dan Jackson wants changes made to the Jackson's Youth Sports Web site. Aly and Chris ask you to incorporate the changes. You will add Web links to the home page and complete the Photos and Videos pages. The Videos page, which will display short video segments of youth sports games, will contain buttons to select from two video clips and will include controls to play and pause the videos and mute the audio. You will also create a page that displays a coupon the user can print to redeem at the store. You will use components to create these interactive elements in Flash. Finally, you will create a sample ad that can be sent to customers' mobile phones.

OBJECTIVES

Session 9.1
- Add Web links using the ComboBox component
- Add photos using the UILoader and Button components
- Add a ProgressBar component
- Add ActionScript to control components

Session 9.2
- Learn the basics of using digital video
- Format video with Adobe Media Encoder
- Import video
- Modify the FLVPlayback component
- Add button components to control video

Session 9.3
- Prepare Flash content for printing
- Control printing with ActionScript
- Create Flash content for mobile devices

STARTING DATA FILES

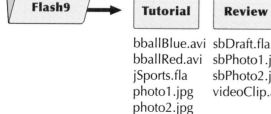

Flash9 →	Tutorial	Review	Case1	Case2	Case3	Case4
	bballBlue.avi	sbDraft.fla	kprDraft.fla	aczDraft.fla	flower1.jpg	mission1.jpg
	bballRed.avi	sbPhoto1.jpg		zooClip1.avi	flower1_sm.jpg	mission2.jpg
	jSports.fla	sbPhoto2.jpg		zooClip2.avi	flower2.jpg	msaDraft.fla
	photo1.jpg	videoClip.avi			flower2_sm.jpg	
	photo2.jpg				flower3.jpg	
					flower3_sm.jpg	
					loadPics.as	
					wcDraft.fla	
					wcLandscape.avi	

FL 443

SESSION 9.1 VISUAL OVERVIEW

A **component** is a prebuilt movie clip installed with Flash that includes a set of user interface and video components. Flash components are located in the Components panel.

The Button component creates a functional button instance. Change the button's text label in its label parameter.

When an instance of the ComboBox component is first placed on the Stage, all of its elements are added to the document's library.

The ComboBox component displays a drop-down list from which the user can make a selection.

The ProgressBar component can display the progress of loading content, such as a photo file, into the UILoader instance.

The UILoader component can be used to load content such as images and SWF files.

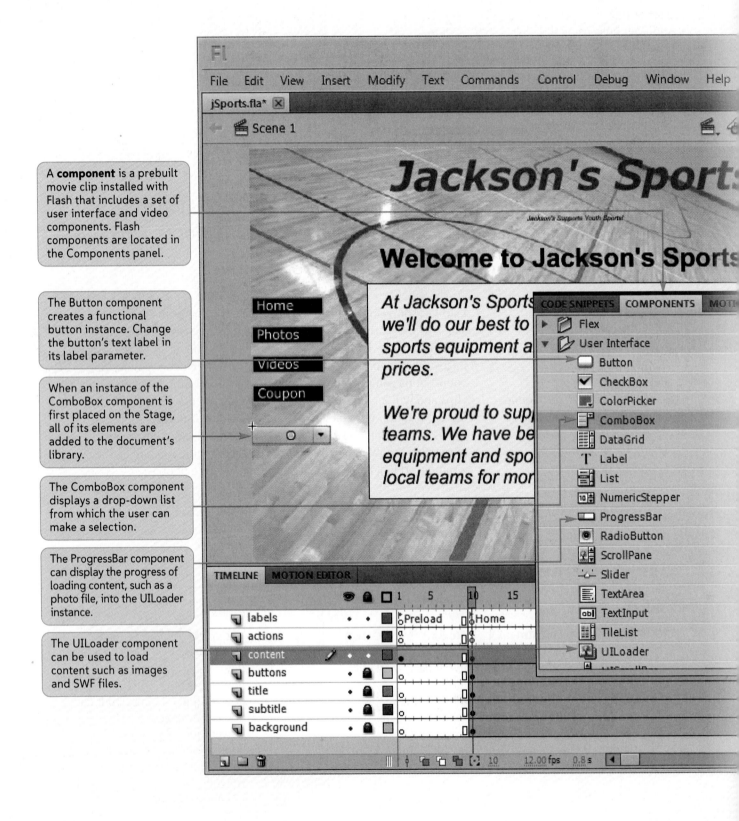

WEB LINKS AND COMPONENTS

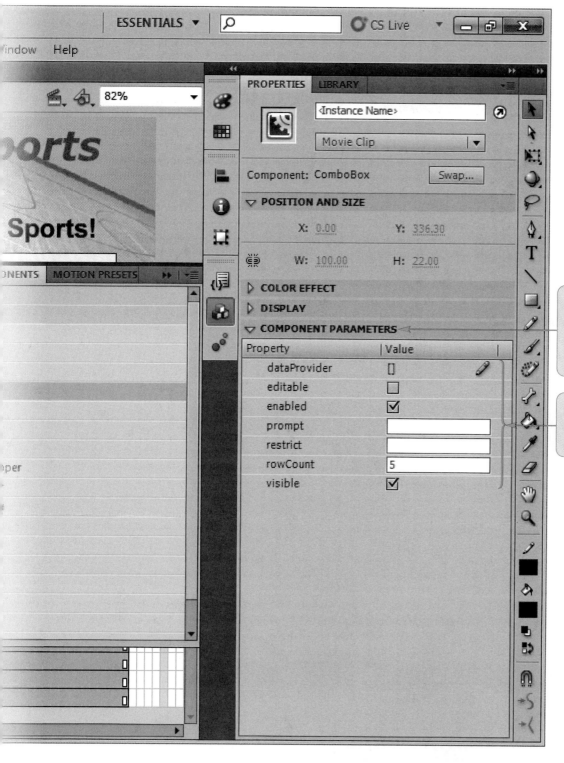

The Component Parameters section of the Property inspector contains the most commonly used parameters based on the selected component.

The values of a component's parameters can be changed in the Property inspector.

Using Flash Components

Components are movie clips that have been exported with the .swc extension. Some components installed with Flash can be used to create user interface elements in documents. For example, you can use the CheckBox component to create check boxes with options that a user can select on a form. When the user clicks a check box, a check mark appears in the check box. This information can then be processed using ActionScript. Using a component such as the CheckBox component means you don't have to create the necessary graphics and functionality because they're already built into the component. Other user interface components include the ComboBox and the ProgressBar, which displays the loading progress of content loading into the Flash Player.

INSIGHT

Downloading Additional Components

You can add more components by downloading them from Web resources such as the Flash Exchange, which is an Adobe Web site with resources for Flash developers. You can purchase components from other sources such as *www.flashloaded.com*. You can also create your own components by exporting a movie clip symbol from the document's Library panel. Downloaded components are installed using the Adobe Extension Manager. The Flash Exchange and the Adobe Extension Manager are both accessible from the Help menu.

The first time you add a component to a document, simply drag an instance of the component from the Components panel to the Stage. The component's movie clip and other elements are added to the document's library. Then, you can add more instances of the same component by dragging them from the Library panel to the Stage and then assigning each instance a different name. A component contains parameters that can be viewed or changed in the Component Parameters section of the Property inspector.

REFERENCE

Adding a Flash Component

- In the docked panel group, click the Components button.
- In the Components panel, double-click a category to expand its list, if necessary.
- Drag an instance of the component from the Components panel to the Stage.
- Reposition and align the component instance on the Stage as needed.
- In the Property inspector, name the instance and enter width and height values.
- In the Component Parameters section of the Property inspector, enter the appropriate values.

Using the ComboBox Component

The ComboBox component displays a list from which the user can make a selection. In place of the Resources page you created previously for the Jackson's Youth Sports Web site, you will add a drop-down list of Web links to the home page based on Aly's instructions, shown in Figure 9-1. The user can then click an item on the list to navigate to another Web site.

Figure 9-1 | Home page with Web links

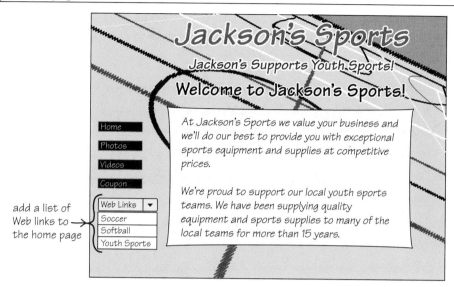

You will create the Web links by adding an instance of the ComboBox component to the Jackson's Youth Sports Web site home page, setting its parameters, and adding ActionScript code to make the items in the ComboBox functional.

To add a ComboBox instance to the home page:

1. Open the **jSports.fla** file located in the Flash9\Tutorial folder included with your Data Files, save the file as **jsWebSite.fla** in the same folder, reset the workspace to the **Essentials** layout, and then change the zoom to **Fit in Window**.

2. In the Timeline, select **Frame 10** of the content layer, if necessary. The Home page content appears on the Stage.

3. In the docked panel group, click the **Components** button. The Components panel opens.

4. In the Components panel, double-click **User Interface** to expand its list of components, if necessary.

5. Drag an instance of the **ComboBox** component from the Components panel to the Stage.

6. On the Stage, if necessary, reposition the ComboBox instance below the Coupon navigational button.

7. In the Property inspector, name the instance **webLinks_mc**, change the width of the instance to **120** pixels, and then make sure the height is **22** pixels. The ComboBox instance is positioned and sized for the Home page.

The ComboBox component instance has properties, called parameters, which can be modified in the Component Parameter section of the Property inspector. The dataProvider parameter defines the labels that appear on the drop-down list and the values that are associated with each item. The editable parameter, when set to true, enables the user to edit the items in the list. The contents of the prompt parameter appear on the ComboBox instance on the Stage. The rowCount parameter determines how many rows to allocate to the drop-down list.

You will enter values for the prompt and dataProvider parameters.

To set parameter values for the ComboBox instance:

▶ **1.** In the Component Parameters section of the Property inspector, type **Web Links** in the prompt box, and then press the **Enter** key. The Web Links text appears in the ComboBox instance on the Stage.

▶ **2.** In the Component Parameters section of the Property inspector, click the **Value** column next to the dataProvider parameter. The Values dialog box opens.

▶ **3.** Click the **Add value** button ⊕. A label and data without values are inserted.

▶ **4.** In the label Value column, click **label0**, and then type **Soccer**. The label value is added.

▶ **5.** Press the **Tab** key to move the insertion point to the data Value box, and then type **1** to add the data value. The first value is added to the dataProvider parameter.

▶ **6.** Repeat Steps 3 through 5 to add two more values to the dataProvider parameter, using **Softball** and **2** for the second label and value, and **Youth Sports** and **3** for the third label and value. See Figure 9-2.

Figure 9-2 Values dialog box

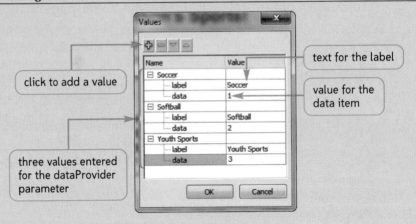

click to add a value

text for the label

value for the data item

three values entered for the dataProvider parameter

▶ **7.** Click the **OK** button. The Values dialog box closes.

With the ComboBox component instance added to the Stage and its parameters set, you need to add ActionScript code to make the ComboBox instance operational. When the user clicks an item in the drop-down list, the value associated with the item can be checked using ActionScript code. For example, if a user clicks the Soccer item, the value of the ComboBox instance is 1 because that value is associated with Soccer.

ActionScript uses the ComboBox value to determine which URL to use to navigate to a Web site. To check which of the three URLs will be used, you can use a switch statement, which is helpful when you need to execute one of several statements or blocks of statements based on the value of the same expression. Each block of statements that may be executed is enclosed between a case statement and a break statement. Each case statement has a value associated with it, as shown in Figure 9-3.

| Figure 9-3 | Sample switch statement |

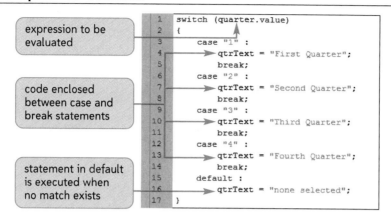

The expression is evaluated, and its value is compared with the values in each case statement. If a match exists, the statements following the case statement are executed. The break statement is used to exit the switch statement. The default statement executes when there is no match.

You will add a switch statement to check the value of the selected ComboBox item, which can be 1, 2, or 3. When a match is found, the associated code within the case statement assigns a Web site URL to a string variable. No default value is needed because a user can select only three possible values. After the switch statement, the value in the string variable is used to navigate to the corresponding Web site.

Written Communication: Accurately Entering and Testing Code

PROSKILLS

Programming code can be complex and lengthy. One minor syntax error can yield unexpected or inaccurate results. It is, therefore, very important to be as accurate as possible when you enter the programming code in the Actions panel. This will help reduce the possibility of syntax errors, which can be difficult to find. You should also format the code for readability—not only to help you see how the code is structured, but also to help someone else who might need to work with the code later. It is also very critical to test the code you enter to ensure that it works correctly. Be sure to test the code whenever you make any changes to it.

You'll use ActionScript to add functionality to the ComboBox instance.

To add functionality to the ComboBox instance using ActionScript:

1. In the Timeline, select **Frame 10** of the actions layer, open the **Actions** panel, and then, if necessary, click the **collapse** button in the vertical bar between the Actions toolbox and the Script pane. The Actions toolbox collapses and the Script pane, which contains the code for the Web site's navigational buttons, expands.

2. In the Script pane, place the insertion point at the end of the last line, and then press the **Enter** key to insert a blank line.

3. Starting in the blank line, type the following lines of code, pressing the **Enter** key after each line to create an event listener. When a change occurs in the ComboBox instance, webLinks_mc, the gotoSite function is called.

```
// Function to assign URL based on selected option
webLinks_mc.addEventListener(Event.CHANGE, gotoSite);
```

TIP

You can click the Auto format button in the Actions panel to align and apply indentation to the code to improve readability.

4. In the Script pane, type the following lines of code after the last line to create the function that determines which URL will be used.

```
// Function to assign URL based on selected option
function gotoSite(event:Event):void
{
      // Variable that will hold the URL
      var linkText:String;
      // Switch statement determines which URL to assign
      switch (webLinks_mc.value)
      {
      case "1" :
            linkText = "http://www.usyouthsoccer.org/";
            break;
      case "2" :
            linkText = "http://www.softball.org/";
            break;
      case "3" :
            linkText = "http://www.nays.org/";
            break;
      }
```

5. In the Script pane, type the following line of code after the last line to create the URLRequest object that is used in the navigateToURL function. The URLRequest uses the URL assigned to the linkText variable in the switch statement.

```
//Open Web site using the selected URL
navigateToURL(new URLRequest(linkText), "_blank");
```

6. In the Script pane, type the following lines of code after the last line to change the value displayed in the ComboBox instance after the Web site is opened. Without this statement, the ComboBox instance will display the label of the item selected by the user. The last line closes the function.

```
//Set ComboBox to display the prompt, Web Links
webLinks_mc.selectedIndex = -1;
}
```

7. In the Actions panel, click the **Check syntax** button ✔ to check for syntax errors in the code. The script is checked. If no errors are displayed in the Compiler Errors panel, the script is correct.

Trouble? If your code contains errors, the errors will be listed in the Compiler Errors Panel at the bottom of the screen. Review your script to compare it to the code you modified in the previous steps, make any necessary corrections, and then repeat Step 7 until no errors are encountered.

8. Close the Actions panel, and then save the jsWebSite.fla document.

You will test the links you added to the ComboBox on the Home page by opening the movie in the Flash Player and clicking each link in the ComboBox.

To test the ComboBox instance on the Home page:

1. On the Application bar, click **Control**, point to **Test Movie**, and then click **in Flash Professional**. The Home page appears in the Flash Player window.

2. On the Home page, click the **Web Links** button to display the link selections, and then point to **Softball**. See Figure 9-4.

Figure 9-4   Web links on the Home page

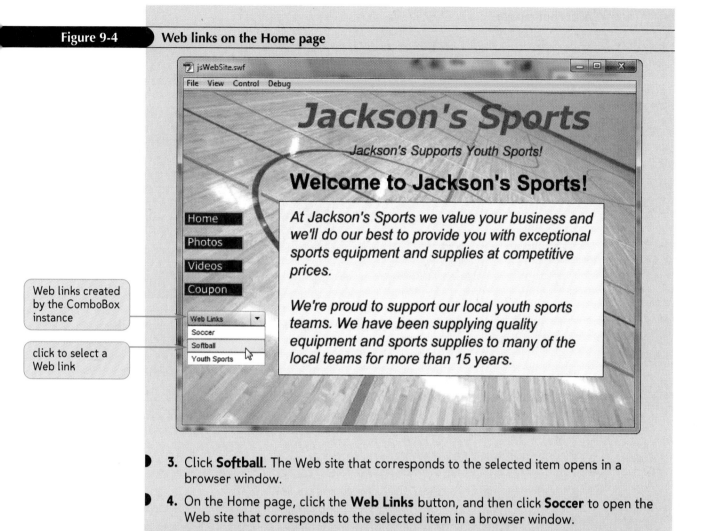

Web links created by the ComboBox instance

click to select a Web link

3. Click **Softball**. The Web site that corresponds to the selected item opens in a browser window.

4. On the Home page, click the **Web Links** button, and then click **Soccer** to open the Web site that corresponds to the selected item in a browser window.

5. On the Home page, click the **Web Links** button, and then click **Youth Sports** to open the Web site that corresponds to the selected item in a browser window.

6. Close the Flash Player window and the browser windows.

Using the UILoader Component to Display Photos

The UILoader component can be used to load content such as images and SWF files to a Web page. The revised Web site created by Aly and Chris contains a Photos page that displays youth sports team photos, as shown in Figure 9-5. You will add an instance of the UILoader component to the page. The youth sports photos can be loaded into an instance of the UILoader component. You will then use the Button component to add buttons that control which pictures are loaded into the UILoader instance.

Figure 9-5   Photos page

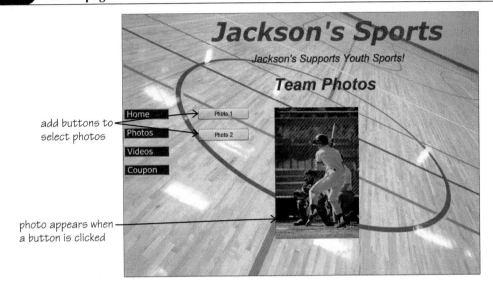

You will add instances of the UILoader and Button components to complete the Photos page.

To add the UILoader and Button components to the Photos page:

1. In the Timeline, select **Frame 20** of the content layer. The Photos page appears on the Stage.

2. Display the rulers, and then click the **Components** button 🔲 in the docked panel group to open the Components panel.

3. Drag an instance of the **UILoader** component from the Components panel to the Stage, and then position the UILoader instance about **180** pixels from the top of the Stage and **300** pixels from the left of the Stage.

4. In the Property inspector, name the instance **loader_mc**, change the width of the instance to **165** pixels, and then change the height to **250** pixels.

5. In the docked panel group, click the **Components** button 🔲 to open the Components panel, and then drag an instance of the **Button** component from the Components panel to the Stage, positioning it about **180** pixels from the top of the Stage and **150** pixels from the left of the Stage.

6. Repeat Step 5 to add another instance of the **Button** component to the Stage, positioning it about **220** pixels from the top of the Stage and **150** pixels from the left of the Stage.

7. Select the first Button instance on the Stage and name the instance **photo1_btn** in the Property inspector, and then repeat to name the second Button instance on the Stage **photo2_btn**.

8. On the Edit bar, change the zoom magnification to **100%** to magnify the view of the buttons.

9. On the Stage, select the **photo1_btn** instance, and then, in the Component Parameters section of the Property inspector, type **Photo 1** in the label box and press the **Enter** key. The Button instance on the Stage changes to reflect the new label.

10. Repeat Step 9 to select the **photo2_btn** instance and change its label to **Photo 2**. The second Button instance on the Stage changes to reflect its new label. See Figure 9-6.

Figure 9-6	UILoader and Button instances

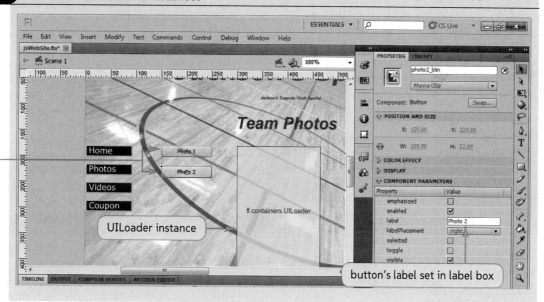

button instances with new labels

UILoader instance

button's label set in label box

The UILoader and Button components are added to the document. To make the component instances operational, you need to add ActionScript code similar to the code you used for the Web links on the Home page. You create a function with the URLRequest object that contains the name of the photo file to be loaded. Then, instead of using the navigateToURL function, you use the load function of the UILoader instance. You also add an event listener to each button instance to listen for the CLICK event and to run the respective function that will load the photo.

To make the UILoader and Button instances operational:

1. In the Timeline, select **Frame 20** of the actions layer, and then open the Actions panel.

2. In the Script pane, type the following lines of code to create the functions that will create a URLRequest object with the photo's filename. The object will then be used in the load method of the UILoader instance, loader_mc, to load the photo.

```
// Function to load the first photo
photo1_btn.addEventListener(MouseEvent.CLICK, loadPhoto1);

function loadPhoto1(event:MouseEvent):void
{
    loader_mc.load(new URLRequest("photo1.jpg"));
}
// Function to load the second photo
photo2_btn.addEventListener(MouseEvent.CLICK, loadPhoto2);
```

```
function loadPhoto2(event:MouseEvent):void
{
    loader_mc.load(new URLRequest("photo2.jpg"));
}
```

3. In the Actions panel, click the **Check syntax** button ✅ to check for syntax errors in the code. The script is checked. If no errors are displayed in the Compiler Errors panel, the script is correct.

   Trouble? If your code contains errors, the errors will be listed in the Compiler Errors Panel at the bottom of the screen. Review your script to compare it to the code you modified in the previous steps, make any necessary corrections, and then repeat Step 3 until no errors are encountered.

4. Close the Actions panel, and then save the document.

5. On the Application bar, click **Control**, point to **Test Movie**, and then click **Flash Professional**. The Home page appears in the Flash Player window.

6. On the Home page, click the **Photos** navigation button to display the Photos page.

7. On the Photos page, click the **Photo 1** button to load the first photo, and then click the **Photo 2** button to load the second photo. Each photo, in turn, is loaded into the UILoader instance and appears on the Stage. See Figure 9-7.

| Figure 9-7 | UILoader instance operational |

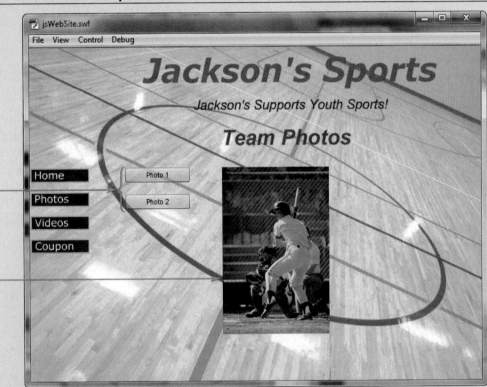

click a button to load a photo into the UILoader instance

photo loaded into the UILoader instance

8. Close the Flash Player window.

Using the ProgressBar Component

The Photos page now displays photos in the UILoader instance each time a photo button is clicked. To improve the user experience with the Photos page, you will add a preloader that provides visual feedback when the photos are loading. This is helpful to someone using a slow Internet connection. To create a preloader that requires only a minimal amount of ActionScript and that shows the progress of the photos loading into the Flash Player, use the ProgressBar component.

The ProgressBar component can work together with the UILoader component to display the progress of loading the photo file into the UILoader instance. As the photo file loads into the UILoader instance, the ProgressBar instance displays an animation that depicts the loading progress. For the ProgressBar to detect the loading of the content, you enter the name of the UILoader instance into the source parameter of the ProgressBar instance. This establishes a connection between the two component instances.

You will add a ProgressBar component to display a preloader animation for the Photos page.

To add an instance of the ProgressBar component to the Stage:

1. Set the zoom magnification to **Fit in Window**, and then, in the Timeline, select **Frame 20** of the content layer.

2. Open the Components panel, and then drag an instance of the **ProgressBar** component from the Components panel to the center of the UILoader instance on the Stage.

> The instance name must be in the source parameter to be associated with the ProgressBar component.

3. In the Property inspector, name the instance **progressBar_mc** and change the height to **10** pixels.

4. In the Component Parameters section of the Property inspector, type **loader_mc** in the source box, and then press the **Enter** key. See Figure 9-8.

| Figure 9-8 | ProgressBar instance added to the Stage |

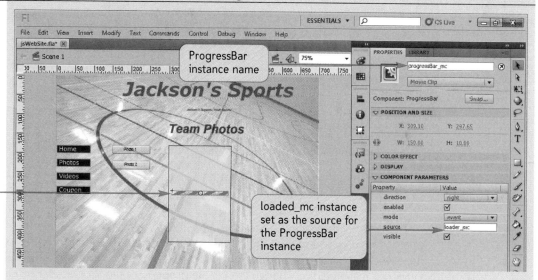

ProgressBar instance added to center of the UILoader instance

ProgressBar instance name

loaded_mc instance set as the source for the ProgressBar instance

The ProgressBar instance will use the contents of the UILoader instance as the source of the content whose progress will be tracked. As the content loads into the loader_mc movie clip, the progressBar_mc instance will display a preloader animation.

5. Save the document, and then test the movie. The Home page appears in the Flash Player window.

6. On the Flash Player menu bar, click **View**, point to **Download Settings**, and then click **DSL (32.6 KB/s)** to select the download speed for the simulation.

7. On the Flash Player menu bar, click **View**, and then click **Simulate Download**. The Home page appears after a few moments.

8. On the Home page, click the **Photos** navigational button to display the Photos page. The ProgressBar instance appears on the Photos page.

9. On the Photos page, click the **Photo 1** button to load the first photo. The ProgressBar instance displays an animation indicating the content is being loaded. When the photo appears, the ProgressBar animation stops but remains visible. See Figure 9-9.

Figure 9-9 ProgressBar instance on the photo

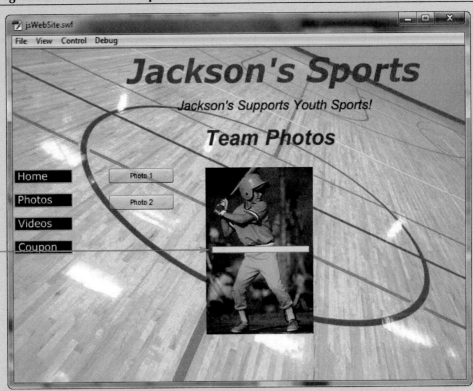

ProgressBar instance remains visible after the photo has loaded

10. Close the Flash Player window.

The ProgressBar instance works as expected; however, it appears before and after a photo is loaded. To hide the ProgressBar instance before a photo is being loaded, you need to change its visible property to false. When a photo is about to be loaded into the UILoader instance, you change the visible property of the ProgressBar instance to true so that it appears. After the photo loading is complete, you change the visible property back to false. You also need to add an event listener that will check for the COMPLETE event of the UILoader instance, which indicates that the loading of the content into the UILoader is complete. When the COMPLETE event is detected, the event listener will run a function to set the visible property of the ProgressBar instance to false so the instance disappears from the Stage.

To add ActionScript code to control the ProgressBar instance:

1. In the Timeline, select **Frame 20** of the actions layer, and then open the Actions panel.

2. In the Script pane, place the insertion point at the beginning of the first line, press the **Enter** key to add a blank line, and then, starting in the blank line, type the following lines of code to hide the progressBar_mc instance when the Photos page is displayed.

```
// Hide the ProgressBar instance
progressBar_mc.visible = false;
```

3. In the Script pane, place the insertion point after the opening curly brace within the loadPhoto1 function, press the **Enter** key to add a blank line, and then, in this blank line, type the following line of code to display the progressBar_mc instance before the first photo is loaded.

```
progressBar_mc.visible = true;
```

4. In the Script pane, place the insertion point after the opening curly brace within the loadPhoto2 function, press the **Enter** key to add a blank line, and then, in this blank line, type the following line of code to display the progressBar_mc instance before the second photo is loaded. See Figure 9-10.

```
progressBar_mc.visible = true;
```

Figure 9-10 Visibility set for the ProgressBar instance

visible property set to false

visible property set to true

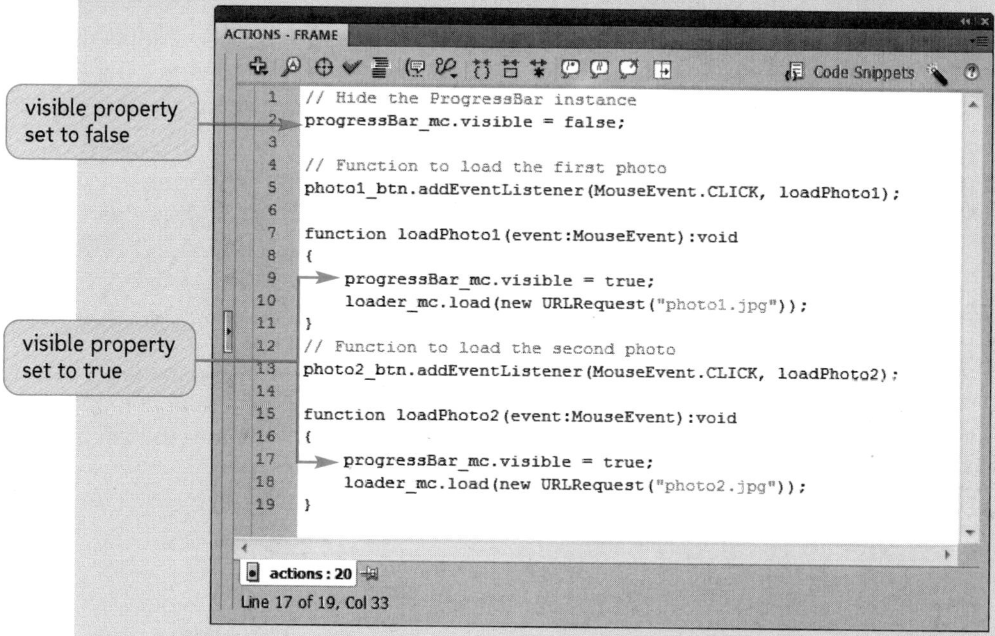

5. In the Script pane, place the insertion point after the closing curly brace of the loadPhoto2 function, press the **Enter** key to add a blank line, and then, starting in this blank line, type the following lines of code to create a function that will hide the progressBar_mc instance when the loading of a photo is completed. The event listener will run the hideBar function when the COMPLETE event occurs for the loader_mc instance.

```
// When the loading is complete, hide the ProgressBar instance
loader_mc.addEventListener(Event.COMPLETE, hideBar);
function hideBar(event:Event)
{
       progressBar_mc.visible = false;
}
```

6. In the Actions panel, click the **Check syntax** button to check for syntax errors in the code. The script is checked. If no errors are displayed in the Compiler Errors panel, the script is correct.

Trouble? If your code contains errors, the errors will be listed in the Compiler Errors Panel at the bottom of the screen. Review your script to compare it to the code you modified in the previous steps, make any necessary corrections, and then repeat Step 6 until no errors are encountered.

7. Close the Actions panel, save the document, and then test the movie. The Home page appears in the Flash Player window.

8. On the Flash Player menu bar, click **View**, and then click **Simulate Download**. The Home page appears after a few moments.

9. On the Home page, click the **Photos** navigational button to display the Photos page, and then click the **Photo 1** button to load the first photo. The ProgressBar animation appears, followed by the photo. The ProgressBar instance disappears after the photo is loaded.

10. Click the **Photo 2** button to load the second photo. The ProgressBar animation appears, followed by the photo. The ProgressBar instance disappears after the photo is loaded.

11. Close the Flash Player window. The Photos page is complete.

In this session, you learned about components and how to use them in Flash documents. You used the ComboBox, Button, UILoader, and ProgressBar components along with ActionScript to add Web links to the Home page and buttons to load photos on the Photos page.

REVIEW

Session 9.1 Quick Check

1. What is a Flash component?
2. What is the purpose of the dataProvider parameter of the ComboBox component?
3. In the ComboBox component, the contents of the _____ parameter appear on the ComboBox instance on the Stage.
4. Which statement is used to exit a block of code in a switch statement?
5. Write the ActionScript code to hide a ProgressBar component instance named progress_mc.
6. For a ProgressBar instance to detect the loading of content into a UILoader instance, you enter the name of the UILoader instance into the _____ parameter of the ProgressBar instance.

SESSION 9.2 VISUAL OVERVIEW

The Adobe Media Encoder export settings dialog box provides a preview of the source video file and of the video file that will be exported.

Export settings including the preset settings can be changed in this section.

The Video tab includes options such as video frame size and information such as the codec used to encode the video.

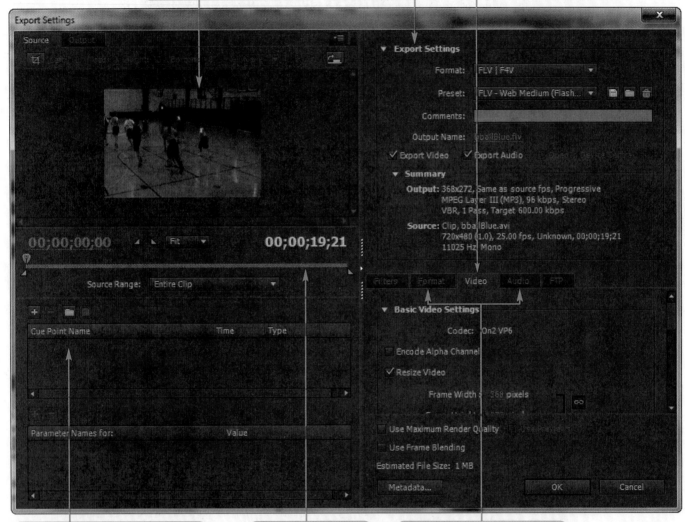

Cue points are markers you set in the video to synchronize the video with animation, graphics, or text in the Flash document.

You can select how much of the video clip will be exported.

Other tabs enable the user to change the file format and the audio settings.

DIGITAL VIDEO

The FLVPlayback component is used to play the video when the video file is loaded externally during playback.

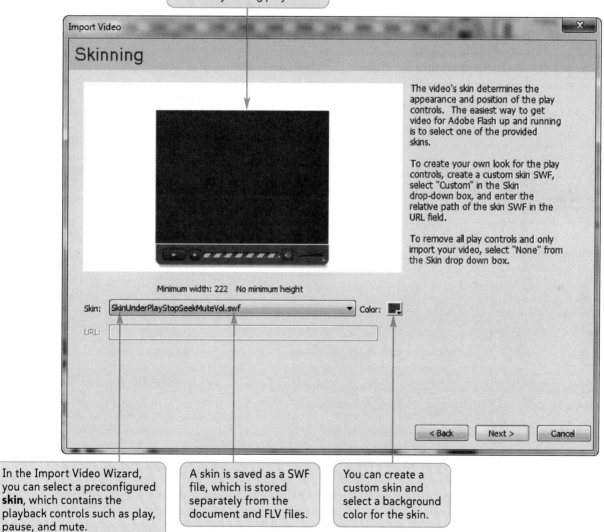

Import Video

Skinning

The video's skin determines the appearance and position of the play controls. The easiest way to get video for Adobe Flash up and running is to select one of the provided skins.

To create your own look for the play controls, create a custom skin SWF, select "Custom" in the Skin drop-down box, and enter the relative path of the skin SWF in the URL field.

To remove all play controls and only import your video, select "None" from the Skin drop down box.

Minimum width: 222   No minimum height

Skin: SkinUnderPlayStopSeekMuteVol.swf   ▼   Color:

URL:

< Back   Next >   Cancel

In the Import Video Wizard, you can select a preconfigured **skin**, which contains the playback controls such as play, pause, and mute.

A skin is saved as a SWF file, which is stored separately from the document and FLV files.

You can create a custom skin and select a background color for the skin.

Adding Video to a Flash Document

So far, the Flash documents you have created include a variety of multimedia elements, such as graphics, bitmaps, and sounds. You can also add video to Flash documents to make them more visually appealing and exciting. Before you work with video in Flash, you should understand some basic terminology and concepts about how video is prepared and in what format video can be imported into Flash. You need to consider the frame size, frame rate, and file size of video files. You also need to understand that using video on your Flash Web site can significantly increase a site's overall download time.

Selecting the Frame Rate and Frame Size

A video's **frame rate**, which is similar to the frame rate of a document in Flash, represents how many frames play each second. Video frame rates vary, depending on where the video is played. For example, video played on television in many countries plays at 29.97 frames per second, whereas video on film plays at 24 frames per second. Video played on the Web, however, often plays at lower frame rates, such as 12 to 18 frames per second. Frame rate also affects the size of the file. The higher the frame rate, the larger the file size of the video. For example, a 10-second video clip formatted at 30 frames per second contains 300 frames. The same 10-second video clip formatted at 12 frames per second contains 120 frames. Of course, a higher frame rate means better video quality.

PROSKILLS

Decision Making: Deciding on a Video's Frame Rate

Deciding on the frame rate to use is a balance between the quality of the video and the size of the file. Lowering the frame rate lowers the quality of the video but decreases the video's file size. Keep in mind the following factors when deciding the appropriate frame rate to select for a video:

- **Content.** Video with a minimal movement, such as someone talking in front of the camera, can be played on the Web at rates of 10 or fewer frames per second. Video with more movement, such as children playing a sport, is best played at a higher frame rate, such as 15 frames per second.
- **Internet connection of target users.** High frame rates do not play well with a dial-up connection because the connection speed cannot download the frames fast enough to play smoothly on the client computer. A faster broadband connection can better handle higher frame rates.
- **Client computer.** A slow computer with minimal capabilities might not be able to support videos with high frame rates.

Choosing an appropriate frame rate ensures a positive experience for all users.

When editing video clips and preparing them for use in Flash, you should also determine what frame size to use. The **frame size** refers to a video's width and height dimensions. You can decide the frame size by considering the type of Internet access that target users will have and the length of the video. If you are targeting users with dial-up connections, limit the frame size of videos to a smaller size, such as 164 pixels wide by 120 pixels high. If the majority of the target users have faster connections, you can set the video's frame size to higher dimensions, such as 360 pixels wide by 264 pixels high or even 640 pixels wide by 480 pixels high.

Using a High-Quality Video Source File

The quality of the source, or original, file is critical to consider when using video in Flash. The better the quality of the source file, the better the result when the video is imported into Flash. You should start with a high-quality video file before importing the video into Flash.

You can use a digital camcorder to record video and then transfer the video from the camcorder's media to the computer. You can also connect the camcorder to a computer and record video directly to the computer. Another method is to convert video from an analog format into a digital format that you can store on a computer. However, whenever possible, it is best to use a digital source file. Converting from analog to digital can produce lower-quality video compared to video that is captured in a digital format.

Regardless of the video source, you should edit the video using a video-editing program such as Adobe Premiere after it is transferred to the computer but before it is imported into Flash. Although Flash provides some editing options when video is imported, the options are limited. A video-editing program allows you to trim unwanted parts of the video or select part of the video, depending on how you plan to use it. You can also change other attributes of the video, such as its frame rate and frame size.

Using Compression and Decompression

Another factor affecting the use of video over the Web is the size of the video file. The amount of data required to represent a few seconds of video can make downloading the video over the Internet a slow process. As a result, compression, which removes redundant data, can be used to reduce the size of the video file. You can specify how much to compress a video when you edit it using a video-editing program or by using an encoder program that uses compression, also known as a **compressor**. Before the compressed video can be played, it needs to be decompressed with a decoder program that uses decompression, also known as a **decompressor**.

A video coder/decoder program is called a **codec**. Various codecs are available to work with video. The codecs used by Flash are On2 VP6, Sorenson Spark, and H.264. These codecs compress the video, and the Flash Player contains the corresponding decompressor to decompress the video for playback. By default, Flash uses the On2 VP6 codec when you publish video content to Flash Player 8 or higher. The H.264 codec, introduced with Flash Player 9, produces higher-quality video with smaller file sizes but requires that you publish the video to Flash Player 9 or higher. If you publish video content to Flash Player 6 or 7, Flash uses the Sorenson Spark codec. Videos published for older versions of the Flash Player will also run on more recent versions of the plug-in, but those published for Flash Player 8 or higher will not work on earlier versions. Because Flash uses codecs that compress video, it is best to avoid compressing the video before bringing it into Flash.

Using Adobe Media Encoder

After video is captured and prepared using a video-editing program, preparing the video for Flash requires two basic steps. First, convert the video to one of the Flash video file formats: FLV or F4V for videos encoded using the H.264 codec. Second, import the video file into a Flash document. To convert the video into a Flash video file format, you can use **Adobe Media Encoder**, an encoder program installed with Flash. Adobe Media Encoder is a separate program that accepts several video file formats, including .mpg, .avi, and .dv. Other formats such as .mov can also be used if your computer has the QuickTime plug-in installed. When you bring a video file into Adobe Media Encoder, you select options for how you want the video to be encoded, and then you encode the video to produce a file in the FLV or F4V format.

Aly prepared two short video clips of local youth sports to add to the Video page, as requested by Dan. You will use the Adobe Media Encoder to encode and convert the videos into the FLV format.

To encode the sports video clips using the Adobe Media Encoder:

1. If you took a break after the previous session, make sure the jsWebSite.fla document is open, the workspace is reset to the Essentials layout, and the Stage magnification is set to Fit in Window.

2. Click the **Start** button on the taskbar, click **All Programs**, and then click **Adobe Media Encoder CS5**. The Adobe Media Encoder program window opens.

TIP

You can also drag files from the storage location and drop them into the queue.

3. Click the **Add** button, navigate to the **Flash9\Tutorial** folder included with your Data Files, click **bballBlue.avi**, press and hold the **Ctrl** key, click **bballRed.avi** to select both files at the same time, release the **Ctrl** key, and then click the **Open** button to add the selected video files to the queue.

   Trouble? If the encoding process starts automatically, click the Pause button, and then continue with Step 4.

4. Make sure both files are selected in the queue, and then in the Preset column, click the **arrow** button ▼ for the bballBlue.avi file to open a list of presets. See Figure 9-11.

Figure 9-11   Select a preset format in Adobe Media Encoder

click the Preset arrow button to display file formatting options

video files in the queue ready to be encoded

select a preset option for the video files

message that files in the queue will start encoding automatically

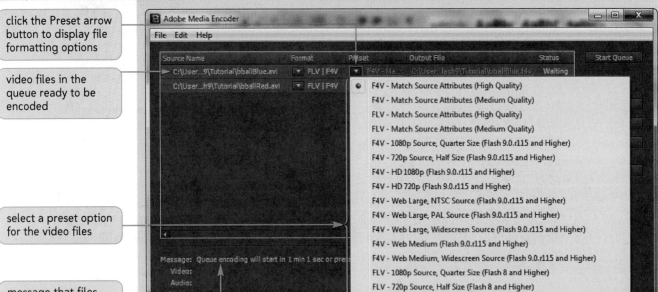

5. Click **FLV - Web Medium (Flash 8 and Higher)**. The selected preset is set for both files and listed in the Preset column.

6. Click the **Settings** button. The Export Settings dialog box opens.

   Trouble? If a dialog box opens to confirm that you are about to edit multiple selected files, click the OK button.

Export settings can be used to modify the way the video will be encoded. You can change the format of the output video to FLV or F4V, change the video's frame rate, change the way the audio is formatted, crop and resize the video clip, as well as add cue points.

To modify export settings in the Adobe Media Encoder:

1. In the Export Settings dialog box, click the **Video** tab, scroll down within the Video panel, and then click the **Frame Rate [fps]** button. See Figure 9-12.

Figure 9-12   Frame rate options

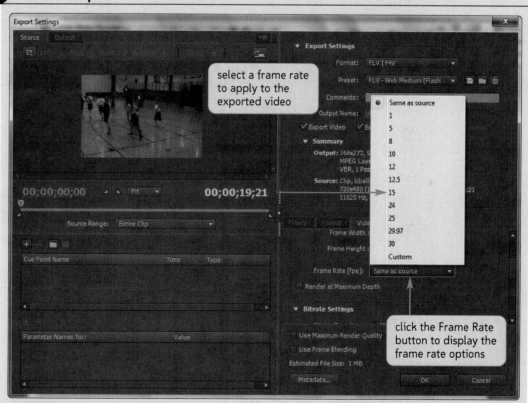

2. On the Frame Rate list, click **15**. The output video file's frame rate is reduced to 15 frames per second.

3. In the Export Settings dialog box, click the **Audio** tab, and then click the **Mono** option button in the Output Channels section. Mono creates a smaller output file than Stereo.

   Trouble? If no codec is listed in the Audio tab under Basic Audio Settings, ask your instructor or technical support person for help. A codec is needed to ensure proper encoding of the audio.

4. Click the **OK** button to close the Export Settings dialog box.

5. Click the **Start Queue** button to start the encoding process for both video files. The encoding process starts for the first file. The encoding progress is displayed at the bottom of the program window. See Figure 9-13.

Figure 9-13   Video files being encoded

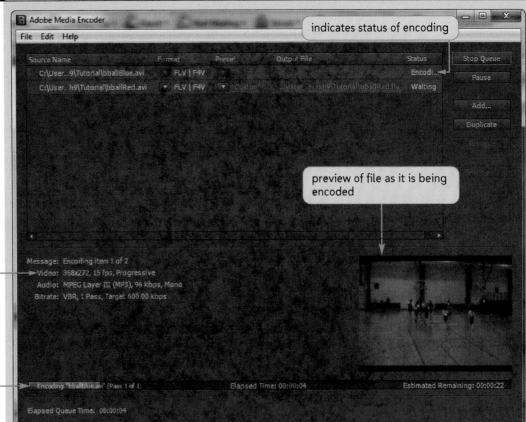

6. After both files have finished encoding, close Adobe Media Encoder. The bballBlue.flv and bballRed.flv files are stored in the Flash9\Tutorial folder included with your Data Files, ready to be imported into your Flash document.

TIP

You can press the Ctrl+Q keys to exit Adobe Media Encoder.

Each converted file is placed in the same location as the original file unless you specify a different location by clicking the file's path link in the Output File column. The encoding process can be time consuming, depending on the size of the video files and the capabilities of the computer. If you have multiple files to encode, you can encode all the files in a batch mode by adding them to the queue, setting the export settings for each file, and then starting the encode process. Adobe Media Encoder encodes each file in turn until all the files in the queue are converted.

Delivering Video

For video to be available as part of a Web site, it must be uploaded to a Web server, just like the site's Web pages and SWF files. When you import video into Flash, you need to know the type of Web server to which the video will be uploaded and how the video will be delivered to a client computer. You can deliver video using Flash in three ways: stream the video using Adobe Flash Media Server, progressively download the video from a Web server, or embed the video in a Flash document.

Video streaming requires that the video file be uploaded to a Web server running **Adobe Flash Media Server**, the server software that provides Web developers features to add interactive audio and video to Web sites. With video streaming, only the part of the video file to be viewed, not the entire video file, is downloaded to the user's computer. This also enables the user to select any part of the video to view without having to wait for the entire video to be downloaded.

Progressive downloading downloads the entire video file, which is stored on a Web server, to the user's computer for viewing. This method is best for shorter videos that are accessed infrequently or by only a few users at the same time. With video streaming and progressive downloading, the video file is saved separately from the Flash SWF file you create to play the video. This makes it easier to change video content without having to change or republish the SWF file.

Embedded video places the entire video in the Flash document, similar to the way that bitmaps are imported and become part of the document. When you publish the Flash file, the video is published as part of the SWF file and can significantly increase the size of the published file. Embedding video is recommended only when you are targeting site visitors with slow Internet connections or visitors using older versions of the Flash Player, or when the video clip is fewer than 10 seconds in length. Embedded video must be in the FLV format, not in the F4V format.

Using the Import Video Wizard

After you convert videos into the FLV or F4V format using Adobe Media Encoder, you can use the Import Video wizard in Flash to embed or link the video in the Flash document. The Import Video wizard presents a series of dialog boxes that guide you through the import process. You first select the video file, and then you choose if the video is to be loaded externally during playback, or if it will be embedded in the Flash document. If the video is to be loaded externally during playback using video streaming or progressive downloading, Flash creates an instance of the FLVPlayback component on the Stage that serves as the video player. If you are using embedding, the video can be embedded directly on the Stage or within a movie clip symbol. By default, the Timeline expands to match the number of frames in the video.

You will use the Import Video wizard to create an instance of the FLVPlayback component, which will serve as the video player for the sports video clips in the Jackson's Youth Sports Web site. You will then modify the FLVPlayback parameters and add two Button components to enable playing the two video clips in the same player, as shown in Figure 9-14. Finally, you will add the necessary ActionScript code to make the buttons operational.

Figure 9-14   Videos page

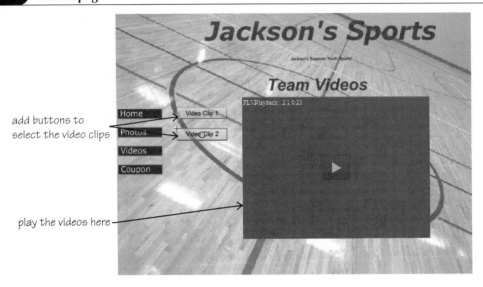

add buttons to
select the video clips

play the videos here

You'll start by adding the bballBlue.flv video to the Videos page.

To import the bballBlue.flv video clip using the Import Video wizard:

1. In the Timeline, select **Frame 30** of the content layer. The Videos page content starts in this frame.

2. On the Application bar, click **File**, point to **Import**, and then click **Import Video** to start the Import Video wizard. The Select Video dialog box opens, prompting you to specify the location of the video file to be imported, which is on your computer or on a Web server. In this case, the video file is located on your computer.

3. Click the **Browse** button, navigate to the **Flash9\Tutorial** folder included with your Data Files, and then double-click **bballBlue.flv**. The video file is selected.

4. Click the **Load external video with playback component** option button, if necessary, to select it. See Figure 9-15.

Be sure to select the FLV file, which you previously encoded with the Adobe Media Encoder, and not the AVI file.

| Figure 9-15 | Select Video dialog box in the Import Video wizard |

FLV video file
selected to import

option to load
playback component

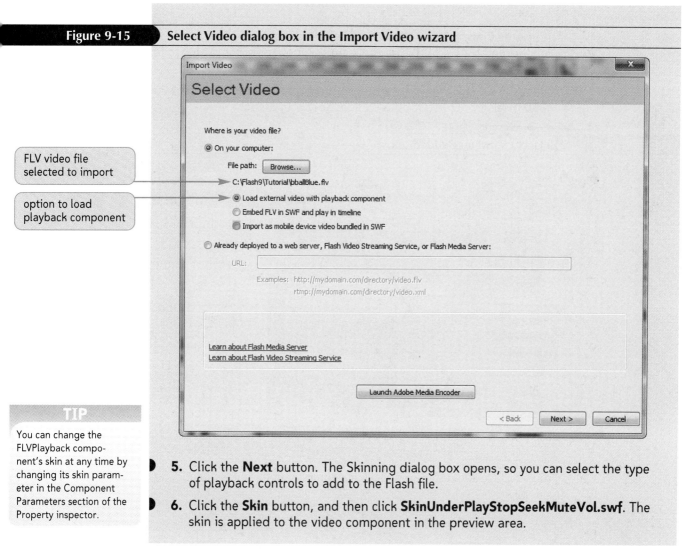

5. Click the **Next** button. The Skinning dialog box opens, so you can select the type of playback controls to add to the Flash file.

6. Click the **Skin** button, and then click **SkinUnderPlayStopSeekMuteVol.swf**. The skin is applied to the video component in the preview area.

After you select a skin, the final dialog box in the wizard shows a summary of your selections and indicates what will be done when you click the Finish button. When you use progressive download or video streaming, an FLV file is created and an instance of the FLVPlayback component with the selected playback controls is added to the Stage. The FLVPlayback component provides the display area in which the video is viewed.

To complete the import process for the bballBlue.flv video clip:

1. Click the **Next** button. The Finish Video Import dialog box displays a summary of the import process, including the location of the bballBlue.flv file.

2. Click the **After importing video, view video topics in Flash Help** check box, if necessary, to remove the check mark.

3. Click the **Finish** button. A Getting metadata dialog box opens, showing the importing progress of the video. When the process is complete, an instance of the FLVPlayback component is placed on the Stage.

4. Reposition the FLVPlayback instance to **160** pixels from the top of the Stage and **250** pixels from the left of the Stage. See Figure 9-16.

Figure 9-16   **FLVPlayback instance added to the Stage**

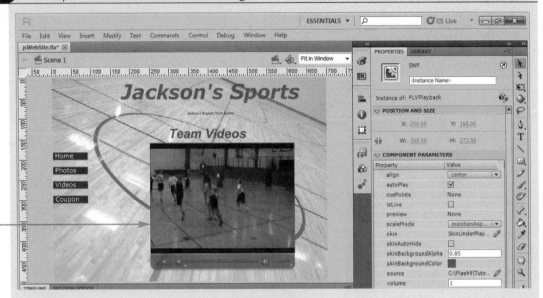

FLVPlayback instance

You will save and test the FLVPlayback component instance you added to the Videos page.

To test the FLVPlayback component instance on the Videos page:

1. Save the jsWebSite.fla document, and then test the movie. The Home page opens in the Flash Player window.

2. In the Flash Player window, click the **Videos** button to advance to the Videos page. The Videos page appears and the video clip starts to play.

3. After the video stops playing, on the video controls click the **Play/Pause** button to play the video again, and then click the **Play/Pause** button to pause the video. As the video plays, the small triangle under the seek bar moves to indicate the progress of the video. See Figure 9-17.

Figure 9-17   Video playing on the Videos page

Play/Pause button controls the playing of the video

seek bar shows the video's progress as it plays

▶ **4.** Close the Flash Player window to return to the Flash document.

The Videos page displays the bballBlue.flv video clip and includes controls to play, pause, and mute the video. To enable the FLVPlayback component to also play the bballRed.flv video, you will add two buttons and ActionScript code so that when each button is clicked, a different video plays, enabling users to choose between the two videos. Because the video you added to the page uses the FLVPlayback component, you can modify the component's parameters so that the video played is determined by ActionScript.

To modify the FLVPlayback's parameters:

▶ **1.** On the Stage, select the **FLVPlayback** instance, if necessary, and then, in the Component Parameters section of the Property inspector, click the **Edit** button 🖉 for the skin parameter. The Select Skin dialog box opens.

▶ **2.** Click the **Skin** button, and then click **None** to remove the skin from the FLVPlayback instance. See Figure 9-18.

Figure 9-18   Changing the skin selection

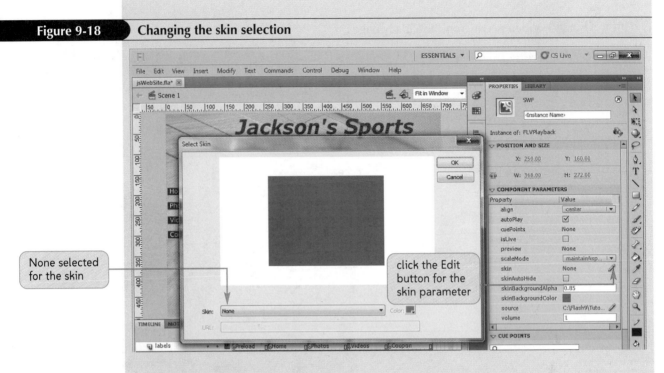

None selected for the skin

click the Edit button for the skin parameter

▶ **3.** Click the **OK** button. The dialog box closes, and the skin with the player controls is removed from the Stage.

▶ **4.** In the Component Parameters section of the Property inspector, click the **Edit** button 🖉 for the source parameter. The Content Path dialog box opens, and the bballBlue.flv filename is selected. See Figure 9-19.

Figure 9-19   Content Path dialog box

delete the filename

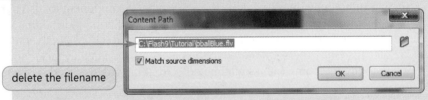

▶ **5.** Press the **Delete** key to delete the filename and path, and then click the **OK** button. The source file is removed.

▶ **6.** In the Property inspector, name the FLVPlayback instance **videoPlayer**. The name assigned to the FLVPlayback instance can be referenced with ActionScript.

Because you previously added an instance of the Button component to the document, the Button component is already in the document's library. You can add instances of the same Button component by dragging them from the Library panel.

To add Button instances to the Videos page:

▶ **1.** In the Timeline, insert a keyframe at **Frame 30** of the buttons layer, and then unlock the layer. You will add Button instances in this frame.

2. Drag an instance of the **Button** component from the Library panel to the Stage, and then position the instance approximately **180** pixels from the top of the Stage and **120** pixels from the left of the Stage.

3. On the Stage, select the **Button** instance, if necessary, and then, in the Property inspector, name the instance **videoButton1_btn**.

4. In the Component Parameters section of the Property inspector, type **Video Clip 1** in the label box and then press the **Enter** key. The videoButton1_btn instance on the Stage is relabeled as Video Clip 1.

5. Repeat Steps 2 through 4 to create a second Button instance approximately **220** pixels from the top of the Stage and **120** pixels from the left of the Stage with the instance name **videoButton2_btn** and the label **Video Clip 2**. The videoButton2_btn instance on the Stage is relabeled as Video Clip 2. See Figure 9-20.

Figure 9-20 ▶ **Buttons and video player in the Flash Player**

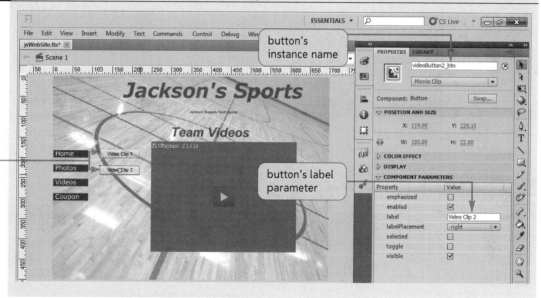

Next, you will add the ActionScript code that controls the loading of the video clips into the FLVPlayback component. The code will include two functions, one for each video. Each function will assign the name of the video clip to the source parameter of the FLVPlayback instance, and it will assign SkinUnderPlaySeekMute.swf to the skin parameter. Event listeners will be added so that when a button is clicked, the associated function will run.

You will add ActionScript code to make the video clip buttons operational on the Videos page.

To add ActionScript code to play the two videos on the Videos page:

1. In the Timeline, select **Frame 30** of the actions layer, and then open the **Actions** panel.

2. In the Script pane, type the following lines of code to define the functions that load a video clip file and a skin into the FLVPlayback instance.

```
// Functions to add video clips and skin to FLVPlayback component
videoButton1_btn.addEventListener(MouseEvent.CLICK, playVideo1);
function playVideo1(event:MouseEvent):void
{
     videoPlayer.source = "bballBlue.flv";
     videoPlayer.skin = "SkinUnderPlayStopSeekMuteVol.swf";
}
videoButton2_btn.addEventListener(MouseEvent.CLICK, playVideo2);
function playVideo2(event:MouseEvent):void
{
     videoPlayer.source = "bballRed.flv";
     videoPlayer.skin = "SkinUnderPlayStopSeekMuteVol.swf";
}
```

3. In the Actions panel, click the **Check syntax** button ☑ to check for syntax errors in the code. The script is checked. If no errors are displayed in the Compiler Errors panel, the script is correct.

   Trouble? If your code contains errors, the errors will be listed in the Compiler Errors Panel at the bottom of the screen. Review your script to compare it to the code you modified in the previous steps, make any necessary corrections, and then repeat Step 3 until no errors are encountered.

4. Close the Actions panel, save the document, and then test the movie. The Home page opens in the Flash Player.

5. On the Home page, click the **Videos** button to advance to the Videos page, and then click the **Video Clip 1** button to play the first video clip. The video plays in the FLVPlayback instance, and the video controls appear under the video. See Figure 9-21.

Figure 9-21   Buttons and video player in the Flash Player

click a button to play a video

video plays in the FLVPlayback instance

video controls appear under the video

▶ **6.** Click the **Video Clip 2** button to play the second video.

▶ **7.** Close the Flash Player window to return to the Flash document. The Videos page is complete, and the Web site can showcase video clips of youth sports teams.

In this session, you learned basic concepts involved in using video and importing it into Flash. You reviewed the video formats you can use with Flash and different types of compression techniques. You encoded videos using the Adobe Media Encoder, and then you imported a video file using the Video Import wizard in Flash. Finally, you modified the parameters of the FLVPlayback component and added ActionScript code to play two videos. In the next session, you will prepare content for printing and for displaying on mobile devices.

REVIEW

Session 9.2 Quick Check

1. List three video formats that can be imported into a Flash document.
2. Why is it important to compress video files?
3. _____ video places the video in the Flash document, similar to the way that bitmaps are imported and become part of the document.
4. What is a codec?
5. Which codecs are used by Flash?
6. _____ are markers you can set in the video to synchronize the video with animation, graphics, or text in the document.
7. Which option in the Import Video wizard creates an instance of the FLVPlayback component on the Stage?

SESSION 9.3 VISUAL OVERVIEW

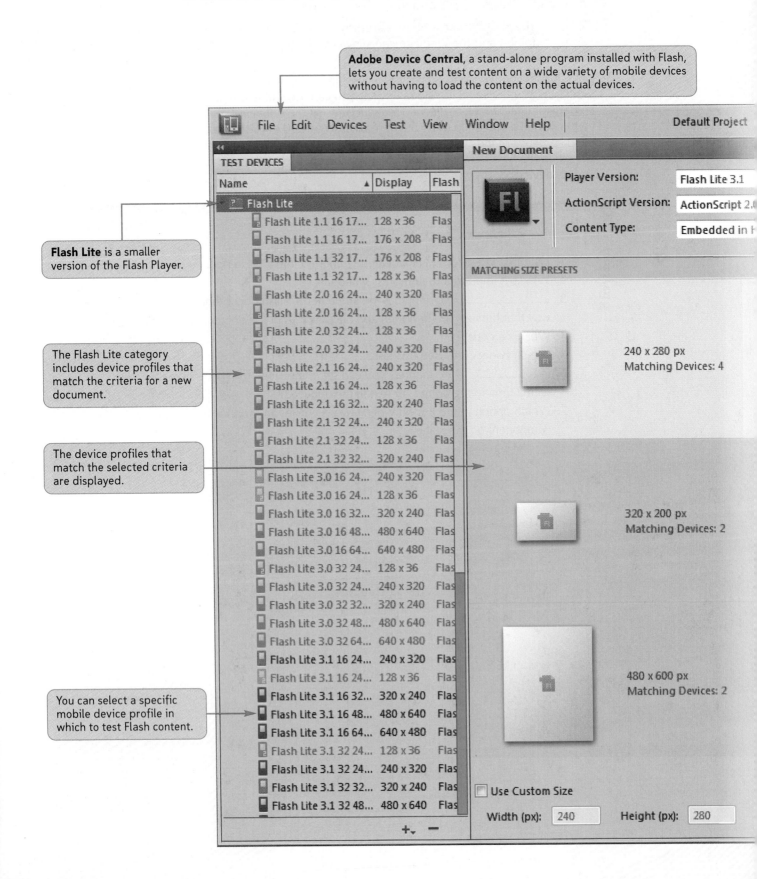

Adobe Device Central, a stand-alone program installed with Flash, lets you create and test content on a wide variety of mobile devices without having to load the content on the actual devices.

Flash Lite is a smaller version of the Flash Player.

The Flash Lite category includes device profiles that match the criteria for a new document.

The device profiles that match the selected criteria are displayed.

You can select a specific mobile device profile in which to test Flash content.

MOBILE CONTENT

The Emulate option is used to test Flash content on a targeted mobile device.

The Browse option is used to view available device profiles located on the computer's storage and online.

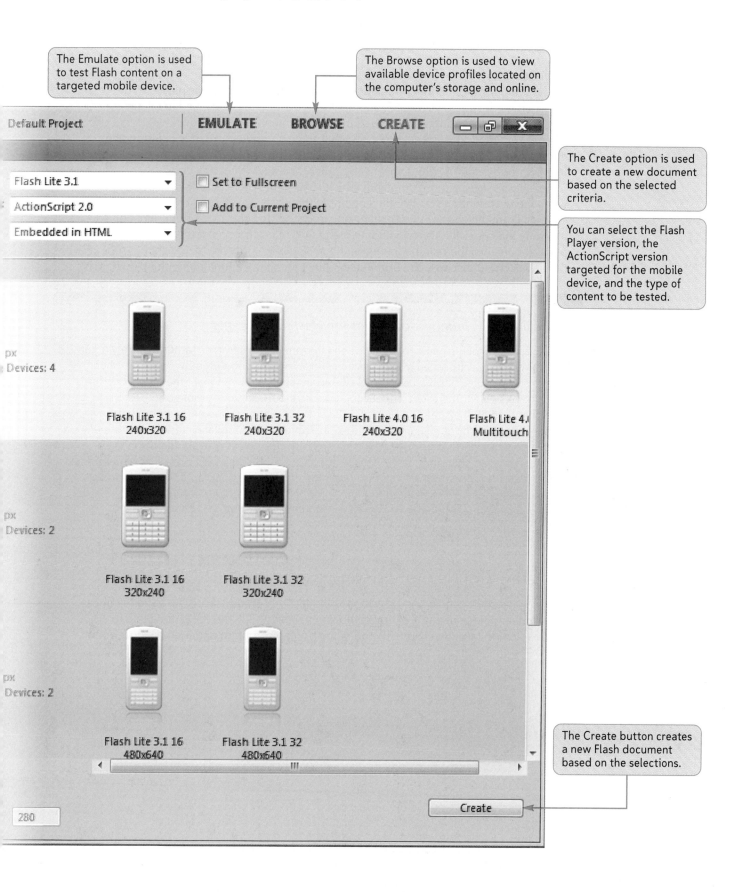

Default Project   EMULATE   BROWSE   CREATE

The Create option is used to create a new document based on the selected criteria.

Flash Lite 3.1

ActionScript 2.0

Embedded in HTML

☐ Set to Fullscreen

☐ Add to Current Project

You can select the Flash Player version, the ActionScript version targeted for the mobile device, and the type of content to be tested.

px
Devices: 4

Flash Lite 3.1 16
240x320

Flash Lite 3.1 32
240x320

Flash Lite 4.0 16
240x320

Flash Lite 4.0
Multitouch

px
Devices: 2

Flash Lite 3.1 16
320x240

Flash Lite 3.1 32
320x240

px
Devices: 2

Flash Lite 3.1 16
480x640

Flash Lite 3.1 32
480x640

The Create button creates a new Flash document based on the selections.

280

Create

Creating Printable Content

The graphics and animations created with Flash are meant to be displayed on computer screens and are usually not designed to be printed on paper. However, users can print the content of a Flash Web site using the Print command in the Web browser or the Flash Player. The Print command in the Flash Player can be disabled when the document is published.

The Web browser's Print command sends the content currently displayed in the Web page to the printer. However, if the content of the SWF file is designed to occupy most of the width of the computer screen, part of the content might be truncated, or cut off, when it is printed. This is because the layout of the computer screen is in **landscape orientation**, which means it is wider than it is tall. The printed page, however, is usually in **portrait orientation**, which means it is taller than it is wide.

The Flash Player's Print command, which is available on the context menu that opens when the user right-clicks SWF file content in the Flash Player, provides several printing options. From the context menu, the user can choose to print the current selection so that only the currently displayed frame of the SWF file is printed. If the user chooses to print all contents, then all the frames of the SWF file are printed. This might not produce the desired result because the SWF file can contain a long animation with many frames.

INSIGHT

Designing Printing Capabilities for Flash Documents

A Flash document should include options to print specific frames rather than relying on the Web browser or the Flash Player to control the printing of the SWF file. You should provide buttons that the user can click to print specific elements of the Web site. This helps to prevent the user from becoming frustrated with undesirable print results. Depending on the site requirements, you should design certain parts of the Web site specifically for printing. For example, a store might want to place a map of the store's location on the Web site. The map can be designed to print on a standard sheet of paper. Or, a restaurant might want to include a coupon on its Web site that the user can print and redeem at the restaurant. Also, you can link to documents that are saved as Adobe Acrobat PDF files that are already formatted for printing. In any case, if a Flash document contains elements that a user might want to print, be sure to design the printing capabilities into the document.

Creating Content for Printing

Dan requested that a coupon be added to the Jackson's Youth Sports Web site that a user can print and redeem at the store, as shown in Figure 9-22. The coupon will be for 15% off any item in the store. You will modify the printable coupon and then create a button to control the printing of the coupon.

Figure 9-22   Coupon page

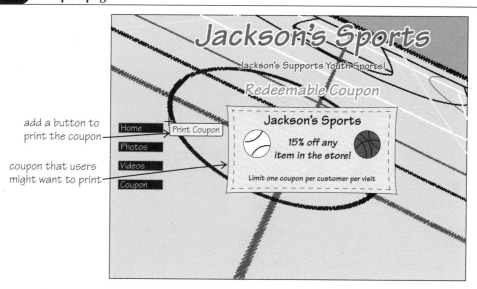

add a button to print the coupon

coupon that users might want to print

Aly has created the coupon as a movie clip with content and a yellow background. However, when the user prints the coupon, you don't want the background to print. You will modify the coupon by adding a second frame to the coupon movie clip that will contain the contents of the coupon but not the background rectangle. The second frame will contain the content to print.

To modify the Coupon movie clip:

1. If you took a break after the previous session, make sure the jsWebSite.fla document is open, the workspace is reset to the Essentials layout, and the Stage magnification is set to Fit in Window.

2. Open the **Coupon** symbol in symbol-editing mode.

3. In the Timeline, select **Frame 2** of the content layer, and then insert a regular frame. The text and graphics appear in Frame 2, but the background rectangle does not.

4. In the Timeline, insert a new layer, name it **action**, and then, in the action layer, select **Frame 1**.

5. Open the **Actions** panel, and then type the following line in the Script pane to add a stop() action to the first frame that keeps the playhead from advancing to the second frame.

   ```
   stop();
   ```

6. Close the Actions panel, and then exit symbol-editing mode.

The coupon is complete. You are ready to add an instance of the coupon to the Coupon page. You will also add an instance of the Button component that will be used to control the printing of the coupon.

To create instances of the Coupon and Button symbols:

▶ 1. In the Timeline, insert a keyframe at **Frame 40** on the buttons layer. The navigation and video buttons are copied to this frame.

▶ 2. Delete the **Video Clip 2** button instance. You will change the properties of the first video button in a later step.

▶ 3. In the Timeline, select **Frame 40** of the content layer, and then drag an instance of the **Coupon** symbol from the Library panel to the Stage.

▶ 4. Reposition the instance about **250** pixels from the left of the Stage and **180** pixels from the top of the Stage. The Coupon instance is in the correct position on the Coupon page.

▶ 5. In the Property inspector, name the Coupon instance **coupon_mc**.

▶ 6. On the Stage, select the **Video Clip 1** button, and then, in the Property inspector, change the name of the instance to **printCoupon_btn**. The video button on the Videos page has a different instance name than the button on the Coupon page.

▶ 7. In the Component Parameters section of the Property inspector, type **Print Coupon** in the label box. The Button instance is named and labeled. See Figure 9-23.

Figure 9-23	Coupon and button in Coupons page

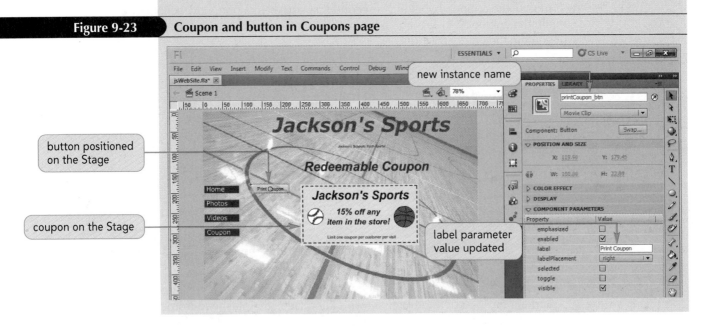

Using the PrintJob Class to Control Printing

The Coupon page contains the coupon and button. Next, you need to add the ActionScript so that when the Print Coupon button is clicked, the coupon prints. The Flash Player can communicate with a computer's operating system's printing interface so that pages can be passed to the print spooler. The **print spooler** manages the print jobs that are sent to the printer by the various programs running on the computer. To control printing within the Flash Player, you use the ActionScript PrintJob class and follow these steps in sequence:

1. Create an instance of the PrintJob class.
2. Initiate the printing process.
3. Add pages to the print job.
4. Send the pages to the operating system's printer.

You will create a function for the coupon that will create an instance of the PrintJob class using the new operator, start the print process using the `start()` method, add a page to the print job using the `addPage()` method, and then send the print job to the computer's operating system using the `send()` method. You should also include code to prevent an error from being generated by the Flash Player if the user cancels the printing process. You can use an `if()` statement that checks if the printing process has been initiated. If the printing process has been initiated, the steps to print the coupon run. Otherwise, the steps do not run.

To add ActionScript code to print the coupon:

1. In the Timeline, select **Frame 40** of the actions layer, and then open the Actions panel.

2. In the Script pane, type the following lines of code to define the function that will print a coupon. The var statement defines a variable named myPrintJob of type PrintJob and assigns the variable an instance of the PrintJob class using the new operator. The `start()` method is then called for the myPrintJob instance. If the `start()` method is successful, the `addPage()` method adds the movie clip contents to the print job and the `send()` method sends the print job to the operating system.

TIP
You can click the Apply line comment button in the Actions panel to add the // comment characters to the Script pane.

```
// Print the coupon when the Print Coupon button is clicked
printCoupon_btn.addEventListener(MouseEvent.CLICK, printCoupon);
function printCoupon(event:MouseEvent):void
{
    var myPrintJob:PrintJob = new PrintJob();
    if (myPrintJob.start())
    {
        myPrintJob.addPage(coupon_mc);
        myPrintJob.send();
    }
}
```

3. In the Actions panel, click the **Check syntax** button ✔ to check for syntax errors in the code. The script is checked. If no errors are displayed in the Compiler Errors panel, the script is correct.

   Trouble? If your code contains errors, the errors will be listed in the Compiler Errors Panel at the bottom of the screen. Review your script to compare it to the code you modified in the previous steps, make any necessary corrections, and then repeat Step 3 until no errors are encountered.

4. Close the Actions panel, save the jsWebSite.fla document, and then test the movie. The Home page appears in the Flash Player.

5. On the Home page, click the **Coupon** button to advance to the Coupon page, and then click the **Print Coupon** button to print the coupon. The operating system's print dialog box opens.

6. Select the appropriate printer, and then click the **Print** button if you are instructed to print the coupon; otherwise, click the **Cancel** button.

7. Close the Flash Player window to return to the Flash document.

The first frame of the coupon movie clip printed. You want only the second frame to print because it contains the coupon without the filled rectangle as a background. To print the second frame of the movie clip, you need to specify the frame number as a parameter in the `addPage()` method. You can include three optional parameters in the `addPage()` method in addition to the name of the movie clip to print. The first optional parameter specifies the area to print, which can be defined by specifying rectangular coordinates. The second optional parameter specifies whether the content prints as a vector or a bitmap. By default, the content is printed as a vector. If the content to print includes a bitmap, you can set this parameter to {printAsBitmap:true}. The third optional parameter is a number that specifies which frame to print. If you want to use this optional parameter without specifying the two other optional parameters, you need to use null as the middle parameters. The method to print the second frame of the coupon_mc movie clip is:

```
myPrintJob.addPage(coupon_mc, null, null, 2);
```

You will add the parameters to the addPage() method for the coupon.

To add the parameters to the addPage() method:

1. Open the **Actions** panel, and then, in the Script pane, revise the addPage() method on line 8 to include the additional parameters.

```
myPrintJob.addPage(coupon_mc, null, null, 2);
```

2. In the Actions panel, click the **Check syntax** button ✔ to check for syntax errors in the code. The script is checked. If no errors are displayed in the Compiler Errors panel, the script is correct.

   Trouble? If your code contains errors, the errors will be listed in the Compiler Errors Panel at the bottom of the screen. Review your script to compare it to the code you modified in the previous steps, make any necessary corrections, and then repeat Step 2 until no errors are encountered.

3. Close the Actions panel, save the document, and then test the movie. The Home page opens in the Flash Player window.

4. On the Home page, click the **Coupon** button to display the Coupon page.

5. On the Coupon page, click the **Print Coupon** button to print the coupon, select a printer in the operating system's print dialog box, and then click the **Print** button if you are instructed to print; otherwise, click the **Cancel** button. The second frame of the coupon movie clip prints.

6. Close the Flash Player window to return to the Flash document.

Aly wants you to modify the ActionScript code so that the size of the printed coupon is larger than the coupon's original size. To print a coupon in a larger format, you need to temporarily scale the movie clip to a larger size, print the coupon, and then scale it back to the size originally set on the Stage.

You use the scaleX and scaleY properties to scale a movie clip. The scaleX property is the scale factor of the width of the movie clip, and the scaleY property is the scale factor of the height of the movie clip. A scale factor of 1 represents 100%. To enlarge the size of the coupon movie clip to twice its original size requires a scale factor of 2, which represents 200%, for both the scaleX and scaleY properties. After the coupon is printed, you need to return the coupon to its original size of 100% as it was originally set on the Stage by setting the scale factor back to 1. The statement to change a movie clip's scaleX property to 200% is:

```
coupon_mc.scaleX = 2;
```

You will add the ActionScript code to the print functions so that the coupon prints at twice its original size.

To scale the coupon movie clip for printing:

1. Open the **Actions** panel, and then, in the Script pane, place the insertion point after the opening curly brace for the `if` statement in the printCoupon function, press the **Enter** key to add a blank line, and, starting in the blank line, type the following lines of code to increase the size of the coupon.

```
// Increase the size of the coupon to 200%
coupon_mc.scaleX = 2;
coupon_mc.scaleY = 2;
```

2. In the Script pane, place the insertion point at the end of the `addPage()` statement in the printCoupon function, press the **Enter** key to add a blank line, and then, starting in the blank line, type the following lines of code to reduce the size of the coupon. See Figure 9-24.

```
// Reduce the size of the coupon to 100%
coupon_mc.scaleX = 1;
coupon_mc.scaleY = 1;
```

Figure 9-24   ActionScript code to scale the Coupon movie clip

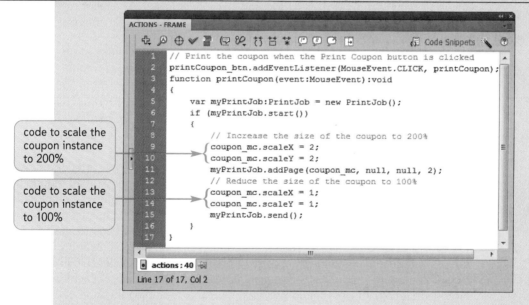

code to scale the coupon instance to 200%

code to scale the coupon instance to 100%

3. In the Actions panel, click the **Check syntax** button to check for syntax errors in the code. The script is checked. If no errors are displayed in the Compiler Errors panel, the script is correct.

    Trouble? If your code contains errors, the errors will be listed in the Compiler Errors Panel at the bottom of the screen. Review your script to compare it to the code you modified in the previous steps, make any necessary corrections, and then repeat Step 3 until no errors are encountered.

4. Close the Actions panel, save the document, and then test the movie. The Home page opens in the Flash Player window.

▶ **5.** On the Home page, click the **Coupon** button to display the Coupon page, click the **Print Coupon** button to print the coupon, select the appropriate printer in the operating system's print dialog box, and then click the **Print** button if you are instructed to print; otherwise, click the **Cancel** button. The coupon prints in a larger size.

▶ **6.** Close the Flash Player window to return to the Flash document.

The Coupon page for the Jackson's Youth Sports Web site is complete, and site visitors can print the coupon. Aly will show the completed Web site to Dan Jackson at their next meeting. She is confident he will be pleased with the finished site.

Creating Mobile Content

Flash content can be played on a wide variety of mobile devices using Flash Lite, which is a smaller version of the Flash Player. Flash Lite comes in various versions, including Flash Lite 2.0 and 2.1, which are based on Flash Player 7. These versions support many of the features in Flash Player 7 and include features specific to mobile development. Flash Lite 3.0 and Flash Lite 3.1 are also based on Flash Player 7 but have support for Flash video and provide improved Web browsing on mobile devices. The latest version, Flash Lite 4, is based on Flash Player 10 and supports the processing and playback of ActionScript 3.0.

Developing content to play on a mobile device using Flash Lite is similar to developing content for a Web site. However, several factors need to be considered. The main factor is screen size. Content developed for a mobile device must fit on a much smaller screen than content developed for a Web site. Mobile devices also don't have the same processing power or memory as desktop or laptop computers, so complex animations using bitmaps and videos may not work as well on a mobile device as they do on a Web site viewed on a larger device.

Another factor to consider is that mobile devices come in many varieties and with varying capabilities. Testing content to make sure it works properly on all mobile devices can be a daunting and time-consuming task. Because there are many different mobile devices from many manufacturers and each device has different characteristics, you need to target a specific device or group of devices for which you will create Flash content.

Adobe Device Central lets you create and test content on a wide variety of mobile devices without having to load the content on all the actual devices. Device Central provides an online library of mobile devices from which to choose. Each device has a profile that contains information about the device, including the type of media and content it supports, such as wallpaper and screensavers. You can view one or more device profiles at one time, and you can compare several targeted devices to help you determine the best screen size to use for the content. Device Central emulates what each device looks like and how the Flash content will appear on the device. It also provides information on how content on a device will affect the device's performance levels, memory, battery power, or even how the content is affected by different types of lighting.

Designing Content for Mobile Devices

When designing Flash content for mobile devices, keep in mind that the processors in mobile devices are not as powerful as those on desktop or laptop computers. SWF movies that play smoothly on larger computers may not play as well on mobile devices. You should avoid creating Flash content that uses complex graphics, has many motion tweens, or uses transparency because these elements place a greater burden on a mobile device's processor and negatively impact its performance. You should limit the number of simultaneous tweens and sequence animations so that they don't overlap. You should also avoid certain visual effects, such as masks or extensive gradients, to reduce the demands on the processor.

Creating Content for the Flash Lite Player

To create a document for a mobile device, you can select Flash Lite 4 or Adobe Device Central within Flash when you create a new document. If you select Flash Lite 4, a new document is created in Flash with dimensions of 240 x 320 pixels. If you select Adobe Device Central, the Adobe Device Central program opens. You can choose which devices to target and then create a new document. The new document will open in Flash with the Stage size matching the screen size of the mobile device you selected. After you create the content in Flash, you test it in Device Central.

Creating Flash Documents for Mobile Devices

- In Flash, create a new document, selecting Flash Lite 4 as the document type.
- In Flash, create the content and then test the movie in Device Central.
- In Adobe Device Central CS5, on the New Document tab, select the player version, the ActionScript version, and the content type.
- In Device Central, click a test device to target and then click the Create button.
- In Flash, create content as usual.

Dan wants advertisements that his customers can view on their mobile devices. Aly asks you to create a sample ad for an upcoming baseball tournament that is targeted for several mobile devices. This ad will give Dan an idea of the type of marketing he can explore to expand his business.

You'll start by creating a new document targeted for mobile devices and specify the devices on which the ad will be tested.

To create a new mobile Flash file:

1. On the Application bar, click **File**, click **New** to open the New Document dialog box, and then click the **General** tab, if necessary.

2. In the Type box, click **Adobe Device Central**. See Figure 9-25.

Figure 9-25   New mobile device document

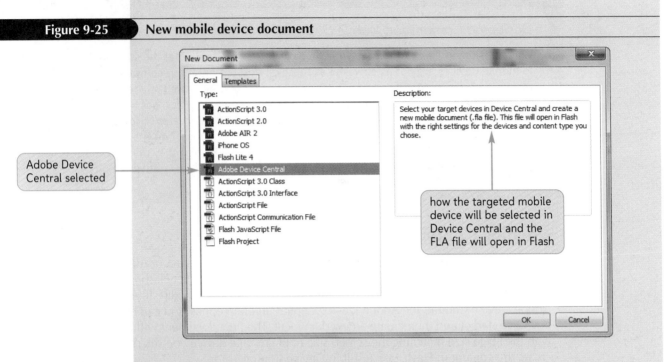

Adobe Device
Central selected

how the targeted mobile
device will be selected in
Device Central and the
FLA file will open in Flash

3. Click the **OK** button to open Adobe Device Central CS5.

4. On the Device Central Application bar, click **Browse** to display the Device Library.
   If necessary, click the **Home** button 🏠 to display a list of device profiles. See
   Figure 9-26.

Figure 9-26   Device profiles in the Device Library

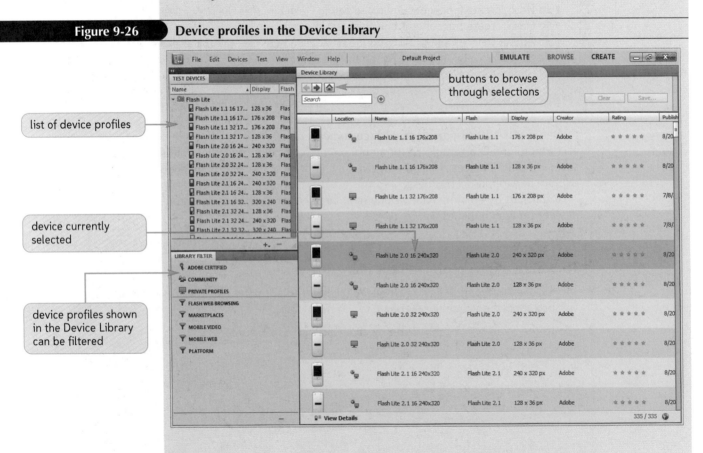

list of device profiles

buttons to browse
through selections

device currently
selected

device profiles shown
in the Device Library
can be filtered

5. In the Device Library, double-click the **Flash Lite 2.0 16 240x320** device. The profile details for the select mobile phone are displayed. See Figure 9-27.

Figure 9-27 | **Details for the selected device**

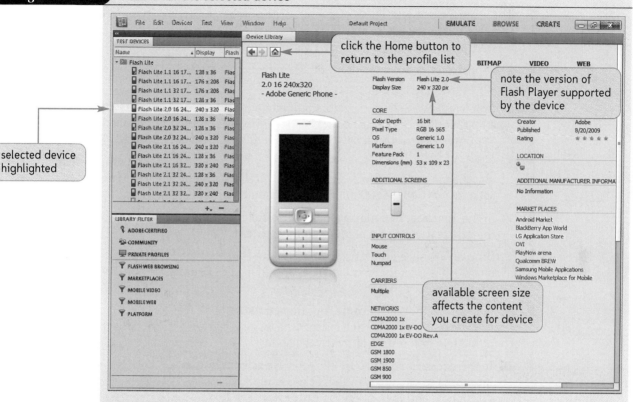

6. On the Application bar, click **Create** to display the New Document tab, change the Player Version to **Flash Lite 3.1**, change the ActionScript Version to **ActionScript 2.0**, and change the Content Type to **Embedded in HTML**, if necessary.

7. In the Test Devices panel, select the **Flash Lite** category. The preset profiles that match the criteria selected in Step 6 display.

8. On the New Document tab, click the first row of matching presets, which includes the **Flash Lite 3.1 16, 240x320** device profile.

9. In the lower-right corner of the New Document tab, click the **Create** button. A new document is created in Flash with the same dimensions as the screen area of the mobile device selected in Device Central.

After you select the mobile device profile in which you will test the mobile content, you are ready to create the content in Flash. You create the content for a mobile device in the same way you create other Flash documents. You'll create the content for the Jackson's Sports Store ad in a new document targeted for the selected mobile device profile.

To create the Jackson's Sports ad for mobile devices:

1. Save the new document as **jsMobileAd.fla** in the Flash9\Tutorial folder included with your Data Files.

2. In the Tools panel, select the **Text** tool T, and then, in the Property inspector, set the font family to **Arial**, set the font style to **Regular**, set the point size to **20**, set the text color to **black** (#FFFFFF), and set the paragraph format to **Align center**.

3. Create a static text block at the top of the Stage and type **Citywide Baseball**, press the **Enter** key to start a new line, type **Tournament**, press the **Enter** key to start a new line, and then type **This Weekend!**.

4. Reposition the text block so that it is centered at the top of the Stage, if necessary.

5. Create a new movie clip symbol and name it **text**. In symbol-editing mode, create a text block at the center of the editing window and type **Sponsored by**, press the **Enter** key to start a new line, and then type **Jackson's Sports!**.

6. In the Tools panel, click the **Selection** tool, and then, in the Property inspector, change the text block's font style to **Italic**, its point size to **24**, and its text color to **maroon** (#660000). Exit symbol-editing mode.

7. In the Timeline, rename Layer 1 to **title text**, and then insert a new layer above the title text layer and name it **animated text**.

8. Drag an instance of the text symbol to the center of the Stage below the title text block, right-click the text instance, and then click **Create Motion Tween** on the context menu. A tween span is created.

9. In the Timeline, click **Frame 1** of the animated text layer to select it, and then, on the Stage, click the text instance, if necessary, to select it. You'll decrease the size of the text in the start of the tween span.

10. In the docked panel group, click the **Transform** button, click the **Constrain** button to change it to the locked icon, if necessary, type **20** in the Scale Width box, and then press the **Enter** key. The text instance decreases in size. See Figure 9-28.

Figure 9-28   **Text block size decreased**

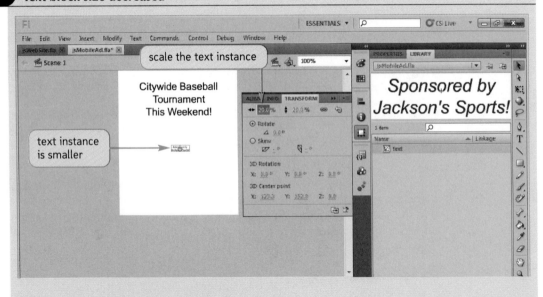

11. In the Timeline, click **Frame 12** of the animated text layer, and then, in the Transform panel, type **100** in the Scale Width box and press the **Enter** key. The text instance increases to its original size. The motion tween is complete.

12. In the Timeline, add regular frames at **Frame 40** of both layers.

The last part of the ad is an animation of a baseball graphic. You'll copy the Baseball symbol from the jsWebSite.fla library to the current document and then create a new animated baseball symbol.

To add a graphic animation to the Jackson's Sports ad:

1. In the Timeline, insert a new layer above the animated text layer, name it **graphic**, and then select **Frame 1** of the graphic layer.

2. In the Library panel, click the button with the **jsMobileAd.fla** name at the top of the panel to display a list of active documents, and then click the **jsWebSite.fla** name. The contents of the jsWebSite.fla library appear in the panel.

3. Drag an instance of the **Baseball** symbol from the Library panel to the Stage and center it at the bottom of the Stage below the animated text instance. A copy of the symbol is also placed in the jsMobileAd.fla document's library.

4. Convert the Baseball symbol to a movie clip symbol named **animated baseball**.

5. Open the animated baseball symbol in symbol-editing mode, right-click the **baseball** instance on the editing window, and then click **Create Motion Tween**.

6. In the Timeline, select **Frame 1** of Layer 1, and then, in the Property inspector, enter **1** in the Rotate text box to rotate the baseball graphic once clockwise.

7. Exit symbol-editing mode, click an empty area of the Stage to deselect the symbol, and then, in the Property inspector, change the Stage background color to **light yellow** (#FFFF99). The ad is complete. See Figure 9-29.

Figure 9-29   **Mobile ad completed**

ad will fit the
selected
mobile devices

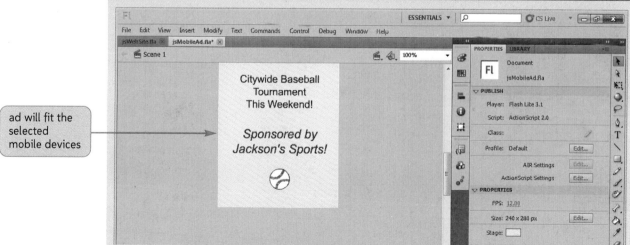

8. Save the document, and then, on the Application bar, click **Control**, point to **Test Movie**, and click **in Device Central**. Adobe Device Central opens with the Flash ad displayed in the targeted mobile device.

When you test a Flash document published for the Flash Lite Player, Adobe Device Central opens to the Emulate mode and the Flash document is displayed on the screen of the selected mobile device. You can use any of the devices listed in the Test Devices panel to test how the Flash content will appear on different screens. You can then use the testing panels to see how the Flash movie impacts the mobile device's performance or how the content is affected by different types of lighting.

PROSKILLS

Problem Solving: Testing Flash Content on Targeted Devices

Whenever possible, test the Flash content you created on the targeted devices to ensure that the audience experiences the content in the way you intended. Adobe Device Central emulates a mobile device, but it doesn't truly emulate all aspects of the device, such as its processor speed or the color depth of its screen. For example, a color gradient that appears smooth in the emulator within Device Central may be displayed differently when viewed on the actual device. Testing helps identify problems that need to be solved. After you test the Flash content on a device, you might need to modify the document's design in Flash, and then retest it. Thoroughly testing the content on the targeted devices enables you to solve any problems that arise, and helps to ensure a positive experience for the target audience.

You will test the Flash ad in several mobile devices and under different lighting conditions.

To test the Jackson's Sports mobile ad in Adobe Device Central:

1. In the Test Devices panel of Adobe Device Central, double-click **Flash Lite 3.0 32 320x240** in the Flash Lite category to make it the active device. The device in the Emulate screen changes to reflect the new selection.

   Trouble? If the Flash Lite 3.0 32 320x240 profile is not listed, double-click another profile in the Flash Lite category.

2. Click the **Display** panel tab to display the panel. See Figure 9-30.

| Figure 9-30 | Jackson's Sports ad displayed on the Flash Lite device |

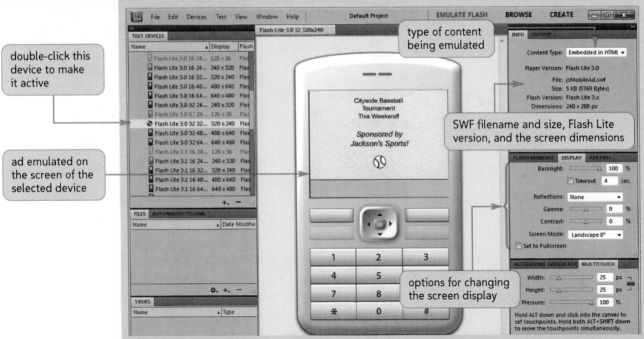

double-click this device to make it active

type of content being emulated

SWF filename and size, Flash Lite version, and the screen dimensions

ad emulated on the screen of the selected device

options for changing the screen display

3. In the Display panel, click the **Reflections** arrow, and then click **Indoor**. The display changes to simulate how the content will appear if indoor lighting is reflected on the device. See Figure 9-31.

| Figure 9-31 | Content on screen with indoor reflection |

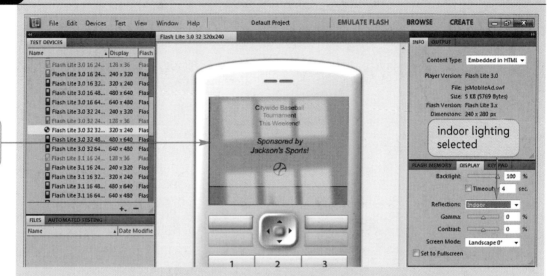

how the ad will look on the mobile device when viewed indoors

4. In the Display panel, click the **Reflections** arrow, and then click **Outdoor**. The display changes to simulate how the content will appear if outdoor lighting is reflected on the device. The testing is complete.

5. On the Application bar, click **File**, and then click **Return to Flash**.

6. In Flash, close the jsMobileAd.fla and jsWebSite.fla files.

TIP

You can also press the Ctrl+ Shift+O keys to return to Flash.

The mobile ad for the Jackson's Youth Web site is complete. Aly will show the completed ad to Dan Jackson at their next meeting. In this session, you created Flash content for printing. You used the PrintJob class to enable printing from within the Flash Player. You also specified which frames in the document to print and how to scale the content to print. Finally, you created and tested content to play on mobile devices using the Flash Lite Player.

Session 9.3 Quick Check

REVIEW

1. What two methods can be used to print Flash content?

2. Write an `addPage()` statement that adds the third frame of the map_mc movie clip to the print job.

3. Write the ActionScript statements to scale both the width and the height of the map_mc movie clip so that it is 150% of its original size.

4. True or False. If the Flash Player's Print command is used, only the current frame of the SWF file can be printed.

5. The print _____ manages the print jobs that are sent to the printer by the various programs running on the computer.

6. List two factors to consider when developing content for mobile devices.

7. How do you make mobile device profiles available to test Flash content in Adobe Device Central?

PRACTICE

Review Assignments

Data Files needed for the Review Assignments: sbDraft.fla, sbPhoto1.jpg, sbPhoto2.jpg, videoClip.avi

Aly wants you to complete a new version of the Softball site she started for Jackson's Sports. You need to add Web links to the site's Home page in the form of a drop-down list. You will also add a Photos page with softball team photos, a Videos page to showcase team videos, and a Coupons page with printable coupons for softball equipment.

1. Open the **sbDraft.fla** file located in the Flash9\Review folder included with your Data Files, and then save the file as **jSoftball.fla** in the same folder.

2. In the Timeline, select Frame 10 of the content layer, drag an instance of the ComboBox component from the Components panel to the Stage, position the ComboBox instance 320 pixels from the left of the Stage and 350 pixels from the top of the Stage, name the instance **softballLinks_mc**, and then change the width of the instance to 150 pixels. Do not change its height.

3. With the ComboBox instance selected, in the Component Parameters section of the Property inspector, enter **Softball Links** for the prompt parameter, and then enter the following label/data value pairs in the dataProvider parameter: **ASA Youth Softball**, **1**; **USA Softball**, **2**; and, **Softball Team Web Sites**, **3**.

4. In the Timeline, select Frame 10 of the actions layer, place the insertion point after the last line of the existing code in the Actions panel, and then type the following lines of code to make the Web links operational.

```
// Function to open Web site based on selection
softballLinks_mc.addEventListener(Event.CHANGE, gotoWebsite);
function gotoWebsite(event:Event):void
{
    // String variable that will hold the URL
    var weblink:String;
    // Switch statement determines which URL to assign to weblink
    switch (softballLinks_mc.value)
    {
        case "1" :
            weblink = "http://www.softball.org/youth/";
            break;
        case "2" :
            weblink = "http://www.usasoftball.com";
            break;
        case "3" :
            weblink = "http://www.eteamz.com/websites/softball/";
            break;
    }

    //Open Web site using the selected URL
    navigateToURL(new URLRequest(weblink), "blank");

    //Reset the ComboBox instance to display the prompt, Web Links
    softballLinks_mc.selectedIndex = -1;
}
```

5. In the Timeline, select Frame 20 of the content layer, and then drag one instance of the UILoader component and two instances of the Button component from the Components panel to the Stage. Position the UILoader instance 300 pixels from the left of the Stage and 180 pixels from the top of the Stage. Position the first Button instance 160 pixels from the left of the Stage and 180 pixels from the top of the Stage, and then position the second Button instance 160 pixels from the left of the Stage and 220 pixels from the top of the Stage.

6. Name the first Button instance **sbPhoto1_btn**, name the second Button instance **sbPhoto2_btn**, name the UILoader instance **photoLoader_mc**, and then change the dimensions of the UILoader instance to 165 pixels wide by 250 pixels high.

7. On the Component Parameters section of the Property inspector, change the label parameter of the first Button instance to **Photo 1** and the label parameter of the second Button instance to **Photo 2**.

8. In the Timeline, select Frame 20 of the actions layer, and then, in the Actions panel, type the following lines of code so that when a button is clicked, the corresponding softball photo will load into the UILoader instance.

```
// Function to load the first photo
sbPhoto1_btn.addEventListener(MouseEvent.CLICK, loadPhoto1);

function loadPhoto1(event:MouseEvent):void
{
    photoLoader_mc.load(new URLRequest("sbPhoto1.jpg"));
}
// Function to load the second photo;
sbPhoto2_btn.addEventListener(MouseEvent.CLICK, loadPhoto2);

function loadPhoto2(event:MouseEvent):void
{
    photoLoader_mc.load(new URLRequest("sbPhoto2.jpg"));
}
```

9. In Adobe Media Encoder, add the **videoClip.avi** file located in the Flash9\Review folder included with your Data Files to the queue.

10. Select the FLV – Web Medium (Flash 8 and Higher) preset for the file, change the audio output channel to Mono and the frame rate to 15, and then encode the file.

11. In Flash, select Frame 30 of the content layer, and use the Import Video wizard to import the **videoClip.flv** video file. For the delivery option, select Load external video with playback component. In the Skinning dialog box, select SkinUnderPlayMute.swf for the skin.

12. On the Stage, position the FLVPlayback instance about 250 pixels from the left of the Stage and 170 pixels from the top of the Stage. In the Component Parameters section of the Property inspector, deselect the autoPlay check box.

13. In the Timeline, insert a keyframe at Frame 40 of the labels layer, and then, in the Property inspector, assign the label name **Coupons**. Select Frame 40 of the content layer, drag an instance of the coupon1 movie clip from the Library panel to the Stage, reduce the size of the instance by 50%, and name the instance **coupon1_mc**. Drag an instance of the coupon2 movie clip from the Library panel to the Stage, reduce the size of the instance by 50%, and name the instance **coupon2_mc**.

14. Position the coupon1_mc instance 220 pixels from the left of the Stage and 180 pixels from the top of the Stage. Position the coupon2_mc instance 420 pixels from the left of the Stage and 180 pixels from the top of the Stage.

15. Drag two instances of the Button component movie clip from the Library panel to the Stage. Place one button below the coupon1_mc instance, and place the second button below the coupon2_mc instance. Name the first Button instance **printCoupon1_btn** and change its label parameter to **Print Coupon**. Name the second Button instance **printCoupon2_btn** and change its label parameter to **Print Coupon**.

16. In the Timeline, insert a keyframe at Frame 40 of the actions layer. In the Script pane of the Actions panel, type the following lines of code so that clicking the buttons will print the corresponding coupon. Frame 2 of each coupon is printed at 200% of its original size.

```
// Function to print the first coupon
printCoupon1_btn.addEventListener(MouseEvent.CLICK, printCoupon1);

function printCoupon1(event:MouseEvent):void
{
    var myPrintJob1:PrintJob = new PrintJob();
    if (myPrintJob1.start())
    {
        // Increase the size of the coupon to 200%
        coupon1_mc.scaleX = 2;
        coupon1_mc.scaleY = 2;
        myPrintJob1.addPage(coupon1_mc, null, null, 2);
        myPrintJob1.send();
        // Reduce the size of the coupon to 50%;
        coupon1_mc.scaleX = .5;
        coupon1_mc.scaleY = .5;
    }
}
// Function to print the second coupon
printCoupon2_btn.addEventListener(MouseEvent.CLICK, printCoupon2);

function printCoupon2(event:MouseEvent):void
{
    var myPrintJob2:PrintJob = new PrintJob();
    if (myPrintJob2.start())
    {
        // Increase the size of the coupon to 200%
        coupon2_mc.scaleX = 2;
        coupon2_mc.scaleY = 2;
        myPrintJob2.addPage(coupon2_mc, null, null, 2);
        myPrintJob2.send();
        // Reduce the size of the coupon to 50%
        coupon2_mc.scaleX = .5;
        coupon2_mc.scaleY = .5;
    }
}
```

17. Save the jSoftball.fla file and test the Web site to make sure the Web links work, the photos load, the video plays, and the coupons print. (If the Web site links do not work, the URLs for the sites might have changed since the printing of this book.)

18. Submit the finished files to your instructor.

Add Web links with a ComboBox component and a printable coupon with a Button component.

APPLY

Case Problem 1

Data File needed for this Case Problem: kprDraft.fla

Katie's Pet Resort   Katie wants to add links to the Resources page of the resort's Web site without cluttering the page with individual buttons. She also wants to add a coupon for 20% off the cost of boarding for one night to the Boarding page. You will add these new elements to the Resources and Boarding pages of the Web site, which are shown in Figure 9-32.

Figure 9-32 Completed Resources and Boarding pages

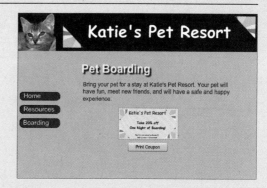

1. Open the **kprDraft.fla** file located in the Flash9\Case1 folder included with your Data Files, and then save the file as **katiesWeb.fla** in the same folder.

2. In the Timeline, insert two layers above the buttons layer and name them **actions** and **labels**, respectively. In the labels layer, insert keyframes at Frame 10 and Frame 20, and then add the label **Home** to Frame 1, the label **Resources** to Frame 10, and the label **Boarding** to Frame 20. In the actions layer, insert keyframes at Frame 10 and Frame 20.

3. On the Stage, select the Home button and name the instance **home_btn**. Repeat to name the Resources button instance **resources_btn** and the Boarding button instance **boarding_btn**.

4. Select Frame 1 of the actions layer, and then, in the Script pane of the Actions panel, type the following lines of code so that clicking the navigational buttons advances the playhead to the corresponding label.

```
//Keep the playhead from advancing
stop();
// Functions for navigational buttons
home_btn.addEventListener(MouseEvent.CLICK, onHomeClick);
function onHomeClick(event:MouseEvent):void
{
      gotoAndStop("Home");
}
resources_btn.addEventListener(MouseEvent.CLICK, onResourcesClick);
function onResourcesClick(event:MouseEvent):void
{
      gotoAndStop("Resources");
}
boarding_btn.addEventListener(MouseEvent.CLICK, onBoardingClick);
function onBoardingClick(event:MouseEvent):void
{
      gotoAndStop("Boarding");
}
```

5. Select Frame 10 of the content layer, drag an instance of the ComboBox component from the Components panel to the Stage, place the instance 240 pixels from the left of the Stage and 270 pixels from the top of the Stage, name the instance **resourceLinks**, and then change the width of the instance to 170 pixels. Do not change its height.

6. With the ComboBox instance selected, in the Component Parameters section of the Property inspector, enter **Pet Adoption Links** for the prompt parameter and enter the following label/data value pairs in the dataProvider parameter: **Adopt a Pet**, **1**; **Best Friends, 2**; and **SPCA**, **3**.

7. Insert a keyframe at Frame 10 of the actions layer, and then, in the Script pane of the Actions panel, type the following lines of code to make the ComboBox operational.

```
// Function to open selected Web site
resourceLinks.addEventListener(Event.CHANGE, gotoWebsite);
function gotoWebsite(event:Event):void
{
        // Variable that will hold the URL
        var weblink:String;
        // Switch statement determines which URL to assign to weblink
        switch (resourceLinks.value)
        {
            case "1" :
                weblink = "http://www.adoptapet.com/";
                break;
            case "2" :
                weblink = "http://www.bfpa.org/";
                break;
            case "3" :
                weblink = "http://www.spca.org/";
                break;
        }
        //Open Web site using the selected URL
        navigateToURL(new URLRequest(weblink), "blank");
        //Reset ComboBox to display the intial prompt
        resourceLinks.selectedIndex = -1;
}
```

8. Create a new movie clip symbol named **Coupon**. In symbol-editing mode, draw a rectangle at the center of the Stage using light green (#CCFF99) for the fill color and black for the stroke color. Select a dotted line for the stroke style, and use a stroke height of 2. Change the rectangle's width to 300 pixels and its height to 150 pixels. If necessary, change its X and Y coordinates to 0. Rename Layer 1 to **background** and lock the layer.

9. Insert a new layer and name it **graphics**. Add four instances of the triangle symbol. Place each instance in a separate corner of the rectangle. Use the Free Transform tool to rotate the instances so that the long side of each triangle faces the center of the rectangle.

10. Insert a new layer and name it **text**. Create a static text block at the top part of the rectangle. Use Comic Sans MS for the font family, Regular for the font style, 22 for the point size, dark blue (#000066) for the text color, and Align center for the paragraph format. Type **Katie's Pet Resort** in the text block. If necessary, center the text block in the top part of the rectangle.

11. Create another text block in the center of the rectangle. Change the point size to 16, the font style to Bold, and the text color to black. Type **Take 20% off**, press the Enter key, and then type **One Night of Boarding!**. If necessary, center the text block within the rectangle.

12. Create a text block at the bottom of the rectangle. Change the point size to 8 and the font style to Regular. Type **Must be redeemed by March 31** in the text block, press the Enter key, and then type **Call to make a reservation!** in the text block. If necessary, center the text block in the bottom part of the rectangle.

13. In the Timeline, insert keyframes at Frame 5 of the text layer and graphics layer and insert a regular frame in Frame 5 of the background layer. In Frame 5 of the text layer, add a text block below the rectangle. Change the point size to 16. Type **Clip this coupon for great savings!** in this text block. In Frame 5 of the graphics layer, add an instance of the scissors symbol, and place it on the lower-left corner of the rectangle so that its midpoint is over the rectangle's stroke.

14. In the Timeline, insert a new layer above the text layer and name it **action**. Select Frame 1 of the action layer, open the Actions panel, and then enter the following line so the playhead will stop at Frame 1. Exit symbol-editing mode.

```
stop();
```

15. In the main document Timeline, select Frame 20 of the content layer, add an instance of the coupon symbol to the center of the Stage, use the Transform panel to reduce the size of the instance by 50%, and then assign the instance the name **coupon_mc**.

16. In Frame 20 of the content layer, drag an instance of the Button component from the Components panel to below the coupon instance on the Stage. Name the Button instance **print_btn**, and then change its label parameter to **Print Coupon**.

17. Insert a keyframe at Frame 20 of the actions layer, and then, in the Script pane of the Actions panel, type the following lines of code so that when the button is clicked, the size of the coupon instance is increased to 100%, the fifth frame of the coupon instance is printed, and then the size of the coupon instance is reduced to 50%.

```
// Function to print the coupon
print_btn.addEventListener(MouseEvent.CLICK, printCoupon);
function printCoupon(event:MouseEvent):void
{
    var myPrintJob:PrintJob = new PrintJob();
    if (myPrintJob.start())
    {
        // Increase the size of the coupon to 100%
        coupon_mc.scaleX = 1;
        coupon_mc.scaleY = 1;
        myPrintJob.addPage(coupon_mc, null, null, 5);
        myPrintJob.send();
        // Reduce the size of the coupon to 50%
        coupon_mc.scaleX = .5;
        coupon_mc.scaleY = .5;
    }
}
```

18. Save the katiesWeb.fla file, and test it to make sure the navigational buttons work, the resource links work, and the coupon prints. (If the Web site links do not work, the URLs for the sites might have changed since the printing of this book.)

19. Submit the finished files to your instructor.

Case Problem 2

Add a video clip with the FLVPlayback component, a printable schedule with a Button component, and a mobile ad.

CHALLENGE

Data Files needed for this Case Problem: aczDraft.fla, zooClip1.avi, zooClip2.avi

Alamo City Zoo   Janet requests that video clips be incorporated into the Exhibits page of the zoo's Web site to show examples of animals on exhibit. She also wants a schedule of tours added to the site that can be printed so visitors can plan tours ahead of time. In addition, she wants an ad to send to the mobile devices of registered zoo members. Alex instructs you to add two video clips to the Exhibits page, add the printable schedule to the Education page, and create an ad targeted to a mobile device. You will encode the video clips and then import them into the document so they load as external FLV files and are displayed on the Exhibits page. You will add buttons to control the playing of the videos. Then you will create the printable schedule and add a button to the Education page to control printing of the schedule. Finally, you will create an ad with animation that can be displayed on a mobile device. Figure 9-33 shows the completed Exhibits and Education pages and the mobile ad.

Figure 9-33	Completed Exhibits and Education pages and mobile ad

1. Open the **aczDraft.fla** file located in the Flash9\Case2 folder included with your Data Files, and then save the file as **aczWeb.fla** in the same folder.
2. In the Timeline, insert two layers above the content layer and name them **actions** and **labels**, respectively. In the labels layer, insert keyframes at Frame 10 and Frame 20, and then add the label **Home** to Frame 1, the label **Exhibits** to Frame 10, and the label **Tours** to Frame 20. In the actions layer, insert keyframes at Frame 10 and Frame 20.
3. On the Stage, name the Home button instance **home_btn**, name the Exhibits button instance **exhibits_btn**, and then name the Tours button instance **tours_btn**.
4. In the Timeline, select Frame 1 of the actions layer, and then, in the Script pane of the Actions panel, type the following lines of code so that clicking the navigational buttons advances the playhead to the corresponding label.

```
//Keep the playhead from advancing
stop();
// Navigational button functions
home_btn.addEventListener(MouseEvent.CLICK, onHomeClick);
function onHomeClick(event:MouseEvent):void
{
    gotoAndStop("Home");
}
exhibits_btn.addEventListener(MouseEvent.CLICK, onExhibitsClick);
function onExhibitsClick(event:MouseEvent):void
{
    gotoAndStop("Exhibits");
}
tours_btn.addEventListener(MouseEvent.CLICK, onToursClick);
function onToursClick(event:MouseEvent):void
{
    gotoAndStop("Tours");
}
```

5. In Adobe Media Encoder, add the **zooClip1.avi** and **zooClip2.avi** files located in the Flash9\Case2 folder included with your Data Files to the queue.
6. Select the FLV – Web Medium (Flash 8 and Higher) preset for both files. For each file, change the audio output channel to Mono and the frame rate to 15 and then encode both files.
7. In Flash, select Frame 10 of the content layer. Use the Import Video wizard to import the **zooClip1.flv** video file. For the delivery option, select Load external video with playback component.

⊕ EXPLORE

8. In the Skinning dialog box, select SkinUnderPlayStopSeekMuteVol.swf for the skin, and then change the skin color to tan (#FFCC66) with an alpha amount of 50%.

⊕ EXPLORE 9. After you import the video, open the Transform panel, select the constrain button, and change the width of the FLVPlayback component instance to 70%. Reposition the FLVPlayback instance below the Alamo City Zoo Exhibits inside the rectangle on the Stage. In the Property inspector, name the FLVPlayback instance **videoPlayer** and in the Component Parameters section, deselect the autoPlay check box and select skinAutoHide.

⊕ EXPLORE 10. Drag two instances of the Button component from the Component panel to the Stage. Place the instances below the rectangle containing the FLVPlayback instance. Align the two Button instances horizontally. In the Component Parameters section of the Property inspector, change the label of the first Button instance to **Bear Video**, change the label of the second Button instance to **Alligator Video**, and select the emphasized check box for each button.

11. In the Property inspector, assign the first button instance the name **video1_btn** and the second Button instance the name **video2_btn**.

12. In the Timeline, select Frame 10 of the actions layer, and then, in the Script pane of the Actions panel, type the following lines of code so that clicking the video clip buttons plays the corresponding videos.

```
// Functions to add video source to FLVPlayback component
video1_btn.addEventListener(MouseEvent.CLICK, addVideo1);
function addVideo1(event:MouseEvent):void
{
     videoPlayer.source = "zooClip1.flv";
}
video2_btn.addEventListener(MouseEvent.CLICK, addVideo2);
function addVideo2(event:MouseEvent):void
{
     videoPlayer.source = "zooClip2.flv";
}
```

13. In the Timeline, select Frame 20 of the content layer. Add an instance of the Button component from the Library to the Stage. Place the button below the text block on the center of the Stage. Name the instance **print_btn**. In the Parameters tab of the Component inspector, change the button's label to **Print Tour Schedule**. In the Property inspector, change the width of the button to 120 pixels. Keep its height at 22 pixels.

14. Create a new movie clip symbol named **Tour Schedule**. In the symbol's Timeline, rename Layer 1 **schedule**, and then add a new layer and name it **action**. In the Actions panel, add the following line to stop the playhead at Frame 1 of the action layer.

```
stop();
```

15. In the schedule layer, draw a rectangle at the center of the Stage with an orange (#FF9900) fill and a black stroke. Make the rectangle 90 pixels wide and 40 pixels high and set its X and Y coordinates to 0. Add a text block at the center of the rectangle. Use Arial for the font family, 12 for the point size, bold for the font style, black for the text color, and align center for the paragraph format. Type **Tour**, press the Enter key, and then type **Schedule**. If necessary, realign the text block over the rectangle.

16. In the schedule layer, insert a blank keyframe at Frame 2, and then change the zoom level of the Stage to 50%. In Frame 2, draw a rectangle with no fill, a black stroke, a stroke height of 2, and a solid stroke style. Make the rectangle 550 pixels wide and 600 pixels high. Set the rectangle's X and Y coordinates to 0.

17. In Frame 2, add a text block inside the top of the rectangle. Use Monotype Corsiva for the font family (the font is listed with the C fonts), 54 for the point size, black for the text color, align center for the paragraph format, and then type **Alamo City Zoo**. Center the text block at the top of the rectangle, if necessary.

18. Drag an instance of the group tour text from the library and place it inside the rectangle below the first text block.

19. Drag an instance of the bear.jpg bitmap from the library to the lower-left corner of the rectangle. Drag an instance of the rhino.jpg bitmap from the library to the lower-right corner of the rectangle. Exit symbol-editing mode.

20. In Frame 20 of the content layer, add an instance of the Tour Schedule symbol to the Stage. Place it below the Print Tour Schedule button instance. Name the instance **tour_mc**.

21. In the Timeline, select Frame 20 of the actions layer, and then, in the Script pane of the Actions panel, type the following lines of code so that when the button is clicked, the second frame of the Tour Schedule movie clip prints.

```
// Function to print the schedule
print_btn.addEventListener(MouseEvent.CLICK, printSchedule);
function printSchedule(event:MouseEvent):void
{
    var myPrintJob:PrintJob = new PrintJob();
    if (myPrintJob.start())
    {
        myPrintJob.addPage(tour_mc, null, null, 2);
        myPrintJob.send();
    }
}
```

22. Save the aczWeb.fla file, and then test it to make sure the video clips play and the tour schedule prints.

23. Create a new **Adobe Device Central** document. In Adobe Device Central, on the New Document tab, change the Player Version to **Flash Lite 2.1**, change the ActionScript Version to **ActionScript 2.0**, and change the Content Type to **Embedded in HTML**.

24. Select the Flash Lite 2.1 16 240x320 test device profile located in the Test Devices panel, and then create a new document in Flash.

25. In Flash, change the Stage color to light orange (#FFCC99). Draw a rectangle with a maroon (#660000) stroke color, a stroke height of 2, a ragged stroke style, rounded corners, and no fill. The rectangle should form a frame around the inside of the Stage. Rename Layer 1 to **background** and lock the layer.

26. Insert a new layer and name it **title**. In this layer, create a text block at the top of the Stage and inside the rectangle. Use Times New Roman for the font, bold italic for the font style, 28 for the point size, and black for the font color. Type **Alamo City Zoo** in the text block.

27. Insert a new layer and name it **animation**. In this layer, create a second text block below the title text. Use Times New Roman for the font, regular for the font style, 16 for the point size, and black for the font color. Type **Dine with the Animals!** in the text block, press the Enter key, type **April 3rd!** in the text block, press the Enter key, and then type **6:00 pm** in the text block.

28. Create a motion tween on the text block. In Frame 12 of the animation layer, move the text block to the bottom of the Stage to create an animation where the text block moves from the top of the Stage to the bottom. In Frame 1 of the animation layer, change the size of the text block to 50% of its original size. In Frame 12 of the animation layer, change the size back to 100%. The text block will increase in size as it moves to the bottom of the Stage.

29. Insert a new layer and name it **graphic**. In this layer, insert a keyframe at Frame 12 and then drag an instance of the bear.jpg bitmap from the aczWeb.fla file library to the center of the Stage.

30. Add a regular frame at Frame 40 of each layer to expand all the layers.

31. Save the file as **aczMobileAd.fla** in the Tutorial.09\Case2 folder included with your Data Files, and then test the file in Adobe Device Central to see it in the Sony Ericsson phone.
32. Submit the finished files to your instructor.

Add photos and buttons using ProgressBar and UILoader components and import a video to complete a nursery Web site.

CHALLENGE

Case Problem 3

Data Files needed for this Case Problem: wcDraft.fla, flower1_sm.jpg, flower2_sm.jpg, flower3_sm.jpg, flower1.jpg, flower2.jpg, flower3.jpg, loadPics.as, wcLandscape.avi

Westcreek Nursery   Alice tells Amanda that she wants a short video clip of a sample landscape added to the Weekly Specials page of the Web site to give potential customers an idea of the nursery's landscaping work. She also wants the Photos page to display thumbnails of the flower pictures to make it easier for potential customers to know what is on sale. Amanda asks you to import the short video and to complete a new Photos page. She has prepared the small versions of the pictures to use as thumbnails. Figure 9-34 shows the completed Weekly Specials and Photos pages.

Figure 9-34	Completed Weekly Specials and Photos pages

 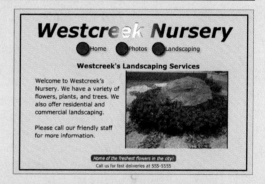

1. Open the **wcDraft.fla** file located in the Flash9\Case3 folder included with your Data Files, and then save the file as **wcWebSite.fla** in the same folder.
2. On the Stage, name the Home button instance **home_btn**, name the Photos button instance **photos_btn**, and then name the Landscaping button instance **landscaping_btn**.
3. In the Timeline, insert two layers above the content layer and name them **actions** and **labels**, respectively. In the labels layer, insert keyframes at Frame 10 and Frame 20, and then add the label **Home** to Frame 1, the label **Photos** to Frame 10, and the label **Landscaping** to Frame 20. In the actions layer, insert a keyframe at Frame 10.
4. Select Frame 1 of the actions layer, and then type the following lines of code in the Script pane of the Actions panel to keep the playhead from advancing and to make the navigational buttons operational.

```
//Keep the playhead from advancing automatically
stop();
// Make the navigational buttons operational
home_btn.addEventListener(MouseEvent.CLICK, onHomeClick);
function onHomeClick(event:MouseEvent):void
{
      gotoAndStop("Home");
}
photos_btn.addEventListener(MouseEvent.CLICK, onPhotosClick);
function onPhotosClick(event:MouseEvent):void
```

```
{
        gotoAndStop("Photos");
}
landscaping_btn.addEventListener(MouseEvent.CLICK,
onLandscapingClick);
function onLandscapingClick(event:MouseEvent):void
{
        gotoAndStop("Landscaping");
}
```

5. Select Frame 10 of the content layer, import the **flower1_sm.jpg** picture onto the Stage, and place it 70 pixels from the left of the Stage and 170 pixels from the top of the Stage. Import the **flower2_sm.jpg** picture onto the Stage and place it below the first picture. Import the **flower3_sm.jpg** picture onto the Stage and place it below the second picture. Align the pictures by their left sides and space them evenly.

6. Convert each picture into a button symbol, using the names **flower1 button**, **flower2 button**, and **flower3 button**, respectively. Name the button instances **flower1_btn**, **flower2_btn**, and **flower3_btn**, respectively.

7. For each button symbol, edit the symbol, insert a keyframe in its Over frame, and add a text block on the center of the picture. Use Verdana for the font family, bold italic for the font style, 12 for the point size, white for the font color, and align center for the paragraph format. Type **Click Me!** in the text block.

8. In the document's main Timeline, select Frame 10 in the content layer, and then drag an instance of the UILoader component from the Components panel to the center of the Stage. Resize the UILoader instance to 250 pixels wide by 187 pixels high. Name the instance **picLoader_mc**. Center the instance below the Westcreek's Photos of the Week text block.

9. Drag an instance of the ProgressBar component from the Components panel to the Stage and place it in the center of the UILoader instance. Name the ProgressBar instance **progressBar_mc**, and change its height to 10. Do not change its width. In the Component Parameters section of the Property inspector, change the source parameter to **picLoader_mc**.

⊕ **EXPLORE** 10. In the Library panel, open the ProgressBar component symbol in symbol-editing mode, double-click the small rectangle to the left of the Bar Skin label to edit the ProgressBar barSkin symbol, and then increase the zoom level to 800%. Double-click the blue stroke of the rectangle to edit it, and then change its color to green (#006600). On the Edit bar, click ProgressBar barSkin, double-click the fill of the rectangle, and then change the fill color to bright green (#00FF00). Exit symbol-editing mode.

⊕ **EXPLORE** 11. Select Frame 10 of the actions layer, open the Actions panel, click the Actions panel options menu, and click Import Script. Open the **loadPics.as** file located in the Flash9\Case3 folder included with your Data Files to add its code to the Script pane.

12. In the Script pane of the Actions panel, type the following lines of code after the last line to complete the script and make the picture buttons operational. Clicking a picture button loads the corresponding picture into the picLoader instance. The ProgressBar instance appears temporarily, indicating the picture is loading.

```
flower3_btn.addEventListener(MouseEvent.CLICK, loadPic3);
function loadPic3(event:MouseEvent):void
{
        progressBar_mc.visible = true;
        picLoader_mc.load(new URLRequest("flower3.jpg"));
}
// When the loading is complete, hide the ProgressBar instance
picLoader_mc.addEventListener(Event.COMPLETE, hideBar);
function hideBar(event:Event) {
        progressBar_mc.visible = false;
}
```

13. In Adobe Media Encoder, add the **wcLandscape.avi** file located in the Flash9\Case3 folder included with your Data Files to the queue.

14. Select the FLV – Web Medium (Flash 8 and Higher) preset, change the audio output channel to Mono, change the frame rate to 15, and then encode the file to output the wcLandscape.flv file.

15. Select Frame 20 of the content layer, and then use the Import Video wizard to import the **wcLandscape.flv** video file located in the Flash9/Case3 folder. For the delivery option, select Load external video with playback component.

⊕ EXPLORE 16. In the Skinning dialog box, select SkinOverPlaySeekStop.swf for the skin, and then change the skin color to blue (#0099CC) with an alpha amount of 70%.

17. After you import the video, open the Transform panel, select the constrain button, if necessary, and change the width of the FLVPlayback component instance to 80%. Reposition the FLVPlayback instance below the Westcreek's Landscaping Services text block in the lower-right side of the Stage. In the Component Parameters section of the Property inspector, click the skinAutoHide check box to select it.

⊕ EXPLORE 18. Save and test the wcWebSite.fla file. Use the Simulate Download command with a download setting of DSL (32.6 KB/s) to test the photos' ProgressBar. Click each photo thumbnail to display the ProgressBar. After a photo loads, the ProgressBar instance is hidden. Also, make sure the video clip plays in the Landscaping page.

19. Submit the finished files to your instructor.

Add photos, Web links and a calculation to a Web site.

C R E A T E

Case Problem 4

Data Files needed for this Case Problem: msaDraft.fla, mission1.jpg, mission2.jpg

Missions Support Association   Brittany wants a new Web site developed that includes a page with links to sites related to the missions as well as a page that displays photos of some of the missions. She also wants to include a page where visitors can select the type of tour and enter the number of people in the tour to calculate the cost of a tour. Anissa developed a revised version of the association's Web site that you will complete by adding Web links, a page with photos, and a tour cost calculator page. You will also create an ad for mobile devices that promotes the association's tours. Figure 9-35 shows one possible solution for the Photos and Tour cost pages and the mobile ad.

Figure 9-35   **Sample Photos and Tour pages and mobile ad**

1. Open the **msaDraft.fla** file located in the Flash9\Case4 folder included with your Data Files, and then save the file as **msaWebsite.fla** in the same folder.

2. Use the Home navigational button to create duplicate buttons for the Web Links, Photos, and Tour Calc pages. Add the buttons to the buttons layer and assign instance names to the buttons.

3. In the Timeline, add a layer with descriptive labels in Frames 1, 10, 20, and 30 to correspond to the Web site pages.

4. In the Timeline, add a layer for the actions, and in Frame 1 of this layer add the ActionScript code to make the navigational buttons operational.

5. In the Timeline, select Frame 1 of the content layer, and add a title for the Home page. Repeat to add appropriate titles for each of the other pages in their respective frames in the content layer.

6. In the Timeline, select the frame in the content layer for the Web links page, and then use a ComboBox component to provide a list of three URL links. (*Hint*: You can use the San Antonio Missions Web site, **http://www.nps.gov/saan**, plus two other links from within the same site or other missions-related sites.)

7. In the corresponding frame of the actions layer, add code in the Script pane to make the ComboBox instance operational so that selecting an item in the ComboBox list opens the corresponding Web link.

8. In the Timeline, select the frame in the content layer for the photos page, and then drag two instances of the Button component and one instance of the UILoader component to the Stage. Use the UILoader to display the **mission1.jpg** (300×225) photo when the first Button instance is clicked and the **mission2.jpg** (300×225) photo when the second Button instance is clicked. Add an instance of the ProgressBar component to the UILoader instance so that the progress bar is displayed as the photos are being loaded.

9. In the corresponding frame of the actions layer, add code in the Script pane to make the Button instances operational so that clicking a button displays the corresponding photo in the UILoader instance. The ProgressBar component instance should not be displayed until a photo is loading and it should not be displayed after a photo has completely loaded.

10. In the Timeline, select the frame in the content layer for the tour calculator page, and then use the ComboBox component to list the type of tours (30-Minute Tour, 1-Hour Tour, Bus Tour). Create an input text block for the number of people in the group, create a dynamic text block for the base cost of the tour, and another dynamic text block for the total cost of the tour. Add Label component instances to label the input and dynamic text blocks. Add an instance of the Button component to use as a Calculate button. Name all of the instances.

11. In the corresponding frame of the actions layer, add code in the Script pane to make the ComboBox instance and Button instance operational so that when a visitor selects a type of tour, enters the number of people in the group, and clicks the Calculate button, the base cost of the tour and total cost will be displayed. Assign a base cost to each type of tour and a cost for each person in the tour.

12. Save and test the msaWebsite.fla file. Make sure the navigational buttons are operational. Also, use the Simulate Download command to test the photos and the ProgressBar. Make sure the Web links work and the tour calculator calculates the correct cost.

13. Create a new mobile Flash file targeted for a mobile device(s) of your choice that uses Flash Lite 3.0 and ActionScript 2.0 for content Embedded in HTML, and then save the document as **msaMobileAd.fla** in the Flash9\Case4 folder included with your Data Files.

14. Create appropriate content for the mobile ad, and then test the Flash ad in the mobile device(s) you selected and under different lighting conditions.

15. Submit the finished files to your instructor.

ENDING DATA FILES

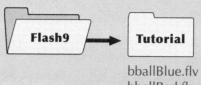

Tutorial

bballBlue.flv
bballRed.flv
jsMobileAd.fla
jsMobileAd.swf
jsWebSite.fla
jsWebSite.swf
photo1.jpg
photo2.jpg
SkinUnderPlayStopSeekMuteVol.swf

Review

jSoftball.fla
jSoftball.swf
sbPhoto1.jpg
sbPhoto2.jpg
SkinUnderPlayMute.swf
videoClip.flv

Case1

katiesWeb.fla
katiesWeb.swf

Case2

aczMobileAd.fla
aczMobileAd.swf
aczWeb.fla
aczWeb.swf
SkinUnderPlayStopSeekMuteVol.swf
zooClip1.flv
zooClip2.flv

Case3

flower1.jpg
flower2.jpg
flower3.jpg
SkinOverPlaySeekStop.swf
wcLandscape.flv
wcWebSite.fla
wcWebSite.swf

Case4

mission1.jpg
mission2.jpg
msaMobileAd.fla
msaMobileAd.swf
msaWebsite.fla
msaWebsite.swf

ProSkills

 # Written Communication

Conveying Information with a Web Site

A Web site is a common way to share information with others—whether those people are work colleagues, potential customers, classmates, friends, or family. No matter what the purpose of the Web site or its intended audience, the planning process is the same. Developing a Web site includes identifying the site goals and objectives, determining your target audience, developing the site's content, designing the navigation system and site pages, and then building and testing the Web site.

Identify the Site Goals and Objectives

The site goals are a list of what you want the Web site to accomplish. Ideally the site should have at least one goal and no more than five goals. These goals should be clearly defined so that you can develop a site that effectively accomplishes its goals. For example, your site goals might be to promote yourself to potential employers and showcase your skills and accomplishments. The site objectives more clearly define the information the Web site will contain, the types of media that are required, and the number of pages needed to provide the information needed to fulfill the site goals. For example, your site objectives might be to present your resume, provide references and testimonials, showcase your writing skills, and highlight your personal interests. To accomplish these, you could use written text, photos, video, and other graphics.

Determine the Target Audience

The target audience is the group of people you intend to use the Web site. Be sure to take the time to think about your intended audience. Who are they? What knowledge do they already have? What attitudes might they have about your site's topic? What types of content will be interesting to them? Into what demographic information such as age, education, or economic level does your target audience fall? These characteristics impact how you present information on the Web site. For example, if your target audience is potential employers, you should look for a common factor that connects them, such as their intended field.

Develop the Site Content and Organization

The content of the site's pages is determined by the site's goals and target audience. Determine the pages and media you want to use to best accomplish the site goals. Then, create an outline with categories and subcategories to further determine the site's content. Each category can correspond to a page that will be developed for the site. Based on the outline, you can gather and organize the information and media that you will include on the site. Then you can create a storyboard to show how the site's pages are organized and linked. From this, you can determine the navigation system you want to use. For example, you can use different pages for your resume, references and testimonials, writing, and interests, which will include written content, bitmaps of pictures and videos, and other graphics.

ProSkills

Create and Test the Site

With the site content developed, you can build the Web site. You start by creating the main page and navigation system. Then you can create a Flash template to use to develop the remaining documents for the pages in the Web site. After compiling all the pages, you should test the site to be sure it works as expected.

Create a Flash Web Site

Adobe Flash is a professional authoring environment for creating rich, interactive content for the Web, including interactive graphics and advertisements with animation, sound, and video. You can even create entire Web sites using Flash, create online forms to gather data, and display photos in online galleries.

In this exercise, you will use Flash to create a Flash Web site with interactive graphics containing information of your choice, using the Flash skills and tools presented in Tutorials 1 through 9. Use the following steps as a guide to completing your Flash Web site and graphics.

Note: Do *not* include any personal information of a sensitive nature in any graphics or content that you create to be submitted to your instructor for this exercise. Later, you can update the content with such information.

1. Create a list of at least three goals for the Flash Web site.
2. Based on the goals of the Flash Web site, develop a list of objectives. Include the use of audio, video, and bitmaps as part of the objectives for your site.
3. List three characteristics of the site's target audience.
4. Develop an outline with categories and subcategories to correspond to the site's objectives.
5. Develop a storyboard that shows how the site's content and navigation will be organized.
6. Gather relevant graphics for the site's background and banner. Write the headings and content for each of the pages. Gather and prepare the relevant photos, obtain any sound effect clips you plan to use, and obtain and prepare any video clips you plan to show.
7. Sketch the site's design to show how the banner, navigational buttons, page headings, and site graphics will be organized.
8. Create a new document that is at least 600 pixels wide and 400 pixels high. Extend the layer in the document's Timeline to include 10 frames for the site's preloader animation plus an additional 10 frames for each of the site's pages.
9. Make Layer 1 the background layer and insert additional layers, as needed, for content that will be the same on each page of the site, such as the site's navigational buttons.
10. Insert a layer for the content that will be different on each page, insert a layer for the actions, and insert a layer for the labels that identify each page in the site. Rename each layer appropriately.

ProSkills

11. In the labels layer, add labels to identify the preloader section, the home page, and each of the other pages of the site.

12. Based on the site's design, in Frame 10 of the background layer, add a background graphic or image as well as other graphics to the document that will be the same in each page of the site.

13. Create a banner as a movie clip and include the site's title, a bitmap graphic, and a gradient. In Frame 10 of the background layer in the document's main Timeline, add an instance of the banner to the Stage and align it attractively on the banner.

14. Create a movie clip with a motion tween animation of an appropriate graphic and add an instance to the background layer. This animation may be of a rectangle, circle, star, or other shape that appears on all pages of the Web site.

15. Create a Home button symbol. Include a graphic or simple animation in the button's Timeline that is displayed when the pointer is moved over the button. Add a sound effect that plays when the button is clicked.

16. Duplicate and modify the Home button to create buttons for each of the other pages of the site. Add an instance of each button to Frame 10 of the document's main Timeline. Align and space the button instances on the Stage.

17. Assign names to the button instances and then add the ActionScript code to Frame 10 of the actions layer to make the navigational buttons operational.

18. Create a preloader animation in the first frame of the site that includes a graphic and a dynamic text field to display the percentage of the movie's content that has been loaded. Add the ActionScript code to Frame 1 of the actions layer to make the preloader animation work.

19. For each page in your site, create an appropriate page heading and add content and graphics pertinent to that page. Add animated text to one of the pages and a graphic or animation to another page.

20. In one of the site's pages, add a component to display multiple photos saved as JPEG or GIF files. Add buttons that enable the user to choose which photo to display. Include a component to display a progress bar animation as each photo is loaded. Add the ActionScript code to make the buttons and components functional.

21. In one of the site's pages, create a form using input text and dynamic text to enable the user to enter data, click a button, and receive a result based on the data. Add the ActionScript code to process the input values and display the appropriate result.

22. In one of the site's pages, create at least three URL links using a Flash component. The links should be to Web sites related to the site's content based on the objectives you identified for the site. Add the ActionScript code to make the component functional.

23. If you are including video in the site, use Adobe Media Encoder to encode the video clip and to export it in the FLV format. In Flash, import the FLV video, and then add an instance of the video to an appropriate page using the FLVPlayback component and a skin with playback controls.

24. Save the pages, and test them in the Flash Player. Adjust the pages, as needed.

25. Publish the finished document in at least one format other than FLV.

26. Save and close the files, and then submit the completed Web site to your instructor.

OBJECTIVES

- Create a new Flash document
- Add text and shapes
- Import bitmap graphics
- Create movie clip and button symbols
- Create motion tweens
- Insert layers and keyframes
- Use ActionScript to insert actions, functions, and event listeners

Creating an Interactive Banner for a Web Site

FLASH

Case | *Metro Children's Museum*

The Metro Children's Museum is a nonprofit organization dedicated to providing information and exhibits of special interest to children. The museum has been in operation for more than 15 years and is accredited by the American Museum Association. The museum is open year-round and has recently redesigned its Web site. Cecilia Fuentes, museum director, wants to add a new banner to the Web site to promote an upcoming space shuttle exhibit at the museum. The banner will display several space shuttle pictures and have a link for more information at NASA's Space Shuttle Web site.

STARTING DATA FILES

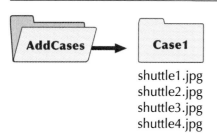

shuttle1.jpg
shuttle2.jpg
shuttle3.jpg
shuttle4.jpg

Complete the following:

1. Create a new document with dimensions of 500 pixels by 300 pixels and a background color of teal (#007D7D), and then save the file as **shuttlePromo.fla** in the AddCases\Case1 folder included with your Data Files.

2. Insert a regular frame at Frame 40 to extend Layer 1. Create a rectangular border around the inside edges of the Stage, using a stroke color of peach (#FFCC99), a solid stroke style, a stroke height of 3, no fill color, and a corner radius of -15.

3. Create a title for the banner by adding a text block at the top of the Stage, using peach (#FFCC99) text and a large font, with the text **Metro Children's Museum**. Center the text block horizontally, and apply a drop shadow. Change the name of Layer 1 to **background**.

4. Import the **shuttle1.jpg**, **shuttle2.jpg**, **shuttle3.jpg**, and **shuttle4.jpg** bitmap files located in the AddCases\Case1 folder included with your Data Files into the document's library.

5. Create a new movie clip symbol named **shuttle1_fade**. In this symbol, insert an instance of the shuttle1.jpg bitmap and use the Info panel to center it in the editing window. Select the shuttle1.jpg bitmap instance and convert it into a movie clip symbol named **shuttle1_mc**.

6. In the shuttle1_fade movie clip Timeline, create a motion tween to fade in the shuttle1_mc instance from a starting alpha amount of 50% to an ending alpha amount of 100%. Change the name of Layer 1 to **picture**.

7. Insert a new layer and name it **rectangle**. In this layer, draw a filled rectangle with rounded corners over the shuttle1_mc instance. Make the rectangle slightly smaller than the shuttle1_mc instance. Convert the rectangle layer to a mask layer so that the picture layer becomes a masked layer. The picture is displayed through the mask.

8. Insert a new layer and name it **action**, and then add a stop() action to Frame 12 of this layer so that the motion tween is only played once.

9. Repeat Steps 5 through 8 to create a movie clip symbol with a mask and a fade-in effect for each bitmap image that is named based on the bitmap it contains: **shuttle2_fade**, **shuttle3_fade**, and **shuttle4_fade**.

10. In the document's main Timeline, insert a new layer and name it **content**. In Frame 1 of this layer, add an instance of the shuttle1_fade symbol to the center of the Stage below the title text.

11. In the content layer, insert keyframes at Frame 10, Frame 20, and Frame 30. In Frame 10, swap the movie clip instance on the Stage with an instance of the shuttle2_fade movie clip. In Frame 20, swap the instance on the Stage with a shuttle3_fade instance. In Frame 30, swap the instance on the Stage with a shuttle4_fade instance.

12. Insert a new layer and name it **labels**, and then, in the labels layer, add the frame label **shuttle1** at Frame 1; add the frame label **shuttle2** at Frame 10, add the frame label **shuttle3** at Frame 20, and add the frame label **shuttle4** at Frame 30.

13. Create a new button symbol named **picture1 button**. In symbol-editing mode, draw a small triangle about 36 pixels in width and height for the button shape using a white fill and black stroke, and center the triangle in the editing window. In the button's Over frame, change the color of the triangle's fill and flip the triangle shape vertically to create a rollover effect. Insert a new layer and add a text block with the number **1**. The text block should be inside the triangle.

14. Create a duplicate of the picture1 button named **picture2 button**, and then change the text in the symbol to **2**. Repeat to create two more duplicates of the button named **picture3 button** and **picture4 button** with the text **3** and **4**, respectively.

15. In the document's main Timeline, insert a new layer and name it **buttons**. Insert an instance of each button along the bottom of the Stage, inside the border, and below the picture. Align the button instances horizontally and name the instances **pic1_btn**, **pic2_btn**, **pic3_btn**, and **pic4_btn**.

16. Insert a new layer and name it **actions**, and then, in Frame 1, type the following ActionScript code to make the first picture button operational. When the pointer moves over the pic1_btn instance, the onButton1 function is called, which moves the playhead to the frame with the shuttle1 label. The stop() action keeps the playhead from advancing automatically.

```
stop();
pic1_btn.addEventListener(MouseEvent.MOUSE_OVER, onButton1);
function onButton1(event:MouseEvent):void
{
gotoAndStop("shuttle1");
}
```

17. Add the appropriate functions and event listeners to the code to make the rest of the picture button instances functional. When the pointer moves over a picture button instance, the playhead should move to the frame with the corresponding label and stop.

18. Create a new button symbol named **webLink button**. In symbol-editing mode, add a text block using a small point size, type **Web Link** in the text block, and then center the text. Insert a keyframe in the Over frame and change the font style to Italic. Add a keyframe in the Hit frame and draw a rectangle to cover the text block.

19. In the document's main Timeline, select the buttons layer, and then add an instance of the webLink button to the left side of the Stage. Assign the name **weblink_btn** to the instance.

20. Select Frame 1 of the actions layer, and in the Script pane type the following ActionScript code to make the button operational. The gotoShuttleSite function is called when the webLink button is clicked.

```
weblink_btn.addEventListener(MouseEvent.CLICK, gotoShuttleSite);
function gotoShuttleSite(event:MouseEvent):void
{
   navigateToURL(new
   URLRequest("http://www.nasa.gov/mission_pages/shuttle/main/"),
   "blank");
}
```

21. Save the banner, and then test it in the Flash Player.

22. Submit the finished files to your instructor.

ENDING DATA FILES

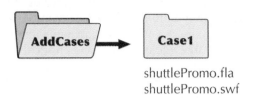

shuttlePromo.fla
shuttlePromo.swf

OBJECTIVES

- Duplicate and modify symbols
- Use ActionScript to insert actions, functions, and event listeners
- Create movie clip symbols
- Create a custom gradient
- Insert layers and keyframes
- Create a text animation
- Create a mask effect
- Add the UILoader, ProgressBar, and Button components
- Use Adobe Media Encoder to add video
- Create input text blocks and dynamic text blocks
- Add the ComboBox component

Creating a Web Site with a Banner, Calculator, Photos, and Video

Case | Discount Autos

Discount Autos of San Antonio has been in business for more than 15 years providing quality used vehicles. Located on the corner of Highway 151 and Alamo Parkway, Discount Autos' sales have been steadily increasing. To continue this trend in sales, owner Allen Bidwell has developed a new marketing campaign. As part of this new campaign, Allen wants to improve the company's Web site by adding a new banner as well as a tool that potential customers can use to calculate their monthly loan payments based on a loan amount, the number of months for the loan, and the interest rate. He also wants the site to include an area to showcase auto specials, using pictures of vehicles and a page to display a video of vehicles for sale.

STARTING DATA FILES

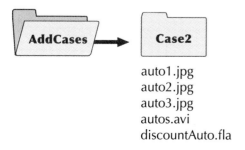

AddCases → Case2

auto1.jpg
auto2.jpg
auto3.jpg
autos.avi
discountAuto.fla

Complete the following:

1. Open the **discountAuto.fla** file located in the AddCases\Case2 folder included with your Data Files, and save the file as **autoWebsite.fla** in the same folder.
2. In the labels layer, add the label **Video** at Frame 20 and the label **Calculator** at Frame 30.
3. Create two duplicates of the Home button symbol named **Video button** and **Calculator button**. Change the text in the Up and Over frames of the Video button to **Video**. Change the text in the Up and Over frames of the Calculator button to **Calculator**.
4. In the document's main Timeline, select the buttons layer, and then place an instance of the Video button on the Stage to the right of the Photos button and place an instance of the Calculator button to the right of the Video button. Name the Video button instance **video_btn** and name the Calculator button instance **calculator_btn**. Horizontally align and evenly space the four button instances on the Stage.
5. Select Frame 1 of the actions layer, and then, in the Script pane of the Actions panel, after the last line, type the following lines of code exactly as shown to create the functions for the Video and Calculator buttons.

```
video_btn.addEventListener(MouseEvent.CLICK, onVideoClick);
function onVideoClick(event:MouseEvent):void
{
      gotoAndStop("Video");
}
calculator_btn.addEventListener(MouseEvent.CLICK, onCalcClick);
function onCalcClick(event:MouseEvent):void
{
      gotoAndStop("Calculator");
}
```

6. Test the movie in the Flash Player, clicking each button to make sure it displays its associated page.
7. Create a new movie clip symbol named **autoBanner**. Rename Layer 1 as **background**, and add a regular frame at Frame 60 to extend the layer.
8. Use the Color panel to create a linear gradient. Set the color of the left gradient pointer to light blue (#6188AF) and the right gradient pointer to white. Create a rectangle 604 pixels wide and 100 pixels high using the new gradient as its fill and no stroke. The rectangle will serve as a background for the banner. If necessary, reposition the rectangle so it is centered on the editing window.
9. Create a new layer and name it **title** for the title text block. Select a font family such as Impact, a text color such as maroon (#660000), and a large point size, and then type **DI$COUNT AUTO$** in the text block. Increase the line spacing slightly for the text, and then center the text within the background rectangle. The text should extend the width of the rectangle.
10. Create a text animation with the dollar sign so that it alternately increases and then decreases in size for a pulsating effect. Start by breaking the title text block into its individual letters and then converting the left $ character into a graphic symbol named **dollar sign**.
11. Edit the dollar sign graphic symbol in symbol-editing mode and create a motion tween. Extend the tween through Frame 20. In Frame 5, use the Transform panel to increase the size of the dollar sign to 110% of its original size, being sure to constrain its width and height. In Frame 10, decrease the size of the dollar sign to 100%. In Frame 15, increase its size to 110%. In Frame 20, decrease its size to 100% so that the dollar sign exhibits a pulsating effect throughout the motion tween.

12. In the title layer of the autoBanner Timeline, delete both $ text blocks, and then create a new layer and name it **dollar signs**. In the dollar signs layer, insert an instance of the dollar sign graphic symbol between the letters I and C on the banner, being sure to align the $ with the rest of the letters.

13. In the dollar signs layer, insert another instance of the dollar sign graphic after the letter O in AUTO, being sure to align the $ with the rest of the letters in AUTO. In the Looping section of the Property inspector, change the first frame of the instance to 10.

14. Add a mask effect to the banner using a gradient that moves horizontally across the text. Select all the letters in the title layer (the $ symbols should not be selected) at the same time, and then convert the letters to fills. Copy all the letters at the same time and paste the copies into a new layer above the title layer in the same relative position as the original letters, and then name the new layer **title2**.

15. Insert a new layer between the title and the title2 layers and name the layer **gradient**. In this layer, draw a rectangle that is 600 pixels wide and 100 pixels high. The rectangle should have a linear gradient as its fill and no stroke. The linear gradient should be black on the ends and have a narrow white strip in the middle.

16. Convert the rectangle into a movie clip symbol and then move the rectangle to the left of the letter D. Create a motion tween in Frame 1 of the gradient layer, and in Frame 30, move the rectangle to the right of the $ in AUTO. In Frame 60, move the rectangle back to the left of the letter D. The rectangle should move from the left side of the title text horizontally across to the right side of the title text for 30 frames and then back to the left side of the title text for the next 30 frames.

17. Convert the title2 layer into a mask layer. The gradient layer with the rectangle should be masked. Press the Enter key to test the banner animation. The animation creates a highlight effect on the title text in which the highlight moves across the text and back.

18. Return to the document's main Timeline, and in Frame 1 of the background layer, delete the title text block. Add an instance of the autoBanner to the top of the Stage and align the instance with the left and top sides of the Stage.

19. In the Timeline, select Frame 10 of the content layer and add an instance of the UILoader component to the center of the Stage. Name the instance **photos_mc** and set its width and height at 130 pixels. This is where the auto photos will be loaded.

20. Add a ProgressBar component instance below the UILoader instance. Name the instance **pBar_mc**, and in the Component Parameters section of the Property inspector, type **photos_mc** as its source parameter.

21. Add a Button component instance below the ProgressBar instance. Name the button instance **next_btn** and change its label parameter to **Next Picture**.

22. Insert a keyframe at Frame 10 of the actions layer, and then, in the Script pane of the Actions panel, add the following ActionScript code. When the Next button is clicked, a photo will be loaded into the UILoader instance. The photo filenames used are auto1.jpg, auto2.jpg, and auto3.jpg. The ActionScript code uses the variable num for the value (1, 2, 3) in the filename. The ProgressBar instance is displayed only while a photo is being loaded.

```
// Code to load photos; set initial value of num to 1
var num:Number = 1;
// Hide the ProgressBar instance
pBar_mc.visible = false;
// Load photos function
next_btn.addEventListener(MouseEvent.CLICK, loadPics);
function loadPics(event:MouseEvent):void
{
pBar_mc.visible = true;
// Create the photo file name using the value in num
var pic:String = "auto" + num + ".jpg";
// Load the photo into the Loader instance
```

```
photos_mc.load(new URLRequest(pic));
// Increment the value in num
num += 1;
// If num is greater than 3, set it back to 1
if (num > 3)
{
  num = 1;
}
}
// When the loading is complete, hide the ProgressBar instance
photos_mc.addEventListener(Event.COMPLETE, hideBar);
function hideBar(event:Event)
{
pBar_mc.visible = false;
}
```

23. Test the movie. In the Photos page, click the Next Picture button three times to display each of the three auto pictures.

24. In Adobe Media Encoder, add the **autos.avi** file located in the AddCases\Case2 folder included with your Data Files to the queue.

25. Select the FLV – Web Medium (Flash 8 and Higher) preset for the file, change the audio output channel to Mono and the frame rate to 15, and then encode the file.

26. In Flash, in the Timeline, select Frame 20 of the content layer, and use the Import Video wizard to import the **autos.flv** video file. For the delivery option, select Load external video with playback component. In the Skinning dialog box, select SkinUnderPlaySeekMute.swf for the skin.

27. On the Stage, center the FLVPlayback instance on the Stage below the Video text block. In the Component Parameters section of the Property inspector, deselect the autoPlay value.

28. Test the movie. Click the Video button to display the autos.flv video. Click the video's Play button to play the video.

29. In the Timeline, select Frame 30 of the content layer. Create four text blocks using the font family of your choice and a small point size. Type **Loan Amount** for the first text block, **Interest Rate** for the second text block, **Length of Loan** for the third text block, and **Monthly Payment** for the fourth text block. Align the text blocks vertically by their right edges and space them evenly.

30. Create an input text block to the right of the Loan Amount text to be used to enter the amount of the loan. Create another input text block to the right of the Interest Rate text block to be used to enter a rate. Make each input text block 60 pixels wide and 30 pixels high. In the Property inspector, for each text block, select the Show border around text option, select black (#000000) for the text color, and select Align right for the paragraph format. Name the first input text block instance **loanAmount_txt** and name the second input text block instance **interestRate_txt**.

31. Add an instance of the ComboBox component to the right of the Length of Loan text block to be used to select the number of months for the loan. Name the ComboBox instance **lengthOfLoan_mc** and make the instance 100 pixels wide. In the Component Parameters section of the Property inspector, enter **No. of Months** for the prompt parameter. Add the following labels and data value pairs for the dataProvider parameter: label:**36 mo.**, data:**1**, label:**48 mo.**, data:**2**, label:**60 mo.**, and data:**3**.

32. Create a dynamic text block to the right of the Monthly Payment text block. Make the text block 60 pixels wide and 30 pixels high. In the Property inspector, deselect the Show border around text option, select black (#000000) for the text color, and select Align right for the paragraph format. Name the text block instance **monthlyPayment_txt**.

33. Add an instance of a Button component to the bottom of the Stage and assign the name **calc_btn** to the instance and change its width to 110 pixels. In the Component Parameters section of the Property inspector, type **Calculate Payment** for the label parameter.

34. In the Timeline, insert a keyframe in Frame 30 of the actions layer. In the Script pane of the Actions panel, type the following ActionScript code to calculate the monthly payment and place the result in the Monthly Payment dynamic text block.

```
// Function to calculate the monthly payment
calc_btn.addEventListener(MouseEvent.CLICK, calculatePayment);
function calculatePayment(event:MouseEvent):void
{
        var numberOfMonths:Number;
        switch (lengthOfLoan_mc.value)
        {
            case "1" :
                    numberOfMonths = 36;
                    break;
            case "2" :
                    numberOfMonths = 48;
                    break;
            case "3" :
                    numberOfMonths = 60;
                    break;
        }
        // Convert input values into Integer numbers
        var Loan:Number = int(loanAmount_txt.text);
        var Rate:Number = int(interestRate_txt.text);
        // Determine the monthly interest rate
        var monthlyRate:Number = (Rate/12)/100;
        // Calculate part of the formula using the Math power
        function
        var factor:Number = 1 - Math.pow(1 + monthlyRate, -
        numberOfMonths);
        // Calculate the payment; round to the nearest dollar
        var payment:Number = Math.round((monthlyRate/factor)*Loan);
        // Display the resulting monthly payment
        monthlyPayment_txt.text = String(payment);
        //Set ComboBox to display the initial prompt, No. of Months
        lengthOfLoan_mc.selectedIndex = -1;
}
```

35. Save the document, and then test the monthly payment calculator in the Flash Player. Enter **20000** for the loan amount, enter **5** for the interest rate, and select **48 mo**. for the No. of Months. Click the Calculate Payment button. The Monthly Payment amount is 461.

36. Submit the finished files to your instructor.

ENDING DATA FILES

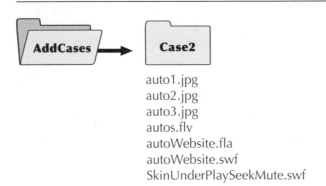

auto1.jpg
auto2.jpg
auto3.jpg
autos.flv
autoWebsite.fla
autoWebsite.swf
SkinUnderPlaySeekMute.swf

Becoming an Adobe Certified Associate

OBJECTIVES

- Learn about the Adobe Certified Associate credential
- Review the Adobe Certified Associate objectives for Flash Professional CS5
- Learn where objectives are discussed in the tutorials
- Find additional training resources

Preparing for the Adobe Rich Media Communication Using Adobe Flash Professional CS5 Exam

Case | *Adobe Certified Associate*

Adobe offers an Adobe Certified Associate (ACA) credential that certifies individuals as having demonstrated the entry-level skills needed to plan, design, build, and maintain effective communications using Flash Professional CS5. The Adobe Certified Associate objectives for Flash Professional CS5 are listed in this appendix. Each objective is followed by a brief discussion of the objective and a reference to the tutorial session in this book where the objective is discussed. For additional training resources, go to *www.adobe.com/education/instruction/ace* and *www.adobe.com/training*.

STARTING DATA FILES

There are no starting Data Files needed for this appendix.

ACA Certification Objectives

Setting Project Requirements

1.1   Identify the purpose, audience, and audience needs for rich media content.

Before adding rich media content such as animations, audio, or video to a project, you should determine the purpose that the content will serve based on the project's goals. Is rich media content necessary to communicate the intended message? Can the message be effectively communicated without rich media content? When starting a new project, develop a plan that includes the goals and objectives of the project to determine whether rich media content is needed and what purpose it will serve.

It is also important to know about the intended audience for the project. You should consider demographic information about the intended audience such as age, gender, education, occupation, and computer literacy, and then use this information in designing the content. The average age of the audience, for example, affects that audience's expectations in terms of rich media content. A younger audience might expect more interactivity, animations, or video than an older, more mature audience.

See Session 7.1 for a discussion of planning a Web site.

1.2   Identify rich media content that is relevant to the purpose of the media in which it will be used (Web sites, mobile devices, and so on).

After outlining the purpose of the project and where the project will be used such as on a Web site or a mobile device, you can identify the appropriate content that fits the media in which it will be used. For example, if the project is for a Web site whose purpose is entertainment, you should identify rich media content such as Flash movies with audio or video to include in the project. An educational Web site, on the other hand, might require interactive rich media content such as Flash movies that present the user with options to choose from based on the information displayed.

See Session 7.1 for a discussion of planning a Web site and developing relevant content. See Session 9.3 for a discussion of creating content for a mobile device.

1.3   Understand options for producing accessible rich media content.

People with disabilities may use assistive technology such as screen readers to read the content on Web pages. A screen reader is a software program that reads the content on the screen so that a visually impaired person can hear it. For Flash media to be interpreted correctly by a screen reader, you should provide accessibility information in Flash using either the Accessibility panel or ActionScript. From the Accessibility panel, you can enter text to describe elements in a Flash movie, which the assistive technology can then read when the movie is played in the Flash Player.

Including accessible rich media content is important to both the client and the target audience. The client, who is providing information, a service, or a product through a Web site, wants the content to be accessible to all members of the target audience. Otherwise, the goals and objectives of the Web site are not met and the needs of members of the target audience with disabilities are not met.

Accessibility elements can be applied to individual objects or to the entire document using the Accessibility panel. Some of the ways to make rich media content accessible include adding keyboard access to all controls such as buttons, adding captions to audio content, or adding alternative text to buttons and images. You can also control the order of tabbing so that pressing the Tab key moves the cursor within the Flash document in an intuitive manner.

See Session 7.1 for a discussion of creating accessible content. For more information, see the Adobe Accessibility Resource Center at *www.adobe.com/accessibility*. You can also find information on Adobe Flash Professional CS5 accessibility at *www.adobe.com/accessibility/products/flash*.

1.4 Demonstrate knowledge of standard copyright rules (related terms, obtaining permission, and citing copyrighted material).

Copyright protects "original works of authorship," including literary, dramatic, musical, artistic, and other intellectual property, or derivative works such as unique compilations or collections of existing content as long as they are fixed in some tangible form, such as on paper or in electronic memory. Since January 1, 1978, copyright in the United States extends for the life of the author plus 70 years. So, works created before January 1, 1923, are now in the public domain, which means they are public property and can be reproduced without permission or charge. Works created after that date may or may not be in the public domain, and should be verified through the Copyright Office. Works created outside the United States are protected in their own countries generally for the life of the author plus 50 or 70 years, depending on the country. A copyright notice includes (1) the symbol © or the word "copyright", (2) the year of first publication, and (3) the name of the copyright owner.

Elements such as pictures, sound files, and video files are usually copyrighted. To use copyrighted work, whether published or unpublished, you must obtain the copyright owner's permission unless the intended use is "fair use." Generally, the fair use doctrine allows you to reproduce small amounts of an original work specifically for a review, criticism, or illustration of a point. When creating commercial work, you must be careful to get permission to include anything that is someone else's work. It is a good idea to get permission to reuse anything that you didn't create yourself or that is not owned by the client. Most material on the Internet is copyrighted even if that fact is not explicitly stated.

Whenever you reuse someone else's work—including Web sites, images, sounds, video, and text from the Internet—you should indicate that the content is copyrighted and give credit to the original source. When you obtain permission, ask the copyright holder(s) for the specific information they want included with the work. If they don't specify the information or the content falls under fair use, include the name of the copyright holder(s), the copyright year, the work's title, and the source. For works found online, list the URL and the date accessed.

See Session 5.3 for a discussion of acquiring sound files. Also, for more information about copyright issues and laws, visit the U.S. Copyright Office site at *www.copyright.gov*.

1.5 Understand project management tasks and responsibilities.

Large projects often involve a team of designers and developers working together to produce a product. Different team members work on various parts of the project. One person might develop the graphic design of a project, while another person works on the programming requirements of the project. It is important to manage this team to ensure that each member of the team understands his or her role. One way to manage a project and the team is to create a project plan, which outlines the project's scope and goals, lists all the tasks required to complete the project, presents the timeline for completing the tasks, and identifies the resources needed for the project. The project leader assigns tasks to team members along with the timelines or due dates for the tasks. Areas of responsibility must be clearly defined. The plan may be divided into different phases, such as planning, designing, creating, testing, implementing, and launching. The plan should also list what items need to be produced at each phase, such as design specifications, storyboards, flowcharts, Flash files, HTML files, and so on. These items are often referred to as deliverables. Common problems in project management such as scope creep also need to be avoided. Scope creep occurs when project managers don't recognize small changes to a project's scope. And then a large number of small changes become too large to manage and they negatively impact the project team.

1.6   Communicate with others (such as peers and clients) about design and content plans.

Communication with both the client and team members is essential throughout the life of a project. As you plan a project such as a Web site that incorporates rich media content, you need to meet with the client to establish the project's goals and objectives, including its design and content. Goals that are clearly defined help to ensure that the finished project will meet the client's needs. Also, with open communication during a project, changes can be discussed and implemented as needed. If a team is involved in the project's development, communication among team members is vitally important to ensure that all parts of the project are developed based on the established goals and objectives.

See Session 7.1 for a discussion of working with a client to design a Web site and meeting the client's needs.

Identifying Rich Media Design Elements

2.1   Identify general and Flash-specific best practices for designing rich media content for a Web site.

As you develop Flash content for a Web site, you need to keep in mind how it will be used in the Web site and how the intended user will view the content. Any bitmap images included in the project should be sized and optimized in a program such as Adobe Photoshop before being imported into Flash to ensure that the file size of the bitmap is as small as possible while maintaining the image's desired quality. Sound files and video files embedded in a Flash movie should also be made as small as possible while meeting the goals and objectives of the Web site. When designing rich media content for a Web site, keep in mind the target audience, the type of Internet connection they most likely will have, and their ability to easily interact with rich media (such as audio, video, and so on). The overall goal should be to keep the size of the published SWF files as small as possible to reduce the download time for the user.

Web sites should have consistent elements throughout the site. For example, a consistent navigation system would provide buttons in the same location of each page to make it easy for users to navigate from one part of the Web site to another. You can create consistent buttons by creating a symbol and then duplicating it for the required buttons. Other elements of a Web site that should be uniform are the colors and fonts used throughout the site. You can achieve this consistency in a Web site by using a template. The template created for the Web site, which includes the consistent placement of elements, symbols, fonts, colors, and so on, is then used to create additional pages for the Web site. Using templates reduces the time it takes to develop the pages for a Web site and makes it easier to maintain the Web site. Development of a Web site can be made easier by using motion presets to animate objects. Using motion presets cuts down the time required to achieve certain animation effects.

Before developing content for a Web site, you should determine whether implementing the content by using rich media is appropriate by considering criteria such as the following:

- Will using rich media improve the effectiveness of the message being delivered?
- Will rich media help attract the attention of the user?
- Does the use of rich media improve how information is presented?
- What platforms will the content be delivered to, and how can the rich media be developed so that it is compatible across various platforms?

Using rich media elements such as an interactive menu for selecting multiple levels of information can make it easier for the user to understand how to access the information. Also, if three-dimensional structures are part of the content, using rich media can enhance the user's ability to visualize the structure. Rich media content can also make the user's experience more engaging and improve the likelihood that the content's message will be delivered successfully.

When developing rich media content for other platforms such as Adobe AIR or Adobe Integrated Runtime, you can leverage the skills you learned using Flash. Adobe AIR uses the same technology as used in the Flash Player to play rich media content, except that you can develop content to run on a client computer's desktop rather than a Web browser. When creating video for Adobe AIR applications, you can encode the video files in the FLV format. You can then develop an AIR application using Flash and with the video files in the FLV format, you can use the same process to import the video into the AIR application as you do to import the video into a Flash movie. As a result, developing video in the FLV format means you can use the same video in both a Flash movie and an Adobe AIR application.

Metadata can be included in a SWF file in the form of Extensible Metadata Platform (XMP) data. The metadata contains information about a file such as its contents, author, title, and copyright status. You can also include metadata specifically for SWFs created for mobile devices. Metadata is entered in the File Info dialog box accessed through the File menu in Flash.

See Session 1.2 for a discussion of colors. See Session 2.2 for a discussion of using library objects and symbols. See Session 3.2 for a discussion of using motion presets to animate objects. See Session 7.2 for a discussion of creating templates for a Web site.

2.2   Demonstrate knowledge of design elements and principles.

Each type of media, such as bitmaps, sound, and video, included in a Flash movie has its own set of characteristics that impact how it is used. As you design a project with rich media content, be aware of these characteristics and design content appropriately. Graphic design principles are important to consider when designing rich media content. These principles guide how you arrange elements on the Stage and help determine the colors you select for the elements. For example, you can use the rule of thirds to arrange graphic elements on the Stage. The rule of thirds method divides the page into three equal sections both vertically and horizontally to form a grid. The lines and intersections of the grid are where you should place the key graphical elements. As you place elements, be aware of how the eye moves along the content, what gets emphasized, how the page is balanced, and what unity and symmetry (horizontal, vertical, diagonal, radial, or asymmetric) is presented. You can improve the legibility of text by using consistent alignment and including margins and white space to delineate different sections of the Web page. Overall, maintain consistency in the design and avoid extraneous elements, overcrowded layout designs, and distracting colors. Also, to avoid having to adapt a design to fit specific content, consider all content that will be included when designing the site to maintain the site's consistency.

2.3   Identify general and Flash-specific techniques to create rich media elements that are accessible and readable.

Many of the elements in a Flash movie can be made accessible and readable for screen readers by setting options in the Accessibility panel. You can select an instance of a movie clip, button, or component on a document's Stage, and then, in the Accessibility panel, specify that the object be made accessible. You can assign a name and a description to the object in the panel. You can also assign a name and description to the entire Flash movie to make it accessible. For keyboard access, you can assign tab order specifying the order in which elements are selected using the Tab key. You can also assign keyboard shortcuts to buttons to provide an option for users to use the keyboard instead of the mouse.

You can improve readability of text by using consistent fonts, avoiding small font sizes, and using proper spacing and appropriate indentation. In the Property inspector, you can specify how anti-aliasing is applied to text depending on whether the text will or will not be animated. For example, for text that will not be animated, select the Anti-alias for readability option.

See Session 7.1 for a discussion of making content accessible using the Accessibility panel.

2.4   Use a storyboard to produce rich media elements.

A storyboard is a diagram that shows a project's major elements and the way these elements are organized. A storyboard may show the state of an animation from one frame to another. A storyboard for a Web site may show a sketch of each page with lines indicating how each page links to other pages in the site. The way the pages link to each other determines the navigation system for the site. You can also include information about specific animations, navigation, images, text, transitions and interactions that will be included in the project. Placement of different elements such as buttons and links can also be identified in a storyboard.

See Session 7.1 for an example of using a storyboard during the development of a Web site.

2.5   Organize a Flash document.

A Flash document may consist of many different elements and can easily become complex and unwieldy if you don't organize its contents in a consistent manner. For example, the layers in the Timeline should be named appropriately and similar layers, such as text layers, can be grouped together in layer folders. ActionScript should be placed in one layer at the top of the Timeline and not mixed with other content. Appropriately named labels, such as Start or Loop, should be used when referencing frames rather than using frame numbers. Similar objects in the Library panel should also be arranged in folders to make them easy to find.

See Sessions 1.1, 3.1, and 5.2 for discussions of elements commonly used to organize Flash documents, including folders, scenes, layers, and frame labels.

Understanding the Adobe Flash Professional CS5 Interface

3.1   Identify elements of the Flash interface.

The main elements of the Flash interface include the Stage, pasteboard, Tools panel, Timeline, Property inspector, and panels such as the Library. You create the content on the Stage, use the pasteboard as a staging area for content to be animated onto the Stage, use the Timeline to control the frames that make up an animation, and use the Property inspector to set a tool's properties or to change a selected object's attributes. You use the Edit bar to access a document's scenes and symbols as well as to change the magnification of the Stage. The Edit bar displays the name of the current scene. You can show and hide panels individually by double-clicking their title bars, by selecting them in the Windows menu or by pressing the F4 key to hide or show all currently displayed panels at the same time.

Another key element of the Flash interface is the Motion Editor which displays all the properties and property keyframes for a selected motion tween and enables you to control individual motion tweens more precisely and to easily create complex animations. In the Motion editor, you can modify a tween's properties and the animated object's position, rotation, and ease values.

See Sessions 1.1 and 1.2 for an overview of the Flash interface including the Stage, pasteboard, Tools panel, Timeline, and Property inspector. See Session 4.1 for an overview of the Motion Editor.

3.2   Use the Property inspector.

The Property inspector provides easy access to the most common attributes of the currently selected tool or object. For example, when you select the Text tool, the Property inspector contains options to select the font, the font style, the text size, text color, and other text attributes. When an object such as text, an image, or a symbol instance is selected, the Property inspector displays properties specific to that object, and enables you to set the object's properties such as its name, color style, coordinates, or dimensions. You can also use the Property inspector to add a filter, such as a drop shadow, to instances of symbols.

See Session 1.2 for an overview of the Property inspector. The Property inspector is used extensively in all tutorials in this book.

3.3 Use the Timeline.

The Timeline contains layers and frames that make up a Flash document. Layers are used to organize the images, animations, and other objects that are part of a document. You can add, delete, and rename layers as needed. Use separate layers to hold different parts of the Stage content to make it easier to manipulate the content. You can also arrange a group of related layers into a layer folder. Frames represent units of time in an animation and may contain different images or different states of the same image. The frame rate determines how many frames are played per second, creating the illusion of motion, and affects the movie's final file size. The Timeline contains the playhead, a marker that indicates which frame is currently selected in the Timeline. You can preview a movie within Flash to see how an animation changes as the playhead moves from one frame to the next in the Timeline. You can hide or lock layers as you work on a document. Locking a layer protects its content from being accidently modified as you work with the content of the document. You can also change a layer's properties such as adjusting its height or outline color.

The Timeline is introduced in Session 1.2, and it is used extensively in Tutorial 3 where animation is discussed.

3.4 Adjust document properties.

To adjust a document's properties, use the Document Settings dialog box, which is accessible through the Modify command on the Application bar or through the Edit button in the Property inspector. The Document Settings dialog box enables you to set the dimensions, background color, frame rate, and ruler units of a Flash document. You can also change the frame rate and Stage background color in the Property inspector.

See Session 1.2 for a discussion of changing a document's properties.

3.5 Use Flash guides and rulers.

You can add vertical and horizontal guides on the Stage as you work with a document. Guides are lines that help you to align objects on the Stage. You drag guides from the rulers onto the Stage. To remove a guide, you can drag it off the document window or you can clear all guides at one time. You can also change the guide colors, lock the guides, and set the snap accuracy. The snap accuracy determines how close an object needs to be to a guide before it snaps to the guide. Rulers display the document's measurement units, such as pixels, and can be used to place objects on the Stage according to specific coordinates. You can show or hide the rulers through the View menu on the Application bar.

See Session 1.2 for more information about guides and rulers.

3.6 Use the Motion Editor.

A motion tween is considered an object in Flash and its properties can be modified using the Motion Editor. The Motion Editor displays all properties and property keyframes for a selected motion tween and enables you to control the target object's coordinates, rotation, and transformation properties at each property keyframe. You can use the Motion Editor to more precisely modify a motion tween, including changing the timing of the animation and applying easing to create more natural motion. A motion path can be selected on the Stage using the Subselection tool to display its Bezier controls, which you can adjust to modify the path of the object in the motion tween.

See Session 4.1 for a discussion of the Motion Editor and modifying motion paths.

3.7 Understand Flash file types.

A document created in Flash is saved in the FLA format, which contains all of the different elements created in Flash. To revise the document, you edit the FLA file. A published document is saved in the SWF file format and is called a Flash movie. The SWF file requires the Flash Player plug-in to play in a Web browser. Flash files can also be exported in various other file formats, including JPG, GIF, and PNG. You can use the Adobe Media Encoder program to convert video files into the Flash video formats of FLV or F4V files so you can import them into a Flash document.

Other file types in Flash include XMP and XFL files. XMP files contain metadata such as file content information, author, title, and copyright status. XFL files store the same information as FLA files, but the information is in XML (Extensible Markup Language) format. XFL files can be exported from an application such as InDesign or After Effects and opened in Flash, allowing you to start a project in a separate application and then continue with the project in Flash.

See Session 1.1 for a discussion of bitmap and vector graphic file formats. See Session 2.2 for a discussion of Flash file formats. See Session 5.2 for a discussion of sound file formats that can be used in Flash documents. See Session 6.1 for a discussion of bitmap file formats. See Session 9.2 for a discussion of video file formats that can be imported into Flash.

3.8   Identify best practices for managing the file size of a published Flash document.

It is important to keep the size of a published Flash document as small as possible because the larger the file size, the longer it takes to download to a user's computer. A Flash document's file size increases as you add more graphic elements as well as bitmap, audio, and video elements.

Keep the number of bitmap images in a document to a minimum and optimize bitmap images before importing them into Flash. You can also break apart a bitmap graphic to convert it to a smaller vector format. Also keep the number and size of sound and video files to a minimum, and do not embed video files into a Flash document unless it is a very short video. When adding graphics that are similar to each other, convert the graphic to a symbol and then use multiple instances of the symbol. In addition, keep shape tweens to a minimum because they can be processor-intensive and can affect the movie's performance.

See Session 6.1 for a discussion of bitmap files. See Session 9.2 for a discussion of video files.

Building Rich Media Elements by Using Flash Professional CS5

4.1   Make rich media content development decisions based on your analysis and interpretation of design specifications.

The rich media elements you create for a project should be based on the design specifications developed as part of the planning process. Otherwise, the resulting project may not meet the needs of the client and may not be accepted by the client. This could lead to having to re-create the rich media elements from scratch and a loss of time and/ or money. Consider the technical requirements for the rich media content you create and how it impacts the capability of the user to view the content. Technical factors that impact how the target audience receives the rich media content include download speed, screen resolution, operating system, and type of browser used.

See Session 7.1 for a discussion of the planning process and developing design specifications for a Web site. See Session 9.3 for a discussion of designing and creating content for a mobile device.

4.2   Use tools on the Tools panel to select, create, and manipulate graphics and text.

The Tools panel, located on the right side of the Flash workspace in the Essentials layout, contains the tools that you use to draw, paint, select, and modify Flash graphics. The Tools panel also contains tools to change the magnification level of the Stage and to select colors. Tools can be selected in the Tools panel by clicking the tool's button or by pressing the tool's keyboard shortcut. Some tools in the Tools panel are hidden behind other tools and can be accessed by clicking and holding the visible tool button to open a pop-up menu, and then clicking the hidden tool. You can also collapse the display of the Tools panel by clicking the double-arrow icon above the Tools panel. The Selection and Subselection tools are used to select fills and strokes. The Subselection tool enables you to modify specific points on a line or curve. With the Selection tool, you can select just the fill or stroke of a graphic by clicking the object or you can select both the fill and the stroke at the same time by double-clicking the object. The Lasso tool can be used to make irregular selections.

Tools used to draw or create shapes include the Rectangle, Oval, Brush, Pencil, and Deco tools. You can modify the shapes using the Selection, Paint Bucket, or Free Transform tools. You can use the Color panel to select and apply colors to fills and to strokes.

See Session 1.1 for a discussion of bitmap and vector images. See Session 1.2 for more information about using the Tools panel and its tools, and for a discussion of using the selection tools and techniques. See Session 2.1 for a discussion of using the various drawing tools and tools for working with shapes. See Sessions 1.3 and 6.2 for a discussion of using the Color panel to apply and create colors.

4.3   Import and modify graphics.

Flash Professional CS5 can use graphics created in other applications such as Adobe FreeHand, Adobe Fireworks, Adobe Illustrator, and Adobe Photoshop. Vector graphics and bitmaps can be imported in a variety of file formats such as PNG, JPG, and PSD. PNG images usually have large blocks of color. The JPG file format is usually used for photographs. The PSD file format is for files created in Photoshop. When importing files, the Import dialog box includes options you can select to preserve elements of the imported file such as Photoshop layers. You can import graphics into the Library panel or directly onto the Stage. You can break apart a bitmap, which separates the bitmap from its symbol in the library and treats the image as a shape. You can also trace a bitmap to convert it to a vector graphic.

See Session 1.1 for a discussion of graphic file types. See Sessions 6.1 and 6.2 for a discussion of importing and working with bitmaps. See Session 3.3 for information on how to swap a bitmap on the Stage with one stored in the library. Also, in the Flash Help system, see the Using imported artwork topics.

4.4   Create text.

In Flash, you can create text blocks in a variety of colors, sizes, and fonts using the Text tool. You can create static text blocks, which contain text that doesn't change after the document is published. You can also create dynamic text blocks or input text blocks. A dynamic text block can be updated while the Flash movie is playing as a result of a calculation or from external data. An input text block allows the user to enter text in forms or surveys. Text can be created in a fixed-width text block that doesn't change as you type or in a single-line text block that extends as you type. You can check the spelling of text using the Check Spelling command. You can use the Text Layout Framework (TLF) engine to create text and have extensive formatting options including the ability to create columns of text and to link text blocks. The TLF text engine also provides support for character styles such as ligatures, highlighting, strikethrough, and underlining and the ability to create right-to-left text.

See Session 2.2 for a discussion of creating text.

4.5   Adjust text properties.

After you have created a text block, you can change the text properties by selecting the text block and adjusting settings in the Property inspector. You can change the text block's font, size, color, font style, and alignment. You can also select a font-rendering method, which allows you to specify an anti-alias method for text that is to be animated. Text that will not be animated can be rendered differently for improved readability. In addition, text properties such as the text size can be changed using the commands on the Text menu, the Property inspector, or by using the Free Transform tool. Also, graphic filters, such as a drop shadow, can be applied to text using the Property inspector. The Property inspector includes more extensive options for adjusting the properties of TLF text than for Classic text. TLF text is the default text format in Flash Professional CS5.

See Session 2.2 for a discussion of setting text properties and adding graphic filters.

4.6   Create objects and convert them to symbols, including graphics, movie clips, and buttons.

Existing graphic objects such as shapes and lines drawn with Flash can be converted to symbols. You can also create new symbols from scratch within the symbol-editing window. Symbols have one of three types of behavior: movie clip, graphic, or button. You can easily change a symbol's behavior type at any time. Movie clips contain their own Timeline and operate independently of the document's main Timeline. A graphic symbol's Timeline operates in sync with the Timeline of the movie in which it appears. A button symbol has its own four-frame Timeline with Up, Over, Down, and Hit frames that can be used to make a symbol into an interactive button. You can also create invisible buttons by creating a new button symbol with content only in its Hit frame. However, you should avoid invisible buttons when creating accessible documents. You can also use symbols from other Flash documents in the current document.

See Session 2.2 for a discussion of creating symbols. See Sessions 5.1 and 7.2 for a discussion of creating button symbols.

4.7   Understand symbols and the library.

Each document has a library whose contents can be viewed and managed using the Library panel. Symbols are stored in the document's library and instances of the symbols are then added to the Stage. Multiple instances of the same symbol can be used in a document, but only one copy of the symbol is stored. This reduces the ultimate file size, ensures consistency of a symbol, and allows editing multiple instances of a symbol at once. In addition, you can incorporate symbols created in one document into other documents. To add an instance of a symbol, you drag it from the Library panel to the Stage. Symbols can also be used with the Spray Brush tool as patterns that can be applied to objects. You can select a symbol to use for the Spray Brush tool from the Property inspector.

See Session 2.2 for a discussion of the Library panel, symbols, and instances of symbols.

4.8   Edit symbols and instances.

Each symbol instance in a document can be edited without changing the symbol in the document's Library. For example, you can change the size, orientation, or color tint of one instance without affecting other instances of the same symbol or the symbol. If you modify the symbol, however, all the instances of that symbol also change. You modify a symbol by placing it in symbol-editing mode. A symbol can be edited by itself in symbol-editing mode, or it can be edited in place with the rest of the graphics on the Stage dimmed.

See Session 2.2 for a discussion of editing symbols and instances.

4.9   Create masks.

A mask is created using a mask layer, which hides the contents of the layer below it, called the masked layer. The contents of the masked layer are hidden except for the area covered by the object on the mask layer. The object can be a filled shape such as an oval or it can be text. The content of the masked layer shows through only when the object is over it. You can convert any layer into a mask layer. You can also create an animation in a mask layer to show different areas of the masked layer throughout the animation.

See Session 4.1 for a discussion of creating masks.

4.10   Create animations (changes in shape, position, size, color, and transparency).

Objects in a Flash document can be animated by creating different states of an object in different keyframes and playing the frames over time. An animation can be created by changing the object's shape, size, color, or transparency over time. In Flash, you can create a frame-by-frame animation or a tween animation (which can be a motion tween, a classic motion tween, or a shape tween). In a frame-by-frame animation, you create or modify the objects in multiple keyframes. In a motion tween, you change the object's properties in any frame, called property keyframes, within its tween span. You can also adjust a motion tween's motion path with the Selection tool or by using the Motion Editor. In a classic tween animation, you change the objects in the starting and ending frames, and then Flash creates the content in the in-between frames. In a shape tween, you create the graphic shape in the starting and ending frames, and Flash creates the tweened frames. Shape tweens should be created with simple shapes and used sparingly because shape tweens tend to be processor-intensive.

When creating animation effects, assign frame labels in the Timeline to refer to key points in the animation to help organize content on the Timeline and to provide documentation. You can use inverse kinematics to animate one or more objects in relation to each other. With inverse kinematics, you can easily create complex animations and natural movement by animating objects that are connected to each other with bones. Bones are created using the Bone tool and can be added to connect one symbol instance to another, or they can be added to the interior of a shape object so that you can move or animate parts of the shape without having to draw the shape multiple times.

Motion tweens are relatively easy to create, but errors can still occur. One example of a tweening error is when you accidently remove the target object from the tween span. You can detect this error by looking at the layer in the Timeline that contains the tween span. Usually, a black dot represents the initial keyframe containing the target object. If a white dot appears in the tween span's beginning frame, the target object is missing. You can correct this error by selecting the layer that contains the tween span and then adding an instance of the target object to the layer. When working with classic tweens, a common tweening error occurs when a keyframe is not added to the end of the tween. This error is indicated by a dotted line in the layer that contains the tween. You can correct this error by adding a keyframe to the end of the classic tween.

See Tutorial 3 for discussions of the elements of an animation; using the Timeline to create frames and layers for an animation; creating Timeline effects, frame-by-frame animations, and tween animations; and using motion presets. See Tutorial 4 for a discussion of motion paths, the Motion Editor, animating text blocks, and using inverse kinematics. See Tutorial 5 for a discussion of frame labels.

4.11 Add simple controls through ActionScript 3.0.

ActionScript 3.0 is the latest version of the programming language in Flash Professional CS5, which you can use to add interactive elements to a Flash movie. With ActionScript, you can add functionality to buttons as well as control the sequence in which a movie's frames are played. You add ActionScript code through the Script pane in the Actions panel.

ActionScript code consists of actions, event listeners, and other programming statements to control how the actions are executed. An action is a statement, such as `gotoAndStop`, that instructs the Flash file to do something. Events are things that happen when a movie is playing, such as when the user clicks a button or presses a key. ActionScript can carry out instructions based on the event. The code to handle events consists of the event source, the event, and the response. An event listener is a method that the Flash Player executes in response to a specific event. Every object that has an event has an event listener. Event listeners establish a connection between a function and an event source, such as a button instance.

The Code Snippets panel provides snippets of prewritten ActionScript 3.0 code that can be added to a Flash document. You can add code snippets to affect the behavior of objects on the Stage, to enable navigation within the Timeline, to load and unload images and other SWF files, to control audio and video elements, or to handle events such as mouse clicks. When code snippets are applied to a Flash document, the ActionScript code is added to the current frame on the Timeline. The code snippets also contain instructions on how to customize the code to achieve the desired results.

See Session 8.1 for an introduction to ActionScript 3.0, using simple actions, object-oriented programming, event-handling concepts, and the Code Snippets panel.

4.12 Import and use sound.

Flash offers several ways to use sounds. You can add sounds that play continuously, such as a background sound. You can add sound effects to instances of buttons to make them more interactive. For example, you can add a sound that plays when a user clicks a button. You can add sounds that are synchronized with the animation, such as a sound simulating a clap of thunder that coincides with an animation of a lightning bolt. Sound files must first be imported into Flash. Sound file formats that are compatible with Flash include Windows Waveform (WAV), Audio Interchange File Format (AIFF), MPEG-3 (MP3), and Adobe Soundbooth (ASND). Because Flash has limited options for editing sounds, you should edit sound files in a sound-editing program before importing them into Flash.

There are two types of sounds in Flash. One type of sound is an event sound which does not play until the entire sound has downloaded completely and is not synchronized with the Timeline. The other type is a stream sound which is synchronized with the Timeline and begins playing as soon as enough data has downloaded. You add a sound from the document's Library panel into the Stage. The sound is added to the current frame in the Timeline and a waveform is displayed in the Timeline. You can also edit a sound file to add fade in or fade out effects.

See Session 5.2 for a discussion of importing and using sounds in Flash.

4.13 Add and export video.

Various video formats may be imported into a Flash document. After video is captured and prepared using a video-editing program, it can be encoded using Adobe Media Encoder to create a Flash video file in an FLV or F4V format. The Flash video file can then be imported into a Flash document using the Import Video wizard, which presents a series of dialog boxes in which you select the video file, select playback options, and select a skin or prebuilt playback controls. The Video Import wizard creates an instance of the FLVPlayback component on the Stage.

See Session 9.2 for a discussion of importing and using video in Flash.

4.14 Publish and export Flash documents.

Documents created in Flash are usually made available for use on the Web and must be published or exported into a format readable by a Web browser. A Flash document is published in the SWF file format and plays in the Flash Player plug-in. You can also publish or export a Flash document in a different file format such as JPEG, GIF, or PNG, depending on where and how the file is to be used. You specify how you want an FLA document published in the Publish Settings dialog box. The Formats tab lists the many file formats in which you can publish a Flash document, such as Flash (.swf), HTML (.html), or JPEG Image (.jpg). Each file format selected on the Formats tab has a corresponding tab in the Publish Settings dialog box with additional options and settings for that file type.

Flash Player detection may be added to a Web page to detect for the installation of the Flash Player plug-in on the user's computer. If the Flash Player is not installed or if the version installed is older than that required to display the SWF file, the user will be prompted to install the plug-in. The detection of Flash Player is important because you want to ensure that the site viewer can view the SWF movie. If the SWF movie does not play, you want to user to know why. You can have Flash create the code needed for Flash Player detection in the Publish Settings dialog box. Select the HTML (.html) tab; in the HTML publish settings, select Detect Flash Version, and then specify the version you want detected. When you publish the document, the code is created in the HTML file.

See Session 6.2 for a discussion of publishing Flash documents.

4.15 Make a document accessible.

A Flash document or an individual object in a document can be made accessible to a screen reader using the Accessibility panel by assigning a name and description to the document or selected object. Select an object on the Stage, such as a movie clip, to make it accessible. Select no objects on the Stage to make the entire Flash document accessible. You can also hide objects from screen readers by selecting the object on the Stage, and then deselecting Make object accessible in the Accessibility panel. You hide objects that convey no content or are repetitive, in which case you don't want the screen reader to read the same object's name and description repeatedly.

See Sessions 7.1 and 7.2 for a discussion of accessibility issues and the Accessibility panel.

Evaluating Rich Media Elements

5.1 Conduct basic technical tests.

After you have completed a Flash document, you should test it to ensure that the published movie works as designed and doesn't cause any errors. You should test it on the most common Web browsers, especially those you expect the target audience to use. You should also test it in both the Windows and Macintosh computer platforms. When conducting a test of the Flash movie, be sure to navigate to all parts of the movie, to play all sounds and videos, and to test all interactive elements of the movie. You can also use the Simulate Download command in the Flash Player to simulate how the movie plays at different download speeds. If part of the movie loads too slowly based on a target download speed, you can make changes to improve performance.

The Bandwidth Profiler is another option in the Flash Player you can use to test a movie. The Bandwidth Profiler graphically displays how much data is sent for each frame based on the download speed you select. You can use this information to make changes to the content in frames that are slowing playback of the movie.

When you test a movie using the Test Movie command, a new SWF file is created and played. However, if you preview the movie in HTML, you get to see how the SWF movie is displayed in a Web browser, which better simulates the experience of the user.

Textual content in a Flash document should be checked for correct spelling. This can easily be done using the Check Spelling command on the Text menu, which opens a dialog box with suggestions for potentially misspelled words.

See Session 2.2 for a discussion of checking text for spelling errors. See Sessions 3.2 and 6.2 for a discussion of previewing and testing a movie.

5.2 Identify techniques for basic usability tests.

Usability, as it relates to Flash, means that the user can use the finished Flash movie easily and quickly. The focus of usability testing is on the user experience. You can conduct a usability test by observing a group of users as they perform various tasks with the Flash movie to see how effectively they interact with it. As a result of this observation, as well as interviews with the users, you might determine that certain aspects of the Flash movie need to be changed to improve its usability.

For more information on usability testing, see *www.useit.com*.

GLOSSARY/INDEX

input text field A field in which a user can enter text in forms or surveys. FL 86

instance A copy of a symbol. FL 84, FL 276
    editing, FL A10
    of symbols, creating, FL 10–103

interactive When a user has some level of control, such as being able to stop or play a movie's animation. FL 231

Internet Explorer
    allowing blocked content, FL 7, FL 312
    viewing SWF files in, FL 6–8

inverse kinematics An animation method used to create bone structures so that when one bone moves, the other bones move in relation to it. FL 204
    using to create animations, FL 212–216

J

JavaScript The Web language used to add interactive elements to Web pages. FL 250

JPEG files, FL 4, FL 278

JPG file format, FL 91

K

keyframe A frame that contains a new symbol instance or a new graphic object; in the Timeline, a keyframe has a white dot when empty and a black dot when it has content. FL 114
    adding sounds to, FL 249
    property, FL 126

keyword A word that has a specified use or meaning in ActionScript and cannot be used in another context in a statement; also called a reserved word. FL 384

kilobyte Approximately 1000 bytes. FL 408

L

labels
    frame, FL 248
    for input text boxes, FL 418

landscape orientation A layout that is wider than it is tall. FL 478

Lasso tool The tool used to select an object, to select several objects at one time, or to select an irregularly shaped area of an object by drawing a free-form marquee. FL 15, FL 25, FL 42–44

layer An element used to organize the content (images, animations, and other objects) of a Flash document. FL 114
    distributing objects to individual, FL 198–201
    locking, unlocking, FL 93, FL 114, FL 116
    mask, masked, FL 166, FL 177–185
    organizing actions using, FL 254
    repositioning frames within, FL 147
    and the Timeline, FL 13
    tween, FL 126
    viewing properties, FL 119

layer folder A container in the Timeline in which to place layers. FL 114
    adding, FL 120–121
    organizing distributed layers in, FL 199

layouts, workspace, FL 3

letters
    animating individual, FL 195–201
    converting to symbols, FL 200–201

levels Different planes in which the Flash Player can load SWF files or other content such as images. FL 322

library The place that stores symbols created for a document; symbols stored in the library can be viewed, organized, and edited from the Library panel. FL 85, FL A10
    using, FL 97–100
    using external, FL 341–348

Library panel, FL 97–100

licensing issues for sounds, FL 258

linear gradient A gradient that blends the colors from one point to another in a straight line. FL 296

Line tool The tool used to draw straight lines (strokes) of varying lengths, widths, and colors. FL 15, FL 55, FL 77

lines, drawing, FL 56–71

links to Web sites, creating, FL 402–408

loadedBytes value, FL 401

loading external image files, FL 362–369

loop An animation effect in which a group of frames plays repeatedly by having the playhead return to an earlier frame. FL 248, FL 253

lossless compression Compression that retains all the original data in an image, but is limited to 256 colors. FL 278

lossy compression Compression that removes some of the original data in an image to achieve a smaller file size. FL 278

M

magnifying glass (Zoom tool), FL 16

magnifying view of the Stage, FL 26–27

marquee An outline that encloses an area to be selected. FL 26
    creating free-form, FL 42
    and Selection tool, FL 37

mask layer A layer that contains a graphic element that hides the content of the masked layer. FL A10, FL 166
    using in animations, FL 177–185

masked layer The layer below the mask layer; the contents of the masked layer are hidden except for the area covered by the element on the mask layer. FL 166

Merge Drawing mode The default drawing mode in which objects drawn or moved on top of other objects merge with or segment the existing objects on the same layer. FL 33–34, FL 59, FL 63

method A function specific to a particular object; built-in capabilities of the object that perform certain actions or respond to certain events. FL 389–390

mobile
    content, creating, FL 484–491
    devices, testing Flash content on, FL 477–478

modifiers, tool, FL 14

TASK REFERENCE

TASK	PAGE #	RECOMMENDED METHOD
Action, add to button using Behaviors panel	FL 367	Select button instance, open Behaviors panel, click ⊞., point to behavior type, click behavior, modify values in dialog box, click OK
Action, add using Actions panel in Script Assist mode	FL 251	*See* Reference box: Using the Actions Panel in Script Assist Mode
Actions, check for syntax errors	FL 359	In Actions panel, click ✔, click OK, check errors in Compiler Errors panel
Actions toolbox, collapse or expand	FL 391	In Actions panel, click ⦂
ActionScript code, add using Code Snippets panel	FL 393	Click ⊞, expand Code Snippet category, double-click code snippet to add it to the Script pane; modify code in Actions panel
Adobe Media Encoder, start program	FL 464	Click Start button, click All Programs, click Adobe Media Encoder CS5
Animation, test	FL 138	*See* Reference box: Testing a Document's Animation
Bitmap, change properties	FL 279	In Library panel, select bitmap, click 🛈
Bitmap, convert to symbol	FL 280	Select bitmap instance, click Modify, click Convert to Symbol, set options, click OK
Bitmap, convert to vector	FL 290	Select bitmap instance, click Modify, point to Bitmap, click Trace Bitmap, set options, click OK
Bitmap, import to library or Stage	FL 276	*See* Reference box: Importing a Bitmap
Bone, add to an instance or shape	FL 219	In Tools panel, click 🦴, click and drag to connect instance or object on Stage
Button, add ActionScript code	FL 357	*See* Reference box: Adding ActionScript Code to a Button
Button, add from Buttons library	FL 232	Click Window, point to Common Libraries, click Buttons, expand button category, drag button from Buttons library panel to Stage or library
Button, create	FL 238	*See* Reference box: Creating a Custom Button
Button, test within program window	FL 234	Click Control, click Enable Simple Buttons, click button on Stage
Classic tween animation, create	FL 142	*See* Reference box: Creating a Classic Tween Animation
Colors, select	FL 36	In Property inspector, click ✎ ▭ or ⬥ ▬ to open color palette, or in Tools panel, click ⬜ or ⬛ to open color palette, click desired color swatch
Comment, add multiple lines to ActionScript code	FL 398	In Actions panel, type /* followed by comment text and then type */
Comment, add single line to ActionScript code	FL 398	In Actions panel, type // followed by comment text
Component, create instance	FL 446	*See* Reference box: Adding a Flash Component
Component, set parameters	FL 448	Select component on Stage, in Component Parameters section of Property inspector, set parameter values
Dynamic text box, create type	FL 422	In Tools panel, click **T**; in Property inspector, click Text engine button, click Classic Text, click Text type button, click Dynamic Text, create text block on Stage, set properties
External library, copy symbol	FL 341	*See* Reference box: Copying Symbols from an External Library
Fill, apply with Paint Bucket tool	FL 72	In Tools panel, click 🪣, select fill properties, click modifier, click object on Stage

TASK	PAGE #	RECOMMENDED METHOD
Filter, apply to object	FL 103	In Filters section of Property inspector, click ⬛, click filter, set properties
Filter, copy and paste	FL 104	In Filters section of Property inspector, click ⬛, click Copy All, select object to apply filter to, click ⬛, click Paste
Flash, exit program	FL 47	Click File, click Exit
Flash, start program	FL 8	Click Start button, click All Programs, click Adobe Flash Professional CS5
Flash document, close	FL 23	Click File, click Close
Flash document, create from template	FL 343	Click File, click New, click Templates tab, select category, select template, click OK, add content and save as usual
Flash document, export as image	FL 309	Click File, point to Export, click Export Image, select destination, type filename, select file type, click Save, set options, click OK
Flash document, make accessible	FL 334	Click Window, point to Other Panels, click Accessibility, select options, type name and description
Flash document, modify properties	FL 31	Click Modify, click Document
Flash document, open	FL 9	Click File, click Open, select file, click Open
Flash document, preview by scrubbing	FL 13	Drag playhead in Timeline header
Flash document, preview in Flash Player window	FL 10	Click Control, point to Test Movie, click in Flash Professional
Flash document, preview in Flash program window	FL 10	Click Control, click Play; or press Enter
Flash document, preview in Web page	FL 11	Click File, point to Publish Preview, click HTML
Flash document, publish	FL 304	Click File, click Publish
Flash document, save with current name	FL 23	Click File, click Save
Flash document, save with new name	FL 9	Click File, click Save As, select folder, type filename, click Save
Flash document, test download in different settings	FL 414	Click Control, click Test Movie, click View, point to Download Settings, click desired setting, click View, click Simulate Download
Flash Web site, develop	FL 327	*See* Reference box: Developing a Flash Web Site
Frame, copy	FL 121	Select frame or frames, right-click selected frames, click Copy Frames
Frame, make Frame 1 current	FL 20	Click Control, click Rewind
Frame, make last current	FL 22	Click Control, click Go To End
Frame, paste	FL 121	Select frame or frames, right-click selected frames, click Paste Frames
Frame action, test within Flash	FL 256	Click Control, click Enable Simple Frame Actions, click Control, click Play
Frame-by-frame animation, create	FL 151	Insert graphic object in initial frame, add keyframe and new content or properties at each place the object changes
Frame label, add	FL 255	Select keyframe; in Property inspector, type label in Name box, press Enter
Gradient fill, apply to text	FL 300	Select text block, Click Modify, click Break Apart, click Modify, click Break apart, select gradient for fill color
Gradient fill, transform	FL 302	In Tools panel, click ⬛; click gradient on Stage, adjust gradient

TASK	PAGE #	RECOMMENDED METHOD
Gradient, create, edit, save	FL 297	*See* Reference box: Creating, Editing, and Saving a Gradient
Grid, display	FL 28	Click View, point to Grid, click Show Grid
Grid, hide	FL 32	Click View, point to Grid, click Show Grid
Grid, modify appearance	FL 29	Click View, point to Grid, click Edit Grid
Grouped object, edit	FL 36	Double-click grouped object
Grouped object, exit edit mode	FL 37	Click Edit, click Edit All; or on the Edit bar, click Scene 1
Guide, create	FL 30	Display rulers, drag guide from a ruler to Stage
Guides, clear	FL 65	Click View, point to Guides, click Clear Guides
Guides, hide	FL 32	Click View, point to Guides, click Show Guides
Guides, modify appearance	FL 31	Click View, point to Guides, click Edit Guides
Help, display contents	FL 44	*See* Reference box: Using the Flash Help System
History panel, open	FL 93	Click Window, point to Other Panels, click History
Image, export	FL 91	Click File, point to Export, click Export Image, select location, enter filename, click Save as type button to select file format, click Save
Input text box, create	FL 420	In Tools panel, click $\boxed{\text{T}}$; in Property inspector, click Text engine button, click Classic Text, click Text type button, click Input Text, create text block on Stage, set properties
Instance behavior, change	FL 149	Select instance on Stage; in Property inspector, click Instance behavior button, click desired type
Instance name, add	FL 387	Select instance on Stage, enter name in Instance name box in Property inspector
Keyframe, insert	FL 144	Select frame in Timeline, click Insert, point to Timeline, click Keyframe
Layer, insert	FL 121	In Timeline, click ▣
Layer, move into layer folder	FL 120	In Timeline, drag layer over the layer folder
Layer, rename	FL 121	In Timeline, double-click layer name, type new name, press Enter
Layer, select	FL 121	In Timeline, click layer name
Layer folder, insert	FL 120	In Timeline, click ▢
Layer folder, rename	FL 120	In Timeline, double-click folder name, type new name, press Enter
Letter animations, create	FL 203	*See* Reference box: Animating Individual Letters
Library panel, open	FL 98	Click Window, click Library or click Library tab
Lines, draw with Line tool	FL 77	In Tools panel, click ＼, set stroke properties, draw on Stage
Lines, draw with Pencil tool	FL 68	In Tools panel, click ✐, click modifier, set stroke properties, draw on Stage
Mask layer, create	FL 184	*See* Reference box: Creating a Mask Layer Animation
Merge Drawing mode, select or deselect	FL 64	In Tools panel, click ▣
Mobile Flash file, create	FL 485	*See* Reference box: Creating Flash Documents for Mobile Devices
Mobile Flash file, test	FL 490	Click Control, point to Test Movie, click in Device Central
Motion path, add to motion tween	FL 130	Drag instance to new location
Motion path, modify	FL 175	*See* Reference box: Modifying a Tween's Motion Path
Motion preset, apply	FL 134	Select symbol instance on Stage; in Motion Presets panel, click desired motion preset in Default Presets folder, click Apply

TASK	PAGE #	RECOMMENDED METHOD
Motion tween, create	FL 128	Add instance of a symbol or text block in beginning frame, right-click frame, click Create Motion Tween, modify instance in ending frame
Motion tween, modify properties	FL 132	Select tweened object on Stage; in Property inspector, change settings
Motion tween, modify properties in Motion Editor	FL 179	Select Motion Tween, click Motion Editor tab, modify tween's properties
Movie Explorer, use	FL 223	Click Window, click Movie Explorer, click Show buttons to select and deselect as needed
Object, change orientation	FL 222	Click Modify, point to Transform, click option
Object, copy and paste	FL 81	Select object, click Edit, click Copy, click Edit, click a paste command
Object, flip horizontally	FL 154	Select object, click Modify, point to Transform, click Flip Horizontal
Object, manipulate in 3D	FL 208	Select frame with object, in Tools panel, click 🔵, drag red line to rotate x axis, drag green line to rotate y axis, drag blue circle to change z axis, drag orange circle to change all axes
Object, modify anchor points	FL 41	*See* Reference box: Using the Subselection Tool
Object, modify with Selection tool	FL 39	In Tools panel, click �. , drag a line or a corner of the object to change its shape
Object, modify with Subselection tool	FL 41	In Tools panel, click ▷ , click stroke of object, drag an anchor point of the object to change its shape
Object, move	FL 39	In Tools panel, click ▶ , click object, drag object
Object, orient to curved motion path	FL 176	Click starting frame of motion tween span, in Properties inspector, click Orient to path check box
Object, reposition on Stage	FL 16	Drag object with ▶ , or change object's X and Y values in Property inspector
Object, scale on Stage	FL 22	Select object with ▶ ; in Property inspector, change object's W and H values
Object, select with Selection tool	FL 39	In Tools panel, click ▶ , click object or draw marquee around object(s)
Object, transform	FL 79	*See* Reference box: Transforming an Object Using the Free Transform Tool
Object Drawing mode, select or deselect	FL 64	In Tools panel, click 🔘
Objects, align on Stage	FL 246	Select several objects at one time, open Align panel, click align button(s)
Objects, distribute to layers	FL 206	Select objects, click Modify, point to Timeline, click Distribute to Layers
Objects, group	FL 35	Click ▶ , draw marquee around objects, click Modify, click Group
Objects, select with Lasso tool	FL 42	In Tools panel, click 🔾 , click and drag to select objects or click 🔾 , click points around objects, double-click to complete selection
Onion marker, set number of frames	FL 213	In the Timeline, click [·] , click option
Onion skinning, toggle on or off	FL 213	In the Timeline, click 🔲
Oval, draw	FL 64	In Tools panel, click ⚪ , set stroke and fill properties, click and drag pointer on Stage
Panel, close panel group	FL 26	Click panel's title bar, click panel menu button ▤ , click Close Group
Panel, collapse to icons	FL 19	Click Collapse to Icons button ▶▶

TASK	PAGE #	RECOMMENDED METHOD
Panel, display	FL 18	Click Window, click panel name
Panels and panel groups, organize	FL 18	*See* Reference box: Organizing Panels and Panel Groups
Primitive oval, draw	FL 75	In Tools panel, click [icon], set stroke and fill colors, click and drag pointer on Stage
Publish profile, save	FL 307	In Publish Settings dialog box, click [+], enter publish profile name, click OK
Publish settings, change	FL 307	Click File, click Publish Settings, select types and enter filenames on Formats tab, select options on file type tabs, click Publish, click OK
Rectangle, draw	FL 59	In Tools panel, click [icon], set stroke and fill properties, click and drag pointer on Stage
Rectangle, set rounded corners	FL 62	In Tools panel, click [icon]; in Property inspector, enter Rectangle corner radius values
Regular frame, insert	FL 129	Select frame in Timeline; on Application bar, click Insert, point to Timeline, click Frame
Rulers, display or hide	FL 30	Click View, click Rulers
Scene, duplicate	FL 125	In Scene panel, select scene, click [icon]
Scene, rename	FL 123	In Scene panel, double-click scene, type new name, press Enter
Scene, select	FL 124	On Edit bar, click [icon], select scene
Scenes, reorder	FL 124	In Scene panel, drag scene to new location
Shape tween, create	FL 155	Create graphic content in beginning and ending frames of animation, right-click frame, click Create Shape Tween
Snap to Objects, select or deselect	FL 62	In Tools panel, click [icon]
Sound, add effect	FL 264	Select keyframe with sound; in Property inspector, click Effect button, click sound effect
Sound, add to button	FL 259	*See* Reference box: Adding a Sound to a Button
Sound, change Sync setting	FL 263	Select keyframe with sound, if necessary; in Property inspector, click Sync button, click setting, click Sound loop button, click options, set number of times to repeat
Sound, import to library	FL 258	Click File, point to Import, click Import to Library, select file, click Open
Spelling checker, set options	FL 88	*See* Reference box: Setting Options for the Spelling Checker
Stage, change view	FL 26	*See* Reference box: Changing the View of the Stage
Stage, move its view	FL 27	In Tools panel, click [icon], drag Stage to new position
Static text box, create	FL 87	In Tools panel, click [T]; in Property inspector, click Text engine button, click Classic Text, click Text type button, click Static Text, set text properties, create text block on Stage
Steps, replay	FL 94	Select steps in History panel, select object on Stage, click Replay button in History panel
Steps, undo	FL 95	Click Edit, click Undo or move slider to previous steps in History panel
Stroke or fill properties, copy	FL 73	*See* Reference box: Using the Eyedropper Tool
Symbol, change type	FL 99	In Library panel, select symbol, click [icon], select Type, click OK
Symbol, create	FL 97	*See* Reference box: Creating a Symbol

TASK	PAGE #	RECOMMENDED METHOD
Symbol, create duplicate	FL 100	In Library panel, select symbol, click ▼, click Duplicate, type name, click OK
Symbol, edit	FL 101	*See* Reference box: Editing a Symbol
Symbol instance, create	FL 102	Drag copy of symbol from Library panel to Stage
Symbol instance, swap	FL 146	Select symbol instance on Stage; in the Property inspector, click Swap button, select symbol, click OK
Template, create	FL 339	*See* Reference box: Creating a Flash Template
Text, create	FL 87	In Tools panel, click **T**; in Property inspector, set text properties, click or click and drag on Stage to create text block, type text
Text, spell check	FL 90	Click Text, click Check Spelling
Text, split letters into individual text blocks	FL 205	Select text block, click Modify, click Break Apart
Text animations, create	FL 193	*See* Reference bpx: Creating Text Animations
Text box, set type	FL 420	In Tools panel, click **T**; in Property inspector, click Text type button, click Input Text or Dynamic Text or Static Text, create text block on Stage
Timeline, change view	FL 118	In Timeline, click ▼, click desired view
Timeline, show or hide	FL 56	Click Window, click Timeline
Tool, select	FL 14	Click tool's button in the Tools panel or press tool's shortcut key
Toolbar, open or close	FL 9	Click Window, point to Toolbars, click toolbar
Tween span, extend or reduce	FL 129	In Timeline, drag right side of tween span right or left
Tween span, move	FL 133	In Timeline, drag frame within tween span right or left
Video, encode	FL 464	In Adobe Media Encoder, click Add button, select file, click Open; set export settings, click OK, click Start Queue
Video, import	FL 468	Click File, point to Import, click Import Video, follow steps in Import Video wizard
Web page, preview	FL 6	Start Internet Explorer or another Web browser, click File, click Open, click Browse, select HTML file, click Open, click OK
Workspace, select or reset layout	FL 9	Click Window, point to Workspace, click layout
Workspace, show all	FL 10	Click View, point to Magnification, click Show All
Workspace, switch layouts or reset layout	FL 9	Click the workspace switcher button, click layout or click Reset layout
Zoom level, change	FL 27	Click 🔍, click 🔍 or 🔍, click specific area of Stage